Conquering Complexity

Mike Hinchey · Lorcan Coyle

Editors

Conquering Complexity

Foreword by Roger Penrose

 Springer

Editors
Mike Hinchey
Lero, Irish Software Eng Research Centre
University of Limerick
Limerick, Ireland
mike.hinchey@lero.ie

Lorcan Coyle
Lero, International Science Centre
University of Limerick
Limerick, Ireland
lorcan.coyle@lero.ie

ISBN 978-1-4471-5826-4   ISBN 978-1-4471-2297-5 (eBook)
DOI 10.1007/978-1-4471-2297-5
Springer London Dordrecht Heidelberg New York

British Library Cataloguing in Publication Data
A catalogue record for this book is available from the British Library

Printed on acid-free paper

Springer is part of Springer Science+Business Media (www.springer.com)

Today, "complexity" is a word that is much in fashion. We have learned very well that many of the systems that we are trying to deal with in our contemporary science and engineering are very complex indeed. They are so complex that it is not obvious that the powerful tricks and procedures that served us for four centuries or more in the development of modern science and engineering will enable us to understand and deal with them...

... We are learning that we need a science of complex systems and we are beginning to develop it.

– Herbert A. Simon

Foreword

The year 2012—of publication of this book *Conquering Complexity*—is particularly distinguished by being the centenary year of Alan Turing, whose theoretical analysis of the notion of "computing machine", together with his wartime work in deciphering German codes, has had a huge impact on the enormous development of electronic computers, and the consequent impact that these devices have had on our lives, particularly with regard to science and technology. It is now possible to model extremely complex systems, whether they be naturally occurring physical processes or the predicted behaviour of human-constructed machinery. The complexity that can now be handled by today's electronic computers has completely transformed our understanding of many different kinds of physical behaviour, such behaviour being taken to act in accordance with the known physical laws. The extreme precision of these laws, as ascertained in numerous delicate experiments, allows us to have very considerable confidence in the results of these computations, and when the computations are done correctly, we may have a justified trust in the expectation of agreement between the computationally predicted outcomes and the details of observed behaviour. Conversely, such agreement between calculated predictions and actual physical behaviour reflects back as further confirmation on the very accuracy of the laws that are employed in the calculations.

However, the very possibility of reliably performing calculations of the extreme complication that is frequently required raises numerous new issues. Many of these issues would not have been evident before the advent of modern electronic computer technology, which has rendered it possible—and indeed commonplace—to enact the vast computations that are frequently needed. Whereas, our modern computers can be trusted to perform the needed calculations with enormous speed and accuracy, the machines themselves have no understanding of what they are doing nor of the purposes to which the results of these computations are to be put. It is *we* who must supply this understanding. Our particular choices of the actual computations that are to be performed need to be correct ones that do actually reflect the physical processes that are intended to be simulated. In addition, there are frequently many different ways of achieving the same ends, and insight and subtle judgements need to be employed in the decisions as to which procedures are the most effective to be deployed. In my own extremely limited experience, in early 1956, when computer technology was still in its infancy, I obtained some direct experience of the vast simplification, even then, that could sometimes be achieved by the reformulation of a particular calculation into a subtly different one. How much greater is the potential, now, to improve the speed, accuracy—and indeed the very feasibility—of an intended simulation. The very enormity of the complexity of so many currently required computations vastly increases the role of such general considerations, these often leading to reliable computations that might have otherwise appeared not to be feasible, and frequently providing a much better understanding of what can indeed be achieved in practise. Many such matters are considered in this book, which address the issue of computational complexity from a great many different points of view. It is fascinating to see the variety of different types of argument that are here brought to bear on the issues involved, which so frequently indeed provide the taming of complexity in its multifarious forms.

Roger Penrose

Preface

Software has long been perceived as complex, at least within Software Engineering circles. We have been living in a recognised state of crisis since the first NATO Software Engineering conference in 1968. Time and again we have been proven unable to engineer software as easily/cheaply/safely as we imagined. Cost overruns and expensive failures are the norm.

The problem is fundamentally one of complexity—translating a problem specification into a form that can be solved by a computer is a complex undertaking. Any problem, no matter how well specified, will contain a baseline of intrinsic complexity—otherwise it is not much of a problem. Additional complexities accrue as a solution to the problem is implemented. As these increase, the complexity of the problem (and solution) quickly surpasses the ability of a single human to fully comprehend it. As team members are added new complexities will inevitably arise.

Software is fundamentally complex because it must be precise; errors will be ruthlessly punished by the computer. Problems that appear to be specified quite easily in plain language become far more complex when written in a more formal notation, such as computer code. Comparisons with other engineering disciplines are deceptive. One cannot easily increase the factor of safety of software in the same way that one could in building a steel structure, for example. Software is typically built assuming perfection, often without adequate safety nets in case the unthinkable happens. In such circumstances it should not be surprising to find out that (seemingly) minor errors have the potential to cause entire software systems to collapse. A worrying consideration is that the addition of additional safety or fault protection components to a system will also increase the system's overall complexity, potentially making the system *less safe*.

Our goal in this book is to uncover techniques that will aid in overcoming complexity and enable us to produce reliable, dependable computer systems that will operate as intended, and yet are produced on-time, in budget, and are evolvable, both over time and at run time. We hope that the contributions in this book will aid in understanding the nature of software complexity and provide guidance for the control or avoidance of complexity in the engineering of complex software systems. The book is organised into three parts: Part I (Chaps. 1 and 2) addresses the sources and types of complexity; Part II (Chaps. 3 to 9) addresses areas of significance in dealing with complexity; Part III (Chaps. 10 to 17) identifies particular application areas and means of controlling complexity in those areas.

Part I of the book (Chaps. 1 and 2) drill down into the question of how to recognise and handle complexity. In tackling complexity two main tools are highlighted: abstraction and decomposition/composition. Throughout this book we see these tools reused, in different ways, to tackle the problem of *Controlling Complexity*.

In Chap. 1 José Luiz Fiadeiro discusses the nature of complexity and highlights the fact that software engineering seems to have been in a permanent state of crisis, a crisis might better be described as one of complexity. The difficulty we have in conquering it is that the nature of complexity itself is always changing. His sentiment that we cannot hope to do more than "shift [. . .] complexity to a place where it can be managed more effectively" is echoed throughout this book.

In Chap. 2 Michael Jackson outlines a number of different ways of decomposing system behaviour, based on the system's constituents, on machine events, on requirement events, use cases, or software modules. He highlights that although each offers advantages in different contexts, they are in themselves not adequate to master behavioural complexity. In addition he highlights the potential for oversimplification. If we decompose and isolate parts of the system and take into account only each part's intrinsic complexities we can easily miss some interactions between the systems, leading to potentially surprising system behaviour.

Part II of the book outlines different approaches to managing or controlling complexity. Chapters 3 and 4 discuss the need to tackle complexity in safety-critical systems, arguing that only by simplifying software can it be proven safe to use. These chapters argue for redundancy and separation of control and safety systems respectively.

Gerard Holzmann addresses the question of producing defect-free code in Chap. 3. He argues that rather than focusing on eliminating component failure by producing perfect systems, we should aim to minimise the possibility of system failure by focusing on the production of fallback redundant systems that are much simpler—simple enough to be verifiably correct. In Chap. 4, Wassyng et al. argue that rather than seeking to tame complexity we should focus our efforts on avoiding it altogether whenever reliability is paramount. The authors agree with Holzmann in that simpler systems are more easy to prove safe, but rather than using redundant systems to take control in the case of component failure they argue for the complete separation of systems that must be correct (in this case safety systems) from control systems.

In Chap. 5, Norman Schneidewind shows how it is possible to analyse the tradeoffs in a system between complexity, reliability, maintainability, and availability *prior to implementation*, which may reduce the uncertainty and highlight potential dangers in software evolution. In Chap. 6, Bohner et al argue that change tolerance must be built into the software and that accepting some complexity today to decrease the long term complexity that creeps in due to change is warranted.

Chapters 7 to 9 discuss autonomous, agent-based, and swarm-like software systems. The complexity that arises out of these systems comes from the interactions between the system's component actors or agents.

In Chap. 7 Hinchey et al. point out that new classes of systems are introducing new complexities, heretofore unseen in (mainstream) software engineering. They describe the complexities that arise when autonomous and autonomic characteristics are built into software, which are compounded when agents are enabled to interact with one another and self-organise. In Chap. 8 Mike Hinchey and Roy Sterritt discuss the techniques that have emerged from taking inspiration from biological systems. The autonomic nervous system has inspired approaches in autonomic computing, especially in self-managing, self-healing, and other self-* behaviours. They consider mechanisms that enable social insects (especially ants) to tackle problems as a colony (or "swarm" in the more general sense) and show how these can be applied to complex tasks. Peña et al. give a set of guidelines to show how complexity derived from interactions in agent-oriented software can be managed in Chap. 9. They use the example of the Ant Colony to model how complex goals can be achieved using small numbers of simple actors and their interactions with each other.

Part III of the book (Chaps. 10 to 17) discusses the control of complexity in different application areas. In Chap. 10, Tiziana Margaria and Bernhard Steffen argue that classical software development is no longer adequate for the bulk of application programming. Their goal is to manage the division of labour in order to minimise the complexity that is "felt" by each stakeholder.

The use of formal methods will always have a role when correct functioning of the software is critical. In Chap. 11, Jonathan Bowen and Mike Hinchey examine the attitudes towards formal methods in an attempt to answer the question as to why the software engineering community is not willing to either abandon or embrace formal methods. In Chap. 12 Filieri et al. focus on how to manage design-time uncertainty and run-time changes and how to verify that the software evolves dynamically without disrupting the reliability or performance of applications. In Chap. 13, Wei et al. present a timebands model that can explicitly recognise a finite set of distinct time bands in which temporal properties and associated behaviours are described. They demonstrate how significantly their model contributes to describing complex real-time systems with multiple time scales. In Chap. 14 Manfred Broy introduces a comprehensive theory for describing multifunctional software-intensive systems in terms of their interfaces, architectures and states. This supports the development of distributed systems with multifunctional behaviours and provides a number of structuring concepts for engineering larger, more complex systems.

In Chap. 15, John Anderson and Todd Carrico describe the Distributed Intelligent Agent Framework, which defines the essential elements of an agent-based system and its development/execution environment. This framework is useful for tackling the complexities of systems that consist of a large network of simple components without central control. Margaria et al. discuss the difficulties in dealing with monolithic ERP systems in Chap. 16. As the business needs of customers change the ERP system they use must change to respond to those needs. The requirements of flexibility and customisability introduce significant complexities, which much be overcome if the ERP providers are to remain competitive. In Chap. 17 Casanova et al. discuss the problem of matching database schemas. They introduce procedures to test strict satisfiability and decide logical implication for extralite schemas with role hierarchies. These are sufficiently expressive to encode commonly-used Entity-Relationship model and UML constructs.

We would like to thank all authors for the work they put into their contributions. We would like to thank Springer for agreeing to publish this work and in particular Beverley Ford, for her support and encouragement. We would like to thank all of our friends and colleagues in Lero.[1]

Limerick, Ireland   Mike Hinchey
                                                                                     Lorcan Coyle

---

[1]This work was supported, in part, by Science Foundation Ireland grant 03/CE2/I303_1 to Lero–the Irish Software Engineering Research Centre (www.lero.ie).

Contents

Contributors

John A. Anderson Cougaar Software, Inc., Falls Church, VA, USA, janderson@cougaarsoftware.com

Steve Boßelmann TU Dortmund, Dortmund, Germany, steve.bosselmann@cs.tu-dortmund.de

Shawn Bohner Rose-Hulman Institute of Technology, Terre Haute, USA, bohner@rose-hulman.edu

Jonathan P. Bowen Museophile Limited, London, UK, jonathan.bowen@lsbu.ac.uk

Karin K. Breitman Department of Informatics, PUC-Rio, Rio de Janeiro, RJ, Brazil, karin@inf.puc-rio.br

Manfred Broy Institut für Informatik, Technische Universität München, München, Germany, broy@in.tum.de

Alan Burns Department of Computer Science, University of York, York, UK, burns@cs.york.ac.uk

Todd Carrico Cougaar Software, Inc., Falls Church, VA, USA, tcarrico@cougaarsoftware.com

Marco A. Casanova Department of Informatics, PUC-Rio, Rio de Janeiro, RJ, Brazil, casanova@inf.puc-rio.br

Markus Doedt TU Dortmund, Dortmund, Germany, markus.doedt@cs.tu-dortmund.de

José Luiz Fiadeiro Department of Computer Science, University of Leicester, Leicester, UK, jose@mcs.le.ac.uk

Antonio Filieri DeepSE Group @ DEI, Politecnico di Milano, Milan, Italy, filieri@elet.polimi.it

Barry D. Floyd Orfalea College of Business, California Polytechnic University, San Luis Obispo, CA, USA, bfloyd@calpoly.edu

Antonio L. Furtado Department of Informatics, PUC-Rio, Rio de Janeiro, RJ, Brazil, furtado@inf.puc-rio.br

Carlo Ghezzi DeepSE Group @ DEI, Politecnico di Milano, Milan, Italy, ghezzi@elet.polimi.it

Mike Hinchey Lero—the Irish Software Engineering Research Centre, University of Limerick, Limerick, Ireland, mike.hinchey@lero.ie

Gerard J. Holzmann Laboratory for Reliable Software, Jet Propulsion Laboratory, California Institute of Technology, Pasadena, CA, USA, gholzmann@acm.org

Michael Jackson The Open University, Milton Keynes, UK, jacksonma@acm.org

Mark Lawford McMaster University, Hamilton, ON, Canada, lawford@mcmaster.ca

Renato Levy Intelligent Automation Inc., Rockville, USA, rlevy@i-a-i.com

José A. F. de Macêdo Department of Computing, Federal University of Ceará, Fortaleza, CE, Brazil, jose.macedo@lia.ufc.br

Tom Maibaum McMaster University, Hamilton, ON, Canada, tom@maibaum.org

Tiziana Margaria Chair Service and Software Engineering, University of Potsdam, Potsdam, Germany, margaria@cs.uni-potsdam.de

Andrew Milluzzi Rose-Hulman Institute of Technology, Terre Haute, USA, milluzaj@rose-hulman.edu

Raffaela Mirandola DeepSE Group @ DEI, Politecnico di Milano, Milan, Italy, mirandola@elet.polimi.it

Joaquin Peña University of Seville, Seville, Spain, joaquinp@us.es

James L. Rash NASA Goddard Space Flight Center, Emeritus Greenbelt, MD, USA, james.l.rash@nasa.gov

Ramya Ravichandar CISCO Inc., San Jose, CA, USA, ramyar@vt.edu

Christopher A. Rouff Lockheed Martin Advanced Technology Laboratories, Arlington, VA, USA, christopher.rouff@lmco.com

Antonio Ruiz-Cortés University of Seville, Seville, Spain, aruiz@us.es

Norman F. Schneidewind Department of Information Science, Graduate School of Operational and Information Sciences, Monterey, CA, USA, ieeelife@yahoo.com

Bernhard Steffen Chair Programming Systems, TU Dortmund, Dortmund, Germany, steffen@cs.tu-dortmund.de

Roy Sterritt School of Computing and Mathematics, University of Ulster, Newtownabbey, Northern Ireland, r.sterritt@ulster.ac.uk

Giordano Tamburrelli DeepSE Group @ DEI, Politecnico di Milano, Milan, Italy, tamburrelli@elet.polimi.it

Walter F. Truszkowski NASA Goddard Space Flight Center, Emeritus Greenbelt, MD, USA, walter.f.truszkowski@nasa.gov

Vânia M.P. Vidal Department of Computing, Federal University of Ceará, Fortaleza, CE, Brazil, vvidal@lia.ufc.br

Alan Wassyng McMaster University, Hamilton, ON, Canada, wassyng@mcmaster.ca

Kun Wei Department of Computer Science, University of York, York, UK, kun@cs.york.ac.uk

Jim Woodcock Department of Computer Science, University of York, York, UK, jim@cs.york.ac.uk

Abbreviations

ABAP	Advanced Business Application Programming
ACM	Association for Computing Machinery
ADL	Architecture Description Language
ADT	Abstract Data Type
AE	Autonomic Element
ANS	Autonomic Nervous System
ANTS	Autonomous Nano-Technology Swarm
AOP	Aspect Oriented Programming
AOSE	Agent-Oriented Software Engineering
APEX	Adaptive Planning and Execution
API	Application Programming Interface
AUML	Agent UML
BAPI	Business Application Programming Interface
BB	Black-Box
BOR	Business Object Repository
BP	Business Process
BPEL	Business Process Execution Language
BPM	Business Process Management
BPMS	Business Process Management System
CACM	Communications of the ACM
CAS	Complex Adaptive System
CASE	Computer-Aided Software Engineering
CBD	Component-Based Development
CCF	Common Cause Failure
CCFDB	Common-Cause Failure Data Base
CE	Capabilities Engineering
CMDA	Cougaar Model-Driven Architecture
COM	Computation Independent Model
COP	Common Operating Picture
CORBA	Common Object Request Broker Architecture
COTS	Component Off The Shelf

CPR	Core Plan Representation
CSP	Communicating Sequential Processes
CTMCs	Continuous Time Markov Chains
DARPA	Defense Advanced Research Projects Agency
DoD	Department of Defense
DL	Description Logic
DSL	Domain Specific Language
DST	Decision Support Tool
DTMCs	Discrete Time Markov Chains
EDAM	EMBRACE Ontology for Data and Methods
EMBRACE	European Model for Bioinformatics Research and Community Education
EMBOSS	European Molecular Biology Open Software Suite
EMF	Encore Modelling Language
ER	Entity-Relationship
ERP	Enterprise Resource Planning
FAST	Formal Approaches to Swarm Technologies
FD	Function Decomposition
FLG	Feature Level Graph
FDR	Failures-Divergences Refinement
FIFO	First In First Out
FPGA	Field-Programmable Gate Array
GB	Grey-Box
GCAM	General Cougaar Application Model
GCME	Graphical Cougaar Model Editor
GDAM	General Domain Application Model
GEF	Graphical Editing Framework
GPAC	General-Purpose Autonomic Computing
GRASP	General Responsibility Assignment Software Patterns
GUI	Graphical User Interface
HITL	Human In The Loop
HOL	Higher Order Logic
HPRC	High-Performance Reconfigurable Computing
HRSM	Hubble Robotic Servicing Mission
IEC	International Electrotechnical Commission
IEEE	Institute of Electrical and Electronics Engineers
IP	Intellectual Property
IT	Information Technology
IWIM	Idealised Worked Idealised Manager
jABC	Java Application Building Centre
JC3IEDM	Joint Consultation, Command and Control Information Exchange Data Model
JDBC	Java Database Connectivity
JDL	Joint Directors of Laboratories
JET	Java Emitter

jETI	Java Electronic Tool Integration Platform
JVM	Java Virtual Machine
JMS	Java Message Service
KLOC	Thousand (k) Lines of Code
LARA	Lunar Base Activities
LOC	Lines of Code
LOGOS	Lights-Out Ground Operating System
MAPE	Monitor-Analyse-Plan-Execute
MAS	Multi-Agent System
MBE	Model-Based Engineering
MBEF-HPRC	Model-Based Engineering Framework for High-Performance Reconfigurable Computing
MBSE	Model-Based Software Engineering
MDA	Model-Driven Architecture
MDD	Model-Driven Development
MDPs	Markov Decision Processes
MDSD	Model-Driven Software Development
MGS	Mars Global Surveyor
MIL	Module Interconnection Language
MIP	Multilateral Interoperablity Programme
MLM	Military Logistics Model
MPS	Meta Programming System
MOF	Meta Object Facility
MTBF	Mean-Time Between Failure
NASA	National Aeronautics and Space Administration
NATO	North Atlantic Treaty Organisation
NOS	Network Object Space
OASIS	Organisation for the Advancement of Structured Information Standards
OCL	Object Constraint Language
OMG	Object Management Group
OO	Object-Oriented
OOP	Object-Oriented Programming
OOram	Object Oriented Role Analysis and Modelling
OSMA	NASA Office of Systems and Mission Assurance
OTA	One-Thing Approach
OWL	Web Ontology Language
PAM	Prospecting Asteroid Mission
PARSY	Performance Aware Reconfiguration of software SYstems
PCTL	Probabilistic Computation Tree Logic
PDA	Personal Digital Assistant
PIM	Platform Independent Model
PLD	Programmable Logic Device
PSM	Platform Specific Model
PTCTL	Probabilistic Timed Computation Tree Logic

PVS	Prototype Verification System
QNs	Queueing Networks
QoS	Quality of Service
QSAR	Quantitative Structure Activity Relationships
R2D2C	Requirements-to-Design-to-Code
RC	Reconfigurable Computing
RFC	Remote Function Call
RMI	Remote Method Invocation
RPC	Remote Procedure Call
RSL	RAISE Specification Language
SASSY	Self-Architecting Software SYstems
SBS	Service-Based Systems
SC	Situation Construct
SCA	Service Component Architecture
SCADA	Supervisory Control and Data Acquisition
SDE	Shared Data Environment
SDR	Software-Defined Radio
SIB	Service-Independent Building block
SLA	Service Level Agreement
SLG	Service Level Graph
SNA	Social Networking Application
SNS	Semantic Network Space
SOAP	Simple Object Access Protocol
SOA	Service-Oriented Architecture
SOC	Service-Oriented Computing
SOS	Situational Object Space
SRF	Situational Reasoning Framework
SRML	SENSORIA Reference Modelling Language
SSA	Shared Situational Awareness
SWS	Semantic Web Service
TA	TeleAssistence
TCO	Total Cost of Ownership
TCTL	Timed Computation Tree Logic
$TCSP_M$	Timed CSP with the Miracle
UID	Unique Object Identifier
UML	Unified Modelling Language
URL	Uniform Resource Locator
UTP	Unifying Theories of Programming
VDM	Vienna Development Method
VHDL	VHSIC hardware description language
VLSI	Very-Large-Scale Integration
W3C	World Wide Web Consortium
WB	White-Box
WBS	White-Box Shared
WSDL	Web Service Definition Language

xADL	Extensible Architecture Description Language
XMDD	Extreme Model-Driven Development
XMI	XML Metadata Interchange
XML	Extensible Markup Language
XP	Extreme Programming
XPDL	XML Process Definition Language
3GL	Third Generation Languages

Part I
Recognizing Complexity

Chapter 1
The Many Faces of Complexity in Software Design

José Luiz Fiadeiro

1.1 Introduction

Complexity, not in the formal sense of the theory of algorithms or complexity science, but in the more current meaning of "the state or quality of being intricate or complicated", seems to be unavoidably associated with software. A few quotes from the press over the last 10 years illustrate the point:

- *The Economist*, 12/04/2001—In an article aptly called "The beast of complexity", Stuart Feldman, then director of IBM's Institute for Advanced Commerce, is quoted to say that programming was "all about suffering from ever-increasing complexity"
- *The Economist*, 08/05/2003—A survey of the IT industry acknowledges that "computing has certainly got faster, smarter and cheaper, but it has also become much more complex"
- *Financial Times*, 27/11/2004—The British government's chief information officer gives the following explanation for the Child Support Agency IT project failure: "Where there's complexity, there will, from time to time, be problems"
- *The Economist*, 06/09/2007—In an article called "The trouble with computers", Steven Kyffin, then senior researcher at Philips, is quote to concede that computer programmers and engineers are "compelled by complexity"
- *Financial Times*, 27/01/2009—"It is very easy to look at the IT industry and conclude that it is fatally attracted to complexity"

But why are we so bothered about complexity? The following quote from the Financial Times of 27/01/2009 summarises the point quite effectively:

Complexity is the enemy of flexibility. It entangles us in unintended consequences. It blocks our attempts to change. It hides potential defects, making it impossible to be sure our systems will function correctly. Performance, transparency, security—all these highly desirable attributes leak away in the face of increasing complexity.

J.L. Fiadeiro (✉)
Department of Computer Science, University of Leicester, Leicester, UK
e-mail: jose@mcs.le.ac.uk

M. Hinchey, L. Coyle (eds.), *Conquering Complexity*,
DOI 10.1007/978-1-4471-2297-5_1, © Springer-Verlag London Limited 2012

In this chapter, we argue that, although the public in general would readily accept that software is 'complicated', complexity in the sense of the quotes above has lurked under many guises since the early days of programming and software engineering, which explains why software seems to be in a permanent 'crisis'. We also discuss the ways that we, computer scientists, have been devising to tackle "the beast of complexity", which we classify into two main activities: abstraction and decomposition.

1.1.1 Abstraction

Abstraction is an activity that all of us perform on a daily basis without necessarily realising so. Abstraction is one of the ways we use to go around the complexity of the world we live in and simplify the way we interact with each other, organisations, systems, and so on.

Bank accounts provide a rich and mundane example of the way we use abstraction, as the following 'story' illustrates. In "A Visit to the Bank", Paddington Bear goes to Floyds Bank to withdraw money for his holiday. He decides to leave the interest in for a rainy day but is horrified to learn that it only amounts to three pence. Tension mounts when he finds out that he cannot have back the very same notes that he deposited in the first place: he knew perfectly well that he had spilled marmalade over them...

We (or most of us) have learnt that an account is not a physical storage of bank notes that we manipulate through the cashier just as we would do with a safe box or a piggy bank. However, the advantages (and dangers?) of working with bank accounts as abstractions over the physical manipulation of currency are not restricted to avoiding handling sticky bank notes (or other forms of 'laundering'). Indeed, a bank account is not (just) a way of organising the storage of money, but of our business interactions: it solves a good part of the complexity involved in business transactions by decoupling our ability to trade from the manipulation of physical bank notes.

Much the same can be said about the way we use computers. Abstraction pervades computing and much of the history of computer science concerns precisely the development of abstractions through which humans can make full usage of the (computational) power made available by the machines we call computers by tackling the complexity of programming them. In the words of Peter Denning [16]:

> Most computing professionals do not appreciate how abstract our field appears to others. We have become so good at defining and manipulating abstractions that we hardly notice how skilfully we create abstract 'objects', which upon deployment in a computer perform useful actions.

Paddington's view of his bank account may make us smile because these are abstractions that we have learnt to live with a long time ago. However when, not long ago, we tried to organise a transfer from Leicester to Lisbon, it turned out that providing the clerk with the SWIFT and IBAN codes was not sufficient and that a full postal address was indispensable. (No, this was not at Floyds Bank but a major high-street bank in the UK.) What is more, when given a post code that, for some reason, did not look credible enough to his eyes, the clerk refused to go ahead with the transfer on the grounds that "the money might get lost in the post"...

This example from 'real life' shows that the fact that abstraction is such a routine activity does not mean that we are all equally and well prepared to perform it in a 'professional' way—see [47] for a discussion on how abstraction skills in computer science require education and training. The following paragraph from the 27/01/2009 article of the Financial Times quoted above can help us understand how abstraction relates to complexity:

> Most engineers are pretty bright people. They can tolerate a lot of complexity and gain a certain type of power by building systems that flaunt it. If only we could get them to focus their intellect instead on eliminating it. The problem with this message is that, for all our best efforts, we almost never eliminate complexity. Most of the time, when we create a system that appears simple, what we have actually done is shift the complexity somewhere else in the technology stack.

Indeed, operating systems, compilers and, more recently, all sorts of 'clever' middleware support the layers of abstraction that allow us to program software systems without manipulating directly the code that the machine actually understands (and we, nowadays, rarely do). The current emphasis on model-driven development is another example of this process of abstraction, this time in relation to programming languages, avoiding that IT specialists spread marmalade over lines of code...

Why is it then that, in spite of phenomenal progress in computer science for at least three decades, which the quote from P. Denning acknowledges, is complexity still haunting software as evidenced by the articles cited at the beginning of this section? Expanding the quote from the 08/05/2003 edition of The Economist:

> Computing has certainly got faster, smarter and cheaper, but it has also become much more complex. Ever since the orderly days of the mainframe, which allowed tight control of IT, computer systems have become ever more distributed, more heterogeneous and harder to manage. [...] In the late 1990s, the internet and the emergence of e-commerce "broke IT's back". Integrating incompatible systems, in particular, has become a big headache. A measure of this increasing complexity is the rapid growth in the IT services industry. [...]

What is the significance of the internet to the complexity of software? In this chapter, we will be arguing that the reason for the persistence of the 'complexity crisis' is in the change of the nature of complexity, meaning that programming and software engineering methodology often lags behind advances in more technological areas (such as the internet) and, therefore, fails to develop new abstractions that can be used for tackling the complexity of the systems that are being built.

1.1.2 Decomposition

Although we started this chapter with quotes that have appeared in the press during the last 10 years, the threat of complexity was the topic of a famous article published in the Scientific American 10 years before that, in 1994, following on the debacle of the Dallas international airport baggage handling system—glitches in the software controlling the shunting of luggage forced the airport to sit empty for nine months:

> The challenge of complexity is not only large but also growing. [...] When a system becomes so complex that no one manager can comprehend the entirety, traditional development processes break down. [...] To keep up with such demand, programmers will have to change the way that they work. [...] Software parts can, if properly standardised, be reused at many different scales. [...] In April [1994], NIST announced that it was creating an Advanced Technology Program to help engender a market for component-based software.

Nothing very surprising, one could say. Indeed, another way of managing complexity that we use in our day to day is embedded in the Cartesian principle of divide and conquer—breaking a complicated problem down into parts that are easier to solve, and then build a solution to the whole by composing the solutions to the parts.

The literature on component-based software development (CBD) is vast (e.g., [10, 15]). Therefore, what happened to component-based software if, according to the sources quoted by The Economist in 08/05/2003, the challenge of complexity was still growing in 2003? A couple of years later, an article in the 26-01-2005 edition of the Financial Times reported:

> "This is the industrial revolution for software," says Toby Redshaw, vice-president of information technology strategy at Motorola, the US electronics group. He is talking about the rise of service oriented architectures (SOAs) a method of building IT systems that relies not on big, integrated programs but on small, modular components.

"Small, modular components"? How is this different from the promise reported in the Scientific American? What is even more intriguing is that the article in the Scientific American appeared almost 20 years after Frank DeRemer and Hans H. Kron wrote [17]:

> We distinguish the activity of writing large programs from that of writing small ones. By large programs we mean systems consisting of many small programs (modules), possibly written by different people.[...] We argue that structuring a large collection of modules to form a 'system' is an essentially distinct and different intellectual activity from that of constructing the individual modules.

Why didn't these modules fit the bill given that, in 1994, component-based software was being hailed as the way out of complexity? DeRemer and Kron's article itself appeared eight years after the term 'software crisis' was coined at the famous 1968 NATO conference in Garmisch-Partenkirschen which Douglas McIlroy's addressed with a talk on Mass Produced Software Components.

Given that, today, we are still talking about 'the crisis' and 'components' as a means of handling complexity, did anything change during more than 40 years? As argued in the previous subsection, our view is that it is essentially the nature of the crisis that has been changing, prompting for different forms of decomposition and, therefore, different notions of 'component'. Whereas this seems totally uncontroversial, the problem is that it is often difficult to understand what exactly has changed and, therefore, what new abstractions and decomposition methods are required. For example, the fact that component-based development is now a well-established discipline in software engineering makes it harder to argue for different notions of component. This difficulty is well apparent in the current debate around service-oriented computing.

The purpose of this chapter is to discuss the nature of complexity as it arises in software design, review the progress that we have achieved in coping with it through abstractions and decomposition techniques, and identify some of the challenges that still remain. Parts of the chapter have already been presented at conferences or colloquia [21–24]. The feedback received on those publications has been incorporated in this extended paper. Sections 1.2, 1.3 and 1.4 cover three different kinds of programming or software design— 'programming in-the-small', 'programming in-the-large' and 'programming in-the-many', respectively. Whereas the first two have been part of the computer science jargon for many years, the third is not so well established. We borrow it from Nenad Medvidović [53] to represent a different approach to decomposition that promotes *connectors* to the same status as *components* (which are core to programming in-the-large) as first-class elements in software architectures [65]. Section 1.5 covers service-oriented computing and contains results from our own recent research [26, 27, 29], therefore presenting a more personal view of an area that is not yet fully mature.

The chapter is not very technical and does not attempt to provide an in-depth analysis of any of the aspects that are covered—several chapters of this volume fulfil that purpose.

1.2 Programming In-the-small

The term programming in-the-small was first used by DeRemer and Kron [17] to differentiate between the activity of writing 'small' programs from those that, because of their size, are best decomposed into smaller ones, possibly written by different people using programming-in-the-small techniques. To use an example that relates to current programming practice, writing the code that implements a method in any object-oriented language or a web service would be considered as programming in-the-small.

Precisely because they are 'small', discussing such programs allows us to illustrate some of the aspects of complexity in software development that do not relate to size. For example, the earlier and more common abstractions that we use in programming relate to the need for separating the software from the machine that runs it. This need arises from the fact that programming in machine code is laborious (some would say complicated, even complex). The separation between program and code executable on a particular computer is supported by machine-independent programming languages and compilers. This separation consists of an abstraction step in which the program written by the programmer is seen as a higher-level abstraction of the code that runs on the machine.

High-level programming languages operate two important abstractions in relation to machine code: control execution and memory. Introduced by E. Dijkstra in the 70s [18], structured programming promoted abstractions for handling the complexity of controlling the flow of execution; until then, control flow was largely defined in terms of *goto* statements that transferred execution to a label in the program text, which meant that, to understand how a program executed, one had to chase goto's across the text and, inevitably, would end tangled up in complex control flows (hence the term 'spaghetti' code). The three main abstractions are well known to all programmers today—sequence, selection, and repetition. As primitives of a (high-level) programming language, they transformed programs from line-oriented to command-oriented structures, opening the way to formal techniques for analysing program correctness.

Another crucial aspect of this abstraction process is the ability to work with data structures that do not necessarily mirror the organisation of the memory of the machine in which the code will run. This process can be taken even further by allowing the data structures to reflect the organisation of the solution to the problem. This combination of executional and data abstraction was exploited in methodologies such as JSP—Jackson Structured Programming [42]—that operate a top-down decomposition approach. The components associated with such a decomposition approach stand for blocks of code that are put together according to the executional abstractions of structured programming (sequential composition, selection and iteration). Each component is then developed in the same way, independently of the other components. The criteria for decomposition derive from the structure of the data manipulated by the program.

JSP had its own graphical notation, which we illustrate in Fig. 1.1 for a run-length encoder—a program that takes as input a stream of bytes and outputs a stream of pairs consisting of a byte along with a count of the byte's consecutive occurrences in the input stream. This JSP-diagram includes, at the top level, a box that represents the whole program—*Encode run lengths*. The program is identified as an iteration of an operation—*Encode run length*—that encodes the length of each run as it is read from the input. The input is a stream of bytes that can be viewed as zero or more runs, each run consisting of one or more bytes of the same value. The fact that the program is an iteration is indicated by the symbol * in the right hand corner of the corresponding box. This operation is itself identified as the sequential composition of four more elementary components. This is indicated by the sequence of boxes that decompose *Encode run length*. The second of these boxes—*Count remaining bytes*—is itself an iteration of an operation—*Count remaining byte*—that counts bytes.

An advantage of structured programming is that it simplifies formal verification of program correctness from specifications, for example through what is known as the Hoare calculus [40] (see also [39, 59]). Typically, we consider a specification to be a pair $[p, q]$ of state conditions.[1] A program satisfies such a specification if,

---

[1] A frame—the set of variables whose values may change during the execution of the program—can be added as in [59]. For simplicity, we only consider partial correctness in this chapter; techniques for proving that the program terminates, leading to total correctness, also exist [39, 59].

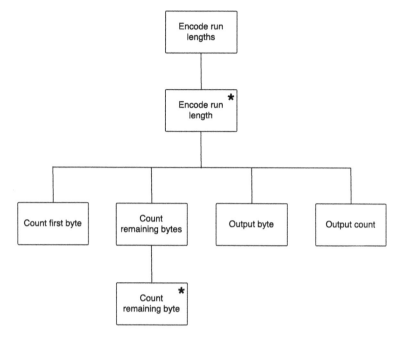

Fig. 1.1 Example of a JSP-diagram

Fig. 1.2 A program module

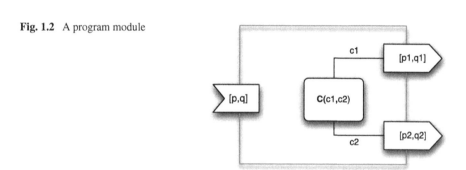

whenever its execution starts in a state that satisfies p (called the 'pre-condition') and terminates, the final state satisfies q (called the 'post-condition').

In order to illustrate how, together with the Hoare calculus, we can define a notion of 'module' (or component) through which we can define a compositional (bottom-up) approach to program construction, we introduce another graphical notation that we will use in other sections to illustrate similar points in other contexts.

An example of what we will call a program module is given in Fig. 1.2. Its meaning is that if, in the program expression $C(c1, c2)$, we bind $c1$ to a program that satisfies the specification $[p1, q1]$ and $c2$ to a program that satisfies the specification $[p2, q2]$, then we obtain a program that satisfies the specification $[p, q]$.

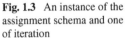

Fig. 1.3 An instance of the
assignment schema and one
of iteration

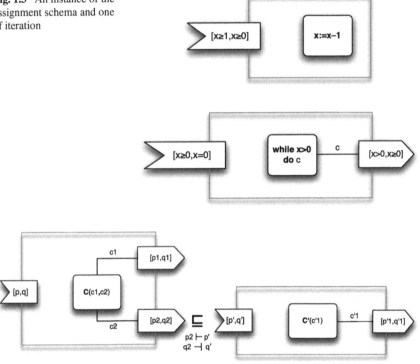

Fig. 1.4 Binding two modules

One can identify $[p, q]$ with the interface that is *provided* by the module, and $[p1, q1]$ and $[p2, q2]$ with those of 'components' that are *required* by the module so that, upon binding, the expression forms a program that meets the specification $[p, q]$. Notice that the module does not need to know the inner workings of the components that implement $[p1, q1]$ and $[p2, q2]$ in order to make use of them, thus enforcing a form of encapsulation.

Using this notation, we can define a number of module schemas that capture the rules of the Hoare calculus and, therefore, define the basic building blocks for constructing more complex programs. In the Appendix (Fig. 1.30) we give the schemas that correspond to assignments, sequence, iteration, and selection. Two instances of those schemas are presented in Fig. 1.3: one for assignment and one for iteration.

Modules can be composed by binding a requires-interface of one module with the provides-interface of another. Binding is subject to the rules of *refinement* [59]: $[p, q] \sqsubseteq [p', q']$ iff $p' \dashv p$ and $q' \vdash q$. That is, $[p', q']$ refines $[p, q]$ if its precondition p' is weaker than p and its post-condition q' is stronger than q. This is illustrated in Fig. 1.4.

The result of the binding is illustrated in Fig. 1.5: the body of the right-hand-side module is used to (partially) instantiate the program expression of the left-hand-side module; the resulting module has the same provides-interface as the left-hand-side

Fig. 1.5 The result of the binding in Fig. 1.4

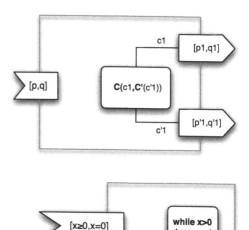

Fig. 1.6 The result of binding the modules in Fig. 1.3

module, and keeps the unused requires-interface of the left-hand-side module and the requires-interface of the right-hand-side module. A concrete example is given in Fig. 1.6 for the binding of the two modules depicted in Fig. 1.3 (notice that, x being an integer program variable, the condition $x > 0$ entails $x \geq 1$).

These notions of program module and binding are, in a sense, a reformulation of structured programming intended to bring out the building blocks or component structure that results from the executional abstractions. Notice that, through those modules, it is the program as a syntactic expression that is being structured, not the executable code: there is encapsulation with respect to the specifications as argued above—the interface (specification) provided by a module derives only from the interfaces (specifications) of the required program parts—but not with respect to the executable code: in the second module in Fig. 1.3, one cannot reuse code generated for c to generate code for *while $x > 0$ do c*. Other programming abstractions exist that allow for code to be reused, such as procedures.

Procedural abstractions are indeed a way of developing resources that can be reused in the process of programming an application. Resources can be added to program modules through what we would call a uses-interface. Examples are given in Fig. 1.7, which correspond to two of the schemas discussed in [59] (see also [39]): one for substitution by value and the other for substitution by result. Uses-interfaces are different from requires-interfaces in the sense that they are preserved through composition, i.e., there is no syntactic substitution like in binding. Like before, the module does not need to know the body of the procedure in order to make use of it, just the specification, thus enforcing a form of encapsulation.

JSP-diagrams can be viewed as providing an architectural view (*avant la lettre*, as the notion of software architecture emerged only much later) of programs. To make the connection with other architectural views reviewed in later sections of this chapter, it is interesting to notice JSP-diagrams can be combined with the notion

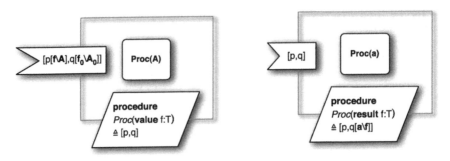

Fig. 1.7 Two schemas for procedural abstraction (see [59] for details). By A_0 we denote the value of the expression A before the execution of the command (procedure call)

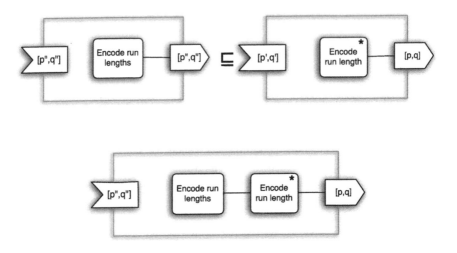

Fig. 1.8 Building JSP-diagrams through program-module composition

of program module that we defined above. Essentially, we can replace the syntactic expressions inside the modules by JSP-diagrams as illustrated in Fig. 1.8. Binding expands the architecture so that, as modules are combined, the JSP-architecture of the program is built.

1.3 Programming In-the-large

1.3.1 Modules and Module Interconnection Languages

Whereas the program modules and JSP-diagrams discussed in the previous section address the complexity of understanding or developing (correct) executional structures, they do not address the complexity that arises from the size of programs (measured in terms of lines of code). This is why the distinction between programming in-the-small and programming in-the-large was introduced in [17]:

> By large programs we mean systems consisting of many small programs (modules), possibly written by different people. We need languages for programming-in-the-small, i.e., languages not unlike the common programming languages of today, for writing modules. We also need a "module interconnection language" for knitting those modules together into an integrated whole and for providing an overview that formally records the intent of the programmer(s) and that can be checked for consistency by a compiler.

Notice that, as made clear by the quote, the term programming in-the-small is not derogatory: 'small' programs whose correctness can be formally proved will always play an essential role in building 'large' software applications that we can trust to operate safely in mission-critical systems (from avionics to power plants to healthcare, *inter alia*). The problem arising at the time was that, as the scope and role of software in business grew, so did the size of programs: software applications were demanded to perform more and more tasks in all sorts of domains, growing very quickly into millions of lines of code. Sheer size compromised quality: delivery times started to suffer and so did performance and correctness due to the fact that applications became unmanageable for the lone programmer.

To address this problem, programming in-the-large offered a form of decomposition that addressed the global structure of a software application in terms of what its modules and resources are and how they fit together in the system. The main difference with respect to programming in-the-small is in the fact that one is interested not in structuring the *computational* process, but the *software-construction* (and evolution) process.[2] Hence, the resulting components (modules) are interconnected not to ensure that the computation progresses towards the required *final state* (or postcondition, or output), but that, in the *final application*, all modules are provided with the resources they need (e.g., the parsing module of a compiler is connected to the symbol table). In other words, it is the flow of resources among modules, not of control, that is of concern.

The conclusions of Parnas' landmark paper [61] are even clearer in this respect:

> [...] it is almost always incorrect to begin the decomposition of a system into modules on the basis of a flowchart. We propose instead that one begins with a list of difficult design decisions or design decisions which are likely to change. Each module is then designed to hide such a decision from the others. Since, in most cases, design decisions transcend time of execution, modules will not correspond to steps in the processing. To achieve an efficient implementation we must abandon the assumption that a module is one or more sub-routines, and instead allow subroutines and programs to be assembled collections of code from various modules.

That is to say, we cannot hope and should not attempt to address the complexity of software systems as products with the mechanisms that were developed for structuring complex computations. That is why so-called module interconnection

---

[2]Procedural abstractions, as mentioned at the end of Sect. 1.2, do offer a way of simplifying program construction by naming given pieces of program text that would need to be repeated several times, but they are not powerful enough for the coarse-grained modularity required for programming in-the-large.

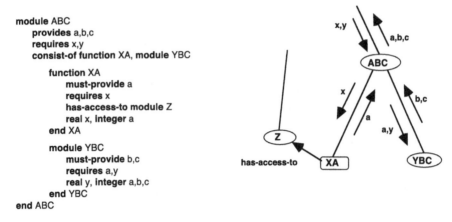

```
module ABC
    provides a,b,c
    requires x,y
    consist-of function XA, module YBC

        function XA
            must-provide a
            requires x
            has-access-to module Z
            real x, integer a
        end XA
        module YBC
            must-provide b,c
            requires a,y
            real y, integer a,b,c
        end YBC
end ABC
```

Fig. 1.9 An example of a MIL description taken from [62]

languages (MILs) were developed for programming in-the-large [62]. Indeed, the quote from [17] makes clear that the nature of the abstraction process associated with programming in-the-large is such that one can rely on a compiler to link all the modules together as intended by the programmer(s). Hence, MILs offered primitives such as *export/provide/originate* and *import/require/use* when designing individual modules at the abstract level so as to express the dependencies that would need to be taken into account at the lower level when "knitting the modules together".

Module-interconnection structures are essential for project management, namely for testing and maintenance support: they enforce system integrity and inter-module compatibility; they support incremental modification as modules can be independently compiled and linked, and thus full recompilation of a modified system is not needed; and they enforce version control as different versions (implementations) of a module can be identified and used in the construction of a system. Figure 1.9 illustrates the kind of architecture that is described in such languages. The dependencies between components concern access to and usage of resources.

In order to illustrate how notions of module can be formalised, we use a very simple example in which modules consist of procedures, variables and variable initialisations (similar to [59][3]). Procedures can be abstract in the sense that they are not provided with a fully-developed body (code). Some of those procedures or variables are exported and some are imported (imported procedures are abstract); the interface of the module consists of the specifications of exported and imported resources. An example, also borrowed from [59], is given in Fig. 1.10 where frames are added to pre-/post-condition specifications.

[3]Notions of module were made available in the wave of programming languages that, such as Modula-2 [70], followed from structured programming.

Fig. 1.10 Example of a
module borrowed from [59]

module *Tag*
   export *Acquire, Return;*
   import *Choose;*

   var u : set $\mathbb{N}$;

   procedure *Acquire* (**result** $t : \mathbb{N}$)
   $\,\hat{=}\,$ *Choose* $(\mathbb{N} - u, t)$;
     $u := u \cup \{t\}$

   procedure *Return* (**value** $t : \mathbb{N}$)
   $\,\hat{=}\, u := u - \{t\}$;

   procedure *Choose* (**value** s : set $\mathbb{N}$; **result** $e : \mathbb{N}$)
   $\,\hat{=}\, e: [s \neq \{\} ,\ e \in s]$;

   initially $u = \{\}$
end

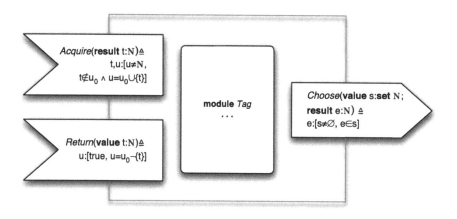

Fig. 1.11 An interface for the module in Fig. 1.10

Using a diagrammatic notation similar to that used in Sect. 1.2, we could represent the module *Tag* and its interface as in Fig. 1.11. We say that a module is *correct* if, assuming that resources (e.g., a procedure *Choose*) are provided that satisfy the specifications that label the import-interfaces, the body of the module (e.g., *Tag*) implements resources (e.g., procedures *Acquire* and *Return*) that satisfy the specifications that label the export-interfaces.

Binding two such modules together consists in identifying in one module some of the resources required by the other. This process of identification needs to obey certain rules, namely that the specification that labels the export-interface of one module refines the specification of the import-interface of the other module. This is illustrated in Fig. 1.12 where the specification of *Choose* is refined by that of *Pick* (*Pick* will accept a set of natural numbers and return a natural number).

Typically, in MILs, the result of the binding is a configuration as depicted in Fig. 1.13. In our case, the edge identifies the particular resource that is being imported. In MILs, the link is represented by a direct reference made in the code inside the module (which is interpreted by the compiler as an instruction to link the corresponding implementations) and, in diagrams, the edge may be used to represent other kinds of relationships as illustrated in Fig. 1.9. Notice the similarity with the program modules defined in Sect. 1.2 where binding defines an operation over JSP-diagrams, which we can identify with program configurations (or architectures). The difference between the two notions is that MILs do not operate at the level of control structures (as JSP-diagrams do) but organisational ones.

Another important aspect of modules is reuse, which can be supported by a notion of refinement between modules. In the case of our example, and following [59] once again, we say that a refinement of a module $\langle Exp, Imp, Loc, Init \rangle$—where *Exp*, *Imp* and *Loc* stand for the sets of exported, imported and local resources, respectively, and *Init* is an initialisation command—by another module $\langle Exp', Imp', Loc', Init' \rangle$ consists of two injective functions $exp : Exp \to Exp'$ and $imp : Imp \to Imp' \cup Loc'$ such that, for every $e \in Exp$ (resp. $i \in Imp$), $e \sqsubseteq exp(e)$ (resp. $imp(i) \sqsubseteq i$), and $init \sqsubseteq init'$. Notice that exported interfaces of the refined module can promise more (i.e., they refine the original exported resources) but the imported interfaces of the original module cannot require less (i.e., they refine the corresponding resources in the refined module). Moreover, imported resources of the original module can be mapped to local resources of the refined one.

1.3.2 Object-Oriented Programming

Object-oriented programming (OOP)[4] can be seen to define a specific criterion for modularising code: objects group together around methods (variables, functions, and procedures) all the operations that are allowed on a given piece of the system state—"Object-oriented software construction is the software development method which bases the architecture of any software system on modules deduced from the types of objects it manipulates (rather than the function or functions that the system is intended to ensure)" [56].

This form of state encapsulation offers a mechanism of data abstraction in the sense that what is offered through an object interface is a collection of operations that hide the representation of the data that they manipulate. This abstraction mechanism is associated with so-called abstract data types [49]—"Object-oriented software construction is the building of software systems as structured collections of possibly partial abstract data type implementations" [56].

---

[4]We follow Meyer [56] throughout most of this section and recommend it for further reading not just on object-oriented programming but modularity in software construction as well.

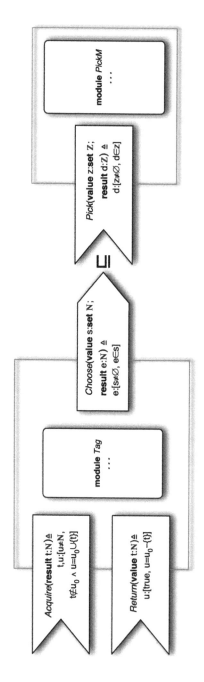

Fig. 1.12   Binding modules through refinement

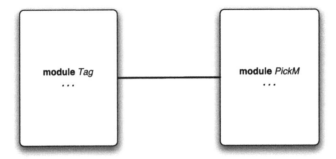

Fig. 1.13 Linking modules

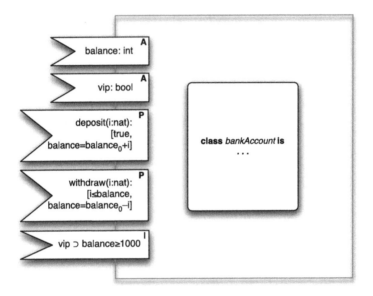

Fig. 1.14 The interface of the class *bankAccount*

In OOP, modules are classes. A class interface consists of the specifications associated with the features that it provides to clients—attributes (A), functions (F),
or procedures (P)—and a set of invariants (I) that apply to all the objects of the
class. A class is correct with respect to its interface if the implementations of the
features satisfy their specifications and the execution of the routines (functions or
procedures) maintains the invariants. An example, using a diagrammatic notation
similar to the one used in previous sections, is given in Fig. 1.14.

As modules, classes do not include an explicit import/require interface mechanism similar to the previous examples, which begs the question: how can modules be interconnected? OOP does provide a mechanism for interconnecting objects:
clientship—an object can be a client of another object by declaring an attribute (or

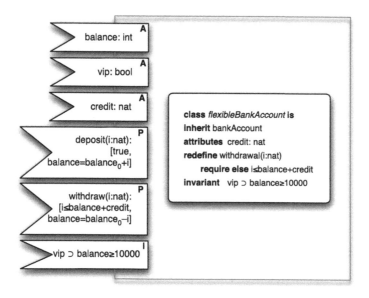

Fig. 1.15   The interface of the class *flexibleBankAccount*, which inherits from *bankAccount*

function) whose type is an object class; methods of the client can then invoke the features of the server as part of their code.[5] For example, *bankAccount* could be a client of a class *customer* through an attribute *owner* and invoke *owner.addDeposit(i)* as part of the code that executes *deposit(i)* so as to store the accumulated deposits that customers make on all the accounts that they own.

The difference in relation to an import (or required) interface is that clientship is programmed in the code that implements the classes, not established through an external interconnection language. In a sense, clientship is a more sophisticated form of procedure invocation in which the code to be executed is identified by means of a pointer variable. That is, clientship is essentially an executional abstraction in the sense of programming in-the-small.

Classes do offer some 'in-the-large' mechanisms (and therefore behave as modules) through the mechanism of *inheritance*. Inheritance makes it possible for new classes to be defined by adding new features to, or re-defining features of, existing classes. This mechanism is controlled by two important restrictions: extension of the set of features is constrained by the need to maintain the invariants of the source class; redefinition is constrained by the need to refine the specifications of the features. An example of a class built by inheriting from *bankAccount* is given in Fig. 1.15. These restrictions are important for supporting dynamic binding and polymorphism, which are run-time architectural techniques that are typically ab-

---

[5]Import statements can be found in OOP languages such as Java, but they are used in conjunction with packages in order to locate the classes of which a given class is a client.

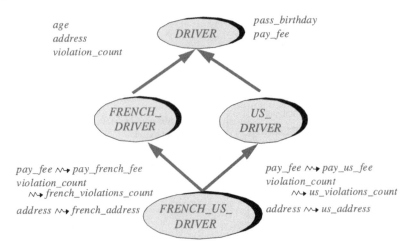

Fig. 1.16 An example of repeated inheritance borrowed from [56]

sent from MILs (where binding is essentially static, i.e., performed at compile time).

Formally, inheritance can be defined as a mapping ρ between the interfaces of the two classes, say $\langle A, F, R, I \rangle$ and $\langle A', F', R', I' \rangle$, such that

1. for every routine $r : [p, q] \in F \cup R$, if $\rho(r) : [p', q']$ then
   a. $p' \dashv \rho(p)$
   b. $q' \vdash \rho(p_0) \supset \rho(q)$
2. $I' \vdash \rho(I)$

Notice that the first condition is a variation on the notion of refinement used in Sect. 1.2 in which the post-condition of the redefined routine needs to imply the original post-condition only when the original pre-condition held before execution. On the other hand, the original invariant cannot be weakened (it needs to be implied by the new one). Together, these conditions ensure that an instance of the refined class can be used where an instance of the original class was expected. Notice the similarity between this formalisation of inheritance and that of module refinement discussed in Sect. 1.3.1.

Multiple and repeated inheritance offer a good example of another operation on modules: composition, not in the sense of binding as illustrated previously, but on building larger modules from simpler ones. An example of repeated inheritance (copied from [56]) is shown in Fig. 1.16: repeatedly inherited features that are not meant to be shared (for example, *address*) need to be renamed.

Formally, repeated inheritance can be defined over a pair of inclusions $C_1 \overset{l_1}{\leftarrow} C \overset{l_2}{\rightarrow} C_2$ between sets of features (inheritance arrows usually point in the reverse direction of the mappings between features) where C contains the features that are meant to be shared between C_1 and C_2; these inclusions give rise to another pair of mappings $C_1 \overset{\rho_1}{\rightarrow} C' \overset{\rho_2}{\leftarrow} C_2$ that define an amalgamated union of the original pair. An amalgamated union is an operation on sets and functions that renames the features of C_1 and C_2 that are not included in C when calculating their union. In relation to the specifications of the shared routines, i.e., routines $r' : [p', q'] \in F' \cup R'$ such that there is $r \in F \cup R$ with $r' = \rho_1(\iota_1(r)) = \rho_2(\iota_2(r))$, we obtain:

1. $p' = \rho_1(p_1) \vee \rho_2(p_2)$
2. $q' = \rho_1(p_{1_0} \supset q_1) \wedge \rho_2(p_{2_0} \supset q_2)$

where $\iota_n(r) : [p_n, q_n]$. These are the combined pre-/post-condition rules of Eiffel, which give the semantics of interface composition.

The reason we detailed these constructions is that they allow us to discuss the mathematical semantics of refinement (including inheritance) and composition. We have already seen that logic plays an essential role in the definition of specifications and refinement or inheritance. Composition (in the sense of repeated inheritance) can be supported by category theory, a branch of mathematics in which notions of structure can be easily expressed and operations such composition can be defined that preserve such structures. For instance, one can express refinement (or inheritance) as a morphism that preserves specifications (i.e., through refinement mappings), from which composition operations such as repeated inheritance result as universal constructions (e.g., pushouts in the case at hand). Amalgamated union is an example of a universal construction and so are conjunction and disjunction—composition (in the sense of repeated inheritance) operates as disjunction on pre-conditions but as conjunction on post-conditions precisely because the inheritance morphism is co-variant on post-conditions but contra-variant on pre-conditions. Several other examples are covered in [20], some of which will be discussed in later sections.

The use of category theory in software modularisation goes back many years and was pioneered by J. Goguen—see, for example, [38] for an overview of the use of category theory in computer science and [12] for one of the first papers in which the structuring of abstract data type specifications was discussed in mathematical terms.[6] Abstract data types (ADTs) are indeed one of the pillars of object-oriented programming but it would be impossible to cover in this chapter the vast literature on ADT specification. See also [37] on how ADTs can be used in the formalisation of MILs. Finally, it is important to mention that ADTs, specifications (pre-/post-conditions and invariants) as well notions of abstraction and refinement/reification, are also at the core of languages and methods such as VDM [43], B [1] and Z [71], each of which offer their own modularisation techniques.

1.3.3 Component-Based Software Development

The article of the Scientific American quoted in Sect. 1.1.2 offers component-based software explicitly as a possible way out of the 'software crisis'. However, one prob-

---

[6]See also [36] on the applications of category theory to general systems theory.

lem with the term 'component' is that, even in computer science, it is highly ambiguous. One could say that every (de)composition method has an associated notion of component: *ça va de soi*. Therefore, one can talk of components that are used for constructing programs, or systems, or specifications, and so on. In this section, we briefly mention the specific notion of component-based software that is usually associated with the work of Szyperski [66][7] because, on the one hand, it does go beyond MILs and object-oriented programming as discussed in the previous two sub-sections and, on the other hand, it is supported by dedicated technology (e.g., Sun Microsystem's Enterprise JavaBeans or Microsofts's COM+) and languages and notations such as the UML (e.g., [15]), thus offering a layer of abstraction that is available to software designers.

Indeed, component-based development techniques are associated with another layer of abstraction that can be superposed over operating systems. So-called component frameworks make available a number of run-time layers of services that enforce properties such as persistence or transactions over which one can rely on when developing and interconnecting components to build a system. By offering interconnection standards, such frameworks also permit components to be connected without knowing who designed them, thus promoting reuse.

Components are not modules in the sense of programming in-the-large (cf. Sect. 1.3): a component is a software implementation that can be executed, i.e., a resource; a module is a way of hiding design decisions when organising the resources that are necessary for the construction of a large system such as the usage of components. Components also go beyond objects in the sense that, on the one hand, components can be developed using other techniques than object-oriented programming and, on the other hand, the interconnection mechanisms through which components can be composed are also quite different from clientship.

More specifically, one major difference between a component model and an object-oriented one is that all connections in which a component may be involved are made explicit through provides/exports or requires/imports interfaces that are *external* to the code that implements the component—"in a component setting, providers and clients are ignorant of each other" [66]. In the case of OOP, connections are established through clientship and are only visible by inspecting the code that implements the objects—the client holds an explicit reference to and calls the client, i.e., the connections are not mediated by an interface-based mechanism that is external to the code. That is, one could say that objects offer a white-box connection model whereas components offer a black-box one.

Whereas components in the sense discussed above are essentially a way of modularising implementation (and promoting reuse), there is another important aspect that is often associated with components—their status as architectural elements and the way they modularise change, i.e., the focus is on "being able to manage the total system, as its various components evolve and its requirements change, rather than

---

[7]"A software component is a unit of composition with contractually specified interfaces and explicit context dependencies only. A software component can be deployed independently and is subject to composition by third parties".

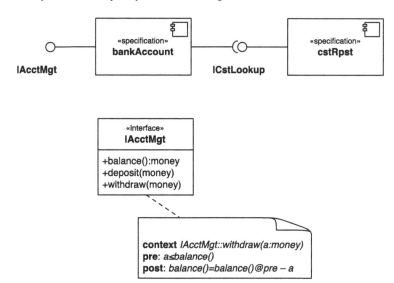

Fig. 1.17   An example of a component specification architecture using UML notation

seeking to ensure that individual components are reusable by multiple component systems" [15].

From the point of view of complexity, the aspects of component-based software that interest us are the notions of interface and binding/composition of a component model. Typically, a component specification is defined in terms of the interfaces that the component provides (or realises) and those that it requires (or uses), and any dependencies between them. An interface is, as before, a set of operations, each specified via pre-/post-conditions, and an 'information model' that captures abstract information on the state of the component and the way the operations relate to it. Specific notations have been proposed within the UML for supporting the definition of components or component specifications, including the 'lollipop' for provided interfaces and the 'socket' for required interfaces. An example is shown in Fig. 1.17, using the stereotype 'specification' to indicate that the architecture applies to component specifications, not to instances (implementations) [15].

Connections between components are expressed through 'assembly connectors' by fitting balls into sockets—they bind the components together but do not compose them. However, components can have an internal structure that contains subcomponents wired together through assembly connectors. The rules and constraints that apply to such forms of composition are not always clear, especially in what relates to specifications.

1.4 Programming In-the-many

We borrow the term 'programming in-the-many' from Nenad Medvidović [53] and use it to mark the difference between the concern for size that is at the core of programming in-the-large and the complexity that arises from the fact that systems are ever more distributed and heterogeneous, and that software development requires the integration and combination of possibly 'incompatible' systems. An important driver for this more modern emphasis comes from the pressures that are put on systems to be flexible and agile in the way they can respond to change. As put in [31], "[...] the ability to change is now more important than the ability to create [e-commerce] systems in the first place. Change becomes a first-class design goal and requires business and technology architectures whose components can be added, modified, replaced and reconfigured".

This is not to say that research in component-based development has not addressed those challenges. For example, design mechanisms making use of event publishing/subscription through brokers and other well-known patterns [33] have found their way into commercially available products that support various forms of agility in the sense that they make it relatively easy to add or remove components without having to redesign the whole system. However, solutions based on the use of design patterns are not at the level of abstraction in which the need for change arises and needs to be managed. Being mechanisms that operate at the design level, there is a wide gap that separates them from the application modelling levels at which change is better perceived and managed. This conceptual gap is not easily bridged, and the process that leads from the business requirements to the identification and instantiation of the relevant design patterns is not easily documented or made otherwise explicit in a way that facilitates changes to be operated. Once instantiated, design patterns code up interactions in ways that, typically, requires evolution to be intrusive because they were not conceived to be evolvable: most of the times, the pattern will dissolve as the system evolves.

Therefore, the need arises for semantic primitives founded on first principles through which interconnections can be externalised, modelled explicitly, and evolved directly, leading to systems that are 'exoskeletal' in the sense that they exhibit their configuration structure explicitly [46]. This is why, in this section, we would like to emphasise a different form of abstraction and decomposition that promotes 'connectors' to the same status as components as first-class elements in software architectures[8] [65].

Connector abstractions [55] and the architectural styles that they promote are also supported by developments in middleware [57, 58], including the use of reflection [45]. An important contribution to this area comes from so-called coordination languages and models [35]. These languages promote the separation between 'computation' and 'coordination', i.e., the ability to address the computations that need to take place locally within components to implement the functionalities that they

---

[8]As could be expected, the term 'architecture' is as ambiguous as 'component'. We have argued that every discipline of decomposition leads to, or is intrinsically based on, a notion of part (component) and composition. The way we decompose a problem, or the discipline that we follow in the decomposition, further leads to an architecture, or architectural style, that identifies the way the problem is structured in terms of its sub-problems and the mechanisms through which they relate to one another.

advertise through their interfaces separately from the coordination mechanisms that need to be superposed on these computations to enable the properties that are required of the global behaviour of the system to emerge. An example is *Linda* [34], implemented in *Java* through *JavaSpaces*, part of the *Jini* project (see also IBM's *TSpaces* as another example of coordination middleware). Another example is *Manifold* [5]. Whereas, in *Linda*, components communicate over shared tuple-spaces [7], *Manifold* is based on an event-based communication paradigm—the *Idealized Worker Idealized Manager* (IWIM) model [3].

The importance of this separation in enabling change can be understood when we consider the complexity that clientship raises in understanding and managing interactions. For example, in order to understand or make changes to the way objects are interconnected, one needs to examine the code that implements the classes and follow how, at run time, objects become clients of other objects. This becomes very clear when looking at a UML collaboration diagram for a non-trivial system. In a sense, clientship brings back the complexity of 'spaghetti' code by using the equivalent of goto's at the level on interactions.

Several architectural description languages (ADLs) have emerged since the 90s [54]. Essentially, these languages differ from the MILs discussed in Sect. 1.3.1 in that, where MILs put an emphasis on how modules *use* other modules, ADLs focus instead on the organisation of the *behaviour* of systems of components interconnected through protocols for communication and synchronisation. This explains why, on the semantic side, ADLs tend to be based on formalisms developed for supporting concurrency or distribution (Petri-nets, statecharts, and process calculi, *inter alia*). Two such ADLs are *Reo* [4], which is based on data streams and evolved from the coordination language *Manifold* mentioned above, and *Wright* [2], based on the process algebra CSP—Communicating Sequential Programs [41].

In order to illustrate typical architectural concepts and their formalisation, we use the basic notion of connector put forward in [2]: a set of *roles*, each of which identifies a component type, and a *glue* that specifies how instances of the roles are interconnected. The example of a *pipe* is given in Fig. 1.18 using the language COMMUNITY [30] (CSP is used in [2]).

The roles and the glue of the connector are COMMUNITY 'designs', which provide specifications of component behaviour that can be observed over communication channels and actions. A COMMUNITY design consists of:

- A collection of channels, which can be output (written by the component, read by the environment), input (read by the component, written by the environment), or private (local to the component)—denoted O, I and Pc, respectively.
- A collection A of actions. Every action a is specified in terms of
  - The set W_a of output and private channels that the action can write into (its write-frame); for example, the action *prod* of *asender* can write into the channels *val* and *rd*, but not into *cl*, i.e., $W_{prod} = \{val, rd\}$.
  - A pair L_a, U_a of conditions—the lower (or safety) guard and the upper (or progress) guard—that specify a necessary (L_a) and a sufficient (U_a) condition for the action to be enabled, respectively; for example, action *close* of *areceiver* is only enabled when *cl* is false—$L_{close} \equiv \neg cl$—and is enabled if *eof* is true

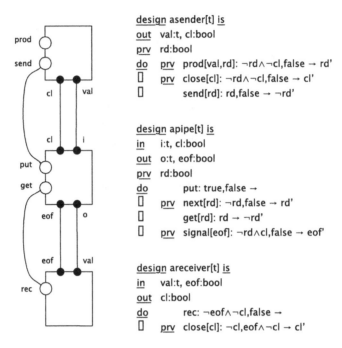

```
design asender[t] is
out  val:t, cl:bool
prv  rd:bool
do    prv  prod[val,rd]: ¬rd∧¬cl,false → rd'
☐     prv  close[cl]: ¬rd∧¬cl,false → cl'
☐          send[rd]: rd,false → ¬rd'


design apipe[t] is
in    i:t, cl:bool
out   o:t, eof:bool
prv   rd:bool
do         put: true,false →
☐     prv  next[rd]: ¬rd,false → rd'
☐          get[rd]: rd → ¬rd'
☐     prv  signal[eof]: ¬rd∧cl,false → eof'


design areceiver[t] is
in    val:t, eof:bool
out   cl:bool
do         rec: ¬eof∧¬cl,false →
☐     prv  close[cl]: ¬cl,eof∧¬cl → cl'
```

Fig. 1.18 An example of a connector (pipe) in *CommUnity*

and *cl* is false—$U_{close} \equiv eof \wedge \neg cl$. When the two guards are the same, we write only one condition as in the case of action *get* of *apipe*.

– A condition R_a that describes the effects of the action using primed channels to denote the value taken by channels after the action has taken; for example, action *signal* of *apipe* sets *cl* to true—$R_{signal} \equiv cl'$.

Actions can also be declared to be private, the set of which is denoted by *Pa*.

Each role is connected to the glue of the connector by a 'cable' that establishes input/output communication and synchronisation of non-private actions. Notice that all names are local, meaning that there are no implicit interconnections based on the fact that different designs happen to use the same names for channels or actions. Therefore, the cable that connects *apipe* and *areceiver* identifies *eof* of *apipe* with *eof* of *areceiver*, *o* with *val*, and *get* with *rec*. This means that *areceiver* reads *eof* from the channel *eof* of *apipe* and *val* from *o*, and that *apipe* and *areceiver* have to synchronise to execute the actions *get* and *rec*.

Designs can be abstract (as in the examples in Fig. 1.18) in the sense that they may not fully determine when actions are enabled or how they effect the data made available on channels. For example, action *prod* of *asender* has *val* in its write-frame but its effects on *val* are not specified. Making the upper (progress) guard false is another example of underspecification: the lower guard defines a necessary condition for the action to be enabled but no sufficient condition is given. Such abstract designs can be refined until they are fully specified, in which case the design is called a program. A program is, essentially, a collection of guarded commands.

```
design rpipe[t] is
in    i:t, cl:bool
out   o:t, eof:bool
prv   q:queue(t); rd:bool
do         put[q]: ¬full(q) → q'=enqueue(i,q)
☐    prv  next[rd,q]: ¬empty(q)∧¬rd → o'=head(q) ∧ q'=tail(q) ∧ rd'
☐         get[rd]: rd → ¬rd'
☐    prv  signal[eof]: ¬rd∧cl∧empty(q) → eof'
```

Fig. 1.19 A refinement of the design *apipe*

Non-private actions are reactive in the sense that they are executed together with the environment; private actions are active because their execution is only under the control of the component.

An example of a refinement of *apipe* is given in Fig 1.19. Formally, refinement consists of two mappings—one on channels, which is co-variant, and the other on actions, which is contra-variant. In the example, the refinement mapping introduces a new private channel—a queue—and is the identity on actions. The mappings need to preserve the nature of the channels (input, output, or private) and of actions (private or non-private). Private actions do not need to be refined but non-private ones do, in which case their effects need to be preserved (not weakened), lower guards can be weakened (but not strengthened) and upper can be strengthened (but not weakened), i.e., the interval defined by the two guards must be preserved or shrunk. For example, for all actions of *rpipe*, the lower and upper guards coincide. A given action can also be refined by a set of actions, each of which needs to satisfy the same constraints. Finally, new actions introduced during the refinement cannot include output channels of the abstract design in their write frames. A full formal definition can be found in [30].

COMMUNITY encapsulates one of the principles that have been put forward for modularising parallel and distributed programs—superposition or superimposition [14, 32, 44]. Indeed, programming in-the-many arose in the context of the advent of concurrency and distribution, i.e., changes in the operating infrastructure that emphasise cooperation among independent processes. Programmers find concurrency 'complicated' and, therefore, a source of complexity in software design. For example, it seems fair to say that extensions of OOP with concurrency have failed to make a real impact in engineering or programming practice, one reason being that the abstractions available for OOP do not extend to concurrency in an intuitive way. In contrast, languages such as *Unity* [14], on which COMMUNITY is based, have put forward proper abstractions and modularisation techniques that follow on the principles of structured programming.

In Fig. 1.20 we present a COMMUNITY design for a luggage-delivery cart. The context is that of a simplified airport luggage delivery system in which carts move along a track and stop at designated locations for handling luggage. Locations in the track are modelled through natural numbers modulo the length of the circuit. Pieces of luggage are also modelled through natural numbers, zero being reserved to model the situation in which a cart is empty. According to the design *cart*, a cart is able

```
design cart is
in     nbag, ndest:nat
out    loc,dest:nat
prv    bag:nat
do     move[loc]: loc≠dest → loc'>loc
☐      load[bag,dest]: loc=dest ∧bag=0 → bag'=nbag ∧ dest'=Dest(nbag)
☐      unload[bag,dest]: loc=dest ∧bag≠0 → bag'=0 ∧ dest'=Dest(nbag)
```

Fig. 1.20 A COMMUNITY design of an airport luggage-delivery cart

to *move*, *load* and *unload*. It moves by incrementing *loc* while it has not reached its destination (the increment is left unspecified). The current destination is available in *dest* and is retrieved from the bag each time the cart stops to load, using a function *Dest* that we assume is provided as part of a data type (e.g., abstracting the scanning of a bar code on the luggage), or from the environment, when unloading, using the input channel *ndest*. Loading and unloading take place only when the cart has reached its destination.

In Fig. 1.21 we present a superposition of *cart*: on the one hand, we distinguish between two modes of moving—slow and fast; on the other hand, we count the number of times the cart has docked since the last time the counter was reset. Notice that *controlled_cart* is not a refinement of *cart*: the actions *move_ slow* and *move_fast* do not refine *move* because the enabling condition of *move* (which is fully specified) has changed. Like refinement, superposition consists of a co-variant mapping on channels and a contra-variant mapping on actions. However, unlike refinement, the upper guard of a superposed action cannot be weakened—this is because, in the superposed design, actions may occur in a more restricted context (that of a controller in the case at hand). In fact, superposition can be seen to capture a 'component-of' relationship, i.e., the way a component is part of a larger system. Another difference in relation to refinement is the fact that input channels may be mapped to output ones, again reflecting the fact that the part of the environment from which the input could be expected has now been identified. Other restrictions typical of superposition relations apply: new actions (such as *reset*) cannot include channels of the base design in their write-frames; however, superposed actions can extend their write-frames with new channels (e.g., *load* and *unload* now have *count* in their write-frames).

COMMUNITY combines the modularisation principles of superposition with the externalisation of interactions promoted by coordination languages. That is, although superposition as illustrated in Fig. 1.21 allows designs to be extended (in a disciplined way), it does not externalise the mechanisms through which the extension is performed—the fact that the cart is subject to a speed controller and a counter at the docking stations. In COMMUNITY, this externalisation is supported by allowing designs to be interconnected with other designs. In Figs. 1.22 and 1.23, we show the designs of the speed controller and the counter, respectively.

Neither the speed controller nor the counter make reference to the cart (as with refinement, names of channels and actions are treated locally). Therefore, they can be reused in multiple contexts to build larger systems. For example, in Fig 1.24 we

<u>design</u> controlled_cart <u>is</u>
<u>in</u>   nbag, ndest:nat
<u>out</u>   count,loc,dest:nat
<u>prv</u>   bag:nat
<u>do</u>   move_slow[loc]: 0<|loc-dest|≤2 → loc'=loc+1
◻   move_fast[loc]: |loc-dest|>2 → loc'>loc
◻   load[bag,dest,count]: loc=dest ∧bag=0 → bag'=nbag ∧ dest'=Dest(nbag) ∧ count'=count+1
◻   unload[bag,dest,count]: loc=dest ∧bag≠0 → bag'=0 ∧ dest'=Dest(nbag) ∧ count'=count+1
◻   reset[count]: true,false → count'=0

Fig. 1.21 A superposition of the COMMUNITY design *cart* shown in Fig. 1.20

Fig. 1.22 A
COMMUNITY design
of a speed controller

<u>design</u> speed <u>is</u>
<u>in</u>   dest,loc:nat
<u>do</u>   slow[loc]: 0<|loc-dest|≤2 → loc'=loc+1
◻   fast[loc]: |loc-dest|>2 → loc'>loc

Fig. 1.23 A
COMMUNITY design
of a counter

<u>design</u> counter <u>is</u>
<u>out</u>   count:nat
<u>do</u>   inc[count]: true,false → count'=count+1
◻   reset[count]: true,false → count'=0

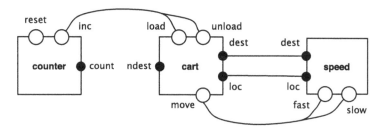

Fig. 1.24 The COMMUNITY architecture of the controlled cart

depict the architecture of the controlled cart as a system of three components inter-connected through cables that, as in the case of connectors, establish input/output and action synchronisation.

The design *controlled_cart* depicted in Fig. 1.21 is the result of the composition of the components and connections depicted in Fig. 1.24. This operation of compo-sition can be formalised in category theory [50], much in the same way as repeated inheritance (cf., Sect. 1.3.2) except that the morphisms in COMMUNITY capture superposition. The notion of refinement discussed above can also be formalised in category theory and refinement can be proved to be compositional with respect to composition—for example, one can refine *speed* by making precise the increment on the location; this refinement carries over to the controlled cart in the sense that the composition using the refined controller yields a refinement of the controlled cart. Full details of this categorical approach to software systems can be found in [20].

Extensions of COMMUNITY supported by the same categorical formalisations can be found in [51] for location-aware mobile systems (where location is defined as an independent architectural dimension) and in [25] for event-based architectures. Notions of higher-order architectural connectors were developed in [52] and dynamic reconfiguration was addressed in [68].

Finally, notice that, as most ADLs, COMMUNITY does not offer a notion of module in the sense of programming in-the-large, i.e., it does not provide coarser structures of designs (though the notion of higher-order architectural connectors presented in [52] goes in that direction by offering a mechanism for constructing connectors). Through channels and actions, COMMUNITY offers an explicit notion of interface through which designs can be connected, but neither channels nor actions can be seen as provided or required interfaces.

1.5 Programming In-the-universe

Given the tall order that the terms 'small', 'large' and 'many' have created, we were left with 'universe' to designate yet another face of complexity in software design, one that is more modern and sits at the core of the recent quotes with which we opened this chapter. The term 'universe' is also not too far from the designation 'global (ubiquitous) computing' that is often used for characterising the development of software applications that can run on 'global computers', i.e., "computational infrastructures available globally and able to provide uniform services with variable guarantees for communication, co-operation and mobility, resource usage, security policies and mechanisms" (see the Global Computing Initiative at cordis.europa.eu/ist/fet/gc.htm). It is in this context that we place service-oriented architectures (SOA) and service-oriented computing (SOC).

1.5.1 Services vs Components

SOC is a new paradigm in which interactions are no longer based on the exchange of products with specific parties—clientship as in object-oriented programming—but on the provisioning of services by external providers that can be procured on the fly subject to a negotiation of service level agreements (SLAs). A question that, in this context, cannot be avoided, concerns the difference between component-based and service-oriented design. Indeed, the debate on CBD vs. SOC is still out there, which in our opinion reflects that there is something fundamental about SOC that is not yet clearly understood.

A basic difference concerns the run-time environment that supports both approaches. Component models rely on a homogeneous framework in which components can be plugged in and connected to each other. Services, like components, hide their implementations but, in addition to components, they do not reveal any implementation-platform or infrastructure requirements. Therefore, as put in [66], services are more self-contained than typical components. However, as a consequence, interactions with services are not as efficient as with objects or components, a point that is very nicely put in [64]: where, in OO, clientship operates through a direct mapping of method invocation to actual code and, in CBD, invocation is performed via proxys in a slower way but still within a communication environment that is native to the specific component framework, SOC needs to bridge between different environment boundaries and rely on transport protocols that are not necessarily as performant.

Indeed, where we identify a real paradigm shift in SOC—one that justifies new abstractions and decomposition techniques—is in the fact that SOAs provide a layer of middleware in which the interaction between client and provider is mediated by a broker, which makes it possible to abstract from the identity of the server or of the broker when programming applications that need to rely on an external service. Design patterns or other component-oriented solutions can be used for mediating interactions but abstraction from identity is a key feature of SOC: as put in [19], services respond to the necessity for separating "need from the need-fulfilment mechanism".[9]

Another difference between components and services, as we see it, can be explained in terms of two different notions of 'composition'. In CBD, composition is integration-oriented—"the idea of component-based development is to industrialise the software development process by producing software applications by assembling prefabricated software components" [19]; "component-based software engineering is concerned with the rapid assembly of systems from components" [6]. The key aspect here is the idea of assembling systems from (reusable) components, which derives from the principle of divide-and-conquer.

Our basic stance is that what we are calling programming in-the-universe goes beyond this assembly view and abandons the idea that the purpose of programming or design is to build a software system that is going to be delivered to a customer; the way we see this new paradigm is that (smaller) applications are developed to run on global computers (like the Web) and respond to business needs by engaging, dynamically, with services and resources that are globally available at the time they are needed. Because those services may in turn require other services, each such application will create, as it executes, a system of sub-systems, each of which implements a session of one of the services that will have been procured.

For example, a typical business system may rely on an external service to supply goods; in order to take advantage of the best deal available at the time the goods are needed, the system may resort to different suppliers at different times. Each of those suppliers may in turn rely on services that they will need to procure. For instance, some suppliers may have their own delivery system but others may prefer

---

[9]Notice that mechanisms that, as SOAP, support interconnections in SOAs, do not use URLs (universal resource locators) as identities: "there is no built-in guarantee that the URL will indeed refer back to an object actually live at the sending process, the sending machine, or even the sending site. There is also no guarantee that two successive resolution requests for the same URL will yield the same object" [66].

to outsource the delivery of the goods; some delivery companies may have their own transport system but prefer to use an external company to provide the drivers; and so on. In summary, the structure of an application running on a global computer, understood as the components and connectors that determine its configuration, is intrinsically dynamic.

Therefore, the role of architecture in the construction of a service-oriented system needs to go beyond that of identifying, at design time, components that developers will need to implement or reuse. Because these activities are now performed by the SOA middleware, what is required from software architects is that they identify and model the high-level business activities and the dependencies that they have on external services to fulfil their goals. A consequence of this is that, whereas the notion of a 'whole' is intrinsic to CBD—whether in managing construction (through reuse) or change (through architecture)—SOC is not driven by the need to build or manage such a whole but to allow applications to take advantage of a (dynamic) universe of services. The purpose of services is not to support reuse in construction or manage change of a system as requirements evolve, but to allow applications to compute in an open-ended and evolving universe of resources. In this setting, there is much more scope for flexibility in the way business is supported than in a conventional component-based scenario: business processes need not be confined to fixed organisational contexts; they can be viewed in more global contexts as emerging from a varying collection of loosely coupled applications that can take advantage of the availability of services procured on the fly when they are needed.

1.5.2 Modules for Service-Oriented Computing

A number of 'standards' have emerged in the last few years in the area of Web Services promoted by organisations such as OASIS[10] and W3C.[11] These include languages such as WSDL (an XML format for describing service interfaces), WS-BPEL (an XML-based programming language for business process orchestration based on web services) and WS-CDL (an XML-based language for describing choreographies, i.e., peer-to-peer collaborations of parties with a common business goal).

A number of research initiatives (among them the FET-GC2 integrated project SENSORIA [69]) have been proposing formal approaches that address different aspects of the paradigm independently of the specific languages that are available today for Web Services or Grid Computing. For example, recent proposals for service calculi (e.g., [9, 13, 48, 67]) address operational foundations of SOC (in the sense of how services compute) by providing a mathematical semantics for the mechanisms that support choreography or orchestration—sessions, message/event correlation, compensation, *inter alia*.

---

[10]www.oasis-open.org.

[11]www.w3.org.

Whereas such calculi address the need for specialised language primitives for *programming* in this new paradigm, they are not abstract enough to address those aspects (both technical and methodological) that concern the way applications can be developed to provide business solutions independently of the languages in which services are programmed and, therefore, control complexity by raising the level of abstraction and adopting coarser-grained decomposition techniques. The Open Service Oriented Architecture collaboration[12] has been proposing a number of specifications, namely the Service Component Architecture (SCA), that address this challenge:

> SCA is a model designed for SOA, unlike existing systems that have been adapted to SOA. SCA enables encapsulating or adapting existing applications and data using an SOA abstraction. SCA builds on service encapsulation to take into account the unique needs associated with the assembly of networks of heterogeneous services. SCA provides the means to compose assets, which have been implemented using a variety of technologies using SOA. The SCA composition becomes a service, which can be accessed and reused in a uniform manner. In addition, the composite service itself can be composed with other services [...]
>
> SCA service components can be built with a variety of technologies such as EJBs, Spring beans and CORBA components, and with programming languages including Java, PHP and C++ [...]
>
> SCA components can also be connected by a variety of bindings such as WSDL/SOAP web services, Java^{TM} Message Service (JMS) for message-oriented middleware systems and J2EE^{TM} Connector Architecture (JCA) [60].

In Fig. 1.25 we present an example of an SCA component and, in Fig. 1.26, an example of an SCA composite (called 'module' in earlier versions). This composite has two components, each of which provides a service and has a reference to a service it depends on. The service provided by component A is made available for use by clients outside the composite. The service required by component A is provided by component B. The service required by component B exists outside the composite.

Although, through composites, SCA offers coarser primitives for decomposing and organising systems in logical groupings, it does not raise the level of abstraction. SCA addresses low-level design in the sense that it provides an assembly model and binding mechanisms for service components and clients programmed in specific languages, e.g., Java, C++, BPEL, or PHP. So far, SOC has been short of support for high-level modelling. Indeed, languages and models that have been proposed for service modelling and design (e.g., [11, 63]) do not address the higher level of abstraction that is associated with business solutions, in particular the key characteristic aspects of SOC that relate to the way those solutions are put together dynamically in reaction to the execution of business processes—run-time discovery, instantiation and binding of services.

The SENSORIA Reference Modelling Language (SRML) [29] started to be developed within the SENSORIA project as a prototype domain-specific language for modelling service-oriented systems at a high level of abstraction that is closer to business concerns. Although SRML is inspired by SCA, it focuses on providing a

---

[12]www.osoa.org.

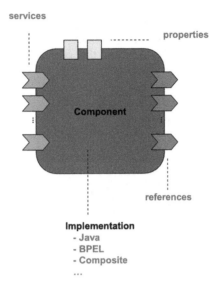

services

properties

Component

references

Implementation
- Java
- BPEL
- Composite
...

Fig. 1.25 An example of an SCA component. A component consists of a configured instance of an implementation, where an implementation is the piece of program code providing business functions. The business function is offered for use by other components as services. Implementations may depend on services provided by other components—these dependencies are called references. Implementations can have settable properties, which are data values which influence the operation of the business function. The component configures the implementation by providing values for the properties and by wiring the references to services provided by other components [60]

formal framework with a mathematical semantics for modelling and analysing the business logic of services independently not only of the hosting middleware but also of the languages in which the business logic is programmed.

In SRML, services are characterised by the conversations that they support and the properties of those conversations. In particular:

- messages are exchanged, asynchronously, through 'wires' and are typed by their business function (requests, commitments, cancellations, and so on);
- service interface behaviour is specified using message correlation patterns that are typical of business conversations; and
- the parties engaged in business applications need to follow pre-defined conversation protocols—requester and provider protocols.

On the other hand, the difference between SRML and more generic modelling languages is precisely in the fact that the mechanisms that, like message correlation, support these conversation protocols do not need to be modelled explicitly: they are assumed to be provided by the underlying SOA middleware. This is why SRML can be considered to be a domain-specific language: it frees the modeller from the need to specify aspects that should be left to lower levels of abstraction and concentrate instead on the business logic.

The design of composite services in SRML adopts the SCA assembly model according to which new services can be created by interconnecting a set of elementary

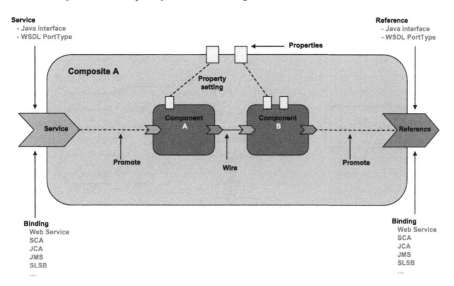

Fig. 1.26 An example of an SCA simple composite. Composites can contain components, services, references, property declarations, plus the wiring that describes the connections between these elements. Composites can group and link components built from different implementation technologies, allowing appropriate technologies to be used for each business task [60]

components to a set of external services; the new service is provided through an interface to the resulting system. The business logic of such a service involves a number of interactions among those components and external services, but is independent of the internal configurations of the external services—the external services need only be described by their interfaces. The actual external services are discovered at run time by matching these interfaces with those that are advertised by service providers (and optimising the satisfaction of service level agreement constraints).

The elementary unit for specifying service assembly and composition in SRML is the *service module* (or just *module* for short), which is the SRML equivalent to the SCA notion of composite. A module specifies how a set of internal components and external required services interact to provide the behaviour of a new service. Figure 1.27 shows the structure of the module *TravelBooking*, which models a service that manages the booking of a flight, a hotel and the associated payment. The service is assembled by connecting an internal component *BA* (that orchestrates the service) to three external services (for booking a flight, booking a hotel and processing the payment) and the persistent component *DB* (a database of users). The difference between the three kinds of entities—internal components, external services and persistent components—is intrinsic to SOC: internal components are created each time the service is invoked and killed when the service terminates; external services are procured and bound to the other parties at run time; persistent components are part of the business environment in which the service operates—they are not created nor destroyed by the service, and they are not discovered but directly invoked as

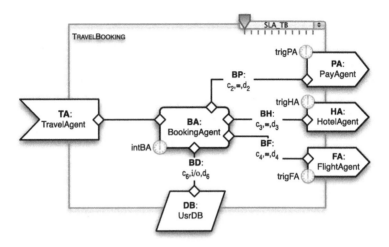

Fig. 1.27 The structure of the module *TravelBooking*. The service is assembled by connecting a component *BA* of type *BookingAgent* to three external service instances *PA*, *HA* and *FA* with interface types *PayAgent*, *HotelAgent* and *FlightAgent* (respectively) and the persistent component (a database of users) *DB* of type *UsrDB*. The wires that interconnect the several parties are *BP*, *BH*, *BF*, and *BD*. The interface through which service requesters interact with the *TravelBooking* service is *TA* of type *TravelAgent*. Internal configuration policies (indicated by the symbol ⊙) are specified, which include the conditions that trigger the discovery of the external services. An external configuration policy (indicated by the symbol ▼...SLA...▶), specifies the constraints according to which service-level agreements are negotiated (through constraint optimisation [8])

in component-based systems. By *TA* we denote the interface through which service requesters interact with *TravelBooking*. In SRML, interactions are peer-to-peer between pairs of entities connected through wires—*BP*, *BH*, *BF* and *BD* in the case at hand.

Each party (component or external service) is specified through a declaration of the interactions the party can be involved in and the properties that can be observed of these interactions during a session of the service. Wires are specified by the way they coordinate the interactions between the parties.

If the party is an internal component of the service (like *BA* in Fig. 1.27), its specification is an orchestration given in terms of state transitions—using the language of *business roles* [29]. An orchestration is defined independently of the language in which the component is programmed and the platform in which it is deployed; the actual component may be a BPEL process, a C++ or a Java program, or a wrapped up legacy system, *inter alia*. An orchestration is also independent of the parties that are interconnected with the component at run time; this is because the orchestration does not define invocations of operations provided by specific co-parties (components or external services); it simply defines the properties of the interactions in which the component can participate.

If the party is an external service, the specification is what we call a *requires-interface* and consists of a set of temporal properties that correlate the interactions in which the service can engage with its client. The language of *business protocols* [29] is used for specifying the behaviour required of external services not in terms of their internal workflow but of the properties that characterise the interactions in which the service can engage with its client, i.e., their interface behaviour. Figure 1.28 shows the specification of the business protocol that the *HotelAgent* service is expected to follow.

The specification of the interactions provided by the module (at its interface level) is what we call the *provides-interface*, which also uses the language of business protocols. Figure 1.29 shows the specification of the business protocol that the composite service declares to follow, i.e., the service that is offered by the service module *TravelBooking*. A service module is said to be correct if the properties offered through the provides-interface can be guaranteed by the (distributed) orchestration performed by components that implement the business roles assuming that they are interconnected to external services that ensure the properties specified in the requires-interfaces.

Persistent components can interact with the other parties synchronously, i.e., they can block while waiting for a reply. The properties of synchronous interactions are in the style of pre/post condition specification of methods as discussed in Sect. 1.3.2.

The specifications of the wires consist of *connectors* (in the sense of Sect. 1.4) that are responsible for binding and coordinating the interactions that are declared locally in the specifications of the two parties that each wire connects. In a sense, SRML modules are a way of organising interconnected systems in the sense of programming in-the-many, i.e., of offering coarser-grained abstractions (in the sense of programming in-the-large) that can respond to the need for addressing the complexity that arises from the number of interactions involved in the distributed systems that, today, operate at the larger scale of global computers like the Web. This matches the view that services offer a layer of organisation that can be superposed over a component infrastructure (what is sometimes referred to as a 'service overlay'), i.e., that services are, at a certain level of abstraction, a way of using software components and not so much a way of constructing software. We have explored this view in [27] by proposing a formalisation of services as interfaces for an algebra of asynchronous components understood as configurations of components and connectors.

Through this notion of service-overlay, such configurations of components and connectors expose conversational, stateful interfaces through which they can discover and bind, on the fly, to external services or expose services that can be discovered by business applications. That is, services offer an abstraction for coping with the run-time complexity of evolving configurations. A mathematical semantics for this dynamic process of discovery, binding and reconfiguration has been defined in [28], again using the tools of category theory: modules are used for typing configurations understood as graphs; such graphs evolve as the activities that they implement discover and bind to required services.

```
BUSINESS PROTOCOL HotelAgent is
───────────────────────────────────────────

    INTERACTIONS
        r&s lockHotel
            ⏣ checkin,checkout:date,
               name:usrData
            ⊠ hconf:hcode
    BEHAVIOUR
        initiallyEnabled lockHotel⏣?

        lockHotel✓? enables
                lockHotel⚕? until date(time)≥lockHotel.checkin
```

Fig. 1.28 The specification of the service interface of a *HotelAgent* written in the language of
business protocols. A *HotelAgent* can be involved in one interaction named *lockHotel* that models
the booking of a room in a hotel. Some properties of this interaction are specified: a booking request
can be made once the service is instantiated and a booking can be revoked up until the check-in
date. The specification language makes use of the events associated with the declared interactions:
the initiation event (⏣), the reply event (⊠), the commit event (✓), the cancellation event (✗) and
the revoke event (⚕)

```
BUSINESS PROTOCOL TravelAgent is
───────────────────────────────────────────

    INTERACTIONS
        r&s login
            ⏣ usr:usrName, pwd:password
        r&s bookTrip
            ⏣ from,to:airport,
               out,in:date
            ⊠ fconf:fcode,
               hconf:hcode,
               amount:moneyValue
        snd payNotify
            ⏣ status:bool
        snd refund
            ⏣ amount:moneyValue
    BEHAVIOUR
        initiallyEnabled login⏣?

        login⊠! ∧ login.reply enables
            bookTrip⏣? until time≥login.useBy

        bookTrip✓? ensures payNotify⏣!

        payNotify⏣! ∧ payNotify.status enables
            bookTrip⚕? until date(time)≥dayBefore(bookTrip.out)

        bookTrip⚕? ensures refund⏣!
```

Fig. 1.29 The specification of the provides-interface of the service module *TravelBooking* written
in the language of business protocols. The service can be involved in four interactions (*login*,
bookTrip, *payNotify* and *refund*) that model the login into the system, the booking of a trip, the
sending of a receipt and refunding the client of the service (in case a booking is returned). Five
properties are specified for these interactions

An example of this process is shown in the Appendix. Figure 1.31 depicts a run-time configuration (graph) where a number of components execute business roles and interact via wires with other components. The sub-configuration encircled corresponds to a user-interface *AUI* interacting with a component *ant*. This sub-configuration is typed by the activity module *A_ANT0* (an activity module is similar to a service module but offering a user-interface instead of a service-interface). Because the activity module has a requires-interface, the sub-configuration will change if the trigger associated with *TA* occurs. This activity module can bind to the service module *TravelBooking* (depicted in Fig. 1.27) by matching its requires-interface with the provides-interface of *TravelBooking* and resolving the SLA constraints of both modules (see Fig. 1.32). Therefore, if the trigger happens and *TravelBooking* is selected, the configuration will evolve to the one depicted in Fig. 1.33: an instance *AntBA* of *BookingAgent* is added to the configuration and wired to *Ant* and *DB* (no new instances of persistent components are created). Notice that the type of the sub-configuration has changed: it now consists of the composition of *A_ANT0* and *TravelBooking*. Because the new type has several requires-interfaces, the configuration will again change when their triggers occur.

Typing configurations with activity modules is a form of reflection, a technique that has been explored at the level of middleware to account for the evolution of systems [45]. In summary, we can see SOC as providing a layer of abstraction in which the dynamic reconfiguration of systems can be understood in terms of the business functions that they implement and the dependencies that those functions have on external services. This, we claim, is another step towards coping with the complexity of the systems that operate in the global infrastructures of today.

1.6 Concluding Remarks

This chapter is an attempt to make sense of the persistent claim that, in spite of the advances that we make on the way we program or engineer software systems, software is haunted by the beast of complexity and doomed to live in a permanent crisis. Given the complexity of the task (pun intended), we resorted to abstraction— we did our best to distill what seemed to us to have been key contributions to the handling of complexity—and decomposition by organising these contributions in four kinds of 'programming': in-the-small (structured programming), in-the-large (modules, objects, and components), in-the-many (connectors and software architectures), and in-the-universe (services). The fact that, to a large extent, these forms of programming are organised chronologically, is not an accident: it reflects the fact that, as progress has been made in computer science and software engineering, new kinds of complexity have arisen. We started by having to cope with the complexity of controlling execution, then the size of programs, then change and, more recently, 'globalisation'.

What remains constant in this process is the way we attempt to address complexity: abstraction and decomposition. This is why we insisted in imposing some degree of uniformity in terminology and notation, highlighting the fact that notions of module, interface, component, or architecture have appeared in different guises to support different abstraction or decomposition techniques. Although we chose not to go too deep into mathematical concepts and techniques, there is also some degree of uniformity (or universality) in the way they support notions of refinement or composition—for example, through the use of categorical methods—even if they are defined over different notions of specification—for example, pre/post-conditions for OO/CBD and temporal logic for SOC.

As could be expected, we had to use a rather broad brush when painting the landscape and, therefore, we were not exhaustive and left out many other faces of complexity. For example, as put in the 27/01/2009 edition of the Financial Times, cloud computing is, today, contributing to equally 'complex' aspects such as management or maintenance:

> *Cloud computing doesn't work because it's simpler than client-server or mainframe computing. It works because we shift the additional complexity to a place where it can be managed more effectively. Companies such as Amazon and Google are simply a lot better at managing servers and operating systems than most other organisations could ever hope to be. By letting Google manage this complexity, an enterprise can then focus more of its own resources on growth and innovation within its core business.*

To us, this quote nails down quite accurately the process through which complexity has been handled during the last fifty years or so: "we shift the additional complexity to a place where it can be managed more effectively". That is, we address complexity by making the infrastructure (or middleware) more 'clever' or by building tools that translate between levels of abstraction (e.g., through compilation or model-driven development techniques). For example, the move from objects to components to services is essentially the result of devising ways of handling interactions (or clientship): from direct invocation of code within a process (OO), to mediation via proxys across processes but within a single component framework (CBD), and across frameworks through brokers and transport protocols (SOA) [64].

Unfortunately (or inevitably), progress on the side of science and methodology has been slower, meaning that abstractions have not always been forthcoming as quickly as they would be needed to take advantage of new layers of infrastructure, which justifies that new levels of complexity arise for humans (programmers, designers, or analysts) when faced with new technology: notions of module tend to come when the need arises for managing the complexity of developing software over new computation or communication infrastructures. The answer to the mystery of why, in spite of all these advances, software seems to live in a permanent crisis, is that the beast of complexity keeps changing its form and we, scientists, do take our time to understand the nature of each new form of complexity and come up with right abstractions. In other words, like Paddington Bear, we take our time to abstract business functions from the handling of bank notes (with or without marmalade).

Acknowledgements Section 1.4 contains material extracted from papers co-authored with Antónia Lopes and Michel Wermelinger, and Sect. 1.5 from papers co-authored with Antónia Lopes, Laura Bocchi and João Abreu. I would like to thank them all and also Mike Hinchey for giving me the opportunity (and encouraging me) to contribute this chapter.

Appendix

Fig. 1.30 Module schemas for assignment, sequence, iteration, and selection

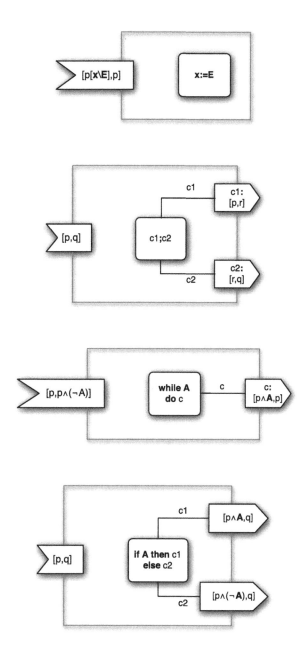

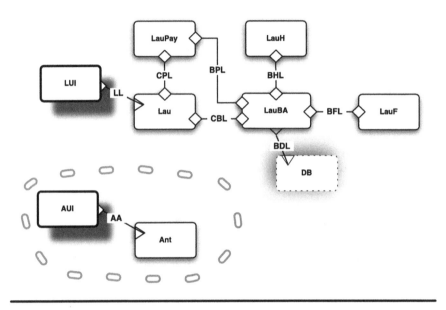

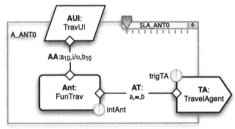

Fig. 1.31 A configuration, a sub-configuration of which is typed by an activity module

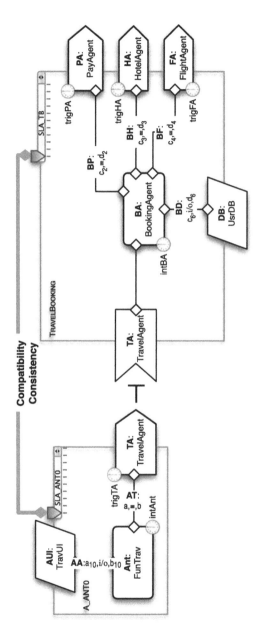

Fig. 1.32 Matching the activity module of Fig. 1.31 with the service module *TravelBooking*

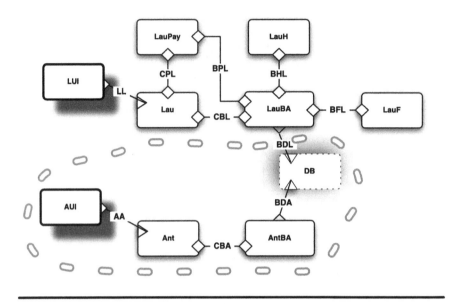

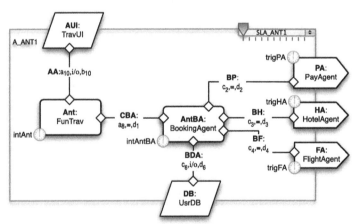

Fig. 1.33 The reconfiguration resulting from the binding in Fig. 1.32

References

1. Abrial, J.-R.: The B-book: Assigning Programs to Meanings. Cambridge University Press, New York (1996)
2. Allen, R., Garlan, D.: A formal basis for architectural connection. ACM Trans. Softw. Eng. Methodol. **6**(3), 213–249 (1998)
3. Arbab, F.: The IWIM model for coordination of concurrent activities. In: Ciancarini, P., Hankin, C. (eds.) Coordination. LNCS, vol. 1061, pp. 34–56. Springer, Berlin (1996)
4. Arbab, F.: Reo: a channel-based coordination model for component composition. Math. Struct. Comput. Sci. **14**(3), 329–366 (2004)
5. Arbab, F., Herman, I., Spilling, P.: An overview of manifold and its implementation. Concurr. Comput. **5**(1), 23–70 (1993)
6. Bachmann, F., Bass, L., Buhman, C., Comella-Dorda, S., Long, F., Robert, J., Seacord, R., Wallnau, K.: Volume II: technical concepts of component-based software engineering. Technical report CMU/SEI-2000-TR-008 ESC-TR-2000-007 (2000)
7. Banâtre, J.-P., Métayer, D.L.: Programming by multiset transformation. Commun. ACM **36**(1), 98–111 (1993)
8. Bistarelli, S., Montanari, U., Rossi, F.: Semiring-based constraint satisfaction and optimization. J. ACM **44**(2), 201–236 (1997)
9. Boreale, M., et al.: SCC: a service centered calculus. In: Bravetti, M., Núñez, M., Zavattaro, G. (eds.) WS-FM. LNCS, vol. 4184, pp. 38–57. Springer, Berlin (2006)
10. Brown, A.W.: Large-Scale, Component Based Development. Prentice-Hall, Upper Saddle River (2000)
11. Broy, M., Krüger, I.H., Meisinger, M.: A formal model of services. ACM Trans. Softw. Eng. Methodol. **16**(1) (2007)
12. Burstall, R.M., Goguen, J.A.: Putting theories together to make specifications. In: IJCAI, pp. 1045–1058 (1977)
13. Carbone, M., Honda, K., Yoshida, N.: Structured communication-centred programming for web services. In: De Nicola, R. (ed.) Programming Languages and Systems. LNCS, vol. 4421, pp. 2–17. Springer, Berlin (2007)
14. Chandy, K.M., Misra, J.: Parallel Program Design: A Foundation. Addison-Wesley, Boston (1988)
15. Cheesman, J., Daniels, J.: UML Components: A Simple Process for Specifying Component-Based Software. Addison-Wesley, Boston (2000)
16. Denning, P.J.: The field of programmers myth. Commun. ACM **47**(7), 15–20 (2004)
17. DeRemer, F., Kron, H.H.: Programming-in-the-large versus programming-in-the-small. IEEE Trans. Softw. Eng. **2**(2), 80–86 (1976)
18. Dijkstra, E.W.: A Discipline of Programming, 1st edn. Prentice-Hall, Upper Saddle River (1976)
19. Elfatatry, A.: Dealing with change: components versus services. Commun. ACM **50**(8), 35–39 (2007)
20. Fiadeiro, J.L.: Categories for Software Engineering. Springer, Berlin (2004)
21. Fiadeiro, J.L.: Software services: scientific challenge or industrial hype? In: Liu, Z., Araki, K. (eds.) ICTAC. LNCS, vol. 3407, pp. 1–13. Springer, Berlin (2004)
22. Fiadeiro, J.L.: Physiological vs. social complexity in software design. In: ICECCS, p. 3. IEEE Comput. Soc., Los Alamitos (2006)
23. Fiadeiro, J.L.: Designing for software's social complexity. Computer **40**(1), 34–39 (2007)
24. Fiadeiro, J.L.: On the challenge of engineering socio-technical systems. In: Wirsing, M., Banâtre, J.-P., Hölzl, M.M., Rauschmayer, A. (eds.) Software-Intensive Systems and New Computing Paradigms. LNCS, vol. 5380, pp. 80–91. Springer, Berlin (2008)
25. Fiadeiro, J.L., Lopes, A.: An algebraic semantics of event-based architectures. Math. Struct. Comput. Sci. **17**(5), 1029–1073 (2007)
26. Fiadeiro, J.L., Lopes, A.: A model for dynamic reconfiguration in service-oriented architectures. In: Babar, M.A., Gorton, I. (eds.) ECSA. LNCS, vol. 6285, pp. 70–85. Springer, Berlin (2010)

27. Fiadeiro, J.L., Lopes, A.: An interface theory for service-oriented design. In: Giannakopoulou, D., Orejas, F. (eds.) FASE. LNCS, vol. 6603, pp. 18–33. Springer, Berlin (2011)

28. Fiadeiro, J.L., Lopes, A., Bocchi, L.: An abstract model of service discovery and binding. Form. Asp. Comp. **23**(4), 433–463 (2011)

29. Fiadeiro, J.L., Lopes, A., Bocchi, L., Abreu, J.: The SENSORIA reference modelling language. In: Wirsing, M., Hölzl, M.M. (eds.) Rigorous Software Engineering for Service-Oriented Systems. LNCS, vol. 6582, pp. 61–114. Springer, Berlin (2011)

30. Fiadeiro, J.L., Lopes, A., Wermelinger, M.: A mathematical semantics for architectural connectors. In: Backhouse, R.C., Gibbons, J. (eds.) Generic Programming. LNCS, vol. 2793, pp. 178–221. Springer, Berlin (2003)

31. Fingar, P.: Component-based frameworks for e-commerce. Commun. ACM **43**(10), 61–67 (2000)

32. Francez, N., Forman, I.R.: Superimposition for interacting processes. In: Baeten, J.C.M., Klop, J.W. (eds.) CONCUR. LNCS, vol. 458, pp. 230–245. Springer, Berlin (1990)

33. Gamma, E., Helm, R., Johnson, R., Vlissides, J.: Design Patterns: Elements of Reusable Object-Oriented Software. Addison-Wesley, Boston (1995)

34. Gelernter, D.: Generative communication in linda. ACM Trans. Program. Lang. Syst. **7**(1), 80–112 (1985)

35. Gelernter, D., Carriero, N.: Coordination languages and their significance. Commun. ACM **35**(2), 96–107 (1992)

36. Goguen, J.A.: Categorical foundations for general systems theory. In: Pichler, F., Trappl, R. (eds.) Advances in Cybernetics and Systems Research, pp. 121–130. Transcripta Books, London (1973)

37. Goguen, J.A.: Reusing and interconneccting software components. Computer **19**(2), 16–28 (1986)

38. Goguen, J.A.: A categorical manifesto. Math. Struct. Comput. Sci. **1**(1), 49–67 (1991)

39. Gries, D.: The Science of Programming, 1st edn. Springer, Secaucus (1981)

40. Hoare, C.A.R.: An axiomatic basis for computer programming. Commun. ACM **12**, 576–580 (1969)

41. Hoare, C.A.R.: Communicating Sequential Processes. Prentice-Hall, Upper Saddle River (1985)

42. Jackson, M.A.: Principles of Program Design. Academic Press, Orlando (1975)

43. Jones, C.B.: Systematic Software Development Using VDM, 2nd edn. Prentice-Hall, Upper Saddle River (1990)

44. Katz, S.: A superimposition control construct for distributed systems. ACM Trans. Program. Lang. Syst. **15**(2), 337–356 (1993)

45. Kon, F., Costa, F.M., Blair, G.S., Campbell, R.H.: The case for reflective middleware. Commun. ACM **45**(6), 33–38 (2002)

46. Kramer, J.: Exoskeletal software. In: ICSE, p. 366 (1994)

47. Kramer, J.: Is abstraction the key to computing? Commun. ACM **50**(4), 36–42 (2007)

48. Lapadula, A., Pugliese, R., Tiezzi, F.: A calculus for orchestration of web services. In: De Nicola, R. (ed.) Programming Languages and Systems. LNCS, vol. 4421, pp. 33–47. Springer, Berlin (2007)

49. Liskov, B., Zilles, S.: Programming with abstract data types. In: Proceedings of the ACM SIGPLAN Symposium on Very High Level Languages, pp. 50–59. ACM, New York (1974)

50. Lopes, A., Fiadeiro, J.L.: Superposition: composition vs refinement of non-deterministic, action-based systems. Form. Asp. Comput. **16**(1), 5–18 (2004)

51. Lopes, A., Fiadeiro, J.L.: Adding mobility to software architectures. Sci. Comput. Program. **61**(2), 114–135 (2006)

52. Lopes, A., Wermelinger, M., Fiadeiro, J.L.: High-order architectural connectors. ACM Trans. Softw. Eng. Methodol. **12**(1), 64–104 (2003)

53. Medvidović, N., Mikic-Rakic, M.: Programming-in-the-many: a software engineering paradigm for the 21st century

54. Medvidović, N., Taylor, R.N.: A classification and comparison framework for software architecture description languages. IEEE Trans. Softw. Eng. **26**(1), 70–93 (2000)

55. Mehta, N.R., Medvidovic, N., Phadke, S.: Towards a taxonomy of software connectors. In: ICSE, pp. 178–187 (2000)
56. Meyer, B.: Object-Oriented Software Construction, 2nd edn. Prentice-Hall, Upper Saddle River (1997)
57. Mikic-Rakic, M., Medvidović, N.: Adaptable architectural middleware for programming-in-the-small-and-many. In: Endler, M., Schmidt, D.C. (eds.) Middleware. LNCS, vol. 2672, pp. 162–181. Springer, Berlin (2003)
58. Mikic-Rakic, M., Medvidović, N.: A connector-aware middleware for distributed deployment and mobility. In: ICDCS Workshops, pp. 388–393. IEEE Comput. Soc., Los Alamitos (2003)
59. Morgan, C.: Programming from Specifications. Prentice-Hall, Upper Saddle River (1990)
60. OSOA: Service component architecture 2007. Version 1.00
61. Parnas, D.L.: On the criteria to be used in decomposing systems into modules. Commun. ACM **15**, 1053–1058 (1972)
62. Prieto-Diaz, R., Neighbors, J.M.: Module interconnection languages. J. Syst. Softw. **6**, 307–334 (1986)
63. Reisig, W.: Modeling- and analysis techniques for web services and business processes. In: Steffen, M., Zavattaro, G. (eds.) FMOODS. LNCS, vol. 3535, pp. 243–258. Springer, Berlin (2005)
64. Sessions, R.: Fuzzy boundaries: objects, components, and web services. ACM Queue **2**, 40–47 (2004)
65. Shaw, M., Garlan, D.: Software Architecture: Perspectives on an Emerging Discipline. Prentice-Hall, Upper Saddle River (1996)
66. Szyperski, C.: Component Software: Beyond Object-Oriented Programming, 2nd edn. Addison-Wesley, Boston (2002)
67. Vieira, H.T., Caires, L., Seco, J.C.: The conversation calculus: a model of service-oriented computation. In: Drossopoulou, S. (ed.) ESOP. LNCS, vol. 4960, pp. 269–283. Springer, Berlin (2008)
68. Wermelinger, M., Fiadeiro, J.L.: A graph transformation approach to software architecture reconfiguration. Sci. Comput. Program. **44**(2), 133–155 (2002)
69. Wirsing, M., Hölzl, M. (Eds.): Rigorous Software Engineering for Service-Oriented Systems. LNCS, vol. 6582. Springer, Berlin (2011)
70. Wirth, N.: Programming in Modula-2, 3rd corrected edn. Springer, New York (1985)
71. Woodcock, J., Davies, J.: Using Z: Specification, Refinement, and Proof. Prentice-Hall, Upper Saddle River (1996)

Chapter 2
Simplicity and Complexity in Programs and Systems

Michael Jackson

2.1 Introduction

The topic of this chapter is complexity in an informal sense: difficulty of human comprehension. Inevitably this difficulty is partly subjective. Some people have more experience, or more persistence, or simply more intellectual skill—agility, insight, intelligence, acuity—than others. The difficulty of the subject matter to be mastered depends also on the intellectual tools brought to bear on the task.

These intellectual tools include both mental models and overt models. An overt model is revealed in an explicit public representation, textual or graphical. Its purpose is to capture and fix some understanding or notion of its subject matter, making it reliably available to its original creator at a future time and to other people also. A mental model is a private possession held in its owner's mind, sometimes barely recognized by its owner, and revealed only with conscious effort. A disdain for intuition and for informal thought may relegate a mental model—which by its nature is informal—to the role of a poor relation, best kept out of sight. Such disdain is misplaced in software development.

Complexity is hard to discuss. A complexity, once mastered, takes on the appearance of simplicity. In the middle ages, an integer division problem was insuperably complex for most well-educated Europeans, taught to represent numbers by Roman numerals; today we expect children in primary school to master such problems. Taught a better model—the Hindu-Arabic numerals with positional notation and zero—we learn a fast and reliable route through the maze: its familiarity becomes so deeply ingrained in our minds that we forget why it ever seemed hard to find.

To master a fresh complexity we must understand its origin and its anatomy. In software development a central concern is behavioral complexity, manifested at every level from the behavior of a small program to the behavior of a critical system. Behavioral complexity is the result of combining simple behaviors, sometimes

M. Jackson (✉)
The Open University, Milton Keynes, UK
e-mail: jacksonma@acm.org

M. Hinchey, L. Coyle (eds.), *Conquering Complexity*,
DOI 10.1007/978-1-4471-2297-5_2, © Springer-Verlag London Limited 2012

drawn from such different dimensions as the program invocation discipline imposed by an operating system, the behavior of an external engineered electromechanical device, and the navigational constraints of a database.

To master behavioral complexity we must identify and separate its simple constituents, following the second of Descartes's four rules [3] for reasoned investigation:

> "...to divide each of the difficulties under examination into as many parts as possible, and as might be necessary for its adequate solution."

But this rule alone is quite inadequate. Leibniz complained [8]:

> "This rule of Descartes is of little use as long as the art of dividing remains unexplained... By dividing his problem into unsuitable parts, the inexperienced problem-solver may increase his difficulty."

So we must devise and apply systematic criteria of simplicity, allowing us to know when we have identified a simple constituent of the complexity that confronts us. But it is not enough to identify the constituent simplicities. We must also understand the origins and anatomy of their existing or desired combination. Developers should not hamper their understanding of a problem by assuming a uniform discipline and mechanism of composition, whether derived from a program execution model or from a specification language.

The complexities to be mastered in software development arise both in tasks of analysis and of synthesis. In analysis, the task is to tease apart the constituents of a given complex whole, identifying each distinct constituent and the ways in which they have been reconciled and brought together. Such analysis may be applied to an existing program, to a requirement, or to any given subject matter of concern. In synthesis the task is to construct an artifact to satisfy certain requirements. For a program, the requirements themselves may be simple and immediately comprehensible: synthesis can then proceed directly. For a realistic computer-based system, requirements are almost always complex, given *a priori* or to be discovered in a process that may be partly concurrent with the synthesis itself. In either case, synthesis can proceed only to the extent that the relevant complexities of the requirement have been successfully analysed and understood.

In this chapter we first consider an example of a small integer program, and go on to discuss small programs that process external inputs and outputs. Then we turn to a consideration of complexities in computer-based systems. At the end of the chapter we recapitulate some general propositions about complexities in software development and techniques for mastering them. The approach throughout is selective, making no attempt to discuss complexity in all its software manifestations, but focusing on complexity of behavior. In programming, it is this complexity that surprises us when a program that we had thought was simple produces an unexpected result. In a realistic computer-based system, behavior is harder to understand, and its surprises can be far more damaging. In a critical system the surprises can be lethal.

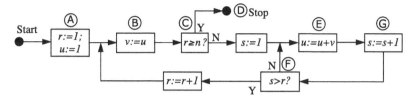

Fig. 2.1 A flowchart of a program designed by Alan Turing

2.2 A Small Integer Program

The pioneers of electronic computing in the 1940s recognized the difficulty of the programmer's task. Figure 2.1 shows a flowchart designed by Alan Turing, slightly modified to clarify a minor notational awkwardness. Turing used it as an illustration in a paper [16] he presented in Cambridge on 24th June 1949.

The program was written for a computer without a multiplier. It calculates *factorial*(*n*) by repeated addition. The value *n* is set in a local variable before the program starts; on termination the variable $v = factorial(n)$. Other local variables are r, s and u. Turing began his talk by asking: "How can one check a routine in the sense of making sure that it is right?" He recommended that "the programmer should make assertions about the various states that the machine can reach." Assertions are made about the variable values at the entries and exits of the named flow graph nodes. For example, on every entry to node B, $u = r!$; on exit from C to E, $v = r!$, and on exit from C to D, $v = n!$. The program is correct if the assertion on entry to the Stop node is correctly related to the assertion "*n* contains the argument value" on entry to node A from Start.

Along with the flowchart, Turing presented a table containing an entry for each marked block or point in the program: the entry shows "the condition of the machine completely," including the asserted precondition and postcondition, and the next step, if any, to be executed. The table entries are fragments which can be assembled into a correctness proof of the whole program by checking them in sequence while traversing the flowchart. Further discussion of this program, focusing particularly on the proof, can be found in [7] and in an interesting short paper [9] by Morris and Jones.

A careful reading of the flowchart shows that the program is essentially structured as an initialisation and two nested loops. The outer loop iterates multiplying by each value from 2 to *n*; the inner loop iterates to perform each multiplication. However, the flowchart does not express this structure in any systematic way, and Turing's explanation of the program is difficult to follow. Turing no doubt had a clear *mental* model of the process executed by his program: "multiply together all the integers from 1 to *n* in ascending order"; but his *overt* model of the computation—that is, the flowchart—does not show it clearly. We might even be bold enough to criticise Turing's program for specific design faults that make it hard to understand. The roles of the variables *u* and *v* are not consistently assigned. On one hand, *v* is the result variable in which the final result will be delivered. On the other hand, *v* is a parameter of the inner loop, specifying the addend by which the multiplication develops its product in the variable u. The awkwardness of the exit at block C from the middle of the outer loop is associated with this ambivalence. A further point, made in [9], is that the value of *factorial*(0) is correctly calculated, but this appears almost to be the result of chance rather than design.

Even after a reading of the formal proof has shown the program to be correct in that it delivers the desired result, the program remains complex in the sense that it is hard to understand. One aspect of the difficulty was well expressed by Dijkstra in the famous letter [4] to the editor of CACM: "we can interpret the value of a variable only with respect to the progress of the process." Flowcharts offer little or no support for structuring or abstracting the execution flow, and hence little help in understanding and expressing what the values of the program variables are intended to mean and how they evolve in program execution. This lack of support does not make it impossible to represent an understandable execution flow in a flowchart. It means that the discipline inherent in flowcharts helps neither to design a well-structured flow nor to capture the structure clearly once it has been designed.

Such support and help was precisely what structured programming offered, by describing execution by a nested set of sequence, conditional and loop clauses in the form now familiar to all programmers. In the famous letter, Dijkstra argued that this discipline, unlike unconstrained flowcharting, provides useful "coordinates in which to describe the progress of the process," allowing us to understand the meaning of the program variables and how their successive values mark the process as it evolves in time. Every part, every variable, and every operation of the program is seen in a nested closed context which makes it easily intelligible. Each context has an understandable purpose to which the associated program parts can be seen to contribute; and this purpose itself can be seen to contribute to an understandable purpose visible in the text at the next higher level. These purposes and the steps by which they are achieved are then expressible by assertions that fit naturally into the structure of the text.

This explanation of the benefits of structured programming is compelling, but there is more to say. Structured programming brings an additional benefit that is vital to human understanding. In a structured program text the process, as it evolves in execution, can become directly comprehensible in an immediate way. It becomes captured in the minds of the writer and readers of the text, as a vivid mental model. Attentive contemplation of the text is almost a physical enactment of the process itself; this comprehension is no less vital for being intuitive and resistant to formalisation.

2.3 Programs with Multiple Traversals

The problem of computing *factorial*(n) by repeated multiplication is simple in an important respect. The behavior of Turing's solution program is a little hard to understand, but this complexity is gratuitous: a more tidily structured version—left as an exercise for the reader—can be transparently simple. Only one simple behavior need be considered: the behavior of the program itself in execution. This behavior can be regarded as a traversal of the factors $1, 2, \ldots, n$ of $n!$, incorporating each factor into the result by using it as a multiplier when it is encountered in the traversal. The problem world of the program, which is the elementary arithmetic of small integers, imposes no additional constraint on the program behavior. The argument n, the result $v!$, the multipliers, and any local integer values in the other variables can all be freely written and read at will. The program as designed visits the factors of $n!$ in ascending numerical order, but descending order is equally possible and other orders could be considered.

More substantial programs, however, usually demand consideration of more than one simple behavior. For example, a program computing a result derived from an integer matrix may require to traverse the matrix in both row and column order. Both the input and output of a program may be significantly structured, and these structures may restrict the traversal orders available to the program. An input stream may be presented to the program as a text file, or as a time-ordered stream of interrupts or commands. A collection of records in a database, or an assemblage of program objects may afford only certain access paths for reading or writing, and the program must traverse these paths. For example, a program that summarises cellphone usage and produces customer bills must read the input data of call records, perhaps from a database or from a sequential file, and produce the output bills in a format and order convenient for the customers. The traversal of a program's input may involve some kind of navigation or parsing, and production of the output may demand that the records be written in a certain order to build the required data structure.

Multiple behaviors must therefore be considered for input and output traversals. The behavior of the program in execution must somehow combine the input and output traversals with the operations needed to implement the input-output function—that is, to store and accumulate values from the input records as they are read, and to compute and format the outputs in their required orders. This need to combine multiple behaviors is a primary potential source of software complexity.

A program encompassing more than one behavior is not necessarily complex if it is well designed. In the cellphone usage example, each customer's call records may be accessible in date order, each giving details of one call; the corresponding output bill may simply list these calls in date order, perhaps adding the calculated cost of each call, and appending summary information about total cost and any applicable discount. It will then be easy to design the program so that it traverses the input, calculates output values, and produces the output while doing so. The two behaviors based on the sequential structures of the two data streams fit together perfectly, and can then be easily merged [6] to give the dynamic structure of the program. The program text shows clearly the two synchronised traversals, with the operations on the program's local variables fitting in at the obviously applicable points. The program has exactly the clarity, simplicity, and immediate comprehensibility that are the promised benefits of structured programming.

2.4 Programs with Multiple Structures

Sometimes, however, there is a conflict—in the terminology of [6], a *structure clash*—between two sequential behaviors both of which are essential to the program. One particular kind of conflict is a *boundary clash*. For example, in a business reporting program, input data may be grouped by weeks while output data is grouped by months. The behaviors required to handle input and output are then in conflict, because there is a conflict between weeks and months: it is impossible to merge a traversal by weeks with a traversal by months to give a single program structure. In a similar example of a different flavour, variable-length records must be constructed and written to fixed length disk sectors, records being split if necessary across two or more sectors. The record building behavior conflicts with the sector handling behavior, because the record structure is in conflict with the sector structure. The general form of the difficulty posed by such a conflict is clear: no single structured program text can represent both of the required behaviors in the most immediate, intuitive, and comprehensible way.

To deal effectively with a complexity it must be divided into its simple constituents. In these small programming examples the criterion of simplicity of a proposed division is clear: each constituent behavior should be clearly described by a comprehensible structured program text. Now, inevitably, a further concern demands attention: How are the simple constituents to communicate? This concern has two aspects—one in the requirement world, the other in the implementation world. One is more abstract, the other more concrete. We might say that one is the communication between behaviors, while the other is the combination of program executions. Here we will consider the communication between the conflicting behaviors. The combination of program executions will be the topic of the next section.

For the business reporting problem, the conflicting behaviors must communicate in terms of days, because a day is the highest common factor of a week and a month: each consists of an integral number of days. Similarly, in the disk sector problem, communication must be in terms of the largest data elements—perhaps bytes—that are never split either between records or between sectors. Ignoring much detail, each problem then has two simple constituent conflicting but communicating behaviors:

- For the business problem: (a) *by-week* behavior: analysing the input by weeks and splitting the result into days; (b) *by-month* behavior: building up the output by months from the information by days.
- For the disk sector problem: (a) *by-record* behavior: creating the records and splitting them into bytes; (b) *by-sector* behavior: build up the sectors from bytes.

The communication concern in the requirement world demands further consideration, because the constituent behaviors are not perfectly separable. For example, in the processing of monthly business data it may be necessary to distinguish working days from weekend days. The distinction is defined in terms of weeks, but the theme of the separation is to keep the weeks and the months apart. The concern can be addressed by associating a *working/weekend* tag with each day's data. The tag is set in the context of the *by-week* behavior, and communicated to the *by-month* behavior.

Effectively, the tag carries forward with the day's data an indication of its context within the week. In the same way, the *record* behavior can associate a tag with each byte to indicate, for example, whether it is the first or last, or an intermediate byte of a record. We will not pursue this detail here.

2.5 Combining Programs

The program combination concern arises because a problem that required a solution in the form of one executable programmed behavior has been divided into two behaviors. Execution of the two corresponding programs must be somehow combined in the implementation to give the single program execution that was originally demanded. Possible mechanisms of combination may be found in the program execution environment—that is, in programming language features and in the operating system—or in textual manipulation of the program texts themselves.

The *by-week* and *by-month* behaviors for the business reporting problem communicate by respectively writing and reading a sequential stream of tagged days. An obvious combination mechanism introduces an intermediate physical file of day records on disk or tape. The *by-week* program is run to termination, writing this intermediate file; then the *by-month* program is run to termination, reading the file. This implementation is primitive and simple, and available in every execution environment. But it is also unattractively inefficient and cumbersome: execution time is doubled; use of backing store resources is increased by one half; and the first output record is not available until after the last input record has been read.

In a better combination design, the two programs are executed in parallel, each day record being passed between them to be consumed as soon as it is produced. Having produced each day record, the *by-week* program suspends execution until the *by-month* program has consumed it; having consumed each day record, the *by-month* program suspends execution until the *by-week* program has produced the next day. The two programs operate as *coroutines*, a programming construct first described by Conway as a machine-language mechanism [1], and adopted as a programming language feature [2] in Simula 67. In Simula, a program P suspends its own execution by executing a *resume*(Q) statement, Q being the name of the program whose execution is to be resumed. Execution of P continues at the point in its text following the *resume* statement when next another program executes a *resume*(P) statement.

A restricted run-time form of the coroutine combination is provided by the Unix operating system. For a linear structure of programs Unix allows the *stdout* output stream of a program to be either sent to a physical file or piped to another program; similarly, the *stdin* input stream of a program can either be read from a physical file or piped from another program's *stdout*. If the intermediate file of day records is written to *stdout* in the *by-week* program, and read from *stdin* by the *by-month* program, then the Unix shell command:

```
InW < ByWeek | ByMonth > OutM
```

specifies interleaved parallel execution of the programs *by-week* and *by-month*, the day records being passed between them in coroutine style.

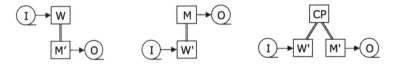

Fig. 2.2 Three ways of combining two small programs into one

2.6 Transforming a Program

Conway explains the coroutine mechanism [1] in terms of input and output operations:

> "…each module may be made into a *coroutine*; that is, it may be coded as an autonomous program which communicates with adjacent modules as if they were input or output subroutines. … There is no bound placed by this definition on the number of inputs and outputs a coroutine may have."

From this point of view, the *by-week* program can regard the *by-month* program as an output subroutine, and the *by-month* program can regard the *by-week* program as an input subroutine. If the programming language provides no *resume* statement and the operating system provides no pipes, the developer will surely adopt this point of view at least to the extent of writing one of the two programs as a subroutine of the other. Another possibility is to write both programs as subroutines, calling them from a simple controlling program. These possibilities are pictured in Fig. 2.2.

In the diagrams a tape symbol represents a physical file: I is the input data file; O is the output report file. W and M are the *by-week* and *by-month* programs written as autonomous (or 'main') programs; W′ and M′ are the same programs written as subroutines; CP is the controlling program, which loops, alternately reading a day record from W′ and writing it to M′. A double line represents a subroutine call, the upper program calling the lower program as a subroutine.

The behaviors evoked by one complete execution of the main program W and by one complete sequence of calls to the subroutine W′ are identical. This identity is clearly shown by the execution mechanisms of Simula and the Unix pipes, which demand no change to the texts of the executed programs. Even in the absence of such execution mechanisms, the subroutine W′ is mechanically obtainable from the program W by a transformation such as *program inversion* [6], in which a main program is 'inverted' with respect to one of its input or output files: that it, it is transformed to become an output or input subroutine for that file. Ignoring some details, the elements of the transformation are these:

- a set of labels identifying those points in the program text at which program execution can begin or resume: one at the start, and one at each operation on the file in question;
- a local variable *current-resume-point*, whose value is initialised to the label at the start of the program text, and a switch at the subroutine entry of the form "go to *current-resume-point*";
- implementation of each operation on the file in question by the code:

```
current-resume-point:=X; return; label X:
```

- the subroutine's local variables, including the stack and the *current-resume-point*, persist during the whole of the programmed behavior.

The essential benefit of such a transformation is that the changes to the text are purely local. The structured text of the original program is retained intact, and remains fully comprehensible. Essentially this transformation was used by Conway in his implementation of coroutines [1]. Applying the transformation to the development of interrupt-handling routines for a computer manufacturer [10] produced a large reduction in errors of design and coding.

Unfortunately, in common programming practise, instead of recognising that W' and W are behaviourally identical, the programmer is likely to see them as different. Whereas the behavior span of W is correctly seen as the complete synchronised behavior in which the whole day record file is produced in parallel with the traversal of the whole input data file, the behavior span of W' is seen as bounded by the production of a single day record. Treating the behavior span of W' in this way, as bounded by the production of a single day record, casts the behavior in the form of a large case statement, each limb of the case statement corresponding to some subset of the many different conditions in which a day record could be produced. This is the perspective commonly known as *event-driven programming*. Gratuitously, it is far more complex—that is, both harder to program correctly and harder to comprehend—than the comprehensible structured form that it mistakenly supplants.

2.7 Computer-Based Systems

The discussion in the preceding sections suggests that behavioral complexities in small programs may yield to several intellectual tools. One is a proper use of structured programming in its broadest sense: that is, the capture and understanding of behavior in its most comprehensible form. Another is the decomposition of a complex behavior into simple constituent parallel behaviors. Another is the careful consideration of communication between separated behaviors by an identified highest common factor and its capacity to carry any additional detail necessary because the behaviors can be only imperfectly separated. And another is the recognition that the task of combining program executions within an operating system environment is distinct from the task of satisfying the communication requirement between the separated programmed behaviors.

Computer-based systems embody programs, so the intellectual tools for their analysis and development will include those needed for programs. The sources of complexity found in small programs can also be recognized, writ large, in computer-based systems; but for a realistic system there are major additional sources and forms of complexity. These arise in the *problem world* outside the *machine*—that is, outside the computing equipment in which the software is executed. The expression *problem world* is appropriate because the purposes of the system lie in the world outside the machine, but must be somehow achieved by the machine through its

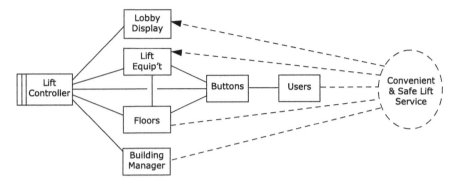

Fig. 2.3 Problem diagram of a lift system

interactions with the world. Systems for avionics, banking, power station control, welfare administration, medical radiation therapy and library management are all of this kind. The problem is to capture and understand the *system requirement*, which is a desired behavior in the problem world, and to devise and implement a behavior of the computer that will ensure the required behavior of the world.

The problem world comprises many *domains*: these are the parts of the human and physical world relevant to the system's purposes and to their achievement. It includes parts directly interfaced to the machine through its ports and other communication devices, parts that are the subject of system requirements, and parts that lie on the causal paths between them. Together with the computer, the problem domains constitute a system whose workings are the subject matter of the development. Figure 2.3 is a sketch of a system to control the lifts in a large building.

The machine is the Lift Controller; plain rectangles represent problem domains; solid lines represent interaction by such shared phenomena as state and events. The dashed oval represents the required behavior of the whole system. The dashed lines link the oval to the problem domains referenced by the requirement; an arrowhead on a dashed line to a problem domain indicates that the machine must, directly or indirectly, constrain the behavior of that domain. Here the requirement constrains only the Lobby Display and the Lift Equipment; it refers to, but does not constrain, the Users, the Building Manager (who can specify lift service priorities to suit different circumstances), and the Floors. All problem domains are constrained by their *given properties* and their interactions with other problem domains. For example: by the properties of the Lift Equipment, if the lift direction is set *up*, and the motor is set *on*, the lift car will rise in the shaft; by the properties of the Floors domain the rising car will encounter the floors successively in a fixed vertical sequence. The requirement imposes further constraints that the machine must satisfy. For example: if a user on a floor requests lift service, the lift car must come to that floor, the doors must open and close, and the car must go to the floor desired by the user.

The problem world is an assemblage of interacting heterogeneous problem domains. Their properties and behaviors depend partly on their individual constitutions, but they depend also on the context in which the system is designed to operate. The context sets bounds on the domain properties and behaviors, constraining them further beyond the constraints imposed by physics or biology. For example, the vertical floor sequence would not necessarily be preserved if an earthquake caused the building to collapse; but the system is not designed to operate in such conditions. On the other hand, the system is required to operate safely in the presence of faults in the lift equipment or the floor sensors. If the system is designed for an office building, the time allowed for users to enter and leave the lift will be based on empirical knowledge of office workers' behavior; in a system designed for an old age home the expected users' behavior will be different.

2.8 Sources of Complexity

The system requirements are complex because they combine several functions. The lift system must provide normal lift service according to the priorities currently chosen by the building manager. Some facility must be provided to allow the building manager to specify priority schemes, to store them, and to select a scheme for current use. The lobby display must be controlled so that it shows the current position and travel direction of each lift in a clear way. A system to administer a lending library must manage the members' status and collect their subscriptions; control the reservation and lending of books; calculate and collect fines for overdue loans and lost books; maintain the library catalogue; manage inter-library loans; and enable library staff to ensure that new and returned books are correctly identified and shelved, and can be easily found when needed.

In a critical system fault-tolerance adds greatly to complexity because it demands operation in different subcontexts within the overall context of the whole system, in which problem domains exhibit subsets of the properties and behaviors that are already constrained by the overall context. The lift system, for example, must ensure safe behavior in the presence of equipment malfunctions ranging from a stuck floor sensor or a failed request button to a burned-out hoist motor or even a snapped hoist cable. At the same time, lift service—in a degraded form—must be available, subject to the overriding requirement that safety is not compromised.

Further complexity is added by varying modes of system operation. The lift control system must be capable of appropriate operation in ordinary daily use; it must also be capable of operation according to priorities chosen by the building manager to meet unusual needs such as use of the building for a conference. It must also be capable of operating under command of a maintenance engineer, of a test inspector certifying the lift's safety, or of fire brigade personnel fighting a fire in the building.

System functions, or features, are not, in general, disjoint: they can interact both in the software and in the problem domains. In the telecommunications area, *feature interaction* became recognized as a major source of complexity in the early 1990s, giving rise to a series [14] of dedicated workshops and conferences. Feature interaction is also a source of complexity and difficulty in computer-based systems more generally. The essence of feature interaction is that features whose individual behaviors are relatively simple in isolation may interfere with each other. Their combination may be complex, allowing neither to fulfil its individual purpose by exhibiting its own simple behavior. In principle the potential complexity of feature interaction is exponential in the number of features: all features that affect, or are affected by, a common problem domain have the potential to interact.

2.9 Candidate Behaviour Constituents

In a small program, such as the business reporting program briefly discussed in earlier sections, requirement complexity can be identified by considering the input stream traversal necessary to parse the input data, the output stream traversal necessary to produce the output in the required order, and the input-output mapping that the machine must achieve while traversing the input and output streams. If a structure clash is found, the behavior is decomposed into simpler constituents, their communication is analysed, and the corresponding programs are combined. Clear and comprehensible simple constituents reward the effort of considering their communication and combination. The approach can be seen as a separation of higher-order concerns: we separate the intrinsic complexity of each constituent from the complexity of composing it with its siblings.

Various proposals have been made for decomposing system behavior, and have furnished the basis of various development methods:

- *Objects*: each constituent corresponds to an entity in the problem world, capturing its behavior and evolving state as it responds to messages and receives responses to messages it sends to other objects. For example, in the library system one constituent may capture the behavior of a library member, another constituent the behavior of a book, and so on.
- *Machine events*: each constituent corresponds to an event class caused by the machine and affecting the problem world. For example, in the lift system one constituent may correspond to switching on the hoist motor, one to applying the emergency brake, and so on. Each constituent captures an event and the resulting changes in the problem world state.
- *Requirement events*: each constituent corresponds to an event or state value change caused by a problem domain. For example, in the lift system one constituent may correspond to the pressing of a lift button, another to the closing of a floor sensor on arrival of the lift car, and so on. Each constituent captures an event and specifies the required response of the machine.
- *Use cases*: each constituent corresponds to a bounded episode of interaction between a user and the machine. For example, in the library system one constituent may capture the interaction in which a member borrows a book, another the interaction in which a user searches for a book in the library catalogue, and so on. In the lift system one constituent may capture the interaction in which a user successfully summons the lift.
- *Software modules*: each constituent corresponds to an executable textual constituent of the machine's software. For example, in the library system one constituent may capture the program procedure that the machine executes to charge

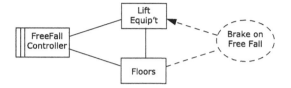

Fig. 2.4 Problem diagram of a lift system constituent

a member's subscription to a credit card, another the procedure of adding a newly acquired book to the library catalogue.

Each of these proposals can offer a particular advantage in some facet or phase of developing a particular system. They are not mutually exclusive, but neither singly nor in any combination are they adequate to master behavioral complexity.

2.10 Functional Constituent Behaviours

In the famous phrase of Socrates in the Phaedrus, a fully intelligible decomposition of system behavior must "carve nature at the joints" [11]. The major joints in a system's behavior are the meeting places of the system's large functions or features. In a decomposition into functions the constituents will be projections of the system and of its overall behavior.

Each constituent projection of system behavior has a requirement, a problem world, and a machine; each of these is a projection of the corresponding part of the whole system. To illustrate this idea, Fig. 2.4 shows a possible behavior constituent of the lift control system.

The behavior constituent shown corresponds to a lift control feature introduced by Elisha Otis in 1852. The lift is equipped with an emergency brake which can im-mobilise the lift car by clamping it to the vertical steel guides on which it travels. If at any time the hoist cable snaps, the hoist motor is switched off and the emergency brake is applied, preventing the lift car from falling freely and suffering a disastrous impact at the bottom of the shaft. A suitably designed Free Fall Controller might achieve the required behavior by continually measuring the time from floor to floor in downwards motion of the lift car, applying the brake if this time is small enough to indicate a snapped cable or a major malfunction having a similar effect.

A behavioral constituent is not necessarily a subsystem in the sense that implies implementation by distinct identifiable constituents that will remain recognisable and distinguishable in the complete developed system. In general, the combination of separated simple constituents in a computer-based system is a major task, and must exploit transformations of many kinds. However, for purposes of analysis and understanding, each simple constituent can be regarded as a closed system in its own right, to be understood in isolation from other simple constituents, and having no interaction with anything outside itself. In the analysis, the omitted domains— the Users, Buttons, Lobby Display and Building Manager—play no part. The other behaviors of the Lift Controller machine, too, play no part here: although in the complete system the motion of the lift is under the control of the Lift Controller machine, here we regard the lift car as travelling autonomously in the lift shaft on its own initiative.

By decomposing system behavior into projections that take the form of subsystems, we bring into focus for each projection the vital question: How can the machine achieve the required behavior? That is, we are not interested only in the question: What happens? We are interested also in the question: How does it work? To understand each behavior projection we must also understand its genesis in the workings of the subsystem in which it is defined. This operational perspective affords a basis for assessing the simplicity of each behavior projection by assessing the simplicity of the subsystem that evokes it. We consider each projection in isolation. We treat it as if it were a complete system, although in fact it is only a projection of the whole system we are developing. This view is far from new. It was advanced by Terry Winograd over thirty years ago [17]:

> "In order to successfully view a system as made up of two distinct subsystems, they need not be implemented on physically different machines, or even in different pieces of the code. In general, any one viewpoint of a component includes a specification of a boundary. Behaviour across the boundary is seen in the domain of interactions, and behaviour within the boundary is in the domain of implementation. That implementation can in turn be viewed as interaction between subcomponents."

We will turn in a later section to the interactions between distinct constituents. Here we consider the intrinsic complexity—or simplicity—of each one considered in isolation. The criteria of simplicity provide a guide and a check in the decomposition of system behavior.

2.11 Simplicity Criteria

Each behavior constituent, regarded as a subsystem, is what the physical chemist and philosopher Michael Polanyi calls a *contrivance* [12]. A contrivance has a set of characteristic parts, arranged in a configuration within which they act on one another. For us these are the machine and the problem domains. The contrivance has a purpose: that is, the requirement. Most importantly, the contrivance has an *operational principle*, which describes how the parts combine by their interactions to achieve the purpose.

Simplicity of a contrivance can be judged by criteria that are largely—though not, of course—entirely—objective: failure on a simplicity criterion is a forewarning of a development difficulty. The criteria are not mutually independent: a proposed constituent failing on one criterion will probably fail on another also. Important criteria are the following:

- *Completeness*: The subsystem is closed in the sense that it does not interact with anything outside it. In the Free Fall projection the behavior of the Lift Equipment is regarded as autonomous.

- *Unity of Context*: Different contexts of use demand different modes of operation. An aircraft may be taxiing, taking off, climbing, cruising, and so on. Not all context differences are relevant to all behaviors: differences between climbing and cruising are not relevant to the functioning of the public address system. The context of a simple behavior projection is constant over the span of the projection.
- *Simplicity of Purpose*: The purpose or requirement of a simple behavior constituent can be simply expressed as a specific relationship among observable phenomena of its parts. The requirement of the Free Fall constituent is that the emergency brake is applied when the lift car is descending at a speed above a certain limit.
- *Unity of Purpose*: A behavior projection is not simple if its purpose has the form: "Ensure P1, but if that is not possible ensure P2." This kind of cascading structure may arise in a highly fault-tolerant system. The distinct levels of functional degradation can be distinct behavior projections.
- *Unity of Part Roles*: In any behavior constituent each part fulfils a role contributing to achieving the purpose. In a simple behavior constituent each part's role, like the overall purpose, exhibits a coherence and unity.
- *Unity of Part Properties*: In a simple behavioral constituent each part's relevant properties are coherent and consistent, allowing a clear understanding of how the behavior is achieved. In a Normal Lift Service behavioral projection, the properties of the Lift Equipment domain are those on which the lift service function relies.
- *Temporal Unity*: A simple behavioral constituent has an unbroken time span. When a behavior comprises both writing and reading of a large data object, it is appropriate to separate the writing and reading unless they are closely linked in time, as they are in a conversation. In the lift system, the Building Manager's creating and editing of a scheme of priorities should be separated from its use in the provision of lift service.
- *Simplicity of Operational Principle*: In explaining how a behavior constituent works, it is natural to trace the causal chains in the problem diagram. An explanation of the free fall constituent would trace a path over Fig. 2.4:
  - From the Lift Equipment domain to the Floors domain: "the lift car moves between floors;"
  - At the Floors domain: "lift car arrival and departure at a floor changes the floor sensor state;"
  - From the Floors domain to the Free Fall Controller machine: "the lift car movement is detected by the machine's monitoring the floor sensors;"
  - At the Free Fall Controller machine: "the machine evaluates the speed of downward movement; excessive speed is considered to indicate free fall"
  - From the Free Fall Controller machine to the Lift Equipment: "if the downward movement indicates free fall the machine applies the brake".

  Satisfaction of the requirement is explained in a single pass over the causal links, with no backtracking and no fork or join. The complexity of an operational principle is reflected in the number and complexity of the causal paths in the problem diagram that trace out its explanation.

- *Machine Regularity*: The machine in a simple behavioral constituent achieves its purpose by executing a regular process that can be adequately understood in the same way as a structured program.

These criteria of simplicity aim to characterise extreme simplicity, and a developer's reaction to the evaluation of simplicity must depend on many factors. It remains true in general that major deviations from extreme simplicity warn of difficulties to come.

2.12 Secondary Decompositions

The simplicity criteria motivate behavioral decompositions beyond those enjoined by recognising distinct system functions. One important general class is the introduction of an *analogic model*, with an associated separation of the writer and reader of the model.

Correct behavior of a computer-based system relies heavily on monitoring the problem world to detect significant states and conditions to which the machine must respond. In the simplest and easiest cases the machine achieves this monitoring by recognising problem world signals or states whose meaning is direct and unambiguous. For example, in the Lift System the Lift Controller can detect directly that the lift car has arrived at a desired floor by observing that the floor sensor state has changed to *on*.

Often, however, the monitoring of the problem world, and the evaluation of the signals and states it provides, is more complex and difficult, and constitutes a problem that merits separate investigation in its own right. For example, in an employee database in a payroll system, information about the hiring, work and pay of each employee becomes available to the computer as each event occurs. The information is stored, structured and summarised in the database, where it constitutes an *analogic model* of the employee's attributes, history, and current state. This model is then available when needed for use in calculating pay, holiday entitlement, and pension rights, and also for its contribution to predictive and retrospective analyses. The model, of course, is not static: it is continually updated during the working life of the employee, and its changes reflect the employee's process evolving in time.

For a very different example, consider a system [15] that manages the routing of packages through a tree structure of conveyors. The destination of each package is specified on a bar-coded label that is read once on entry at the root of the tree. The packages are spatially separated on the conveyors, and are detected by sensors when they arrive at each branch point and when they leave. For each package, the machine must set the switch mechanism at each branch point so that the package follows the correct route to its specified destination.

The analogic model is needed because although the sensors at the switches indicate that some package has arrived or left, they cannot indicate the package destination, which can be read only on entry to the tree. In the model the conveyors are represented as queues of packages, each package being associated with its barcoded destination. The package arriving at a switch is the package at the head of the

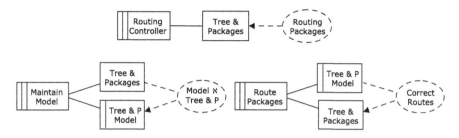

Fig. 2.5 Behaviour decomposition: introducing an analogic model

queue in the incoming conveyor; on leaving by the route chosen by the machine, it becomes the tail of the queue in the outgoing conveyor.

The upper part of Fig. 2.5 shows the problem diagram of the whole system; the lower left diagram shows the projection of the system in which the analogic model is built and maintained; the lower right diagram shows the packages being routed through the tree using the analogic model. The analogic model is to be understood as a latent local variable of the Routing Controller machine, exposed and made explicit by the decomposition of the machine's behavior.

2.13 The Oversimplification Strategy

A source of system complexity is feature interaction. The complexity of an identified behavioral constituent has two sources. One is the inherent complexity of the constituent considered in isolation; the other is the additional complexity due to its interaction with other constituents. It is useful to separate these two sources. For this purpose a strategy of *oversimplification* should be adopted in initially considering each projection: the projection is oversimplified to satisfy the simplicity criteria of the preceding section. The point can be illustrated by two behavior constituents in a system to manage a lending library. The library allows its paying members in good standing to borrow books, and the system must manage both membership and book borrowing.

For each member, membership is a behavior evolving in time. Between the member's initial joining and final resignation there are annual renewals of membership. There are also vicissitudes of payment and of member identity and accessibility: credit card charges may be refused or disputed; bankruptcy, change of name, change of address, promotion from junior to senior member at adulthood, emigration, death, and many other possibly significant events must be considered for their effect on the member's standing.

For each book, too, there is a behavior evolving in time. The book is acquired and catalogued, shelved, sent for repair when necessary, and eventually disposed of. It can be reserved, borrowed for two weeks, and returned, and a current loan may be renewed before its expiry date. The book may be sent to another library in an inter-library loan scheme; equally, a book belonging to another library may be the

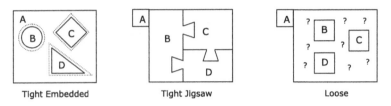

Fig. 2.6 Decomposition techniques

subject of a loan to a member. At any point in a book's history it may be lost, and may eventually be found and returned to the library.

A projection that handles both membership and book borrowing cannot satisfy the machine regularity criterion: there is a structure clash between the book and member behaviors. From reservation to final return or loss a loan can stretch over a long time, and in this time the member's status can undergo more than one change, including membership expiry and renewal. So it is desirable to separate the two behaviors, considering each in isolation as if the other did not exist. To isolate the book behavior we may assume that membership status is constant for each member and therefore cannot change during the course of the member's interaction with the book. The membership behavior is isolated by assuming that interaction with a book process consists only of the first event of the interaction—perhaps *reserve* or *borrow*. Each process can then be studied and understood in isolation, taking account only of its own intrinsic complexities.

When each behavior is adequately understood, and this understanding has been captured and documented, their interaction can be studied as a distinct aspect of the whole problem. The questions to be studied will be those that arise from undoing the oversimplifications made in isolating the processes. For example: Can a book be borrowed by a member whose membership will expire during the expected currency of the loan? Can it be renewed in this situation? How do changes in a member's status affect the member's rights in a current loan? How and to what extent is a resigning member to be relieved of membership obligations if there is still an unreturned loan outstanding on resignation? What happens to a reservation made by a member whose status is diminished? The result of studying the interaction will, in general, be changes to one or both of the behaviors.

2.14 Loose Decomposition

The strategy of oversimplification fits into an approach to system behavior analysis that we may call *loose decomposition*. Three classes of decomposition technique are pictured in Fig. 2.6. Each picture shows, in abstract form, the decomposition of a whole, A, into parts B, C and D.

Embedded decomposition is familiar from programs structured as procedure hierarchies. A is the procedure implementing the complete program; B, C and D are procedures called by A. Each called procedure must fit perfectly, both syntactically and semantically, into its corresponding 'hole' in the text and execution of the calling procedure A. The conception and design of each of the parts B, C and D must therefore simultaneously address any complexity of the part's own function and any complexity arising from its interaction with the calling procedure A and its indirect cooperation, through A, with A's other parts.

Jigsaw decomposition is found, for example, in relational database design. A is the whole database, and B, C and D are tables within it. Essentially, A has no existence except as the assemblage formed by its parts, B, C and D. The parts fit together like the pieces of a jigsaw puzzle, the tabs being formed by foreign keys—that is, by common values that allow rows of different tables to be associated. The process decomposition of CSP is also jigsaw decomposition, the constituent processes being associated by events in the intersection of their alphabets. In jigsaw decomposition, as in embedded decomposition, both the part's own function and its interaction with other parts must be considered simultaneously.

In *loose decomposition*, by contrast, the decomposition merely identifies parts that are expected to contribute to the whole without considering how they will make that contribution or how they will fit together with each other. The identified parts can then be studied in isolation before their interactions are studied and their recombination designed.

In general, it can be expected, as the picture suggests, that there will be gaps to be filled in assembling the whole from the identified parts. Further, the decomposition does not assume that the identified parts can be designed in full detail and subsequently fitted, unchanged, into the whole. On the contrary: the primary motivation for using loose decomposition is the desire to separate the intrinsic complexities of each part's own function from any additional complexities caused by its interaction with other parts. After the parts have been adequately studied, their interactions will demand not only mechanisms to combine them, but also modifications to make the combination possible.

2.15 Recombining Behaviours

The purpose of loose decomposition is to separate the intrinsic complexity of each behavioral projection from the complexity added by its interactions with other projections. The recombination of the projections must therefore be recognized as a distinct development task: their interactions must be analysed and understood, and a recombination designed that will support any necessary cooperation and resolve any conflicts. In a spatial dimension, two behavioral projections can interact if their problem worlds include a common domain. In a temporal dimension, they can interact if their behavior spans overlap or are contiguous.

A very well known recombination problem concerns the potential interference between two subproblem contrivances that interact at a shared problem domain. To manage this potential interference some kind of mutual exclusion must be specified at an appropriate granularity. For interference in a lexical domain such as a database, mutual exclusion is effectively achieved by a transaction structure.

An important class of recombination concern arises when the control of a problem domain is transferred from one subsystem to another. Consider, for example, an automotive system in which the required behavior of the car while driven on the road is substantially different from its required behavior when undergoing a regular servicing. If the two behaviors have been separated out into two behavior projections, then at some point when the car is taken in for servicing, or, conversely, taken back from servicing to be driven on the road, control of the car must pass from one to the other. The former, currently active, subproblem machine must suspend or terminate its operation, and the latter, newly active, must resume or start. The problem of managing this transfer of control has been called a *switching concern* [5].

The focus of a switching concern is the resulting concatenated behavior of the problem world. This concatenated behavior must satisfy two conditions. First, any assumptions about the initial problem world state on which the design of the latter contrivance depends must be satisfied at the point of transfer. For example, in the automotive system the latter subproblem design might assume that the car is stationary with the handbrake on, the engine stopped, and the gear in neutral. Second, the concatenated behavior must satisfy any requirements and assumptions whose scope embraces both the former and the latter subproblem.

Two behavior projections' lifetimes may be coterminous: for example, the free fall constituent is always in operation and so is the constituent that displays the current location of the lift car. In general, the operational lifetimes of distinct subproblem contrivances are not coterminous. One may begin operation only when a particular condition has been detected by another that is monitoring that condition: for example, a contrivance that shuts down the radiation beam in a radiotherapy system may be activated only when the emergency button is pressed. A set of subproblem contrivances may correspond to successive phases in a defined sequential process: for example, taxi, take-off, climb, and cruise in an avionics system. One contrivance's operational lifetime may be nested inside another's: for example, a contrivance that delivers cash from an ATM and the contrivance that controls a single session of use of the ATM.

In discussing small programs we distinguished the required communication between separated simple constituents from recombining their execution to fit efficiently into the operational environment. For computer-based systems, the recombining the execution of separated simple behaviors is a large task in its own right, often characterised as software architecture.

2.16 Some Propositions About Software Complexity

This section recapitulates some propositions about software complexity, summarising points already made more discursively in earlier sections.

(a) Success in software development depends on human understanding. We perceive complexity wherever we recognise that we do not understand. Complexity is the mother of error.

(b) Behavioral complexity is of primary importance. A complex behavior is a combination of conflicting simple behaviors. In analysis we identify and separate the constituent simple behaviors. In synthesis we clarify their communication and recombine the execution of the programs that realise them.

(c) For small programs there are three obvious categories of required behavior: traversing the inputs—that is, parsing or navigating them; traversing the outputs—that is, producing them in the required order and structure; and computing the output data values from the input.

(d) In each category of required behavior of a small program, a behavior is simple if it can be represented by a labelled regular expression, as it is in a structured program text. In general, a structured program is more understandable than a flowchart.

(e) A structured program is understandable because it localises the demand for understanding at each level of the nested structure. More importantly, the described behavior is comprehensible in an intuitive way that is closely related to a mental enactment of the behavior. The importance of this comprehension is not lessened by its intuitive nature, which resists formalisation.

(f) Complexity in a small program can be mastered by separating the conflicting behaviors into distinct simple programs. Communication between these programs demands explicit clarification and design because they may be only imperfectly separable. This design task is concerned to satisfy the behavior requirement.

(g) The task of combining simple program executions is concerned with implementation within the facilities and constraints of the programming language and execution environment. Parallel execution facilities such as coroutines or Unix pipes may make this task easy.

(h) In the absence of parallel execution facilities the simple programs must often be combined by textual manipulation. Systematic manipulation can convert a program into a subroutine with persistent state; this subroutine can then play the role of an input routine for one of its output files, or an output routine for one of its input files.

(i) Requirements for a computer-based system stipulate behaviors of the problem world. The system is an assemblage of interacting heterogeneous parts, or domains, including the machine, which is the computer equipment executing the software.

(j) The software development problem for a system includes: clarifying and capturing the requirements; investigating and capturing the given properties and behaviors of the problem domains; and devising a behavior of the machine to evoke the required behavior in the problem world.

(k) Realistic systems have multiple functions, operating in various modes and contexts. These functions, modes and contexts provide a basic structure for understanding the system behavior.

(l) Like a complex behavior of a small program, a complex behavior of a system is a combination of simple behaviors, each a projection of the whole. Each is a behavior of an assemblage of problem domains and the machine. These simple behaviors can interact both within the machine and within common problem domains.

(m) For a system, the behaviors of interest are not input or output streams or computing the values of output from inputs. They are joint behaviors of parts of the problem world evoked by the machine. They must therefore be understood as behaviors of contrivances, comparable to the behaviors of such mechanical devices as clocks and motor cars.

(n) In addition to its interacting parts, a contrivance has a purpose and an operational principle. The purpose is the behavioral requirement to be satisfied by the contrivance. The operational principle explains how the purpose is achieved: that is, how the contrivance works. Understanding of the operational principle is essentially an informal and intuitive comprehension, resistant to formalisation.

(o) Some criteria of simplicity in a contrivance can be understood as unities: unity of requirement; unity of the role played by each domain in satisfying the requirement; unity of context in which the contrivance is designed to operate; unity of domain properties on which the contrivance depends; and unity of the contrivance's execution time.

(p) An overarching criterion is simplicity of the operational principle. Any operational principle can be explained by tracing the operation along causal links in the configuration of domains and their interactions. An operational principle is simple if it can be explained in a single pass over the configuration, with no backtracking and no fork or join.

(q) As in a small program, a criterion of simplicity for a contrivance is that the behavior of the machine can be adequately represented by a labelled regular expression, as it is in a structured program text.

(r) The criteria of simplicity enjoin further decompositions. In particular, many system functions can be decomposed into the maintenance of a dynamic model of some part of the problem world, and the use of that model. Similarly, where the system transports data over time or place or both, the writing should be separated from the reading.

(s) Communication between separated behaviors, and combination of the executions of the machines that evoke them, are a major source of complexity in systems. Loose decomposition is therefore an effective approach: consideration of communication and combination is deferred until the constituent behaviors are well enough understood.

(t) Because separation into simple behaviors can rarely be perfect, understanding of constituent behaviors usually demands initial oversimplification. The oversimplification can be reversed later, when the communication between the simple behaviors is considered.

(u) For a system, combining the machine executions of constituent behaviors is—or should be—the goal of software architecture after the constituent behaviors have been adequately understood.

2.17 Understanding and Formalism

The discussion of software complexity in this chapter has focused on human understanding and has ignored formal aspects of software development. Formal reasoning, calculation, and proof are powerful tools, but they are best deployed in the context of an intuitive, informal, comprehension that provides the necessary structure and guiding purposes. Polanyi stresses the distinction between science and engineering [13]:

> "Engineering and physics are two different sciences. Engineering includes the operational principles of machines and some knowledge of physics bearing on those principles. Physics and chemistry, on the other hand, include no knowledge of the operational principles of machines. Hence a complete physical and chemical topography of an object would not tell us whether it is a machine, and if so, how it works, and for what purpose."

A similar distinction applies to software development and formal mathematical reasoning. The historic development of structured programming illustrates the point clearly. Rightly, the original explicit motivation was human understanding of program executions. Later it proved possible to build formal reasoning on the basis of the intuitively comprehensible program structure. Correctness proofs exploited this structure, using loop invariants and other formal techniques. This is the proper role of formalism: to add strength, precision and confidence to an intuitive understanding. Unfortunately, advocates of formal and informal techniques often see each other as rivals. It would be better to seek means and opportunities of informed cooperation in the mastery of software complexity.

References

1. Conway, M.E.: Design of a separable transition-diagram compiler. Commun. ACM **6**(7), 396–408 (1963)
2. Dahl, O.-J., Hoare, C.A.R.: Chapter III: Hierarchical program structures. In: Dahl, O.J., Dijkstra, E.W., Hoare, C.A.R. (eds.) Structured Programming, pp. 175–220. Academic Press, San Diego (1972)
3. Descartes, R.: Discourse on the Method of Rightly Conducting the Reason, and Seeking Truth in the Sciences (1637)
4. Dijkstra, E.W.: A case against the GO TO statement; EWD215, published as a letter (Go To statement considered harmful) to the editor. Commun. ACM **11**(3), 147–148 (1968)
5. Jackson, M.: Problem Frames: Analysing and Structuring Software Development Problems. Addison-Wesley, Reading (2001)
6. Jackson, M.A.: Constructive methods of program design. In: Goos, G., Hartmanis, J. (eds.) 1st Conference of the European Cooperation in Informatics, pp. 236–262. Springer, Berlin (1976)
7. Jones, C.B.: The early search for tractable ways of reasoning about programs. IEEE Ann. Hist. Comput. **25**(2), 26–49 (2003)
8. Leibniz, G.W.: Philosophical Writings (Die Philosophischen Schriften) vol. VI (1857–1890). Edited by C.I. Gerhardt
9. Morris, F.L., Jones, C.B.: An early program proof by Alan Turing. IEEE Ann. Hist. Comput. **6**(2), 139–143 (1984)
10. Palmer, P.F.: Structured programming techniques in interrupt-driven routines. ICL Tech. J. **1**(3), 247–264 (1979)
11. Plato: Phaedrus. Oxford University Press, Oxford (2002). Translated by Robin Waterfield
12. Polanyi, M.: Personal Knowledge: Towards a Post-critical Philosophy. Routledge and Kegan Paul, London (1958), and University of Chicago Press, 1974

13. Polanyi, M.: The Tacit Dimension. University of Chicago Press, Chicago (1966); republished with foreword by Amartya Sen, 2009
14. Reiff-Marganiec, S., Ryan, M. (eds.): Feature Interactions in Telecommunications and Software Systems, ICFI'05, 28–30 June 2005, Leicester, UK, vol. VIII. IOS Press, Amsterdam (2005)
15. Swartout, W., Balzer, R.: On the inevitable intertwining of specification and implementation. Commun. ACM **25**(7), 438–440 (1982)
16. Turing, A.M.: Checking a large routine. Report of a Conference on High Speed Automatic Calculating Machines, 67–69 (1949). Also discussed in Refs. [7, 9]
17. Winograd, T.: Beyond programming languages. Commun. ACM **22**(7), 391–401 (1979)

Part II
Controlling Complexity

.

Chapter 3
Conquering Complexity

Gerard J. Holzmann

3.1 Introduction

Outside software engineering, the main principles of reliable system design are commonly practiced, and not just for safety critical systems. If, for instance, a kitchen-sink leaks, one can close a valve that stops the flow of water to that sink. The valve is there because experience has shown that sinks do occasionally leak, no matter how carefully they are constructed. If an electrical outlet short-circuits in someone's home, a fuse will melt. The fuse is there to prevent greater disaster in case the unanticipated happens. The presence of the fuse or valve does not signify an implicit acceptance of sloppy workmanship: they are an essential part of reliable system design.

Most software today is built without any valves and fuses. We try to build perfect parachutes or sinks or outlets that do not need backup. When software fails, we blame the developer for failing to be perfect. It would be wiser to assume from the start that even carefully constructed and verified software components, like all other things in life, may fail in sometimes unpredictable ways, and to use this knowledge to construct assemblies of components that provide independently verifiable system reliability. Studying how this can be accomplished is the focus of this chapter.

3.2 Reliable Systems from Unreliable Parts

Non-critical software applications are often designed in a monolithic fashion. When the application crashes, for instance when it hits a divide by zero error, the only

G.J. Holzmann (✉)
Laboratory for Reliable Software, Jet Propulsion Laboratory, California Institute of Technology, Pasadena, CA, USA
e-mail: gholzmann@acm.org

M. Hinchey, L. Coyle (eds.), *Conquering Complexity*,
DOI 10.1007/978-1-4471-2297-5_3, © Springer-Verlag London Limited 2012

recourse one then has is to restart the application from scratch. This approach is not adequate to use in the construction of systems that are safety critical, for instance when human life depends on its correct and continued functioning. When, for instance, a spacecraft experiences an unexpected failure of one of its components during a launch or landing procedure, a complete restart of the software may lead to the loss of the mission. In manned space flight, a few minutes spent in rebooting the crew's life support system can have undesired consequences. Systems like this must be reliable, even if some of their software parts are not. The wise course is to assume that no software components are fail-proof, not even those that have been verified exhaustively. Note, for instance, that in software verification we can only prove that a system has, or does not have, specific properties. If we omit a property, or verify the wrong properties, the verification effort will be of limited value. Alas, in practice we often only realize in retrospect (after a failure occurs) that the documented and carefully vetted requirements for a system were incomplete, or too vaguely stated to prevent subtle or even catastrophic problems later.

3.3 Simplicity and Redundancy

There are two commonly used strategies for achieving system reliability. The first is to use a design that achieves robustness through *simplicity* and the second is to protect against unanticipated failure by using *redundancy*.

A simple design is easier to understand, easier to verify, and easier to operate and maintain in good working order. The argument for redundancy in *hardware* (not software) components is also readily made. If the probability of failure of individual components is statistically independent, the chance of having both a primary and a backup component fail at the same time can be small. If, for instance, all components have the same independent probability p of failure, then the probability that all N components fail in an N-redundant system would be p^N. The use of simplicity reduces the value of p, and the use of redundancy increases the value of N. Trivially, for all values of $N \leq 1$ and $0 < p < 1$ both techniques can lower the probability of failure p^N for the system.

One of the basic premises used in the redundancy argument is the statistical independence of the failure probabilities of components. Although this independence can often be secured for hardware components, it can be very hard to achieve in software. Well-known are the experiments performed in the eighties by Knight and Leveson with N-version programming techniques, which demonstrated that different programming teams can make the same types of design errors when working from a common set of (often imperfect) design requirements [3]. Independently, Sha also pointed out that a decision to apply N-version programming is never independent of budget and schedule decisions. With a fixed budget, each of N independent development efforts will inevitably receive only $1/N$-th of the project resources. If we compare the expected reliability of N development efforts, each pursued with $1/N$-th of the project resources with a single targeted effort that can consume all available resources, the tradeoffs can become very different [11].

Another commonly used method to improving system reliability is the *recovery block approach* [7], in which several alternative systems are constructed, and all are subjected to a common acceptance test. For a given input, the system attempts each alternative in turn (possibly in a fixed order), until one of the alternatives produces a response that passes the acceptance test. In this case, the system must be designed so that it is possible to rollback the effects of an alternative if its result fails the acceptance test. While the recovery block approach has the advantage over N-version programming that only one of the alternatives needs to be correct (as opposed to a majority of them), it has the same disadvantage that the implementation budget is divided across several teams.

Redundancy in the traditional sense, in the way that has proven to work well with hardware systems, therefore, cannot be duplicated easily in safety critical software systems. A further complication is that traditional redundancy assumes that system failures are normally cause by individual component failures. Although this may be true in relatively small systems, more complex systems tend to fail in entirely different ways. We will discuss this phenomenon first before we explore new strategies for reliable system design that can be based on these observations.

3.4 The Nature of Failure in Complex Systems

In a 1984 book [6], sociologist Charles Perrow wrote about the causes of failure in complex systems, concluding that they were of a different nature than most people normally assume. Perrow argued that when seemingly unrelated parts of a larger system fail in some unforeseen combination, dependencies can become apparent that are rarely accounted for in the original design. In safety critical systems the potential impact of each possible component or sub-system failure is normally studied in detail and remedied with backups. But failure *combinations* are rarely studied in detail; there are just too many of them and most of them can be shown to have a very low probability of occurrence. A compelling example in Perrow's book is a description of the events leading up to the partial meltdown of the nuclear reactor at Three Mile Island in 1979. The reactor was carefully designed with multiple backups that should have ruled out what happened. Yet a small number of relatively minor failures in different parts of the system (an erroneously closed valve in one place and a stuck valve in another) conspired to defeat all protections and allowed a major accident to occur. A risk assessment of the probability of the scenario that unfolded would probably have concluded that it had a vanishingly small chance of occurring and need not be addressed in the overall design.

To understand the difficulty of this problem, consider a complex system with M different components, each of which has a small and independent probability of failure p. The probability that any one component will fail is p, and we can protect ourselves against this with a backup. The probability that N arbitrarily chosen components fail in combination is p^N (assuming $1 \leq N \leq M$). Clearly, with increasing values for N the probability of this event decreases exponentially fast with the value of N, but at the same time the total number of possible combinations that can trigger this type of failure rises exponentially fast with N. As a first order approximation, there are M^N possible combinations of N components. For a moderately complex system with one thousand components, there are close to one million possible combinations of two components, and one billion possible combinations of three components. It is virtually impossible to test the potential consequences of each possible (though unlikely) combination of component failures.

Examples of this phenomenon are not hard to find. The loss of contact with the Mars Global Surveyor (MGS) spacecraft is a recent example that has all the elements of a Perrow-style failure.

The MGS Spacecraft failure.

The failure scenario started with a routine check of the contents of the RAM memories in the two CPUs of the dual-redundant control system of the spacecraft. One CPU in the spacecraft is designated the primary CPU, and it controls all functions of the spacecraft. The other CPU is designated as a standby, ready to take over control when the primary CPU fails. The memory contents of the two CPUs are meant to be identical. In the routine check it was found that the two memories differed in a few locations. The difference was of no major consequence, it merely reflected that some flight parameters had been updated with slightly more precise versions while the standby CPU was offline, and thus unable to accept the new values.

A correction to this problem was planned for a routine update. One of the parameters was stored as a double-word value, and erroneously the address of the parameter was taken to be the second word, instead of the first word. (Only the second word differed between the two memories.) This meant that the update of this parameter actually turned out to corrupt the correct value. The update was done simultaneously in both memories (to make sure the two memories would now match), which meant that both copies of the parameter were now corrupted. This parameter recorded a soft-stop value for the rotation of the solar-arrays. No harm would be done to the spacecraft if the soft-stop value was incorrect, though, because there was also a hardware protection mechanism in case the physical hard-stop was reached. Here then is the first coincidence of an unsuspected coupling. By coincidence the parameter immediately adjacent to the soft-stop parameter was the parameter that recorded the correct position of the space-craft for earth-pointing. Because the update of the soft-stop parameter was off by one word, it corrupted not just that parameter but also the parameter adjacent to it in memory.

What had gone wrong so far could easily have been caught in routine checks at any point later. Several months after these events, without these routine checks having been performed yet, the solar arrays were adjusted from their summer to their winter position—again a routine operation performed twice each year. In this case, though, the adjustment triggered a fault, which was caused by the incorrect value for the soft stop parameter. The fault automatically put the spacecraft into, what is called, Safe Mode, where all normal operations are suspended until controllers on earth can determine what happened and take corrective actions. Even at this point, only a sequence of relatively minor problems had occurred.

The top two priorities for the spacecraft in Safe Mode are to be power-positive (i.e., to make sure that the batteries are charged) and to communicate with earth. The MGS spacecraft could not do both of these functions at the same time, given the perceived problem with the solar arrays (a conservative approach, given that the solar arrays had reach a hard-stop unexpectedly). Pointing the presumed stuck solar panels at the sun, by rotating the spacecraft itself, however, also pointed the batteries at the sun—something that had not been anticipated, and was caused by another hidden coupling, in this case of Safe Mode priorities and the perceived failure mode of the solar panels. The exposure to the sun quickly overheated the batteries, which the fault protection software interpreted as a signal that the batteries were overcharging. This is still not a major problem, until it combines yet again in an unforeseen way with the remaining problem. Communicating with earth required pointing the antennas at earth, but that required access to the one extra parameter that had been corrupted in the original update. Now the cycle was complete: a series of relatively small problems lined up to cause a big problem that prevented the spacecraft *both* from communicating with earth *and* from charging its batteries. Within a matter of hours the spacecraft exhausted all charge on its batteries and was lost. Taking away any one of the smaller problems could have prevented the loss. What makes this example extra interesting is that some of the dependencies were introduced by the fault protection system itself—which functioned as designed. The part of the design that was meant to prevent failure in this case helped to bring it about. This is not uncommon in complex systems. In a sense, the addition of fault protection mechanisms increases a system's complexity. The increase in complexity itself carries risk, which can in some cases decrease rather than increase a system's reliability.

Although Perrow's observations were originally intended primarily for hardware system designs, they also have relevance to the study of complex *software* systems. There are many other examples of the phenomenon that combinations of relatively small defects can cause large problems in software systems. It is for instance known that residual software defects (i.e., those defects that escape all phases of testing and only reveal themselves once a system is in operation) tend to hide most successfully in rarely executed code. A good example of rarely executed code is error-handling and fault-protection code: precisely that code that is added for handling the relatively rare cases where the main application experiences a problem. This means that a defect in the error-handling code will normally be triggered in the presence of an unpredictable other type of defect: the classic Perrow combination of two or more independent failures with often unpredictable results. A misbehaving component (be it software or hardware) can reveal or even introduce a dependency into the system that would not exist if the component was behaving as designed, which can therefore be very hard to anticipate by the designers in their evaluation of the overall system reliability.

The remedies that follow from Perrow's analysis will be clear. We can try to reduce the number of all defects, including what may seem to be benign or minor defects, we can try to reduce overall system complexity by using simpler designs, and most of all we can try to reduce opportunities for unrelated problems to combine by using standard decomposition and decoupling techniques.

Although all observations we have made so far are basic, they are rarely if ever taken into account in reliable software system design. In the remainder of this chapter we will consider how we can build upon them. One specific issue that we will consider is how the basic principle of redundancy can be combined with the need for simplicity.

3.5 Redundancy and Simplicity

One simple method to exploit redundancy that can be used in the design of software systems is familiar to most programmers, but too often ignored: the aggressive use of assertions in program text. The assertions are technically redundant, but only if the program is completely free of defects. It is generally unwise, though, to assume zero-defect software at any stage of program development, which means that the use of assertions is one of the best and simplest defenses available to software bugs.

In a sense, an assertion works like the fuse in an electrical circuit. The fuse formalizes the claim that current will never exceed a preset level. The fuse is not expected to melt, because the circuit is designed to keep the current level in check. But in case of an unexpected defect (a short-circuit), the fuse will detect the anomaly and protect the system against wider damage by disabling the sub-system with the malfunctioning component. A software assertion can work in the same manner, although it is not always used as such. First, the assertion formalizes a claim that the developer intends to hold at specific points in a program text. The assertion can formalize a pre-condition, a post-condition, or an invariant for key pieces of code. When the assertion fails it means that the code cannot be executed safely. Often this is interpreted to mean that the entire program must be aborted, but this is not necessarily the case. It is often sufficient to terminate only the sub-system with the newly discovered defect, and to allow the system as a whole to continue, to recover from the mishap, or to develop a work-around for the problem. What the nature of this work-around can be is explored in the next few sections. A disciplined use of assertions is key to reliable software development. Assertion density has been shown to be inversely correlated with defect density in large software projects [4].

Similar to assertions in scope and in ability to recognize erroneous program execution are *property monitors*. Monitors are more powerful than assertions, and can be designed to catch more insidious types of defects. A monitor can be executed as a special purpose process that is analogous to a hardware fault-monitor; it verifies that critical system invariants are satisfied during system execution. Property monitors can follow an execution over a longer period, and can, for instance, be derived from temporal logic formulae. The main disadvantage of monitors is the runtime overhead that they could impose on a system. For safety critical systems this is often justified by the additional protection that is provided. A further exploration of assertions or property monitors should be considered outside the scope of the current chapter though. Instead, we will focus on methods for handling the defects that are flagged by failing assertions or monitors, and explore a methodology that is not yet commonly practiced.

3.6 Architecture

Consider a standard software architecture consisting of software modules with well-defined interfaces. Each module performs a separate function. The modules are defined in such a way that information flow across module boundaries is minimized. We will assume, for simplicity but without loss of generality, that modules interact through message passing, and that the crash of one module cannot affect other modules in any other way than across its module interface. A failed module can stop responding, or fail to comply with the interface protocols by sending erroneous requests or responses. We will make a further assumption that module failures can be detected either through consistency checks that are performed inside a module, or by peer modules that check the validity of messages that cross module boundaries. It is, for instance, common in space craft software systems for modules to send periodic heart-beat messages to a health-monitor. The absence of the heart-beat message can then signal module failure, and trigger counter-measures. Similarly, a health-monitor can verify the sanity of critical system components by sending queries that require a specific type of response that can be verified for consistency.

We now provide each software module with a backup, but not a backup that is simply a copy of the module. The backup is a deliberately *simplified* version of the main module that is meant to provide only basic keep-alive functionality. During normal system operation, this backup module is idle. When a fault is detected in a module, though, the faulty module is switched offline and the simplified backup module is used to replace it. Naturally, the backup module can have its own backup, and so on, in a hierarchical fashion, to provide different layers of system functionality and system protection, but we will not pursue this generalization here.

The backup, due to the fact that it is a simplified version of the main module, may offer fewer services, or it may offer them less efficiently. The purpose of the backup, though, is to provide a survival and recovery option to a partially failed system. It should provide the minimally necessary functionality that is required for the system as a whole to "stay alive" and to maintain basic functionality until the fault can be repaired.

Note that in a traditional system any failing module is its own backup. Upon failure one simply restarts the module that failed (possibly as part of a complete system reboot) and hopes that the cause for failure was transient. We can, however, defend against a substantially larger class of defects if the backup module is *distinct* from the primary module and deliberately constructed to be *simpler*.

As indicated earlier, if the primary and backup modules are constructed within an N-version programming paradigm, we do not necessarily gain additional reliability. This system structure will not adequately defend against design and coding errors. Some of the same design errors may be made in the construction of both modules, and if the two modules are of similar size and complexity, they should be expected to contain a similar number of residual coding defects (i.e., coding defects that escape code testing and verification). By making the backup modules significantly simpler than the primary modules we can succeed in more effectively increasing system reliability.

3.7 Hierarchical Redundancy

The backup modules in the approach we have sketched are constructed as deliberately *simplified* versions of the primary modules. It is important to note that these backup modules can be designed and built by the same developers that design and build the primary modules. The primary module is build for *performance* and the backup module is build for *correctness*. We gain reliability by making sure that the backup modules are easier to *verify*. The statistically expected number of residual defects in a backup module may still not be zero, but it should be lower than that of the module it is designed to replace.

A simplified backup module is used to guarantee continuity of operation, though in a possibly degraded state of operation (e.g., slower or with reduced functionality). The backup gives the system the opportunity to recover from unexpected failures: the primary module is offline and can be diagnosed and possibly restarted, while the backup module takes care of the most urgent of tasks in the most basic of ways. If code is developed in a hierarchical fashion, using a standardized software refinement approach, the backup module could encapsulate a higher level in the refinement of the final module: a simpler version of the code that is not yet burdened with all features, extensions, and optimizations that support the final version, but that does perform basic duties in the most straightforward and robust way.

Generally, a backup module will be smaller, measured in lines of code, than a primary module. By virtue of being smaller and simpler, the expected number of residual defects in its code should also be smaller. We will tacitly assume here that the number of design and coding defects is proportional to the size of a module, just like the assumption that the number of syntax and grammar mistakes in English prose is proportional to the length of that prose. If the primary module has a probability of failure p and the backup has a probability of failure q, we should have $1 > p > q > 0$ (ignoring the boundary cases where we have either certainty of failure or absolute perfection). Because the backup module contains less code, and implements less functionality, it offers fewer opportunities for defects to hide. The module with its backup now fails with probability $p \times q$.

3.7.1 Replace and Resume

When a software fault has been detected and the module that caused the fault can reliably be identified, the next step is to transfer control to its backup module. There are two possibilities:

- *Active*: The backup module is already running as a shadow module, either in a separate thread of control or as a separate process
- *Passive*: The backup module needs to be initialized and started, either in the same thread of control as the failed module, or as a separate thread or process.

An *active* backup strategy simplifies the handoff, since no further processing or initialization is required. The module interface is reconfigured within the system so that the backup becomes the active module. The *passive* approach, on the other hand, uses fewer resources, but requires the initialization of the backup module to a state that is consistent with the operation of the primary module up until the point of failure. There are two possible ways to achieve this. The first is to require all modules to set *checkpoints* on their state at regular intervals, and to use these checkpoints to initialize a backup module to a valid state. A second method is to design the modules to be *stateless*. This is generally the preferred strategy in a distributed system with many active components, since it avoids the need for initialization and it avoids the complications of distributed state information.

Once the handoff process has been completed, system execution resumes without requiring any further action. In special cases, though, it is an explicit notification to other modules to record that module reset may be needed.

3.8 Synopsis

To achieve software reliability we have argued in this chapter that it is unwise to focus all our attention on ways to achieve zero-defect *code*. Instead, we have proposed to investigate methods that can secure fail-proof *systems*, despite the possibility of *component* failures. Remarkably, this is largely unexplored territory in the design of reliable software systems.

The principal method of structuring code we have discussed is deliberately simple and can be summarized as follows. The system is structured into modules that can fail independently. Modules communicate via well-defined interfaces, and each critical module is provided with one or more backups that can take over basic operations when the primary module fails. The backup modules are constructed to be simpler, smaller, and more robust than the primary modules that they support, possibly performing less efficiently and providing less functionality.

We can recognize this basic mode of operation in *hardware* design for safety critical systems, e.g., of spacecraft. Spacecraft typically do not just have redundant components, but also components of different type and designs providing different grades of service. Most current spacecraft, for instance, have both a high-gain and a low-gain antenna. When the high-gain antenna becomes unusable, the more reliable low-gain antenna is used, be it at a significantly reduced bit-rate. The same principle can also be found on a more modest scale in the design of certain key software functions for spacecraft. Spacecraft software is normally designed to support at least two main modes of operation: the fully functional mode with all features and functions enabled, and a minimal basic mode of operation that has become known as *Safe Mode*. Safe mode is automatically engaged on any mission anomaly, though it typically requires a system reboot as well [9]. The principles we have outlined hold promise for a much broader routine use in the design of reliable software systems.

Acknowledgements The research described in this chapter was carried out at the Jet Propulsion Laboratory, California Institute of Technology, under a contract with the National Aeronautics and Space Administration.

References

1. Anderson, T., Barrett, P.A., Halliwell, D.N., Moudling, M.L.: An evaluation of software fault tolerance in a practical system. In: Fault Tolerant Computing Symposium, pp. 140–145 (1985)
2. Avižienis, A.A.: Software fault tolerance. In: The Methodology of N-Version Programming, pp. 23–46. Wiley, New York (1995)
3. Knight, J.C., Leveson, N.G.: An experimental evaluation of the assumption of independence in multi-version programming. IEEE Trans. Softw. Eng. **12**(1), 96–109 (1986)
4. Kudrjavets, G., Nagappan, N., Ball, T.: Assessing the relationship between software assertions and code quality: an empirical investigation. Tech. rep. MSR-TR-2006-54, Microsoft Research (2006)
5. Lions, J.-L.: Report of the inquiry board for the Ariane 5 flight 501 failure (1996). Joint Communication, European Space Agency, ESA-CNES, Paris, France
6. Perrow, C.: Normal Accidents: Living with High Risk Technologies. Princeton University Press, Princeton (1984)
7. Randell, B., Xu, J.: The evolution of the recovery block concept. In: Lyu, M.R. (ed.) Software Fault Tolerance, pp. 1–21. Wiley, New York (1995)
8. Rasmussen, R.D., Litty, E.C.: A voyager attitude control perspective on fault tolerant systems. In: AIAA, Alburquerque, NM, pp. 241–248 (1981)
9. Reeves, G.E., Neilson, T.A.: The mars rover spirit FLASH anomaly. In: IEEE Aerospace Conference, Big Sky, Montana (2005)
10. Rushby, J.: Partitioning in avionics architectures: requirements, mechanisms, and assurance. Technical report, Computer Science Laboratory, SRI (1999). Draft technical report
11. Sha, L.: Using simplicity to control complexity. IEEE Softw. **18**(4), 20–28 (2001)
12. Weber, D.G.: Formal specification of fault-tolerance and its relation to computer security. In: Proceedings of the 5th International Workshop on Software Specification and Design, IWSSD'89, pp. 273–277. ACM, New York (1989)

Chapter 4
Separating Safety and Control Systems to Reduce Complexity

Alan Wassyng, Mark Lawford, and Tom Maibaum

4.1 Introduction

This book is about complexity in the context of analyzing, designing and implementing software intensive systems. Actually, there are three different kinds of complexity that are of direct relevance. It is thus important to define the terminology we will use so that we may be as clear as possible as to exactly what kind of complexity is under discussion at any one time.

> *Problem complexity*—the inherent complexity of the simplest but still complete and accurate version of the application (problem) to be built.
> *Programming complexity*—the complexity of the implementation of the application.
> *Computational complexity*—the performance cost of an algorithm.
> *Complexity*—if we use the generic term, 'complexity', we mean both problem and programming complexity.

At the moment there is a vast difference in what we know about the three kinds of complexity. There is a growing body of knowledge related to computational complexity, including terminology that describes how complex an algorithm is. There are also accepted measures of this kind of complexity. Unfortunately, we cannot claim the same for problem complexity and programming complexity. We speak about these (related) complexities often. We proclaim that they are an important cause of software errors. However, we do not even know how to measure them effectively, which seriously impacts our ability to design experiments to study them. Even more unfortunate is that, in the context of developing safe and dependable

T. Maibaum (✉)
McMaster University, Hamilton, ON, Canada
e-mail: tom@maibaum.org

M. Hinchey, L. Coyle (eds.), *Conquering Complexity*,
DOI 10.1007/978-1-4471-2297-5_4, © Springer-Verlag London Limited 2012

systems, it is problem complexity and programming complexity that are of primary importance.

Complexity is important to Software Engineers because we have anecdotal evidence that systems of high problem complexity are extremely difficult to build so that they are suitably dependable [15]. And we have enormous amounts of evidence that systems with high programming complexity are extremely hard to maintain, in the full general sense of maintenance. Computer Scientists and Software Engineers have spent years developing techniques for dealing with complexity. The most important of these techniques are *abstraction* and *modularization* (as a specific and somewhat limited form of separation of concerns).

Abstraction is a common and useful practice which is used to focus attention on a simplified view of the system/component. The idea is that the view should retain relevant information but ignore 'irrelevant' details that make the system/component more complex. Abstraction is an essential tool in our toolkit. It helps us understand, model and analyze complex systems. Problem complexity cannot be reduced by abstraction, though it, and some related notions, such as views, may help us cope with complex systems. What is definitely reduced by abstraction is programming complexity. Abstraction is not unique to the software world. It has been used effectively for ages by anyone who has had to build mathematical models of complex systems—physicists, engineers, economists, ecologists, and many others. Sometimes, we are so expert in abstraction that we do not notice that we have abstracted away essential details of the real system! So, abstraction can genuinely reduce complexity, but the reduction is usually temporary. At some stage, most of the details have to be reintroduced into the solution. However, we should not underestimate the usefulness of abstraction while we develop our understanding of the system that has to be built.

Modularization is a special case of *separation of concerns*. We do this, i.e., modularize, at many stages in software development. For example, we may modularize the requirements so that the required behavior is easier to understand. Typically this is done along functional lines. We can modularize the software design (and the code) so that it has some desirable properties. For example, *information hiding* was postulated by Parnas [21, 22] so that the software design would be easy to maintain under classes of foreseen changes. And, speaking of 'classes', *object oriented design/programming* was developed to further enhance our ability to modify existing design modularization when subjected to change. In all these cases, modularization has come to mean *encapsulation* of behavior and/or data in *modules*. Each module is relatively simple and the modules communicate with each other through public interfaces. This is not only an example of separation of concerns, it is also an example of an old standby in dealing with complexity—*divide-and-conquer*. Modularization lies at the very heart of modern Software Engineering. It has proved to be extremely effective in providing a mechanism for structuring software designs in particular.

Modularization has become so useful, in fact, that software experts proclaim that it is possible to **reduce** complexity through the use of modularization and other similar software engineering techniques and principles. We now think that this view is flawed. There is a very good reason why it is useful to differentiate between problem complexity and programming complexity. If we are correct in supposing that there is such a concept as problem complexity, it suggests a principle we can formulate as *conservation of complexity*. Simply put, our conjecture is that we cannot reduce the programming complexity of a system to the extent that it is 'less than' the problem complexity of that system, whatever measure we use for complexity. In the case of modularization, for example, we might say that the individual program components are simplified while their interactions are made more complex. In fact, it is often observed that the (programming) complexity of modern systems is not in their components, but in the interactions between components.

So, if we cannot really reduce the programming complexity of a safety-critical system below its problem complexity, and if the dependability of the system is adversely affected by high problem/programming complexity, how can we build highly dependable safety-critical systems?

There are a number of good answers to this question—and this book contains many of them. Our answer focuses on an idea that supersedes the concept of modularization, namely separation of concerns. This approach has provided excellent solutions in a number of instances in the past. Our suggested approach is an extreme case of separation of concerns. What if we can partition the system so that we have components with no (or very little) interaction between them? For example, Canadian regulations for nuclear power generation state that safety systems in nuclear power plants have to be completely separated from the control systems in that plant, and isolated as much as possible from each other (where there is more than one safety system). Similar regulation is actually common in other countries [18, 19], as well as in the process control domain. A significant difference seems to be how strictly the regulation is enforced across countries and between the domains. A decade or so ago, there was general adherence to this principle of separation. There is now pressure to relax/remove this restriction. The pressure comes from manufacturers of these systems, *not* from regulators!

Analogous principles are used in other settings: operating systems kernels, communication kernels, etc. In recent years we have found that there are advantages in building dynamically adaptive embedded systems. These systems often have to react to malfunctions and/or changes in the environment. It seems to us that this principle of separation may be just as important for these systems as it is for many current safety-critical systems. Many adaptive and reconfigurable embedded systems integrate safety-critical and mixed-criticality components. We believe that these systems should be designed so that the safety and adaptive components must be separated for the same reasons that safety and control systems are separated. This could even cover separation of components such as those for communication from components corresponding to application features [7].

A recent paper on separation of concerns and its usefulness in relation to dependability of systems makes similar points about the usefulness of separation of concerns in relation to establishing the dependability of systems. [10]. The paper focuses on the idea of simplicity as the underlying basis for the feasibility of establishing dependability. We revisit a few of the arguments in this paper below and add our own. Most importantly, we replace the undefinable notion of simplicity (a call to arms proclaimed for several decades by Tony Hoare [8], and now reissued by Lui Sha [24] and others), by the definable and scientific concept of *problem* complexity.

For the remainder of this chapter we will use separation of safety and control systems in the context of the nuclear power domain to illustrate the concepts and principles, referring to other examples as and when necessary. We first introduced the idea of *conservation of complexity* in an invited paper [27] specific to adaptive systems, which served as the basis for this chapter.

4.2 Reducing Complexity

A fundamental reason for separating control and safety systems is that we believe that, at least in the nuclear domain, fully isolated safety systems are inherently less complex than are the systems that control the reactor ("fully" here means one extreme of separation, what we might call *physical separation*). The safety subsystem is literally isolated from the control system and each safety subsystem (there were two at Darlington) is totally separated from the other. The disparity in complexity is even greater between safety systems and integrated safety and control systems. We also believe that this reduced problem complexity enables us to design, build, and certify the behavior of the safety system to a level of quality that would be difficult to achieve for an integrated, and thus more complex, system.

The safety systems at Darlington were of the order of tens of thousands of lines of code, whereas the control system was of the order of hundreds of thousands. Now, given extant criticisms of the lines of code metric for complexity, we do not want to use this essentially qualitative measure for anything other than to emphasize the difference in size and, therefore, the likely significant difference in programming complexity—and by inference, problem complexity as well. This order of magnitude difference in programming complexity alone indicates the impact on analyzability of the two pieces of software. As we know, more or less any verification approach (testing based or proof based) suffers from exponential growth in the size of the search space in relation to 'size'. Hence, the control system, and similarly an integrated control and safety system, will not be an order of magnitude more difficult to analyze, but exponentially harder.

At this point, it may be useful to discuss the principle that we have called *the conservation of complexity*. We assert that systems and their requirements have some level of inherent complexity. Sometimes, systems are designed so that they are more complex than necessary, ditto requirements. However, for a particular system, there is some level below which its complexity cannot be reduced. Principles like modularity do not reduce this inherent complexity; they simply redistribute it. Modularity may reduce complexity of parts. However, if we want to consider the complexity of the complete system we must 'add' the complexity of interactions between parts.

Modularization in the usual sense is taken to mean division into parts in relation to the functionality or features to be delivered by the application. The *divide and conquer* strategy in problem solving is often taken as the pattern on which to base such functional decompositions. What is often forgotten in such discussions is that the decomposition of a problem into subproblems that are easier to solve must be accompanied by a recomposition operation that is not 'free'. This recomposition involves some level of complexity. The complexity of interaction mentioned above is a direct reflection of this cost of recomposition. In fact, it has often been observed that the complexity of modern, large systems is down to the interaction between components, whilst components themselves tend to be trivial. Very few would argue that modern large systems are not complex, though some might argue that they have somehow reduced the complexity of the application. If there is any truth to this latter claim, it must, in our view, be related to programming complexity: surely no one would disagree with the assertion that the programming complexity of a modularized design is significantly lower than that of a monolithic design. So, this line of argument does not provide evidence for having lowered problem complexity in any way; in fact, our use of the word conservation in this context implies that it cannot be reduced.

Now, separating safety and control in a system is *not* an example of modularization in the usual sense, because, surely, we are not taming complexity by moving complexity to interaction. Separation, in this example, creates two independent systems, at least one of which is going to be inherently lower in problem complexity than that of the original problem. Of course, the other part, the control system, may also be inherently less complex than the original requirements, but the two systems, taken together, are no less complex than the original integrated system because of the conservation of complexity. This separation is an example of separation of concerns that cuts across functional hierarchies. In fact one might characterize it as doing the opposite of aspect weaving! It disentangles safety concerns from the various parts of the system and packages them up in a separate subsystem, never to be weaved again into the application.

Of course, such a complete separation may not be possible in all systems. Adaptive and dynamically reconfigurable systems may be examples of such systems. For these, we need to develop a better understanding of the separation that *is* feasible and how this contributes to a division that still enables the development of greater confidence in the safety component, because its problem complexity is significantly lower than that of the original problem and, further, its interactions with the rest of the system are also of less complexity than the original. The differences in complexity still have to be significant enough to enable the claim of simpler analysis. An example of such a system, where complete separation is not possible, is that of operating systems and trusted kernels. One of the motivations for building operating systems using trusted kernels is exactly the issue of low complexity and analyzability. The kernel is significantly simpler than the whole operating system and its interactions, usually defined through a small interface with the rest of the operating system, are also significantly less complex than interactions in the other parts of the operating system.

4.2.1 The Effect of Reduced Complexity on Quality and Dependability

In our context, it is the effect of complexity on dependability and the quality of the software that is of primary interest. Surprisingly perhaps, we have not yet in this chapter discussed any sort of definition for *'complex system'*. This is not an oversight. It seems to be a fact of life that people instinctively know what complexity means, but defining it has occupied the minds of countless philosophers and researchers from many domains over many years—and we still do not have a widely accepted definition of what constitutes a complex system. In a very recent paper, Ladyman, Lambert and Wiesner [14] list many 'definitions' of a complex system, including the following one that we found to be the most appropriate in our context. This definition originally appeared in [29]:

"In a general sense, the adjective 'complex' describes a system or component that by design or function or both is difficult to understand and verify. [...] complexity is determined by such factors as the number of components and the intricacy of the interfaces between them, the number and intricacy of conditional branches, the degree of nesting, and the types of data structures".

This statement seems to fit our notion of programming complexity. It is directly related to the notion of "aggregate complexity", which 'concerns how individual elements work in concert to create systems with complex behavior' [16]. There have been many attempts to create practical and representative metrics for programming complexity, and some of them use the components of this definition (see [6] for representative examples). However, none has met with any significant success, and the metric most commonly used in practice is an old and simple one that we referred to earlier—*lines of code (LOC)*. There are many documented problems with using *LOC* as a metric for programming complexity [11], but alternatives seem to fare no better [5]. This brings us to our first point.

1. *Reduction in size.* The crucial fact here is that we use the resulting code size of the system as a measure of programming complexity. Size can be measured in *LOC* as discussed above. This assumes that *LOC* is typically correlated with the number of system inputs and outputs, the number of classes/modules, and even the state space of the system. Thus *LOC* provides us with an indication of programming complexity. The specific 'size' does not matter. We are interested in the size merely as an indication of the programming complexity of the system, and hence the feasibility of using rigorous (mathematical) methods and tools to complement more typical approaches, and to be able to retain sufficient intellectual control over the design and implementation of the system to achieve the required dependability. At this stage in the history of software engineering, we are capable of using formal techniques to specify the requirements and design of 'small' systems, and thus be able to mathematically verify designs against

requirements and code against designs with a level of rigor that is not yet possible for larger systems [26]. One conclusion to draw here is that reduction in programming complexity may not really be effective unless the resulting system is small enough to be amenable to a variety of validation and verification methods, not just testing. Constructing and certifying safety systems that are smaller than a hundred thousand *LOC* is a very different task compared with systems that are hundreds of thousands of *LOC*, let alone millions of *LOC*. Note that verification is just one of the activities adversely affected by the size of the system (programming complexity of the system), but it is a pivotal one.

Returning to the point at issue: if we can achieve a significant reduction in the size of the application, we believe that it is possible to reduce the *problem* complexity of that application. Put another way, the only way to reduce the size of an application by a significant amount is to reduce the problem complexity of the application. There is a trite but important assumption implicit here, and that is that the application has not been so poorly designed that we could achieve a significant reduction in programming complexity simply by doing a better job.

We believe that we can reduce the problem complexity of the system in a number of ways:

- we can scale back the number of features planned for the system;
- we may be able to reduce the number of inputs and/or outputs;
- scaling back efficiency requirements often reduces the complexity inherent in the system;
- we can require a rudimentary user interface rather than a sophisticated one;
- we can reduce or eliminate concurrency;
- we can restrict or eliminate interfaces to other systems;
- we can remove error handling;
- we can relax timing requirements.

Most readers will be quite familiar with the above list—or one very much like it. We see some or all of these actions all the time in industry. We may even have resorted to using these 'simplifications' ourselves. If we further examine each of these 'cuts', we can envision quite easily that each of them would result in a reduction in the size of the implemented system, measured by *LOC*. This would seem to confirm that these 'cuts' would reduce the problem complexity of the system. This fits in well with our suggestion that one way to reduce the problem complexity of a system is to partition the system. If we partition the system into two parts, for example, and if we can isolate a small, cohesive subset of the original requirements into a separate system, then that system will have significantly fewer features, inputs and/or outputs, than did the original, integrated system. There are usually two reasons for making the above 'cuts' to a system under development. The first is that we are far behind schedule and the schedule has to be met (not always true), so that if we do not reduce the scope of the system, we will not meet the schedule. The second is that if we try and get everything done, the quality (correctness, dependability) of the resulting system will be inadequate. In other words, experience has taught us that if we are struggling with maintaining the quality of the system under development, reducing the number of features, inputs and/or outputs may allow us to achieve the target quality of the system. This shows that we have, for years, instinctively linked problem complexity with system dependability. The greater the complexity, the more difficult it is to achieve the required dependability.

2. *Reduction in algorithmic complexity.* Simple algorithms and data structures are easier to construct correctly in the first place, and subsequently are easier to verify as being correct. Manual verification poses few challenges and automated verification is often quite straightforward. On the other hand, proving that complex algorithms achieve desired results and that they are implemented correctly, presents us with significant challenges. This is easy to see when we examine the progress we have made in certifying scientific computation software packages. Scientific computation packages (as well as statistical packages) have a long history, going back to the 1960s. These early versions were surprisingly reliable in spite of the lack of sophistication regarding their development—by today's standards. An advantage that they enjoyed was that each method was based on strong mathematical knowledge about the algorithms and also about tests that should be performed to confirm that the methods were working correctly. As scientific computation grew more ambitious, the problem complexity of the packages grew tremendously. Today, many researchers are deeply concerned about the dependability of scientific computation [12]. The increase in algorithm complexity has led directly to an increase in problem complexity so that development and verification of large scientific computation software suites remains an open and extremely challenging research field [4]. To reduce problem complexity in a system with considerable algorithmic complexity, it is not sufficient to simply partition the system into two parts. We have to partition the system in such a way that one part will have significantly reduced algorithmic complexity. Fortunately this is possible in many of the systems we are interested in. Later, in Sect. 4.2.3, we will show why we believe that separation of safety and control is likely to result in a safety system that has much less algorithmic complexity than either the associated control system, or the integrated system.

4.2.2 Modularization and Abstraction Cannot Reduce Problem Complexity

Modularization is often touted as a way of reducing complexity. In fact modularization (and abstraction) cannot reduce problem complexity, but may actually increase programming complexity, in order to, for example, improve maintainability. Still, "conquering complexity" is a common phrase used to describe how modularization supposedly makes things simple enough for designers to be able to cope with the potential complexity of an application. The motivation for this comes from the *divide and conquer* problem solving techniques used in many areas of mathematics, engineering and science [23]. As noted above, the divide and conquer tactic is intended to reduce the solution of some problem to the solution of several subproblems, each of which is a 'simpler' problem than the original. But an often unstated part of this tactic is the necessity to find a way of composing the solutions of the subproblems to provide the solution to the whole problem. So the overall problem complexity of the solution to the problem is a function of the complexity of the solutions to the subproblems and the complexity of the composition mechanism used to 'aggregate' the overall solution. The same may be said about programming complexity, though the function used to compute this overall complexity will likely be different from the one used for problem complexity. This function may differ from problem to problem and from one composition function to another. In modern large systems, the 'composition' operator on subproblem solutions may be extremely complex, and inherently so.

In fact, many modern systems may have little programming complexity in any particular module, but the numbers of modules and the variety of interactions and behaviors possible as a result of their combination boggle the mind. There is no obvious reduction in overall complexity as compared with the system's problem complexity. In fact, the real tactic behind the divide and conquer method is to reduce the solution of an 'unknown' to that of a number of known problems and a known technique for combining their solutions. The overt purpose of the tactic is not reduction of overall problem complexity, but a reduction in the complexity of the solution process undertaken to solve the problem—reducing the solution problem to known patterns of solutions. If (inherent) problem complexity is to mean anything, then no tactic will have the effect of reducing it. In fact, one might say that engineering methods address the issue of solution complexity—the problem of finding a solution to an application problem—by systematizing the tactics used to solve a specific class of application problems. One might conjecture that programming complexity, as discussed above, somehow reflects this solution complexity. However, we do not plan to go further in this direction in this chapter.

In respect of programming complexity, it may be conjectured that modularization techniques sometimes act to increase it. The pattern of solutions to sub problems and their composition may well act to introduce 'artificial complexities' (non-essential complexities) in relation to basic problem complexity. This is perhaps best exemplified by the problems of entanglement in object oriented implementations. As an example, in a recent investigation of a three tiered application (database, generic application software, and company specific application software), three functions of interest at the database level were potentially called by more than 80,000 functions at the generic application level, but this was again reduced to five functions at the company specific level. The enormous numbers associated with the middle layer were largely the result of the use, perhaps inappropriate, of inheritance structures. This kind of programming complexity does not appear to be uncommon in the object oriented world. We should note here that the problem of analysis in relation to dependability is clearly more a function of programming complexity than problem complexity, assuming that the former is always greater than the latter. However, problem complexity defines a minimum analysis complexity to be expected for the application.

We now come to the consideration of abstraction in relation to complexity. While modularization is often said to reduce complexity by reducing a complex system to its parts, abstraction is said to reduce complexity by 'forgetting' unnecessary details. Certainly, we would agree with this statement if the complexity referred to in the last sentence was programming complexity. The 'unnecessary details' referred to above are always intended to be those necessary to make the problem solution executable on a computer. However, it is not clear to us why abstraction should reduce problem complexity. An abstract model that captures the essence of a problem must also inherit its complexity.

Having said that, there may be one abstraction technique (and perhaps others) that appears to reduce problem complexity, namely the use of *views* or *viewpoints* [17, 20]. A view of an application is a partial specification that not only leaves out unnecessary details, but also leaves out aspects of the application problem. The view might be seen as presenting a subproblem, and the inherent problem complexity of this subproblem may well be less than that of the whole. The analysis of the view may then indeed be simpler than that of the whole. However, as for modularization, we may well have difficulties in putting views together and performing the analysis related to this 'view composition'. So we find that again, the technique does not really reduce problem complexity. The use of views is an example of separation of concerns in the more general sense discussed above. As such, when it comes to establishing dependability properties of an application, it may be quite efficacious in reducing the complexity of performing an analysis by dividing the analysis into parts that may require differing levels of rigor. An example of this will be discussed next: separating safety subsystems from control subsystems. However, for this to happen, there also has to be a commensurate reduction in programming complexity related to the core dependability concerns. If, as is usual in implementing applications, the views developed at the abstract level have no direct correspondences with parts of the application, then the programming complexity introduced by the implementation completely overwhelms the reduced complexity of individual views.

It is possible that a catastrophic example of this kind of complexity leading to disaster was the integration of patient billing information with the control of clinical X-ray therapy machines such as those reported in the articles in the New York Times [1, 2]. We have no written documentation confirming this, but have been told that this happened. Whether it is accurate or not, the possibility is very real. The medical device in question had no separate safety system; it was integrated with the control features. A very serious error occurred when the settings for the shields used to focus and aim the X-rays were accidentally left fully open leading to a serious overdose of radiation applied to a patient. Although the machine was regularly checked and calibrated, because the machine's software was directly linked to the billing system, the next time the patient came in for therapy, the device's software recovered patient information from the billing system and set the device to the configuration used in the previous overdose. So, it is possible to conjecture that a serious error imparting profound harm to the patient, which could have been prevented by a separate safety system, was compounded as a result of increased problem complexity caused by linking the device to billing subsystems. The initial error could be said to have been caused by combining safety and control features into a complex whole, resulting in a highly complex system that was too complex for proper safety analysis. The second (and subsequent errors) were the result of making the dependability problem even more complex by introducing the link to the billing system.

4.2.3 Why Control Is More Complex than Safety

The shutdown system in a Canadian nuclear power plant is designed to monitor whether safety limits are exceeded, and in such cases to initiate the shutdown of the plant. The shutdown must be irrevocable once started, which simplifies the logic— but this principle is sometimes relaxed if the additional logic required is minimal. A nuclear reactor operates by initiating and then controlling a nuclear chain reaction. This reaction is constantly changing and so the nuclear control system algorithms initiate actions that are definitely not irrevocable. These control system algorithms are designed to keep the reactor operating within safe limits, but their purpose is to maximize productivity by maximizing the power level, and so they are far more complex than the simple checks against safety limits implemented in the shutdown systems.

The difference between control and safety systems is reflected in the mathematical analyses that are performed for these two classes of systems. The nuclear safety analysis always assumes that trips are taken to completion, and this simplifies the required behavior. The same assumption is clearly not appropriate for the control systems. Partly as a result of this assumption, in our experience, almost all the algorithms required in nuclear shutdown systems are extremely simple. This is certainly not true of the control systems. Note that we are not saying that the mathematical nuclear safety analyses performed to obtain requirements for the shutdown systems are simple. They are not, and correctness of the scientific computation code used to perform these analyses is an ongoing research topic.

There are at least two primary reductions in complexity that we expect to see in safety systems. The first is a reduction in size, and the second is a reduction in algorithmic complexity.

1. *Reduction in size.* The shutdown system is responsible for monitoring reactor attributes (neutronics, pressure, temperature, flow of coolant, etc), checking them against pre-determined limits, and initiating a shutdown if necessary. It has to be able to accept a very limited set of operator inputs, and may have limited communication functions to perform. If we use the number of lines of source code as an indication of complexity, we expect that it should be of the order of tens of thousands, and the number of system inputs and outputs under a hundred for each. These are then relatively small programs by modern standards, and tend to be more amenable to the application of rigorous software engineering techniques in ways and at a level that would not be possible for more complex systems, which typically require hundreds of thousands of *LOC*. As an example, the shutdown systems for the Darlington Nuclear Generating Station in Ontario

are of the order of 30,000 to 40,000 *LOC*. The control system for the same plant is upwards of 500,000 *LOC*. Alternatively, there may be other measures of size that are more meaningful in this context and do not correspond directly to *LOC*, but relate to complexity of analysis.

2. *Reduction in algorithmic complexity.* The control systems in nuclear power plants contain algorithms that are designed to control the nuclear chain reaction such that the plant operates at maximum power and still maintains all its monitored parameters within safe operating limits. These algorithms are also designed so that the controlled behavior is stable. By comparison, most of the algorithms in the shutdown systems are incredibly simple. A huge proportion of the algorithms implement simple checks of monitored values against predefined limits. Some of the algorithms have to cope with simple timing behaviors, while others implement very basic hysteresis behavior, and signal calibrations. The complexity of these algorithms is demonstrably orders of magnitude less than those required for the control systems.

As noted above, by reducing both size and algorithmic complexity, we have directly addressed the two main complicating factors in the analysis of software. By reducing the size of the program and by reducing algorithmic complexity, we will have reduced analysis complexity exponentially. In the ongoing battle to build dependable systems, this should be considered a signal achievement.

4.3 Separation of Concerns

There is a long-standing principle in software engineering that we can use *separation of concerns* to control complexity in software systems. Separation of control and safety systems can be viewed as a special case of separation of concerns, and there is at least one recent example in the software literature indicating that people are recognizing the importance of this [10]. Again, there is a case to be made that this separation of concerns is not the same as modularization. It is more like the splitting of the system into parts in a way that does not respect the rules of modularization. The ideas behind aspects come to mind. It seems to us that work in adaptive and reconfigurable systems has failed to consider adequately the use of such separation mechanisms to affect better control of safety functions. There is a real opportunity, in exploring these ideas, to improve safety mechanisms for this emerging class of systems.

4.3.1 Physical Separation: Reducing Complexity

A fundamental safety principle is to maintain physical separation and independence between safety systems and control systems. This helps limit the impact of common cause failures and systemic errors, and provides protection against sabotage and cyber-attacks. These are important principles that establish the requirements to assure that high reliability requirements are met. Physical separation as a primary safety principle has been a standard requirement throughout the process control industry for decades, and *independent protection layers* are mandated in international standards such as IEC 61508 [9]. As noted above, this is also a requirement in the regulation of nuclear power plants in both Canada and the USA. The only engineering arguments against this principle come from considerations of efficiency rather than safety. However, where such an argument arises, safety always trumps efficiency. If a safe system is not efficient enough, design engineers need to find a different solution. The question of where to draw the line between integration and strict separation of safety and control systems has gained some traction in recent years. Some manufacturers of nuclear power station control systems do not wish to separate safety systems from control systems, and, compounding the problem, wish to integrate plant management systems and even billing systems into the critical software controlling the power generation. Others wish to weaken the physical and logical separation of redundant control systems by allowing communication and interaction between them, to save cost by reducing the number of parts. As a consequence, there is, unfortunately (in our opinion), a recent and deleterious trend to weakening the physical separation between shutdown systems, and between shutdown and control systems. We address this development in Sect. 4.5.

So how does this relate to our discussion on complexity? If we look again at our opening sentence in Sect. 4.2, we see that we described the separated systems as 'fully' isolated, meaning physically separated. There was a good reason for this. Physical separation of the systems helps us show that there is minimum, hopefully zero, interaction along interfaces between the systems. We need to show that any interaction between the systems is restricted to those interactions possible in their environments. This is not the same as having to cope with interactions through a common interface. To achieve this, the systems must be logically separate from each other. Demonstrating this conclusively is sometimes nontrivial. Actual physical separation makes this a much easier task. Logical connections are only possible where there are physical connections, and these would then be clearly visible—or, even better, non-existent.

As an aside, and not connected to our discussion on complexity, there are additional reasons that physical and logical separation of safety systems from each other and from control systems benefits the cause of dependability and safety.

The first of these is related to *common cause failures* [19]. Common cause failures occur when more than one component in a system fails due to a single shared cause. This is clearly not limited to software and has been studied over a significant period of time. Prevention of common cause failure is a staple of international standards and regulations related to high-dependability systems, for example, the *Common-Cause Failure Database and Analysis System: Event Data Collection, Classification, and Coding* [18], and *Guidelines on Modeling Common-Cause Failures in Probabilistic Risk Assessment* [19], nuclear regulatory documents published by the Nuclear Regulatory Commission in the USA. The *Common Cause Failure*

Database[1] is a data collection and analysis system that is used to identify, code and classify common cause failures events.

Separation on its own is not enough to prevent common cause design errors. In this case we need to add *diversity* and *independence* to our toolset. Diversity and independence are sound arguments (for software, enforced diversity [3] should be preferred), and are reflected in all international standards that apply to high-dependability systems. Diversity and independence do not make sense unless the systems are physically and conceptually separated from each other. Any commonality between the systems would serve to reduce the efficacy of these principles.

The second reason why standards and regulations mandate separation of control and safety systems is that future maintenance of an integrated system would be much more difficult. This is actually somewhat affected by the complexity of the system. Changes to the system would have to be 'guaranteed' not to adversely affect existing safety functions. If the separation between control and safety is effected through the software design/logic and not through physical and logical separation, it is much more difficult to demonstrate/prove that changes to the control system cannot affect the safety functions. A carefully constructed *information hiding design* can alleviate but cannot eliminate this concern. The situation can be made even more difficult if the control and safety systems are treated as an integrated system. These issues are particularly pertinent to adaptive and reconfigurable systems, in which the principles of separation are not well understood.

4.3.2 Ideas for Separate Safety Systems in Other Domains

We have seen that separation of control and safety is not confined to the nuclear domain. It is enforced throughout the process control industry as well. It seems clear to us that we should be considering using this principle in domains such as automotive and medical devices. Microkernels are a good example of a less drastic separation of safety and other functions. The nucleus keeps the system safe (memory checks and messaging as core functionalities) and the rest of the operating system provides the main functionality. Here we do not have physical separation, but design separation enforced through the mechanisms associated with layered architectures. Microkernels have been certified and/or verified: QNX certified for SIL3, and seL4 has been verified [13].

We have recently had occasion to consider software-driven radiation machines. These devices are effective life-savers in the fight against cancer, but they also can be devastatingly harmful if they malfunction. Two thoughts come to mind with these devices:

1. Manufacturers/vendors seem to be more concerned with including features that will help sell the devices rather than with controlling the complexity of the device so that they can be more confident that the device is fail-safe; and

---

[1]The US Nuclear Regulatory Commission's Common-Cause Failure Data Base (CCFDB): http://nrcoe.inel.gov/results/index.cfm?fuseaction=CCFDB.showMenu.

2. It should be possible to add a low-complexity safety system that will 'guarantee' that the device does not deliver an overdose to any patient.

The safety system could, for example, require simple inputs from the doctor that limit the allowable dosage for a specific patient, and then monitor the radiation to ensure this dosage is not exceeded. This safety system would be completely independent of the control system that 'drives' the device. It would also be independent of any billing system that might compromise safety features, preventing accidents such as the ones noted above.

There are currently a number of *active safety* functions included in modern cars. These include automatic braking, adaptive cruise control, lane departure warning systems, adaptive high beam and adaptive headlamps. Typically, these are implemented as self-contained, isolated units, although some of them clearly have to be integrated with other functions—braking for instance. Although the auto industry seems to have realized that keeping such components as isolated as possible helps to deal with complexity issues and increases our ability to engineer extremely dependable systems, this objective is undermined by the need to interconnect some subsystems, e.g., braking and throttle subsystems, and the fact that subsystems may share processors and communication buses with other subsystems. It may be that we can further improve the dependability and maintainability of the systems by isolating safety from control again, rather than by relying on functional modularization.

4.4 Reducing Programming Complexity: The Engineering Approach

Engineers are continually faced with the issue of problem complexity and its impact on engineering design. For most situations met by engineers in their every day work, engineers have developed a way of dealing with this issue: the engineering method, or what Vincenti calls *normal design* [25]. Over time, as engineers solve specific problems in some domain, the successful approaches are incorporated into a standard engineering method specific for those kinds of *devices* [25]. Devices in this sense are the subject of normal design methods. Engineers know that if they follow the prescriptions of the method, including which analyses to do when and which decision to make in light of results of analysis, they are likely to design a safe and effective product. As we have noted elsewhere [28], this also forms the basis of the prescriptive regulatory regimes in classical engineering. Radical design involves design problems that are not within the normal envelope associated with a normal design method. Some new element is introduced, e.g., untried technology, or some new combination of technologies, which takes the design problem outside the incremental improvement normal design supports. This makes the achievement of safe and effective designs more problematic and requires much more serious attention to justification of safety properties. From the point of view of problem complexity, normal design helps to tame this complexity, but not reduce it, by systematizing standard solutions to design problems. In analogy with divide and conquer techniques, the motivation behind normal design is not that of reducing problem complexity, but the reduction of programming complexity. This also sheds some light on the ongoing discussion of process based standards in software certification versus product based standards [28]. Engineers put a lot of store in normal design methods providing a higher level of assurance of safety and effectiveness of products. A process based standard for software development standardizes the process to be used in developing a new software product, but does not propose a normal design method for software, either generally or for a specific domain. This is the missing ingredient required to enable a process based claim for the product to be safe and/or effective. Until such process standards evolve to be the equivalent of normal design methods, we cannot give them much credit for reducing programming complexity, and such process based claims probably should be mistrusted.

One of the principles we would expect/hope to see in a software process standard based on normal design, is the guidance for how to separate control and safety systems so as to reduce the problem complexity of the safety system.

4.5 Conclusion

Separation of control and safety systems can be viewed as a special case of separation of concerns. This is not the same as modularization. It is a strict partitioning of the system into at least two parts, one of which contains the safety related behavior. The idea is that the separated and isolated safety system will have lower problem complexity than would the integrated system. Unlike the dangerous practice in aspect oriented programming, it is not our intention to weave the separated concern back into the application software.

We believe that separation of control systems and safety systems in the nuclear power industry is not only a good principle to follow, but that rigorous adherence to this principle should make it possible to analyze the system to an extent where we develop much greater confidence in the safety of the plant. The reasons are presented above, but the primary reason is that the reduction in complexity allows us to employ techniques that currently would not be possible for more complex systems. Without these mathematically based techniques we would be reduced to relying on testing alone to show conformance with requirements and correctness. It would also be much more difficult to apply techniques such as model checking, to confirm safe behavior at the requirements level. Recent trends in the nuclear industry would seem to indicate that manufacturers wish to abandon, at least to some degree, the need for separation of safety and control functions, and, arguably even worse, they want to abandon the basic principle of physical and logical separation between replicated safety functions. This trend is dangerous, because it moves complexity from elsewhere in the system, back into the safety function, thus significantly increasing the complexity of the safety function without significant reduction in the complexity of the control function. There appears to be no gain here, except an economic one. We are concerned that manufacturers seem to think that one time cost savings in the original development of these systems would be more important than the increased assurance we could realize in the dependability and safety of these systems. In fact, it is quite likely that adherence to this principle of separation will result in a long-term cost reduction, since the safety components in the overall system will be less likely to require corrective modification over the life of the system. Other modifications/enhancements can typically be made with reduced re-verification since the simpler safety systems can be pre-verified with ranges for constants, and information hiding designs on these smaller systems can help us prove the localization of changes.

The nuclear power domain is but one example domain in which this technique of separating control and safety should be common practice—preferably mandated by regulatory authorities. It also seems clear to us, that this same principle can be applied to building highly dependable, *cyber-physical systems*, such as medical devices and 'smarter cars'.

Acknowledgements This work is supported by the Ontario Research Fund, and the National Science and Engineering Research Council of Canada.

References

1. Bogdanich, W.: Radiation offers new cures, and ways to do harm. The New York Times Online (2010). Published January 23, 2010. Available online: http://www.nytimes.com/2010/01/24/health/24radiation.html
2. Bogdanich, W., Rebelo, K.: A pinpoint beam strays invisibly, harming instead of healing. The New York Times Online (2010). Published December 28, 2010. Available online: http://www.nytimes.com/2010/12/29/health/29radiation.html
3. Caglayan, A., Lorczak, P., Eckhardt, D.: An experimental investigation of software diversity in a fault-tolerant avionics application. In: Proceedings Seventh Symposium on Reliable Distributed Systems, pp. 63–70 (1988)
4. Easterbrook, S., Johns, T.: Engineering the software for understanding climate change. Comput. Sci. Eng. **11**(6), 65–74 (2009)
5. Fenton, N., Neil, M.: Software metrics: successes, failures and new directions. J. Syst. Softw. **47**(2–3), 149–157 (1999)
6. Fenton, N.E., Pfleeger, S.L.: Software Metrics: A Rigorous and Practical Approach. PWS Publishing Co., Boston (1998)
7. Fischmeister, S., Sokolsky, O., Lee, I.: A verifiable language for programming real-time communication schedules. IEEE Transactions on Computers 1505–1519 (2007)
8. Hoare, C.A.R.: The emperor's old clothes. Commun. ACM **24**(2), 75–83 (1981)
9. IEC 61508: Functional safety of electrical/electronic/programmable electronic (E/E/EP) safety-related systems: Parts 3 and 7. International Electrotechnical Commission (IEC) (2010)
10. Jackson, D., Kang, E.: Separation of concerns for dependable software design. In: Proceedings of the FSE/SDP Workshop on Future of Software Engineering Research, FoSER'10, pp. 173–176. ACM, New York (2010)
11. Jones, C.: Software metrics: good, bad and missing. Computer **27**(9), 98–100 (1994)
12. Kelly, D.F.: A software chasm: software engineering and scientific computing. IEEE Softw. **24**(6), 119–120 (2007)
13. Klein, G., Elphinstone, K., Heiser, G., Andronick, J., Cock, D., Derrin, P., Elkaduwe, D., Engelhardt, K., Kolanski, R., Norrish, M., Sewell, T., Tuch, H., Winwood, S.: seL4: formal verification of an OS kernel. In: Proceedings of the ACM SIGOPS 22nd Symposium on Operating Systems Principles, SOSP '09, pp. 207–220. ACM, New York (2009)

14. Ladyman, J., Lambert, J., Wiesner, K.: What is a complex system? http://philsci-archive.pitt. edu/8496/ (2011). Preprint

15. Lee, L.: The Day the Phones Stopped. Donald I. Fine Inc., New York (1991)

16. Manson, S.M.: Simplifying complexity: a review of complexity theory. Geoforum **32**(3), 405–414 (2001)

17. Niskier, C., Maibaum, T., Schwabe, D.: A pluralistic knowledge-based approach to software specification. In: Ghezzi, C., McDermid, J. (eds.) ESEC '89. Lecture Notes in Computer Science, vol. 387, pp. 411–423. Springer, Berlin (1989)

18. NRC Staff: Common-cause failure database and analysis system: event data collection, classification, and coding. Tech. rep. NUREG/CR-6268, US Nuclear Regulatory Commission (1998)

19. NRC Staff: Guidelines on modeling common-cause failures in probabilistic risk assessment. Tech. rep. NUREG/CR-5485, US Nuclear Regulatory Commission (1998)

20. Nuseibeh, B., Kramer, J., Finkelstein, A.: A framework for expressing the relationships between multiple views in requirements specification. IEEE Trans. Softw. Eng. **20**, 760–773 (1994)

21. Parnas, D.: On the criteria to be used in decomposing systems into modules. Commun. ACM **15**(12), 1053–1058 (1972)

22. Parnas, D.L., Clements, P.C., Weiss, D.M.: The modular structure of complex systems. IEEE Trans. Softw. Eng. **SE-11**(3), 66–259 (1985)

23. Polya, G., Stewart, I.: How to Solve It. Princeton University Press, Princeton (1948)

24. Sha, L.: Using simplicity to control complexity. IEEE Software, 20–28 (2001). http://doi. ieeecomputersociety.org/10.1109/MS.2001.936213

25. Vincenti, W.G.: What Engineers Know and how They Know It: Analytical Studies from Aeronautical History. Johns Hopkins University Press, Baltimore (1993)

26. Wassyng, A., Lawford, M.: Lessons learned from a successful implementation of formal methods in an industrial project. In: Araki, K., Gnesi, S., Mandrioli, D. (eds.) FME 2003: International Symposium of Formal Methods Europe Proceedings. Lecture Notes in Computer Science, vol. 2805, pp. 133–153. Springer, Pisa (2003)

27. Wassyng, A., Lawford, M., Maibaum, T., Luxat, J.: Separation of control and safety systems. In: Fischmeister, S., Phan, L.T. (eds.) APRES'11: Adaptive and Reconfigurable Embedded Systems, Chicago, IL, pp. 11–14 (2011)

28. Wassyng, A., Maibaum, T., Lawford, M.: On software certification: we need product-focused approaches. In: Choppy, C., Sokolsky, O. (eds.) Foundations of Computer Software. Future Trends and Techniques for Development. Lecture Notes in Computer Science, vol. 6028, pp. 250–274. Springer, Berlin (2010)

29. Weng, G., Bhalla, U., Iyengar, R.: Complexity in biological signaling systems. Science **284**(5411), 92 (1999)

Chapter 5
Conquering System Complexity

Norman F. Schneidewind

5.1 Complexity and System Evolution

Software development can be thought of as the evolution of abstract requirements into a concrete software system. Development, achieved through a successive series of transformations, is inherently an evolutionary process. Software evolution is often sub-optimal, because requisite information, like reliability and complexity, may be missing during the transformations. While some understanding of software may be reasonably clear at a given time, future dependencies may not be fully understood or accessible. The clarifications obtained over time make the system more concretely understood, but there may be loss of relevant information. Some may be lost due to failure to be fully acquainted with dependencies between various software artifacts [6].

As pointed out by Munson and Werries [14], as systems change through successive builds, the complexity characteristics of the individual modules that make up the system also change. Changes to systems are measured to provide indicators of potential problems, or mitigation of problems, introduced by the changes. For example, the evolution of the elevator system in Fig. 5.1 from undecomposed to decomposed modules actually results in reduction in complexity and increase in reliability. In addition, establishing a complexity baseline permits the comparison of a sequence of successive configurations. The baseline in Fig. 5.1 is the number of nodes and edges in the undecomposed system that is compared with this metric for the decomposed modules, thus permitting the reduction in complexity to be assessed. We investigate elevator floor travel distance, as a metric of complexity that can be mapped to elevator system reliability. When this mapping is achieved with the desired degree of accuracy, the approach is judged a success [20].

N.F. Schneidewind (✉)
Department of Information Science, Graduate School of Operational and Information Sciences, Monterey, CA, USA
e-mail: ieeelife@yahoo.com

M. Hinchey, L. Coyle (eds.), *Conquering Complexity*,
DOI 10.1007/978-1-4471-2297-5_5, © Springer-Verlag London Limited 2012

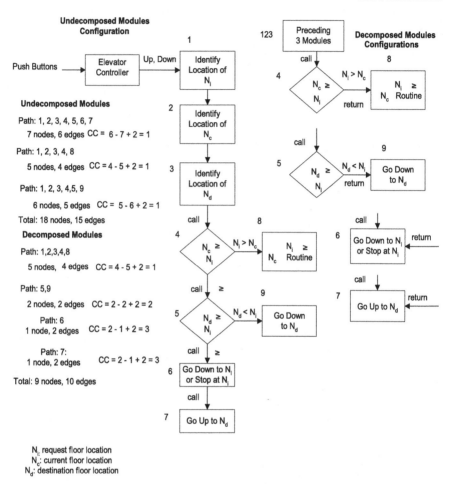

Fig. 5.1 Elevator system logic diagrams

As Lehman mentions, it is beneficial to determine the number of distinct additions and changes to systems and constituent modules of the system per release in order to assess system volatility. This can assist evolution release planning in a number of ways, for example by pointing to system areas that are ripe for restructuring because of high defect rates [10]. Some authors have suggested that if the IT industry used standardized and interchangeable software components, the problem of unreliable systems would largely disappear [4]. Unfortunately, for one-of-a-kind space systems that are addressed to solving unique research problems, the COTS solution will not work. In space systems, reliability and complexity across systems will show considerable variation. Therefore, complexity reduction efforts cannot be limited to a single system; it must address multiple systems.

When dealing with complex systems, it is unrealistic to assume that the system will be static, as the evolution from undecomposed to decomposed modules in Fig. 5.1 attests. Complex systems evolve over time, and the architecture of an evolving system will change even at run time, as the system implements self-configuration, self-adaptation, and meets the challenges of its environment. An evolving system can be viewed as multiple versions of the same system. That is, as the system evolves it represents multiple instances of the same system, for example, in Fig. 5.1, decomposed modules represent multiple instances of the original undecomposed system [16]. We consider the evolution of systems as progressing to the point where a system has met the reliability goal as a function of number of tests time and can be released for operational usage. As long as this goal is not satisfied, the systems continue to evolve, as the result of continuing testing. Reliability models are used to assess whether reliability is increasing over operational time and number of tests.

Software developers can benefit from an early warning of their complexity and resultant reliability while there is still time to react. This early warning can be built from a collection of internal and external metrics. An internal metric, such as the node and edge counts in Fig. 5.1, is a measure derived from the product itself. An external measure is a measure of a product derived from assessment of the behavior of the system. For example, the number of defects found in test is an external measure [15].

5.2 Complexity Tradeoffs

Complexity affects functionality, reliability, and cost. In addition, there is design complexity and operational complexity, with the former leading to the latter. The greater the complexity, the greater the functionality and cost and the lower the reliability. Therefore, there are tradeoffs among these system attributes. If the user wants a lot of functionality, it will cost a lot and have lower reliability than with a simpler system. Interestingly, different users can have different expectations with respect to complexity. For example, in an elevator system, one mode of operation would be to go directly to the floor with the oldest request by user x, by passing floors with a more recent request by user y. This policy would reduce complexity and provide great functionality for user x, but would result in poor functionality for user y. Which policy should be used? Manufacturers of general purpose systems, such as elevator systems, will opt for a great deal of functionality in order to achieve large market share, whereas specific system providers, such as space system developers, are motivated to achieve only the functionality required by the application, with high cost and reliability, because of the limited market served and the willingness of customers to pay for safety attributes in mission critical applications.

5.3 Complexity Metrics

5.3.1 Program Slicing

There is a plethora of complexity metrics that can be used to increase program comprehension and thereby improve reliability. One metric is program slicing that aims to increase program comprehension by focusing on a sliver of the program rather than the complete code [18]. Slices can also be used to increase the understandability of specifications [3]. A slice corresponds to the mental abstractions that people make when they debug a program [25]. If debugging can be improved by using slicing, then this would aid reliability. Slices are useful in identifying changes that may ripple through to other computations.This is particularly important in maintaining software, but because changes dominate this function. If software is not maintainable, it will not be reliable. Despite these theoretical benefits of slicing, computing the slice for an arbitrary predicate is known to be intractable in general [12]. Thus, this is not a useful metric for *quantitatively* estimating software reliability.

5.3.2 Symbolic Execution

This procedure involves taking a user's existing code, adding semantic declarations for some primitive variables, symbolically executing the user's code, and recognizing code structure from the symbolic expressions generated. This analysis provides high-level, semantic information and detects errors in a user's code [23]. Since we are dealing with the complexity of program configurations as an indicator of program complexity, it is appropriate to mention how symbolic execution can aid white-box testing methods based on the analysis of program configuration. For this method, an important problem is to determine the complexity of configurations by finding appropriate paths to execute the configurations [26], as shown in Fig. 5.1.

5.4 Design Complexity

Having stated that there are complexity tradeoffs, there are some design approaches that can achieve desired functionality, accompanied by lower complexity and cost, and high reliability. We explore these approaches at the system, hardware, and software levels.

5.5 System and Software Complexity

For example, consider Fig. 5.1 that compares system configurations for an elevator system. If we compare the configuration that is not decomposed with the one that is divided into short software routines that can be called, we see that the latter is considerably less complex than the former in terms of node and edge counts. Now, McCabe [11] developed the cyclomatic complexity metric that measures the complexity of a system represented by nodes and edges in a directed graph. While it is useful for identifying critical paths to test, it does not always yield accurate representations of complexity, as Fig. 5.1 attests. According to McCabe, cyclomatic complexity $= CC =$ number of edges (e) − number of nodes (n) + 2. The calculations of CC in Fig. 5.1 suggest that the undecomposed modules are less complex than the decomposed ones, but this is clearly not the case. Therefore, we suggest that a better quantification of complexity is node count and edge count for each path. Using this formulation, yields consistent representations of complexity in Fig. 5.1. Thus, this characterization of complexity can be used in deciding on system configuration alternatives during the design process.

5.6 Cost of Complexity

Using the complexity quantification developed in the preceding section, the cost of complexity for a configuration of modules, such as those shown in Fig. 5.1, can be formulated as follows:

$$C = \sum_{j=1}^{N}(n_j * cn) + \sum_{k=1}^{E}(e_k * ce),$$

where C is cost of the configuration, n_j is the jth node, N is the number of nodes in the configuration, cn is the cost per node, e_k is the kth edge, E is the number of edges in the configuration, and ce is the cost per edge.

For example, referencing Fig. 5.1 and using the undecomposed Path: 1, 2, 3, 4, 5, 6, 7, with 7 nodes and 6 edges,

$$C = 7 * cn + 6 * ce.$$

Comparing this result with the decomposed Path: 1, 2, 3, 4, 8, with 5 nodes and 4 edges,

$$C = 5 * cn + 4 * ce.$$

Thus even without knowing node and edge cost, configuration complexity-based costs can be estimated *prior* to implementation, demonstrating that reduced complexity results in reduced cost.

5.7 Hardware Complexity

De Morgan's Theorem [7] is used to simplify complex logic equations, which are used in the design of hardware, and the resultant digital logic. By simplifying the digital logic complexity, reliability is increased and cost is decreased, as the number of components is decreased. The theorem is used to simplify relatively simple expressions, as contrasted with Karnaugh Maps, described in the next section. The application of this theorem is shown in the following example:

De Morgan's Theorem: $\overline{A + B} = \bar{A}\bar{B}$ and $\overline{AB} = \bar{A} + \bar{B}$

Table 5.1 Truth table to demonstrate equivalence between F and AB

A	B	$\overline{AB}$	$(\overline{AB})(\overline{AB})$	$F = (\overline{(\overline{AB})(\overline{AB})})$	AB
0	0	1	1	0	0
0	1	1	1	0	0
1	0	1	1	0	0
1	1	0	0	1	1

Table 5.2 K-map for $F = \bar{A}\bar{B}\bar{C} + A\bar{B}\bar{C} + \bar{A}\bar{B}C + A\bar{B}C$. Each of the table entries (in italics) represents a boolean expression, clockwise from top left they are: $\bar{A}\bar{B}\bar{C}$, $\bar{A}\bar{B}C$, $A\bar{B}C$, and $A\bar{B}\bar{C}$

Boolean expression		$\bar{B}\bar{C}$	$\bar{B}C$	BC	$B\bar{C}$
	Boolean representation	00	01	11	10
$\bar{A}$	0		*1*	*1*	
A	1		*1*	*1*	

Suppose it is required to simplify $F = (\overline{(\overline{AB})(\overline{AB})})$, where F is the digital output of inputs A and B. Applying the theorem:

$$\overline{AB} = \bar{A} + \bar{B},$$

$$(\overline{AB})(\overline{AB}) = (\bar{A} + \bar{B})(\bar{A} + \bar{B})$$

$$= \bar{A}\bar{A} + \bar{A}\bar{B} + \bar{A}\bar{B} + \bar{B}\bar{B}$$

$$= \bar{A} + \bar{A}\bar{B} + \bar{B}$$

$$= \bar{A} + (\bar{A} + 1)\bar{B}$$

$$= \bar{A} + \bar{B}$$

demonstrate the equivalence

$$F = \overline{(\bar{A} + \bar{B})(\bar{A} + \bar{B})} = \overline{(\bar{A} + \bar{B})} = AB$$

Then, use Table 5.1 to demonstrate equivalence between $F = (\overline{(\overline{AB})(\overline{AB})})$ and AB.

A Karnaugh Map (K-map) in Table 5.2 is used to minimize a complex Boolean expression [17]. Each square of a K-map represents a minterm (i.e., product terms). The process proceeds by listing the binary equivalents of the terms A and BC on the axes of Table 5.2, ordering them so that there is only a one bit difference between adjacent cells. Then, the minimum number of cells is enclosed. Next, minterms are identified according to terms that are common to all cells in the enclosure. Notice what a clever method this is. Minimization is achieved by noting the combination of terms that yields the minimum difference!

Example: Simplify $F = \bar{A}\bar{B}\bar{C} + A\bar{B}\bar{C} + \bar{A}\bar{B}C + A\bar{B}C$.

Table 5.3 F function truth table

A	B	C	$F = \bar{A}\bar{B}\bar{C} + A\bar{B}\bar{C} + \bar{A}\bar{B}C + A\bar{B}C$	$F = \bar{B}$
0	0	0	1	1
0	0	1	1	1
0	1	0	0	0
0	1	1	0	0
1	0	0	1	1
1	0	1	1	1
1	1	0	0	0
1	1	1	0	0

Now, simplify F, demonstrating that it reduces to $\bar{B}$.

$$F = \bar{A}\bar{B}\bar{C} + A\bar{B}\bar{C} + \bar{A}\bar{B}C + A\bar{B}C$$
$$= \bar{B}\bar{C}(\bar{A} + A) + \bar{B}C(\bar{A} + A)$$
$$= \bar{B}\bar{C} + \bar{B}C$$
$$= \bar{B}(\bar{C} + C)$$
$$= \bar{B}$$

In the K-map, $\bar{B}$ is common to the enclosed minterms. Therefore, $F = \bar{B}$. Table 5.3 demonstrates this result. The considerable reduction from the original function would result in significant savings in circuitry to implement the function.

5.8 Complexity and Reliability

In the NASA Space Shuttle, program size and complexity, number of conflicting requirements, and memory requirements have been shown to be significantly related to reliability (i.e., increases in these risk factors are associated with decreases in reliability) [21]. Therefore, organizations should conduct studies to determine what factors are contributing to reliability degradation.

One view of complexity that it is the degree to which a system is difficult to analyze, understand, or explain [2]. If a system lacks structure, it will be difficult to understand, test, and operate. Therefore, complexity has a direct bearing on reliability. We bring structure and complexity into our elevator system reliability examples by designating elevator floor travel distance and time as reliability-dependent complexity metrics.

Why study complexity in relation to reliability? The answer is that complexity breeds bugs. The more complex the system, the harder it is to make it reliable [22]. Thus, building a reliability model for predicting the failure-proneness of systems can help organizations make early decisions on the quality of their

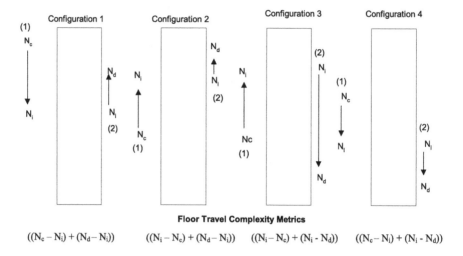

Fig. 5.2 Elevator floor travel configurations

systems. Such early estimates can be used to help inform decisions on testing, refactoring, code inspections, design rework, etc. This has been demonstrated by the efficacy of building failure-proneness models, based on code complexity metrics, across the Microsoft Windows operating system [2]. The ability of such models to estimate failure-proneness and provide feedback on complexity metrics helps guide the evolution of the software to higher-and-higher plateaus of reliability.

The first consideration in developing complexity-based reliability predictions is to formulate the equations for configuration probability. Configurations for elevator systems are generated based on the number of distinct combinations of floor locations (N_i: request floor, N_c: current floor, N_d: destination floor), and their travel directions. These configurations are representative of complexity because the longer the elevator traversal distance, the greater the complexity. The possible floor travel configurations are shown in Fig. 5.2. Configuration operation numbers (1) and (2) in the list below, and in Fig. 5.2, correspond to the order of floor traversals. Note, if the elevator is already at the request floor ($N_c = N_i$), there is zero travel time from N_c to N_i. Also note that the relative locations of the elevator, the request floor, and the destination floor, are important in computing the elevator travel distances for the configurations.

The probability of configuration traversal P_c is proportional to length and direction of elevator travel, using the differences in floor location values to account for the relative locations of current floor, request floor, and destination floor, as shown in the sequence list below. Since we have no prior knowledge of elevator traversal distances, we generate their values using uniformly distributed random numbers, multiplied by 100, the assumed number of floors. Then, these values are used in predicting configuration probability according the following equations:

Configuration 1

(1) Elevator goes *down* from current floor N_c to request floor N_i then (2) goes *up* from request floor N_i to destination floor N_d ($N_c \geq N_i$, $N_d \geq N_i$):

$$P_c = \frac{N_d - N_i}{(N_c - N_i) + (N_d - N_i)}$$

Configuration 2

(1) Elevator goes *up* from current floor N_c to request floor N_i then (2) goes *up* from request floor N_i to destination floor N_d ($N_i \geq N_c$, $N_d \geq N_i$):

$$P_c = \frac{N_d - N_i}{(N_i - N_c) + (N_d - N_i)}$$

Configuration 3

(1) Elevator goes *up* from current floor N_c to request floor N_i then (2) goes *down* from request floor N_i to destination floor N_d ($N_i \geq N_c$, $N_i \geq N_d$):

$$P_c = \frac{N_i - N_d}{(N_i - N_c) + (N_i - N_d)}$$

Configuration 4

(1) Elevator goes *down* from current floor N_c to request floor N_i then (2) goes *down* from request floor N_i to destination floor N_d ($N_c \geq N_i$, $N_i \geq N_d$):

$$P_c = \frac{N_i - N_d}{(N_c - N_i) + (N_i - N_d)}$$

5.9 Configuration Response Time

The next step in arriving at reliability prediction equations is to quantify configuration response time because this is the time during which the reliability goal must be achieved. A real-time system is one in which the time of output is significant. This may be the case because the input occurs while there is movement in the physical world, and the output has to relate to the same movement. For example, in an elevator system, user input occurs while the elevator is moving, and subsequently, the resultant output is movement to respond to the user request, as depicted in Fig. 5.1. The lag from input time to output time (i.e., response time) must be sufficiently small for acceptable timeliness [9].

Since real-time systems have stringent end-to-end timing requirements [5], we focus on response time in elevator systems, wherein we consider response time as being "end-to-end": difference between the time of completing a user request to reach the destination floor and the start time of the request.

The reliability analysis of real-time complex systems is a very important engineering issue for guaranteeing their functional behavior. Most of the critical failures are generated by the interactions between components. Therefore the analysis of the system as a whole is not enough and it is necessary to study interactions between components in order to predict system reliability [8]. Thus, in our elevator system example, floor traversal configurations are the components whose interactions are modeled.

The probability, P_c, of configuration c traversal, is combined with single floor travel time, t_f, and door opening and closing time, t_{oc}, to produce configuration c traversal response time, T_c. The response times, corresponding to the travel distances in the four configurations, are computed as follows:

Configuration 1

$$T_c = (t_f * ((N_d - N_i) + (N_c - N_i))) * P_c + t_{oc}$$

Configuration 2

$$T_c = (t_f * ((N_i - N_c) + (N_d - N_i))) * P_c + t_{oc}$$

Configuration 3

$$T_c = (t_f * ((N_i - N_c) + (N_c - N_d))) * P_c + t_{oc}$$

Configuration 4

$$T_c = (t_f * ((N_c - N_i) + (N_i - N_d))) * P_c + t_{oc}$$

5.10 Configuration Failure Rate

In order to predict configuration reliability, it is necessary to estimate configuration c failure rate, λ_c, a parameter that is used in the prediction of configuration c reliability. This parameter is estimated using the number of failures, nf, which is assumed to occur during n tests of configuration c, and configuration c response time, T_c, computed over n tests. A key determinate of configuration failure rate is whether there are failures in delivering information from source to destination [13], such as push buttons generating signals that are delivered to the elevator controller in Fig. 5.1. Thus, this type of failure is included in the assumed failure count n_f.

In addition, we postulate that the *expected* number of failures in configuration c is proportional to configuration c floor traversal distance for test i, n_i, with respect to total floor traversal distance over n tests for configuration c, based on the premise that the larger the floor traversal distance, the higher the probability of failure. Putting these factors together, we arrive at the following:

$$\lambda_c = n_f \frac{(\frac{n_i}{\sum_{i=1}^{n} n_i})}{(\sum_{i=1}^{n}(T_c))}$$

5.11 Reliability Model and Predictions

5.11.1 Reliability Model

Because a system that lacks structure is likely to have poor reliability, we provide structure in our elevator design in Fig. 5.1 by using decomposed modules. In order to identify beneficial system evolutionary steps, as they relate to reliability and complexity, we develop our complexity-based reliability model with the aim of reducing complexity and thereby increasing reliability. Therefore, we include the effect of floor traversal complexity in the computation of the above configuration failure rate.

In developing complex real-time reliability predictions, it is important that the predictions reflect *operational reliability* [24]. That is, reliability must be cast in the context of operational conditions, such as differences in floor traversal times in the elevator system. Otherwise, the predictions will not represent user requirements. We adhere to this principle by using configuration response time, which represents operational conditions, in the formulation of reliability.

The *unreliability* of configuration c, UR_c, is predicted by using the probability of configuration c, P_c, configuration failure rate λ_c, and sequence c response time, T_c, assuming exponentially distributed response time.

$$UR_c = P_c(1 - e^{-\lambda_c T_c})$$

Then, configuration c reliability R_c can be predicted as follows:

$$R_c = 1 - P_c(1 - e^{-\lambda_c T_c})$$

The distinction between normal and complex operations is important in characterizing reliability [19]. Thus, we assume exponentially distributed response time that is based on the premise that reliability degrades fast with increases in response time caused by increasing complexity of operations.

Because numerous predictions of reliability are made due to the fact that sequences are simulated n times, it is appropriate to predict the mean value of configuration c reliability, as follows:

$$MR_c = \frac{\sum_{j=1}^{n} R_c}{n}$$

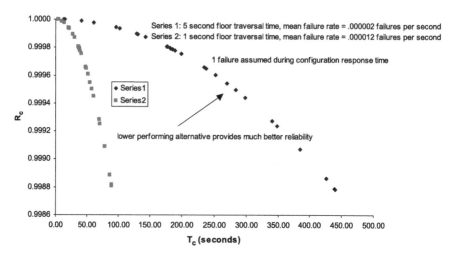

Fig. 5.3 Elevator system: configuration 1 predicted reliability R_c vs. configuration response time T_c

5.11.2 Predictions

Figure 5.3 demonstrates that it is infeasible to achieve both high performance and high reliability because the higher performing alternative has a much higher mean failure rate, resulting in lower reliability for this performance alternative. The higher failure rate results from the assumed single failure occurring over a shorter operational (response) time. Thus, in choosing a system, a decision must be made between lower performing-higher reliability and higher performing-lower reliability alternatives. Interestingly, when reliability is compared by configuration for the same floor traversal time and assumed number of failures in Fig. 5.4, there is no significant difference evident. We might expect a difference because, presumably, different configurations could represent different degrees of complexity. However, the four configurations in Fig. 5.2 that were used in developing the plots in Fig. 5.4, exhibit essentially the same complexity. This would not be the case in assessing the complexity of different web sites, for example, Google and Yahoo. Thus in analyzing reliability by configuration, it is essential to consider configuration characteristics.

5.12 Maintainability

A key objective of addressing maintainability is to develop maintainability predictions that would be used to *anticipate* the need for maintenance actions (i.e., preventive maintenance [1]). Preventive maintenance would also be achieved by reducing system complexity, leading to increasing reliability, assuming that reduced complexity would not violate customer functionality requirements. Since there are

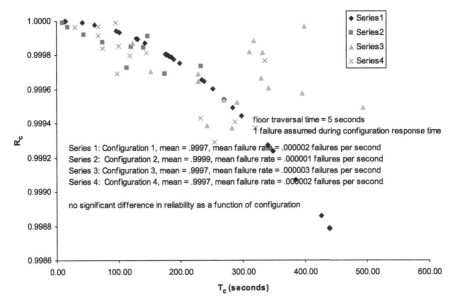

Fig. 5.4 Elevator system: configuration c predicted reliability R_c vs. configuration c response time T_c

many situations in which the foregoing approach is infeasible, maintainability can be implemented by performing maintenance actions on configurations that have experienced failures, with the objective of eliminating or reducing the failures. Since there is no assurance that maintenance actions will be successful, the probability of successful maintenance, P_m, for configuration c, is applied to the number of failures, n_c, that occur on configuration c, as follows:

$$n_m = P_m n_c,$$

where n_m is the revised failure count on configuration c and P_m and n_c are uniformly distributed random numbers that are used because we have no knowledge a priori of the probability of successful maintenance or of the incidence of failures on a configuration. Then, the configuration c failure rate is revised by computing $\lambda_c = \frac{n_m}{T_c}$. Next, the predicted reliability of configuration c, R_c, is revised by using $\frac{n_m}{T_c}$ as the failure rate. Once the revised failure count has been estimated, the failure rate can be revised, and reliability predictions can be repeated.

Figure 5.5 provides dramatic proof of the effectiveness of maintenance actions in improving reliability for configuration 1 for both performance options. Thus, this type of plot is useful for predicting in advance of implementation, the likely effect of maintainability policies, and it could be combined with configuration complexity reduction, if the latter were feasible from a functionality standpoint.

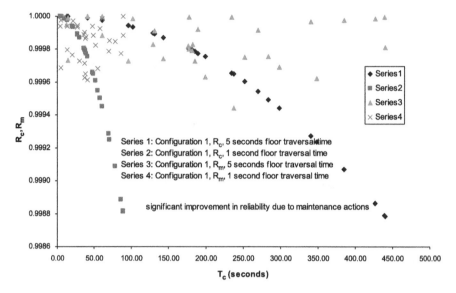

Fig. 5.5 Elevator system: comparison of original configuration c reliability R_c with revised reliability due to maintenance R_m vs. configuration c response time T_c

5.12.1 Availability

In order to predict configuration c availability, A_c, we use configuration c response time, T_c, and maintenance time, T_m, as follows:

$$A_c = \frac{T_c}{T_c + T_m}$$

Maintenance time T_m is predicted by considering the two factors that affect it: revised failure count due to maintenance actions, n_m, and configuration c response time, T_c. The concept is that maintenance time is proportional to both the failure reduction effort, as represented by n_m, and length of response or operational time, T_c, because the longer this time, the more complex the maintenance action, and, hence, the longer the required maintenance time. Thus, $T_m = n_m * T_c$.

In addition, we can predict the mean value of availability by using the mean values of configuration c response time, MT_c, and maintenance time MT_m:

$$MA_c = \frac{MT_c}{MT_c + MT_m}$$

The result of applying these principles is Fig. 5.6 that shows the need for more effective maintenance in the form of reduced maintenance time with respect to operational time (response time). Maintenance time, in turn, can be reduced by increasing reliability through additional fault removal, or reduction in complexity, if feasible, with respect to customer functionality requirements. The figure also shows

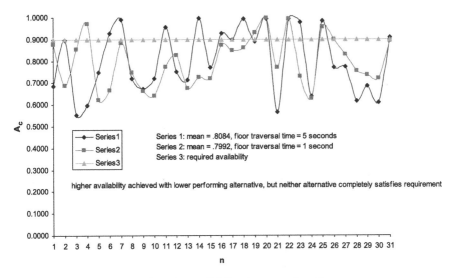

Fig. 5.6 Elevator system: configuration availability A_c vs. number of tests n

that, as in the case of reliability, the lower performing alternative achieves higher availability, due to greater operational time relative to maintenance time.

5.13 Summary

This chapter has shown that there is an intimate relationship among complexity, reliability, maintainability, and availability. This relationship should be exploited by reducing complexity, where feasible, to increase reliability, maintainability, and availability. As we noted, it is not always feasible to reduce complexity because customers may expect high functionality that results in high complexity. We also noted that high complexity results in high cost. Thus, there are tradeoffs that must be analyzed to achieve balance among the competing objectives. We presented a number of models, using an elevator system example, which can be used *prior to implementation* to analyze the tradeoffs.

References

1. Azem, S., Aggoune, R., Dauzère-Pérès, S.: Disjunctive and time-indexed formulations for non-preemptive job shop scheduling with resource availability constraints. In: IEEE International Conference on Industrial Engineering and Engineering Management, pp. 787–791 (2007)
2. Bohner, S.: An era of change-tolerant systems. IEEE Comput. **40**(6), 100–102 (2007)

3. Bollin, A.: The efficiency of specification fragments. In: 11th Working Conference on Reverse Engineering, pp. 266–275. IEEE Comput. Soc., Washington (2004)
4. Fiadeiro, J.L.: Designing for software's social complexity. IEEE Comput. **40**(1), 34–39 (2007)
5. Fu, X., Wang, X., Puster, E.: Dynamic thermal and timeliness guarantees for distributed real-time embedded systems. In: 15th IEEE International Conference on Embedded and Real-Time Computing Systems and Applications, RTCSA '09, pp. 403–412. IEEE Comput. Soc., Washington (2009)
6. George, B., Bohner, S.A., Prieto-Diaz, R.: Software information leaks: a complexity perspective. In: Ninth IEEE International Conference on Engineering Complex Computer Systems, pp. 239–248 (2004)
7. Greenfield, S.E.: The Architecture of Microcomputers. Winthrop Publishers, Inc., Cambridge (1980)
8. Guerin, F., Barreau, M., Morel, J.-Y., Mihalache, A., Dumon, B., Todoskoff, A.: Reliability analysis for complex industrial real-time systems: application on an antilock brake system. In: Second IEEE International Conference on Systems, Man and Cybernetics (SMC'02), October 6–9, 2002, Hammamet, Tunisia, vol. 7. IEEE Comput. Soc., Los Alamitos (2002)
9. Kurki-Suonio, R.: Real time: further misconceptions (or half-truths) [real-time systems]. IEEE Comput. **27**, 71–76 (1994)
10. Lehman, M.M.: Rules and tools for software evolution planning and management. In: International Workshop on Feedback and Evolution in Software and Business Processes (2000). Revised and extended version in Annals of Software Engineering, vol. 11, Nov. 2001, pp. 15–44
11. McCabe, T.J.: A complexity measure. In: 2nd International Conference on Software Engineering, ICSE '76, p. 407. IEEE Comput. Soc., Los Alamitos (1976)
12. Mittal, N., Garg, V.K.: Computation slicing: techniques and theory. In: 15th International Conference on Distributed Computing, DISC '01, pp. 78–92. Springer, London (2001)
13. Mizanian, K., Yousefi, H., Jahangir, A.H.: Modeling and evaluating reliable real-time degree in multi-hop wireless sensor networks. In: 32nd International Conference on Sarnoff Symposium, SARNOFF'09, pp. 568–573. IEEE Press, Piscataway (2009)
14. Munson, J.C., Werries, D.S.: Measuring software evolution. In: 3rd International Symposium on Software Metrics: From Measurement to Empirical Results, METRICS '96, p. 41. IEEE Comput. Soc., Washington (1996)
15. Nagappan, N.: Toward a software testing and reliability early warning metric suite. In: 26th International Conference on Software Engineering, ICSE '04, pp. 60–62. IEEE Comput. Soc., Washington (2004)
16. Peña, J., Hinchey, M.G., Resinas, M., Sterritt, R., Rash, J.L.: Designing and managing evolving systems using a MAS product line approach. Sci. Comput. Program. **66**(1), 71–86 (2007)
17. Rafiquzzaman, M.: Fundamentals of Digital Logic and Microcomputer Design. Wiley-Interscience, New York (2005)
18. Rilling, J., Klemola, T.: Identifying comprehension bottlenecks using program slicing and cognitive complexity metrics. In: 11th IEEE International Workshop on Program Comprehension, IWPC '03, p. 115. IEEE Comput. Soc., Washington (2003)
19. Russ, N., Peter, G., Berlin, R., Ulmer, B.: Lessons learned: on-board software test automation using IBM rational test realtime. In: IEEE International Conference on Space Mission Challenges for Information Technology, p. 305. IEEE Comput. Soc., Los Alamitos (2006)
20. Schneidewind, N.F.: Requirements risk and software reliability. In: Madhavji, N.H., Fernández-Ramil, J.C., Perry, D.E. (eds.) Software Evolution and Feedback, pp. 407–421. Wiley, New York (2006)
21. Schneidewind, N.F.: Risk-driven software testing and reliability. Int. J. Reliab. Qual. Saf. Eng. **14**(2), 99–132 (2007)
22. Sha, L.: Using simplicity to control complexity. IEEE Softw. **18**(4), 20–28 (2001)
23. Stewart, M.E.M.: Towards a tool for rigorous, automated code comprehension using symbolic execution and semantic analysis. In: 29th Annual IEEE/NASA on Software Engineering Workshop, pp. 89–96. IEEE Comput. Soc., Washington (2005)

24. Sun, Y., Cheng, L., Liu, H., He, S.: Power system operational reliability evaluation based on real-time operating state. In: 7th International Power Engineering Conference, Nov. 29–Dec. 2, 2005, pp. 722–727 (2005)
25. Weiser, M.: Program slicing. IEEE Trans. Softw. Eng. **10**(4), 352–357 (1984)
26. Zhang, J.: Symbolic execution of program paths involving pointer and structure variables. In: Fourth International Conference on Quality Software, QSIC '04, pp. 87–92. IEEE Comput. Soc., Washington (2004)

Chapter 6
Accommodating Adaptive Systems Complexity with Change Tolerance

Shawn Bohner, Ramya Ravichandar, and Andrew Milluzzi

6.1 Introduction

Just as complex structures of matter are fundamental to chemistry and physics, complex compositions of software (both from component and language perspectives) and their response to changes are fundamental to computer science and software engineering. Complexity in software is a bit like complexity in music. Both software and music are languages that get read by another practitioner and executed on instruments (computing and musical instruments respectively). Both have logical, if not mathematical, underpinnings. Take a piece of music by Johann Sebastian Bach; it is complex largely because of the intricacy of the elements woven into the music. Johann Strauss Jr., on the other hand, has music complex in the abundance of detail it exhibits. Others such as Wolfgang Mozart have both types of complexity with the overall level of sophistication in their work. No matter the composer, the properly orchestrated music fulfills its purpose as it inspires and entertains audiences around the world.

Similarly, software can be complex for intricacy and abundance of detail. To examine these, we have posed two projects later in this chapter. The first was to conquer intricacy by looking how Model-Based Engineering (MBE) approaches could be applied to a particularly sophisticated agent-based system called "Cougaar." The second was to address the abundance of detail shown in reconfigurable computing with Field-Programmable Gate Arrays (FPGA). Both projects show how complexity can be dealt with using abstraction, and managing complexity with coupling and cohesion.

6.1.1 Faces of Software System Complexity

Robert Glass masterfully distinguishes the complexity of the problem from the complexity of the solution—solution complexity increases about four times as fast as the

S. Bohner (✉)
Rose-Hulman Institute of Technology, Terre Haute, USA
e-mail: bohner@rose-hulman.edu

M. Hinchey, L. Coyle (eds.), *Conquering Complexity*,
DOI 10.1007/978-1-4471-2297-5_6, © Springer-Verlag London Limited 2012

problem complexity [21]. Highly dynamic problem spaces often require intermediary technologies to reduce the cognitive load of the "many" to allow focus on the "important."

The nature of software and its concomitant complexity turned a corner over the past decade with the advent of agent-based systems, social networking, autonomic and self-healing systems, reconfigurable computing, web services, and the like [5]. José Luiz Fiadeiro describes this as "social complexity" arising from the number and intricacy of interactions [16]. Software complexity compounds volume (structure) and interaction (social) properties as modern applications increasingly use agents to carry out collaborative tasking and the use of the Internet enables software functionality to be delivered as services. Yet, most technologies that we use to develop and evolve software systems do little to accommodate these notions of interaction-oriented complexity and dynamic change.

The range of sophistication in software applications is on the rise. Individually we use it for everything from doing our taxes to automating our home security to obtaining news from the web. Collectively, we use it to manage information in corporations (and even across industries) and for collaborative efforts across the web through online meetings.

Workflow automation in the logistics community has become an exemplar for large, sophisticated applications. Substantial knowledge about assets flowing through an organization requires relevant intelligence that must be flexible enough to respond to complex situations and changing environments [1]. In the small, agents routinely make decisions about routing and scheduling (relieving humans of these tasks). In the large, agents augment and expedite key management tasks by acquiring requisite information for corporate decision-makers.

Traditionally, we respond to complexity by decomposing systems into manageable parts to accommodate the number of elements and their structure. Collaborative agents are inherently social and interactions stem from a range of dependencies and values. Manifold dependencies involved in sophisticated systems warrant new ways of structuring the problem space and allowing solutions to evolve and flex with knowledge introduced after the system is deployed. Agent-based systems and Service-Oriented Architectures (SOA) reflect the need for flexibility and self-assembly more than size and structure.

6.1.2 Models Help Conquer Complexity

Software systems are supposed to change—otherwise, we would have put the software capabilities in the hardware. While, this is true for the most part, the convenience of a software solution for a general processor is often preferred to the specially designed circuits that render an optimal solution. Why? The precision of a specific solution induces complexity and time to the solution. That is, the time to produce an optimal solution exceeds the available resources. Further, today's computing solutions entail heterogeneous computing platforms with varying configurations (even within the individual processing types). Increasingly, the complexity of the application domain requires solutions that entail use of even more adaptable components that the software reflects in the language (e.g., intelligent agents or adaptable hardware like dynamically reconfigurable hardware). These induce even more complexity.

How do we accommodate the added complexity that solution approaches might induce? Part of the answer lies in what principles we use to bring visibility and predictability to the solution. Model-Based Engineering uses classical complexity control through abstractions, coupled with provable transformations between the levels of understanding. Hence, modularity measures like coupling and cohesion apply.

At its core, system development can be thought of as the systematic progression from abstract requirements to a concrete system implementation. This process, achieved through a successive series of transformations (i.e., elaborations and refinements), is inherently complex and models are used to understand relevant areas of concern [19, 31].

It is important to recognize that we use models at each level of abstraction to separate key concerns and hide unnecessary details that are not relevant to the abstraction (the elements of the abstraction are balanced in their level of reasoning—e.g., reason about problem space objects to the exclusion of design). If a higher-level representation is overly complex, this is not fixable at subsequent levels without substantial effort. This means that as we move from analysis, to design, to implementation, etc. we "accumulate complexities" that impact both the ability to produce the final product and especially to evolve it. This chapter examines how to, from a first-principles perspective, control the accumulation of undue complexity. At the same time, we examine how capturing models as intermediate forms allow us to accumulate intellectual simplifications that can ease the generation of the systems specified. These entail formalisms and rigor that at first induce complexity, but later enable simplifications that outweigh the initial cost as subsequent uses provide returns.

Again, models provide abstractions that allow us to decompose problems/solutions into manageable pieces, focus on the appropriate level of detail, separate concerns, and formalize solution space for validation. Models enable people working together to reason about systems using a medium that is convenient for different disciplines. However, the convenience can lead to losses in precision and recall, as information is necessarily omitted for various levels of interaction. This must be managed in order to conquer complexity.

6.1.3 Systems Capabilities and Change Tolerance

Capabilities—functional abstractions that are neither as amorphous as user needs nor as rigid as system requirements—are intended to assist in architecting systems to accommodate change [37]. These entities are designed to exhibit desirable characteristics of high cohesion, low coupling, and balanced abstraction levels—criteria derived from the reconciliation of a synthesis and decomposition approach to capability definition [38]. Using this approach in the early stages of defining the problem domain to produce key elements of the computationally independent models can lead to longer-lived architectural components. We leverage this in our approach as we move forward towards managing complexity and change-tolerance of systems that are produced using model-based engineering.

The low coupling, high cohesion, and balanced abstraction levels applies to each level of detail as we move from analysis to understand the problem domain and specify the requirements, to architecture and design to specify the solution space, to implementation using appropriate language abstraction so that the design is conveyed both to the future maintainer as well as the computing platform. In this chapter, we submit this concept as a key element for understanding and controlling complexity as software evolves.

A key aspect of software is its capacity or tolerance for change. Inspired by aspects of fault tolerance, the term "change tolerance" connotes the ability of software to evolve within the bounds that it was designed—that software change is intentional [5]. There is a range of ways to reason about the notion of software change. One can take a maintenance view of corrective, adaptive, and perfective change. But this doesn't really deal with managing the variant and invariant nature found in Bertrand Meyer's Open/Closed Principle (open for extension, closed for modification) or the Lisksov Substitution Principle (notion of a behavioral subtype defines notion of substitutability for mutable objects). These and others are necessary principles to evolve software effectively.

One can design for change at the product level (e.g., reconfigurable computing) or at the process level (e.g., reuse of models). Industry addresses software change from top-down model-based engineering (e.g., Object Management Group's Model-Driven Architecture) and bottom-up agile method (e.g., Extreme Programming) perspectives. Both address risks of producing large volumes of software on shorter time-lines, but from different perspectives.

From a practical perspective, change tolerance can be reasoned about through coupling, cohesion, and balance of the abstraction. In this treatment, we examine the models used to proceed from analysis to architecture in these terms.

6.1.4 Model-Based Engineering (MBE)

We use MBE in the broadest sense to mean those model-based approaches used in various engineering disciplines to develop products. For most engineering disciplines that have tangible products, MBE is used largely for simulation and verification purposes. Note in software, our simulation goes further and becomes operational. In software MBE comes in the forms of Model-Based Software Engineering (MBSE), Model-Driven Architecture (MDA), Model-Driven Development (MDD), Model-Driven Software Development (MDSD), Domain Specific Languages (DSL), and the like.

MBE strategies are emerging technologies that show promise to improve productivity both during initial development and subsequent maintenance. These approaches use modeling to abstract and separate concerns about system behaviors and performance so that they can be reasoned about and conveyed to subsequent levels of elaboration and refinement. Each transition to a more detailed level must abide by coupling and cohesion principles to have balanced abstractions and guarantees regarding their properties.

The application of model-based strategies on the system, technical, and configuration levels can be challenging. With the shift towards distributed systems of systems, service-oriented architectures, and the like, complex interaction between control and reactive parts of a system, and the increasing number of variants introduced by product lines, the complexity continues to rise. However, with populated model repositories containing canonical domain-level capabilities and application-level components, the complexities can be managed with some level of discipline. Further, if the components and their integration can be examined in light of coupling, cohesion, and balance of abstraction, we should have a rational model for understanding adaptive system complexity.

As expressed earlier, we applied an MBE approach to a sophisticated agent-based collaborative agent architecture that is known to be powerful, but difficult to program [8]. The objective was to investigate model-driven architecture [6, 10] as a means of raising the level of abstraction for development teams and improving productivity in the generation of these systems. One important observation from this empirical exercise was that most of the reusable components were discovered opportunistically and the team needed to be mindful to identify elements of the system that would have high utility and be tolerant of changes that would be imposed on the system over the system's lifetime. This led us to explore the concept of capabilities engineering for change tolerant systems and using it as a means for managing complexity.

Through a series of elaborations and refinements, model-based approaches systematically move from abstract computationally independent models, to platform independent models, to concrete platform specific models—organizing knowledge and leveraging reuse at appropriate levels. The complexities are interactions, mappings, and transforms in the populated models repositories that evolve over time.

Armed with an approach for identifying those capabilities that bound relevant architectural components, we investigated the application of MBE to the Reconfigurable Computing (RC) development environment problem. As with the development of agent-based systems, the RC development environments are geared for the RC specialist working on FPGAs and other Programmable Logic Devices (PLD). The demand for RC applications is growing at a much faster rate than the RC specialists entering the field and productivity improvement is needed to meet the demand. In some sense, the RC development community is in a very similar position to software engineering in the mid-1980s. The hardware technologies are progressing at a faster rate than the RC developers can take advantage of them and one way that this gap can be reduced is to explore ways to move the level of programming up using model abstractions and reuse.

Building upon the previous work, we took the concepts to the classroom. Social networks are popular among people of many ages and provide an interesting platform for examining MBE for product-lines. While capabilities of today's Social Networking Applications (SNA) are not sophisticated or complex at a detailed level, they are evolving and growing at an unprecedented rate. So, to examine this complex property of SNAs, we investigated what how the MBE approach would serve in a project that involved a team of students who were given about six weeks to build a simple SNA. Complexities of the added scaffolding coupled with the additional tasking were considered, then an additional version of the application development environment was developed using a DSL oriented environment, showing considerable simplification in the development and change tolerance for future changes.

6.2 Background

The nature of software systems and their concomitant complexity has turned a corner with the advent of agent-based systems, autonomic and self-healing systems, reconfigurable computing, web services, and the like. Software complexity has compounded volume (structure) and interaction (social) properties as modern applications increasingly use agents to carry out collaborative tasking and the use of the Internet has enabled software functionality to be delivered as services. Unlike our engineering ancestors, we have a number of technologies that can bring insight into decisions we make in developing and evolving systems to respond to a changing environment. We have various adaptive technologies such as software agents that can sense their situations and alter the behaviors accordingly. We have modeling technologies that help us understand the structural information about the functional abstractions for determining the most effective composition of capabilities and decomposition of components to support them.

To better understand the elements that went into this work, we present a perspective on complex engineering, some background on model-based engineering via MDA, key concepts of Capabilities Engineering, and introduce the challenges with reconfigurable computing development environments.

6.2.1 Model-Driven Architecture

The projects discussed later in this chapter involved the use of MDA, a software-oriented variant of MBE. Models are not merely aids for understanding; they are intermediate forms to implement applications. Using models in the development of systems has been practiced for decades, and even for centuries in other engineering disciplines (e.g., mechanical engineering, building architecture). MDA provides a way to create models, systematically refine and elaborate them, and provide automatic (or semi-automatic) translation to one or more execution platforms. Perhaps the most telling transition in mindset is how modeling in MDA takes a model (typically an abstraction of a reality) and creates an executable form through a series of predictable transformations. Since the computer uses a conceptual medium developed by a software engineer (i.e., a model or series of models), transforms now make abstractions of the real world accessible and even executable on a computer.

In some respects, MDA is an advanced perspective on well-known essential systems development concepts practiced over the years (albeit frequently practiced poorly). The Object Management Group[1] (OMG) promotes MDA advocating Unified Modeling Language (UML) as the modeling technology at the various levels [23]. MDA endeavors to achieve high portability, interoperability, and reusability through architectural separation of concerns; hinging on the long-established concept of separating the operational system specification from the details of how that system implements those capabilities on its respective platform(s). That is, separate the logical operational models (external view) from the physical design for platform implementations.

Starting with an often-abstract Computation Independent Model (CIM) such as a process workflow or functional description, the Platform Independent Model (PIM) is derived through elaborations and mappings between the original concepts and the PIM renderings. Once the PIM is sufficiently refined and stable, the Platform Specific Models (PSM) are derived through further elaborations and refinements. The PSMs are transformed into operational systems.

The CIM layer is where vernacular specific to the problem domain is defined, constraints are placed on the solution, and specific requirements illumined. Artifacts in the CIM layer focus largely on the system requirements and their environment to provide appropriate vocabulary and context (e.g., domain models, use case models, conceptual classes). The CIM layer contains no processing or implementation details. Instead, it conveys non-functional requirements such as business constraints, deployment constraints, and performance constraints as well as functional constraints.

The PIM provides the architecture, the logical design plan, but not the execution of the plan in a tangible form. Beyond high-level services, the problem domain itself must be modeled from a processing perspective. The PIM is where the logical components of the system, their behaviors, and interactions are modeled. PIM artifacts focus on modeling what the system should do from an external or logical perspective. Structural and semantic information on the types of components and their interactions (e.g., design classes, interaction and state diagrams) are rendered in UML, the de facto modeling language for MDA.

Mapping from the PIM to the PSM, is a critical element of MDA's approach. Mappings from PIM representations to those that implement the features or functions directly in the platform specific technologies are the delineation point where there is considerable leverage in MDA. This mapping allows an orderly transition from one platform to another. But the utility does not stop there. Like the PIM,

---

[1]The OMG's MDA website is here: www.omg.org/mda.

there are opportunities to have layers within the PSM to produce intermediate-transformations on the way to the executable system. These models range from detailed behavior models to source code used in constructing the system. Each of these layers offer opportunities to employ change tolerance as a guide for controlling complexity.

6.2.2 Capabilities Engineering

In MBE, productivity gains are a direct result of forming models that will be reused in subsequent development activities and efforts. It has been shown that higher-level reuse (i.e., analysis and design models) is more likely to result in productivity increases than lower-level code reuse [18]. Domain analysis has been effectively applied over the years to ensure that the developed system maps well to the application domain, reusable concepts are captured, and software change is accommodated [18]. Similarly, Capabilities Engineering (CE) starts at the problem domain engineering level and using structure and semantics applies rules to determine capabilities in the needed system that will be change tolerant. For this reason, we explored how CE can be used to formulate the requisite elements of the system early in the effort so that change tolerant components will be modeled and used to expresses the architecture.

Lehman's first law of software evolution [30] asserts that if a system is to function satisfactorily then it must constantly adapt to change. To key approaches to reconcile the dynamics of change are to adopt a strategy to minimize it or attempt to incorporate the change with minimum impact. Traditional requirements engineering attempts to minimize change by baselining requirements prior to design and implementation. However, empirical research evidence indicates the failure of this approach to cope with the attendant requirements evolution when building complex emergent software-based systems [2, 32]. Consequently, in the case of many systems today such failures are extremely expensive in terms of cost, time, and human life [12].

At the other end of the spectrum on this issue, many of today's software processes now accommodate requirements change in one way or another. The Unified Process uses an iterative strategy to accommodate emerging requirements in various releases of the software. Agile methods accommodate changing requirements by keeping the iterations small and refactoring the product as incongruences arise. Both of these have challenges trying to establish a good starting point for composing the component architectures of systems. We believe that the CE approach offers a substantial solution that can readily be applied in most any process. Further, for MBEs such as model-driven architecture, this is particularly helpful as canonical capabilities for a domain can help establish the basis for the architecture.

As expressed earlier, the CE process strives to accommodate change (as opposed to minimizing it). We deduce that changes can be accommodated with minimum impact if systems are architected using aggregates that are embedded with change-tolerant characteristics—we call such aggregates as "capabilities." Specifically, capabilities are functional abstractions that exhibit high cohesion, low coupling, and balanced abstraction levels. The property of high cohesion helps localize the impact of change to within a capability. Also, the ripple effect of change is less likely to propagate beyond the affected capability because of its reduced coupling with neighboring capabilities. The ripple effect is the phenomenon of propagation of change from the affected source to its dependent constituents [27]. An optimum level of abstraction assists in the understanding of the functionality in terms of its most relevant details.

Capabilities are determined mathematically from a Function Decomposition (FD) graph. This is an acyclic directed graph that represents system functionality that has been implicitly derived from user needs. Thus, capabilities originate after the elicitation of needs, but prior to the formalization of technical system requirements. This unique spatial positioning permits the definition of capabilities to be independent of any particular development paradigm. More specifically, although capabilities are derived from user needs, they are imbued with design characteristics of cohesion and coupling. This introduces aspects of a solution formulation. On the other hand, capabilities are less detailed than entities that belong to the solution space. Consequently, capabilities fit more naturally in the space in-between—the transition space. Furthermore, their formulation from the user needs and mapping to requirements implies that they have the potential to bridge the complexity gap; thus assisting the traceability between needs and requirements. Moreover, the inherent ability of capabilities-based systems to accommodate change with minimum impact enhances the efficacy of traceability; random, unstructured ripple-effects impair the strength of regular traceability techniques.

Capabilities are generated in a two-phased process. The first phase determines the change-tolerant capability set that exhibits high cohesion, low coupling, and balanced abstraction levels. The second phase optimizes these capabilities to accommodate the constraints of technology feasibility and implementation schedule. Figure 6.1 illustrates the two major phases of the CE process. Phase I implicitly derives expected system functionality from needs and decomposes them to directives; directives are similar to requirements but have domain information associated with them. The decomposition activity results in the construction of the FD graph. Then, the algorithm for identifying capabilities—based on the criteria of cohesion, coupling, and abstraction level—is executed on this graph, as a part of the formulation activity. The resulting set of capabilities are the required change-tolerant entities. Phase II employs a multi-disciplinary optimization approach on the capabilities obtained from Phase I to accommodate the constraints of technology and schedule. The resulting set of capabilities is then transformed into requirements as dictated by an incremental development process. The final set of capabilities and their associated requirements constitute the output of the CE process.

While the first phase of capabilities engineering is detailed later in the chapter, it is important to note at this point that much of this is algorithmic and repeatable. Hence, when establishing the computationally independent models that will help form the architecture of the system, a predictable approach can be employed to establish the base set of model boundaries that will drive the components generated via the model-based approach. Phase II involves metrics for assessing the sched-

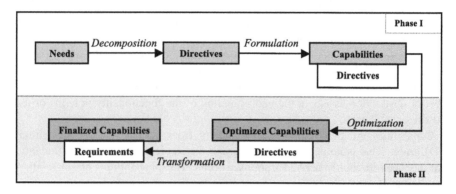

Fig. 6.1 Capabilities engineering phased process

ule/technology trade-offs to arrive at finalized capabilities. These are beyond the scope of this treatment but can be found in [37, 38].

6.3 Change Tolerance Starts with Capabilities

As expressed earlier, change tolerance can be reasoned about through coupling, cohesion, and balance of the abstraction. Traceability models tell us this is true at most levels of abstraction—needs, capabilities, requirements, architecture, logical design, physical design, and various levels of implements. Each of these levels of abstraction represents models when considered from a software engineering perspective. Even the source code is a model! This is useful as we consider how to conquer complexity. In analysis, we tend to capture information about the problem domain and organize it in domain models and accompanying textual specifications. We move from the abstract, ambiguous, inconsistent, and incomplete to the more defined, clarified, consistent, and complete, as we elaborate and refine our understanding. Formal methods certainly bring the computer to bear on this problem with formal specifications and provers [29]. The more dependence and structure information that we have, the more we can predict the complexity and potentially control it.

MBE approaches express the computation independent models early in the development as it provides the relevant problem domain structure for the logical models. This is where we needed a mechanism to define model constructs that would reflect long-lived elements of the system and begin the characterization of change tolerance. We exploit the semantics of the functional decomposition (FD) graph to compute the change-tolerant characteristics of a capability.

Decomposition is the process of recursively partitioning a problem until an atomic level is reached. We begin with user needs because they help determine what problem is to be solved; in the context of software engineering this means what functionality is expected of the system to be developed. Different techniques such as interviews, questionnaires, focus groups, introspection, and others [22] are employed to gather information from users. Often, because of the informality of the problem domain language, needs are expressed at varying levels of abstraction.

A function derived from a need at the highest level of abstraction is the mission or overarching goal of the system. An abstraction presents information essential to a particular purpose, ignoring irrelevant details. In particular, a functional abstraction indicates the functionality expected of the system from a high-level perspective while ignoring minute details. We use the vertices (or nodes) of an FD graph to represent functional abstractions of the system, and its edges to depict the relationship between the various functionalities. The construction of this graph is a core component of the decomposition activity.

High cohesion, low coupling, and balanced abstraction levels are basic characteristics that define change-tolerant capabilities. Recall that change tolerance connotes the ability of software to evolve within the bounds that it was designed—that software change is intentional. Cohesion, coupling, and balanced abstraction offer reasonable measures to identify change tolerant capabilities. Much in the same way these concepts have been successfully used in design, the same principles work at the more abstract levels between the problems space (bounding the needs) and the solution space (composing the solution). In this subsection, we examine the rationale underlying this definition of a capability, and subsequently, present measures that are specifically constructed to compute each criterion. Figure 6.2 depicts an example of an FD graph of a Course Evaluation System that we use to make more concrete these concepts.

6.3.1 Cohesion

Cohesion characterizes a stable structure and depicts the "togetherness" of elements within a unit. Every element of a highly cohesive unit is directed toward achieving a single objective. For MBE this is important to identify the domain level elements of the system that can form capabilities. We focus on maximizing functional cohesion, the strongest level of cohesion [3] among all the other types (coincidental, logical, temporal, procedural, communicational, and sequential) [45] and therefore, is most desirable. In particular, a capability has high functional cohesion if all its constituent elements, viz. directives (later transformed to requirements), are devoted to realizing the principle function represented by the capability.

By virtue of construction, in the FD graph the function of each child node is essential to achieving the function of its immediate parent node. Note that, neither the root nor the leaves of an FD graph can be considered as a capability. This is because the root indicates the mission or main goal of the system, which is too holistic, and the leaves symbolize directives, which are too reductionistic in nature. Both of these entities lie on either extreme of the abstraction scale, and thereby, conflict with the objective of avoiding such polarity when developing complex emergent systems [28]. Hence, only the internal nodes of an FD graph are considered as potential capabilities. In addition, these internal nodes depict functionalities at different

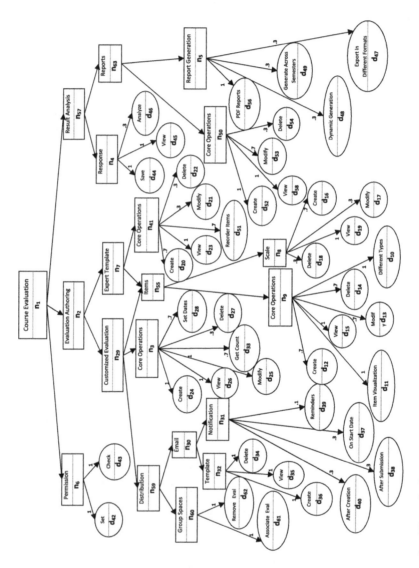

Fig. 6.2 Example of an FD graph of a course evaluation system

levels of abstraction, and thereby, provide a representative sample for formulating capabilities.

We develop the cohesion measure for internal nodes by first considering nodes whose children are only leaves. We then generalize this measure for any internal node in the graph.

(a) Measure for Internal Nodes with Only Leaves as Children

Internal nodes with only leaves as children represent potential capabilities that are linked directly to a set of directives. In Fig. 6.2 example of such nodes are n_{60}, n_5, n_3, n_{41}, and n_9. Directives are necessary to convey and develop an in-depth understanding of the system functionality and yet, by themselves, lack sufficient detail to dictate system development. Failure to implement a directive can affect the functionality of the associated capability with varying degrees of impact. We reason that the degree of impact is directly proportional to the relevance of the directive to the functionality. Consequently, the greater the impact, the more crucial the directive. This signifies the strength of relevance of a directive and is symptomatic of the associated capability's cohesion. Hence, the relevance of a directive to the functionality of a unit is an indicator of the unit's cohesion.

The failure to implement a directive can be interpreted as a risk. Therefore, we use existing risk impact categories: Catastrophic, Critical, Marginal, and Negligible [4] to guide the assignment of relevance values. Each impact category is well defined and has an associated description. This is used to estimate the relevance of a directive on the basis of its potential impact. For example, negligible impact is described to be an inconvenience, whereas a catastrophic impact implies complete failure. This signifies that the relevance of a directive with negligible impact is much lower when compared to a directive with catastrophic impact. Intuitively, the impact categories are ordinal in nature. However, we conjecture that the associated relevance values are more than merely ordinal. The issue of determining the natural measurement scales [42] of cohesion and other software metrics is an open problem [9]. Therefore, we refrain from subscribing both the attribute in question (i.e. cohesion) and its metric (i.e. function of relevance values), to a particular measurement scale. Rather than limiting ourselves to permitted analysis methods as defined by Stevens [42], we let the objective of our measurement—computing the cohesion of a node to reflect the relevance of its directives—determine the appropriate statistic to be used [44]. We assign values to indicate the relevance of a directive based on the perceived significance of each impact category; these values are normalized to the [0, 1] scale (e.g., Marginal is a reduction in performance at a relevance of 0.30, while Negligible is a non-operational impact at a relevance of 0.10). We estimate the cohesion of an internal node as the average of the relevance values of all its directives. The arithmetic mean is used to compute this average as it can be influenced by extreme values. This thereby captures the importance of directives with catastrophic impact or the triviality of directives with negligible impact, and affects the resulting average appropriately, to reflect the same.

Every parent-leaf edge is associated with a relevance value $Rel(v, n)$ indicating the contribution of directive v to the cohesion of parent node n. For an FD graph

$G = (V, E)$ we denote relevance of a directive d to its parent node n as $Rel(d, n)$ where $d, v \in V$, $(n, d) \in E$, $outdegree(d) = 0$ and $outdegree(n) > 0$. Formally, the cohesion measure of a potential capability that is directly associated with a set of directives (i.e. the cohesion measure of an internal node $n \in V$ with t leaves as its children $[t > 0]$) is given by computing the arithmetic mean of relevance values:

$$Ch(n) = \frac{\sum_{i=1}^{t} Rel(d_i, n)}{t}$$

The cohesion value ranges between 0 and 1. A capability with a maximum cohesion of 1 indicates that every constituent directive is of the highest relevance.

(b) Measure for Internal Nodes with only Non-leaf Children

The cohesion measure for internal nodes with only non-leaf children is computed differently. This is because the relevance value of a directive is valid only for its immediate parent and not for its ancestors. For example, the functionality of node n_{30} in Fig. 6.2 is decomposed into nodes n_{31} and n_{32}. This implies that the functionality of n_{30} is directly dependent on the attainment of the functionality of both n_{31} and n_{32}. Note that n_{30} has only an indirect relationship to the directives of the system. In addition, the degree of influence that n_{31} and n_{32} each have on parent n_{30} is influenced by their size (number of constituent directives). Therefore, the cohesion of nodes that are parents with non-leaf children is a weighted average of the cohesion of their children. Here, the weight is the size of a child node in terms of its constituent directives. This indicates the child's contribution towards the parent's overall cohesion. The rationale behind this is explained by the definition of cohesion, which states that a node is highly cohesive if every constituent element is focused on the same objective, i.e. the node's functionality.

Formally, the cohesion measure of an internal node n with $t > 1$ non-leaf children is:

$$Ch(n) = \frac{\sum_{i=1}^{t} (size(v_i) . Ch(v_i))}{\sum_{i=1}^{t} size(v_i)}$$

such that $(n, v_i) \in E$ and,

$$size(n) = \begin{cases} \sum_{i=1}^{t} size(v_i) & (n, v_i) \in E, outdegree(v_i) > 0 \\ 1 & outdegree(n) = 0 \end{cases}$$

6.3.2 Coupling

Why should capabilities exhibit low coupling? We restate the reasons advanced by Page-Jones [34] for minimizing coupling, in the context of capabilities. Fewer interconnections between capabilities reduces:

- the chance that changes in one capability affects other capabilities, thus promoting reusability,
- the chance that a fault in one capability will cause a failure in other capabilities, and
- the labor of understanding the details of other capabilities

Thus, coupling is a measure of interdependence between units [43] and thereby, is the other indicator of stability of a capability. We desire that units accommodate change with minimum ripple effect. Ripple effect is the phenomenon of propagation of change from the affected source to its dependent constituents [27]. Specifically, the dependency links between units behave as change propagation paths. The higher the number of links, the greater is the likelihood of ripple effect. Therefore, we strive to design minimally coupled capabilities.

Capability p is coupled with capability q if a change in q affects p. Note that $Cp(p,q)$ is the measure that p is coupled with q and so, $Cp(p,q) \neq Cp(q,p)$. In particular, a change in q implies a change in one or more of its constituent directives. Therefore, the coupling measure for capabilities is determined by the coupling between their respective directives.

We assume that the coupling between directives is a function of two components: distance and probability of change.

1. Distance: Directives are associated with their parent capabilities through decomposition edges; recall, a decomposition edge signifies that the functionality of the parent is a union of its children. Thus, the directives of a capability are highly functionally related; this is represented by leaves that share the same parent node. However, relatedness between directives decreases as the distance between them increases. We define the distance between directives $u, v \in V$ as the number of edges in the shortest undirected path between them and denote it as $dist(u, v)$. By choosing the shortest path we account for the worst-case scenario of change propagation. Specifically, the shorter the distance, the greater the likelihood of impact due to change propagation.

2. Probability of Change: The other factor that influences the coupling measure is the probability that a directive will change and thereby, cause a ripple effect. Minimal interconnections reduce the likelihood of a ripple effect phenomenon. We know that coupling between capabilities is a function of coupling between their respective directives. As mentioned earlier, if u and v are directives then $Cp(u, v)$ can be quantified by measuring the effect on u when v changes. However, we still need to compute the probability that such a ripple effect will occur. This requires us to compute the likelihood that a directive might change. Therefore, $Cp(u, v)$ also needs to factor in the probability of directive v changing: $P(v)$. We use a simplistic model to determine the probability that a directive will change. Specifically, we consider the likelihood that exactly one directive changes among all other directives in a given capability.

Formally, coupling between two directives u and $v \in V$ is computed as:

$$CP(u, v) = \frac{P(v)}{dist(u, v)}$$

This metric computes the coupling between directives u and v as the probability that a change in v propagates through the shortest path and affects u. We denote the set of leaves (directives) associated with an internal node $n \in V$ as:

$$D_n = \{x \mid \exists path(n, x); outdegree(x) = 0; n, x \in V\}$$

where $path(n, x)$ is a set of directed edges connecting n and x.

Generalizing, the coupling measure between any two internal nodes $p, q \in V$, where $outdegree(p) > 1$, $outdegree(q) > 1$ and $D_p \cap D_q = \varphi$ is:

$$Cp(p, q) = \frac{\sum_{d_i \in D_p} \sum_{d_j \in D_q} Cp(d_i, d_j)}{|D_p||D_q|}$$

where

$$Cp(d_i, d_j) = \frac{P(d_j)}{dist(d_i, d_j)}$$

and

$$P(d_j) = \frac{1}{|D_q|}$$

6.3.3 Abstraction Level

The third criterion requires that capabilities be defined at balanced abstraction levels. Given that holism and reductionism lie on the extremes of the abstraction scale, we seek a balance that is most desirable from a software engineering perspective. Specifically, we identify a balanced abstraction level as that point where the node is of an optimum size (size is the number of associated directives), and at the same time, whose implementation as an independent entity does not result in increased dependencies. For example, in Fig. 6.2, n_2 representing the functionality Evaluation Authoring is of size 30 (number of associated directives); its children, Customized Evaluation (n_{29}) and Expert Template (n_7), are smaller-sized nodes. Based on size, let us say we consider the children instead of the parent as capabilities. This implies that nodes n_{29} and n_7 are independent entities. However, we see from Fig. 6.2, that the functionality Items (n_{55}) is common to both these capabilities. This, in some sense, is a manifestation of content coupling, the least desirable among all types of coupling. Consequently, the dependency between n_{29} and n_7 is increased by deploying them as separate capabilities, because they share a common functionality in n_{55}. This trade off between the convenience of developing smaller sized units and the long-term advantages of reduced dependencies, characterizes a balanced abstraction level. Thus, based on certain heuristics we use the level of abstraction to determine which nodes in an FD graph are capabilities.

We are interested in measuring the cohesion, coupling, and abstraction level of various functional abstractions of a system to identify capabilities. It is generally observed that as the cohesion of a unit increases the coupling between the units decreases. However, this correlation is not exact. Therefore, we develop specific metrics to measure the coupling and cohesion values of the internal nodes in an FD graph. Most existing coupling and cohesion measures focus on evaluating the quality of design or code. These measures have access to information regarding function calls, data parameters and other design or implementation details, which are abundantly available to construct their metric computations. In contrast, measures for capabilities are based on the fundamental definitions of cohesion and coupling, and rely on the limited information provided by the FD graph. To determine balanced abstraction levels, we compute the sizes of nodes and examine the levels in terms of their distances from the root. In addition, the FD graph helps us visually understand the commonalities between potential capabilities. We use this information to construct heuristics to evaluate the abstraction levels.

Abstraction is instrumental in successful architecture, design patterns, object-oriented frameworks, and the like. High abstraction level is key in the development and evolution of complex emergent systems [6, 36, 39]. As we apply CE in the CIM, we strive to identify nodes at balanced levels of abstraction as capabilities. According to the FD graph in Fig. 6.2, the node at the highest level is the overall mission. If we implement this as a capability, then the entire system is composed of exactly one large-sized capability—a retrograde to the original requirements engineering approach. Instead, we need to identify capabilities of a size such that its functionality is comprehensible by the human mind. For this we consider nodes at lower levels of abstraction, that depict more specifically, what functionality is expected of the system.

From the FD graph in Fig. 6.2 we observe that as the abstraction level becomes lower, the node sizes decrease but the coupling values increase. We estimate the size of a capability as the number of its associated directives, for example, $size(n_1) = 43$, and $size(n_9) = 6$. In fact, size estimates determined from non-code entities such as requirements are known to be fairly representative of the actual functional size.

Given a choice between two nodes of different sizes, we choose to implement the smaller-sized node as a capability. This is in agreement with Miller's observation about the limited processing capacity of the human mind [33] (cf. [35]). A large-sized capability may encompass too much functionality for a developer to process. Intuitively, the implementation of a smaller sized Capability is less complex. Like components, for capabilities the relation between the size and number of defects or defect density could also be an issue. However, with capabilities that exist in a realm even prior to requirements specification, the assumption of small-sized capabilities being less complex and more easily maintainable than their large-sized counterparts may not be invalid. With insufficient information, it is premature to question fundamental principles of modularization.

Two possible scenarios may arise when lowering the abstraction level of a node in order to decrease its size:

- **Common Functionality**: In the former case, lowering the abstraction level of the large capability results in nodes that share a common functionality. For example, in Fig. 6.2, the FD graph of the Course Evaluation System, this is illustrated by decreasing the level of Evaluation Authoring (n_2) to Expert Template (n_7) and Customized Evaluation (n_{29}); both share the common node Items (n_{55}).
- **No Common Functionality**: This case involves the reduction of a single aggregate to smaller nodes that have no commonalities.

Thus for each scenario, balanced abstraction levels are determined by examining the trade-space of two aspects: node size and coupling values. While this treatise defines the concepts for purposes of this research, the details of the slices and algorithms for analyzing these are detailed in [36]. As indicated earlier, the details of the phase two can also be found there. However, in the next section we provide a short overview.

6.3.4 Optimization

Phase II of the CE process (shown in Fig. 6.1) further optimizes change-tolerant capabilities to accommodate the constraints of schedule and technology. In fact, aspects of schedule and technology are closely intertwined, and thus, need to be considered as different dimensions of a single problem, rather than separate individual concerns. We discuss our interpretation of schedule and technology constraints.

We examine two possible scenarios when incorporating technology in a system—obsolescence and infusion. The former involves replacing obsolete technology with new technology and the latter introduces new technology in the system, as a result of building new capabilities. The set of capabilities can be optimized to accommodate different scenarios of technology advancement. For example, if a particular technology needed to develop a capability requires additional time to mature then one may examine alternate configurations where the development of the concerned capability can be postponed with minimal impact on related entities. In the case of technology obsolescence, the change-tolerant characteristics of a capability mitigate the effects of replacing the underlying technology. Specifically, high cohesion implies that the constituent elements of a capability are strongly tied to the underlying technology. In addition, the minimal coupling between capabilities reduces the impact relative to technology replacement.

Scheduling has been empirically identified as a key risk component in software development [12]. It is often discussed with respect to global project management aspects such as the distribution of personnel effort, allocation of time, determination of milestones, and others. However, in the context of the CE process we view schedule as a function of implementation order and time. Order is the sequence in which capabilities are to be developed. Time is the period within which a capability of the system is to be delivered. This definition of scheduling capabilities is reflective of the principle of incremental development, a risk mitigation strategy for large-scale system development. The permutations of a set of capabilities generate different sequences in which capabilities can be developed. Thus, as discussed earlier, in the case of a necessary delay in implementing a particular capability, one may examine other potential ordering of nodes.

6.3.5 Transition Space for Change-Tolerant Capabilities

A concept of CE that is key to the MBE approaches is the idea of "transition space"—the space between user needs in the problem space and system requirements in the solution space. Capabilities occupy a position that is neither in the problem space nor in the solution space. More specifically, although Capabilities are derived from user needs, they share design characteristics of cohesion and coupling. This introduces aspects of a solution formulation, and thus, discourages the membership of a Capability in the problem space. On the other hand, Capabilities are less detailed than entities that belong to the solution space. Consequently, Capabilities fit more naturally in the transition space. Furthermore, their formulation from the user needs and mapping to requirements imply that they have the potential to bridge the complexity gap; thus assisting the traceability between needs and requirements [39]. Moreover, the inherent ability of Capabilities-based systems to accommodate change with minimum impact enhances the efficacy of traceability; random, unstructured ripple-effect impairs the strength of many traceability techniques.

The use of the transition space facilitates the capture of domain information, and preserves relationships among needs and their associated functionalities during the progression between spaces. On the other hand, the characteristics of high cohesion and low coupling of Capabilities, support traceability in evolving systems by localizing and minimizing the impact of change. The ability to trace is unhindered by the system magnitude when utilizing a capabilities-based development approach because traceability techniques are embedded into the process.

From an MBE perspective, this early start to establishing boundaries for subsystems and components is very important. Recognizing the structure of the application domain often dominates the system architecture. Take for example the application domain for business systems—Enterprise Resource Planning (ERP) systems reflect the canonical business processes they support. While ERP systems changed the way that companies worked by reducing the administrative tasks of manually conveying information for business decisions, it retained the key structures of the domain that it supports (e.g., financial, human resource, and asset management). Similarly, most applications domains when modeled will have these canonical functional abstractions. While we model them in the CIM, up to this point, we did not have a mechanism for identifying these aspects that CE terms capabilities. Now, capabilities give way to modeling the logical architecture design in the PIM.

In the transition space, with capabilities defined, we can reason about the major subsystems and components that will be comprised in the architecture and ultimately in the design. We can do this while it is still relatively inexpensive to make

Table 6.1 Four layer metamodel architecture

Layer	Description	Examples
M3: Metametamodel	Foundation for a metamodeling architecture. Defining the language to describe metamodels	MetaClass, MetaAttribute, MetaOperation
M2: Metamodel	An instance of a metametamodel. Defining the language to describe models	Class, Attribute, Operation, Component
M1: Model	An instance of metamodel. Defining a language to describe the information object domain	Product, Unit Price, Customer, Sale, Detail
M0: User objects	An instance of a model. Defines specific information domain	\<Chair>, \<Desk>, $100, $200

changes. And we can have a reasonable justification for the capabilities that are defined both from structural and semantic perspectives.

6.3.6 Coupling and Cohesion in Solution Space Models and MBE

Most treatments of software architecture and design describe and use coupling, cohesion, and balanced abstraction as key measures for effective software design [11, 15]. Hence, we will defer to them for detailed discussions. However, here we want to indicate the importance of these three measures as they pertain to change tolerance as one moves through the process of elaboration and refinement of the software system into more detailed representations, ultimately to be generated into source code. In MBE, this process is described in the Metamodel. For many MDA projects, this uses a four layer Metamodel Architecture like that shown in Table 6.1 and the Meta Object Facility (MOF) [40] to describe the transition between representation forms. Note that a higher-level meta-layer defines the structure of the lower layer, but is not the abstraction of that layer. Rather, meta-layer relationships are more like grammar-layer relationships found in transformation systems. This helps govern the complexity from a transformation standpoint and aids in moving from manual to automated generation of software.

Software knowledge often starts out as abstract and informal, but the more we know about the system, the more canonical and formal we can become in our representation forms. The more formal the representations, the more likely that transformations from abstract levels to concrete levels can be reliably conveyed through automation. This is key to conquering complexity. Once the canonical design elements associated with the capabilities can be captured in a form that is accessible through a specification and reliably transformable to more concrete form(s), the computer is then handling the complexity. In a large part, this is what happens with a compiler and a programming language—complexities of control and data flow are accommodated in the language and transformed to forms that can be executed by the computer. Ideally, we would like to have model compilers where the models map reliably to the application domain and systems would be generated from specifications that the domain experts would produce.

At this point, it is important to recognize that computing languages are like models. Arguably, general-purpose languages like Java and C++ provide an abstraction for software engineers to reason through implementing a solution using a computer. This relatively low-level abstraction was not always considered low. Early on, micro-coding was the dominant programming approach. As more convenient machine (processor) structures emerged, assembly languages provided machine abstraction that substantially improved productivity by abstracting away the complex details. Then, as programming domains such as business and scientific applications were established, third generation languages (3GL) like Cobol and Fortran with control and data flow abstractions gave way to significant productivity progress.

Moving from assembly to 3GLs is an example of increasing abstraction. More recently, MBE approaches aim to increase the level of abstraction to manage complexity and improve productivity [13, 41]. For example, in developing Reconfigurable Systems with FPGAs, traditional systems required knowledge of low-level languages like Verilog or VHDL. More recently, we have seen the rise of block intellectual property (IP) and model based environments like National Instrument's LabVIEW FPGA where we see increases in productivity in producing these RC systems. Moving some of the programming tasks to end-users through key abstractions reduced the programming load, freeing staff for engineering tasks relevant to their skills.

A technology that bridges the language oriented programming and model-based software engineering communities are DSLs. DSLs have been around for a long time and most practitioners do not realize it! A DSL is a language targeted at an application domain and expressive in domain terms. Examples of DSLs include SQL, LaTeX, Pic, HTML, VHDL, Lexx/Yacc, Diesel, and Groovy. Note that the languages are often small and tailored to the domains.

According to Martin Fowler [17], there are three primary types of DSLs: (1) External, (2) Internal, and (3) Language Workbenches for building DSLs. External DSLs use a different syntax than the main language that uses them (e.g., make, flex, bison, SQL, sed, and awk). These may or may not be embedded in the code and often can be used separately for their specific domain purpose. Internal DSLs share the same syntax as the main language that uses them—a subset of the host language that is congruent with the development environment, but may have some expressivity limitations due to constraints of host language. From a complexity tradeoff perspective, the internal DSLs do not require a new language to be learned, but they will not have the expressivity gains of external DSLs.

Language workbenches such as JetBrains Meta Programming System (MPS) and openArchitectureWare offer yet another perspective much like the use of Software Refinery in the 1990s. That is, having an environment that provides the framework and tools to generate a system from components and a specification language can be very effective and productive since much of the complexity of scaffolding around building a repository of software artifacts, developing a language to express the system, and ultimately generating software for a range of applications are all accommodated with a predictable framework. Later in this chapter, we will examine projects that each developed a small social networking development environment using a DSL workbench (JetBrains MPS), an existing MBE framework (Eclipse Modeling Framework), and a team that rolled their own (using Microsoft Visual Studio without the DSL support). The upshot of using these types of technologies is that abstraction is used to simplify the reasoning about the system, enable effective decomposition (divide and conquer—a well-known means of reducing complexity), and provide cues on how to organize the solution space for making changes in the future.

6.4 Model-Based Engineering Experience Dealing with Complexity

Capabilities and change tolerance are effective ways of starting out on the right path to deal with complexity, and complementary to these are the use of models in the production of software. In this section, we examine two MBE projects: one sophisticated agent-based system and one with an abundance of detail—a reconfigurable system. Then we examine three strategies for developing an MBE for a social networking system to understand some implications of the approaches discussed in the previous section. Note that the Capabilities Engineering work was performed separately from this, but theoretically, the principles of coupling, cohesion, and balanced abstraction hold with MBE. The objective in this section is to examine how MBE could be used to reduce complexity over time for some classes of systems development.

6.4.1 Cougaar Model-Driven Architecture (CMDA)

Certain classes of problems lend themselves to the use of collaborative agents. While DARPA explored them in large-scale logistics programs [1], others have looked at them in intelligent swarms for BioTracking, unmanned underwater vehicles, and autonomous nanotechnology swarms (ANTS) [29]. Agent-based systems provide a means to embed complex behaviors in applications where tasking or decisions are vital. Yet, they are notoriously difficult to program and produce reliable implementations [20]. Cognitive Agent Architecture (COUGAAR) is an open-source, agent architecture framework resulting from almost a decade of research by DARPA.

What makes Cougaar complex for development is largely the range of capabilities provided and the types of situations that Cougaar is designed to support.

Cougaar systems are usually deployed as agent "societies" where agents collaborate to solve a common class of problems. If a problem can be partitioned, then subsets of agents, called a "community," work on partitions of the problem (often autonomously and opportunistically). The society can directly contain both agents and communities. While these Cougaar capabilities are designed to aid engineers in thinking of the problem and solution space more along the lines of collaborative resources organized to support planning and tasking, the implementation of the systems using Cougaar agents is complex with an array of agent configurations and processing rules. The typical Cougaar developer takes months to become proficient with the facilities and development environment.

The concept of a Cougaar agent is relatively simple, but the details of the behaviors and how they are manifest in peer-to-peer interactions between agents through a blackboard are challenging. A Cougaar agent, a first-class member of a Cougaar Society, consists of a blackboard, a set of Plugins, and logic providers that are referentially uncoupled (i.e., they do not know about each other). The blackboard is a container of objects that adheres to publish/subscribe semantics. Plugins provide business logic and logic providers translate both incoming and outgoing messages. The Blackboard serves as the communications backbone connecting the plugins together. When an agent receives a message, it is published on the blackboard. The logic provider observes this addition and transforms the message into an object that plugins can work on. All instance-specific behavior of the agent is implemented within the plugin. Plugins create subscriptions to get notified when objects of its interest are added, removed or changed.

The CMDA approach simplifies the development of Cougaar-based applications by facilitating the generation of key software artifacts using models [7]. The CMDA partitions the modeling space into domain and applications. The domain level is referred to as the General Domain Application Model (GDAM), while the application level is named the General Cougaar Application Model (GCAM).

The domain layer, GDAM, encompasses the representations of domain specific components found in the domain workflow [24]. The application layer GCAM, encompasses the representations of Cougaar, its specifications, and environment [20]. Models are at the center of the approach, with even source code considered as a model.

Figure 6.3 illustrates the transformations and mappings in the CMDA [6] abstraction layers as they reflect the MDA approach. As with MDA, at CIM level, the user specifies the workflow of the intended Cougaar system. Then the user maps the workflow of the intended system into its PIM and PSM using GDAM and GCAM components respectively. An assembly approach is used, whereby the developer assembles the system and implementation models of the intended system by choosing, configuring, and connecting various predefined GDAM and GCAM components [25]. Once completed, the models are fed into a transformer, which then parses through this assembled set of models to produce the actual software artifacts such as requirements, design, code, and test cases. The generation of software artifacts is controlled by predefined mapping rules and template structures.

As the models mature, increasing use of transformations in the generation of software are employed. An application may not be completely generated from mod-

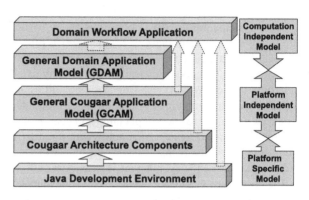

Fig. 6.3 CMDA abstraction layers

els and specifications. Earlier in the development, when the repository is not yet populated with models and components, and the detailed mappings have not been produced, there is a considerable human-in-the-loop (HITL) element. However, as development progresses, more of the models and components are reused and/or evolved systematically—reducing the cycle time and improving productivity. This was a fundamental finding in CMDA—early models needed to mature along with the representations that populate the repository of model components. Early models were often incomplete with only some components and transformation rules. As the understanding increased, both the fidelity of the models and the transformations/mappings grew until there was minimal HITL needed. This follows the iterative nature of development in software.

6.4.1.1 CMDA Environment

We explored relevant ways to automate Cougaar system development so that interdisciplinary team of domain experts and Cougaar developers could work effectively to produce sophisticated agent-based applications. Ideally, this would entail an exclusively transformational architecture as outlined by OMG. However, with healthy skepticism we embarked on a more pragmatic approach that started with assembly of mapped components and introduced transformations where there were opportunities to leverage configurations and optimizations. This architecture served us well as the domain and application models were derived and connected via a common meta-model.

Strongly leveraging the Eclipse[2] IDE, the CMDA framework allows domain experts to specify the intended Cougaar system using a combination of a custom UML profile, Object Constraint Language (OCL), and Java Emitter (JET) Templates. The UML profile is used to delineate the domain and application models of the intended system. The OCL is used to describe the domain and application specific constraints that the intended application must adhere. The JET templates form the base structure for the code and documentation artifacts. In essence, required software artifacts

---

[2]The Eclipse main website is here: http://www.eclipse.org/.

are generated by populating the templates with requisite parameters obtained from the domain and application models of the intended system. The key components in CMDA architecture are (details of which can be found in [8]):

- Graphical Editor: The Graphical Editing Framework (GEF) based Graphical Cougaar Model Editor (GCME) allows users to create and edit domain and application models of the intended system.
- Component Repository: Manages components with version control and storage support (SVN). Facilitates a collaborative development environment in which a user can publish components for use by other users.
- ModelManager: Provides a comprehensive view of all the components in a model.
- OCL Interpreter: Language interpreter for OCL built on top of ANTLR. The interpreter facilitates the validation of constraints specified in the component definitions and supports the evaluation of domain and application level constraints describing system behaviors.
- OCL Profile: Translator taking a configured component, producing OCL expressions for the OCL interpreter.
- OCL Java Generator: Generates Java source code equivalent of OCL constraints.
- Compiler: Translator that converts, with the help of the mapping and OCL profiles, the input high-level description language of the intended system into its equivalent software artifacts.
- Mapping Profile: Translator that takes descriptions of configured components and produces model artifacts.

6.4.1.2 CMDA Meta-model

As this was an early MDA project, we chose to design our own meta-model. Our meta-model facilitates easy translation between the GDAM and GCAM layers. Our meta-model shown in Fig. 6.4 illustrates conceptually how components are instantiated for use by specifying a set of parameters. In order to have smooth translation between GDAM and GCAM and to facilitate multiple sub-layers within the two models, the same meta-model was used to define both models. Hence the meta-model has recursive associations (depicted by the circular arrows in the figure) and allows the users to specify the intended application as a hierarchy of components. A component is said to be fully instantiated when it has roles (connections to other components) and has values defined for its parameters. The leaf components (the component at the lowest level) have additional mapping profiles that references templates used by transformer to generate code artifacts.

The meta-model allows smooth translation between the GDAM and GCAM layers and facilitates multiple sub-layers within them. The meta-model allows the developers to specify the intended model as a hierarchy of components. Each component references instances of other components either at the same or at a lower layer. The models are strictly hierarchical in nature and care is taken to avoid circular dependencies. The lowest layer of the application model consists of templates into

Fig. 6.4 The recursive
meta-model

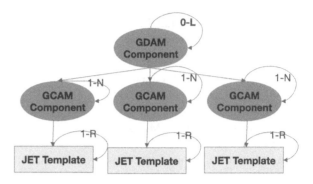

which the system fills in parameters (obtained from top-level components), resulting
in generation of code artifacts.

The CMDA components can range from abstract XPDL-based workflow diagrams, UML Domain model classes, and Sequence Diagrams, down to specific code
modules used to populate the JET Templates during final assembly. Everything is
treated as a model to be used in the generation of the application. In this way, we
hold true to the MDA approach. GDAM and GCAM components are developed systematically as gaps are found in the model transformations. When a subcomponent
does not exist for a higher-level abstraction, an attempt is first made to derive it from
existing models. If that is not possible, then a human in the loop must be employed
to derive the appropriate models.

A key design decision in CMDA was to provide the flexibility through the meta-
model for UML model components as well as code constructs directly. This way,
major portions of existing Cougaar source code could be accessed as relevant abstractions for use in the transformations to generate the Cougaar applications. This
was before MOF was mature and we erred on the side of flexibility. The downside
of this decision is that roundtrip engineering which requires the mappings and transformation for the ability to make changes in one model and it show up in another.
Today, the tools for MDA are far more capable.

We have been more elaborate in this first description of CMDA as it covers many
of the perspectives employed in the Model-Based Engineering Framework for High-
Performance Reconfigurable Computing (MBEF-HPRC) and the ManPages Generator applications covered in the next two sections. These following explorations
build off of the original project, but exploited newer technologies and leveraged
open-source software for MBE development.

6.4.2 Model-Based Engineering Framework for High-Performance Reconfigurable Computing

This second MBE effort built off of the CMDA project; however, the target environment objectives were quite different. Rather than addressing complexity in the application sophistication (complexity in the interactions), the MBEF-HPRC focused on

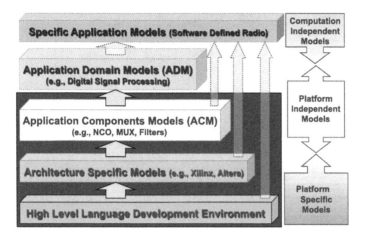

Fig. 6.5 MBE framework for HPRC

the specific implementation details of hardware description languages (complexity in the abundance of details). In some domains such as high-performance computing and embedded systems, the rendering of the system is in circuit designs on an FPGA or other reconfigurable hardware devices.

This project was conducted for the National Science Foundation's Center for High-performance Reconfigurable Computing. As FPGAs continue to increase in logic density (doubling every 18 months), their potential expands to more and more application domains. However, the ability to program FPGA to address the ever-increasing capacity in the logic is only growing at a fraction of the rate of logic density. In short, there is a "productivity gap" hindering the development of reconfigurable computing applications as the development productivity is not keeping pace with the growth in logic density. So, this project was to examine how we could move the abstraction level up for programming FPGAs from low-level circuits to design components and the eventual integration of capabilities.

There has been progress with C mappers (e.g., Handel-C, Mitrion-C, and Impulse-C), but these are not productive enough to keep up with the growth in logic density. The solution we embarked on was to prototype an IDE for reconfigurable computing that can address the productivity problem. Like software development, FPGAs and other reconfigurable technologies are programmable. Hence, they can benefit from software engineering lessons in MBE.

We exploit models that enable systematic elaboration and refinement of specifications into more and more concrete models that ultimately get converted into source for FPGAs and other reconfigurable devices. Figure 6.5 illustrates the basic concept of using models to compose HPRC systems.

While the basic MBE concepts hold for a reconfigurable computing IDE, the details are specific here to a hardware-design approach. Note that much of the emphasis is on the PSM (Application Components Models, Architecture Specific Models, and High Level Language framed at the bottom). At the top, the specific application models reflect the CIM for the Software-Defined Radio (SDR). The CIM

Fig. 6.6 MBE-HPRC
architecture

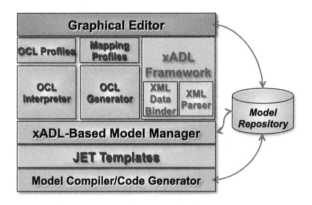

may have several layers of models but is typically specified in the language of the problem domain. Application domain models such as digital signal processing incorporate elements of computation and are typically specified in terms of platform independent models (PIM); these are agnostic towards the underlying technology. The application component model provides the building blocks from which the application domain model is constructed, such as digital filters, multiplexers, and the like. This is where the PIM transitions to the PSM. For this project, we concentrated on these transitions as they represent the most challenging aspect of deriving models for circuit design. The [hardware] architecture specific models specify board specific requirements for configuration such as ports and levels. These differ above the FPGA chip level and must often be accommodated in reconfigurable devices.

Ultimately, the component designs are specified in some implementation form (e.g., VHDL). Note that while the specification decomposes into increasingly detailed elaborations and refinements going from the domain application down to the implementation language(s), using the models, an application is produced/generated from the composite elements specified earlier. While difficult to achieve in the first round, as the CIM, PIM, and PSM are populated at the various levels with more canonical models, the generation of systems becomes increasingly rapid, improving design productivity for applications development. Similar to the CMDA, Fig. 6.6 illustrates the MBE-HPRC architecture elements used to specify and generate the software.

While xADL is still somewhat research oriented, it served our purpose well as did the open-source versions of OCL. The GEF-based graphical editor captured the details through a diagram. This included typical blocks like filters, NCO, and multiplexers. Each block has parameters that can be used to provide configuration detail, trigger component inclusion, transforms, and mappings.

For the resulting SDR designs, the parameters can also be used for including specifications such as Carrier frequency, channel bandwidth, modulation index, and audio response. Additionally, system design parameters for specific FPGA implementation boards can be specified such as system clock rate, sampling frequency, and bit precision. We used largely the same meta-model for the MBE-HPRC approach as we did for the CMDA. Each model consisted of one or more models until they got down to the template level where the JET templates rendered transforms or assemblies.

For example, in a radio a received signal must be filtered to separate out noise. For a hardware engineer, this is solved by a simple low pass filter. In a digital environment, the translation from the circuit to discrete time processing can be complex and forces the engineer to think procedurally. By abstracting out the actual code to create the filter on a RC system, the engineer is able to design the filter (and radio) around the common engineering models. Further, algorithms for identifying efficient placement and sizes for the filters in the signal processing stream can be simulated in models that ultimately produce the digital design through series of transformation rules. By simply focusing on the more abstract models, engineers are able to lower the coupling of the overall RC system applying MBE principals.

The project goals were largely accomplished. In a relatively short time, we were able to demonstrate that even lower-level representations like those in reconfigurable computing could be addressed with MBE and higher-level abstractions provided similar results in enabling non-FPGA professionals to contribute to developing SDR applications. Given that FPGA design environments are substantially below this abstraction level, even without timed comparisons, the evidence is clear that MBE could improve productivity in this domain. Further, it would enable FPGA professionals to incorporate technologies that software engineers currently take for granted. With the complexity in the large and complexity in the small explored in the CMDA and MBE-HPRC approaches respectively, we now turn to the emergent domain of social networking applications.

6.4.3 Model-Based Engineering for Social Network Applications

Recently, social networks have been popular among people of many ages. They offer a platform to stay connected with friends and family. While capabilities of today's social networking applications (SNA) are not sophisticated or complex at a detailed level, they are evolving and growing at an unprecedented rate. So, to experiment with this emergent property of SNAs, this project involved a team of students who were given about six weeks to build a simple SNA called ManPages (based on a FaceBook-like assignment that Mehran Sihami gave his students at Stanford University called "Face Pamphlet"), conduct a basic domain analysis to determine the emerging common capabilities and model them for generation. The application was first developed, exercised, and then analyzed to understand the extensibility and change parameters needed for a product-line system.

Rather than starting with the MBE-HPRC IDE, the team explored the available open-source projects and identified the Eclipse Modeling Project [26]. Figure 6.7 depicts the MBE framework for the ManPages MBE approach.

ManPages is a simple SNA that enables users to stay in touch with their friends. Users can add and remove friends from their profile, change their profile picture, update their status to allow their friends to see what they are doing, allow users

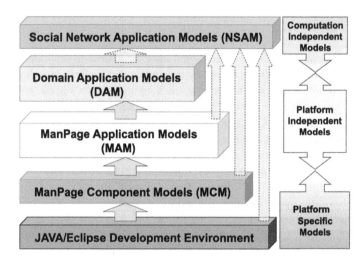

Fig. 6.7 MBE-HPRC architecture

to become members of their groups. Users list their friends that they have on the network.

From the domain perspective, a ManPages profile represents a network entity and can either be an existing ManPages profile or an empty profile. An existing profile will have a profile name, picture, status, and list of friends. If the profile is empty, not all of these components will be present.

Control of a profile is contained within the main display of the system. In Man-Pages there are three areas of control: Persistence Management, Network Management, and Profile Management. ManPages enables a user to save and load a network, which is done through the Persistence Management control panel. The Network Management control panel provides the ability to add or delete users to/from the network, and look up profiles of other users on the network. When users want to change their status, change their picture, or add a friend to their list, the Profile Management control panel provides these capabilities.

The basic design of the MBE for ManPages reflects that of the Eclipse Modeling Project [26]. There is a graphical editor based on EMF (with the Encore Modeling Language) and Graphical Modeling Framework as well model parsers for the various model levels. For example, once a PIM model has been created in the graphical editor, the associated XML file is passed to a parser that reads the file (in XMI format) and generates the abstract classes and interfaces of the system. The parser generates a list of source files that are contained in the repository so they can be moved into a new Java project along with the generated files. The model XML file contains 4 key areas:

1. the location of the source repository,
2. the sources files that instantiate the node objects in the model (e.g., files associated with an entity are contained in a `composedOf` tag with a `name` attribute `manpages:Entity`),

3. system communication is provided via requisite interfaces (e.g., `communi-catesBy` tags), and
4. a list of files that the network contains, but that are not graphical components or an interface.

The ManPages IDE parses the XML and produces the PSM (assembly for nascent components and generated via transforms where the fidelity of the components is mature enough to express the variance reliably). Generated components include all the interfaces required for the event-based assembly of the components as well as a set of abstract classes for the components that contain the implementation required for the event-based design. Event-based design relies on the Provider interface and the Registry interface for each event. Components using a Provider interface implement the handling and firing of events and components using a Registry interface act as the listeners for the events. This allows components to be linked together as specified by associations between the entities in the PIM. The assembly container instantiates and links all the entities. Generation is performed using JET templates, which receives parameters from the parser.

While this project was not as meaty at the others, it focused on something important from the complexity and productivity perspectives. That is, the ability to take a common MBE framework and apply it to a new or emerging product-line often involves considerable scaffolding and infrastructure to produce variants of a product (albeit a simple SNA). By capturing models and components, pre-conditioning them for utilization multiple times, and developing a reliable way of generating the SNA, there is considerable complexity increase to start with along with the associated productivity impacts. However, for future SNA development, the complexity is significantly reduced as crafting the custom applications turns to mass-customization. Like producing cars, the use of a production facility with the variants of the car pre-planned, the generation of the various models can be more readily done predictably and adjusted for normal market changes (i.e., year-to-year styles).

As SNAs mature, there will be more capabilities that become common and need not be reinvented. Rather, they will be improved as software engineers on multidisciplinary teams work together to capture their respective models and refine them for future generation. This opens another question—What happens if you introduce a factory generator for a given product line? If we could constrain the breadth of the application, the language used to specify the systems could be simplified and an environment to generate systems could be employed. In the next subsection on DSLs, we examine briefly that potential to reduce further, the complexities of development for better productivity.

6.4.3.1 FacePamphlet via a Domain Specific Language

Another version of the FacePamphlet environment was developed using a DSL Language Environment by Robert Adams, a student at Rose-Hulman Institute of Technology. While the student's thesis work was not yet published at the time of the writing, the preliminary results are worth mentioning here. Using JetBrains MPS [14], a version of the FacePamphlet environment was produced with significantly less effort than the project with five developers reported above. Indeed, one person produced an equivalent FacePamphlet application generator in less time and with more resulting flexibility. This was enabled by having a language-oriented programming environment for DSLs. This DSL toolkit provided facilities that aid in building up languages, which are then used to specify and generate a domain application.

MPS is a set of tools created to construct a language or set of languages that can be used for some purpose like a DSL. JetBrains MPS uses three principle components (languages) to construct DSLs: a structure language, an editor language, and a generator language. Each of these is itself a DSL.

The structure language is like the abstract syntax of a language that consists of concepts for definition. Like objects, concepts can be inherited, can contain other concepts, and can contain references to other concepts. With this, the DSL-programmer is able to specify the underlying behaviors, properties, and data elements of their languages.

The editor language establishes the concrete syntax of a language. It provides development environment utilities (e.g., as context menus). MPS also provides DSL code completion, hotkey context menus, and protections against creating malformed code. Since the definition of DSL is done in the same DSL generation environment as language creation, all of the capabilities provided for DSL application are available to the custom-created DSLs, reducing the overhead of defining concrete and abstract syntaxes.

The generation language provides for creating sets of mappings from concepts created in the structure language to sets of templates for a lower level language. Since these are written in MPS, extending these templates, or writing templates to target any other language is enabled. Building languages like this provides for building abstraction on abstraction, codifying the complexities of transformations and making things like portability and interoperability simpler.

6.5 Increasing Today's Complexity to Decrease Tomorrow's Complexity

If we look at the additional complexities induced by developing the environment to deliver an application, MBE looks more complex for the short term (high overhead). However, if we examine the knowledge that is codified into that environment to make simpler the tasks of producing said software systems in future systems, the complexity in the long run is certainly decreased. This is especially true for situations where one wants to be responsive to changes and variances that are induced by the environment (market, economy, etc.). This is one of the key lessons that came out of the efforts to explore MBE in software development and evolution.

Table 6.2 outlines the basic characteristics of the four efforts described in the last section to give a baseline for comparison. The staff represents the average number of people on the project over the duration. The duration is the calendar months, but effort would be approximately the duration times the staff divided by 4 (working only

Table 6.2 Basic MBE project characteristics

	CMDA	MBE-HPRC	ManPages MBE	FacePamphlet DSL
Staff	5	4	5	1
Duration	18 months	9 months	1.4 months	1 month
Size	~67 KLOC	~6 KLOC	~3 KLOC	~700 LOC
Reuse of domain components	~40% from Cougaar code; <10% open-source	<5% from HPRC code; <5% open-source	~20% from ManPage code; <0% open-source	~30% from FacePamplet code; <0% open-source
Reuse of MBE components	<5% open-source	~35% from CMDA; <5% open-source	0% from CMDA; <45% open-source	0% from CMDA; ~70% open-source
Abstraction	High	Low	Medium	High
Process	Medium	Low/Medium	Medium	Medium
Automation	High	Medium	Medium	High
Assembly	~65%	~80%	~90+%	~15+%

10 hours a week). The size estimates are based on discussions with the developers and course counts of code. The reuse of domain components (e.g., Cougaar Agent code) and MBE components (e.g., code that constituted contributing to the MBE infrastructure like parsers) are based on module counts (more is better). Process represent the level of attention paid to codifying the reuse and MBE process activities (higher is better). Automation represents opinion of how much of the process was not human-in-the-loop (higher is better). Assembly represents how much of the model components were assembled instead of transformed for generation (less is better).

While we started each project with a healthy dose of skepticism that drove us to take the risk averse assembly approach, we overcame the challenges and ultimately moved to a more transformation-heavy approach in the CMDA approach. While the other two projects did not attain a lower-level of assembly, we believe that the amount of time in the project increases the level of transformation. The more transformation, the more likely the component has a good fit for purpose and less glue code needed, and better productivity.

In all four cases experience developing components (models at various levels) and transformation rules lead to patterns and more effective techniques for populating a project's repository of components. From an economic perspective, speed with which one could produce domain applications rose significantly with the growth in generative components in the repository. Hence, the more populated with high yield components, the low the complexity and the better the productivity.

With the components and templates developed in CMDA, generating Cougaar applications was feasible, reliable, and the resulting system was a near match to the existing open-source Cougaar test code. The CMDA GDAM/GCAM structures based on a single meta-model appears to provide a reasonably good framework for implementing the MDA approach. While this was not as specific as the four level meta-structure of MOF, it was robust and resilient to the changes that were induced by our explorations. The MBE-HPRC used the same approach with similar results. The ManPages MBE employed the MOF successfully and was able to demonstrate better UML-based transformations. The productivity benefit of having the MOF meta-model is the integration of model artifacts with other projects; hence, gaining productivity advantages less glue.

The use of a DSL environment provided the language and automation scaffolding to expedite the development process and even when changes like `AddNon-Friend` were specified, the changes were made in a fraction of the time that the other SNA environment was able to achieve.

True Roundtrip engineering is hard to achieve without a full-bidirectional mapping of all artifacts. There must be enough markers left on the forward trek through transformations to find your way back. Also, until debugging moves up in abstraction (i.e., model level), we believe this will remain a difficult problem except for the less complex cases. While the MOF meta-model makes this more feasible, we were unable to demonstrate the efficacy of roundtrip engineering in the ManPages MBE. Therefore, the potential productivity gains of making changes in the system at any model level and having them propagate to the relevant components is still untried.

While we would like to claim that CMDA, MBE-HPRC, and ManPages MBE were all fully automated, our experience indicates that early on most efforts will require some human in the loop (e.g., verification of domain and system level constraints like UML operation contracts). This is especially true for unpopulated repositories and new components. However, this does point to a key element of productivity with MBE approaches for software—they are expensive to start, but like momentum in physics, the payoff in reduced complexity and increased productivity is once the repository is populated and unto speed.

With the more abstract domain components, it was clear that for many applications, a domain person could generate a Cougaar application with only a little help from the developer. This was shown true for the MBE-HPRC environment too as software people could aid in producing SDRs. This promising insight is one of the key objectives of the first two projects. The domain models and their respective components provided a reasonable interface for a Cougaar novice to be productive in generating domain applications. Of course, the population of models in the repository had a large influence on productivity.

6.6 Conclusions

Software size and complexity continue to increase and the software engineering community must respond to this ever-present risk. In the past, we have used abstraction, reuse, process, and automation to address the productivity concerns that stem from this, but there is still a productivity gap that is substantially caused by our inability to conquer complexity in large software systems. Abstraction plays a key role in our ability to deal with complexity. We presented the capabilities engineering with change tolerance measures (coupling, cohesion, and balanced abstraction) as a starting point to get a handle on complexity early on. We then transitioned these concepts to the models that are produced as one develops a software system—low coupling, high cohesion, and a balance in the modeling abstractions brings clarity to the questions answered at each level of abstraction traversed in developing software models (including coding). To this end, we concentrated on examining model-based engineering approaches for software like Model-Driven Architecture and Domain Specification Languages.

We presented three key projects examining three key themes to complexity: Sophisticated agents with complex interactions, low-level circuit design in reconfigurable FPGAs with complexity in the abundance of details, and Social Network Applications generation with complexity in production. While these three projects ranged from early research prototypes over a longer period to open-source based MBEs completed over a short six weeks, the potential to establish a Model-Based Engineering capability is feasible and potentially beneficial for organizations seeking to get a handle on complexity and improve the productivity of their software organization. While there is not a great deal of validation in our experience, lessons learned coupled with the definitions we provide about coupling and cohesion for change tolerance offer a reasonable substantiation of the leverage that MBE can bring to a software engineering project.

Much of this book on Conquering Complexity centers on using formal methods and rigor to govern complexity. While this chapter does not emphasize formalisms, they are central to the specification and transformation technologies used to generate software systems from models. Like MBE in other disciplines, MBE for software provides a valuable measure of early validation and verification, especially when the models are executable or formal enough for provers. We must not ignore the potential to reduce software faults and the costly rework to improve productivity.

From the perspective of abstraction reducing complexity and improving productivity, we believe that this is the greatest lever that MBEs have to offer—the other three (reuse, process, and automation) stem from it. In some sense, reuse is only an interim step on the way to the next level of language for expressing systems—today's specification language in MBE could be tomorrow's programming language as we begin to program in models. This can be seen readily in DSLs.

Abstraction also brings with it the advantage of employing more than software engineers to develop the system. Complexity can find its way in as a workaround is introduced due to lack of understanding that someone else may possess, but is not conveyed. With models as the expression mechanism, domain experts, and staff from other relevant disciplines can be employed to increase the speed at which we can clarify specifications and produce software systems. This was especially true in the CMDA and MBE-HPRC efforts where moving abstraction up opened doors for better productivity by having the right people involved at the right level—reducing errors early and expediting the effort.

Reuse has been touted for some time as a key productivity enhancer. While reused code is helpful, reused concepts and models at the higher levels are even more precious for productivity. With long-lived systems this is even more potent as the platforms are apt to become obsolete before the system. Hence, separating platform concerns (CIM, PIM, and PSM) offers a key way to reduce long-term complexity.

MBE involves a disciplined process to gain momentum from reusing artifacts in the production of software systems. In this process, however, there is some front-loading needed to establish the infrastructure for reusable components, reuse of the components, and the modeling underpinnings. Making this happen in an organization unaccustomed to the discipline would take longer—at least until the benefits of better productivity begins to result from the populated model repositories and clients being able to work with software staff in producing the systems more quickly and accurately.

Acknowledgements   This work has been supported, in part, by the DARPA grant "AMIIE Phase II—Cougaar Model Driven Architecture Project," (Cougaar Software, Inc.) subcontract number CSI-2003-01. We would like to acknowledge the efforts, ideas, and support that we received from our research team including Michael Hinchey, Todd Carrico, Tim Tschampel, Denis Gracanin, Lally Singh, and Nannan He. We want to thank students at Rose-Hulman Institute of Technology who participated in the FacePamphlet projects, and especially Rob Adams, whose work on the DSL version of FacePamphlet substantiated further our findings.

References

1. Cougaar developers' guide: Version for cougaar 11.4. Tech. rep., BBN Technologies (2004)
2. Bell, T.E., Thayer, T.A.: Software requirements: are they really a problem? In: ICSE, pp. 61–68 (1976)
3. Bieman, J.M., Ott, L.M.: Measuring functional cohesion. IEEE Trans. Softw. Eng. **20**(8), 644–657 (1994)
4. Boehm, B.W.: Software Risk Management. IEEE Comput. Soc., New York (1989)
5. Bohner, S.: An era of change-tolerant systems. IEEE Comput. **40**(6), 100–102 (2007)
6. Bohner, S., Gracanin, D., George, B., Singh, L., He, N.: Active methods project report and CMDA system documentation. Virginia Tech Department of Computer Science (2005), p. 77
7. Bohner, S.A., George, B., Gracanin, D., Hinchey, M.G.: Formalism challenges of the cougaar model driven architecture. In: Formal Approaches to Agent-Based Systems, Third International Workshop, FAABS 2004, Greenbelt, MD, USA, April 26–27, 2004, Revised Selected Papers, pp. 57–71 (2004)
8. Bohner, S.A., Ravichandar, R., Arthur, J.D.: Model-based engineering for change-tolerant systems. Innovations Syst. Softw. Eng. **3**(4), 237–257 (2007)
9. Briand, L., El-Emam, K., Morasca, S.: On the application of measurement theory in software engineering. Empir. Softw. Eng. **1**(1), 61–88 (1996)
10. Brown, A.: An introduction to model driven architecture: Part I: MDA and today's systems. IBM developerWorks (2004). Available from http://www-128.ibm.com/developerworks/rational/library/3100.html.
11. Card, D.N., Glass, R.L.: Measuring Software Design Quality. Prentice Hall, New York (1990)
12. Charette, R.N.: Why software fails. IEEE Spectr. **42**(9), 42–49 (2005)
13. Cuadrado, J.S., Molina, J.G.: Building domain-specific languages for model-driven development. IEEE Softw. **24**, 48–55 (2007)

14. Dmitriev, S.: Language oriented programming: the next programming paradigm (2004). Jetbrains. http://www.onboard.jetbrains.com/articles/04/10/lop/
15. Fenton, N.E., Pfleeger, S.L.: Software Metrics. Pws Publishing, Boston (1996)
16. Fiadeiro, J.L.: Designing for software's social complexity. IEEE Comput. **40**(1), 34–39 (2007)
17. Fowler, M., Parsons, R.: Domain-Specific Languages. Addison-Wesley, Reading (2010)
18. Frakes, W.B., Díaz, R.P., Fox, C.J.: Dare: domain analysis and reuse environment. Ann. Softw. Eng. **5**, 125–141 (1998)
19. George, B., Bohner, S.A., Prieto-Diaz, R.: Software information leaks: a complexity perspective. In: Ninth IEEE International Conference on Engineering Complex Computer Systems, pp. 239–248 (2004)
20. George, B., Singh, H.L., Bohner, S.A., Gracanin, D.: Requirements capture for cougaar model-driven architecture system. In: 29th Annual IEEE/NASA on Software Engineering Workshop, pp. 109–117 (2005)
21. Glass, R.L.: Facts and Fallacies of Software Engineering. Addison-Wesley, Reading (2002)
22. Goguen, J.A., Linde, C.: Techniques for requirements elicitation. In: First International Symposium on Requirements Engineering (RE'93), San Diego, CA, USA, pp. 152–164 (1993)
23. Gracanin, D., Bohner, S.A., Hinchey, M.G.: Towards a model-driven architecture for autonomic systems. In: 11th IEEE International Conference on the Engineering of Computer-Based Systems (ECBS 2004), 24–27 May 2004, Brno, Czech Republic, pp. 500–505 (2004)
24. Gracanin, D., Singh, H.L., Bohner, S.A., Hinchey, M.G.: Model-driven architecture for agent-based systems. In: Hinchey, M.G., Rash, J.L., Truszkowski, W., Rouff, C. (eds.) Formal Approaches to Agent-Based Systems, Third International Workshop, FAABS 2004, Greenbelt, MD, USA, April 26–27, 2004, Revised Selected Papers, pp. 249–261 (2004)
25. Gracanin, D., Singh, H.L., Hinchey, M.G., Eltoweissy, M., Bohner, S.A.: A CSP-based agent modeling framework for the cougaar agent-based architecture. In: 12th IEEE International Conference on the Engineering of Computer-Based Systems (ECBS 2005), 4–7 April 2005, Greenbelt, MD, USA, pp. 255–262 (2005)
26. Gronback, R.C.: Eclipse Modeling Project: A Domain-Specific Language (DSL) Toolkit. The Eclipse Series. Addison-Wesley, Reading (2009)
27. Haney, F.M.: Module connection analysis: a tool for scheduling software debugging activities. In: AFIPS '72: Proceedings of the December 5–7, 1972, Fall Joint Computer Conference, Part I (1927)
28. Heylighen, F.: Self-organization, emergence and the architecture of complexity. In: 1st European Conference on System Science, AFCET (1989)
29. Hinchey, M.G., Sterritt, R., Rouff, C.A.: Swarms and swarm intelligence. IEEE Comput. **40**(4), 111–113 (2007)
30. Lehman, M.M.: Laws of software evolution revisited. In: Proceedings 5th European Workshop, Software Process Technology, EWSPT '96, Nancy, France, October 9–11, 1996, pp. 108–124 (1996)
31. Lehman, M.M.: Software's future: managing evolution. IEEE Softw. **15**(1), 40–44 (1998)
32. Lutz, R.R.: Analyzing software requirements errors in safety-critical, embedded systems. In: First International Symposium on Requirements Engineering (RE'93), San Diego, CA, USA, pp. 126–133 (1993)
33. Miller, G.A.: The magical number seven, plus or minus two: some limits on our capacity for processing information. Psychol. Rev. **63**(2), 81–97 (1956)
34. Page-Jones, M.: Practical Guide to Structured Systems Design. YOURDON Press, New York (1980)
35. Qin, S., Chin, W.-N., He, J., Qiu, Z.: From statecharts to verilog: a formal approach to hardware/software co-specification. Innovations Syst. Softw. Eng. **2**(1), 17–38 (2006)
36. Ravichandar, R.: Capabilities engineering: promoting change-reduction and constructing change-tolerant systems. Ph.D. thesis, Computer Science, Virginia Tech. (2008)
37. Ravichandar, R., Arthur, J.D., Bohner, S.A.: Capabilities engineering: constructing change-tolerant systems. In: 40th Hawaii International Conference on Systems Science (HICSS-40 2007), 3–6 January 2007, Waikoloa, Big Island, HI, USA, p. 278 (2007)

38. Ravichandar, R., Arthur, J.D., Broadwater, R.P.: Reconciling synthesis and decomposition: a composite approach to capability identification. In: 14th Annual IEEE International Conference and Workshop on Engineering of Computer Based Systems (ECBS 2007), 26–29 March 2007, Tucson, AZ, USA, pp. 287–298 (2007)
39. Ravichandar, R., Arthur, J.D., Pérez-Quiñones, M.A.: Pre-requirement specification traceability: bridging the complexity gap through capabilities. In: International Symposium on Grand Challenges in Traceability, TEFSE/GC (2007)
40. Stahl, T., Voelter, M., Czarnecki, K.: Model-Driven Software Development: Technology, Engineering, Management. Wiley, New York (2006)
41. Stensrud, E., Myrtveit, I.: Identifying high performance ERP projects. IEEE Trans. Softw. Eng. **29**(5), 398–416 (2003)
42. Stevens, S.S.: On the theory of scales of measurement. Science **103**(2684), 677–680 (1946)
43. Stevens, W.P., Myers, G.J., Constantine, L.L.: Structured design. IBM Syst. J. **13**(2), 115–139 (1974)
44. Velleman, P.F., Wilkinson, L.: Nominal, ordinal, interval, and ratio typologies are misleading. Am. Stat. **47**(1), 65–72 (1993)
45. Yourdon, E., Constantine, L.L.: Structured Design: Fundamentals of a Discipline of Computer Program and System Design. Prentice Hall, New York (1979)

Chapter 7
You Can't Get There from Here!
Large Problems and Potential Solutions in Developing New Classes of Complex Computer Systems

Mike Hinchey, James L. Rash, Walter F. Truszkowski, Christopher A. Rouff, and Roy Sterritt

7.1 Introduction

Software has become pervasive. We encounter it in our everyday lives: the average electric razor contains the equivalent of more than 100,000 lines of code, several high-end cars contain more software than the onboard systems of the Space Shuttle. We are reliant on software for our transportation and entertainment, to wash our clothes and cook our meals, and to keep us in touch with the outside world via the Internet and our mobile phones.

The Information Technology industry, driven by software development, has made remarkable advances. In just over half a century, it has developed into a trillion-dollar-per-year industry, continually breaking its own records [17, 27].

Some breathtaking statistics have been reported for the hardware and software industries [16, 46]:

- The Price-to-Performance ratio halves every 18 months, with a 100-fold increase in performance every decade.
- Performance progress in the next 18 months will equal *all* progress made to date.
- New storage available equals the sum of all previously available storage *ever*.
- New processing capability equals the sum of all previous processing power.

Simultaneously, a number of flawed assumptions have arisen regarding the way we build both software and hardware systems [38, 46], which include:

- Human beings can achieve perfection; they can avoid making mistakes during installation, maintenance and upgrades.
- Software will eventually be bug-free; the focus of companies has been to hire better programmers, and the focus of universities is to better train software engineers in development lifecycle models.

M. Hinchey (✉)
Lero—the Irish Software Engineering Research Centre, University of Limerick, Limerick, Ireland
e-mail: mike.hinchey@lero.ie

M. Hinchey, L. Coyle (eds.), *Conquering Complexity*,
DOI 10.1007/978-1-4471-2297-5_7, © Springer-Verlag London Limited 2012

Fig. 7.1 Contrasting
availability of telephone
systems, computer systems,
Internet, and mobile phones

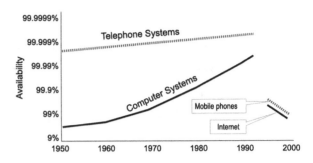

- Mean-time between failure (MTBF) is already very large (approximately 100 years) and will continue to increase.
- Maintenance costs are a function of the purchase price of hardware; and, as such, decreasing hardware costs (price/performance) results in decreases in maintenance costs.

7.2 Software Problems

With the situation stated this way, many flawed assumptions regarding the IT industry come into view. The situation is even worse if we focus primarily on software. The Computing industry has failed to avoid software-related catastrophes. Notable examples include:

- Therac-25, where cancer patients were given lethal doses of radiation during radiation therapy [33].
- Ariane 5, where it was assumed that the same launch software used in the prior version (Ariane 4) could be reused. The result was the loss of the rocket within seconds of launch [34].
- The Mars Polar Lander, where failure to initialize a variable resulted in the craft crash landing on the Martian surface, instead of reverse thrusting and landing softly [29].

Progress in software regularly lags behind hardware. In the last decade, for example, two highly software-intensive applications, namely Internet communications and mobile phone technology, have suffered reduced availability and increased *down time*, while their hardware counterparts, computer hardware and telephony systems, have continued to improve. Figure 7.1 illustrates this trend [17].

7.2.1 An Historic Problem

The realization that software development has lagged greatly behind hardware is hardly a new one [6], nor is the realization that our software development processes have some severe deficiencies.

Brooks, in a widely quoted and much-referenced article [7], warns of complacency in software development. He stresses that, unlike hardware development, we cannot expect to achieve great advances in productivity in software development unless we concentrate on more appropriate development methods. He highlights how software systems can suddenly turn from being well-behaved to behaving erratically and uncontrollably, with unanticipated delays and increased costs. Brooks sees software systems as "werewolves" and rightly points out that there is no single technique, no Silver Bullet, capable of slaying such monsters [6].

On the contrary, more and more complex systems are run on highly distributed, heterogeneous networks, subject to strict performance, fault tolerance, and security constraints, all of which may conflict. Many engineering disciplines must contribute to the development of complex systems in an attempt to satisfy all of these requirements. No single technique is adequate to address all issues of complex system development; rather, different techniques must be applied at different stages of development (and throughout the development process) to ensure unambiguous requirements statements, precise specifications that are amenable to analysis and evaluation, implementations that satisfy the requirements and various (often conflicting) goals, re-use, re-engineering and reverse engineering of legacy code, appropriate integration with existing systems, ease-of-use, predictability, dependability, maintainability, fault tolerance, etc. [6].

Brooks [7] differentiates between the *essence* (that is, problems that are necessarily inherent in the nature of software) and *accidents* (that is, problems that are secondary and caused by current development environments and techniques). He points out the great need for appropriate means of coming to grips with the conceptual difficulties of software development—that is, for appropriate emphasis on specification and design, rather than on coding and testing.

In his article [7], he highlights some successes that have been achieved in gaining improvements in productivity, but points out that these address problems in the current development process, rather than the problems inherent in software itself. In this category, he includes: the advent of high-level programming languages, time-sharing, and unified programming environments. Object-oriented programming, techniques from artificial intelligence, expert systems, automatic programming, program verification, and the advent of workstations, he sees as non-bullets, as they will not help in slaying the werewolf.

He sees software reuse, rapid prototyping, incremental development, and the employment of top-class designers as potential starting points for the Silver Bullet, but warns that none in itself is sufficient.

Brooks' article has been very influential, and remains one of the classics of software engineering. His viewpoint has been criticized, however, as being overly pessimistic and for failing to acknowledge some promising developments [6].

Harel, in an equally influential paper, written as a rebuttal to Brooks [19], points to developments in Computer-Aided Software Engineering (CASE) and visual formalisms [18] as potential *bullets*. Harel's view is far more optimistic. He writes five years after Brooks, and has seen the developments in that period. The last forty years of system development have been equally difficult, according to Harel, and, using a conceptual vanilla framework, the development community has devised means of overcoming many difficulties. As we address more complex systems, Harel argues that we must devise similar frameworks that are applicable to the classes of system we are developing.

Harel, along with many others, including the authors of this paper, believes that appropriate techniques for modeling must have a rigorous mathematical semantics, and appropriate means for representing constructs. This differs greatly from Brooks, who sees representational issues as mainly *accidental*.

7.3 New Challenges for Software Engineering

Clearly there have been significant advances in software engineering tools, techniques, and methods, since the time of Brooks' and Harel's papers. In many cases, however, the advantages of these developments have been mitigated by corresponding increases in demand for greater, more complex functionality, stricter constraints on performance and reaction times, and attempts to increase productivity and reduce costs, while simultaneously pushing systems requirements to their limits. NASA, for example, continues to build more and more complex systems, with impressive functionality, and increasingly autonomous behavior. In the main, this is essential. NASA missions are pursuing scientific discovery in ways that require autonomous systems. While manned exploration missions are clearly in NASA's future (such as the Exploration Initiative's plans to return to the moon and put Man on Mars), several current and future NASA missions, for reasons that we will explain below, necessitate autonomous behavior by unmanned spacecraft.

We will describe some of the challenges for software engineering emerging from new classes of complex systems being developed by NASA and others. We will discuss these in Sect. 7.3.1 with reference to a NASA concept mission that is exemplary of many of these new systems. Then, in Sect. 7.4 we will present some techniques that we are addressing, which may lead towards a Silver Bullet.

7.3.1 Challenges of Future NASA Missions

Future NASA missions will exploit new paradigms for space exploration, heavily focused on the (still) emerging technologies of autonomous and autonomic systems. Traditional missions, reliant on one large spacecraft, are being superseded or complemented by missions that involve several smaller spacecraft operating in collaboration, analogous to swarms in nature. This offers several advantages: the ability to send spacecraft to explore regions of space where traditional craft simply would be impractical, increased spatial distribution of observations, greater redundancy, and, consequently, greater protection of assets, and reduced costs and risk, to name but a few. Planned missions entail the use of several unmanned autonomous vehicles (UAVs) flying approximately one meter above the surface of Mars, covering as much of the surface of Mars in seconds as the now famous Mars rovers did in their entire time on the planet; the use of armies of tetrahedral walkers to explore the Mars and Lunar surface; constellations of satellites flying in formation; and the use of miniaturized pico-class spacecraft to explore the asteroid belt.

These new approaches to exploration missions simultaneously pose many challenges. The missions will be unmanned and necessarily highly autonomous. They will also exhibit all of the classic properties of autonomic systems, being self-protecting, self-healing, self-configuring, and self-optimizing. Many of these missions will be sent to parts of the solar system where manned missions are simply not possible, and to where the round-trip delay for communications to spacecraft exceeds 40 minutes, meaning that the decisions on responses to problems and undesirable situations must be made *in situ* rather than from ground control on Earth.

Verification and Validation (V&V) for complex systems still poses a largely unmet challenge in the field of Computing, yet the challenge is magnified with increasing degrees of system autonomy. It is an even greater open question as to the extent to which V&V is feasible when the system possesses the ability to adapt and learn, particularly in environments that are dynamic and not specially constrained. Reliance on testing as the primary approach to V&V becomes untenable as systems move towards higher levels of complexity, autonomy, and adaptability in such environments. Swarm missions will fall into this category, and an early concern in the design and development of swarms will be the problem of predicting, or at least bounding, and controlling emergent behavior.

The result is that formal specification techniques and formal verification will play vital roles in the future development of NASA space exploration missions. The role of formal methods will be in the specification and analysis of forthcoming missions, enabling software assurance and proof of correctness of the behavior of these systems, whether or not this behavior is emergent (as a result of composing a number of interacting entities, producing behavior that was not foreseen). Formally derived models may also be used as the basis for automating the generation of much of the code for the mission. To address the challenge in verifying the above missions, a NASA project, Formal Approaches to Swarm Technology (FAST), is investigating the requirements of appropriate formal methods for use in such missions, and is beginning to apply these techniques to specifying and verifying parts of a future NASA swarm-based mission.

7.3.2 ANTS: A NASA Concept Mission

The Autonomous Nano-Technology Swarm (ANTS) mission will involve the launch of a swarm of autonomous pico-class (approximately 1 kg) spacecraft that will explore the asteroid belt for asteroids with certain characteristics. Figure 7.2 gives an overview of the ANTS mission [47]. In this mission, a transport ship, launched from Earth, will travel to a point in space where gravitational forces on small objects (such as pico-class spacecraft) are all but negligible. Objects that remain near such

Fig. 7.2 NASA's
Autonomous Nano
Technology Swarm (ANTS)
mission scenario

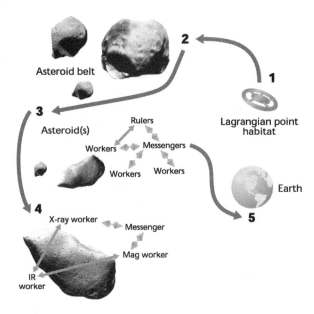

a point (termed a Lagrangian point) are in a stable orbit about the Sun and will have
a fixed geometrical relationship to the Sun-Earth system. From the transport ship
positioned at such a point, 1000 spacecraft that have been assembled en route from
Earth will be launched into the asteroid belt.

Because of their small size, each ANTS spacecraft will carry just one specialized instrument for collecting a specific type of data from asteroids in the belt. As
a result, spacecraft must cooperate and coordinate using a hierarchical social behavior analogous to colonies or swarms of insects, with some spacecraft directing
others. To implement this mission, a heuristic approach is being considered that
provides for a social structure to the swarm based on the above hierarchy. Artificial
intelligence technologies such as genetic algorithms, neural nets, fuzzy logic and
on-board planners are being investigated to assist the mission to maintain a high
level of autonomy. Crucial to the mission will be the ability to modify its operations
autonomously to reflect the changing nature of the mission and the distance and
low-bandwidth communications back to Earth.

Approximately 80 percent of the spacecraft will be workers that will carry the
specialized instruments (e.g., a magnetometer, x-ray, gamma-ray, visible/IR, neutral
mass spectrometer) and will obtain specific types of data. Some will be coordinators
(called rulers) that have rules that decide the types of asteroids and data the mission
is interested in, and that will coordinate the efforts of the workers. The third type
of spacecraft are messengers that will coordinate communication between the rulers
and workers, and communications with the Earth ground station, including requests
for replacement spacecraft with specialized instruments as these are required. The
swarm will form sub-swarms under the direction of a ruler, which contains models
of the types of science that it wants to perform. The ruler will coordinate workers
each of which uses its individual instrument to collect data on specific asteroids

and feed this information back to the ruler who will determine which asteroids are worth examining further. If the data matches the profile of a type of asteroid that is of interest, an imaging spacecraft will be sent to the asteroid to ascertain the exact location and to create a rough model to be used by other spacecraft for maneuvering around the asteroid. Other teams of spacecraft will then coordinate to finish the mapping of the asteroid to form a complete model.

7.3.3 Problematic Issues

7.3.3.1 Size and Complexity

While the use of a swarm of miniature spacecraft is essential for the success of ANTS, it simultaneously poses several problems in terms of adding significantly to the complexity of the mission.

The mission will launch 1000 pico-class spacecraft, many of which possibly will be destroyed by collisions with asteroids, since the craft, having no means of maneuvering other than solar sails, will be very limited in their collision-avoidance capabilities. The several hundred surviving spacecraft must be organized into effective groups that will collect science data and make decisions as to which asteroids warrant further investigation. These surviving spacecraft effectively form a wireless sensor network [23] tens of millions of miles from Earth. The overhead for communications is clearly significant.

To keep the spacecraft small, each craft only carries a single instrument. That is why several craft must coordinate to investigate particular asteroids and collect different types of science data. Again, while miniaturization is important, the use of such a scheme has a major drawback: we have no *a priori* knowledge as to which instruments will be lost during normal operations (where we expect to regularly lose craft due to collisions).

The need to identify lost capabilities and instruments, and then replace them, presents an extremely complex problem. In the case of lost messengers and rulers, other craft may be *promoted* to replace them. It is merely the software that differentiates messengers and rulers from other workers, so mobile code serves to overcome this problem. When an instrument is lost, however, we have a rather different problem. A worker with a damaged instrument can be reserved for use as a ruler, and another spacecraft with an identical instrument can replace it.

An alternative would be add more features (instruments) into each spacecraft, but this would increase both their size (a problem in such a constrained environment) and their power requirements. The addition of features, of course, also increases complexity, as identified by Lawson [32].

7.3.3.2 Emergent Behavior

In swarm-based systems, interacting agents (often homogeneous or near homogeneous agents) are developed to take advantage of their emergent behavior. Each of the agents is given certain parameters that it tries to maximize. Bonabeau et al. [4], who studied self-organization in social insects, state that "complex collective behaviors may emerge from interactions among individuals that exhibit simple behaviors" and describe emergent behavior as "a set of dynamical mechanisms whereby structures appear at the global level of a system from interactions among its lower-level components."

Intelligent swarms [3] use swarms of simple intelligent agents. Swarms have no central controller: they are self-organizing based on the emergent behaviors of the simple interactions. There is no external force directing their behavior and no one agent has a global view of the intended macroscopic behavior. Though current NASA swarm missions differ from true swarms as described above, they do have many of the same attributes and may exhibit emergent behavior. In addition, there are a number of US government projects that are looking at true swarms to accomplish complex missions.

7.3.3.3 Autonomy

Autonomous operation is essential for the success of the ANTS mission concept.

Round trip communications delays of up to 40 minutes, and limited bandwidth on communications with Earth, mean that effective control from the ground station is impossible. Ground controllers would not be able to react sufficiently quickly during encounters with asteroids to avoid collisions with asteroids and even other ANTS spacecraft. Moreover, the delay in sending instructions to the spacecraft would be so great that situations would likely have changed dramatically by the time the instructions were received.

But autonomy implies absence of centralized control. Individual ANTS spacecraft will operate autonomously as part of a subgroup under the direction of that subgroup's *ruler*. That ruler will itself autonomously make decisions regarding asteroids of interest, and formulate plans for continuing the mission of collecting science data. The success of the mission is predicated on the validity of the plans generated by the rulers, and requires that the rulers generate sensible plans that will collect valid science data, and then make valid informed decisions.

That autonomy is possible is not in doubt. What is in doubt is that autonomous systems can be relied upon to operate correctly, in particular in the absence of a full and complete specification of what is required of the system.

7.3.3.4 Testing and Verification

As can be seen from the brief exposition above, ANTS is a highly complex system that poses many significant challenges. Not least amongst these are the complex interactions between heterogeneous components, the need for continuous re-planning, re-configuration, and re-optimization, the need for autonomous operation without intervention from Earth, and the need for assurance of the correct operation of the mission.

As mission software becomes increasingly more complex, it also becomes more difficult to test and find errors. Race conditions in these systems can rarely be found by inputting sample data and checking whether the results are correct. These types of errors are time-based and only occur when processes send or receive data at particular times, or in a particular sequence, or after learning occurs. To find these errors, the software processes involved have to be executed in all possible combinations of states (state space) that the processes could collectively be in. Because the state space is exponential (and sometimes factorial) to the number of states, it becomes untestable with a relatively small number of processes. Traditionally, to get around the state explosion problem, testers have artificially reduced the number of states of the system and approximated the underlying software using models.

One of the most challenging aspects of using swarms is how to verify that the emergent behavior of such systems will be proper and that no undesirable behaviors will occur. In addition to emergent behavior in swarms, there are also a large number of concurrent interactions between the agents that make up the swarms. These interactions can also contain errors, such as race conditions, that are very difficult to ascertain until they occur. Once they do occur, it can also be very difficult to recreate the errors since they are usually data and time dependent.

As part of the FAST project, NASA is investigating the use of formal methods and formal techniques for verification and validation of these classes of mission, and is beginning to apply these techniques to specifying and verifying parts of the ANTS concept mission. The role of formal methods will be in the specification and analysis of forthcoming missions, while offering the ability to perform software assurance and proof of correctness of the behavior of the swarm, whether this behavior is emergent or not.

7.4 Some Potentially Useful Techniques

7.4.1 Autonomicity

Autonomy may be considered as bestowing the properties of self-governance and self-direction, i.e., control over one's goals [15, 26, 43]. Autonomicity is having the ability to self-manage through properties such as self-configuring, self-healing, self-optimizing, and self-protecting. These are achieved through other self-properties such as self-awareness (including environment awareness), self-monitoring, and self-adjusting [45].

Increasingly, self-management is seen as the only viable way forward to cope with the ever increasing complexity of systems. From one perspective, self-management may be considered a specialism of self-governance, i.e., autonomy where the goals/tasks are specific to management roles [46]. Yet from the wider context, an autonomic element (AE), consisting of an autonomic manager and managed component, may still have its own specific goals, but also the additional responsibility of management tasks particular to the wider system environment.

It is envisaged that in an autonomic environment the AEs communicate to ensure a managed environment that is reliable and fault tolerant and meets high level specified policies (where a policy consists of a set of behavioral constraints or preferences that influences the decisions made by an autonomic manager [10]) with an overarching vision of system-wide policy-based self-management. This may result in AEs monitoring or *watching out for* other AEs. In terms of autonomy and the concern of undesirable emergent behavior, an environment that dynamically and continuously monitors can assist in detecting race conditions and reconfiguring to avoid damage (self-protecting, self-healing, self-configuring, etc.). As such, autonomicity becoming mainstream in the industry can only assist in improving techniques, tools, and processes for autonomy [44].

7.4.2 Hybrid Formal Methods

The majority of formal notations currently available were developed in the 1970s and 1980s and reflect the types of distributed systems being developed at that time. Current distributed systems are evolving and may not be able to be specified in the same way that past systems have been developed. Because of this, it appears that many people are combining formal methods into integrated approaches to address some of the new features of distributed systems (e.g., mobile agents, swarms, and emergent behavior).

Integrated approaches have been very popular in specifying concurrent and agent-based systems. Integrated approaches often combine a process algebra or logic-based approach with a model-based approach. The process algebra or logic-based approach allows for easy specification of concurrent systems, while the model-based approach provides strength in specifying the algorithmic part of a system.

Some recent hybrid approaches include:

- CSP-OZ, a combination of CSP and Object-Z [11]
- Object-Z and Statecharts [8]
- Timed Communicating Object Z [13]
- Temporal B [5]
- Temporal Petri Nets (Temporal Logic and Petri Nets) [1]
- ZCCS, a combination of Z and CCS [14]

These and new hybrid formal methods are being investigated to address swarm and other complex NASA missions [41].

7.4.3 Automatic Programming

For many years, automatic programming has referred, primarily, to the use of very high-level languages to describe solutions to problems, which could then be translated down and expressed as code in more traditional (lower level) programming languages. Parnas [36] implies that the term is glamorous, rather than having any real meaning, precisely because it is the solution that is being specified rather than the problem that must be solved. Brooks [7] supports this view, and equally criticizes the field of visual programming, arguing that it will never produce anything of value.

Writing just five years after Brooks, Harel [19] disagrees, faulting Brooks for failing to recognize advances in *visual formalisms*. Now, writing almost two decades after Brooks, we argue that automatic code generation is not only a viable option, it is essential to the development of the classes of complex system we are discussing here, and as exemplified by ANTS.

Autonomous and autonomic systems, exhibiting complex emergent behavior, cannot, in general, be fully specified at the outset. The roles and behaviors of the system will vary greatly over time. While we may try to write specifications that constrain the system, it is clear that not all behavior can be specified in advance. Consequently, the classes of system we are discussing will often require that code is generated, or modified, during execution. As a result, the classes of system we are describing here will *require* automatic code generation.

Several tools already exist that successfully generate code from a given model. Unfortunately, many of these tools have been shown to generate code, portions of which are never executed, or portions of which cannot be justified from either the requirements or the model. Moreover, existing tools do not and cannot overcome the fundamental inadequacy of all currently available automated development approaches, which is that they include no means to establish a provable equivalence between the requirements stated at the outset and either the model or the code they generate.

Traditional approaches to automatic code generation, including those embodied in commercial products such as Matlab [35], in system development toolsets such as the B-Toolkit [31] or the VDM++ toolkit [28], or in academic research projects, presuppose the existence of an explicit (formal) model of reality that can be used as the basis for subsequent code generation. While such an approach is reasonable, the advantages and disadvantages of the various modeling approaches used in computing are well known and certain models can serve well to highlight certain issues while suppressing other less relevant details [37]. It is clear that the converse is also true. Certain models of reality, while successfully detailing many of the issues of interest to developers, can fail to capture some important issues, or perhaps even the most important issues.

That is why, we believe, future approaches to automatic code generation must be based on Formal Requirements-Based Programming [39].

7.4.4 Formal Requirements Based Programming

Requirements-Based Programming refers to the development of complex software (and other) systems, where each stage of the development is fully traceable back to the requirements given at the outset. In essence, Requirements-Based Programming takes Model-Based Development and adds a *front end* [40].

The difference is that Model-Based Development holds that emphasis should be placed on building a model of the system with such high quality that automatic code generation is viable. While this has worked well, and made automatic code generation feasible, there is still the large *analysis-specification* gap that remains unaddressed. Requirements-Based Programming addresses that issue and ensures that there is a direct mapping from requirements to design, and that this design (model) may then be used as the basis for automatic code generation.

There have been calls for the community to address Requirements-Based Programming, as it offers perhaps the most promising approach to achieving *correct* systems [20]. Although the use of Requirements-Based Programming does not specifically presuppose the existence of an underlying formalism, the realization that proof of correctness is not possible without formalism [2] certainly implies that Requirements-Based Programming should be formal.

In fact, Formal Requirements-Based Programming, coupled with a graphical representation for system requirements (e.g., UML use cases) possesses the features and advantages of a visual formalism described by Harel [18].

7.4.4.1 R2D2C

R2D2C, or Requirements-to-Design-to-Code [22, 39], is a NASA patent-pending[1] approach to Requirements-Based Programming.

In R2D2C, engineers (or others) may write specifications as scenarios in constrained (domain-specific) natural language, or in a range of other notations (including UML use cases). These will be used to derive a formal model (Fig. 7.3) that is guaranteed to be equivalent to the requirements stated at the outset, and which will subsequently be used as a basis for code generation. The formal model can be expressed using a variety of formal methods. Currently we are using CSP, Hoare's language of Communicating Sequential Processes [24, 25], which is suitable for various types of analysis and investigation, and as the basis for fully formal implementations as well as for use in automated test case generation, etc.

R2D2C is unique in that it allows for full formal development from the outset, and maintains mathematical soundness through all phases of the development process, from requirements through to automatic code generation. The approach may also be used for reverse engineering, that is, in retrieving models and formal specifications from existing code, as shown in Fig. 7.3. The approach can also be used to "paraphrase" (in natural language, etc.) formal descriptions of existing systems. In addition, the approach is not limited to generating high-level code. It may also be used to generate business processes and procedures, and we have been experimenting with using it to generate instructions for robotic devices that were to be used on

---

[1]Since this paper was originally published, a number of patents have been awarded, including U.S. Patents 7,668,796, 7,739,671, 7,752,608, 7,765,171, 7,886,273, and 7,979,848.

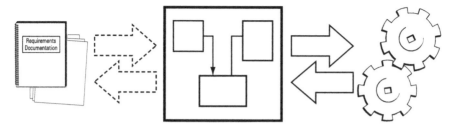

Fig. 7.3 The R2D2C approach, generating a formal model from requirements and producing code from the formal model, with automatic reverse engineering

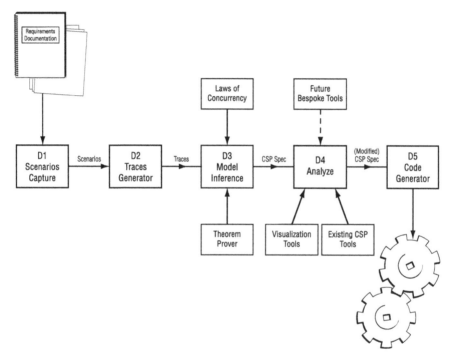

Fig. 7.4 The entire process with D1 through D5 illustrating the development approach

the Hubble Robotic Servicing Mission (HRSM), which, at the time of writing, has not received a final go-ahead. We are also experimenting with using it as a basis for an expert system verification tool, and as a means of capturing domain knowledge for expert systems.

7.4.4.2 R2D2C Technical Approach

The R2D2C approach involves a number of phases, which are reflected in the system architecture described in Fig. 7.4. The following describes each of these phases.

D1 Scenarios Capture: Engineers, end users, and others write scenarios describing intended system operation. The input scenarios may be represented in a constrained natural language using a syntax-directed editor, or may be represented in other textual or graphical forms.

D2 Traces Generation: Traces and sequences of atomic events are derived from the scenarios defined in phase D1.

D3 Model Inference: A formal model, or formal specification, expressed in CSP is inferred by an automatic theorem prover—in this case, ACL2 [30]—using the traces derived in phase D2. A deep[2] embedding of the laws of concurrency [21] in the theorem prover gives it sufficient knowledge of concurrency and of CSP to perform the inference. The embedding will be the topic of a future paper.

D4 Analysis: Based on the formal model, various analyses can be performed, using currently available commercial or public domain tools, and specialized tools that are planned for development. Because of the nature of CSP, the model may be analyzed at different levels of abstraction using a variety of possible implementation environments. This will be the subject of a future paper.

D5 Code Generation: The techniques of automatic code generation from a suitable model are reasonably well understood. The present modeling approach is suitable for the application of existing code generation techniques, whether using a tool specifically developed for the purpose, or existing tools such as FDR [12], or converting to other notations suitable for code generation (e.g., converting CSP to B [9]) and then using the code generating capabilities of the B Toolkit.

7.4.4.3 Advantages of the R2D2C Approach

We have not yet had an opportunity to apply R2D2C to ANTS, although that is certainly our plan.

In addition to applying it to the HRSM procedures [39], we have applied R2D2C to LOGOS, a NASA prototype Lights-Out Ground Operating System, that exhibits both autonomous and autonomic properties [48, 49]. We illustrate the use of a prototype tool to apply R2D2C to LOGOS in [40], and describe our success with the approach.

Here, we summarize some benefits of using R2D2C, and hence of using Formal Requirements-Based Programming in system development. It is our contention that R2D2C, and other approaches that similarly provide mathematical soundness throughout the development lifecycle, will:

- Dramatically increase assurance of system success by ensuring
  - completeness and consistency of requirements
  - that implementations are true to the requirements
  - that automatically coded systems are bug-free; and that
  - that implementation behavior is as expected

---

[2]"Deep" in the sense that the embedding is semantic rather than merely syntactic.

- Decrease costs and schedule impacts of ultra-high dependability systems through automated development
- Decrease re-engineering costs and delays

7.4.5 Tool Support

John Rushby [42] argues that tools are not the *most* important thing about formal methods, they are the *only* important thing about formal methods. Although we can sympathize, we do not support such an extreme viewpoint. Formal methods would not be practical without suitable representation notations, proof systems (whether automated and supported by tools, or not), a user community, and evidence of successful application.

We do agree, however, that tool support is vital, and not just for formal methods. Structured design methods *took off* when they were *standardized*, in the guise of UML. But it is only with the advent of tool support for UML that they became popular. The situation is analogous to high-level programming languages: while the community was well convinced of their benefits, it was only with the availability of commercial compilers that they became widely used.

Tools are emerging for the development of complex agent-based systems such as Java-based Aglets and tools for autonomic systems. For automatic code generation and Formal Requirements-Based Programming to be practical, the development community will need commercial-quality tools.

7.5 Conclusion

The computing industry thrives on the assumption in the marketplace that software is reliable and correct, but many examples from experience over the decades cast doubt on the validity of this assumption. There is no automated, general purpose method for building correct systems that fully meet all customer requirements. This represents a major gap that has yet to be fully addressed by the software engineering community. Requirements-based programming has been described along with new automated techniques recently devised at NASA for ensuring correctness of the system model with respect to the requirements, as a possible way to close this gap.

In future mission concepts that involve advanced architectures and capabilities—such as swarm missions whose individual elements not only can learn from experience but also must pursue science goals cooperatively—NASA faces system development challenges that cannot be met with techniques currently available in the computing industry. The challenges boil down to building reliability and correctness into mission systems, where complexity, autonomous operation, machine adaptation, dangerous environments, and remoteness combine to push such missions far into uncharted territory in systems engineering. With approaches such as autonomic computing and automated requirements-based programming, NASA will have greater possibilities for achieving success with these advanced mission concepts.

Acknowledgements This paper was previously published in Proc. Eighth International Conference on Integrated Design and Process Technology (IDPT), 2005. Reprinted with permission.

This work is funded in part by Science Foundation Ireland grant 03/CE2/I303_1 to Lero—the Irish Software Engineering Research Centre (www.lero.ie); by the NASA Office of Safety and Mission Assurance, under its Software Assurance Research Program project *Formal Approaches to Swarm Technologies* (FAST), administered by the NASA IV&V Facility; by the Office of Technology Transfer, NASA Goddard Space Flight Center; by the NASA Software Engineering Laboratory, NASA Goddard Space Flight Center; and by the University of Ulster Computer Science Research Institute and the Centre for Software Process Technologies (CSPT), funded by Invest NI through the Centres of Excellence Programme under the European Union Peace II initiative.

References

1. Bakam, I., Kordon, F., Page, C.L., Bousquet, F.: Formalization of a spatialized multiagent model using Coloured Petri Nets for the study of an hunting management system. In: Proc. First International Workshop on Formal Approaches to Agent-Based Systems (FAABS I). LNAI, vol. 1871. Springer, Greenbelt (2000)
2. Bauer, F.L.: A trend for the next ten years of software engineering. In: Freeman, H., Lewis, P.M. (eds.) Software Engineering, pp. 1–23. Academic Press, New York (1980)
3. Beni, G., Want, J.: Swarm intelligence. In: Seventh Annual Meeting of the Robotics Society of Japan, Tokyo, Japan, pp. 425–428. RSJ Press, Germering (1989)
4. Bonabeau, E., Théraulaz, G., Deneubourg, J.-L., Aron, S., Camazine, S.: Self-organization in social insects. Trends Ecol. Evol. **12**, 188–193 (1997)
5. Bonnet, L., Florin, G., Duchien, L., Seinturier, L.: A method for specifying and proving distributed cooperative algorithms. In: Proc. DIMAS-95 (1995)
6. Bowen, J.P., Hinchey, M.G.: High-integrity System Specification and Design. FACIT Series. Springer, London (1999)
7. Brooks, Jr., F.P.: No silver bullet: essence and accidents of software engineering. IEEE Comput. **20**(4), 10–19 (1987)
8. Büssow, R., Geisler, R., Klar, M.: Specifying safety-critical embedded systems with statecharts and Z: a case study. In: Astesiano, E. (ed.) Proc. International Conference on Fundamental Approaches to Software Engineering. LNCS, vol. 1382, pp. 71–87. Springer, Berlin (1998)
9. Butler, M.J.: Csp2b: a practical approach to combining Csp and B. Declarative Systems and Software Engineering Group, Department of Electronics and Computer Science, University of Southampton (1999)
10. Fellenstein, C.: On Demand Computing. IBM Press Series on Information Management. Prentice Hall, Upper Saddle River (2005)
11. Fischer, C.: Combination and implementation of processes and data: from CSP-OZ to Java. Ph.D. thesis, Universität Oldenburg, Germany (2000)
12. Formal Systems (Europe), Ltd.: Failures-Divergences Refinement: User Manual and Tutorial. (1999)
13. Gala, A.K., Baker, A.D.: Multi-agent communication in JAFMAS. In: Proc. Workshop on Specifying and Implementing Conversation Policies, Third International Conference on Autonomous Agents (Agents '99), Seattle, Washington (1999)
14. Galloway, A.J., Stoddart, W.J.: An operational semantics for ZCCS. In: Hinchey, M., Liu, S. (eds.) Proc. IEEE International Conference on Formal Engineering Methods (ICFEM-97), pp. 272–282. IEEE Comput. Soc., Los Alamitos (1997)

15. Ganek, A.G., Corbi, T.A.: The dawning of the autonomic computing era. IBM Syst. J. **42**(1), 5–18 (2003)
16. Gray, J.N.: What next? A few remaining problems in information technology. Turing Award Lecture (ACM FCRC) (1999)
17. Gray, J.N.: Dependability in the Internet era. In: Proc. High Dependability Computing Consortium Workshop, Santa Cruz, California (2001)
18. Harel, D.: On visual formalisms. Commun. ACM **31**(5), 514–530 (1988)
19. Harel, D.: Biting the silver bullet: toward a brighter future for system development. IEEE Comput. **25**(1), 8–20 (1992)
20. Harel, D.: Comments made during presentation at "Formal Approaches to Complex Software Systems" panel session. ISoLA-04 First International Conference on Leveraging Applications of Formal Methods (2004)
21. Hinchey, M.G., Jarvis, S.A.: Concurrent Systems: Formal Development in Csp. International Series in Software Engineering. McGraw-Hill International, London (1995)
22. Hinchey, M.G., Rash, J.L., Rouff, C.A.: Requirements to design to code: towards a fully formal approach to automatic code generation. Technical report TM-2005-212774, NASA Goddard Space Flight Center, Greenbelt, MD, USA (2004)
23. Hinchey, M.G., Rash, J.L., Rouff, C.A.: Towards an automated development methodology for dependable systems with application to sensor networks. In: Proc. IEEE Workshop on Information Assurance in Wireless Sensor Networks (WSNIA 2005). IEEE Comput. Soc., Los Alamitos (2005). Proc. International Performance Computing and Communications Conference (IPCCC-05) (Reprinted in Proc. Real Time in Sweden 2005 (RTiS2005), the 8th Biennial SNART Conference on Real-time Systems, 2005)
24. Hoare, C.A.R.: Communicating sequential processes. Commun. ACM **21**(8), 666–677 (1978)
25. Hoare, C.A.R.: Communicating Sequential Processes. Prentice Hall International Series in Computer Science. Prentice Hall, Englewood Cliffs (1985)
26. Horn, P.: Autonomic computing: IBM's perspective on the state of information technology. Presented at agenda 2001, Scotsdale, Arizona, 2001, IBM T. J. Watson Laboratory (October 15, 2001)
27. Horn, P.M.: Meeting the needs, realizing the opportunities. In: Wessner, C.W. (ed.) Capitalizing on New Needs and New Opportunities: Government—Industry Partnerships in Biotechnology and Information Technologies (2001) Board on Science, Technology, and Economic Policy (STEP), pp. 149–152. The National Academies Press, Washington (2001)
28. IFAD: The VDM++ toolbox user manual. Technical report, IFAD (2000)
29. JPL Special Review Board: Report on the Loss of the Mars Polar Lander and Deep Space 2 missions, Pasadena, California, USA (2000)
30. Kaufmann, M., Manolios, P., Moore, J.: Computer-Aided Reasoning: An Approach. Advances in Formal Methods Series. Kluwer Academic, Boston (2000)
31. Lano, K., Haughton, H.: Specification in B: An Introduction Using the B-toolkit. Imperial College Press, London (1996)
32. Lawson, H.W.: Rebirth of the computer industry. Commun. ACM **45**(6), 25–29 (2002)
33. Leveson, N.G.: Medical devices: the Therac-25 story. In: Safeware: System Safety and Computers, pp. 515–553. Addison-Wesley, Reading (1995)
34. Lions, J.L.: ARIANE 5: Flight 501 failure, report by the inquiry board (1996)
35. The MathWorks, Inc., Natick, Massachusettes: Getting Started with MATLAB (2000)
36. Parnas, D.L.: Software aspects for strategic defense systems. American Scientist (1985)
37. Parnas, D.L.: Using mathematical models in the inspection of critical software. In: Applications of Formal Methods. International Series in Computer Science, pp. 17–31. Prentice Hall, Englewood Cliffs (1995)
38. Patterson, D., Brown, A.: Recovery-oriented computing (Keynote talk). In: Proc. High Performance Transaction Systems Workshop (HPTS) (2001)
39. Rash, J.L., Hinchey, M.G., Rouff, C.A., Gračanin, D.: Formal requirements-based programming for complex systems. In: Proc. International Conference on Engineering of Complex Computer Systems. IEEE Computer Society Press, Shanghai (2005)

40. Rash, J.L., Hinchey, M.G., Rouff, C.A., Gračanin, D., Erickson, J.D.: A tool for requirements-based programming. In: Proc. International Conference on Integrated Design and Process Technology (IDPT 2005). The Society for Design and Process Science, Beijing (2005)
41. Rouff, C.A., Truszkowski, W.F., Rash, J.L., Hinchey, M.G.: A survey of formal methods for intelligent swarms. Technical report TM-2005-212779, NASA Goddard Space Flight Center, Greenbelt, Maryland (2005)
42. Rushby, J.: Remarks, panel session on the future of formal methods in industry. In: Bowen, J.P., Hinchey, M.G. (eds.) Proc. 9th International Conference of Z Users. LNCS, vol. 967, pp. 239–241. Springer, Limerick (1995)
43. Sterritt, R.: Towards autonomic computing: effective event management. In: 27th Ann. IEEE/NASA Software Engineering Workshop (SEW), MD, USA, pp. 40–47. IEEE Comput. Soc., Los Alamitos (2002)
44. Sterritt, R.: Autonomic computing. Innovations in Systems and Software Engineering: a NASA Journal **1**(1) (2005)
45. Sterritt, R., Bustard, D.W.: Autonomic computing: a means of achieving dependability? In: IEEE Int. Conf. Engineering of Computer Based Systems (ECBS'03), Huntsville, AL, USA, pp. 247–251 (2003)
46. Sterritt, R., Hinchey, M.G.: Why computer based systems *Should* be autonomic. In: Proc. 12th IEEE International Conference on Engineering of Computer Based Systems (ECBS 2005), Greenbelt, MD, pp. 406–414 (2005)
47. Truszkowski, W., Hinchey, M., Rash, J., Rouff, C.: NASA's swarm missions: the challenge of building autonomous software. IT Prof. **6**(5), 47–52 (2004)
48. Truszkowski, W.F., Hinchey, M.G., Rash, J.L., Rouff, C.A.: Autonomous and autonomic systems: a paradigm for future space exploration missions. IEEE Trans. Syst. Man Cybern., Part C, Appl. Rev. **36**(3), 279–291 (2006)
49. Truszkowski, W.F., Rash, J.L., Rouff, C.A., Hinchey, M.G.: Some autonomic properties of two legacy multi-agent systems—LOGOS and ACT. In: Proc. 11th IEEE International Conference on Engineering Computer-Based Systems (ECBS), Workshop on Engineering Autonomic Systems (EASe), pp. 490–498. IEEE Comput. Soc., Los Alamitos (2004)

Chapter 8
99% (Biological) Inspiration...

Mike Hinchey and Roy Sterritt

8.1 Introduction

Thomas Alva Edison described invention as 1% inspiration and 99% perspiration. This quotation is attributed to him with multiple variations, some describing invention, others describing genius.[1]

We cannot possibly hope to match the inventiveness and genius of nature. We can be *inspired* by nature and influenced by it, but to attempt to mimic nature is likely to have very limited success, as early pioneers of flight discovered.

Icarus attempted to escape the Labyrinth in which he was imprisoned with his father, Daedalus, by building wings from feathers and wax. Despite Deadalus's warning not to fly so low as to get the feathers wet, nor so near the sun as to melt the wax, Icarus flew too high, the wax did indeed melt, and he fell to his death.

In 1809, a Viennese watchmaker named Degen claimed to have flown with similar apparatus. In reality, he only hopped a short distance, and was supported by a balloon. Early attempts at mechanical flight involved the use of aircraft with wings that flapped like a bird's. But clearly, trying to copy birds was not going to work:

> Since the days of Bishop Wilkins the scheme of flying by artificial wings has been much ridiculed; and indeed the idea of attaching wings to the arms of a man is ridiculous enough, as the pectoral muscles of a bird occupy more than two-thirds of its whole muscular strength, whereas in man the muscles, that could operate upon wings thus attached, would probably not exceed one-tenth of his whole mass. There is no proof that, weight for weight, a man is comparatively weaker than a bird... [13].

---

[1] The earliest recorded quotation is from a press conference, quoted by James D. Newton in *Uncommon Friends* (1929): "None of my inventions came by accident. I see a worthwhile need to be met and I make trial after trial until it comes. What it boils down to is one per cent inspiration and ninety-nine per cent perspiration."

R. Sterritt (✉)
School of Computing and Mathematics, University of Ulster, Newtownabbey, Northern Ireland
e-mail: r.sterritt@ulster.ac.uk

M. Hinchey, L. Coyle (eds.), *Conquering Complexity*,
DOI 10.1007/978-1-4471-2297-5_8, © Springer-Verlag London Limited 2012

It was only when inventors such as Otto Lilienthal, building on the work of Cayley, moved away from directly mimicking nature, and adopted fixed wings, originally as gliders and later as monoplanes, and eventually as aircraft with wings and a tail, as Cayley had identified was needed for flight [4], that success was achieved [13]. Even then, early aircraft had very limited success (the Wright brothers' historic first powered flight at Kitty Hawk, North Carolina, in 1903 only lasted 12 seconds and 120 feet [9]), and required the addition of gas-powered engine for thrust and the Wright brothers' identification of an effective means of lateral control, for a feasible heavier-than-air craft to be possible.

Aircraft as we know them now bear very little resemblance to birds. Flight was *inspired* by nature, but hundreds of years were spent trying to copy nature, with little success. Inspiration was vital—otherwise man would never have attempted to fly. But direct mimicry was the wrong direction. Similarly we believe that computing systems may benefit much by being *inspired* by biology, but should not attempt to copy biology slavishly.

> To invent an airplane is nothing.
> To build one is something.
> But to fly is everything.
> *Otto Lilienthal (1848–1896)*

8.2 Biologically-Inspired Computing

> We've discovered the secret of life.
> *Francis Crick (1916–2004)*

The Nobel prize-winning discovery, in 1953, of the double helix structure of DNA and its encoding was revolutionary. It has opened a whole new world of understanding of biology and the way in which nature works. Simultaneously, it has resulted in several new fields of scientific research: genetics, genomics, computational biology, and bioinformatics, to name but a few.

The understanding of how nature encodes biological information and determines how living organisms will develop and evolve has enabled us to improve the quality of life, eliminate certain diseases, cure congenital defects in unborn children, and make significant advances in controlling and eventually eliminating life-threatening conditions.

This greater understanding of the biology of living organisms has also indicated a parallel with computing systems: molecules in living cells interact, grow, and transform according to the "program" dictated by DNA. Indeed, the goal of bioinformatics is to develop "in silico" models of in vitro and in vivo biological experiments [6].

Paradigms of Computing are emerging based on modeling and developing computer-based systems exploiting ideas that are observed in nature. This includes building self-management and self-governance mechanisms that are inspired by the human body's autonomic nervous system into computer systems, modeling evolutionary systems analogous to colonies of ants or other insects, and developing highly-efficient and highly-complex distributed systems from large numbers of (often quite simple) largely homogeneous components to reflect the behavior of flocks of birds, swarms of bees, herds of animals, or schools of fish.

This field of "Biologically-Inspired Computing", often known in other incarnations by other names, such as: Autonomic Computing, Organic Computing, Biomimetics, and Artificial Life, amongst others, is poised at the intersection of Computer Science, Engineering, Mathematics, and the Life Sciences [12]. Successes have been reported in the fields of drug discovery, data communications, computer animation, control and command, exploration systems for space, undersea, and harsh environments, to name but a few, and augur much promise for future progress [12, 26].

8.3 The Autonomic Nervous System

> The nervous system and the automatic machine are fundamentally alike in that they are devices, which make decisions on the basis of decisions they made in the past.
> *Norbert Weiner (1894–1964)*

Inspiration from human biology, in the form of the autonomic nervous system (ANS), is the focus of the Autonomic Computing initiative . The idea is that mechanisms that are "autonomic", in-built, and requiring no conscious thought in the human body are used as inspiration for building mechanisms that will enable a computer system to become self-managing [18].

The human (and animal) body's *sympathetic nervous system (SyNS)* deals with defense and protection ("fight or flight") and the *parasympathetic nervous system (PaNS)* deals with long-term health of the body ("rest and digest"), performing the vegetative functions of the body such as circulation of the blood, intestinal activity, and secretion of chemicals (hormones) that circulate in the blood. So too an autonomic system tries to ensure the continued health and well-being of a computer-based system by sending and monitoring various signals in the system.

The general properties of an autonomic (self-managing) system can be summarized by four objectives: being self-configuring, self-healing, self-optimizing and self-protecting, and four attributes: self-awareness, self-situated, self-monitoring and self-adjusting (Fig. 8.1). Essentially, the objectives represent broad system requirements, while the attributes identify basic implementation mechanisms [21].

In achieving such self-managing objectives, a system must be aware of its internal state (self-aware) and current external operating conditions (self-situated). Changing circumstances are detected through self-monitoring, and adaptations are made accordingly (self-adjusting). As such, a system must have knowledge of its available resources, its components, their desired performance characteristics, their current status, and the status of inter-connections with other systems, along with rules and policies of how these may be adjusted. Such ability to operate in a heterogeneous environment will require the use of open standards to enable global understanding and communication with other systems [12].

Fig. 8.1 Autonomic system properties

These mechanisms are not independent entities. For instance, if an attack is successful, this will necessitate self-healing actions, and a mix of self-configuration and self-optimization, in the first instance to ensure dependability and continued operation of the system, and later to increase self-protection against similar future attacks. Finally, these self-mechanisms should ensure that there is minimal disruption to users, avoiding significant delays in processing.

At the heart of the architecture of any autonomic system are sensors and effectors. A control loop is created by monitoring behavior through sensors, comparing this with expectations (knowledge, as in historical and current data, rules and beliefs), planning what action is necessary (if any), and then executing that action through effectors. The closed loop of feedback control provides the basic backbone structure for each system component [21].

The autonomic environment requires that autonomic elements and, in particular, autonomic managers for these elements communicate with one another concerning self-* activities, in order to ensure the robustness of the environment. Figure 8.2 depicts that the autonomic manager communications (AM ⇔ AM) also includes a reflex signal. This may be facilitated through the additional concept of a pulse monitor—PBM (an extension of the embedded system's heart-beat monitor, or HBM, which safeguards vital processes through the emission of a regular "I am alive" signal to another process) with the capability to encode health and urgency signals as a pulse [19]. Together with the standard event messages on the autonomic communications channel, this provides dynamics within autonomic responses and multiple loops of control, such as reflex reactions among the autonomic managers. This reflex component may be used to safeguard the autonomic element by communicating its health to another AE. The component may also be utilized to communicate environmental health information.

An important aspect concerning the reflex reaction and the pulse monitor is the minimization of data sent—essentially only a "signal" is transmitted. Strictly speaking, this is not mandatory; more information may be sent, yet the additional information must not compromise the reflex reaction. For instance, in the absence of

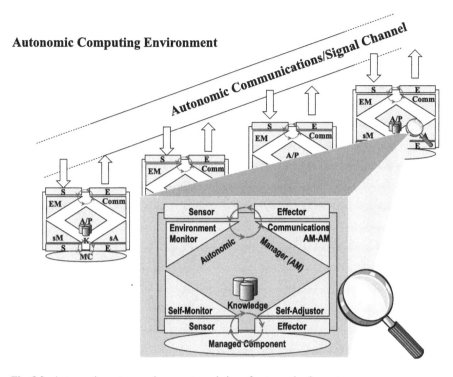

Fig. 8.2 Autonomic system environment consisting of autonomic elements

bandwidth concerns, information that can be acted upon quickly and not incur processing delays could be sent. The important aspect is that the information must be in a form that can be acted upon immediately and not involve processing delays (such as is the case of event correlation) [20].

Just as the beat of the heart has a double beat ("lub-dub", as it is referred to by the medical profession) the autonomic element's pulse monitor may have a double beat encoded—a *self* health/urgency measure and an *environment* health/urgency measure [25]. These match directly with the two control loops within the AE, and the self-awareness and environment awareness properties.

8.4 Inspiration from Human Biology

We still do not know one thousandth of one percent
of what nature has revealed to us.
Albert Einstein (1879–1955)

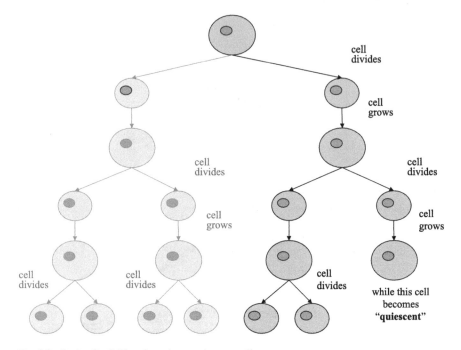

Fig. 8.3 Cycle of cell life—featuring a quiescent cell

8.4.1 New Metaphors

In this emerging field of biologically-inspired computing, we are seeking inspiration for new approaches from (obviously, pre-existing) biological mechanisms, and in fact a whole plethora of further self-* properties are being proposed and developed, leading to the coining of the term *selfware*.

The biological cell cycle is often described as a circle of cell life and division. A cell divides into two "daughter cells" and both of these cells live, "eat", grow, copy their genetic material and divide again producing two more daughter cells. Since each daughter cell has a copy of the same genes in its nucleus, daughter cells are "clones" of each other. This "twinning" goes on and on with each cell cycle. This is a natural process.

Very fast cell cycles occur during development causing a single cell to make many copies of itself as it grows and differentiates into an embryo. Some very fast cell cycles also occur in adult animals. Hair, skin and gut cells have very fast cell cycles to replace cells that die naturally. Scientists now believe that some forms of cancer may be caused by cells not dying quickly enough, rather than cycling out of control.

But there is a kind of "parking spot" in the cell cycle, called "quiescence". A *quiescent* cell has left the cell cycle; it has stopped dividing (Fig. 8.3). Quiescent cells may re-enter the cell cycle at some later time, or they may not; it depends on the type of cell. Most nerve cells stay quiescent forever. On the other hand, some quiescent cells may later re-enter the cell cycle in order to create more cells (for example, during pubescent development) [14].

We have been considering self-destruction as a means of providing an intrinsic safety mechanism against non-desirable emergent behavior from the selfware.

It is believed that a cell knows when to commit suicide because cells are programmed to do so—self-destruction (sD) is an intrinsic property. This sD is delayed due to the continuous receipt of biochemical retrieves. This process is referred to as *apoptosis*, meaning "drop out", used by the Greeks to refer to the Autumn dropping of leaves from trees; i.e., loss of cells that ought to die in the midst of the living structure. The process has also been nicknamed "death by default" where cells are prevented from putting an end to themselves due to constant receipt of biochemical "stay alive" signals.

Further investigations into the apoptosis process have discovered more details about the self-destruct program. Whenever a cell divides, it simultaneously receives orders to kill itself. Without a reprieve signal, the cell does indeed self-destruct. It is believed that the reason for this is self-protection, as the most dangerous time for the body is when a cell divides, since if just one of the billions of cells locks into division the result is a tumor, while simultaneously a cell must divide to build and maintain a body [22–24].

8.4.2 Inspiration

Of course, each of these techniques and mechanisms is useful in achieving autonomicity and in mimicking the autonomic nervous system (ANS). But while the inspiration comes substantially from that of the human (or animal) body, the techniques are not those that the ANS actually uses.

There *are* signals sent around the human body in the form of hormones and pulses, amongst others, in the blood. But in modern computer science and engineering, we have developed many efficient communication mechanisms that do not rely on signals flowing through miles of unnecessary channels (veins and arteries), but may be directly routed or broadcast using wireless communications.

We do not know precisely how apoptosis and quiescence works, nor specifically their roles. But they certainly offer interesting ideas for future security and safety mechanisms in computer-based systems [26].

These techniques are *inspired* by nature, but not necessarily implemented as they are by nature. In many cases, we can make some optimizations or improvements; in other cases we simply do not understand enough of how nature works to implement these directly, but they can certainly inspire interesting metaphors for self-management and self-governance.

8.5 Swarms

> What is not good for the swarm is not good for the bee.
> *Marcus Aurelius (A.D. 121–180)*

We are all familiar with swarms in nature. The mere mention of the word "swarm" conjures up images of large groupings of small insects, such as bees (apiidae) or locusts (acridiidae), each insect having a simple role, but with the swarm as a whole producing complex behavior.

Strictly speaking, such emergence of complex behavior is not limited to swarms, and we see similar complex social structures occurring with higher order animals and insects that don't swarm *per se*: colonies of ants, flocks of birds, packs of wolves, etc. These groupings behave like swarms[2] in many ways [11].

A *swarm* consists of a large number of simple entities that have local interactions (including interactions with the environment) [1]. The result of the combination of simple behaviors (the microscopic behavior) is the emergence of complex behavior (the macroscopic behavior) and the ability to achieve significant results as a "team" [3]. Basing collaborative computing systems on the concept of a swarm allows us to build complex systems, with often surprising behavior, from simple components.

Intelligent swarm technology is based on swarm technology where the individual members of the swarm also exhibit independent intelligence [2]. Intelligent swarms may be homogeneous or heterogeneous, or may start out as homogeneous and evolve as in different environments they "learn" different things, develop new (different) goals, and eventually become heterogeneous, reflecting different capabilities and a societal structure.

Agent swarms have been used as a computer modeling technique and have also been used as a tool to study complex systems [10]. Examples of simulations that have been undertaken include flocks of birds as well as business and economics and ecological systems.

In *swarm simulations*, each of the agents is given certain parameters that it tries to maximize. Swarm simulations have been developed that exhibit unlikely emergent behavior. These emergent behaviors are the sums of often simple individual behaviors, but, when aggregated, form complex and often unexpected behaviors.

Swarm intelligence techniques (note the slight difference in terminology from "intelligent swarms") are population-based stochastic methods used in combinatorial optimization problems, where the collective behavior of relatively simple individuals arises from their local interactions with their environment to give rise to the emergence of functional global patterns.

Swarm robotics refers to the application of swarm intelligence techniques to the analysis of swarms where the embodiment of the "agents" is as physical robotic devices.

---

[2]The term "swarm", as we use it here, refers to a (possibly large) grouping of simple components collaborating to achieve some goal and produce significant results. The term should not be taken to imply that these components fly (or are airborne); they may equally well be on the surface of the Earth, under the surface, under water, or indeed operating on other planets.

8.5.1 Swarm Inspiration

The idea that swarms can be used to solve complex problems has been taken up in several areas of computer science. These include the use of analogies to the pheromone trails used by ants (to leave trails for the colony to follow to stores of food) in software to solve the traveling salesman problem, allowing the software to "find" the shortest route by following the route with the most "digital pheromone", meaning it is the shortest (as on longer routes the concentration of pheromone would be lower due to being spread over a greater distance) [7, 11]. The approach is an example of *Ant Colony Optimization*, a very interesting approach that is inspired by the social behavior of ants, and uses their behavior patterns as models for solving difficult combinational optimization problems [8].

Swarm behavior is also being investigated for use in such applications as telephone switching, network routing, data categorizing, and shortest path optimizations. Swarm radio and "swarmcasting" of television over the internet is an approach to file-sharing that is inspired substantially by swarms. The approach exploits under-utilized uplinks to download part of the file to other users and then allow for the receipt of portions of the file from those users. The result is that streaming video is possible even without a high-speed internet connection.

Research at Penn State University has focused on the use of particle swarms for the development of quantitative structure activity relationships (QSAR) models used in the area of drug design [5]. The research created models using artificial neural networks and k-nearest neighbor and kernel regression. Binary and niching particle swarms were used to solve feature selection and feature weighting problems.

Particle swarms have influenced the field of computer animation also. Rather than scripting the path of each individual bird in a flock, the Boids project [16] elaborated a particle swarm with the simulated birds being the particles. The aggregate motion of the simulated flock is much like that in nature: it is the result of the dense interaction of the relatively simple behaviors of each of the (simulated) birds, where each bird chooses its own path.

8.5.2 Swarms for Exploration

NASA is investigating the use of swarm technologies for the development of sustainable exploration missions that will be autonomous and exhibit autonomic properties [28]. The idea is that biologically-inspired swarms of smaller spacecraft offer greater redundancy (and, consequently, greater protection of assets), reduced costs and risks, and the ability to explore regions of space where a single large spacecraft would be impractical.

ANTS is a NASA concept mission, a collaboration between NASA Goddard Space Flight Center and NASA Langley Research Center, which aims at the development of revolutionary mission architectures and the exploitation of artificial intelligence techniques and the paradigm of biological inspiration in future space exploration. The mission concept includes the use of swarm technologies for both spacecraft and surface-based rovers, and consists of several submissions:

- *SARA: The Saturn Autonomous Ring Array* will launch 1000 pico-class space-craft, organized as ten sub-swarms, each with specialized instruments, to perform *in situ* exploration of Saturn's rings, by which to understand their constitution and how they were formed. The concept mission will require self-configuring structures for nuclear propulsion and control, which lies beyond the scope of this paper. Additionally, autonomous operation is necessary for both maneuvering around Saturn's rings and collision avoidance.
- *PAM: Prospecting Asteroid Mission* will also launch 1000 pico-class spacecraft, but here with the aim of exploring the asteroid belt and collecting data on particular asteroids of interest for potential future mining operations.
- *LARA: ANTS Application Lunar Base Activities* will exploit new NASA-developed technologies in the field of miniaturized robotics, which may form the basis of remote landers to be launched to the moon from remote sites, and may exploit innovative techniques to allow rovers to move in an amoeboid-like fashion over the moon's uneven terrain.

8.5.3 Inspiration and Improvement

ANTS, although a nice acronym, is actually somewhat of a misnomer—other than the LARA submission, the concept mission is more inspired by swarms of bees or flocks of birds than by colonies of ants.

But even then, ANTS is merely *inspired* by birds and bees. As we discussed in Sect. 8.1, the pioneers of flight found that directly attempting to mimic avian flight was the wrong way forward. Similarly, ANTS spacecraft in the PAM and SARA submissions will not attempt to fly like birds (in any case it would not be practical to build them with wings, a short tail, a curved sternum and hollow bones, in the way birds have evolved from *Archaeopteryx*, a dromaeosaurid from the late Jurrasic and Cretaceous periods and the earliest known flying creature).

In PAM, illustrated in Fig. 8.4, a swarm of autonomous pico-class (approximately 1 kg) spacecraft will explore the asteroid belt for asteroids with certain characteristics. In this mission, a transport ship, launched from Earth, will travel to a point in space where gravitational forces on small objects (such as pico-class spacecraft) are all but negligible. From this point, termed a Lagrangian, 1000 spacecraft, which will have been assembled *en route* from Earth, will be launched into the asteroid belt.

Approximately 80 percent of the spacecraft will be workers that will carry the specialized instruments (e.g., a magnetometer or an x-ray, gamma-ray, visible/IR, or neutral mass spectrometer) and will obtain specific types of data. Some will be coordinators (called leaders) that have rules that decide the types of asteroids and data the mission is interested in and that will coordinate the efforts of the workers. The third type of spacecraft are messengers that will coordinate communication between the rulers and workers, and communications with the Earth ground station.

Fig. 8.4 ANTS PAM
(prospecting asteroid
mission) scenario

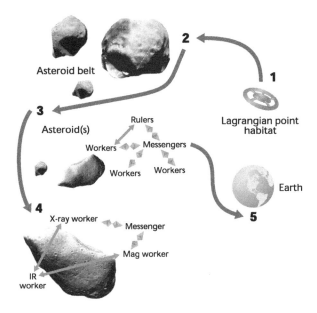

The swarm will form sub-swarms under the control of a ruler, which contains models of the types of science that it wants to perform. The ruler will coordinate workers, each of which uses its individual instrument to collect data on specific asteroids and feed this information back to the ruler, who will determine which asteroids are worth examining further. If the data matches the profile of a type of asteroid that is of interest, an imaging spacecraft will be sent to the asteroid to ascertain the exact location and to create a rough model to be used by other spacecraft for maneuvering around the asteroid. Other teams of spacecraft will then coordinate to finish mapping the asteroid to form a complete model.

This is *not* how birds flock nor bees swarm.[3] Birds form flocks in response to a *flocking call* issued by one of the birds. Birds in the flock continue in the flight pattern by "following" another bird. It is thought that collisions are avoided via *flight calls*, whereby birds let other birds know where they are via sound. In ANTS, the spacecraft do not "broadcast" in this way; spacecraft do not communicate with each other directly, but rather via a *messenger* that coordinates communications between the spacecraft and with Earth. Collision-avoidance (both collisions with other spacecraft and with asteroids) in ANTS is achieved by keeping models of locations, which will be achieved via various means. Since movement will be enabled only by simple thrusters, it is anticipated that many of the spacecraft will be lost due to collisions.

In many senses, this is more efficient than the broadcast mechanism of the flocking calls and flight calls. There is less communication overhead, and the spacecraft are not continually having to update the information on where other spacecraft are

---

[3]Not all species of bee swarm; there are several solitary species.

located relative to them. Of course we can tolerate certain losses of spacecraft (one of the motivations for a swarm-based approach is to have redundancy and avoid mission loss due to a single incident), as long as the number of incidents is within certain boundaries, whereas a flock of birds could not tolerate continual losses due to collisions.

ANTS spacecraft will also need to have protection mechanisms built in, such as going into sleep mode to protect solar sails (used for power) during solar storms. This is analogous to a flock of birds taking shelter in severe weather, but the spacecraft do not have to land and find shelter, they merely have to alter their position and lower their sails to avoid damage from electrical charges, etc.

Similarly, flocks of birds and swarms of bees do not form sub-swarms as is envisioned in ANTS, nor do they take instructions directly from a leader. While flocks and swarms in nature do occasionally allow for an alternate to take over a particular role (e.g., the establishment of a new queen in a hive), this is not so efficient as in ANTS where a worker with a damaged instrument, instead of becoming useless, can take over the role of messenger, or even leader.

The ANTS swarm, collaborating to collect science data from the asteroid belt, is clearly inspired by nature and the biology of birds and bees, but exhibits enhancements over nature by virtue of techniques and approaches known to us from the fields of computing and engineering.

8.6 Conclusions

The human race has gained much from a greater understanding of biology. Understanding how the "program" of life works has made it possible to prevent many undesirable conditions, cure certain diseases and afflictions, devise new treatments and drugs and understand better when they can be used, etc. Notwithstanding this greater understanding of biology, most of these advancements were due to the exploitation of modern computing technology and its application to biological problems, and in particular the ability to develop and explore (search) models of reality. We begin with such models, and enhance them with concepts not seen in nature or the real world [15], but deriving from advancements in computing and engineering.

Such modeling of biological phenomena and nature has enabled us to better understand the behavior patterns of insects, birds, and mammals. Simultaneously, an understanding of biology and nature has enabled the creation of a whole field of biologically-inspired computing. Ingenuity in nature has sparked imaginations and inspired ideas for means of developing complex computer systems that reduce complexity, enable the development of classes of system which we could never have achieved without this inspiration, and move towards self-governance of systems.

Biologically-inspired computing involves looking at biology and nature and models of it, and then adapting it and improving on it with advances made in computing technology and engineering.

Unlike Edison, at least in this context, we see the inspiration as being 99% of the effort, and believe that computing can benefit in many ways from biological inspiration. We believe that biologically-inspired computing should be 99% (biological) inspiration, combined with 1% mimicry.

> Look deep into nature, and you will understand everything better.
> *Albert Einstein (1879–1955)*

Acknowledgements The chapter is based on a keynote talk given at the IFIP Conference on Biologically Inspired Cooperative Computing (BICC 2006) at 19th IFIP WCC 2006, Santiago, Chile, August 2006

First published as: *Hinchey, M.G., Sterritt, R., 2006, in IFIP International Federation for Information Processing, Volume 216, Biologically Inspired Cooperative Computing, eds. Pan, Y., Rammig, F., Schmeck, H., Solar, M. (Boston: Springer), pp. 7–20.* Reprinted with kind permission of Springer Science and Business Media.

We are grateful to the organizers of BICC 2006 for inviting this talk and associated paper.

Autonomic apoptosis was introduced in [22], and quiescence in [26]. More detailed expositions of the ANTS concept mission, and specifically the PAM submission, are given in [17, 27, 28].

Part of this work has been supported by the NASA Office of Systems and Mission Assurance (OSMA) through its Software Assurance Research Program (SARP) project, Formal Approaches to Swarm Technologies (FAST), and by NASA Software Engineering Laboratory, Goddard Space Flight Center (Code 581).

This research is partly supported at University of Ulster by the Computer Science Research Institute (CSRI) and the Centre for Software Process Technologies (CSPT) which is funded by Invest NI through the Centres of Excellence Programme, under the EU Peace II initiative.

Some of the technologies described in this chapter are patented or patent-pending and assigned to the United States government.

References

1. Beni, G.: The concept of cellular robotics. In: IEEE International Symposium on Intelligent Control, pp. 57–62. IEEE Comput. Soc., Los Alamitos (1988)
2. Beni, G., Want, J.: Swarm intelligence. In: Seventh Annual Meeting of the Robotics Society of Japan, Tokyo, Japan, pp. 425–428. RSJ Press, Germering (1989)
3. Bonabeau, E., Théraulaz, G.: Swarm smarts. Sci. Am. **282**(3), 72–79 (2000)
4. Cayley, G.: On aeriel naviation. Nicholson's Journal (1809)
5. Cedeno, W., Agrafiotis, D.K.: Combining particle swarms and k-nearest neighbors for the development of quantitative structure-activity relationships. Int. J. Comput. Res. **11**(4), 443–452 (2003)
6. Cohen, J.: Bioinformatics—an introduction for computer scientists. ACM Comput. Surv. **36**(2), 122–158 (2004)
7. Dorigo, M., Gambardella, L.M.: Ant colonies for the traveling salesman problem. Biosystems **43**, 73–81 (1997)
8. Dorigo, M., Stützle, T.: Ant Colony Optimization. MIT Press, Cambridge (2004)
9. Gates, B.: The Wright brothers. Time (1999). Monday, Mar. 29
10. Hiebeler, D.E.: The swarm simulation system and individual-based modeling. In: Decision Support 2001: Advanced Technology for Natural Resource Management, Toronto, Canada (2001)
11. Hinchey, M.G., Rash, J.L., Truszkowski, W.F., Rouff, C.A., Sterritt, R.: Autonomous and autonomic swarms. In: Autonomic & Autonomous Space Exploration Systems (A& A-SES-1) at 2005 Int. Conf. Software Engineering Research and Practice (SERP'05), Las Vegas, NV, 27–29 June 2005, pp. 36–42. CREA Press, Gent (2005)
12. Hinchey, M.G., Sterritt, R.: Self-managing software. Computer **39**, 107–109 (2006)

13. Lilienthal, O.: Practical experiments for the development of human flight. The Aeronautical Annual, 7–20 (1896)
14. Love, J.: Science explained: the cloning of Dolly. Workshop publication (1999)
15. Peterson, I.: Calculating swarms. Sci. News **158**(20), 314 (2000)
16. Reynolds, C.W.: Flocks, herds, and schools: a distributed behavioral model. Comput. Graph. **21**(4), 25–34 (1987)
17. Rouff, C.A., Hinchey, M.G., Rash, J.L., Truszkowski, W.F.: Experiences applying formal approaches in the development of swarm-based exploration missions. Int. J. Softw. Tools Technol. Transf. **8**(6), 587–603 (2006)
18. Sterritt, R.: Towards autonomic computing: effective event management. In: 27th Ann. IEEE/NASA Software Engineering Workshop (SEW), MD, USA, pp. 40–47. IEEE Comput. Soc., Los Alamitos (2002)
19. Sterritt, R.: Pulse monitoring: extending the health-check for the autonomic GRID. In: IEEE Workshop Autonomic Computing Principles and Architectures (AUCOPA 2003) at INDIN 2003, Banff, AB, Canada, pp. 433–440 (2003)
20. Sterritt, R., Bantz, D.F.: PAC-MEN: personal autonomic computing monitoring environments. In: Proc IEEE DEXA 2004 Workshops—2nd Int. Workshop Self-adaptive and Autonomic Computing Systems (SAACS 04), Zaragoza, Spain (2004)
21. Sterritt, R., Bustard, D.W.: Autonomic computing: a means of achieving dependability? In: IEEE Int. Conf. Engineering of Computer Based Systems (ECBS'03), Huntsville, AL, USA, pp. 247–251 (2003)
22. Sterritt, R., Hinchey, M.G.: Apoptosis and self-destruct: a contribution to autonomic agents? In: FAABS-III, 3rd NASA/IEEE Workshop on Formal Approaches to Agent-Based Systems, 26–27 April 2004, Greenbelt, MD. LNCS, vol. 3228. Springer, Berlin (2004)
23. Sterritt, R., Hinchey, M.G.: Biologically-inspired concepts for self-managing ubiquitous and pervasive computing environments. In: WRAC-II, 2nd NASA/IEEE Workshop on Radical Agent Concepts, Sept. 2005, Greenbelt, MD. LNCS, vol. 3825. Springer, Berlin (2005)
24. Sterritt, R., Hinchey, M.G.: Engineering ultimate self-protection in autonomic agents for space exploration missions. In: IEEE Workshop on the Engineering of Autonomic Systems (EASe 2005) at 12th Ann. IEEE Int. Conf. Engineering of Computer Based Systems (ECBS 2005), Greenbelt, MD, USA, pp. 506–511. IEEE Comput. Soc., Los Alamitos (2005)
25. Sterritt, R., Hinchey, M.G.: SPAACE: Self-properties for an autonomous and autonomic computing environment. In: Software Engineering Research and Practice (SERP'05), Las Vegas, NV. CREA Press, Gent (2005)
26. Sterritt, R., Hinchey, M.G.: Biologically-inspired concepts for autonomic self-protection in multiagent systems. In: Safety and Security in Multiagent Systems: Research Results from 2004–2006, pp. 330–341. Springer, Berlin (2009)
27. Truszkowski, W.F., Hinchey, M.G., Rash, J.L., Rouff, C.A.: NASA's swarm missions: the challenge of building autonomous software. IT Prof. **6**(5), 47–52 (2004)
28. Truszkowski, W.F., Hinchey, M.G., Rash, J.L., Rouff, C.A.: Autonomous and autonomic systems: a paradigm for future space exploration missions. IEEE Trans. Syst. Man Cybern., Part C, Appl. Rev. **36**(3), 279–291 (2006)

Chapter 9
Dealing with Complexity in Agent-Oriented Software Engineering: The Importance of Interactions

Joaquin Peña, Renato Levy, Mike Hinchey, and Antonio Ruiz-Cortés

9.1 Introduction

Complexity has been one of the main problems that science and industry has dealt with from the beginning of the industrial world. It prevents us from understanding and controlling reality, and as a result, significant effort of many scientists and practitioners have been expended on conquering it, with the aim of finally, understanding and controlling our world.

Complexity has been studied by researchers in many fields, ranging from the Social Sciences to Physics, and of course, Software Engineering. But in all of these fields, researchers agree that complexity is caused by the interaction between the parts that conform a system (see Sect. 9.2 for further details). Complex systems expose a behavior that cannot be predicted since it is the consequence of a long chain of cause-effects (interactions) where a small change in a component of the systems affects many others, thus amplifying its effect. This results in an overall behavior of the system—also called macro-level behavior—which cannot be explained by the behavior exposed by each of its component parts, its micro-level behavior. For example, an ant colony is able to feed and protect itself forming a sophisticated social system while the behavior of individual ants remains quite simple, most of the time consisting just of interacting with other ants by following trails of pheromones left by other individuals.

If these ants didn't interact by means of pheromones, the emergent behavior would not be possible, and thus, we would have removed complexity. So, in order to address complexity full-on, we must focus our efforts on studying the interactions, to subsequently understand how the composition of these interactions brings us to the macro-level behavior.

However complexity does not always appear at the same level. There are systems with higher levels of complexity and systems with lower ones, ranging from com-

J. Peña (✉)
University of Seville, Seville, Spain
e-mail: joaquinp@us.es

M. Hinchey, L. Coyle (eds.), *Conquering Complexity*,
DOI 10.1007/978-1-4471-2297-5_9, © Springer-Verlag London Limited 2012

plicated systems, to complex systems, to chaotic systems (see Sect. 9.4 for further details). The level of complexity of a system, however, is not a property derived from the structure and behavior of the system and its parts, but it depends significantly on the tools that we use to study them. For instance, the *computational complexity* for many algorithms is smaller when using a multi-tape or inductive Turing machines than when using a Turing machines with a single tape.

The use of appropriate software engineering tools can open the possibility of understanding and controlling systems that are seen as complex with current tools, but can be designed as merely complicated with the proper ones [27].

Among these tools, the first must be to focus modelling efforts on the main source of complexity—interactions—and not on structural properties as is commonly done in the Software Engineering community, where UML class diagrams or component diagrams are the most commonly used modelling tools.

Hence, we must pay special attention to interactions when developing software systems, but especially so when addressing Multi-Agent Systems (MASs). This focus is possible based on the premise, accepted by researchers of human organizations [23], and later by researchers in the field of agent technology, that an organization can be observed from two different viewpoints: functional/interaction and structural. Roughly speaking, the model of the functional organization is composed of roles and interactions while the model of the structural organization is composed of agents and interactions. Despite their close relationship, both types of organization views can be modelled independently. This fact allows designers to model the interaction process while ignoring the organizational structure until it is clearly understood how it operates. This modelling process reduces the complexity of models to be managed at the early stages of the software process and eases the comprehension of complex behaviors (see Sect. 9.3 for further details on modelling in terms of interactions).

Once we can address the problem in terms of interactions, we find new problems. For example, the number of interactions to be designed may be huge, and the combination of them required until reaching the required macro-level behavior difficult. To address this, in Sects. 9.5, 9.6, 9.7, and 9.8 we present the main principles we can apply in this situation: abstraction, decomposition, composition, reuse, and automation. All of these can be applied to deal with complexity, but we also need guidelines that help us to apply them systematically depending on the kind of system we face. These guidelines and the software process that can be followed to apply these principles systematically are presented in Sect. 9.9. In general, two approaches can be used: a top-down software process where we start at the desired macro-level and we systematically refine models by applying abstraction and decomposition principles; and bottom-up, where we start at the micro-level and we apply systematically composition and abstraction until we reach the desired macro-level behavior.

In addition, in order to show how to apply each principle and how they must be combined to systematically engineer a complex MAS, we employ a case study on what has traditionally been seen as a complex system: an Ant Colony. As a result, we end up showing how this system can be modelled, linking the macro-level behavior with the micro-level behavior systematically from a software engineering point-of-view.

9.2   Related Work on Focusing on Interactions as the Source of Complexity

Several authors agree that the complexity of MASs is a consequence of their interactions [17, 24]: *Complexity is caused by the collective behavior of many basic interacting agents.*

In fact, many authors point out that the complexity of MASs is the consequence of those interactions among agents, and that these interactions can vary at execution time, and cannot be predicted thoroughly at design time, viz., emergent behavior. The reasons for the emergence can be traced to two features present in MASs: self-adaptation, and self-organization [13, pp. 20–21], [17, 24]. It is important to observe that this capability of demonstrating emergent behavior is the key factor that drove us to implement MAS solutions in the first place, since this key capability is essential to address solutions to the targeted domains.

The importance of interactions has been already established in the agent literature as well as in several other fields. In the field of software engineering many authors have seen interactions as a source of complexity, and thus, many solutions has been proposed for dealing with it (see also Chaps. 1, 7, 8, and 15). For example, Larman et al. in [21] presents a set of principles proposed by other authors, from which, many of them focus on reducing the coupling, that is to say, the interactions, between different part of the system, namely Demeter's Law, Liskov's Principle, GRASPs Low Coupling, Indirection, Protected Variations, etc.

In addition, some advanced Object-Oriented Software Engineering approaches, e.g., [32, 35], even traditional sociology, already present a predominant role regarding structural features to interactions, to such a point that all the modelling process is focused on them.

OOram [32] is a good example of an Object-Oriented approach where the whole development cycle is focused on interactions. OOram's authors state that the main advantages of focusing on interactions is the improvement of reuse, traceability and the ability to cope with complexity [31].

Furthermore, in sociology, interactions have been also emphasized by important authors such as the German sociologist Max Weber. Weber in his concept of *ideal bureaucracy* emphasizes the form, or in other words, the interrelationships between the members of an organization. In 1988, Reenskaug, the author of OOram, stated in [31] that object-orientation was born at the hand of Weber. In this reference, Reenskaug concluded that object-oriented methodologies must focus on interactions.

In addition, this fact is also ratified by the research done in other mature fields: (i) in the component world, Szyperski and D'Souza also emphasized the importance of focusing on interactions instead of architecture (structure in MAS) in complex systems [34, p. 124], [6]; (ii) in the distributed field, several authors has also favored approaches that focus on interactions, i.e., Francez who highlight the importance of modelling complex interactions as a singleton and who also work on functional groups of interacting elements [12]; (iii) the latest version of UML also provides modelling artifacts to perform interaction-centered modelling, emphasizing and improving the role concept compared to previous versions.

9.3 The Main Tool for Dealing with Complexity: Modelling the Problem in Terms of Interactions

Given that interactions are the main source of complexity, we conclude that [27]:

if we want to conquer complexity of MASs, we must focus the modelling process on them

In observing any MAS, we can say that no agent is an island, and thus, every MAS has the potential to become a "complex system". Since agents are limited to some environment and have limited abilities, complex problems are usually solved by a set of agents [4]. Hence, an organization represents a group of agents formed in the system in order to get benefits from one to another in a collaborative or competitive manner.

Therefore, a sub-organization emerges only when some kind of interaction between its participants exists, either through direct communication by means of speech acts or through the environment. The structure of an organization is underlined by the nature of their interactions; hence it is vital to clearly understand the interactions within a MAS system in order to determine its sub-organizations.

The Organization of the Agents in a MAS can be observed from two different points of views [3, 8, 36]:

The interaction point of view: it describes the organization by the set of interactions between its roles. The interaction view corresponds to the functional point of view.
The structural point of view: it describes the agents of the system and how they are distributed into sub-organizations, groups, and teams. In this view, agents are also organized into hierarchical structures showing the social architecture of the system.

The former is called the *Acquaintance Organization*, and the later is called the *Structural Organization*. Both views are intimately related, but they show the organization from radically different points of view.

Since any structural organization must include interactions between its agents in order to function, it is safe to say that the acquaintance organization is always contained in the structural organization. Therefore, if we determine first the acquaintance organization, and we define the constraints required for the structural organization, a natural map is formed between the acquaintance organization and the corresponding structural organization. This is the process of assigning roles to agents [36]. Thus, we can conclude that any acquaintance organization can be modelled orthogonally to its structural organization [20].

In Fig. 9.1, we present a simple version of the manufacturing pipeline example presented in [36, p. 10]. In this example, each stage is performed by an agent and the main requirement is that the speed of all stages is coordinated. A set of roles and interactions between them is implied in the Acquaintance Organization. In the structural organization, these roles can be structured to form several organizational structures. For example, as shown in Fig. 9.1, we can map the acquaintance organization into a plain structure, a hierarchical structure, and so on. In addition, starting the analysis with a certain organizational structure in mind (by means of agents), even if based on a real organization, will drive the deployment of the MAS. Consequently, the initial subdivision in interactions and roles may not be optimal.

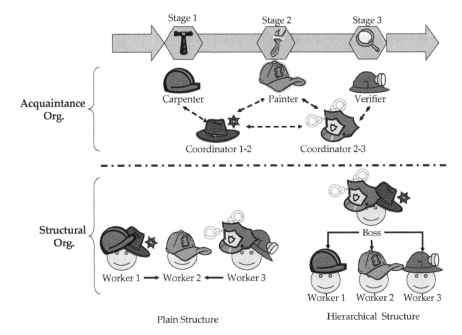

Fig. 9.1 Acquaintance vs. structural organization

Real life organizations are known to present less then optimal structures. The presence of such organizational mistakes has been well studied in economics [23], hence the field of operational research. Using the real life organization as the initial drive for the MAS system without further consideration will mimic its mistakes and may lead to some important misconstructions in terms of agent systems. Some of the common errors that can be induced are: agents coordinated by more than one agent, agents introduced to cover the relations between several sub-organizations, redundant agents with the same profile placed in different sub-organizations, etc.

As we show later, since interactions are the main source of complexity, we should not bother about organization structure at the initial analysis. This approach facilitates the process of understanding the complex behavior of a MAS and minimizes structural mistakes. Thus, when we consider the relationship between real organizations and their constraints in the system architecture, we must abstract the organization and let it be modelled by means of roles and interactions during the analysis phase. Later, these roles can be mapped into concrete agents and structured as the real organization trying to fit the real life organization and trying to minimize structural mistakes.

Interactions and role-to-role relationships are therefore the primary concept of the engineering process of MASs and structural organization arises because of them.

To exemplify these concepts and the tools for conquering complexity, we are going to use a typical case study of an emergent system: the ant colony. An ant colony is defined as a huge number of autonomous agents defined independently. There are many definitions of ant colonies. We have selected the one given by StarLogo.[1] The ants in this implementation follow the set of rules below [24]:

1. Wander randomly.
2. If food is found, take a piece back to the colony and leave a trail of pheromones that evaporates over time; then go back to rule 1.
3. If a pheromone trail is found, follow it to the food and then go to rule 2.

In the emergent behavior that appears at the macro-level of an ant colony, the interactions between ants are the key concept. Notice that if ants move randomly without interacting among each other, no emergent behavior appears. Given this fact, if we were able to put together all ants in a colony and compose them to find out their interdependencies, we could provide a macro-level model of the colony.

To perform this model, where interactions are the main feature of interest, we must focus on the acquaintance organization. Ants are designed to pursue two goals: "search for food" and "carry food home". Considering both functional requirements, two kinds of ants appear, that is to say, ants playing two different roles: *explorer* and *carrier*. An *explorer* behaves as follows:

1. Wanders randomly.
2. If a pheromone trail is found, follows it, and go to rule 4.
3. If food is found directly, go to rule 4.
4. Becomes a *carrier* ant.

A *carrier* should behave as follows:

1. Takes a piece of food back to the colony.
2. Leaves a trail of pheromones that evaporates over time.
3. Becomes an *explorer* ant.

In addition, we can find two more roles representing the environment. In the ants' environment we can find the *ground* and the *anthill* as significant from the interaction point of view. Hence, we can divide the environment into two roles, one for each of them. We can observe that ants interact with these roles by means of pheromone trails, which are used to communicate the food position.

9.4 Characterizing Complexity

Although in Sect. 9.2, we show that interactions are seen as the main source of complexity in MASs, a large MAS is usually composed of many parts which do not present the same features. Some parts of a MAS could be fully predictable not presenting any emergent feature, while some other parts of the same MAS could be highly complex presenting a high-degree of self-adaptation and self-organization. In the field of enterprise organization, Snowden and Kurtz recognize this fact [33].

---

[1] The StarLogo definition is available here: http://education.mit.edu/starlogo/samples/ants.htm.

Fig. 9.2 Complexity and predictability

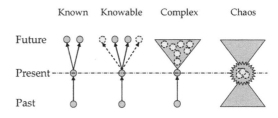

These authors divide an organization into the following domains whose main features are summarized in Fig. 9.2:

(1) *Ordered Domain*: Stable cause and effect relationships exist. In this domain, the sequence of events/actions of the organization can be established as a cause/effect chain. It represents the predictable part of the system. This domain is further divided into:
 (i) *Known Domain*: In this domain, every relationship between cause and effect is known. The part of a MAS in this domain is clearly predictable and can be easily modelled.
 (ii) *Knowable Domain*: This is the domain in which, while stable cause and effect relationships exist, they may not be fully known. In general, relationships are separated over time and space in chains that are difficult to fully understand. The key issue is whether or not we can afford the time and resources to move from the knowable to the known domain. In Fig. 9.2 this is represented by a higher number of future directions given a certain present state.
(2) *Un-ordered*: This domain presents unstable cause and effect relationships between interactions in the system. It represents the unpredictable part of the system. This domain is divided into:
 (i) *Complex Domain*: There are cause and effect relationships between the agents, but both the number of agents and the number of relationships defy categorization or analytic techniques. Relationships between cause and effect exist but they are not predictable. This domain presents retrospective coherence. That is to say, coherence can be only established by analyzing the past history of the system. Unfortunately, future directions, although coherent, cannot be predicted. In Fig. 9.2, the past events/actions can be understood as a single chain of cause/effects, but when we try to extrapolate and predict future changes the solution space is too wide to be analyzed.
 (ii) *Chaos Domain*: There are no perceivable relationships between cause and effect, and the system is turbulent; we do not have the response time to investigate change. Despite some previous work in this area, chaotic domains are still out of reach from the point of control theory. Agents systems have been used to model such domains, but strictly limited to simulation.

The Santa Fe Institute[2] define complexity as *"the condition of the universe that is integrated and yet too rich and varied for us to understand in simple common ways.*

---

[2]The Santa Fe Institute's webpage is here: http://www.santafe.edu/.

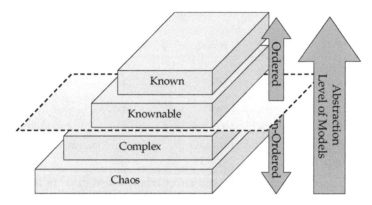

Fig. 9.3 Domain of a problem depending on the abstraction level of models

We can understand many parts of the universe in these ways, but the larger more intricately related phenomena can only be understood by principles and patterns; not in detail."

As the previous fact shows, problems in the complex or chaos domains can be only understood by principles and patterns that summarize their features and omit details; that is to say, that use abstract models. We do not have to know all the details of a problem, but the level of detail needed depends on our purpose. For example, the weather report can predict the temperatures, rain, and so forth, accurately enough for our daily life purposes: for example, to decide whether to pick up the umbrella or not. The model used to predict the weather can be classified in the known domain, but not the weather itself, which is so far chaotic. Depending on our purpose when studying a certain problem, we may need more or fewer details.

Consequently, we can introduce another dimension in the categorization of complexity done in the Cynefin framework: the level of abstraction of models as we have depicted in Fig. 9.3 [33]. Thus, depending on the level of abstraction with which we observe a MAS, each subpart of the model can be categorized in the known domain, using the highest level of abstraction, or even in the chaos domain, using the lowest level of abstraction.

9.4.1 Characterization of Interaction Complexity

Similarly, the complexity level of an interaction depends on the level of abstraction in which its features regarding emergence are observed. This principle can be visualized by the interaction categorization shown in Fig. 9.4.

The complexity of an interaction, or set of interactions, depends on their nature and on the effort taken in understanding its details, such as, their predictability and flexibility, and their level of abstraction. Our proposed interaction categorization is based in the space defined by these two axes. Figure 9.4 shows the classification of interactions in three categories: known, knowable, and complex interactions.

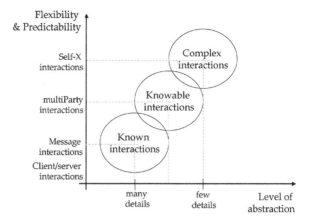

Fig. 9.4 Proposed interactions taxonomy regarding complexity

Known interactions are the least flexible; they do not present emergence, and all their details can be identified. Complex interactions present a higher degree of flexibility and can only be described with higher-level patterns emphasizing most important details. Knowable interactions represent a middle point between both of them.

In addition, agents undertaking complex interactions may present a high degree of autonomy, proactivity, reactivity, and social abilities. The further a subpart of an agent system moves from known into complex interactions the further its abilities, as described above, are intensified. We must observe that the need to describe (and generate) complex behavior from simpler constructs was the reason that drove us to agent based systems in the first place; therefore our goal, must be to describe the system as it is perceived (complex), and increase details until the desired behaviors can be synthesized.

9.5 Principles to Deal with Complexity

In [17], Jennings adapts to agency the three main principles for managing complexity proposed by Booch in the OO context [1]: Abstraction, Decomposition and Organization/Hierarchy[3]:

- *Abstraction*: is based on defining simplified models of the systems that emphasize some details while avoiding others. It is interesting since it limits the designer's scope of interest and the attention can be focused on the most important details at a given time.
- *Decomposition*: is based on the principle of "divide and conquer". It helps to limit the designer's scope to a portion of the problem.

---

[3]Notice that hereafter we call it *Composition* in order to differentiate it from the organization term in AOSE.

Fig. 9.5 Abstraction
principle

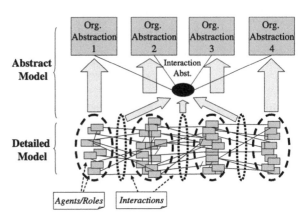

• *Composition*: consists of identifying and managing the inter-relationships between the various subsystems in the problem. It makes it possible to group together various basic agents or organizations and treat them as higher-level units
of analysis. It also provides means of describing the high-level relationships between several units.

In addition, automation and reuse have been presented as two important principles to overcome complexity [6, 19]:

• *Automation*: Automating the modelling process results in lower complexity of
models and reduces effort and errors. Some procedures must definitely be carried
out based on the judgment of the human modeller. However, some steps can be
performed using automatic techniques to transform models which can be carried
out by a software tool.
• *Reuse*: Reuse is based on using previous knowledge in designing MASs. It saves
modellers from redesigning some parts of the system and avoids errors, thus
achieving lower complexity of models. Reuse involves processes, modelling artifacts, techniques, guidelines, and models of previous projects.

However, these authors do not focus on managing the main source of complexity,
as we do in this chapter. In the following, we detail each of the previous principles.

9.6 Abstraction

Abstraction consists of defining simplified models of the systems that emphasize
some details, while avoiding others. The power of abstraction comes from limiting
the designer's scope of interest, allowing the attention to be focused on the most
important details. Abstraction can be applied to interactions that fall in the complex
and knowable domains, enabling us to abstract from how emergence can be obtained
until the designer is ready to address the issue.

As depicted in Fig. 9.5, we can apply abstraction to produce a simple model
of a complex acquaintance organization where most relevant interaction patterns

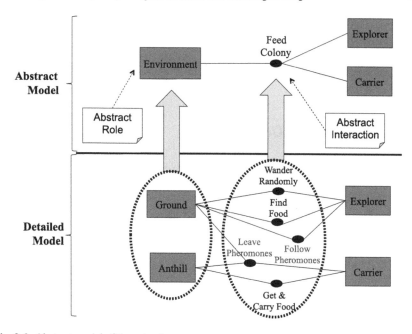

Fig. 9.6 Abstract model of the ant colony

and members of the organization can be abstracted until we bring the model to the known domain. In this model, most relevant patterns of interaction are abstractedly represented, while less important relationships, or even internal details of relevant interaction patterns, are omitted. Abstract interaction patterns, i.e., complex interactions, hide flexibility and emergence of interactions, which take place at lower levels of abstraction.

Consequently, there are two main modelling artifacts, abstractions that include the tools to perform simplified models [17, 19]: organization and interaction abstractions.

First, *organizational abstractions* represent how a system goal or several of them are achieved by a group of roles/agents. Many authors have worked on recursive definitions of agents and organizations, e.g., [2, 7, 9, 14–16, 26].

Secondly, but more importantly, *interaction abstractions* represent a set of interactions between any number of agents/roles. Many authors have proposed these abstractions, e.g., the protocols of Gaia [36], the interactions of MESSAGE [3], or joint intentions in the Belief-Desire-Joint-Intention Architecture [18].

If we consider our case study, the ant colony, we can derive a very abstract model, shown in Fig. 9.6. As shown in the figure, we provide an abstract model where we only consider the roles used by ants to interact, and just one interaction that abstracts all the relationships that takes part between the ground, the anthill, the explorers and the carriers. Given this model, we can observe just the amount of food available in the environment, the probability of finding food depending on the size of the ground, and the mean speed to find and carry food, all of them attributes of the roles involved, to provide a model that ensures that our system operates within the requirements of the system at the macro-level.

Notice that this model is simpler than the one performed based on the structural organization where we should have modelled every ant in the colony.

9.7 Composition and Decomposition

Composition and Decomposition help us to merge or separate interactions and models in order to focus just on a part of the system in order to study it in isolation. In addition, when abstraction is applied to interactions, key for dealing with complexity, these principles help us also to decrease or increase the level of abstraction by dividing an interaction into several or by grouping several interactions into one. These tools are crucial for transiting from complex to knowable or known interactions, and thus understanding complexity.

9.7.1 Decomposition

Excessively large problems may become unmanageable. The decomposition principle helps us to divide large problems and their elements into smaller, more manageable chunks. Decomposition consists of the "divide and conquer" principle, helping to limit the designer's scope to a portion of the problem. Regarding interactions, it may help to decompose complex and knowable interactions into finer grain interactions. These finer grain interactions can be augmented with details, which cannot be applied when more abstract interactions are managed. Hence, using decomposition, the interactions obtained can be implemented with less effort.

Decomposition techniques can be applied to the main abstractions: interactions or organizational models, based on roles, organizations, or agents. On the one hand, as depicted in Fig. 9.7, interaction abstraction can be decomposed to observe them from a lower level of abstraction. The main approach to decompose interactions consists of providing an abstract modelling artifact that can be refined by means of finer grain interaction abstraction, or modelling artifacts designed to provide lower levels of details, such as AUML sequence diagrams where abstract interactions are decomposed into messages-based models [25].

On the other hand, an organizational model that becomes too large and complex can be also decomposed into several models. This allows each sub-problem to be studied in isolation, ignoring the complexity derived from the interactions between sub-problems. Notice also that agents can be indeed decomposed. The materialization of decomposition of agents can be found in the "Role" concept. As depicted in Fig. 9.7, when a complex organization, formed by agents, is decomposed to extract some functional aspect, their agents must also be decomposed to extract only the part that is related with the functionality we desire to observe. Each of these

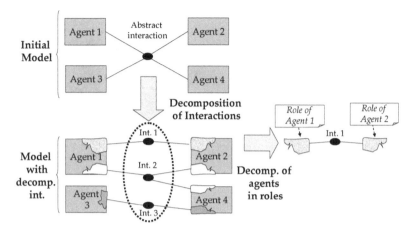

Fig. 9.7 Decomposition principle

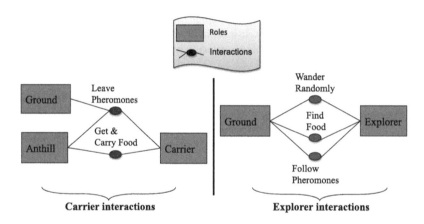

Fig. 9.8 Decomposed models of the ants colony

parts represents the role that the agent plays in the achievement of that functionality, permitting us to observe the acquaintance organization of the system.

For example, we can derive several models of our case study in order to study each of them separately. As shown in Fig. 9.8, we provide two models: one, on the left of the figure, where we can observe the interactions between the carrier and the environment, and another, on the right of the figure, where the interactions between the explorer and the environment are shown. The designer can focus, for example, on how the explorer may find food by means of wandering over the ground until finding it, or by finding a pheromone trail that can follow until reaching the food. In this way, the designer can focus on this problem not taking into account how carriers do their work.

Fig. 9.9 Composition
principle

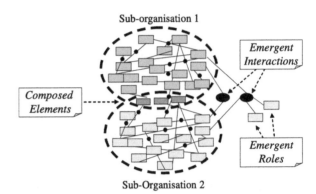

9.7.2 Composition

Composition consists of identifying and managing the inter-relationships between the various subsystems in the problem. It makes it possible to group together various basic components and treat them as higher-level units of analysis. Composition makes it possible to describe the high-level interactions between several units. Composition helps to discover subtle interactions between several sub-organizations of the MAS.

In a sense, composition is the required mechanism in order to recreate the abstract complex interactions from their simpler components. In addition, the composition of acquaintance in a sub-organization can be used as the means to build the structural organization. As the roles of an agent are fused, we can draw a "black box" and overlook its internals based only on the interfaces (roles) that cross the boundaries of the box. This process will also help to view a group of agents as a single unit in itself, and help build the hierarchical structure of the organization.

Figure 9.9 shows that the emergent features that appear at the macro-level are a consequence of the interactions between agents and sub-organizations. Consequently, when several parts of the system are modelled in isolation, we are ignoring the interdependencies between them. That is to say, the whole is greater than the sum of its parts [24]. The lost elements may contain crucial features of the system. For example, the two models of our case study presented in Fig. 9.8 can be composed, but when doing so, we discover that the interactions *Follow Pheromones* and *Leave Pheromones* are related. This drives us to discover a new interaction that represents the fact that carriers communicate the path to find food to explorers. Figure 9.10 shows result of the composition of those models.

The advantage of modelling both problems in isolation abstracts these interactions and makes the modelling process easier. It also improves the reuse of models, since their interdependencies would limit the reuse of a combined solution only into systems where both conditions occur. The same principle applies to role composition. Roles are artifacts that can be combined. These artifacts may result in composed roles, or agents playing several roles. When agents are defined as a result of composition, the definition of a structural organization begins to be formed.

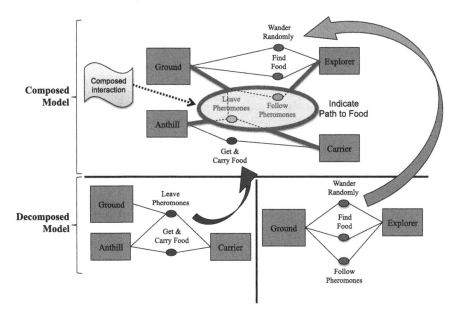

Fig. 9.10 Composition and decomposition of ants case study

9.7.3 Techniques for Decomposition and Composition

Decomposition and composition of the main modelling abstractions requires techniques and guidelines to determine feasible separations and to perform them. There are two main approaches to establish where to draw the limit.

- *Functional Decomposition/Goal-based Decomposition*: One of the most direct ways of determining the frontiers between separable/composable parts is through functional decomposition. As agents, and sub-organizations, are designed to achieve their design objectives, a functional subdivision of the system can be easily used. Functional decomposition, as Jennings argues, and Meyer in the OO field [22], is more intuitive and easier to produce than that based upon data and objects. Using this technique, we can analyze an interaction to observe which sub-goals can be found on it, and determine which decomposed interactions can be found inside it or which interactions can be grouped to pursue a higher level goal. Notice that this can be also used to divide a big role model into several smaller problems or vice-versa. Notice that this kind of decomposition/composition is the one used in Fig. 9.10.
- *Dependency Composition/Decomposition*: The other main approach to decomposition/composition is that based on analyzing dependencies between modelling abstractions [3, 36]. Interactions between roles in a MAS are performed to solve small parts of the problem. Each of these interactions modifies the state of the roles participating in it, which is used later to perform further interactions. Thus, we can say that the results of an interaction are used by the rest of interactions.

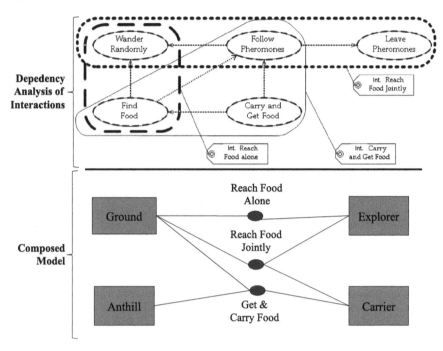

Fig. 9.11 Intermediate abstraction model of the ant colony by dependency analysis

Given that, we can analyze the dependencies between the state of each role and its interactions to find feasible decompositions or compositions. This kind of analysis has been studied in the distributed systems field where Francez et al. propose various techniques to decompose multiparty interactions [11, 12, 28].

This kind of analysis can also be applied to organizational abstractions. As agents/roles are designed to achieve their design objectives and are limited to a specific environment, sometimes the nature of the problem requires working with part of the environment and the capabilities of other agents/roles. Consequently, the achievement of certain goals is determined by dependencies with other agents [4, 5]. This shows how roles can be grouped/separated to form organizations and it is also useful to determine how they can be composed/decomposed.

As shown in Fig. 9.10, the model at the bottom is the one obtained directly from the problem description in terms of the behavior of each individual ant observed from an interaction point of view. Given that model, we can analyze the dependencies between interactions in the less abstract view, shown at the top of Fig. 9.11, to build a more abstract view of the same system obtained by means of interaction composition. From more detailed interactions, we obtain just three of them that abstract the interactions between the explorer and carrier ants with the environmental roles "anthill" and "ground". This view is closer to the macro level of the system.

9.8 Reuse and Automation Principles

Automating the modelling process results in lower complexity of models and reduces effort and errors [19]. Some procedures must be carried out that rely on the judgment of the human modellers. However, in recent years the technique that better represents reuse is model driven engineering (MDE) whose goal is to automatically produce a system from requirements, analysis, and/or design models [10].

Reuse is based on using previous knowledge in designing MASs. It saves modellers from redesigning some parts of the system and avoids errors, thus achieving lower complexity of models [6, 19]. Catalysis and OOram are specially concerned about reuse and, as many authors in the agent field [20], present the role concept as the most appropriate tool to reuse functionality.

Reuse is strongly related to the bottom-up software process. When a set of already developed agents or roles are available, e.g., stored in a repository, they can be reused to cover some of the required aspects of the current project. In these situations, we have a highly detailed model of the micro-level of the part of the system implemented by reuse. From the interactions of these reused agents/roles, the required macro-level may or may not emerge. Using a bottom-up approach has proven to be appropriate to transit from the micro-level functionality of reused assets to the macro-functionality required, cf. *Assemble process* in [6, pp. 512–513].

Regarding reuse, the main techniques appearing in the literature are MAS Product Lines, which focus on massive reuse by analyzing common and variable features of MASs to produce a system with the desired features by reusing common features and adding, as automatically as possible, variable features [29].

9.9 Applying the Principles—Software Process

Although abstract models can provide us with a coherent and simple model, abstract models do not offer enough detail to reach a code model of the system. This problem has been solved in traditional software engineering by maintaining a set of system models structured in several abstraction layers. That is to say, a model of the same problem that is described using a different level of detail. Layered models are presented by Karageorgos as one of the main factors for reducing model complexity [19]. In a layered model, top layers show us abstract models that provide an overview of the system. On the other hand, bottom layers give us the means for detailing top layers, bringing our model nearer to a code model.

As modelling using several abstraction layers usually produces a large amount of models, traceability models are especially important to properly manage such an amount of models as D'Souza shows in [6].

9.9.1 Top-Down and Bottom-Up

In layered models, the completion of layers is usually done in an iterative way where abstract layers are refined to produce bottom layers and bottom layers are abstracted to produce top layers. That is to say, modelling in a top-down approach or in a bottom-up approach [30].

Top-down approaches correlate with reductionism, that is, designing by starting at the macro-level [13, 24]. Development starts with abstract models of the macro-level of the system. This model is refined until all details are discovered. This approach has some disadvantages. The interactions of systems studied with this approach should be fully known and fully predictable since, otherwise, we will not be able to discover all details. In addition, it misses the flexibility and change adaptation obtained in bottom-up designs.

Bottom-up approaches correlate with emergence, that is, designing by starting at the micro-level [13, 24]. In emergence, development starts at the micro-level defining a set of simple agents. Later, in subsequent layers, these agents are successively grouped into sub-organizations, and the latter into organizations, until reaching the macro-level of the system. This approach also has some advantages and disadvantages. It does not require modelling all interactions in the system since agents can be provided with the expertise necessary to decide their interactions with others at run-time, and thus, the macro-level need not be modelled. However, it requires tuning the macro-level behavior by changes in the micro-level. Bottom-up is also a crucial tool for reuse since reusing a set of agents to implement a new system requires reverse engineering to ensure that the goals of the system are met (cf. Sect. 9.8).

We cannot state categorically that one is better than the other; it depends on the requirements of the software that we intend to develop. Notice also that not all sub-parts of a system usually fall in the same Cynefin domain, but tend to spread out in all of them. The best choice in this situation is to apply both, and find a trade-off between them, as Pressman recommends in [30] and Karageorgos in [19].

Finally, note that decomposition and composition can be used to assist top-down and bottom-up approaches, respectively, as we show in the following sections.

9.9.2 Top-Down Refinement by Means of Decomposition

Decomposition is presented as a principle that supports reductionism, that is to say, a top-down software process. Abstraction mechanisms may result insufficient when we model large and complex MASs since abstract models provide us with an overview of the problem, but not the details. In these cases, we can decompose abstract models to obtain a set of simpler ones which can be easily refined [6]. Using decomposition in this way, we can maintain several layers of abstraction where higher-level layers abstractly represent complex problems and bottom layers store detailed descriptions of sub-parts of top layer models obtained by decomposition.

9.9.3 Bottom-Up Abstraction by Means of Composition

Composition is the principle that mainly supports emergence, that is to say, it supports a bottom-up software process. We can find two different ways of applying emergence in the literature.

On the one hand, in [17], Jennings follows an emergence approach. He presents bottom-up as a process that is automatically performed by agents at runtime. As shown previously, they draw MASs as highly decomposed structures where problems are "automatically" solved by agents or sub-organizations and where interactions between agents/organizations appear naturally at runtime. Thus, Jennings does not argue for engineers to apply a systematic bottom-up software process to model the system, but he leaves it to be accomplished by the system itself. However, this automation is not always possible since the degree of unpredictability exposed by this kind of designs may be not acceptable for some domain applications, e.g., real-time systems or critical business applications.

On the other hand, a set of models obtained by the decomposition of sub-parts of the system offers a tour of the system specification but does not offer the big picture of it, that is to say, the macro-level behavior [6]. The same problem occurs when the system is modelled as a set of autonomous, self-organizing agents, where the emergent behavior of the system is not explicitly modelled. Designers/implementers must be able to get an overview of it and, at least, have an approximation of the behavior of the system at the macro-level. Composition can be used to get this overview. We can compose finest-grain models to represent, in conjunction with the use of abstraction, the most relevant features in a simple higher-level model and to discover the emergent features that appear [6, 32]. Hence, model composition is an important tool to discover such elements when isolated problems have been properly studied. This reduces the complexity that we are concerned with. Usually, problems to be composed have been previously studied, making the construction of the composite model less complex, since when modelling it, we have to manage only the interrelationships between models and not the whole problem.

9.9.4 Guidelines for Deciding Between Top-Down and Bottom-Up

We can use three criteria to decide which approach must be applied: (i) the nature of the requirements of the system; (ii) the complexity domain in which each part of the system falls; and, (iii) the available set of reusable agents and models.

Firstly, requirements can be on the macro-level or on the micro-level. On the one hand, typical domain applications, where most requirements can be localized at the macro-level are information systems since requirements show how the overall system should work. On the other hand, typical systems where requirements deal with micro-level are simulation systems. In these systems, the requirements show

Table 9.1 Summary of criteria for applying top-down and bottom-up

Criteria		Requirements		
		Macro	Micro	Macro & Micro
Complexity Domain	Known	↓	↑	↕
	Knowable	↓	↑	↕
	Complex	↓ / ?	↑ / ?	↕

Criteria With reuse		Requirements		
		Macro	Micro	Macro & Micro
Complexity Domain	Known	↕	↑	↕
	Knowable	↕	↑	↕
	Complex	↕	↑/?	↕

Top-down	Both	Bottom-up	Uncertain Success
↓	↕	↑	?

us how individual agents must work, in order to later study the macro-level of the system.

Secondly, as we showed in Sect. 9.4, a system usually presents parts in several complexity domains. Depending on the domain that each part falls in, a different software process will fit better with its features.

Thirdly, the level of reuse in a certain project affects the software process since some agents or even organizations of agents and their respective models can be reused to reduce mistakes and time-to-market. When these assets fit with requirements, no extra work is needed.

In Table 9.1, we show a summary of these criteria. In the following, we show in which situations these criteria point to a top-down or a bottom-up approach, or to both at the same time:

- *Top-down:* must be applied in MASs where most requirements information is concerned with the macro-level. In addition, another reason to apply top-down is that the macro-level required is not usually clear in requirements documents and therefore must be refined to obtain a more accurate model.

  Whenever the requirements scope allows it, top-down should also be applied to such parts of the system that fall in the known or knowable domains since these parts can be fully analyzed by refining abstract descriptions.
- *Bottom-up:* can be used when most requirements information relates to the micro-level, since bottom-up helps us to discover how different micro-level models work together to produce the macro-level.

  Furthermore, if a repository of yet-to-be implemented agents and their models has been constructed because of previous projects, we must primarily apply bottom-up. In this kind of project, the micro-level has to be abstracted to ensure

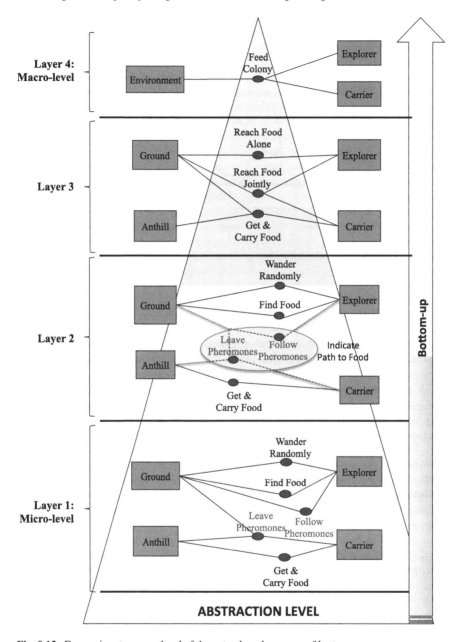

Fig. 9.12   From micro to macro-level of the ant colony by means of bottom-up

that we meet the desired macro-level and this can be done following a bottom-up approach. That is to say, models or code developed for other projects may not fit completely within the new system; thus, by means of bottom-up, we can

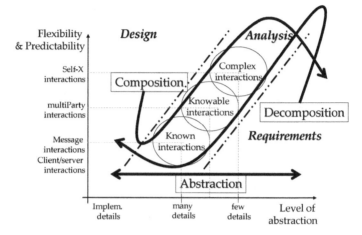

Fig. 9.13 Usage of conceptual tools to manage taxonomy complexity of interactions

integrate it and analyze to determine if the reused chunk produces the desired macro-behavior.

- *Bottom-up in conjunction with top-down:* must be applied when the system presents features that fit with both previous cases. In addition, it must be applied to the parts of the MAS that fall in the complex domain in order to bridge the gap between macro-level and micro-level. Following this process strategy, we can obtain two layered models of the MAS: one set of layered models for the macro-level and another for the micro-level. Thus, when the least abstract model of the macro-level and the most abstract model of the micro-level overlap, we bridge the gap between both levels.

Revisiting our case study, and taking into account previous guidelines, we can determine that the process that better fits with it is "bottom-up". The main reason for this is that we started with requirements at the micro-level of the system and that the macro-level behavior of it can be seen as complex using the classification provided in Sect. 9.4. In Fig. 9.12 we show all the models produced in previous sections by means of compositions of the previous layer until the macro-level behavior of the system is reached. As can be observed, the principles and techniques provided allow us to address a complex system systematically from an engineering point of view.

9.10 Conclusions

As shown, using the proper tools, namely the three principles to deal with complexity, and focusing on the source of complexity, namely interactions, a problem that can be seen as complex, such as an Ant Colony, can be analyzed systematically to perform engineering models that fall in the known domain.

We have shown the importance of interactions and we have outlined how complexity derived from interactions can be managed from an engineering perspective giving a set of guidelines. Given the findings shown in this chapter, we can summarize how these principles can be applied to transit between known, knowable, and complex interactions as shown in Fig. 9.13. As depicted, abstraction is lower for known interactions since their details can be easily modelled, while the level of abstraction required for complex interactions is higher, since they can be only understood when observed by their most important features. In addition, complex interactions modelled abstractly can be transformed into knowable and known interactions by means of decomposition. In the reverse process, known interactions, such as those found in code models, can be transformed into knowable and complex interactions by means of composition. The composition process will uncover emergent behaviors inherent to its internal components. The final resulting complex interaction can be further abstracted.

Acknowledgements   This work has been partially supported by the European Commission (FEDER) and the Spanish Government under the CICYT project SETI (TIN2009-07366), and by the Andalusian Government under the projects ISABEL (P07-TIC-2533 and TIC-5906) and THEOS (TIC-5906).

This work was supported, in part, by Science Foundation Ireland grant 03/CE2/I303_1 to Lero—the Irish Software Engineering Research Centre (www.lero.ie)

References

1. Booch, G.: Object-Oriented Design with Applications. Benjamin/Cummings, Redwood City (1990)
2. Bürckert, H.-J., Fischer, K., Vierke, G.: Teletruck: a holonic fleet management system. In: 14th European Meeting on Cybernetics and Systems Research, pp. 695–700 (1998)
3. Caire, G., Coulier, W., Garijo, F.J., Gómez-Sanz, J.J., Pavón, J., Leal, F., Chainho, P., Kearney, P.E., Stark, J., Evans, R., Massonet, P.: Agent oriented analysis using MESSAGE/UML. In: Proceedings of Agent-Oriented Software Engineering (AOSE'01), Montreal, pp. 119–135 (2001)
4. Castelfranchi, C.: Founding agent's "autonomy" on dependence theory. In: 14th European Conference on Artificial Intelligence, pp. 353–357. IOS Press, Amsterdam (2000)
5. Castelfranchi, C., Miceli, M., Cesta, A.: Dependence relations among autonomous agents. In: Demazeau, I.Y., Werner, E. (eds.) Third European Workshop on Modeling Autonomous Agents in a Multi-agent World. Decentralized AI 3. Elsevier, Amsterdam (1992)
6. D'Souza, D.F., Wills, A.C.: Objects, Components, and Frameworks with UML: The Catalysis Approach. Addison-Wesley, Reading (1999)
7. Ferber, J., Gutknecht, O.: A meta-model for the analysis and design of organizations in multi-agent systems. In: Third International Conference on Multi-agent Systems (ICMAS'98), pp. 128–135. IEEE Comput. Soc., Los Alamitos (1998)
8. Ferber, J., Gutknecht, O., Michel:, F.: From agents to organizations: an organizational view of multi-agent systems. In: Giorgini, P., Müller, J.P., Odell, J. (eds.) IV International Workshop on Agent-Oriented Software Engineering (AOSE'03). LNCS, vol. 2935, pp. 214–230. Springer, Berlin (2003)
9. Fischer, K.: Agent-based design of holonic manufacturing systems. Robot. Auton. Syst. **27**(1–2), 3–13 (1999)
10. Fischer, K., Hahn, C., Madrigal-Mora, C.: Agent-oriented software engineering: a model-driven approach. Int. J. Agent-Oriented Softw. Eng. **1**, 334–369 (2007)

11. Francez, N., Forman, I.: Synchrony loosening transformations for interacting processes. In: Baeten, J., Klop, J. (eds.) Proceedings of Concurr'91: Theories of Concurrency—Unification and Extension. LNCS, vol. 527, pp. 27–30. Springer, Amsterdam (1991)

12. Francez, N., Forman, I.: Interacting Processes: A Multiparty Approach to Coordinated Distributed Programming. Addison-Wesley, Reading (1996)

13. Fromm, J.: The Emergence of Complexity. Kassel University Press, Kassel (2004)

14. Gerber, C., Siekmann, J., Vierke, G.: Flexible autonomy in holonic multi-agent systems. In: AAAI Spring Symposium on Agents with Adjustable Autonomy (1999)

15. Gerber, C., Siekmann, J., Vierke, G.: Holonic multi-agent systems. Technical report RR-99-03, DFKI, Kaiserslautern, Germany (1999)

16. Giret, A., Botti, V.: Towards an abstract recursive agent. Integr. Comput. Aided Eng. **11**(2) (2004)

17. Jennings, N.: An agent-based approach for building complex software systems. Commun. ACM **44**(4), 35–41 (2001)

18. Jennings, N.R.: Specification and implementation of a belief-desire-joint-intention architecture for collaborative problem solving. Int. J. Intell. Coop. Inf. Syst. **2**(3), 289–318 (1993)

19. Karageorgos, A., Mehandjiev, N.: A design complexity evaluation framework for agent-based system engineering methodologies. In: Omicini, A., Petta, P., Pitt, J. (eds.) Fourth International Workshop Engineering Societies in the Agents World. LNCS, vol. 3071, pp. 258–274. Springer, Berlin (2004)

20. Kendall, E.A.: Role modeling for agent system analysis, design, and implementation. IEEE Concurr. **8**(2), 34–41 (2000)

21. Larman, C.: Applying UML and Patterns: An Introduction to Object-Oriented Analysis and Design and the Unified Process, 2nd edn. Prentice Hall, Upper Saddle River (2001)

22. Meyer, B.: Object-Oriented Software Construction. Prentice Hall, Hertfordshire (1988)

23. Mintzberg, H.: The Structuring of Organizations. Prentice Hall, Upper Saddle River (1978)

24. Odell, J.: Agents and complex systems. J. Object Technol. **1**(2), 35–45 (2002)

25. Odell, J., Parunak, H.V.D., Bauer, B.: Representing agent interaction protocols in UML. In: Proceedings of the 1th Int. Workshop on Agent-Oriented Software Engineering (AOSE'00). LNCS, vol. 1957. Springer, Limerick (2000)

26. Parunak, H.V.D., Odell, J.: Representing social structures in UML. In: Müller, J.P., Andre, E., Sen, S., Frasson, C. (eds.) Proceedings of the Fifth International Conference on Autonomous Agents, pp. 100–101. ACM Press, Montreal (2001)

27. Peña, J.: On improving the modelling of complex acquaintance organisations of agents. A method fragment for the analysis phase. PhD thesis, University of Seville (2005)

28. Peña, J., Corchuelo, R., Ruiz-Cortés, A., Toro, M.: Towards an automatic method for detecting synchrony loosening anomalies in the context of multiparty interactions. In: Actas del II taller de trabajo sobre Desarrollo de Software Preciso. VI Jornadas de Ingeniería del Software y Bases de Datos (JISBD'01), Almagro (Ciudad Real, Spain) (2001)

29. Peña, J., Hinchey, M.G., Cortés, A.R.: Multi-agent system product lines: challenges and benefits. Commun. ACM **49**(12), 82–84 (2006)

30. Pressman, R.S.: Software Engineering: A Practitioner's Approach, 2nd edn. McGraw-Hill, New York (1986)

31. Reenskaug, T.: A methodology for the design and description of complex, object-oriented systems. Technical report, Center for Industrial Research, Oslo, Norway (November 1988)

32. Reenskaug, T.: Working with Objects: The OOram Software Engineering Method. Manning Publications, Greenwich (1996)

33. Snowden, D., Kurtz, C.: The new dynamics of strategy: sense-making in a complex and complicated world. IBM Syst. J. **42**(3), 35–45 (2003)

34. Szyperski, C., Gruntz, D., Murer, S.: Component Software: Beyond Object-Oriented Programming, 2nd edn. Addison-Wesley, Reading (2002)

35. Wirfs-Brock, R., McKean, A.: Object-Oriented Design: Roles, Responsibilities, and Collaborations. Addison-Wesley, Reading (1990)

36. Zambonelli, F., Jennings, N.R., Wooldridge, M.: Developing multiagent systems: the GAIA methodology. ACM Trans. Softw. Eng. Methodol. **12**(3), 317–370 (2003)

Part III
Complexity Control: Application Areas

Chapter 10
Service-Orientation: Conquering Complexity with XMDD

Tiziana Margaria and Bernhard Steffen

10.1 Motivation

Industrial practice of application development and integration is increasingly characterized by vaguely defined but urgent IT needs. Following pressure, external (by the market or by changed regulations), or internal (by a merger, or for improvement), it is clear that things (be they products, applications, or the own IT landscape) must be changed, but how? Answering this question is typically impossible before major parts of a realization are in place. This is due to the fact that only concrete artifacts provide a sufficiently stable ground for a common understanding between the involved stakeholders. Moreover, only when the customer has a tangible understanding of the options, can he effectively criticize and decide. One observes over and over again that in today's practice this kind of criticism starts only after a first release of a system, and that it continues along the whole life cycle. This observation makes *agility a* if not *the* central requirement for industrial system design. The problem here is twofold: how to manage the time pressure with adequate early feedback to the process owners, and how to manage the evolution of the systems over a long and very heterogeneous lifetime, where further integration, repurposing, and retargeting continuously changes the requirements on the fly. To do this, we need a sort of agile and lean form of "complexity engineering" that should ideally be intrinsic in the development method and help align the needs of the business customers (the process owners—who know the '*what*') with the resulting implementation (the 'how') [31].

10.1.1 Complexity Engineering

Complexity of systems comes in very different flavors and dimension, e.g.,

- sheer size—of the solution itself or of the entities to be processed;

T. Margaria (✉)
Chair Service and Software Engineering, University of Potsdam, Potsdam, Germany
e-mail: margaria@cs.uni-potsdam.de

M. Hinchey, L. Coyle (eds.), *Conquering Complexity*,
DOI 10.1007/978-1-4471-2297-5_10, © Springer-Verlag London Limited 2012

- conceptual complexity—the difficulty to understand any potential solution;
- and heterogeneity—the problem of integrating numerous partners, (communication) technologies, tools, and devices,

all of which can be again individually distinguished in *inherent* and *actual* complexity. Here, the inherent complexity is due to the tackled problem, and cannot be reduced without changing the problem, whereas the actual complexity refers to the complexity of an actual solution, which often is much higher than the inherent complexity.

The actually *felt* complexity may still be quite a different matter: 'Divide and Conquer', or the 'Separation of Concerns' may split a global complexity into a number of aspect-specific complexities, each of which, individually, may well be comfortably tackled at different times, by different people, with different means, often exploiting powerful standard solutions. For example, designing a complex business process can be done independently of integrating the involved applications and devices, independently of managing the often thousands of corresponding process instances on a network, and in particular, independently of the construction of the Internet, without which worldwide end-to-end processes would be hardly possible.

In this chapter we want to address the importance and the role of the 'felt' complexity/ies, which of course is quite subjective: the 'felt' complexity of any system depends on the individual roles sensing it. Usually, the business process designer does not feel the complexity of the realization and of the enactment, let alone the complexity of the required infrastructure. Conversely, those responsible for the infrastructure may not feel the complexity of the business-critical End-to-End process, its legal and economic consequences, and its vital implications for the company.

The central issue for a good and informed design of complex applications is therefore a method that reconciles the subjective views and competencies of the individual stakeholders into an adequate joint communication and decision-making framework. The goal is to comfortably manage an adequate division of labor and allow to easily exploit standards and available solutions in order to minimize the felt complexity for all stakeholders.

10.1.2 Extreme Model-Driven Development

Extreme Model-Driven Development (XMDD) combines into a coherent paradigm the decisive traits taken from:

- *eXtreme programming*, for providing immediate feedback through requirement and design validation by means of model tracing, simulation, and early testing;
- *service orientation*, for virtualizing the implementation of functionality;
- *aspect orientation*, for treating crosscutting as well as role specific concerns modularly; and
- *model-driven design*, for controlling the overall development at the modeling level.

Of course, XMDD cannot reduce the inherent complexity, but it can help make it explicit and thus improve its understanding and its management. Indeed, XMDD might probably add to the inherent complexity, but with the result that the individually felt complexities are rather low, due to the leveraging of standards, the division of labor, and due to the "80/20" principle, i.e. the approach where the majority of problems can be tackled easily, resorting to standard solutions, while only the few really specific and tough problems are left for special consideration.

Consider Graphical User Interface (GUI) design: 10–20 years ago building a GUI was a major project, involving substantial programming effort and pioneering creativity—it often involved PhD level work. With today's GUI libraries even beginners can produce quite advanced standard GUIs in a matter of hours. The inherent complexity of GUI design has not changed, but the advances in the foundational technologies and standards make today the development of a standard GUI rather easy. Another example is the development of parsers or compilers: in the 1970s, writing a compiler was an art. Today most parsers and compilers are easily generated. Thus an originally major problem turned into commodity without the inherent complexity being changed. To master unchanged and even increasing inherent complexity of a system in such a way that the felt complexity of the solution is understandable, acceptable, and manageable by the different stakeholders is a matter of adequate management of the actually felt complexity: this is the design space that we need to be able to explore and adapt to during the creation of a new application and throughout its lifetime. This is a question of agility and evolution.

10.1.3 Agility and Evolution

Separation of concerns and the lowering of the actually felt complexity are particularly important when agility is required and the solution must be able to react flexibly and quickly to new requirements and changed frame conditions. This agility is particularly necessary in areas like business processes, where the ability to change may be business critical. In the aftermath of the 9/11 terrorist attacks in 2001, airlines suffered immense losses because they were unable to adapt their business processes quickly enough to the changed market conditions and demand, ending in huge operational losses and insolvencies. Of course, situations like this are special, but they happen more often than one realizes: after 9/11 the same industry suffered similar crises in the aftermath of the SARS outbreak in 2006, and the Eyjafjallajokull volcanic eruption in 2010. So, there is no doubt that business processes are under the continuous pressure of change and in demand of powerful methods to manage the corresponding process evolution.

We will therefore focus on process modeling, agility, and evolution: How can large End-to-End processes be seamlessly and immediately adapted to new needs? Here is where ideas from eXtreme Programming (XP) enter the picture, and where our One Thing Approach (OTA) has its major impact. We will show how we achieve (a) application-level control, i.e., the continuous involvement of the customer and application/business expert along the entire systems' life cycle, including software maintenance and evolution, together with (b) continuous and ongoing quality assurance with different means at different levels and phases (requirement validation, simulation, model checking, data flow analysis, testing, and monitoring), and (c) specific support to easily and non-invasively integrate new technologies, in a service-oriented way.

The key to our approach is to view the whole development process simply as a complex hierarchical and interactive decision process, where each stakeholder, including the application expert, is allowed to continuously place his/her decisions in term of constraints, and each development or evolution step can be regarded simply as a *transformation* of this set of constraints. We use constraints to describe all the pieces of knowledge and information that define and thus restrict the set of behaviors of the system. They comprise temporal constraints, loose process models, symbolic typing, as well as the definition of roles and rights. This allows one to continuously and globally monitor the consistency of the development and of the evolution process via varying forms of constraint checking.

In the remainder of the chapter we will elaborate on these ideas in more detail. Section 10.2 points to the importance of compatibility and interoperability as central meta-constraints of any system, then Sect. 10.3 summarizes the XMDD approach. Sections 10.4, 10.5 and 10.6 sketch our technical solution. Finally we will present some case studies in Sect. 10.7, before we conclude in Sect. 10.8.

10.2 Technical Hurdles: Compatibility and Interoperability

Today's systems require an unacceptable effort for deployment, which is typically caused by incompatibilities, feature interactions, and the sometimes catastrophic behavior of component upgrades, which no longer behave as expected. This gets even worse when considering heterogeneous, cross-organizational systems, whose components and interfaces typically evolve independently. Thus it is almost impossible to keep up with the increasing pace of changing market requirements.

This situation arises mainly due to the level on which systems are technically composed: even though high level languages and even model-driven development are used for component development, the system-level point of view is not yet adequately supported. In particular, the deployment of a heterogeneous systems is still a matter of assembly-level search for the reasons of incompatibility, which may be due to minimal version changes, slight hardware incompatibilities, or simply due to bugs, which come to surface only in a new, collaborative context of application. Integration testing and the quest for 'true' interoperability are major cost factors and major risks during a system implementation and deployment.

The hardware industry faced similar problems with even more dramatic consequences a decade ago: hardware is by nature far more difficult to patch, making failure of compatibility a real disaster. The trend since the late 1990s has been to move beyond VLSI towards Systems-on-a-Chip in order to guarantee larger integration in both senses: physically, by compacting complex systems on a single chip

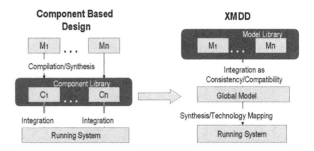

Fig. 10.1 The XMDD process

instead of physically wiring them on a board, but also conceptually, by integrating the components well before the silicon level, namely already at the design level. Rather than combining chips (the classical approach), hardware engineers started to directly combine the component's designs and to produce (in their terms, synthesize) system-level solutions that are homogeneous at the silicon level. Interestingly, they solve the problem of compatibility by moving it to a *higher level of abstraction* and going towards more homogeneous final products.

XMDD is a paradigm for application development that is conceptually closely related to the sketched SoC approach.

10.3 XMDD: Extreme Model-Driven Development

At the larger scale of system development, moving the problem of compatibility to a higher level of abstraction means moving it to the modeling level (see Fig. 10.1): rather than using the models, as is usual in the Component Based Development paradigm, just as a means of specification, which

- need to be compiled to become a 'real thing' (e.g., a component of a software library),
- must be updated (but typically are not), whenever the real thing changes, and
- typically only provide a local view of a portion or an aspect of a system,

models should be put at the center of the design activity, becoming *the* first class entities of the *global* system design process. In such an approach, as shown on the right side of Fig. 10.1,

- libraries should be established at the model level: building blocks should be (elementary) models rather than software components;
- systems should be specified by model combinations (composition, configuration, superposition, conjunction . . .), viewed as a set of constraints that the implementation needs to satisfy;
- global model combinations should be compiled (synthesized, e.g., by solving all the imposed constraints) into a homogeneous solution for a desired environment, which includes the realization of an adequate technology mapping;

- system changes (upgrades, customer-specific adaptations, new versions, etc.) should happen only (or at least primarily) at the model level, with a subsequent global recompilation (re-synthesis);
- optimizations should be kept distinct from design issues, in order to maintain the information on the structure and the design decisions independently of the considerations that lead to a particular optimized implementation.

Using XMDD—which strictly separates compatibility, migration, and optimization issues from model/functionality composition—it would be possible to overcome the problem of incompatibility between

- (global) models and (global) implementations, which is guaranteed and later-on maintained by (semi-)automatic compilation and synthesis, as well as between
- system components, paradigms, and hardware platforms: a dedicated compilation/synthesis of the considered *global* functionality for a specific platform architecture avoids the problems of incompatible design decisions for the individual components.

In essence, delaying the compilation/synthesis until all parameters are known (e.g., all compatibility constraints are available), may drastically simplify this task, as the individual parts can already be compiled/synthesized specifically for the current global context. In a good setup, this should not only simplify the integration issue (rather than having to be open for all eventualities, one can concentrate on precisely given circumstances), but also improve the efficiency of the compiled/synthesized implementations.

XMDD has the potential to drastically reduce the long-term costs due to version incompatibility, system migration and upgrading, and lower risk factors like vendor and technology dependency. Thus it helps protect investment in the software infrastructure. We are convinced that this extreme style of model-driven development will become the development style at least for mass-customized software in the future.

In particular we believe that XMDD, even though drastically different from state of the art industrial system design—which is itself driven right from the beginning by the underlying platform—will change the state of the art: technology moves so fast, and the varieties are so manifold that the classical platform-focused development will find its limits very soon.

10.4 Central Issues to be Addressed

In order to fully leverage the XMDD potential, and by this decrease the felt complexity, a number of issues need to be addressed:

- the design of adequate modeling patterns;
- the adaptation of analysis, verification, and compilation techniques and tools to the XMDD setting; and
- the realization of automatic deployment procedures.

10.4.1 Heterogeneous Landscape of Models

One of the major challenges for software engineering is that software is multi-dimensional: it comprises a number of different (loosely related) dimensions, which typically need to be modeled in different styles in order to be treated adequately. Important for simplifying the software/application development is the reduction of the complexity of this multi-dimensional space, by placing it into some standard scenario. Such reductions are typically application-specific. Besides simplifying the application development they also provide a handle for the required automatic compilation and deployment procedures.

Typical among these dimensions—also called *views*—are the following:

- The *(user) process view*, which describes the dynamic behavior of the system. How does it behave under each circumstance?
- The *architectural view*, which expresses the static structure of the software (dependencies like nesting, inheritance, and references). This should not be confused with the architectural view of the hardware platform, which may indeed be drastically different. The charm of the OO-style was that it claimed to bridge the gap to the user/process view.
- The *exception view*, which addresses the system's behavior under malicious or even unforeseen circumstances.
- The *timing view*, which captures real time aspects.
- The various *thematic views* concerned with roles, specific requirements, and other aspect-like points of view.

Of course, UML already tries to address all these facets in a unifying way. However, UML is currently rather a heterogeneous, expressive sample of languages, which lacks a clear notion of (conceptual) integration like consistency and the idea of global dynamic behavior. Such aspects are currently dealt with independently, e.g., by means of concepts like *contracts* [1] (or more generally, and more complexly, via business-rules oriented programming like e.g., in JRules.[1] The latter concepts are also not supported by systematic means for guaranteeing consistency. In contrast, XMDD views these heterogeneous specifications (consisting of essentially independent models) just as constraints which must be respected during the compilation/synthesis phase (see also [42]).

Another popular approach is Aspect Oriented Programming (AOP) [5, 13]. It has striking success stories for specific purposes (exception handling, access and timing control, insertion of assertions, etc.), but becomes rather intricate when used to solve more general problems. The idea here is to treat different aspects separately in the code, and then to weave the separate code fragments together. In general this requires a precise understanding of the weaving mechanism, which may be more complicated than programming the overall system traditionally. This is due to the fact that the claimed modularity is only in the file structure—not on the conceptual side. In other words, AOP allows one to write down the aspects separately,

---

[1] The JRules website is here: http://www.ilog.com/.

but understanding their mutual global impact may require a deep understanding of weaving, and, even worse, of the result of weaving, which very much reminds of an interleaving expansion of a highly distributed system.

10.4.2 Formal Methods and Tools

There are numerous formal methods and tools addressing validation, ranging from methods for correctness-by-construction/rule-based transformation, correctness calculi, model checkers, and constraint solvers to tools in practical use like PVS [41], Bandera [6], and SLAM [4] to name just a few. On the compiler side there are complex (optimizing) compiler suites, code generators, and controller synthesizers, and other methods to support technology mapping. A complete account of these methods is beyond the purpose of this chapter. Here it is sufficient to note that there is a high potential of available technology waiting to be used.

10.4.3 Automatic Deployment and Maintenance Support

This is the weakest point of the current practice: the deployment of complex systems on a heterogeneous, distributed platform is typically a nightmare, the required system-level testing is virtually unsupported, and maintenance and upgrading very often turn out to be extremely time consuming and expensive, de facto responsible for the slogan "never change a running system".

Still, in the same area there is a lot of technology one can build upon: the development of Java and the JVM or the .NET activities are well-accepted means to help getting models into operation, in particular, when heterogeneous hardware is concerned. Interoperability can be established using CORBA, RMI, RPC, Web services, complex middleware etc., and there are tools for testing and version management. Unfortunately, using these tools requires a lot of expertise, time to detect undocumented anomalies and to develop patches, and this for every application to be deployed.

XMDD differs radically from classical software development, which in our opinion is no longer adequate for the bulk of application programming, particularly when it comes to heterogeneous, cross-organizational systems which must adapt to rapidly changing market requirements. Accordingly, a new approach to system development needs to be developed.

10.5 The One Thing Approach

In XMDD, elaboration and refinement happen until a level is reached, where the classical requirement/implementation gap reduces to service-oriented realization of user/application-level functionalities. Thus rather than building highly complex software architectures, XMDD is characterized by the management of complex hierarchical models that orchestrate/coordinate user/application-level functionalities.

This perspective is now solidified by the One Thing Approach (OTA), which combines the simplicity of the waterfall development paradigm with a maximum of agility [34]. Key to OTA is to view the entire development process simply as a cooperative hierarchical and interactive decision process, which is organized by building and refining one comprehensive model, the 'one thing'. Within this model, each stakeholder, including the application expert, is allowed to continuously place his/her decisions in term of constraints, and each development or evolution step can be regarded simply as a transformation of the current constraint set. These constraints, which may comprise all kinds of aspects, can e.g. be expressed in terms of

- (temporal) formulae expressing the intentions of the application, internal policies, legal constraints or technical frame conditions;
- (loose) process models, specifying the rough distributed workflow from the management perspective without concern for technicalities like type correctness, location or interoperability;
- (symbolic) type information, sufficient to imply executability (later to be enforced by our synthesis technology);
- definitions of roles and rights, timing and localization constraints, and exception handling, which are to be integrated during code generation in an aspect-oriented fashion.

In this view, the waterfall character of the development process is no longer a matter of development phase or a 'before/after', but rather a matter of the chosen decision hierarchy: who can decide/modify what, what is the binding power of which decisions, and how should conflicts be resolved. This approach, conceptually, allows one (1) to monitor globally the consistency of the development or evolution process simply via constraint checking, and (2) to impose a kind of decision hierarchy by mapping areas of competencies to roles of individuals, in order to identify required actions in case of constraint violation.

Like XP for programming in the small, this approach revolutionizes the process/application development process. It replaces the typically long (interaction-free) intervals between contract-and-requirements time and delivery-and-acceptance time, with all its pitfalls, with a continuous, cooperative development process. Misconceptions are revealed and can dealt with as they arise, and the understanding of the application under construction (the user experience) naturally builds up along the way. The new cooperative development and evolution style supports the agile adjustment by

- keeping the customer continuously up to date: the impact of each design decision on the application logic becomes apparent via the shared model, 'One Thing', which provides the customer with a continuously updated user experience;
- focusing on the application logic, which allows one to repair and modify right at the same level as where the need appears;

Fig. 10.2 The XMDD
process in the jABC

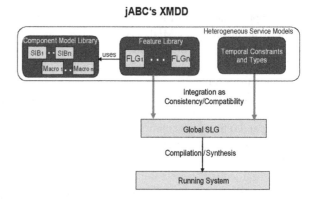

- following the service-oriented paradigm making it is easy to exchange/integrate (third party) functionality in a non-invasive fashion.

10.6 The jABC as an XMDD Environment

The jABC [47, 48] is a framework designed to support systematic development according to the XMDD paradigm within the One Thing Approach. Developed at METAFrame Technologies in cooperation with the TU Dortmund, it is intended to promote the XMDD-style of development in order to move the responsibility and control of application development for certain classes of applications towards the application expert. In its current version[2] the jABC supports an agile and cooperative development of service-oriented systems along the lines of the One-Thing Approach. Technically it comprises the three features discussed above (cf. Fig. 10.2):

1. *Heterogeneous landscape of models*: the central model structure of the jABC are hierarchical Service Logic Graphs (SLGs) [30, 43]. SLGs are flowchart-like graphs. They model the application behavior in terms of the intended process flows, based on coarse granular building blocks called Service-Independent Building blocks (SIBs). These are intended to be understood directly by the application experts [43] i.e., independently of the structure of the underlying code, which in our case is typically written in Java/C/C++. The component models (SIBs or hierarchical subservices called GraphSIBs), the feature-based service models—called Feature Logic Graphs (FLGs)—and the Global SLGs modeling applications are all hierarchical SLGs.
   The jABC also supports model specification in terms of
   a. modal logics, to abstractly and loosely characterize valid behaviors: semantic linear time logic (SLTL) [32, 44] is used for synthesis and the branching time logic modal μ-calculus [14] for model checking,

---

[2]We refer to version 3.5 of jABC here.

b. a classification scheme for building blocks and types, and
c. high level type specifications, used to specify compatibility between the building blocks of the SLGs.

The granularity of the building blocks is essential here, as it determines the level of abstraction all the subsequent reasoning is based upon: the verification tools directly consider the SLGs as formal models, the names of the (parameterized) building blocks as (parameterized) events, and the branching conditions as (atomic) propositions. Thus the jABC focuses on the level of *component (SIB) composition* rather than on component construction: its compatibility, its type correctness, and its behavioral correctness are under formal methods' control [30].

2. *Formal methods and tools*: the jABC comprises a high-level type checker, two model checkers, a model synthesizer, a compiler for SLGs, an interpreter, and a view generator. The model synthesizer, the model checkers, and the type checker take care of the consistency and compatibility conditions expressed by the four kinds of constraints/models mentioned above.

3. *Automatic deployment and maintenance support*: an automated deployment process, system-level testing [39], regression testing, version control, and online monitoring [7] support the phases following initial deployment. In particular the automatic deployment service needs some meta-modeling in advance; that has been realized using the jABC itself. Likewise the testing services and the online monitoring are themselves strong formal methods-based [40] and have been realized via the jABC.

The jABC can be regarded as a first framework for XMDD. It is designed to continuously involve the customer/application expert throughout the whole systems' life cycle according to the OTA [34].

10.7 XMDD Case Studies in jABC

The XMDD paradigm has been successfully used in several contexts, at different abstraction levels. We will now illustrate how the jABC uniformly supports all the abstraction levels, from the requirements/design by non-IT experts in Sect. 10.7.1, to application design in Sect. 10.7.2, to middleware-level configurations in Sect. 10.7.3, complex, semantic web-enhanced processes in bioinformatics in Sect. 10.7.4, and the application to the construction of a family of re-targetable compilers in Sect. 10.7.5.

10.7.1 Requirements and Specification: Supply Chain Management

In [8] we concentrate on the collaborative design of complex embedded systems in the jABC, that has proven to be effective and adequate for team cooperation with *non-IT personnel.* We show how our approach to model-driven collaborative design was applied to the requirement and specification phase of part of IKEA's P3 Document Management Process (part of a new Supply Chain Management system), where it complemented the Rational Unified Process development process already in use. The central contribution of our approach is two-dimensional support of consistency at the user process level:

- *vertical consistency* of models, e.g., across abstraction layers, as well as
- *horizontal model consistency*, which is needed, e.g. across organizational borders within a same abstraction level.

In this particular case we had to bridge between various business process specifications provided by business analysts on one side and use case/activity diagram views needed as specifications by the IT designers on the other side. Based on OTA, horizontal consistency was guaranteed by maintaining the global perspective throughout the refinement process, down to the code level, and vertical consistency by the simple discipline for refinement.

10.7.2 Application Construction: The SWS Challenge Mediation Scenario

A case study that demonstrates a wide span of XMDD features, from the design by modeling to the deployment and test, is our solution with jABC of the Mediation scenario of the Semantic Web Service (SWS) Challenge, as described in [16].

There, we show how we solved the Mediation task (a benchmark scenario of the Challenge, described in [23]) in a model driven, service oriented fashion using the jABC framework for model driven development and its jETI extension [44] for seamless integration of remote (Web) services. In particular we illustrate:

- how atomic services and orchestrations are modeled in the jABC;
- how legacy services and their proxies are represented within our framework, and how they are imported into our framework;
- how the mediators arise as orchestrations of the testbed's remote services and of local services;
- how vital properties of the Mediator are verified via model checking in the jABC; and
- how jABC/jETI orchestrated services are exported as Web services.

Besides providing a solution to the mediation problem, this also illustrates the *agility* of jABC-based solutions, since in the Challenge each scenario comprises a set of problems that come in different levels that build on top of each other. One of the central assessments is the ability of a methodology and of the corresponding technologies and tools to leverage on the first-level solutions to accommodate the changes/extensions required by the subsequent levels with minimal intrusion (in the solution and platforms) and effort (of a modeler/programmer).

The flexibility of the approach has been recently shown in two orthogonal directions:

- the flexibility of the automatic service composition via orchestration synthesis, which had been shown in [29, 32, 44] and demonstrated on the concrete case of the mediation scenario with a number of different construction principles, tools and algorithms in [15, 26];
- the flexibility in coping with changed platform realities—as is common in business evolution—that has been shown in [36] along two different directions of migration/extension of the underlying ERP platform.

10.7.3 Middleware Services: MaTRICS

In [3] we present how we realize in jABC the remote configuration and fault tolerance of the Online Conference Service [24] with our service oriented framework MaTRICS [2]. MaTRICS is our model-based service-oriented platform for remote intelligent configuration and management of systems and services. It is built on top of the jABC, thus it inherits the XMDD perspective. One of the central services offered by MaTRICS is the provision of low-overhead high-availability mechanisms for complex applications that run on distributed platforms. Our solution leaves the services untouched and uses the open source cluster management software, *heartbeat*[3] [38], to provide the high availability features. We showed there how jABC's XMDD approach supports the management services at, or close to, the middleware and operating system level, providing a user-friendly level of service models (implemented as SLGs according to the XMDD paradigm) for the monitoring (sensing of correct functionality) and the reconfiguration/service migration (actuating the changes on the cluster by steering heartbeat functionality). This is in contrast with the usual, script-based, heartbeat working manner, which is strictly code-based.

Reexamining the six issues mentioned in Sect. 10.1, in this case study:

- we structure the high-availability solution from the application perspective, for an application-level definition and management of the high-availability services well above the scripting level (user-centric modeling);
- we enable the model-level validation of the application logic (animation-based requirement validation and model checking), opposed to the sole testing possible in a script-based solution;
- we find an adequate, higher, and more declarative level, where application modeling is handed over to the implementation of (elementary) services. The library of services provided by MaTRICS has been extended by a new, reusable collection that internally uses heartbeat. This establishes a higher-level domain-specific language and service library for high-availability monitoring and enforcement;

---

[3]The Linux high-availability software website is here: http://www.linux-ha.org.

- we automatically deploy the new services, which are complex aggregations and enhanced compositions of the middleware services they embed;
- the new high-availability services and test cases are themselves monitorable at run time; and
- they are easily adaptable according to new requirements and to new platforms.

10.7.4 Bioinformatics Processes: Bio-JETI

Applying XMDD in the field of bioinformatics workflows led to the development of Bio-jETI [25] as a service platform for interdisciplinary work on biological application domains. The following advantages of the approach became evident for bioinformatics workflow management:

- *Integration of heterogeneous resources into a homogeneous environment.* With GeneFisher-P [20], for instance, we built a process-based variant of a software for Polymerase Chain Reaction (PCR) primer design.[4] Within GeneFisher-P we reuse several standard web services and a number of legacy tools that have been integrated with the help of the jETI technology [27] using the jABC modeling framework as the behavioral integration and interoperability layer. Within Bio-jETI, both these remote services and locally available auxiliary functionality (for tasks like file handling) have a uniform appearance (as SIBs) and can be used in the same fashion for workflow/process development.
- *Agility of workflow design.* With XMDD, even complex heterogeneous workflows can be easily changed or extended at the graphical level. In [17] we built several variations of workflows for the frequently needed multiple sequence alignment computation. We provided a set of preconfigured services and workflow snippets on a canvas, so that variations of an alignment workflow, for instance reading the input sequences either from a local file or from a remote database, or calling an alignment service either at the European Bioinformatics Institute or at the Bielefeld Bioinformatics Server, can be built by simply redirecting the branches between the services according to the intended workflow.
- *Deployment to different target platforms.* Using the Genesys code generation framework [9], Bio-jETI models can be compiled into different target languages. We translated a bioinformatics worfklow (performing a homology search and subsequently a multiple sequence alignment with the obtained sequences) into different flavors of native Java code and compared the execution times of the resulting applications, showing that the overhead that is introduced by the model-driven development process is negligible [18].

Moreover, the application of formal methods to support the development process is intended within OTA and has also become part of Bio-jETI: Model checking supports the detection of conceptual errors as well as of type inconsistencies,

---

[4]PCR primers are small nucleic acids that are required for initiating the amplification of DNA fragments.

Fig. 10.3 From MDD to
XMDD: no round trip
engineering

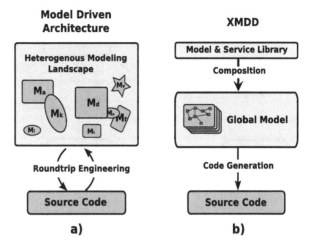

a)   b)

whereas process synthesis methods can be applied to fill gaps within workflows automatically [19]. The bioinformatics community has made significant progress in equipping their services with metadata in terms of Semantic Web technology, and is thus often already providing the information that is needed for proper application of our synthesis techniques. For example, the European Molecular Biology Open Software Suite (EMBOSS) comprises around 350 biological sequence analysis tools, and the EMBRACE Ontology for Data and Methods (EDAM) ontology provides a controlled vocabulary for bioinformatics types and services. We showed in different case studies that (semi-)automatic workflow composition (of EMBOSS tools according to the EDAM ontology) delivers excellent results [18, 21] and can be exploited in practice within the XMDD concept, in what we call a *loose programming* approach [22].

10.7.5 Code Generation: The Genesys Framework

In contrast to the previous application areas, Genesys does not just profit from the XMDD approach, but is itself an important constituent of it: its fully automatic code generation capability allows the users of the jABC to design, control, and modify their process models at the application level, without any need for code-level modification, and consequently, without the burden of round-trip engineering [49] (see Fig. 10.3). Thanks to Genesys, generated code can be considered a "by-product" that must never be touched manually, as it can readily be obtained by full code generation.

Genesys [9, 10, 12] is a framework for the high-level engineering of code generators in XMDD fashion [30, 33, 35]: code generators are modeled as SLGs based on a model and service library that is specifically adapted for the domain of code generation. This library is constantly growing, as any newly developed artifact may immediately contribute to the library, which does not only comprise individual code

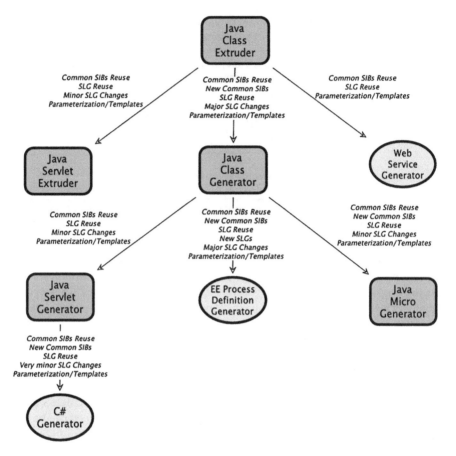

Fig. 10.4 Excerpt of the Genesys product line

generation functionalities, but also complex reusable features like error handling or code beautification, or even entire (models of) code generators. This is a consequence of the fact that SLGs can be truly hierarchical, which grants high reusability not only of the building blocks, but also of the models themselves, independent of their size [45].

Genesys also profits from jABC's clear support of service orientation [37], which allows one to seamlessly integrate third party functionality via SIBs [28]. This could be exploited to enhance Genesys' process-oriented modeling power with AndroMDA's[5] strength for modeling static aspects [11].

The close synergy between jABC and Genesys is best illustrated when looking at Genesys-generated code generators, which target Java, C#, Ruby, Objective-C, as well as BPEL, Lego Mindstorms, Android, iPhone, and more. Figure 10.4 shows an excerpt of this code generation 'product line', which can be extended and main-

---

[5]The AndroMDA website is here: http://www.andromda.org/.

tained within the jABC. This provides the means to validate the code generators at the model-level with respect to an increasing set of temporal properties expressing, e.g., the completeness of the applied tool chain or of the treatment of all involved artifacts, like parameters, local variables, and sub-models [9, 10, 46]. Experience shows that this approach significantly accelerates the development of new code generators by facilitating reuse of SIBs, models, and properties in a way that allows code generators to seamlessly evolve from each other [9, 35, 36].

10.8 Conclusions and Perspectives

We have advocated with XMMD a new direction for mastering of complexity in the service-oriented design of complex applications by combining ideas taken from eXtreme programming, model-driven design, as well as aspect and service orientation. Central is here the 'One-Thing Approach', which works by successively enriching and refining one single artifact, which, throughout the whole life-cycle, maintains a direct link between user-centric high-level models and the corresponding evolving running application. This approach is tailored to address the need for agile and lean development, which is particularly evident when it comes to heterogeneous, cross organizational systems which must adapt to rapidly changing market requirements. We have sketched the impact of this lightweight and cooperative development style that puts the *user process* at the center of development and the *application expert* in control of the process evolution by means of a number of case studies that indicate the breadth of applicability.

XMDD is not intended to replace genuine software development, as it assumes techniques to be able to solve problems (like synthesis or technology mapping) which are undecidable in general. On the other hand, more than 90% of the software development costs that arise worldwide concern a rather elementary software development level—as during routine application programming or software updates—where there are no technological or design challenges. There, the major problem faced is the management and control of software quantity, as it arises, e.g., through fast-evolving product lines, or instant solutions to solve an immediate but short-term need. XMDD is intended to address (a significant part of) this 90% 'niche'.

References

1. Andrade, L., Fiadeiro, J.L.: Architecture based evolution of software systems. In: Formal Methods for Software Architectures. Lecture Notes in Computer Science, vol. 2804, pp. 148–181. Springer, Berlin (2003)
2. Bajohr, M., Margaria, T.: MaTRICS: a service-based management tool for remote intelligent configuration of systems. Innovations Syst. Softw. Eng. **2**, 99–111 (2006)
3. Bajohr, M., Margaria, T.: High service availability in MaTRICS for the OCS. In: Margaria, T., Steffen, B. (eds.) Leveraging Applications of Formal Methods, Verification and Validation. Communications in Computer and Information Science, vol. 17, pp. 572–586. Springer, Berlin (2009)

4. Ball, T., Cook, B., Das, S., Rajamani, S.K.: Refining approximations in software predicate abstraction. In: Tools and Algorithms for the Construction and Analysis of Systems, 10th International Conference, TACAS 2004, Held as Part of the Joint European Conferences on Theory and Practice of Software, ETAPS 2004, Barcelona, Spain, March 29–April 2, 2004. Lecture Notes in Computer Science, vol. 2988, pp. 388–403. Springer, Berlin (2004)

5. Colyer, A., Clement, A., Harley, G., Webster, M.: Eclipse Aspectj: Aspect-Oriented Programming with Aspectj and the Eclipse Aspectj Development Tools. Addison-Wesley, Reading (2004)

6. Corbett, J.C., Dwyer, M.B., Hatcliff, J., Robbie: Bandera: a source-level interface for model checking Java programs. In: ICSE, pp. 762–765 (2000)

7. Hagerer, A., Hungar, H., Niese, O., Steffen, B.: Model generation by moderated regular extrapolation. In: Kutsche, R.-D., Weber, H. (eds.) Fundamental Approaches to Software Engineering, 5th International Conference, FASE 2002, Held as Part of the Joint European Conferences on Theory and Practice of Software, ETAPS 2002, Grenoble, France, April 8–12, 2002. Lecture Notes in Computer Science, vol. 2306, pp. 80–95. Springer, Berlin (2002)

8. Hörmann, M., Margaria, T., Mender, T., Nagel, R., Steffen, B., Trinh, H.: The jABC approach to rigorous collaborative development of SCM applications. In: Margaria, T., Steffen, B. (eds.) Leveraging Applications of Formal Methods, Verification and Validation, Third International Symposium, ISoLA 2008, Porto Sani, Greece, October 13–15, 2008. Communications in Computer and Information Science, vol. 17, pp. 724–737. Springer, Berlin (2008)

9. Jörges, S., Margaria, T., Steffen, B.: Genesys: service-oriented construction of property conform code generators. Innovations Syst. Softw. Eng. 4(4), 361–384 (2008)

10. Jörges, S., Margaria, T., Steffen, B.: Assuring property conformance of code generators via model checking. Form. Asp. Comput. 1–18 (2010). doi:10.1007/s00165-010-0169-9

11. Jörges, S., Steffen, B.: Leveraging service-orientation for combining code generation frameworks. In: 16th Annual IEEE International Conference on the Engineering of Complex Computer Systems (ICECCS), pp. 198–207 (2011)

12. Jörges, S., Steffen, B., Margaria, T.: Building code generators with Genesys: a tutorial introduction. In: 3rd International Summer School Conference on Generative and Transformational Techniques in Software Engineering III. GTTSE'09, pp. 364–385. Springer, Berlin (2011)

13. Kiczales, G., Lamping, J., Mendhekar, A., Maeda, C., Lopes, C.V., Loingtier, J.-M., Irwin, J.: Aspect-oriented programming. In: ECOOP, pp. 220–242 (1997)

14. Kozen, D.: Results on the propositional mu-calculus. Theor. Comput. Sci. 27, 333–354 (1983)

15. Kubczak, C., Margaria, T., Steffen, B.: Mashup development for everybody: a planning-based approach. In: 3rd Int. Worksh. on Service Matchmaking and Resource Retrieval in the Semantic Web, Colocated with ISWC-2009, Washington, DC, USA. CEUR Workshop Proceedings, vol. 525 (2009)

16. Kubczak, C., Margaria, T., Steffen, B., Nagel, R.: Service-oriented mediation with jABC/jETI. In: Petrie, C., Margaria, T., Zaremba, M., Lausen, H. (eds.) Semantic Web Services Challenge: Results from the First Year, pp. 71–99. Springer, Berlin (2009)

17. Lamprecht, A.-L., Margaria, T., Steffen, B.: Seven variations of an alignment workflow—an illustration of agile process design and management in Bio-jETI. In: Mandoiu, I.I., Sunderraman, R., Zelikovsky, A. (eds.) Bioinformatics Research and Applications, Fourth International Symposium, ISBRA 2008, Atlanta, GA, USA, May 6–9, 2008. Lecture Notes in Computer Science, vol. 4983, pp. 445–456. Springer, Berlin (2008)

18. Lamprecht, A.-L., Margaria, T., Steffen, B.: Bio-jETI: a framework for semantics-based service composition. BMC Bioinform. 10(S-10), 8 (2009)

19. Lamprecht, A.-L., Margaria, T., Steffen, B.: Supporting process development in Bio-jETI by model checking and synthesis. In: SWAT4LS-2009, Semantic Web Applications and Tools for Life Sciences. Proceedings of the Workshop on Semantic Web Applications and Tools for Life Sciences, Amsterdam, The Netherlands, November 20, 2009. CEUR Workshop Proceedings, vol. 559 (2009)

20. Lamprecht, A.-L., Margaria, T., Steffen, B., Sczyrba, A., Hartmeier, S., Giegerich, R.: GeneFisher-P: variations of genefisher as processes in Bio-jETI. BMC Bioinform. 9(S-4) (2008). doi:10.1186/1471-2105-9-S4-S13

21. Lamprecht, A.-L., Naujokat, S., Margaria, T., Steffen, B.: Semantics-based composition of EMBOSS services. J. Biomed. Semant. **2**(Suppl 1), 5 (2011)
22. Lamprecht, A.-L., Naujokat, S., Steffen, B., Margaria, T.: Constraint-guided workflow composition based on the EDAM ontology. CoRR arXiv:1012.1640 (2010)
23. Lausen, H., Künster, U., Petrie, C., Zaremba, M., Komazec, S.: SWS challenge scenarios. In: Semantic Web Services Challenge Results from the First Year. Springer, Berlin (2009)
24. Margaria, T., Karusseit, M.: Community usage of the online conference service: an experience report from three CS conferences. In: Monteiro, J.L., Swatman, P.M.C., Tavares, L.V. (eds.) Towards the Knowledge Society: eCommerce, eBusiness, and eGovernment, the Second IFIP Conference on E-Commerce, E-Business, E-Government (I3E 2002), Lisbon, Portugal, October 7–9, 2002, pp. 497–511 (2002)
25. Margaria, T., Kubczak, C., Steffen, B.: Bio-jETI: a service integration, design, and provisioning platform for orchestrated bioinformatics processes. BMC Bioinform. **9**(S-4) (2008). doi:10.1186/1471-2105-9-S4-S12
26. Margaria, T., Meyer, D., Kubczak, C., Isberner, M., Steffen, B.: Synthesizing semantic web service compositions with jMosel and Golog. In: Bernstein, A., Karger, D.R., Heath, T., Feigenbaum, L., Maynard, D., Motta, E., Thirunarayan, K. (eds.) 8th International Semantic Web Conference, ISWC 2009, Chantilly, VA, USA, October 25–29, 2009. Lecture Notes in Computer Science, vol. 5823, pp. 392–407. Springer, Berlin (2009)
27. Margaria, T., Nagel, R., Steffen, B.: jETI: a tool for remote tool integration. In: Halbwachs, N., Zuck, L.D. (eds.) Tools and Algorithms for the Construction and Analysis of Systems, 11th International Conference, TACAS 2005, Held as Part of the Joint European Conferences on Theory and Practice of Software, ETAPS 2005, Edinburgh, UK, 4–8 April 2005, pp. 557–562 (2005)
28. Margaria, T., Nagel, R., Steffen, B.: Remote integration and coordination of verification tools in JETI. In: 12th IEEE International Conference on the Engineering of Computer-Based Systems (ECBS 2005), Greenbelt, MD, USA, 4–7 April 2005, pp. 431–436 (2005)
29. Margaria, T., Steffen, B.: Backtracking-free design planning by automatic synthesis in metaframe. In: FASE, pp. 188–204 (1998)
30. Margaria, T., Steffen, B.: Lightweight coarse-grained coordination: a scalable system-level approach. Int. J. Softw. Tools Technol. Transf. **5**(2–3), 107–123 (2004)
31. Margaria, T., Steffen, B.: From the how to the what. In: Meyer, B., Woodcock, J. (eds.) Verified Software: Theories, Tools, Experiments, First IFIP TC 2/WG 2.3 Conference, VSTTE 2005, Zurich, Switzerland, October 10–13, 2005, Revised Selected Papers and Discussions, pp. 448–459 (2005)
32. Margaria, T., Steffen, B.: LTL guided planning: revisiting automatic tool composition in ETI. In: 31st Annual IEEE / NASA Software Engineering Workshop (SEW-31 2007), Loyola College, Columbia, MD, USA, 6–8 March 2007, pp. 214–226 (2007)
33. Margaria, T., Steffen, B.: Agile IT: Thinking in user-centric models. In: Margaria, T., Steffen, B. (eds.) Leveraging Applications of Formal Methods, Verification and Validation, Third International Symposium, ISoLA 2008, Porto Sani, Greece, October 13–15, 2008, pp. 490–502 (2008)
34. Margaria, T., Steffen, B.: Business process modelling in the jABC: the one-thing approach. In: Cardoso, J., van der Aalst, W. (eds.) Handbook of Research on Business Process Modeling, pp. 1–26. IGI Global, Hershey (2009)
35. Margaria, T., Steffen, B.: Continuous model-driven engineering. IEEE Comput. **42**(10), 106–109 (2009)
36. Margaria, T., Steffen, B., Kubczak, C.: Evolution support in heterogeneous service-oriented landscapes. J. Braz. Comput. Soc. **16**(1), 35–47 (2010)
37. Margaria, T., Steffen, B., Reitenspieß, M.: Service-oriented design: the roots. In: Benatallah, B., Casati, F., Traverso, P. (eds.) Service-Oriented Computing—ICSOC 2005, Third International Conference, Amsterdam, The Netherlands, December 12–15, 2005. Lecture Notes in Computer Science, vol. 3826, pp. 450–464 (2005)
38. Marowsky-Brée, L.: A new cluster resource manager for heartbeat. In: UKUUG LISA/Winter Conf. on High-Availability and Reliability, Bournemouth (UK) (2004)

39. Niese, O., Margaria, T., Hagerer, A., Nagelmann, M., Steffen, B., Brune, G., Ide, H.-D.: An automated testing environment for CTI systems using concepts for specification and verification of workflows. Annu. Rev. Commun. **54**, 927–936 (2001)
40. Niese, O., Steffen, B., Margaria, T., Hagerer, A., Brune, G., Ide, H.-D.: Library-based design and consistency checking of system-level industrial test cases. In: Proceedings of the 4th International Conference on Fundamental Approaches to Software Engineering. FASE '01, pp. 233–248. Springer, London (2001)
41. Shankar, N., Owre, S.: Principles and pragmatics of subtyping in PVS. In: Bert, D., Choppy, C., Mosses, P.D. (eds.) Recent Trends in Algebraic Development Techniques, 14th International Workshop, WADT '99, Château de Bonas, France, September 15–18, 1999, Selected Papers, pp. 37–52 (1999)
42. Steffen, B.: Unifying models. In: Reischuk, R., Morvan, M. (eds.) STACS 97, 14th Annual Symposium on Theoretical Aspects of Computer Science, Lübeck, Germany, February 27–March 1, 1997, pp. 1–20 (1997)
43. Steffen, B., Margaria, T.: METAFrame in practice: design of intelligent network services. In: Olderog, E.-R., Steffen, B. (eds.) Correct System Design, Recent Insight and Advances, pp. 390–415, (to Hans Langmaack on the occasion of his retirement from his professorship at the University of Kiel) (1999)
44. Steffen, B., Margaria, T., Braun, V.: The electronic tool integration platform: concepts and design. Int. J. Softw. Tools Technol. Transf. **1**(1–2), 9–30 (1997)
45. Steffen, B., Margaria, T., Braun, V., Kalt, N.: Hierarchical service definition. Annu. Rev. Commun. **51**, 847–856 (1997)
46. Steffen, B., Margaria, T., Claßen, A., Braun, V.: Incremental formalization: a key to industrial success. Softw. Concepts Tools **17**(2), 78 (1996)
47. Steffen, B., Margaria, T., Nagel, R., Jörges, S., Kubczak, C.: Model-driven development with the jABC. In: Bin, E., Ziv, A., Ur, S. (eds.) Hardware and Software, Verification and Testing, Second International Haifa Verification Conference, HVC 2006, Haifa, Israel, October 23–26, 2006. Revised Selected Papers. Lecture Notes in Computer Science, vol. 4383, pp. 92–108. Springer, Berlin (2006)
48. Steffen, B., Narayan, P.: Full life-cycle support for end-to-end processes. IEEE Comput. **40**(11), 64–73 (2007)
49. Steffen, B., Wagner, C., Margaria, T.: Round-trip engineering vs. one-thing approach. In: Laplante, P.A. (ed.) Encyclopedia of Software Engineering. Auerbach Publications, Boca Raton (2010)

Chapter 11
Ten Commandments of Formal Methods...
Ten Years On

Jonathan P. Bowen and Mike Hinchey

11.1 Introduction

More than a decade ago, in "Ten Commandments of Formal Methods," [2], we offered practical guidelines for projects that sought to use formal methods. Over the years, the article, which was based on our knowledge of successful industrial projects [7], has been widely cited and has generated much positive feedback. However, despite this apparent enthusiasm, formal methods use has not greatly increased, and some of the same attitudes about the infeasibility of adopting them persist.

In 1995, Bertrand Meyer stated that the advancement of software requires a more mathematical approach [12]. Likewise, formal methodists believe that introducing greater rigor will improve the software development process and yield software with better structure, greater maintainability, and fewer errors [6].

But while many acknowledge the existence of formal methods and their continued application in software engineering [9], the software engineering community as a whole remains unconvinced of their usefulness. The myths and misconceptions [1, 4] that surrounded formal methods when we wrote our original article in large part still abound.

One misconception is the basic justification for formal methods—that they are essential to avoid design flaws because software is bad, unique, and discontinuous, and testing is inadequate. Michael Holloway, a proponent of formal methods at NASA, argues that the justification is far simpler: Software engineers want to be real engineers. Real engineers use mathematics. Formal methods are the mathematics of software engineering. Therefore, software engineers should use formal methods.

Yet even with this elegant simplicity, most projects hold formal methods at arm's length unless they involve the design and maintenance of critical systems [15]. Some formal techniques such as program assertions are reasonably popular, but they represent only a tiny slice of the vast formal methods pie.

J.P. Bowen (✉)
Museophile Limited, London, UK
e-mail: jonathan.bowen@lsbu.ac.uk

M. Hinchey, L. Coyle (eds.), *Conquering Complexity*,
DOI 10.1007/978-1-4471-2297-5_11, © Springer-Verlag London Limited 2012

Oddly, despite their spotty application, formal methods continue to appear in the trade literature [16]. Apparently, the software engineering community is not willing to abandon formal methods, given the slight increase in formal methods projects [8], but neither is it willing to embrace them.

Perhaps revisiting our commandments might explain this curious stalemate. Not all our colleagues agreed with our final commandment choices, arguing that some would not stand the test of time. Would a retrospective prove that our colleagues were right?

11.2 I. Thou Shalt Choose an Appropriate Notation

> Notations are a frequent complaint... but the real problem is to understand the meaning and properties of the symbols and how they may and may not be manipulated, and to gain fluency in using them to express new problems, solutions and proofs. Finally, you will cultivate an appreciation of mathematical elegance and style. By that time, the symbols will be invisible; you will see straight through them to what they mean. – *C.A.R. Hoare*

Many blame the use of mathematical notation for formal methods' slow uptake and believe it inhibits industrial application. The common view is that mathematical expressions are beyond normal comprehension. In reality, the mathematics of formal methods is based on notations and concepts that should be familiar to anyone with a computing background, such as set theory and propositional and predicate logics. Of course, customers and end users would need some training and explanation, but the point is that formal methods notations *are* accessible or can be made that way.

But the first commandment addresses a larger issue than user comprehension. "Appropriate" means that the notation has to fit the system it is meant to describe, which can be tricky because some systems are quite large and complex. The more popular notations—B, Calculus of Communicating Systems, Communicating Sequential Processes, and Z, for example—apply to a wide range of systems, but they are not inclusive.

Thus, larger applications often require a combination of languages. Indeed, many argue that no single notation will *ever* address all aspects of a complex system, implying that future systems will require combinations of methods. Process algebras and logics will become particularly important as systems become more sophisticated.

As Table 11.1 shows, the trend over the past decade seems to support the augmenting of notations. The table gives just a flavor of the myriad hybrid formal methods that have emerged, strongly indicating the acceptance of combining notations to address specific system aspects. We see three categories of these combinations:

- *Viewpoints.* In this loose coupling, different notations present different system views, with each notation emphasizing a particular system aspect, such as timing constraints.
- *Method integration.* In a closer coupling, several notations (both formal and informal or semiformal) combine with manual or automatic translation between

Table 11.1 A sampling of hybrid formal methods since 1995

Name	Combines	Advantage
CSP-OZ	Z, CSP	Combines Z and CSP
Object Z	Z, object-oriented principles, temporal logic	Adds object orientation to Z
PiOz	Object-Z, π-calculus	Adds π-calculus style dynamic communication capabilities to Object-Z
Temporal B	B, temporal logic	Adds time to the B method
Timed CSP	CSP, time	Adds time to CSP
TLZ	Z, TLA	Adds temporal aspects plus fairness constraints to Z specification
WSCCS	CCS, probability	Adds probabilistic constraints to CCS specifications
ZCCS	Z, CCS	Combines CCS process algebra and state based aspects of Z

Notes: CCS: Calculus of Communicating Systems; CSP: Communicating Sequential Processes; OZ: Object-Z; PiOZ: π-calculus Object-Z; TLA: Temporal Logic of Actions; WSCCS: Weighted Synchronous CCS

notations. The idea is to provide an underlying semantics for the less formal notations, to enable well-understood graphical (or other) presentations, and to offer the benefits of formal verification.

- *Integrated methods*. In a tight coupling, multiple notations combine within a single framework (such as propositional logic) to give a uniform semantics to each notation.

A decade ago, method integration was hot, and it seemed that integrated methods would become equally popular. Although we see progress in integrated methods [14], the viewpoints approach is the only one that seems to have gained ground. Perhaps this is because of industry's reluctance to take up full formal proofs, which the more tightly coupled approaches would support. But it could also be its general unwillingness to become preoccupied with semantic details.

This unwillingness underlines another misconception—in reality, an appropriate notation can hide unnecessary detail and complexity, and this is a major benefit of formal methods, not a liability. Developers are not only free to concentrate on the essential issues, but they also gain a richer understanding of the system to be developed.

Because formal specifications will often be significantly shorter than their implementation, they are likely to be more understandable. Some argue that a formal specification *must* be significantly shorter, but we disagree. The use of formal methods and formal specification techniques can highlight problems or issues that developers might not see at the coding level. In this case, even a longer formal specification is valuable.

Table 11.2 Formalization levels

Level	Name	Involves
0	Formal specification	Using formal notation to specify requirements only; no analysis or proof
1	Formal development/verification	Proving properties and applying refinement calculus
2	Machine-checked proofs	Using a theorem prover or checker to prove consistency and integrity

11.3 II. Thou Shalt Formalize but not Over-formalize

> Strange as it seems, no amount of learning can cure stupidity, and formal education positively fortifies it. – *Stephen Vizinczey*

In our original article, we advised projects to distinguish between using formal methods appropriately and formalization just for the sake of it. In some areas, such as user interface design, projects *could* apply formal methods, but doing so might not be the best choice.

In fact, a prominent myth (and one we listed in [1]) is that formal methods people always use formal methods. In reality, many highly publicized projects proclaimed as great formal methods successes formalized only 10 percent or less of the system.

Ten years ago, we noted the dearth of toolsets for most formal methods. Not much has changed, although PerfectDeveloper by Escher Technologies and Atelier-B from ClearSy are attempts to develop such tools.

Escher Technologies has even partially applied PerfectDeveloper to the tool's own redevelopment (for all but the graphical user interface), proving around 95 percent of the approximately 130,000 verification conditions the tool generated. For development of simpler systems, it has been used to achieve 100 percent proof checking of the verification conditions. Mistakes are often found to be caused by under-specification in practice. The Spark toolset from Praxis High Integrity Systems (http://www.altran-praxis.com/spark.aspx) is another example of applying an industrial formal methods tool to itself.

The formal methods community seems to have taken the warning not to overformalize somewhat to heart, and there is now more widespread belief that it's best to use formal methods as needed, mainly for key product parts. Cliff Jones introduced "formal methods light," which approximates Level 0 of the three formalization levels in Table 11.2 (taken from [1]).

Even Level 0 formality can accrue many benefits because the importance of getting requirements right at the outset cannot be overstated. Figure 11.1 shows a graph of investment in the requirements phase of NASA projects and missions plotted against the cost of project overruns. The obvious "demand curve" emphasizes that getting requirements right has major payback later—or, conversely, that not getting requirements right will come back to haunt you.

The use of mathematically based approaches has great potential to help eliminate errors early in the design process. It is cheaper than trying to remove them in the

Fig. 11.1 Costs during the requirements phase of NASA projects vs. project overrun costs. The *curves* show the savings of getting requirements right and the price of getting them wrong. Courtesy of W. Gruhl, NASA Comptroller's Office

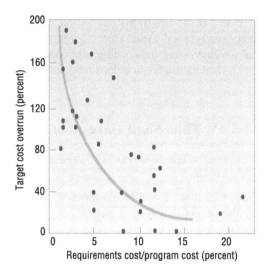

testing phase or, worse, after deployment. Consequently, it is true that using formal methods in the initial stages of the development process can help to improve the quality of the later software, even if formal methods are not used in subsequent phases of development.

11.4 III. Thou Shalt Estimate Costs

> I think that God in creating Man somewhat overestimated his ability. – *Oscar Wilde*

When asked what they'd charge a customer for a software project, software engineers often joke, "As much as we can possibly get away with." Although that's meant to be humor, it reflects a certain mindset that carries over into estimating development costs, where the strategy is often to make the best (usually highest) estimate and then double it.

In the draft of [1], we had "guesstimate costs" instead of "estimate," a term we liked because a hybrid of "guess" and "estimate," more closely captures the imprecision of the exercise. (It did not survive the more precise art of copy editing, however.) Even with several established models, among them CoCoMo II, cost estimation is far from a science. Development costs sometimes grandly exceed estimates: The Darlington power plant and Space Shuttle software had cost overruns that were significantly more than anyone could have foreseen. It was for that reason that we strongly advocated both initial and continuous cost estimation—and we still do.

Research shows that organizations spend 33 percent to 50 percent of their total cost of ownership (TCO) preparing for or recovering from failures [11]. Hardware costs continue to fall, yet TCO continues to rise, and system availability (and hence reliability) is taking a hit. In this light, any cost estimates could be unrealistic, understated, or even unrealistically understated.

However, we still firmly believe in having a cost estimate as well as some idea of anticipated costs if a team elects to forego formal methods. A cost estimate is essential for convincing the development communities—both software and hardware—that formal methods can indeed produce better systems for less.

11.5 IV. Thou Shalt Have a Formal Methods Guru on Call

An expert is a person who has made all the mistakes that can be made in a very narrow field.
– *Niels Bohr*

Part of what we found in our initial research is that most successful projects had regular access to a formal methods expert. Many had several gurus to guide and lead the formal development process and advise on complex aspects. Occasionally, such experts were able to compensate for the development team's lack of experience in applying formal methods.

But access to an expert outside the team is not enough to ensure success. All team members must understand the applicability of formal methods and contribute to rather than inhibit their application. It is too easy for team members, on either the management or technical side, to prevent effective formalization.

Formal methods require the right mix of effort, expertise, and knowledge. Although not every team member needs the same formalization proficiency, at the very least, all must appreciate what formal methods can achieve.

A formally verified program is only as good as its specification. If the specification does not describe what the team truly wants, even a fully formally developed system will be little more than useless. A team that doesn't understand formal methods has only a notion of what they specified using a formal notation and is unclear about how to refine the development process will almost certainly sink the project. Perhaps this is why some quarters are skeptical about the benefits of formal methods.

So we stand by this commandment, although if we were writing the article today, we might tweak it a bit to read, "Thou shalt have both a formal methods guru and a domain expert from the outset." Our experience with industrial projects over the past decade has highlighted the importance of having both kinds of experts early on [6].

11.6 V. Thou Shalt not Abandon Thy Traditional Development Methods

A great many of those who 'debunk' traditional... values have in the background values of their own which they believe to be immune from the debunking process. – *C.S. Lewis*

The software engineering community persists in embracing fads. Each new notation or technique seems to have the unwritten guarantee of painless success. This is a dangerous mindset, particularly when the notational flavor of the month becomes an additional source of problems, not a magical solution. The Unified Modeling Language, which has become ubiquitous in industrial applications over the past decade, is a case in point. UML has some serious flaws, such as its lack of formality and scant guidance on applying the newer graphical notations.

Fortunately, the UML community has recognized the need to address the first flaw. Formal methods research has spent some time considering formalization in the context of UML, which has led to the formation of the precise UML (pUML) group. There is also work at the University of Southampton on the tool-based integration of the B-Method, a formal approach, and UML. Such improvements are likely to show up in future UML developments.

Another caveat to using UML is that it essentially standardizes several existing and emerging graphical notations for system specification. Many of these notations have been around since the 1970s, with only slight variations in their representation, but a wide variety of new graphical notations have recently joined the list. Some of these are there for good reason; others, because they had support from particular quarters. Unfortunately, UML tends to deemphasize the particular development method, so although it provides a range of notations, it gives no guidance for what notations fit best with which system types, which notations conflict when combined, and which notations are good complements.

To be fair, most formal methods and most formal approaches to software or hardware development also fail to address development's methodological aspects. Because they have a specification notation and a reasoning mechanism, formal methods are truly formal. However, they are not truly methodical because they don't offer defined ordered steps and guidance for moving between them. Recent formal approaches like the B-Method have addressed this issue to some extent.

Object-oriented techniques are also popular, and research has produced OO extensions to formalisms, such as Object-Z for the Z notation. Formal methods tools, such as PerfectDeveloper, also target OO development. Software engineers who develop systems with languages such as Java might find such a tool attractive.

Other research at NASA Goddard Space Flight Center [5] is addressing how to increase formality in model-based development and in requirements-based programming. The latter approach aims to transform requirements into executable code systematically and has many of automatic programming's advantages, while avoiding its major deficiency of specifying a solution rather than the problem to be solved.

11.7 VI. Thou Shalt Document Sufficiently

> I have always tried to hide my own efforts and wished my works to have the lightness and joyousness of a springtime which never lets anyone suspect the labors it cost.
> – Henri Matisse

Matisse was a master of abstraction. While most artists prepared rough preliminary drawings for their works and then added detail, Matisse took the opposite approach, making his preliminary drawings extremely detailed. After he had finished working, he would have his assistant photograph what he had done so that he had a record of his decisions and the work he had completed. The next morning he would destroy the work, undoing most (sometimes all) of what he had added the previous day. Consequently, Matisse's final works are often highly abstract, with few lines, but all of what's there is essential to the representation. Perhaps the most compelling example of this is the 1935 edition of James Joyce's *Ulysses*, which Matisse illustrated without even having read it (using Homer's *Odyssey* as a basis instead).

In an attempt to combine abstract documentation with concrete programs, Donald Knuth introduced the idea of *literate programming*. Using this style, programmers connect code fragments to relevant documentation in a way that justifies coding (and hence design) decisions. Literate programming would seem to be an excellent fit with the use of formal methods, since it could also associate code with the relevant formal specification fragments, as well as the requirements that drive those fragments. However, industry did not act on that association. Instead, attempts to build literate programming tools led to the development of eXtreme Programming (XP), which provides little documentation and emphasizes product development and frequent releases.

Formal methods demand quality documentation, some of which can be automated, but someone must fully explain formal specifications so that they are understandable to both nonspecialists and those working on the specification after its initial development. Someone must also record the reasons for various specification, design, and decomposition decisions as a courtesy to future developers.

In addition to the benefits of abstraction, clarification and disambiguation, which accrue from the use of formal methods at Level 0 in Table 11.2, using formal methods at the formal specification level provides invaluable documentation. Experience has shown that quality documentation can greatly assist future system maintenance. In fact, several collaborative European projects have involved the documentation of legacy systems or reverse engineering.

All development involves iteration, and documentation must reflect that. Often, when engineers change the system implementation, they neither record that change nor update the related documentation. True formal development would use formal methods to help avoid such inconsistencies since the formal specification is part of the documentation.

Properly documenting decisions during the formal specification process is also important, which is why we have always advocated augmenting formal specifications with natural language narrative. A proper paper trail is critical. Without it, the organization loses the benefits of abstraction and might even lose useful information.

11.8 VII. Thou Shalt not Compromise Thy Quality Standards

If people knew how hard I worked to get my mastery, it wouldn't seem so wonderful at all.
– *Michelangelo Buonarroti*

According to the National Institute of Standards & Technology, 2002 losses from poor software quality amounted to more than $60 billion [13]. Software quality is still a huge issue that no one has yet addressed adequately. The ISO 9000 quality standards have been in force since 1994, and ISO even revised them in 2000, yet poor software quality still plagues users. Standards could be crucial in changing this destructive trend.

Standards are also critical in high-integrity areas like safety- and security-critical applications. For example, the IEC 61508-3 International Standard on Software Requirements for Safety-Related Systems covers software design, development, and verification. Obviously, formal methods can be part of this process, but most standards merely suggest that a project could use such methods—they don't mandate use. The onus is on the developer to demonstrate that using formal methods makes sense and is worthwhile.

Safety and security standards continue to drive formal methods use at the highest levels of integrity, and this trend is likely to continue. In the UK, for example, the two-part Defence Standard 00-55 from the Ministry of Defence, which regulates defense contracts, has a mandate in the "Requirements" section of part 1 (italics are ours): "Assurance that the required safety integrity has been achieved is provided *by the use of formal methods* in conjunction with dynamic testing and static analysis." The standard also mandates formal methods use for safety-related software: "The methods used in the SRS development process shall include ... : a) *formal methods of software specification and design*; ..." Finally, the "Guidance" section in part 2 mentions formal methods in many places and includes an explicit section under "Required Methods."

However, even standards that mandate formal methods use are not enough to ensure quality. Formal methods practitioners must also adhere to quality standards in the development processes—not only standards for various specification notations (such as Z), but also standards that reflect best practice in software development. Following such standards is the best way to ensure correctness, regardless of whether someone deems that software critical. Formal methods are meant to complement existing quality standards, not supplant them.

Standards documentation itself can use formality, as does the documentation for Prolog, and even formal notations can have associated standards—there are ISO standards for LOTOS, VDM and Z, for example. ISO approved the Z standard in 2002 after nearly a decade of production. Progress was slow and painstaking in part because much effort centered on formalizing a revised version of Z notation. On the other hand, the process did reveal some semantic inconsistencies, so at least in that context it was a success. Regardless of viewpoint, there are lessons for any future efforts to produce a formal method standard.

11.9 VIII. Thou Shalt not Be Dogmatic

... And I am unanimous in that! – Mollie Sugden, a.k.a. Mrs. Slocombe, in "Are You Being Served?" BBC TV (1972–1993)

Perhaps one of the worst misconceptions about formal methods is that they can guarantee correctness [1]. They can certainly offer greater confidence that an organization has correctly developed the software or hardware, but that's all. In fact, it is absurd to speak of correctness without referring to the system specification [1]. If the organization has not built the right system (validation), no amount of building the system right (verification) can overcome that error. In an investigation of failed safety-critical systems, one study found nearly 1,100 deaths attributable to computer error [10]. Many of these errors stemmed from poor or no specifications, not an incorrect implementation.

The danger for many projects is the analysis-specification gap—the space between what is in the procurer's mind (real world entities) and the writing of the specification (notation software professionals choose, either formal or informal). Formal methods—with only a few exceptions—offer very little or no methodological support to close this gap.

The solution for some is to use less formal methods or formal methods augmented with methods that offer greater development support. The argument is that such adaptations would be more intuitive to users. Model-based development aims to address this by placing great emphasis on getting an appropriate model of reality. Likewise, requirements-based programming is attempting to fully integrate requirements in the development process. Both these approaches reduce the analysis-specification gap by ensuring that what is specified (and ultimately implemented) is a true reflection of real-world requirements.

11.10 IX. Thou Shalt Test, Test, and Test Again

> I believe the hard part of building software to be the specification, design and testing of this conceptual construct, not the labor of representing it and testing the fidelity of the representation. – *Frederick P. Brooks, Jr.*

Largely because of formal methods research in the 1960s (before the community had even coined the term), most programs include assertions. The intent of assertions was to prove programs correct, and, at that time, most people believed this was *all* that formal methods were supposed to do [1]. Now, testers use assertions to check if a program's state is correct during runtime. Promising research, centered on the Java Modeling Language, is attempting to broaden the use of assertions to include formal verification as well.

Perhaps some day, a verifying compiler, such as the one Tony Hoare proposed, will be able to verify assertions at compile-time rather than at runtime, eliminating the need to use assertions in testing. A current computer science Grand Challenge proposes the development of such a compiler over the long term.

For the near term, the use of formal methods to improve testing has much potential. A formal specification can aid automatic test-case generation, but the time required to produce a formal specification could be far greater than the time saved at the testing stage. In the UK, researchers are using the Fortest (Formal Methods and Testing) network as a framework (www.fortest.org.uk) to investigate the tradeoffs.

Formal methods also have potential use in clarifying test criteria. The MC/DC (Modified Condition/Decision Coverage) is a criterion in many safety-related applications and standards recommendations, such as the RTCA/DO-178B, Software Considerations in Airborne Systems and Equipment Certification. The criterion is normally defined informally, but the Centre for Applied Formal Methods at London South Bank University has investigated its meaning formally using Z notation and has developed an even stricter criterion.

Although we see formal methods making some inroads into software testing, application is challenging because software is unique in many ways:

- Even very short programs can be complex and difficult to understand.
- Software does not deteriorate with age. In fact, it improves over time because engineers discover and correct latent errors, but the same error correction can introduce defects.
- Changes in software that appear to be inconsequential can result in significant and unexpected problems in seemingly unrelated parts of the code.
- Unlike hardware, software cannot give forewarnings of failure. Many latent errors in software might not be visible until long after the organization has deployed the software.
- Software lends itself to quick and easy changes.

The last characteristic does not translate into quick and easy error location and correction. Rather, organizations must use a structured, well-documented development approach to ensure comprehensive validation. We would never claim that formal methods can or even should eliminate testing. Quite the contrary: The use of formal methods can *reduce* the likelihood of certain errors or help detect them, but formal methods must partner with appropriate testing.

11.11 X. Thou Shalt Reuse

The biggest difference between time and space is that you can't reuse time. – Merrick Furst

Traditionally, organizations have encouraged reuse as a way to reduce costs and boost quality. The idea is to then spend more time improving the quality of components targeted for reuse. Both OO and component-based paradigms exploit the idea of reuse.

Theoretically, formal methods can and should aid in promoting software reuse. One inhibitor to the uptake of software reuse is the inability to identify suitable components in a library and to develop libraries of components that are large enough to give a reasonable return, yet small enough to be broadly reusable.

For some time, practitioners have recognized that they can make searching more effective by having formal specifications of components or at the very least of their pre- and postconditions. (Preconditions specify when to apply the component; postconditions describe the results of using it.) Supplying such conditions lets the component remain a black box, which in turn means that the component is much larger and therefore could have a more significant payoff in reuse.

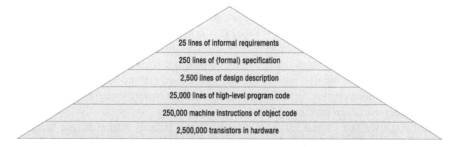

Fig. 11.2 The size explosion as development progresses (numbers are hypothetical)

There are significant returns in applying reuse at the formal specification level. Formal specifications are typically shorter than the equivalent implementation in a programming language. Figure 11.2 provides a comparison of the potential size explosion as development proceeds from specification to hardware implementation. It is obviously easier to search for larger components, while simultaneously getting a sufficient return. Along the same lines, formal specifications could help identify reusable design patterns.

Another way formal specifications can support reuse is in generating implementations on various platforms. This approach essentially reuses the effort expended at earlier development stages and thereby reduces overall cost. The literature reports the successful application of formal specification techniques to developing software product lines—systems (or products) with that have only slight variations. Moreover, formal methods generally result in a cleaner architecture, making a system more efficient and more easily maintainable.

Reusing and porting software is not without pitfalls, however. Ariane 5 is a prime example. Its developers assumed that they could reuse the launch software from Ariane 4. Their assumption resulted in a rocket loss within seconds of launch.

The Therac-25 incidents are arguably the most significant failure of software assurance in a medical or biological application. Therac-25 was a dual-mode linear accelerator that could deliver either photons at 25 MeV or electrons at various energy levels. It was based on Therac-20, which in turn was based on the single-mode Therac-6. The Therac-20 included hardware interlocks for safety, but in Therac-25 these interlocks were software-based. Despite several Therac-25 machines operating, reportedly correctly, for up to four years at various US installations, in six separate incidents the device administered lethal doses of radiation to patients.

Subsequent investigations of both Therac-20 and Therac-25 revealed a software error that caused the machines to act erratically. Students at a radiology school had creatively set parameters that caused the Therac-20 machines to shut down after blowing fuses and breakers. The failures were bothersome, but certainly not life-threatening. However, when the same error perpetuated to Therac-25, which did not have mechanical interlocks, the problem became fatal. If the developers of Therac-25 had fully checked the software using formal methods, possibly, they might have realized the significance of this error.

11.12 Conclusions

Ten years later, we are surprised to find that the original formal methods commandments are still valid. The use of formal methods is not as prevalent as we had hoped, but we are more certain that formal approaches will always have a niche in computer-based systems development, especially when correct functioning is critical [3]. As the final section describes, the next 10 years should see some significant progress in integrating formal methods and traditional development practices. Like any approach, formal methods work best when applied judiciously. It makes the most sense to use them for the software that performs critical operations, but any application should be part of sound engineering judgment that considers both technical feasibility and economics. For such efforts, well-trained personnel of the highest quality will always be needed.

The rewards can be considerable with the right combination of knowledge and expertise, but formal methods are not a panacea. Some, especially those in academia, have oversold formalism's ability. Given that people must apply formal methods, they will never be completely reliable. The logical models must relate to the real world in an informal leap of faith both at the high-level requirements or specification end and at the low-level digital hardware end (which requires belief in Maxwell's equations, for example).

More effort must be devoted to evaluating the effectiveness of formal methods in the software development and maintenance. Hopefully, we have raised issues that others will find worth exploring. Because of the somewhat tarnished reputation of formal methods, largely due to misunderstandings and inappropriate use, a demonstration of how and where formal methods are effective would be well worth the effort.

There are continuing success stories in the industrial use of formal methods [15] and the approach remains in the eye of the press [16]. Studies will help practitioners understand how to ensure that the introduction of formal methods has a positive impact on the software development and maintenance process by reducing overall costs.

Above all, formal methodists must have patience. Sculptor Théophile Gautier once said, "L'ouvre sort plus belle, d'une forme au travail rebelled vers," which translates roughly to "The work is more beautiful from a material that resists the process." If that is true, then formal methods use will eventually emerge in near-perfect form.

11.13 Looking Ahead

Industrial-strength tools for formal methods have always been lacking. A few exist but the demand for a range of compatible tools is growing. In the future, tool support for formal methods will become increasingly important. Some efforts in this direction include:

- Alloy Community based around the Alloy Analyzer (alloy.mit.edu);
- CZT Community Z Tools initiative (czt.sourceforge.net);
- HOL4 Higher Order Logic theorem prover (hol.sourceforge.net);
- Perfect Developer for object-orient software development (www.eschertech.com);
- Rodin Platform, a development environment based on Event B (www.event-b.org);
- Spin model checker (spinroot.com).

Hopefully, tool advances will make formal methods easier to justify and use in an industrial context. Online documentation provides important support. For example, the Formal Methods Wiki (formalmethods.wikia.com), including the Virtual Library formal methods online directory established in the 1990s, continues to be a central resource for formal methods information. Wikipedia, the online encyclopedia, has included increasingly useful and detailed information on formal methods and related topics. Wiki-based resources could be the best path for a repository of collaboratively maintained online information, including for example a Formal Methods Body of Knowledge (FMBoK). Formal Methods Europe (FME, www.fmeurope.org) is the main international organization concerned with formal methods and continues to organize the FM International Symposium on Formal Methods every 18 months that acts as a regular focus for the formal methods community.[1]

Acknowledgements   We are grateful to our many colleagues and friends who provided us with valuable feedback and reactions to our original article. We also acknowledge the contributions of the formal methods community as a whole and thank them for providing us with material on which to base the original commandments. In particular, we thank David Atkinson, Jin Son Dong, Cliff Jones, Tiziana Margaria, Jim Rash, Chris Rouff, Roy Sterritt, and Bernhard Steffen, for their input.

Special thanks go to Tiziana Margaria and Mieke Massink, co-chairs of FMICS 2005, and George Eleftherakis, chair of SEEFM 2005, for inviting earlier conference presentations of this material, in the former case rather aptly to coincide with the tenth anniversary of FMICS.

References

1. Bowen, J.P., Hinchey, M.G.: Seven more myths of formal methods. IEEE Softw. **12**(4), 34–41 (1995)
2. Bowen, J.P., Hinchey, M.G.: Ten commandments of formal methods. IEEE Comput. **28**(4), 56–63 (1995)
3. Bowen, J.P., Hinchey, M.G.: Ten commandments revisited: a ten-year perspective on the industrial application of formal methods. In: 10th International Workshop on Formal Methods for Industrial Critical Systems (FMICS '05), pp. 8–16. ACM, New York (2005)
4. Hall, J.A.: Seven myths of formal methods. IEEE Softw. **7**(5), 11–19 (1990)
5. Hinchey, M.G., Rash, J.L., Rouff, C.A.: Requirements to design to code: towards a fully formal approach to automatic code generation. Technical report NASA Technical Monograph TM-2005-212774, NASA Goddard Space Flight Center (2005)

[1] Section 11.13, *Looking Ahead*, was updated by the authors in March 2011.

6. Hinchey, M.G.: Confessions of a formal methodist. In: Lindsay, P. (ed.) Seventh Australian Workshop Conference on Safety Critical Systems and Software 2002, vol. 15, Adelaide, Australia. Conferences in Research and Practice in Information Technology Series, vol. 139, pp. 17–20. Australian Computer Society, Darlinghurst (2002)
7. Hinchey, M.G., Bowen, J.P. (eds.): Applications of Formal Methods. Prentice Hall, Upper Saddle River (1995)
8. Hinchey, M.G., Bowen, J.P. (eds.): Industrial-Strength Formal Methods in Practice. FACIT Series. Springer, Berlin (1999)
9. Lau, K.-K., Banach, R. (eds.): Formal Methods and Software Engineering, Proceedings 7th International Conference on Formal Engineering Methods, ICFEM 2005, Manchester, UK, November 1–4, 2005. Lecture Notes in Computer Science, vol. 3785. Springer, Berlin (2005)
10. MacKenzie, D.: Mechanizing Proof: Computing, Risk, and Trust. MIT Press, Cambridge (2001)
11. Patterson, D.A., Brown, A., Broadwell, P., Candea, G., Chen, M., Cutler, J., Enriquez, P., Fox, A., Kiciman, E., Merzbacher, M., Oppenheimer, D., Sastry, N., Tetzlaff, W., Traupman, J., Treuhaft., N.: Recovery-oriented computing (ROC): motivation, definition, techniques, and case studies. Technical report Computer Science Technical Report UCB//CSD-02-1175, March 15, 2002, UC Berkeley (2002)
12. Power, D., Meyer, B., Grimes, J., Potel, M., Vetter, R., Laplante, P., Pree, W., Pomberger, G., Hill, M.D., Larus, J.R., Wood, D.A., El-Rewini, H., Weide, B.W.: Where is software headed? A virtual roundtable. Computer **28**(8), 20–32 (1995)
13. Research Triangle Institute: The Economic Impacts of Inadequate Infrastructure for Software Testing. Ed. Dr. Gregory Tassey. RTI Project No. 7007.011. National Institute of Standards and Technology, Washington, DC, May 2002
14. Romijn, J., Smith, G., van de Pol, J. (eds.): Integrated Formal Methods, Proceedings 5th International Conference, IFM 2005, Eindhoven, The Netherlands, November 29–December 2, 2005. Lecture Notes in Computer Science, vol. 3771. Springer, Berlin (2005)
15. Ross, P.E.: The exterminators. IEEE Spectr. **42**(9), 36–41 (2005)
16. Sharpe, R.: Formal methods start to add up again. Computing (2004). 08 Jan 2004. Available online: http://www.computing.co.uk/ctg/feature/1836071/formal-methods-start-add

Chapter 12
Conquering Complexity via Seamless Integration of Design-Time and Run-Time Verification

Antonio Filieri, Carlo Ghezzi, Raffaela Mirandola, and Giordano Tamburrelli

12.1 Introduction

Software is the driving engine of modern society. Most human activities—including critical ones—are either software enabled or entirely managed by software. Examples range from healthcare and transportation to commerce and manufacturing to entertainment and education. As software is becoming ubiquitous and society increasingly relies on it, the adverse impact of unreliable or unpredictable software cannot be tolerated. Software systems are required to be *dependable*, to avoid damaging effects that can range from loss of business to loss of human life.

At the same time, the complexity of modern software systems has grown enormously in the past years with users always demanding new features and better quality of service. Software systems changed from being monolithic and centralized to modular, distributed, and dynamic. They are increasingly composed of heterogeneous components and infrastructures on which software is configured and deployed. When an application is initially designed, software engineers often only have a partial and incomplete knowledge of the external environment in which the application will be embedded at run time. Design may therefore be subject to high uncertainty. This is further exacerbated by the fact that the structure of the application, in terms of components and interconnections, often changes dynamically. New components may become available and published by providers for use by potential clients. Some components may disappear, or become obsolete, and new ones may be discovered dynamically. This may happen, for example, in the case of Web service-based systems [8]. This also happens in pervasive computing scenarios where devices that run application components are mobile [20]. Because of mobility, and more generally context change, certain components may become unreachable, while others become visible during the application's lifetime. Finally, requirements also change continuously and unpredictably, in a way that is hard to anticipate when

A. Filieri (✉)
DeepSE Group @ DEI, Politecnico di Milano, Milan, Italy
e-mail: filieri@elet.polimi.it

M. Hinchey, L. Coyle (eds.), *Conquering Complexity*,
DOI 10.1007/978-1-4471-2297-5_12, © Springer-Verlag London Limited 2012

systems are initially built. Because of uncertainty and continuous external changes the software application is subject to continuous adaptation and evolution. All this is challenging our ability to achieve the required levels of dependability. F.P. Brooks anticipated this when he said, *Complexity is the business we are in and complexity is what limits us* [16].

This chapter focuses on how to manage design-time uncertainty and run-time changes and how to verify that the software evolves dynamically without disrupting the dependability of applications. We refer to *dependability* as broadly defined by the IFIP 10.4 Working Group on Dependable Computing and Fault Tolerance[1] as:

> [...] the trustworthiness of a computing system which allows reliance to be justifiably placed on the service it delivers [...]

Dependability thus includes as special cases such attributes as reliability, availability, performance, safety, security. In this chapter we focus our attention on two main dependability requirements that typically arise in the case of decentralized and distributed applications: namely, *reliability* and *performance*. Both reliability and performance depend on environment conditions that are hard to predict at design time, and are subject to a high degree of uncertainty. For example, performance may depend on end-user profiles, on network congestion, on load conditions of external services that are integrated in the application. Similarly, reliability may depend on the behavior of the network and of the external services that compose the application being built.

Our approach to the development and operation of complex and dynamically evolvable software systems is rooted in the use of formal models. Hereafter we discuss how uncertainty and anticipation of future changes can be taken into account when the system is initially designed. In particular, we focus on the formal models that can be built at design time to support an initial assessment that the application satisfies the requirements. We also show that models should be kept alive at run time and continuously verified to check that the changes with respect to the design-time assumptions do not bring to requirements violations. This requires seamless integration of design-time and run-time verification. If requirements violations are detected, appropriate actions must be undertaken, ranging from off-line evolution to on-line adaptation. In particular, much research is currently investigating the extent to which the software can respond to predicted or detected requirements violation through self-managed reactions, in an autonomic manner. These, however, are out of the scope of this chapter, which only focuses on design-time and run-time verification.

Our contribution is structured as follows. Section 12.2 introduces a running example, which is inspired by a Web-service based *e-Health* application, called Tele-Assistance (TA). Section 12.3 surveys the main formal notations we use to model applications and reason about compliance of its design with respect to its non-functional requirements. We then discuss (Sect. 12.4) how design-time requirements verification may be accomplished in presence of uncertainty. This will be

---

[1]http://www.dependability.org/wg10.4/.

done by first providing high-level models of the running TA example and then by formally verifying requirements satisfaction under some assumptions about the run-time environment in which TA will be embedded. Section 12.5 focuses on monitoring the run-time behavior and performing continuous run-time verification. Finally, Sect. 12.7 provides pointers to on-going work and draws some conclusions.

12.2 A Running Example

This section illustrates the running example adopted in this chapter to illustrate the proposed design and run-time approach. An e-Health application, initially studied in [7] and then further used as a case-study in [29], is designed as a distributed system for medical assistance. The application is built by composing a number of existing Web services. Web-service compositions (and service-oriented architectures in general [27]) make an excellent case for the need to keep models alive at run time. A Web-service composition is an orchestration of Web services aimed at building a new service by exploiting a set of existing ones. The orchestration is performed through the BPEL workflow language [1]. A BPEL composition is, in turn, a service that can be composed with other services in a recursive manner. BPEL instances co-ordinate services that are typically managed by independent organizations, other than the owner of the service composition. This distributed ownership implies that the final functional and non-functional properties of the composed service rely on behaviors of third-party components that influence the obtained results, as we will discuss hereafter.

The running example, called TeleAssistance (TA), focuses on a composite service supporting remote assistance of patients who live in their homes. Figure 12.1 illustrates the TA composite service through a graphical notation into which BPEL constructs are mapped. The mapping between BPEL constructs and the corresponding graphical notation is described in Table 12.1. The reader who wishes to read more about BPEL may find a brief summary in the Appendix at the end of the chapter.

The process starts as soon as a Patient (PA) enables the home device supplied by TA, which sends a message to the process' receive activity *startAssistance*. Then, it enters an infinite loop: every iteration is a pick activity that suspends the execution and waits for one of the following three messages: (1) *vitalParamsMsg*, (2) *pButtonMsg*, or (3) *stopMsg*. The first message contains the patient's vital parameters that are forwarded by the BPEL process to the Medical Laboratory service (LAB) by invoking the operation *analyzeData*. The LAB is in charge of analyzing the data and replies by sending a result value stored in a variable *analysisResult*. A field of the variable contains a value that can be: *changeDrug*, *changeDoses* or *sendAlarm*. The latter message triggers the intervention of a First-Aid Squad (FAS) composed of doctors, nurses, and paramedics, whose task is to visit the patient at home in case of emergency. To alert the squad, the TA process invokes the operation alarm of the FAS. The message *pButtonMsg* caused by pressing a panic button also generates an alarm sent to the FAS. Furthermore, the message *stopMsg* indicates that the patient may decide to cancel the TA service.

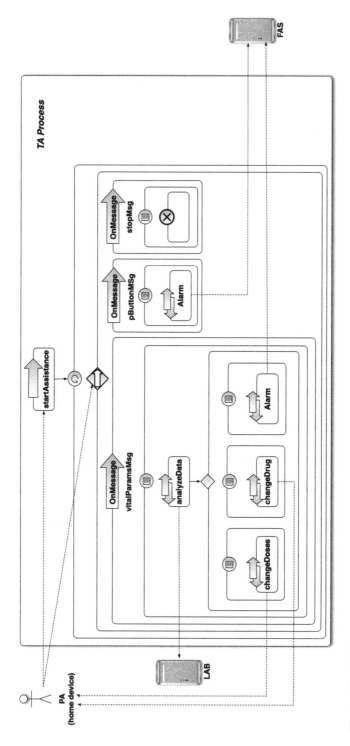

Fig. 12.1 TA BPEL process

Table 12.1 BPEL graphical notation

Activity	Notation	Activity	Notation	Activity	Notation
receive		wait		pick	
invoke		terminate		flow	
reply		sequence		fault handler	
assign		switch		event handler	
throw		while		compensation handler	

The system should be designed to satisfy a number of requirements concerning the Quality of Service (QoS), among which:

- **R1**: *The probability P1 that no failures ever occurs is greater than* 0.7
- **R2**: *If a changeDrug or a changeDoses has occurred the probability P2 that the next message received by the TA generates an alarm which fails (i.e., the FAS is not notified) is less than 0.015*
- **R3**: *Assuming that alarms generated by pButtonMsg have lower priority than the alarms generated by analyzeData, the probability P3 that a high priority alarm fails (i.e., it is not notified to the FAS) is less than 0.012*
- **R4**: *The average response time of the Alarm service (RT_{Alarm}) must be less than 1 second*
- **R5**: *The utilization of the AnalyzeData ($U_{AnalyzeData}$) must be less than 90%*
- **R6**: *The average number of pending requests (i.e., the queue length) to the FAS service (QL_{FAS}) must be less than 60*

Notice that requirements R1–R3 refer to the system's reliability. Conversely, R4–R6 refer to performance.

In the sequel, we will discuss how formal models can support design-time verification that the system being designed satisfies the requirements, under certain assumptions about the behavior of the environment. We will then show how the models can be kept alive at run time to support continuous verification that requirements are not violated despite changes in the assumptions under which the system was initially verified.

12.3 Non Functional Models for Complex Systems

This section provides an introduction to the non-functional models we adopt to express QoS properties. As previously introduced, we focus on reliability and performance. As non-functional models we rely respectively on Discrete Time Markov Chains (DTMCs) ands Queueing Networks (QNs). Let us first introduce Markov models in general and then describe DTMCs and QNs [15].

12.3.1 Markov Models

Several approaches exist in the literature for model-based quality analysis and prediction, spanning the use of stochastic Petri nets, queueing networks, layered queueing network, stochastic process algebras, Markov processes, fault trees, statistical models and simulation models (see [2] for a recent review and classification of models for software quality analysis).

In this work, we focus on Markov models, which are a very general evaluation model that can be used to reason about performance and reliability properties. Furthermore, Markov models include other modeling approaches as special cases, such as queueing networks, stochastic Petri nets [57] and stochastic process algebras [26].

Specifically, Markov models are stochastic processes defined as state-transition systems augmented with probabilities. Formally, a stochastic process is a collection of random variables $X(t)$, $t \in T$ all defined on a common sample (probability) space. $X(t)$ is the state at time t, where t is a value in a set T that can be either discrete or continuous. In Markov models, states represent possible configurations of the system being modeled. Transitions between states occur at discrete or continuous time-steps and the probability of making transitions is given by exponential probability distributions. The Markov property characterizes these models: it means that, given the present state, future states are independent of the past. In other words, the description of the present state fully captures all the information that could influence the future evolution of the process. The most used Markov models include:

- *Discrete Time Markov Chains* (DTMCs), which are the simplest Markovian model where transitions between states happen at discrete time steps;
- *Continuous Time Markov Chains* (CTMCs), where the value associated with each outgoing transition from a state is intended not as a probability but as a parameter of an exponential probability distribution (transition rate);
- *Markov Decision Processes* (MDPs) [62], which are an extension of DTMCs allowing multiple probabilistic behaviors to be specified as output of a state. These behaviors are selected non-deterministically. MDPs are characterized by a discrete set of states representing possible configurations of the system being modeled and transitions between states occur in discrete time-steps, but in each state there is also a non-deterministic choice between several discrete probability distributions over successor states.

The solution of Markovian models aims at determining the system behavior as time t approaches infinity. It consists of the evaluation of the stationary probability π_s of each state s of the model.

The analytical solution techniques for Markov models differ according to the specific model and to the underlying assumptions (e.g., transient or non-transient states, continuous vs. discrete time, etc.). For example, the evaluation of the stationary probability π_s of a DTMC model requires the solution of a linear system whose size is given by the number of states. The exact solution of such a system can be obtained only when the number of states is finite or when the matrix of transition probabilities has a specific form. DTMCs including transient and absorbing states necessitate a more complex analysis for the evaluation of the average number of visits and absorbing probabilities. The detailed derivation is discussed in [15]. A problem of Markov models, which similar evaluation models also face, is the explosion of the number of states when they are used to model real systems [15]. To tackle this problem tool support (e.g., PRISM [52]) with efficient symbolic representations and state space reduction techniques [45, 53] like partial-order reduction, bisimulation-based lumping and symmetry reduction are required.

Given a Markov model it is possible to represent QoS requirements as non-ambiguous properties expressed in an appropriate logic, such as probabilistic temporal logics PCTL (Probabilistic Computation Tree Logic) [40], PCTL* [4], PTCTL (Probabilistic Timed CTL) [54] and CSL (Continuous Stochastic Logic) [5]. The significant benefits of using logic-based requirements specifications include the ability to define these requirements concisely and unambiguously, and to analyze them using rigorous, mathematically-based tools such as model checkers. Furthermore, for logic-based specification-formalism the correct definition of QoS properties is supported with specification patterns [28, 37, 38, 49] and structured English grammars [38, 49, 70].

Markov models are widely used at design time to derive performance and/or reliability metrics. For example, the work presented in [36] discusses in depth the problem of modeling and analyzing the reliability of service-based applications and presents a method for the reliability prediction of service compositions based on the analysis of the implied Markovian models. The analysis of a CTMC implied by a BPEL process is also used in [66] as a way to derive performance and reliability indices of a service composition.

12.3.1.1 Discrete Time Markov Chains

DTMCs are specifically used to model reliability concerns. As introduced before, DTMCs are defined as state-transition systems augmented with probabilities. *States* represent possible configurations of the system. *Transitions* among states occur at discrete time and have an associated probability. DTMCs are discrete stochastic processes with the Markov property, according to which the probability distributions of future states depend only upon the current state.

Formally, a (labeled) DTMC is a tuple (S, s_0, P, L), where

- S is a finite set of states
- $S_0 \subseteq S$ is a set of initial states
- $P : S \times S \to [0, 1]$ is a stochastic transition matrix ($\sum_{s' \in S} P(s, s') = 1 \ \forall s \in S$). An element $P(s_i, s_j)$ represents the probability that the next state of the process will be s_j given that the current state is s_i.
- $L : S \to 2^{AP}$ is a labeling function which assigns to each state the set of *Atomic Propositions* $a \subseteq AP$ holding in s. As discussed in [51], AP formally is a fixed, finite set of atomic propositions used to label states with the properties of interest which can be verified by a stochastic model checker.

A DTMC evolves from the initial state by executing a transition at each discrete time instant. Being at time i in a state s, at time $i + 1$ the model will be in s' with probability $P(s, s')$. The transition can take place only if $P(s, s') > 0$.

A state $s \in S$ is said to be an *absorbing state* if $P(s, s) = 1$. If a DTMC contains at least one absorbing state, the DTMC itself is said to be an *absorbing DTMC*. Furthermore, we assume that every state in the DTMC is reachable from the initial state, that is there exists at least a sequence of transitions from the initial state to every other state.

In an absorbing DTMC with r absorbing states and t transient states, rows and columns of the transition matrix P can be reordered such that P is in the following *canonical form*:

$$\mathbf{P} = \begin{pmatrix} Q & R \\ 0 & I \end{pmatrix}$$

where I is an r by r identity matrix, 0 is an r by t zero matrix, R is a nonzero t by r matrix and Q is a t by t matrix.

Consider now two distinct transient states s_i and s_j. The probability of moving from s_i to s_j in exactly 2 steps is $\sum_{s_x \in S} P(s_i, s_x) * P(s_x, s_j)$. Generalizing the process for a k-steps path and recalling the definition of matrix product, it comes out that the probability of moving from any transient state s_i to any other transient state s_j in exactly k steps corresponds to the entry (s_i, s_j) of the matrix Q^k. By generalization, the probability of moving from s_i to s_j in 0 steps is 1 iff $s_i = s_j$, that is Q^0.

Due to the fact that R must be a nonzero matrix, and P is a stochastic matrix, Q has uniform-norm strictly less than 1, thus $Q^n \to 0$ as $n \to \infty$, which implies that eventually the process will be absorbed with probability 1.

In the simplest model for reliability analysis, the DTMC modeling a task will have two absorbing states, one representing the correct accomplishment of the task, the other representing the failure of the system. The use of absorbing states is commonly extended to represent different failures. For example, a failure state may be associated with each invocation of an external service that may fail. A basic feature of a reasoning system in this framework is to provide an estimate for the probability of reaching an absorbing state or the ability to state whether the probability of reaching an absorbing state associated with a failure is less than a certain threshold.

12.3.2 Queueing Networks

For performance models we exploit QNs. As introduced before, they can be reduced to a Markov model and the solution of a QN might be obtained by solving the underlying Markov process. However, for some classes of QNs, efficient analytical solution techniques exist to determine the average values of the performance metrics (e.g., average response time, utilization, etc.) or, in some cases, also the percentile distribution of the metric of interest.

QNs [15, 55] are a widely adopted modeling technique for performance analysis. QNs are composed by a finite set of: (1) *Service Centers*, (2) *Links*, (3) *Sources and Sinks*, and (4) *Delay Centers*.

Service centers model system resources that process customer request. Each service center is composed of a *Server* and a *Queue*. Queues can be characterized by a finite or an infinite length. In this work we focus on service centers with infinite queues. Service centers are connected through *Links* that form the network topology. Servers process *jobs*—hereafter we refer to requests interchangeably with the term jobs—retrieved from their queue following a specific policy (e.g., FIFO). Each processed request is then routed to another service center through connections provided by links. More precisely, each server, contained in every service center, picks the next job from its queue (if not empty), processes it, and selects one link that routes the processed request to the queue of another service center. It is possible to specify a policy for link selection (e.g., probabilistic, round robin, etc.). The time spent in every server by each request is modeled by continuous distributions such as exponential or Poisson distributions. Jobs are generated by source nodes connected with links to the rest of the QN. Source nodes are also characterized by continuous time distributions that model request inter-arrival times. Sink nodes represent the points where jobs leave the system. Finally, delay centers are nodes of the QN connected with links to the rest of the network exactly as service centers, but they do not have an associated queue. Delay centers are described only by a service time, with a continuous distribution, without an associated queue. They correspond to service centers with infinite servers.

After modeling a software system as a queueing network, the model has to be evaluated in order to determine quantitative performance metrics, such as:

- *Utilization*: the ratio between the server's busy time over the total time.
- *Response Time*: the interval between submission of a request into the QN and output of results.
- *Queue Length*: the average queue length for a given service center.
- *Throughput*: the number of requests processed per unit of time.

The above measures are defined for a single service center, but they can also apply to the whole network. A first step in the evaluation of a QN can be achieved by determining the system bounds; specifically, upper and lower bounds on system throughput and response time can be computed as functions of the system workload intensity (number or arrival rate of customers). Bounds usually require very little computational effort, especially for simple kinds of QN, like single-class networks [22, 48].

More accurate results can be achieved by solving the equations which govern the QN behavior. Solution techniques can be broadly classified as *analytical methods* (which can be *exact* or *approximate*) and *simulation methods*. Analytical methods determine functional relations between model parameters and performance metrics. Queueing networks satisfying the BCMP theorem assumptions (see [10] for further details) are an important class of models also known as *product-form models*. Such models are the only ones that can be solved efficiently, while the solution time of the equations governing non-product-form queueing network grows exponentially with the size of the network. Hence, in practical situations the time required for the solution of non-product-form networks becomes prohibitive and approximate solutions have to be adopted. Analytical solutions often provide only the average values of the performance metrics (e.g., average response time, utilization, etc.). Detailed solutions can be obtained by solving the Markov process underlying the queueing network model (details about the derivation of the Markov process can be found in [15]).

For non-product-form QNs very often simulation is used to evaluate performance metrics. Simulation is a very general and versatile technique to study the evolution of a software system, which is described by a simulation program that mimics the dynamic behavior of the system by representing its components and interactions in terms of functional relations. Non-functional attributes are estimated by evaluating the values of a set of observations gathered in the simulation runs. Simulation results are then obtained by performing statistical analyses of multiple runs [44]. With simulation it is possible to obtain very accurate results but at the cost of a higher computational effort with respect to the analytical solution of QNs.

12.3.2.1 Modeling Complex Systems with Queueing Networks

In modern complex systems, components may fall into different categories. First, they may differ in the way they are used (*use mode*). Their use may be *exclusive*; that is, the component is only used by the currently designed application. In this case, the component may be modeled as a service center, since we have full control of the flows of requests into its input queue. In other cases, the component is *shared* among different applications, which we may not know, although they concurrently access it. The component cannot be modeled as service center because other jobs, which we cannot control, also can access the service. In such a case, the component can be more simply—but less accurately—modeled as a delay center.

As an example of these two cases, consider a component which provides functionalities for video encoding and decoding. In case it is a component-off-the-shelf (COTS), which is deployed within the current application and it is used exclusively by it, the designer has full control and visibility of its activations, and thus it can be modeled by a service center. If, however, the tool is offered by a provider as a Web service, it is potentially accessed by many clients, and the designer has no control nor visibility of the queues of requests.

Another key factor that must be considered by the modeler is *visibility* of the internals of the component. Both accuracy and trust of the component's performance characteristics depend on how detailed the designer's knowledge is of the component's internals. If an accurate description of the component's architecture is available, its performance can be predicted quite accurately, for example using a design-time tool like Palladio [12]. If instead the component is a black-box, like in the case of Web services, the designer must rely on less trustable figures published by the service provider or inferred by past observations. Note that visibility is often related

Table 12.2 QN notation for open systems

Notation	Name	Use Mode	Visibility	Description
	White-Box	exclusive	yes	service center
	Grey-Box	exclusive	no	service center
	White-Box Shared	shared	yes	service center with source node
	Black-Box	shared	no	delay center

to *ownership*. If one owns a component, then normally one also has full access to its internals, and conversely. Furthermore, it is also related with *stability*. Whenever a component is owned, it only evolves under control of the owner. If an accurate model of the component is available, there is no need to monitor the component at run time for possible deviations and, consequently, to update the model.

The above discussion leads to the following main component categories:

- *White-Box (WB)* components. Their internal architecture is fully visible and understood by the designer; for example, they have been developed in-house. In addition, their use is exclusive to the current application.
- *Grey-Box (GB)* components. Their use is exclusive, but their internals are not known; only the executable version of the component is available. COTS are a typical example.
- *White-Box Shared (WBS)* components. The designer has full visibility of the component, which however is not used exclusively within the application being developed. An example is an in-house developed Web-service that is used by the current application, but is also exported for use by others.
- *Black-Box (BB)* components. The designer has no visibility of the internals of the component, whose use is shared with other unknown clients. An example is an externally developed Web service developed by third parties that is available on-line.

Table 12.2 summarizes the previous discussion by showing the main categories of components, the choices we made for modeling them via QNs, and the graphical notation we use.

12.4 Design-Time Modeling and Verification of the TA System

Hereafter we apply the formalisms discussed in the previous section in the initial design and verification of the TA system. The first step of our approach consists of developing models that can be used to reason about our non-functional properties of interest (reliability and performance). To do so, we identify the parts that are subject to uncertainty and which may change in the value of quality attributes. We especially focus on two major sources of uncertainty and volatility: *user profiles*, which describe how system functions will be used by user transactions, and *external components (services)*, which may change their quality of service over time in an unexpected and uncontrolled manner. These may be viewed as black-box components, accessible via an abstract interface that only provides visibility of the stable information upon which we can rely.

We assume that uncertain information can be expressed in probabilistic terms. This may be difficult in practice, but it is a necessary step in our approach if we want to be able to predict and assess non-functional properties at design time. Several practical guidelines may be followed as a guidance through this step. For example, initial estimates may be provided by the designer based on past experience with similar systems. In the case where external components (services) managed by third parties are integrated into the current system, the estimate may be provided by the service-level agreement subscribed by the provider or by ad-hoc tests performed by client stubs.

The next section shows how we model reliability of the TA system via DTMCs. We then show how performance can be modeled by exploiting QNs. Finally we discuss how an initial assessment of requirements satisfaction may be obtained by analyzing the models.

12.4.1 DTMCs at Work

Figure 12.2 illustrates the result obtained by modeling the TA running example introduced in Sect. 12.2. The modeling activity consists of identifying relevant states of the system, assigning probabilities to branches, and failure probabilities to service invocations. Notice that failure states are highlighted in gray. In this example, we adopted numerical values chosen for illustrative purposes; real-world medical applications usually require lower failure probabilities. Usage profiles are also represented in Fig. 12.2 as probabilities associated with transitions. As an example, consider the transitions exiting state 0. With probability 0.3 the user pushes a button to generate an alarm, whose notification to the first-aid squad fails with probability 0.04.

The DTMC derivation can be done either manually or through automatic transformation techniques. Several contributions that appeared in the literature proposed techniques to derive DTMC starting from a formal description of the system's behavior (e.g., [31, 36, 66]).

12.4.2 QNs at Work

Figure 12.3 illustrates the result obtained by modeling the TA example with a QN. Notice that transition probabilities among service centers are consistent with values

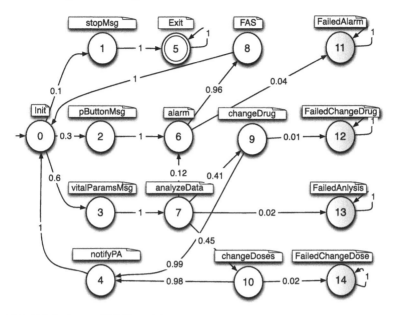

Fig. 12.2 TeleAssistance DTMC model

Table 12.3 QN additional parameters

Component	Parameter	Value
Source 0	Arrival rate	Exponential with $\lambda = 0.5$
Source 1	Arrival rate	Exponential with $\lambda = 0.1$
startAssistance	Service time	Exponential with $\lambda = 1$
startAssistance	Queue	∞
stopMsg	Service time	Exponential with $\lambda = 1$
stopMsg	Queue	∞
FAS	Service time	Exponential with $\lambda = 1.45$
FAS	Queue	∞
Alarm	Service time	Exponential with $\lambda = 1.5$
AnalyzeData	Service time	Exponential with $\lambda = 2.5$
changeDoses	Service time	Exponential with $\lambda = 1.2$
changeDrug	Service time	Exponential with $\lambda = 1.2$

used in Fig. 12.2. Before applying the concepts and the taxonomy illustrated in Sect. 12.3.2, we need to take into consideration some performance data describing the behavior of the components part of the TA system. Such data, as for transition probabilities in DTMCs, might be provided by domain experts or other existing systems. Table 12.3 summarizes this information set.

Concerning the components and services part of the TA system, we assumed the *changeDrug*, *changeDoses* and *sendAlarm* service centers as Web services provided by third-party organizations. Conversely, we considered the FAS service as a service owned by the same organization of the TA system but potentially used by other healthcare functions. According to these assumptions, we model the former as Black-box centers and the latter as White-Box Shared.

To facilitate the software engineer's task, several methodologies can be found in the literature to support transformation techniques that can derive QN-based models (both product and non-product) starting from software models. Some of the proposed methods are reviewed in [6, 11, 71].

12.4.3 Design-Time Verification

Once the models of the application under design are available, they can be analyzed to verify requirements satisfaction. Let us start our discussion from reliability and let us consider the reliability model illustrated in Fig. 12.2.

The reliability requirements R1–R3 can be proven to hold for the composite service. Several instruments are in place to verify stochastic properties on DTMCs, with different pros and cons. The most basic approach is based on probability theory's formulas, which can be solved by means of numerical methods [64]; these approaches are typically fast and very accurate, but most often used for simple properties such as the probability of reaching a certain state. The most popular verification tools nowadays are the probabilistic model checkers. The two most widely adopted are PRISM [42] and MRMC [46]. Model-checkers come with logics expressive enough to assert complex properties over the set of all possible paths through a DTMC, but they typically make use of iterative methods which provide a finite accuracy (though this can be arbitrarily high at the price of a polynomially longer computation time). For very large systems which are hard to be analyzed by means of mathematical methods, it is also possible to apply some verifiers which adopt Monte-Carlo simulation [67].

For example, by using the DTMC probabilistic model checker PRISM [42], we obtain: $P1 = 0.7421$, $P2 = 0.0147$, $P3 = 0.0048$. As we discussed earlier, model parameters (i.e., transition probabilities) might be provided by: (1) domain experts, (2) similar existing systems, or (3) previous versions of the system under design. In any case, such parameters represent only estimates and run-time analyses are in charge of refining them together with a continuous verification of the compliance with the system's requirements, as illustrated later on in Sect. 12.5.

Let us now consider performance and the QN model illustrated in Fig. 12.3. By relying on parameters listed in Table 12.3 and exploiting a QN solver such as JMT [14] we can evaluate the performance requirements R4–R6 and prove to hold for the composite service. In particular, we obtained: $RT_{Alarm} = 0.6667$, $U_{AnalyzeData} = 0.8906$, $QL_{FAS} = 53.4771$. Notice that model parameters might be retrieved as previously mentioned for DTMCs transition probabilities.

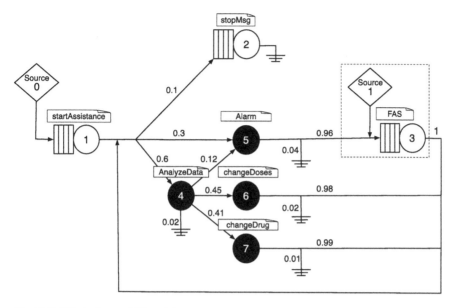

Fig. 12.3 TeleAssistance QN model

12.5 Supporting Run-Time Verification

After an application is developed, it is deployed in the target environment to interact
with the real world. Regrettably, at run time reality may subvert the assumptions
made by software engineers at design time. For example, user profiles may differ
from the expected values, or may later change during operation. Likewise, the performance of an external service integrated in the application may change, due for
example to the deployment of a new version of the service which provides additional features. Similarly, a service's reliability may unexpectedly decrease, due to
the upload of a new, buggier release. For these reasons, it is necessary that verification continues after the application's delivery, to check if changes cause a violation
of requirements. If they do, the application must also change.

We distinguish between two kinds of change: adaptation and evolution [20].
Adaptation refers to the actions taken at run time and affecting the architectural
level, to react to the changing environment in which the application operates. In fact,
changes in the physical context may often require the software architecture to also
change. As an example, a certain service used by the application may become un-
accessible as a new physical context is entered during execution. Conversely, a new
service may become visible. It may also happen that a certain service is changed
unexpectedly by its owner and the change is found to be incompatible with its use
from the current application. *Evolution* instead refers to changes in the application
that are the consequence of changes in the requirements. For example, a new feature
is added to the TA system to support medical diagnosis remotely via video interaction with the patient. Adaptation must be increasingly supported in an autonomic
way. We use the term self-adaptation in this case.

In our approach, evolution and (self) adaptation are triggered by run-time verification, whenever a requirements failure is detected [35]. To support run-time verification, the application's model has to be alive at run time and it must be fed with updated values of the parameters, which reflect the detected changes in environment conditions. To detect changes—in turn—suitable run-time monitors must be activated to collect the relevant data from the environment [9, 33]. In the TA example, a monitor should detect changes in the usage profiles and in the reliability and performance characteristics of the external services. To do so, the data observed at run time must be converted into probabilities that are used to annotate the DTMC and the QN models of the TA example. The conversion can be performed by learning algorithms, typically based on a Bayesian approach, as shown in [29].

In the TA example, let us consider the effect of the following situations that may be occur at run time.

- The service providing the FAS functionality is discontinued for some time (it fails with probability 1). The verification procedure for reliability requirements (a probabilistic model checker) detects a run-time violation of requirement R1.
- The *notifyPA* operation, which was supposed to be completely reliable (failure probability equal to 0) is found out to fail with probability 0.01. The model checker in this case detects a run-time violation of requirement R2.
- The distribution of reactions to *analyzeData* is found to be quite different from the one assumed at design time. The probability discovered at run-time that *changeDoses* is diagnosed is 0.20 instead of 0.45, the probability that *changeDrug* is diagnosed is 0.31 instead of 0.41, the probability that *alarm* is generated is 0.47 instead of 0.12, while the probability that a failure is experienced has exactly the value hypothesized by the designer (0.20). The model checker detects a run-time violation of requirement R3.

Performance requirements can also be checked for possible violation at run time. Hereafter we provide a few examples of cases where the environment's behavior differs from the assumptions made during design and this would lead to requirements violations, detected by the QN analyzer:

- Assuming that due to contextual issues the alarm is able to answer to an average of 0.9 requests per second, instead of the value 1.5 expected, the average response time of the service growths from 0.667 to 1.111, violating requirement R4.
- If from monitoring data the actual measured request processing rate of the data analyzer is 2 requests/sec, slower than the value expected at runtime (2.5), then the utilization of the analyzer becomes 1.1135. Such a value, being larger than 90%, leads to the violation of the requirement R5.
- The FAS component is shared with third parties. Their usage of the component is modeled by Source 1. If those entities, beyond the control of the Tele Assistance company, increase their request rate from 0.1 to 0.2 requests per second, the waiting queue of the FAS saturates (in this model, the number of enqueued requests growths indefinitely) and begins to lose incoming requests. This violates requirement R6 because QL_{FAS} tends to ∞.

12.6 Related Work

In the last years, QoS prediction has been extensively studied in the context of *traditional software systems*. In particular, there has been much interest in model transformation methodologies for the generation of analysis-oriented target models (including performance and reliability models) starting from design-oriented source models, possibly augmented with suitable annotations. Several proposals have been presented concerning the direct generation of performance analysis models. Each of these proposals focuses on a particular type of source design-oriented model and a particular type of target analysis-oriented model, with the former spanning UML, Message Sequence Chart, Use Case Maps, formal language as AEmilia, ADL languages such as Acme, and the latter spanning Petri nets, queueing networks, layered queueing network, stochastic process algebras, Markov processes (see [6] for a thorough overview of these proposals and the WOSP conference series [71] for recent proposals on this topic). A systematization of the current approaches in the framework of MDD and interesting insights on future trends on this topic can be found in [2]. Some proposals have also been presented for the generation of reliability models. All the proposals we are aware of start from UML models with proper annotations, and generate reliability models such as fault trees, state diagrams, Markov processes, hazard analysis techniques and Bayesian models (see [13, 43] for a recent update on this topic).

More recently, with the increasing interest in the topic of reconfigurable and self-adaptive computing systems [25], several papers appeared in the literature dealing with self-adaptation of software systems to guarantee the fulfillment of QoS requirements. Hereafter, we present a short summary of existing work that makes use of models to perform this step. GPAC (General-Purpose Autonomic Computing), for example, is a tool-supported methodology for the model-driven development of self-managing IT systems [17]. The core component of GPAC is a generic autonomic manager capable of augmenting existing IT systems with a MAPE [47] autonomic computing loop. The GPAC tools and the probabilistic model checker PRISM [42] are used together successfully to develop autonomic systems involving dynamic power management and adaptive allocation of data-center resources [18]. KAMI [29] is another framework for model evolution by runtime parameter adaptation. KAMI focuses on Discrete Time Markov Chain models that are used to reason about non-functional properties of the system. The authors adapt the QoS properties of the model using Bayesian estimations based on runtime information, and the updated model allows the verification of QoS requirements. The approach presented in [63] considers the QoS properties of a system in a web-service environment. The authors provide a language called SLAng, which allows the specification of QoS to be monitored.

The Models@Run.Time approach [61] proposes to leverage software models and to extend the applicability of model-driven engineering techniques to the runtime environment to enhance systems with dynamic adapting capabilities. In [68], the authors use an architecture-based approach to support dynamic adaptation. Rainbow [32] also updates architectural models to detect inconsistencies and in this way it is able to correct certain types of faults. A different use of models at runtime for system adaptation is taken in [56]. The authors update the model based on execution traces of the system. In [73] the authors describe a methodology for estimation of model parameters through Kalman filtering. This work is based on a continuous monitoring that provides run-time data feeding a Kalman filter, aimed at updating the performance model.

In [65], the authors propose a conceptual model dealing with changes in dynamic software evolution. Besides, they apply this model to a simple case study, in order to evaluate the effectiveness of fine-grained adaptation changes like service-level degrading/upgrading action considering also the possibility to perform actions involving the overall resource management. The approach proposed in [58] deals with QoS-based reconfigurations at design time. The authors propose a method based on evolutionary algorithms where different design alternatives are automatically generated and evaluated for different quality attributes. In this way, the software architect is provided with a decision making tool enabling the selection of the design alternatives that best fits multiple quality objectives. Menascé et al. [60] developed the SASSY framework for generating service-oriented architectures based on quality requirements. Based on an initial model of the required service types and their communication, SASSY generates an optimal architecture by selecting the best services and potentially adding patterns such as replication or load balancing. In [59] an approach for performance-aware reconfiguration of degradable software systems called PARSY (Performance Aware Reconfiguration of software SYstems) is presented. PARSY tunes individual components in order to maximize the system utility with the constraint of keeping the system response time below a predefined threshold. PARSY uses a closed Queueing Network model to select the components to upgrade or degrade.

In the area of service-based systems (SBS), devising QoS-driven adaptation methodologies is of utmost importance in the envisaged dynamic environment in which they operate. Most of the proposed methodologies for QoS-driven adaptation of SBS address this problem as a service selection problem (e.g., [3, 19, 72]). Other papers have instead considered service-based adaptation through workflow restructuring, exploiting the inherent redundancy of SBS (e.g., [24, 39, 41].) In [21] a unified framework is proposed where service selection is integrated with other kinds of workflow restructuring, to achieve a greater flexibility in the adaptation.

12.7 Conclusions and Future Work

In this chapter we focus on complex, evolvable, and adaptable software applications that live in highly dynamic environments and yet need to provide service in a dependable manner. These requirements affect the way software is designed and operated at run time. The most striking consequence is that models should be kept alive at run time to support a verification activity that extends to run time.

We envision three important directions for future work. First, it is important to investigate how detected requirements violations at run time may drive self-adaptation, to achieve autonomic behavior. In our research group, we achieved some preliminary results for restricted cases of self-adaptation in [23, 34], but much remains to be done.

Another important research direction should investigate the methods that fit the specific requirements of run-time verification. In this chapter, we assumed that the same verification procedures that are used at design time can also be used at run time. This is of course often an unrealistic assumption. Because run-time reactions that lead to self-adaptation are triggered by failures in requirements verification, the time consumed by the verification procedure must be compatible with the time limits within which a reaction must take place. The model checkers available for requirements verification are not designed for on-line use, but rather to explore design-time tradeoffs. Efficient verification algorithms need to be developed to fully support run-time verification. An initial step in this direction is explored in [30].

A third research direction in which we are currently engaging concerns the mechanisms that must support the run-time reconfigurations that are produced as a result of self-adaptation. Dynamic reconfiguration must occur dynamically, as the application is running and providing service. The goal is to preserve correctness and at the same time perform the change in a timely manner, without disrupting the service. Our work is focusing on extending previous work by Kramer and Magee [50], which was further extended by [69].

Acknowledgements This research has been partially funded by the European Commission, Programme IDEAS-ERC, Project 227977-SMScom.

Appendix: BPEL Overview

BPEL, the *Business Process Execution Language*, is an XML-based workflow language conceived for the definition and the execution of service compositions. BPEL processes comprise variables, with different visibility levels, and the workflow logic expressed as a composition of elementary activities. Activities comprise tasks like: *Receive, Invoke,* and *Reply* that are related to the interaction with other services. Moreover it is possible to perform assignments (*Assign*), throw exceptions (*Throw*), pause (*Wait*) or stop the process (*Terminate*).

Branch, loop, while, sequence, and switch constraints manage the control flow of BPEL processes. The pick construct is peculiar to the domain of concurrent and distributed systems, and waits for the first out of several incoming messages, or timer alarms to occur, to execute the activities associated with such an event. Each scope may contain the definition of the several handlers: (1) an Event Handler that reacts to an event by executing a specific activity, (2) a Fault Handler catches faults in the local scope, and (3) a Compensation Handler aimed at restoring the effects of a previously unsuccessful transaction. For a complete description of the BPEL language see [1] and the Organization for the Advancement of Structured Information Standards (OASIS) website.[2] The graphical representation used in this paper is described earlier in Sect. 12.2.

---

[2]The OASIS website is here: http://www.oasis-open.org.

References

1. Alves, A., Arkin, A., Askary, S., Bloch, B., Curbera, F., Goland, Y., Kartha, N., Sterling, König, D., Mehta, V., Thatte, S., van der Rijn, D., Yendluri, P., Yiu, A.: Web services business process execution language version 2.0. OASIS Committee Draft (2006)
2. Ardagna, D., Ghezzi, C., Mirandola, R.: Rethinking the use of models in software architecture. In: 4th International Conference on the Quality of Software-Architectures, QoSA 2008. LNCS, vol. 5281, pp. 1–27. Springer, Berlin (2008)
3. Ardagna, D., Mirandola, R.: Per-flow optimal service selection for web services based processes. J. Syst. Softw. **83**(8), 1512–1523 (2010)
4. Aziz, A., Singhal, V., Balarin, F.: It usually works: the temporal logic of stochastic systems. In: Wolper, P. (ed.) Proc. 7th International Conference on Computer Aided Verification, CAV 95. LNCS, vol. 939, pp. 155–165. Springer, Berlin (1995)
5. Baier, C., Katoen, J.-P., Hermanns, H.: Approximate symbolic model checking of continuous-time Markov chains. In: Baeten, J.C.M., Mauw, S. (eds.) Proc. 10th International Conference on Concurrency Theory, CONCUR 99. LNCS, vol. 1664, pp. 146–161. Springer, Berlin (1999)
6. Balsamo, S., Di Marco, A., Inverardi, P., Simeoni, M.: Model-based performance prediction in software development: a survey. IEEE Trans. Softw. Eng. **30**(5), 295–310 (2004)
7. Baresi, L., Bianculli, D., Ghezzi, C., Guinea, S., Spoletini, P.: Validation of web service compositions. IET Softw. **1**(6), 219–232 (2007)
8. Baresi, L., Di Nitto, E., Ghezzi, C.: Toward open-world software: issue and challenges. Computer **39**(10), 36–43 (2006)
9. Baresi, L., Ghezzi, C., Guinea, S.: Smart monitors for composed services. In: Proceedings of the 2nd International Conference on Service Oriented Computing, ICSOC '04, pp. 193–202. ACM, New York (2004)
10. Baskett, F., Chandy, K.M., Muntz, R.R., Palacios, F.G.: Open, closed, and mixed networks of queues with different classes of customers. J. ACM **22**(2), 248–260 (1975)
11. Becker, S., Grunske, L., Mirandola, R., Overhage, S.: Performance prediction of component-based systems—a survey from an engineering perspective. In: Architecting Systems with Trustworthy Components. LNCS, vol. 3938, pp. 169–192. Springer, Berlin (2006)
12. Becker, S., Koziolek, H., Reussner, R.: Model-based performance prediction with the Palladio component model. In: WOSP '07: Proceedings of the 6th International Workshop on Software and Performance, pp. 54–65. ACM, New York (2007)
13. Bernardi, S., Merseguer, J., Petriu, D.: Adding dependability analysis capabilities to the MARTE profile. In: Model Driven Engineering Languages and Systems, Proceedings 11th International Conference, MoDELS 2008, Toulouse, France, September 28–October 3, 2008. LNCS, vol. 5301, pp. 736–750. Springer, Berlin (2008)
14. Bertoli, M., Casale, G., Serazzi, G.: The JMT simulator for performance evaluation of non-product-form queueing networks. In: Annual Simulation Symposium, pp. 3–10. IEEE Computer Society, Norfolk (2007)
15. Bolch, G., Greiner, S., de Meer, H., Trivedi, K.S.: Queueing Networks and Markov Chains: Modeling and Performance Evaluation with Computer Science Applications. Wiley-Interscience, New York (1998)
16. Brooks, F.P.: The Mythical Man-Month: Essays on Software Engineering. Pearson Education, London (1975)
17. Calinescu, R.: General-purpose autonomic computing. In: Denko, M.K., Yang, L.T., Zhang, Y. (eds.) Autonomic Computing and Networking, pp. 3–30. Springer, Berlin (2009)
18. Calinescu, R., Kwiatkowska, M.: Using quantitative analysis to implement autonomic it systems. In: ICSE '09: Proceedings of the 31st International Conference on Software Engineering, pp. 100–110. IEEE Computer Society, Washington (2009)
19. Canfora, G., Di Penta, M., Esposito, R., Villani, M.L.: A framework for QoS-aware binding and re-binding of composite web services. J. Syst. Softw. **81**(10), 1754–1769 (2008)

20. Caporuscio, M., Funaro, M., Ghezzi, C.: Architectural issues of adaptive pervasive systems. In: Graph Transformations and Model-Driven Engineering, pp. 492–511 (2010)
21. Cardellini, V., Casalicchio, E., Grassi, V., Lo Presti, F., Mirandola, R.: QoS-driven runtime adaptation of service oriented architectures. In: Proceedings ESEC/FSE 2009, pp. 131–140. ACM, New York (2009)
22. Casale, G., Muntz, R., Serazzi, G.: Geometric bounds: a noniterative analysis technique for closed queueing networks. IEEE Trans. Comput. **57**(6), 780–794 (2008)
23. Cavallaro, L., Di Nitto, E., Pelliccione, P., Pradella, M., Tivoli, M.: Synthesizing adapters for conversational web-services from their WSDL interface. In: ICSE Workshop on Software Engineering for Adaptive and Self-Managing Systems, SEAMS '10, pp. 104–113. ACM, New York (2010)
24. Chafle, G., Doshi, P., Harney, J., Mittal, S., Srivastava, B.: Improved adaptation of web service compositions using value of changed information. In: ICWS, pp. 784–791. IEEE Comput. Soc., Los Alamitos (2007)
25. Cheng, B., de Lemos, R., Giese, G., Inverardi, P., Magee, J. (eds.): Software Engineering for Self-Adaptive Systems [outcome of a Dagstuhl Seminar]. LNCS, vol. 5525. Springer, Berlin (2009)
26. Clark, A., Gilmore, S., Hillston, J., Tribastone, M.: Stochastic process algebras. In: 7th Intern. School on Formal Methods, SFM. LNCS, vol. 4486, pp. 132–179. Springer, Berlin (2007)
27. Di Nitto, E., Ghezzi, C., Metzger, A., Papazoglou, M.P., Pohl, K.: A journey to highly dynamic, self-adaptive service-based applications. Autom. Softw. Eng. **15**(3–4), 313–341 (2008)
28. Dwyer, M.B., Avrunin, J.S., Corbett, J.C.: Property specification patterns for finite-state verification. In: Proc. 21th International Conference on Software Engineering (ICSE99), pp. 411–420. ACM, New York (1999)
29. Epifani, I., Ghezzi, C., Mirandola, R., Tamburrelli, G.: Model evolution by run-time parameter adaptation. In: Proc. 31st International Conference on Software Engineering (ICSE09), pp. 111–121. IEEE Comput. Soc., Los Alamitos (2009)
30. Filieri, A., Ghezzi, C., Tamburrelli, G.: Run-time efficient probabilistic model checking. In: Taylor, R.N., Gall, H., Medvidovic, N. (eds.) ICSE, pp. 341–350 (2011)
31. Gallotti, S., Ghezzi, C., Mirandola, R., Tamburrelli, G.: Quality prediction of service compositions through probabilistic model checking. In: QoSA, Quality of Software Architecture. LNCS. Springer, Berlin (2008)
32. Garlan, D., Cheng, S.-W., Huang, A.C., Schmerl, B., Steenkiste, P.: Rainbow: architecture-based self-adaptation with reusable infrastructure. IEEE Comput. **37**(10), 46–54 (2004)
33. Ghezzi, C., Guinea, S.: Run-time monitoring in service-oriented architectures. In: Test and Analysis of Web Services, pp. 237–264. Springer, Berlin (2007)
34. Ghezzi, C., Motta, A., Manna, V.P.L., Tamburrelli, G.: QoS driven dynamic binding in-the-many. In: Heineman, G.T., Kofron, J., Plasil, F. (eds.) Research into Practice—Reality and Gaps, 6th International Conference on the Quality of Software Architectures, QoSA 2010, Prague, Czech Republic, June 23–25, 2010, pp. 68–83. Springer, Berlin (2010)
35. Ghezzi, C., Tamburrelli, G.: Reasoning on non-functional requirements for integrated services. In: RE '09: Proceedings of the 17th International Conference on Requirements Engineering, Atlanta, USA (2009)
36. Grassi, V.: Architecture-based reliability prediction for service-oriented computing. In: Workshop on Architecting Dependable Systems, WADS. LNCS, vol. 3549, pp. 279–299. Springer, Berlin (2004)
37. Gruhn, V., Laue, R.: Patterns for timed property specifications. Electron. Notes Theor. Comput. Sci. **153**(2), 117–133 (2006)
38. Grunske, L.: Specification patterns for probabilistic quality properties. In: Robbie (ed.) 30th International Conference on Software Engineering (ICSE 2008), pp. 31–40. ACM, New York (2008)
39. Guo, H., Huai, J., Li, H., Deng, T., Li, Y., Du, Z.: ANGEL: optimal configuration for high available service composition. In: IEEE International Conference on Web Services (ICWS 2007), pp. 280–287. IEEE Comput. Soc., Los Alamitos (2007)

40. Hansson, H., Jonsson, B.: A logic for reasoning about time and reliability. Form. Asp. Comput. **6**(5), 512–535 (1994)
41. Harney, J., Doshi, P.: Speeding up adaptation of web service compositions using expiration times. In: World Wide Web (WWW), pp. 1023–1032. ACM, New York (2007)
42. Hinton, A., Kwiatkowska, M., Norman, G., Parker, D.: Prism: a tool for automatic verification of probabilistic systems. In: Proc. 12th International Conference on Tools and Algorithms for the Construction and Analysis of Systems (TACAS'06), vol. 3920, pp. 441–444 (2006)
43. Immonen, A., Niemelä, E.: Survey of reliability and availability prediction methods from the viewpoint of software architecture. Softw. Syst. Model. **7**(1), 49–65 (2008)
44. Jain, R.: The Art of Computer Systems Performance Analysis—Techniques for Experimental Design, Measurement, Simulation, and Modeling. Wiley-Interscience, New York (1991)
45. Katoen, J.-P., Kemna, T., Zapreev, I.S., Jansen, D.N.: Bisimulation minimisation mostly speeds up probabilistic model checking. In: Grumberg, O., Huth, M. (eds.) Tools and Algorithms for the Construction and Analysis of Systems TACAS 2007, Proceedings. LNCS, vol. 4424, pp. 87–101. Springer, Berlin (2007)
46. Katoen, J.-P., Khattri, M., Zapreev, I.S.: A Markov reward model checker. In: QEST, pp. 243–244. IEEE Comput. Soc., Los Alamitos (2005)
47. Kephart, J.O., Chess, D.M.: The vision of autonomic computing. IEEE Comput. **36**(1), 41–50 (2003)
48. Kerola, T.: The composite bound method for computing throughput bounds in multiple class environments. Perform. Eval. **6**(1), 1–9 (1986)
49. Konrad, S., Cheng, B.: Real-time specification patterns. In: Roman, G.-C., Griswold, W.G., Nuseibeh, B. (eds.) 27th International Conference on Software Engineering (ICSE 05), pp. 372–381. ACM, New York (2005)
50. Kramer, J., Magee, J.: The evolving philosophers problem: dynamic change management. IEEE Trans. Softw. Eng. **16**, 1293–1306 (1990)
51. Kwiatkowska, M.: Quantitative verification: models, techniques and tools. In: 6th Joint Meeting of the European Software Engineering Conference and the ACM SIGSOFT Symposium on the Foundations of Software Engineering (ESEC/FSE), pp. 449–458. ACM Press, New York (2007)
52. Kwiatkowska, M.Z., Norman, G., Parker, D.: Probabilistic symbolic model checking with PRISM: a hybrid approach. Int. J. Softw. Tools Technol. Transf. **6**(2), 128–142 (2004)
53. Kwiatkowska, M.Z., Norman, G., Parker, D.: Symmetry reduction for probabilistic model checking. In: Ball, T., Jones, R.B. (eds.) Computer Aided Verification, Proceedings 18th International Conference, CAV 2006. LNCS, vol. 4144, pp. 234–248. Springer, Berlin (2006)
54. Kwiatkowska, M.Z., Norman, G., Parker, D., Sproston, J.: Performance analysis of probabilistic timed automata using digital clocks. Form. Methods Syst. Des. **29**(1), 33–78 (2006)
55. Lazowska, E.D., Zahorjan, J., Graham, G.S., Sevcik, K.C.: Quantitative System Performance: Computer System Analysis Using Queueig Network Models. Prentice Hall, New York (1984)
56. Maoz, S.: Using model-based traces as runtime models. IEEE Comput. **42**(10), 28–36 (2009)
57. Marsan, M.A.: Stochastic petri nets: an elementary introduction. In: Advances in Petri Nets, pp. 1–29. Springer, Berlin (1989)
58. Martens, A., Koziolek, H., Becker, S., Reussner, R.: Automatically improve software architecture models for performance, reliability, and cost using evolutionary algorithms. In: 1st Joint WOSP/SIPEW International Conference on Performance Engineering, pp. 105–116. ACM, New York (2010)
59. Marzolla, M., Mirandola, R.: Performance aware reconfiguration of software systems. In: Computer Performance Engineering—Proceedings 7th European Performance Engineering Workshop, EPEW 2010, Bertinoro, Italy, September 23–24, 2010. LNCS, vol. 6342, pp. 51–66. Springer, Berlin (2010)
60. Menascé, D.A., Ewing, J.M., Gomaa, H., Malek, S., Sousa, J.P.: A framework for utility-based service oriented design in sassy. In: Proc. First Joint WOSP/SIPEW Int. Conf. on Performance Engineering, pp. 27–36. ACM, New York (2010)
61. Morin, B., Barais, O., Jézéquel, J.-M., Fleurey, F., Solberg, A.: Models@ run.time to support dynamic adaptation. IEEE Comput. **42**(10), 44–51 (2009)

62. Puterman, M.L.: Markov Decision Processes. Wiley, New York (1994)
63. Raimondi, F., Skene, J., Emmerich, W.: Efficient online monitoring of web-service slas. In: SIGSOFT FSE, pp. 170–180. ACM, New York (2008)
64. Ross, S.M.: Stochastic Processes. Wiley, New York (1996)
65. Salehie, M., Li, S., Asadollahi, R., Tahvildari, L.: Change support in adaptive software: a case study for fine-grained adaptation. In: EASE '09: Proc. Sixth IEEE Conf. and Workshops on Engineering of Autonomic and Autonomous Systems, pp. 35–44. IEEE Comput. Soc., Washington (2009)
66. Sato, N., Trivedi, K.S.: Stochastic modeling of composite web services for closed-form analysis of their performance and reliability bottlenecks. In: ICSOC. LNCS, vol. 4749, pp. 107–118. Springer, Berlin (2007)
67. Sen, K., Viswanathan, M., Agha, G.: On statistical model checking of stochastic systems. In: Etessami, K., Rajamani, S.K. (eds.) Computer Aided Verification. LNCS, vol. 3576, pp. 266–280. Springer, Berlin (2005)
68. Taylor, R.N., Medvidovic, N., Oreizy, P.: Architectural styles for runtime software adaptation. In: WICSA/ECSA, pp. 171–180. IEEE Press, New York (2009)
69. Vandewoude, Y., Ebraert, P., Berbers, Y., D'Hondt, T.: Tranquility: a low disruptive alternative to quiescence for ensuring safe dynamic updates. IEEE Trans. Softw. Eng. 33(12), 856–868 (2007)
70. Wang, L., Dingle, N.J., Knottenbelt, W.J.: Natural language specification of performance trees. In: Thomas, N., Juiz, C. (eds.) Proceedings of the 5th European Performance Engineering Workshop, EPEW 2008. LNCS, vol. 5261, pp. 141–151 (2008)
71. WOSP International Workshops on Software and Performance. ACM, New York (1998–2008)
72. Zeng, L., Benatallah, B., Ngu, A.H., Dumas, M., Kalagnanam, J., Chang, H.: QoS-aware middleware for web services composition. IEEE Trans. Softw. Eng. 30(5), 311–327 (2004)
73. Zheng, T., Woodside, M., Litoiu, M.: Performance model estimation and tracking using optimal filters. IEEE Trans. Softw. Eng. 34(3), 391–406 (2008)

Chapter 13
Modelling Temporal Behaviour in Complex Systems with Timebands

Kun Wei, Jim Woodcock, and Alan Burns

13.1 Introduction

Complex real-time systems exhibit dynamic behaviours on many different time levels. For example, circuits have nanosecond speeds for computation in a component, whereas slower functional units may take seconds to achieve their goals; moreover, the involvement of human activities related to calendar units such as days, weeks, months and even years may take more time. To cope with a wide range of time scales, many approaches [10, 23] have introduced time granularity, so that system specifications and requirements could be naturally described within the best suitable time granularity. However, they usually transform or project all descriptions into the finest granularity in the end. This results in cumbersome formulae and fails to recognise the distinct role that time is taking in the structuring of the system. For example, it is unnecessary to measure the start of a meeting in a millisecond time scale. In fact, most people are usually tolerant of starting a meeting five minutes early or late. Traditional approaches dealing with time granularity sacrifice the separation of concerns in the analysis of complex real-time systems.

To overcome the above weakness when traditional approaches model dynamic temporal behaviours of a system, Burns and Hayes [5] propose a timebands model in which a system is decomposed to reveal different behaviours in different time bands. Apart from defining time bands by granularities, a key aspect of the timebands framework is that *events* are considered to be instantaneous in a band, and then in a finer band they can be mapped into *activities* that have duration. For example, to express a statement that *every month we have a meeting which lasts one hour*, we model the meeting as an instantaneous event in a month band and subsequently map it into an activity in an hour band. This clearly allows dynamic temporal behaviours to be partitioned, but not to be isolated from each other. The mapping

K. Wei (✉)
Department of Computer Science, University of York, York, UK
e-mail: kun@cs.york.ac.uk

M. Hinchey, L. Coyle (eds.), *Conquering Complexity*,
DOI 10.1007/978-1-4471-2297-5_13, © Springer-Verlag London Limited 2012

between different bands leads to more distinct features. For example, precision is introduced to represent the measure of accuracy of events within a band; accordingly, events are *simultaneous* only if, when viewed from a finer band, their corresponding activities are within the precision. Activities may overlap even though their corresponding events in a coarser band are well-ordered. As a result, a formal model of the timebands framework is needed to allow consistency to be asserted between different temporal descriptions that are specified in different time bands.

The concept of time granularity has been well defined in the literature [8, 16] and many approaches have focused on time granularity in different areas of computer science, such as temporal databases, data mining, formal specification and so on. General speaking, the basic idea of time granularity is to partition a universal time domain into differently-grained granules, and a granularity is a set of indexed granules, any one of which is a set of time instants. The choice for time domain is typically between continuous (dense) and discrete. We focus on developing a natural specification language which is able to describe the behaviour of a real-time system whose components engage in different time scales. In other words, we attempt to embed time granularity in a logical specification language. However, adding time granularity to a formalism may give rise to semantic issues like problems of assigning a proper meaning to statements with different time domains and of switching from one domain to a coarser/finer one. So far, most work has been focused on embedding time granularity in temporal logic languages. For example, early exploration [10, 23] consists of translation mechanisms that map a formula associated with different time constraints to the finest granularity. They [7] later revise the simple approach by extending the basic logic language with contextual and projection operators, so that the enhanced semantics can express more general and complete properties. Subsequently, more work [9, 12] uses linear time logic to model and reason about time granularity.

For manipulating the unique feature of mapping events into activities, process algebra approaches are potential candidates for formalising the timebands model. However, there is little work on embedding time granularity in process algebra languages, though there have been many papers [19, 28, 29] on timed process algebra approaches. To formalise the timebands model, we have proposed a new timed model of CSP, called timed CSP with the miracle ($TCSP_M$), which is an extension to timed CSP [28] but whose semantics is based on *Unifying Theories of Programming* (UTP) [15]. This new model uses a complete lattice with respect to the implication order (or the reverse order of the refinement order), which is rather different from previous models such as the complete partial order of CSP [14, 25, 28]. The semantics of the timebands model is built upon $TCSP_M$, fully applying the miracle (the top element of the complete lattice) to express those brand-new features such as simultaneous events and mappings. In this chapter, we use a mine pump example to show how naturally to verify different temporal properties using the timebands model at different time scales. The idea and informal description of the timebands framework has been given in [5], and the formal semantics of the framework is developed in this chapter.

The chapter is structured as follows. We begin with a brief introduction of $TCSP_M$ in Sect. 13.2. Section 13.3 presents how to use the new timed model to formalise the timebands model and how to formally express these distinct features. Then, by means of a rather complex example, we demonstrate how significantly the timebands model contributes to describing a complex real-time system with multiple time scales in Sect. 13.4. Section 13.5 concludes this chapter.

13.2 Timed CSP with the Miracle

Recently, we have proposed a new timed model [32] of *Circus* [26, 33] which is a combination of CSP, Z [34] and the refinement calculus so as to define both data and behavioural aspects of a system. In fact, our timed *Circus* is a compact extension of *Circus* in that it inherits only the CSP part in order to reduce the difficulty of implementing *Circus* programs in practice. Although it does not have the same capability of handling data as the original *Circus* language does, our timed *Circus* preserves local variables for each process that still contains a considerable power to express the change of states. To formalise the timebands model, we further simplify timed *Circus* to $TCSP_M$ by adopting discrete time.

Simply speaking, $TCSP_M$ can also be considered an extension to Schneider's timed CSP [28], but its UTP-style semantics uses a complete lattice in the implication ordering which is different from the complete partial order of timed CSP. With the application of the miracle (the top element of the model), $TCSP_M$ turns out to be able to express some surprising behaviours which, moreover, cannot be described in timed CSP. Additionally, $TCSP_M$ violates some axioms of the standard failures-divergences model of CSP, e.g., traces are not prefix closed any more.

In UTP, Hoare and He use the alphabetised relational calculus to give a denotational semantics that can explain a wide variety of programming paradigms. Hence, the alphabet of a process P in $TCSP_M$ consists of *undashed* variables $(a, b, \ldots)$ and *dashed* variables $(a', x', \ldots)$. The former, written as $in\alpha P$, stands for initial observations, and the latter as $out\alpha P$ for intermediate or final observations. The relation is then called *homogeneous* if $out\alpha P = in\alpha P'$, where $in\alpha P'$ is simply obtained by putting a dash on all the variables of $in\alpha P$. Thus, an observation in $TCSP_M$ is a tuple consisting of $tr, ref, ok, wait, t, v$ and their dashed counterparts, in which tr and tr' are timed traces, ref and ref' are refusals, ok is a boolean variable expressing whether a process has started or not (ok' whether the process has terminated or not), $wait'$ denotes whether the process is in an intermediate state, t is the starting time of the observation (t' is the finishing time), and v and v' denote a set of local variables of the process.

A timed trace is a sequence of timed events which are pairs drawn from $\mathbb{Z}^+ \times \Sigma$,[1] e.g., $\langle (1, pump.on), (3, pump.off) \rangle$ is a timed trace. A refusal is simply a set of events, other than a set of time events in timed CSP, since other variables can assist in representing enough information of when those events are refused. The ok and *wait* observations (and their dashed variables) describe whether a process is started

---

[1] Σ denotes the universal set of events.

(or finished) in a stable state. If ok' is false, the process diverges. If ok' is true, the state of the process depends on the value of $wait'$. If $wait'$ is true, the process is in an intermediate state, otherwise it successfully terminates. Similarly, the values of undashed variables represent the states of the process's predecessor.

Except for the deadline and assignment operators, the syntax of $TCSP_M$ is similar to the one of timed CSP, as described by the following grammar:

$$P ::= \top_R \mid \bot_R \mid SKIP \mid STOP \mid a \rightarrow P \mid P_1; P_2 \mid x :=_A e \mid g\&P \mid$$

$$P_1 \;\square\; P_2 \mid P_1 \sqcap P_2 \mid P_1 \,\|[\,A\,]\| \, P_2 \mid P \setminus A \mid WAIT\, d \mid P_1 \rhd \{d\}P_2 \mid$$

$$P \blacktriangleright d \mid P_1 \triangle \{a\} P_2 \mid \mu X.P$$

13.2.1 Primitive Processes

The miracle $\top_R$ is the top element in the implication ordering, however it cannot be executed since it expresses that a process has not started yet. Of course, an unstarted process satisfies any requirement. The bottom element $\bot_R$ is called *Abort* which can do absolutely anything. The process *STOP* is deadlocked and its only behaviour is to allow time to elapse. The process *SKIP* simply terminates immediately.

13.2.2 Sequential

The sequential composition $P_1; P_2$ behaves as P_1 until P_1 terminates, and then behaves as P_2. In the meanwhile the final state of P_1 is passed on as the initial state of P_2. The prefix process $a \rightarrow P$ is able to execute the event a ($a \in \Sigma$) and then behaves as P. This process can also be represented by a composition of a simple prefix and P itself, written as $(a \rightarrow SKIP); P$. The process $g\&P$ has a boolean expression g, which must be satisfied before P starts.

The notation $(x :=_A e)$ represents that a process simply assigns the value of an expression e to a process variable x, and any other variable in the alphabet A remains unchanged. In practice, we often use a shorthand for the assignment operator. For example, $P(x + 1)$ is actually defined as $(x := x + 1; P)$.

13.2.3 Choice

The process $P_1 \;\square\; P_2$ behaves either like P_1 or P_2, but the first event of which can resolve the choice. Compared with this external choice, the internal choice $P_1 \sqcap P_2$ can also behave either like P_1 or like P_2, but it is out of control of its environment. Both external and internal choices have indexed choices. For example, if I is a finite indexing set such that P_i is defined for each $i \in I$, written as $\square_{i \in I} P_i$. The indexing external choice is also used to define the input operator. For example, if c is a channel name of type T and v is a particular value, the process $c!v \rightarrow P$ outputting v along the channel c is equal to $c.v \rightarrow P$. The inputting process $c?x : T \rightarrow P(x)$ describes a process that is ready to accept any value x of type T, and it is defined as $\square_{x \in T} c.x \rightarrow P(x)$.

13.2.4 Parallel

The process $P_1 \,\|[\, A \,]\|\, P_2$ is the process where all events in the set A must be synchronised, and the events outside A can execute independently. The parallel process terminates only if both P_1 and P_2 terminate, and it becomes divergent after either one of P_1 and P_2 does so. An interleaving of two processes, $P_1 \,\|\|\, P_2$, executes each part independently and is equivalent to $P_1 \,\|[\, \emptyset \,]\|\, P_2$.

13.2.5 Abstraction and Recursion

The hiding operator $P \setminus A$ makes the events in the set A become invisible or internal to the process. The process $P_1 \triangle \{a\} P_2$ behaves as P_1, but at any stage before its termination the occurrence of a will interrupt P_1 and pass the program control to P_2. The recursive process $\mu X.P$ behaves like P with every occurrence of the system variable X in P representing a recursive invocation. For example, to express a simple recursive process $P = a \rightarrow P$, we have a monotonic function F, a variable X, and an equation $F(X) = a \rightarrow X$; and then P is actually represented by $\mu X.F(X)$ which stands for the least fixed point of the above equation.

13.2.6 Timed Operators

The delay process $WAIT\ d$ does nothing except that it allows d time units to pass. The timeout operator $P_1 \triangleright \{d\} P_2$ resolves the choice in favour of P_1 if P_1 is able to execute observable (external) events by d time units, otherwise executes P_2. This operator is defined by the combination of the external choice and hiding operators:

$$P_1 \triangleright \{d\} P_2 = ((P_1 \,;\, e \rightarrow SKIP) \,\square\, (WAIT\,d \,;\, e \rightarrow P_2)) \setminus \{e\}$$

which uses the event e to resolve the external choice, if no external event happens in P_1 by d or P_1 does nothing but terminates before d. Also, e is not included in the alphabet of P_1 and P_2.

The deadline operator $\blacktriangleright$ is similar to the timeout operator, but it uses the miracle to force that P *must* execute observable events by d:

$$P \blacktriangleright d = (((P \,;\, e_1 \to SKIP) \,\square\, (WAIT\; d \,;\, e_2 \to STOP)) \setminus \{e_2\}$$
$$\square\; WAIT\; d \,;\, \top_R) \setminus \{e_1\}$$

where the role of e_1 $(e_1 \notin \alpha P)$ is to resolve both external choices when P quietly terminates before d, and the event e_2 $(e_2 \notin \alpha P)$ is used to resolve the first external choice if P does nothing when d is due. Of course, the miracle $(\top_R)$ forces P to execute external events, otherwise the whole process will behave like the miracle. More detailed explanation of the deadline operator will be found in Sect. 13.2.9 after some algebraic laws are introduced. This is really a very strong requirement in which there is no alternative but to meet the deadline, otherwise P will never start.

Note that our deadline operator is different from the one defined in timed CSP which, in fact, indicates that a process becomes deadlocked if events cannot occur by d. The deadline operator in $TCSP_M$ insists that the process will not start at all if the deadline is missed. In other words, events in P must occur by d, or the process behaves as $\top_R$.

13.2.7 Refinement

Suppose that P_1 and P_2 have the alphabet A of variables. If every observation that satisfies P_1 also satisfies P_2, it is expressed by $\forall v : A \bullet P_1 \Rightarrow P_2$, or $[P_1 \Rightarrow P_2]$. Because the refinement order is the reverse order of implication, it can also be written as $P_2 \sqsubseteq P_1$. The miracle is an unstarted process so that its observation obviously satisfies any other process in the model, i.e., $[\top_R \Rightarrow P]$ or $P \sqsubseteq \top_R$.

13.2.8 The Difference from Timed CSP

Although $TCSP_M$ inherits assumptions of timed CSP such as maximal parallelism and maximal progress, the introduction of the miracle makes $TCSP_M$ different from timed CSP in many aspects. The miracle itself is a very 'strange' process since it can never be executed in practice. However, it is very useful as a mathematical abstraction in reasoning about properties of a system. The semantics of $\top_R$ in $TCSP_M$ is defined as follows:

$$\top_R = (tr \le tr' \wedge t \le t' \wedge \neg ok) \vee (wait \wedge ok' \wedge \mathcal{II})$$

where $\mathcal{II}$ is called relational identity which simply means that all dashed variables in the alphabet are equivalent to correspondingly undashed variables. The observation of the miracle consists of two parts: the left part of the disjunction states that, since *ok* is false, its predecessor diverges and the miracle is in an unstable state; the second one states that the miracle is waiting for its predecessor's termination (e.g., *wait* is true) but in a stable state (e.g., ok' is true). However, in both cases, the miracle has not started yet.

The miracle gives rise to some very strange processes, each of which violates one of axioms of the standard CSP failures-divergences model. For example, we combine the miracle with a simple prefix, and then get the following miraculous process:

$$a \rightarrow \top_R \cong R(true \vdash tr' = tr \wedge a \notin ref' \wedge wait' \wedge v' = v) \qquad (13.1)$$

Let us concentrate on the expression after the symbol $\vdash$, which describes the behaviour if a process starts from a stable state. The reader who is interested in $R, \vdash$ and proof is referred to [31, 32]. The process (13.1) states that, if the process starts stably, then it will wait for interaction with its environment (*wait'* is true), but never actually perform any event ($tr' = tr$) even if the event a has been offered ($a \notin ref'$). This process violates an axiom of the CSP failures-divergences model [25, 28],

$$F3. \ (s, X) \in F \wedge \exists a \in Y \bullet s \frown \langle a \rangle \notin traces_\perp(P) \Rightarrow (s, X \cup Y) \in F$$

saying if at a state an event is not in the refusal set then the process is willing to execute the event.

Another strange process is that the external choice of the miracle with a simple prefix:

$$(a \rightarrow SKIP) \square \top_R = R(true \vdash \neg wait' \wedge tr' = tr \frown \langle (t', a) \rangle \wedge v' = v) \qquad (13.2)$$

In an untimed model this process performs the event a and terminates immediately. There is no state in which the process is waiting for the environment to offer a. It simply occurs instantly; in other words, no empty trace exists for such a process. Obviously, it violates another important axiom of the standard failures-divergences model of CSP where traces are prefix closed. In our timed model, this process reveals more interesting features. Because there is no constraint on timing in (13.2), the event a will occur when the environment is willing to interact with it. However, there is still no state between the start of the process and the occurrence of a, or the time before the occurrence of a has become invisible.

13.2.9 Distinct Features

The combination of the miracle and other operators can further assist us in understanding the role of the miracle. In fact, the key role of the miracle in a process is that the program control should never meet the miracle if the process has started.

This idea can be applies to intuitively get the following laws[2]:

$$L1.\ \mathsf{T}_R\,;P = \mathsf{T}_R$$

$$L2.\ SKIP\,;\mathsf{T}_R = \mathsf{T}_R$$

$$L3.\ STOP\ \Box\ \mathsf{T}_R = \mathsf{T}_R$$

$$L4.\ SKIP\ \Box\ \mathsf{T}_R = SKIP$$

$$L5.\ P\ \sqcap\ \mathsf{T}_R = P$$

$$L6.\ P\ |[\{A\}]|\ \mathsf{T}_R = \mathsf{T}_R$$

For example, the left part in $L2$ should not start and therefore behaves as T_R since *SKIP* allows the program control to meet the miracle immediately if the process starts. Similarly, the process in $L4$ must behave as *SKIP* to discard the miracle. The process in $L6$ states that the parallel of the miracle with any process is the miracle, because all processes engaged in the parallel must start together, however, the miracle cannot start so that the whole parallel cannot too.

13.2.9.1 Deadline

The deadline operator in $TCSP_M$ is different from the one defined in timed CSP. It can be used to specify a property that *something must occur*, rather than that something should occur otherwise the process is deadlocked. For example, $(a \rightarrow SKIP) \blacktriangleright 1$ means that a must occur within one time unit, or the process will not start if the deadline cannot be satisfied. An easy way to understand this property is to note that the process will backtrack to the unstarted state if a cannot happen within the deadline.

We can further clarify how the deadline operator works from its definition. For example, there are three cases in which $P \blacktriangleright d$ will behave: the first one is that P executes external events before d, another two are that P does nothing by d and P does nothing but terminates by d respectively. The first and third cases are straightforward to implement in the definition of $\blacktriangleright$ since the external events and e_1 will resolve both external choices. We focus on the second case and use a simple example to prove its correctness.

$$(WAIT\ 2)\ \blacktriangleright\ 1 = (((WAIT\ 2\,;e_1 \rightarrow SKIP)\ \Box\ (WAIT\ 1\,;e_2 \rightarrow STOP)) \setminus \{e_2\}$$

$$\Box\ WAIT\ 1\,;\mathsf{T}_R) \setminus \{e_1\}$$

$$= WAIT\ 1\,;(((WAIT\ 1\,;e_1 \rightarrow SKIP)\ \Box\ (e_2 \rightarrow STOP)) \setminus \{e_2\}$$

$$\Box\ \mathsf{T}_R) \setminus \{e_1\}$$

$$= WAIT\ 1\,;((e_2 \rightarrow STOP) \setminus e_2)\ \Box\ \mathsf{T}_R$$

---

[2]These laws have been formally proved and the reader is referred to [31].

$$= WAIT \; 1 \; ; (STOP \; \square \; \top_R)$$

$$= WAIT \; 1 \; ; \top_R$$

The result is very interesting. As our previous conclusion that a program control should never meet the miracle during any execution, $WAIT \; 1 \; ; \top_R$ actually means that the process will behave like the miracle unless it can be interrupted before one time unit. As a result, the above example proves that if a process cannot execute external events by the deadline, it behaves as the miracle. In other words, if the process can then it must do so.

13.2.9.2 Atomic Events

In modelling a complex system, it is very convenient to impose a collection of events to happen together. For example, RAISE Specification Language (RSL) [13, 35] has an interlock operator which can prevent the interlocked processes from communicating with other processes until one of them terminates. Of course, the communication can take place between the locked processes if they are able to. Promela/SPIN [17, 18] can define atomic sequences which encapsulate a fragment of code to be executed uninterruptedly and individually. In the interleaving of process executions, no other process can execute statements from the moment that the first statement of an atomic sequence is executed until the last one has completed. Unfortunately, to our best knowledge, neither of the two operators has denotational semantics probably because of the insufficient capability of current languages to express the property that something must occur.

Such 'atomic' events can also be easily defined by the deadline operator with well-defined denotational semantics. For example, setting the value of the deadline as zero can make a process or an event become *instant*. For the sake of convenience, we use the following abbreviations as a shorthand to represent instant events or processes:

$$\ddagger P \; \widehat{=} \; P \; \blacktriangleright \; 0$$

$$P_1 \ddagger P_2 \; \widehat{=} \; P_1 \; ; \; (P_2 \; \blacktriangleright \; 0)$$

$$a \ddagger b \; \widehat{=} \; (a \rightarrow SKIP) \ddagger (b \rightarrow SKIP)$$

Here the instantaneity operator squeezes the 'distance' of events and processes to zero. In addition, none of instant events can happen individually. Moreover, we can define *uninterrupted* events by means of the instantaneity operator. For example, $(a \rightarrow WAIT \; 1) \ddagger (b \rightarrow SKIP)$ means that a can happen only if b can even if there is one time unit delay between them. Such events are extremely useful for dealing with explicit clock-tick events in Sect. 13.3.3.

13.2.10 Discussion

$TCSP_M$ is a discrete-time version of timed *Circus*, which is also considered an extension to timed CSP. Its denotational semantics is based on UTP by embedding the theory of designs in the theory of reactive systems. More detailed introduction to its semantics can be found in [31, 32]. To prove the correctness and consistency of the model, we have done a shallow embedding [30] of the semantics of our timed *Circus* in the theorem prover PVS. The behaviours of our strange processes have been proved by hand and also by PVS. The ongoing work is focusing on the operational semantics of the timed model and the development of efficient tool support.

13.3 Semantics of the Timebands Model

In consideration of the nature of the timebands model, we intend to use $TCSP_M$ to express its semantics. The newly explored process, the miracle, plays a crucial role in the construction of the timebands model to link all time bands as a whole. First, we use a lecture example to explain how to view a simple system in the timebands model. Suppose that one week a lecturer has a lecture which takes two hours and has a five-minute break. To model it, we define three time bands, *Week*, *Hour* and *Minute*, which are given in an increasing finer order and illustrated in Fig. 13.1. In Band *Week*, event *lecture* does not take any time to execute, but it is mapped into activity *L* with duration in Band *Hour*. Furthermore, event *break* in activity *L* is mapped into another activity *B* in Band *minute*. Thus, instead of mapping all events or activities into the finest band, we use some key events (or signature events) to link and integrate different bands into a whole. Meanwhile, the timebands model preserves consistency and coordination of the system in the multiple time scales. The timebands model is developed in a number of stages in this section including time bands, granularity and precision, simultaneous events and durative activities, and mappings between bands.

13.3.1 Time Bands

A system in the timebands model recognises a finite set of distinct time bands, and it always has the highest and the lowest bands that give a temporal system boundary. Each band is defined by a granularity, representing the basic unit of time in that band. This is different from temporal logic approaches which can represent a possibly infinite set of time bands.

The timebands model adopts discrete time, usually represented by non-negative integers. A granule is simply a set of time points and a granularity is a mapping G from integers to a granule. One healthiness condition [4] that granularity must satisfy is

$$\mathbf{G1} : \forall i, j : \mathbb{Z} \mid i < j \land G(i) \neq \emptyset \land G(j) \neq \emptyset \bullet (\forall t : G(i), u : G(j) \bullet t < u)$$

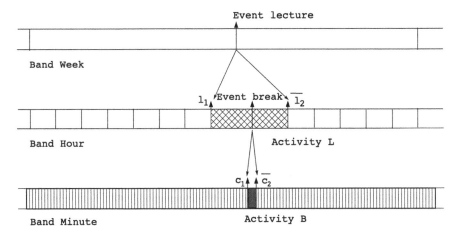

Fig. 13.1 Mapping between different time bands

which states that any two granules of a granularity have no overlap and the elements of granules are ordered the same as their index order. A granule $G(i)$ can be comprised of a single time unit, a set of contiguous units, or even a set of non-contiguous units. For example, the bank holidays for 2009 in England, defined as a collection of several days from different months, can be used as a granule.

Thus, the time bands in the lecture example can be defined as follows:

$$TBI = \{Minute, Hour, Week\}$$

$$Granularity(Hour, Minute) = \{60\}$$

$$Granularity(Week, Hour) = \{7 * 24\}$$

The set *TBI* is a collection of the timeband identities. The function *Granularity* defines conversion factors of different time bands' granularities. These factors can be multiple. For example, a year may have 365 days or 366 days. In addition, the function *Granularity* also satisfies 'finer than' relations of different time bands. A granularity G is *finer than* a granularity H if for each index i, there exists an index j such that $G(i) \subseteq H(j)$. Conversion factors between two bands must be natural numbers, and therefore time bands are not always comparable. For example, a week band is not comparable to a month band.

13.3.2 Events and Precision

Events are instantaneous, but depend on which band they are defined. For example, an event defined in the week band does not take any time to execute, however it might take several hours in the hour band. Indeed, there are a few relationships between events within a band such as instant events defined in Sect. 13.2.9. Instantaneity is the strongest constraint that is used especially to link different time bands via events and activities.

In specification of a system, events may cause an immediate response. For example, we consider such a requirement like 'when the fridge door opens the light must come on immediately'. It actually means that the two events, *door.open* and *light.on*, occur simultaneously but with an order. That is, the response is within the precision of the band. Precision, representing the measure of accuracy of events within that band, can only be expressed using the granularity of finer bands. Accordingly, two *simultaneous* events must, when viewed from a finer band, be within the precision of the current band. In respect to the finite number of time bands in the model, the finest (lowest) band has no precision. Due to precision, two simultaneous events cannot be exactly distinguished because the 'gap' between them is too small to be considered. Here the small gap also results in tolerance of the behaviours when mapping the two events into the corresponding activities of a finer band. For instance, considering the lecture example with three bands, precision can be defined as follows:

$$Precision(Week, Hour) = 2$$

$$Precision(Hour, Minute) = 5$$

If event *break* is supposed to happen in the middle of a lecture, the precision of the hour band restricts the maximal duration of a break to be five minutes, otherwise *break* cannot be considered an instantaneous event in the hour band. Also, the precision allows the break to happen five minutes early or late.

Therefore, similar to the definition of instant events, the simultaneous operator is defined as follows:

$$P_1 \overrightarrow{\#} P_2 \mathrel{\widehat{=}} P_1 \; ; (P_2 \blacktriangleright \rho)$$

where ρ is the precision of that band. Two simultaneous events, e.g., a and b, are expressed as either a is before b or b is before a, but they must occur within the precision. We also use the following abbreviations to represent simultaneous events:

$$a \overrightarrow{\#} b = (a \to SKIP) \overrightarrow{\#} (b \to SKIP)$$

$$a\#b = a \overrightarrow{\#} b \; \square \; b \overrightarrow{\#} a$$

where # denotes that a and b are simultaneous, and $\overrightarrow{\#}$ that they are simultaneous but with an order. This abbreviation is applied to all simultaneous events in this chapter.

Simultaneity is also a very strong constraint which is similar to instantaneity. That is, either simultaneous events occur together or none of them occurs individually. The difference is that two simultaneous events allow one of them to occur within the precision after the other has occurred, even though such a short delay is too small to be considered in this band. Simultaneous events are the same as instant events if these events are not mapped.

We cannot distinguish two simultaneous events in the current band; however, the interval between simultaneous events will be revealed in the form of precision when mapping these events to corresponding activities in a finer band. As a result, the precision basically plays two roles in a band: one is to measure accuracy of events such as simultaneous events, the other is to restrict the duration of activities. Unfortunately, simultaneity is not transitive, i.e., the fact that a and b are simultaneous and so are b and c, does not imply that a and c are simultaneous. This also elegantly explains that a sequence of consecutively simultaneous pairs or repeatedly fast-moving events can be observing durative behaviours. We might not recognise any pair of them because the interval between them is less than the precision, but the whole duration may take a long time.

13.3.3 Punctual Clock-Tick Event

In modelling of real-time systems, we often employ 'clocks' to aid scheduling and coordination. We represent a default abstract clock in a band by defining each granule as a 'clock-tick' event, which is modelled just like any other event. However these clock-tick events are forced to happen at same intervals by the deadline operator. When necessary, more abstract clocks can be defined by the basic unit of time in the band. For example, the clock called *business days* is placed in the day band; however, it is different from the default day clock.

Timed CSP is unlikely to explicitly represent clock-tick events because it can never guarantee that an event is able to happen precisely at a specific time point. The occurrence of events in timed CSP depends on their environment's interaction even if the timeout operator is applied. However, this situation is entirely changed if we use the deadline operator. For example, we may simply define a punctual clock as follows:

$$C = ((tick \rightarrow SKIP) \blacktriangleright 0) \, ; WAIT \ 1 \, ; C$$

where the clock-tick event *tick* must occur precisely every time unit otherwise the punctual clock will not start.

We define clock-tick events for every time band, e.g., the clock-tick events for the lecture example given in previous section can be defined as follows:

$$Event : Minute \ mtick$$

$$Event : Hour \ htick$$

$$Event : Week \ wtick$$

An intuitive way to understand a clock-tick event is that it denotes a start point of a new time unit or the end point of the previous time unit. Therefore, for different clock-tick events in different time bands such as *mtick* and *htick*, we say that the time interval between two *hticks* in the hour band contains 60 *mticks*, rather than that an *htick* can be mapped to an activity in the minute band which includes 60 clock-tick events. That is to say, if a mapping is necessary, a clock-tick event in a higher band is mapped to an activity in a lower band which contains only one clock-tick event.

Punctual clock-tick events provide us with extensive convenience to express clock-related properties. For example, if *tick* is a clock-tick event representing 1:00, *tick* $\ddagger$ *a* denotes that *a* must happen precisely at 1:00 even if we observe it in a finer band; *tick#a* means that *a* must occur at 1:00 too, but *a* is allowed to happen early or late within the bound of the precision; *tick* $\to a \to$ *SKIP* states that *a* occurs only if its environment provides the offer, and *a* occurs exactly at 1:00 only if its environment is friendly.

Note that clock-tick events are just ordinary events and they become meaningful only if we let them happen precisely at intervals of one time unit. Therefore, we attach a local timer to any processes during their life cycles. For example, a process with a timer is defined as follows:

$$P_T = ((P \,;\, e \to SKIP) \,|[\,\{tick, e\}\,]|\, Timer \,\triangle\, \{e\}SKIP) \setminus \{e\}$$

$$Timer = tick \to Timer'$$

$$Timer' = WAIT\ 1 \ddagger (tick \to SKIP)\,;\, Timer'$$

where the event e $(e \notin \alpha P)$ is used to stop the timer by the interrupt operator when P terminates, and one time unit in *WAIT* is a local time unit depending on which band the process is defined in. Notice that such a timer does not record the duration of its whole life cycle, while it starts only if the first clock-tick event of the process starts. By comparison with a globally punctual clock in a band, local timers to processes are able to effectively avoid the deadlock caused by synchronisation of clock-tick events.[3] For the sake of convenience, we directly define a process as usual and subsequently its timer is attached automatically.

We usually use a clock-related process to express a very strong constraint that 'something must occur at certain time points'. For example, a process *tick* $\to a \to$ *tick* $\to$ *SKIP* means that *a* must occur between two clock-tick events. Hence, a well-defined clock-related process is one in which all clock-tick events cannot be blocked. For example, a counterexample can be as follows:

$$P = tick \to tick \to (WAIT\ 2\,;\, (tick \to SKIP))$$

where obviously the third *tick* cannot occur such that the local timer blocks the occurrence of all clock-tick events.

---

[3]One of the approaches to model-check a timed CSP process is to translate it into an untimed CSP one in the form of *timewise refinement* [27]. This idea is quite powerful, but at the cost of dropping all *WAIT d* terms [24] because of the complexity of synchronising clock-tick events in parallel. However, the mechanism of local timers in our model does not require the synchronisation of all clock-tick events so as to avoid an unnecessary deadlock.

13.3.4 Activities

An activity is a special process with clock-tick events. Activities are detailed explanations of events of higher bands, and hence, to maintain consistency of a system, 'qualified' activities must satisfy the following three requirements:

1. An activity must start and also finish with clock-tick events.
2. An activity must have one or more signature events.
3. Duration of an activity must be no longer than the precision of a higher band in which its corresponding event is placed.

Requirement 1 states that an activity should be well placed in the band. If the activity cannot start or finish with clock-tick events, it is supposed to be replaced in a finer time band. For example, an activity may be defined as follows:

$$A = tick\#a_1 \,;\, tick\#\overline{a_2} \,;\, tick\#a_3$$

which means that the events such as a_1, a_2 and a_3 are simultaneous with clock-tick events, and the duration of the activity is two time units. Note that a_1 may actually occur before the event $tick$ in $tick\#a_1$, but we consider that A still starts with the clock-tick event since $tick$ and a_1 cannot be distinguished in this time band. The duration of A is counted from the occurrence of the first $tick$, and not from the start of the activity. That is, the activity may initially wait in silence until the coming of an explicit clock-tick event, and its duration is actually determined by how many clock-tick events it involves.

As Requirement 2, each activity must have one or more signature events, which is not only the major observation of the activity, but also the linking to the corresponding event in a higher band. For example, $\overline{a_2}$ is a signature event in the activity A and an overhead line is used to make it different from other ordinary events. An activity can have more than one signature event, which must be linked to the same event of a coarser band and only one of which can happen during the life cycle of the activity. For example, making a drink by a vending machine may have two choices, tea or coffee, which can be described as follows:

$$Drink = (tick\#hotwater \,;\, tick\#milk \,;\, tick \rightarrow tick\#\overline{tea})$$

$$\square \,(tick\#hotwater \,;\, tick\#milk \,;\, tick\#\overline{coffee})$$

The duration of an activity should be no longer than the precision of a higher band; otherwise it cannot be considered an event of the higher band. This imperative requirement will be fulfilled when the activity is mapped, since the precision for the activity is not yet decided until the link with the event in the higher band has been established. For example, there are two activities, A and B, in a day band, but A and B are linked to two events in a month band and a year band respectively; consequently, their precisions might be different.

When mapping events of a higher band to activities of a lower band, well-defined activities are crucial in maintaining consistency between different time bands. The following three examples are not well-defined activities which violate Requirements 1–3, respectively:

$$A1 = a \rightarrow tick \rightarrow \overline{b} \rightarrow SKIP$$

$$A2 = tick \rightarrow \overline{a} \rightarrow tick \rightarrow \overline{b} \rightarrow tick \rightarrow SKIP$$

$$A3 = tick \rightarrow \overline{a} \rightarrow A3$$

Because an activity is a clock-related process, we can control when the activity will happen by fixing any event of the activity to happen at a specific time. That is, the events in the activity are uninterrupted events, as introduced in Sect. 13.2.9. For example, if we impose the signature event $\overline{a_2}$ of the above activity A to happen at 10:00, a_1 must then happen at 9:00 and A must finish at 11:00. In fact, A starts from the beginning of the system; however a_1, very similar to the event of (13.1) in Sect. 13.2.8, can occur only if the other event must occur later.

13.3.5 Mapping Between Bands

In the components of the model considered so far, all behaviours have been confined to a single band. The essence of the timebands model is to describe the behaviour of each component of a system in a best suitable time band, and compose the multiple-band behaviours regarding the properties to be verified. To achieve this goal, events in one band may need to be mapped into activities in finer bands.

Activities become useful only when they are linked with events in higher time bands. Processes defined in different time bands have no intersection except for the linking of events and activities. Those links are the one and only channel to integrate all behaviours of the timebands model. The establishment of the links is achieved by means of imposing the events and the signature events of the activities to be instant events, so that they are constrained to occur together at all time.

The linked pair of an event and an activity can affect each other to decide when they will occur in their own bands. Recall the lecture example illustrated in Fig. 13.1. Activity B can be given the following behaviour:

Event : *Minute* c_1, c_2

Activity : *Minute* $B = c_1$#*mtick* ; *mtick* $\rightarrow$ *mtick* $\rightarrow$ *mtick* $\rightarrow$ *mtick* $\rightarrow$ $\overline{c_2}$#*mtick*

This activity actually means that students have to take a 5-minute break and any shorter or longer break is not allowed. If we insist that event *break* in the hour band must occur in the middle of the lecture, e.g., around 10:00 (event *break* and the clock-tick event are simultaneous), and then event c_1 in activity B can only happen between 9:50 and 10:00, on account of the five-minute precision. That is to say, the signature event $\overline{c_2}$ can happen only between 9:55 and 10:05. We can also set the time when $\overline{c_2}$ in activity B occurs in the minute band, which alternatively results in the time when event *break* must occur in the hour band. For example, if we say that $\overline{c_2}$ occurs at 9:50, and then *break* in the hour band must occur between 9:00 and 10:00.

To maintain consistency and coordination between different time bands, we simply make events and the signature events of corresponding activities instant. For example, the mapping in the lecture example can be defined as the following processes:

$$Link1 = lecture \ddagger \overline{l_2}$$

$$Link2 = break \ddagger \overline{c_2}$$

And then these processes are synchronised with other processes in the system on all events of the alphabets of *Link1* and *Link2*.

Finally, we use the lecture example, illustrated in Fig. 13.1, to demonstrate the integration of time bands. Granularity, precision and clock-tick events have been defined in previous sections. In the week band, we specify that a lecture must occur within a week:

$$Event : Week\ lecture$$

$$LECTURE = wtick \rightarrow lecture \rightarrow wtick \rightarrow SKIP$$

And activity L, expressing a two-hour lecture with a break, is defined in the hour band as follows:

$$Event : Hour\ l_1, l_2, break$$

$$Activity : Hour\ L = htick\#l_1; htick\#break; htick\#\overline{l_2}$$

Before events and activities are linked together, processes defined in different time bands have no interaction at all. Thus, the system before mapping is expressed by an interleaving process:

$$S = LECTURE \ ||| \ L \ ||| \ B$$

And then the integrated system is constructed by linking events *lecture* and *break* with activities L and B respectively:

$$SYS = S \ |[\ \{lecture, l_2\} \ ]| \ Link1 \ |[\ \{break, c_2\} \ ]| \ Link2$$

In practice, the assumption of maximal progress enables events to occur as soon as possible. For example, the process *LECTURE* in the week band specifies that *lecture* may happen anytime within a week, but without a constraint from other processes or bands it always happens at the beginning of the week. With respect to Fig. 13.1,[4] if the lecture example starts, *wtick*, *htick* and l_1 will initially start

---

[4]The clock-tick events are not directly given in this figure, whereas the reader can easily find out where these events should be placed by the description of the system.

together; *lecture* cannot happen immediately because it is coordinated with $\overline{l_2}$ or the third *htick* in the hour band; c_1 in the minute band cannot happen because it depends on *break* or the second *htick* in the hour band. Subsequently, after one time unit of the hour band, *break* happens; however, $\overline{c_2}$ has occurred five time units (within the precision) of the minute band earlier, since *break* and the second *htick* are simultaneous. Consequently, another hour later, $\overline{l_2}$ and *lecture* happen together.

13.3.6 Discussion

The revolution of the timebands model is to use a mapping between instantaneous events and durative activities to integrate different behaviours described in different time scales into a whole system. The key idea of the mapping is to use instantaneity of the events and the signature events of the corresponding activities, and integrity (uninterrupted events) of the activities to locate right positions for mapped entities. The above two distinct properties are achieved through applying the unique process, the miracle.

The time system of the timebands model is a combination of implicit time and explicit clock-tick events. Here implicit time, similar to time in timed CSP, is a global clock whose granularity is the basic time unit of the finest time band. However, processes themselves do not have read-access to the clock which is rather used in the semantic framework for the analysis and description of processes. A clock-tick event is an observation of a single precise time of the global clock and it can be accessed by any process. Because clock-tick events are punctual, we can specify clock-related events which must occur at specific time points.

Every clock-related process has a local timer (a clock with clock-tick events), which turns out to be able to interfere with the accuracy of its local clock. We do not require that the local clock of a process must be synchronised with the global clock. For example, we let *htick*$\ddagger a$ to express that a must happen at the beginning of an hour such as 1:00, while we make the signature event (such as $\overline{a'}$) of the corresponding activity simultaneous with *mtick* in the minute band. Thus, $\overline{a'}$ must happen at 1:00 because it is instant to a, but *mtick*#$\overline{a'}$ allows its local clock, relative to the clock of the hour band, to quick or slow a little bit within the precision of the minute band. Of course, the local clock of a process can be easily synchronised with the global clock. This property is very useful in modelling the behaviour of a distributed system where components may have asynchronous clocks.

The advantage of the timebands model is the separation of concerns in dealing with different properties with different time scales. Many properties in the timebands model involve only few time bands rather than all of time bands. Obviously, apart from a better description of a complex system, proving such properties is more efficient in the timebands model than the traditional model with a single flat time. In the following section, by means of a complicated example, the mine pump, we demonstrate how significantly the timebands model contributes to describing complex real-time systems with multiple time scales.

13.4 Case Study

The mine pump example was first proposed by Kramer et al. [20] and later used by Burns and Lister [6] as case study for developing dependable systems. The mine pump system is used to control a pump to pump out the water which is collected in a sump. The mine has two sensors to detect when water is above a high level or below a low level. A pump controller switches the pump on when the water level becomes high and off when it goes below the low level. The system also monitors the level of methane, since a pumping operation during a dangerous methane level will cause explosion. Reading from all sensors, the operations of the mine pump should satisfy the following safety requirements:

1. The pump can be used only when the methane level is safe.
2. The pump must be switched on within an interval since the water level has become high.
3. The pump must be switched off within an interval whenever the methane level becomes dangerous.

In a mine, water and methane come from the environment. We assume that the change of the water level is slow, and the methane level is stable in most of the time but can incidentally change very fast. Therefore, we use two time bands, a minute band and a second band, to describe the slow changing of the water level and the dramatic changing of the methane level respectively. For example, a delay of few seconds may have no influence on the change of the water level, while it could be crucial for switching the pump off when the methane level suddenly becomes dangerous. Granularity and precision between the two bands are defined as follows:

$$TBI = \{Minute, Second\}$$

$$Granularity(Minute, Second) = \{60\}$$

$$Precision(Minute, Second) = 5$$

To simplify the modelling of the mine pump, we abstract the state of the water level as Fig. 13.2 by combining the values of two sensors for detecting the water level. That is, the state of the water level is low until water passes the high level, and it stays high until below the low level. This abstraction is reasonable since it is a practical decision to keep the pump on until the water level becomes low, though sometimes the pump has to be switched off due to the dangerous methane level.

We also assume that each component takes some time to react, e.g., updating values of sensors may takes a few seconds, the pump may take some time units to start working and the sampling frequency also brings delay to update fresh values of states. As a result, reaction time will be considered in the light of how much impact it causes on the safety requirements of the system.

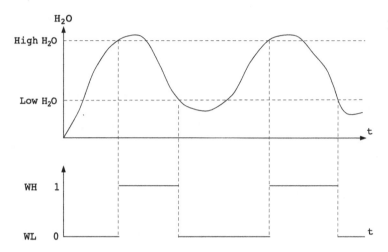

Fig. 13.2 Sample timing diagram for water level

13.4.1 A Pump Controller

Depending on the states of the water and methane levels, a pump controller executes actions on the pump. Therefore, in the following implementation defined in the minute band, the system is basically decomposed into two components: one for monitoring the behaviour of water and the other for the behaviour of methane.

$$Event : Minute \quad water.high, water.low, pump.on, pump.off,$$

$$methane.safe, methane.danger, mtick$$

$$WATER_{low} = water.high \rightarrow (wl := false\,;\, WATER_{high})$$

$$\square\, pump.off \rightarrow WATER_{low} \tag{13.3}$$

$$WATER_{high} = water.low \rightarrow (wl := true\,;\, WATER_{low})$$

$$\square\, pump.on \rightarrow WATER_{high}$$

$$\square\, \neg ms\&pump.off \rightarrow WATER_{high} \tag{13.4}$$

$$METHANE_{safe} = methane.danger \rightarrow METHANE_{danger}$$

$$\square\, pump.on \rightarrow METHANE_{safe}$$

$$\square\, pump.off \rightarrow METHANE_{safe} \tag{13.5}$$

$$METHANE_{danger} = methane.safe \rightarrow METHANE_{safe}$$

$$\square\, pump.off \rightarrow METHANE_{danger} \tag{13.6}$$

We here remove any time constraint from these components in order to make it become a purely logic judgement for proper operations. For example, process

$WATER_{low}$ in (13.3) states that the water level initially stays at the low level, and it can become high through event *water.high* and still remain low if executing *pump.off*. In addition, *ms* and *wl* are two state variables to denote the safe methane and low water respectively. In the process $WATER_{high}$, the event *pump.off* can still happen only if the methane level is dangerous.

These components must agree on when the pump is to be switched on or off. For example, before reaching the low water level during the pumping operation, the pump might be switched off due to the dangerous methane level. Afterwards, the pump has to be switched on again until the water level is below the low level.

$$CONTROL = WATER_{low} \,||[\, \{pump.on, pump.off\}\,]|\, METHANE_{safe} \qquad (13.7)$$

Without considering the timing issues, the above implementation *CONTROL* clearly shows that event *pump.on* can occur only when the water level is high and the methane level is safe (because *pump.on* is executed from processes $WATER_{high}$ and $METHANE_{safe}$). This satisfies the first safety requirement of the system. However, to make this system closer to reality, we will verify the other two more refined properties, which are going to be modelled in different time bands because of the different behaviours when the water and methane levels are changing.

13.4.2 Behaviour of Water and Methane in the Minute Band

Suppose that the change of the water level is slow and hence its behaviour is captured in the minute band. The methane level is stable for most of the time, but can change very fast; e.g., it can reach the dangerous level in just few seconds. Obviously, such a dramatic change of methane is best described in a finer time band such as the second band. In the following modelling, we will specify the different behaviours of the two components in the two time bands, depending on different scenarios.

For modelling the change of the water and methane levels, we use worst-case execution time to describe the worst situations. As illustrated in Fig. 13.3, the worst situation for water is that the water level has reached the high level but the pump cannot be switched on because the methane level just becomes dangerous. Hence, it is unnecessary to consider any operation when the water level is between the low and high levels if the worst case has satisfied the safety requirements. In practice, we always give a good safety margin to the value of the high level in case the pump cannot be switched on immediately. For example, the pump must be on within t_1 time units after the water level becomes high, otherwise the mine fails. And the pump can take the water level below the high level if it has continuously worked for t_2 time units. If assuming that r_1 and r_2 are the rates of change respectively at which water enters and leaves the mine, we can easily get the equation: $r_1 * t_1 = (r_2 - r1) * t_2$.

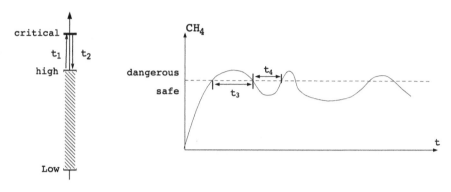

Fig. 13.3 Assumptions on the change of water and methane

Thus, the time constraint of the behaviour of water and the related pump operations in the minute band is modelled as follows:

$$TCW = water.high \rightarrow HIGH(l_1) \tag{13.8}$$

$$HIGH(t_1) = IF \ t_1 == 0 \ THEN \ (pump.on \rightarrow ON(l_1)$$
$$\Box \ flooding \rightarrow STOP)$$
$$ELSE \ (WAIT \ 1 \ ; HIGH(t_1 - 1_1)$$
$$\Box \ pump.on \rightarrow ON(l_1 - t_1)) \tag{13.9}$$

$$ON(t) = OFF(t * r_1/(r_2 - r_1)) \tag{13.10}$$

$$OFF(t_2) = IF \ t_2 == 0 \ THEN \ pump.off \rightarrow water.low \rightarrow TCW$$
$$ELSE \ (WAIT \ 1 \ ; OFF(t_2 - 1_1)$$
$$\Box \ pump.off \rightarrow HIGH(l_1 - t_2 * (r_2 - r_1)/r_1) \tag{13.11}$$

where t, t_1 and t_2 are time variables, and l_1, r_1 and r_2 are constants, e.g., l_1 is the maximal value of the bound of t_1. The operator, *IF b THEN P ELSE Q*, is actually a convenient shorthand of a guarded process, $b \& P \ \Box \ \neg b \& Q$.

The implementation in (13.9) states that *pump.on* should happen within some time units if the water level is high. The value of t_1 in *HIGH*(t_1) is the deadline that *pump.on* must satisfy. If *pump.on* happens before the deadline, the net water level over the high level is recorded and passed to *ON*(t) in the form of time. Thus, the equation in (13.10) calculates how long the pump can lower the water level below the high level in line with the value from *ON*(t). The implementation in (13.11) denotes that the pump might be switched off before water is below the high level because of the dangerous methane level. If the pump is switched off earlier, the program has to go to *HIGH* again to wait for the occurrence of *pump.on*. However, the maximal interval to make the mine fail obviously becomes shorter or is less than l_1.

Accordingly, the timed behaviour of water and the pump is defined by the following parallel composition:

$$A = \{pump.on, pump.off, water.low, water.high\}$$

$$TWATER = WATER_{low} \,\|[\, A \,]\|\, TCW \tag{13.12}$$

The behaviour of methane in the minute band is relatively simple. Under the circumstance of worst-case execution time, we also assume two constants, l_3 and l_4, to be the maximal values of two time variables, t_3 and t_4, as illustrated in Fig. 13.3, to denote the maximal duration of the dangerous methane level and the minimal duration of the safe level respectively.

$$TCM = methane.danger$$

$$\rightarrow WAIT\ l_3\,;\,(methane.safe \blacktriangleright 0)\,;\,WAIT\ l_4\,;\,TCM \tag{13.13}$$

$$TMETHANE = METHANE_{safe} \,\|[\, \{methane.safe, methane.danger\} \,]\|\, TCM \tag{13.14}$$

And then, the system in the minute band can be finally modelled as follows:

$$TCONTROL = TWATER \,\|[\, \{pump.on, pump.off\} \,]\|\, TMETHANE \tag{13.15}$$

Recall the safety properties which are introduced in the beginning of this section. Property 1 can be proved even under the untimed environment. The proof of Property 2 depends on the relationship among those constants. For example, l_1 is obviously greater than l_3, otherwise the mine will fail since the pump cannot be switched on in time. Ideally, l_4 is greater than l_2 or $l_1 * r_1/(r_2 - r_2)$ so that water can be lowered below the high level once the pump is switched on. However, this requirement is too strict to accommodate many patterns of methane's behaviour, e.g., the frequent oscillation around the dangerous level of methane does not satisfy this requirement. Therefore, it is more reasonable to satisfy a looser requirement that l_3/l_4 is less than l_1/l_2 within any interval (whose length should be greater than $l_1 + l_2$).

13.4.3 Behaviour of Methane in the Second Band

Unfortunately, Property 3 is unsuitable to be verified in the minute band. We know that *pump.off* will happen after *methane.danger* if the pump is on, and this logical order can be nicely proved in the minute band. However, in fact, Property 3 is interpreted as a statement that *methane.danger* and *pump.off* must occur simultaneously. To measure the simultaneous actions of two events, we have to consider the influence of various reaction delays such as transmission delay, reaction delay of the pump and so on, whose behaviours can only be captured in the second band. To model and verify Property 3, we need to explore more details in related events of the minute band.

First of all, we specify precision of the minute band to be 5 seconds, which directly determines the definition of simultaneity and the maximal duration of an activity. The delay of updating the state of water is ignored in the minute band, but it is considered in the second band. We assume the delay to be 2 seconds, and *water.high* and *water.low* are mapped into two activities, WH_s and WL_s, in the second band respectively:

$$Activity: Second\ WH_s = stick\#\overline{high}\,;\ stick \rightarrow stick\#whe \qquad (13.16)$$

$$Activity: Second\ WL_s = stick\#\overline{low}\,;\ stick \rightarrow stick\#wle \qquad (13.17)$$

where *stick* is a clock-tick event of the second band, *whe* and *wle* denote the end of the two activities respectively, and *low* and *high* are two signature events. In addition, the activities are annotated for convenience.

Moreover, on account of the costing time on updating states and sampling frequency, *methane.danger* is mapped into the following activity:

$$Activity: Second\ MD_s = stick\#\overline{danger}\,;\ stick \rightarrow stick \rightarrow stick\#mde \qquad (13.18)$$

And then, with regard to reaction delay, *pump.off* is mapped as well:

$$Activity: Second\ PF_s = stick\#command\_off\,;\ stick$$

$$\rightarrow stick\#\overline{action\_off} \qquad (13.19)$$

where the event *action_off* denotes the genuine time when this command takes effect.

Furthermore, we impose a constraint on all of these activities so that none of them can overlap each other because changing states presumably involves some computation:

$$ACT_s = (WH_s\,;ACT_s) \,\square\, (WL_s\,;ACT_s)$$

$$\square\,(MD_s\,;ACT_s) \,\square\, (PF_s\,;ACT_s) \qquad (13.20)$$

To verify Property 3 in the second band, the activities in the above implementation are integrated with the minute band by making their signature events *instant* with the corresponding events of the minute band. For the sake of simplicity, ACT_s is integrated with *CONTROL*, rather than *TCONTROL* with time constraints, because the 'micro' relation of *methane.danger* and *pump.off* is irrelevant with those assumptions on how water and methane change.

$$CONTROL_{second} = (CONTROL \,|||\, ACT_s)$$

$$|[\,\{water.high, high\}\,]|\,Link3$$

$$|[\,\{water.low, low\}\,]|\,Link4$$

$$|[\,\{methane.danger, danger\}\,]|\,Link5$$

$$|[\,\{pump.off, commmand\_off\}\,]|\,Link6 \qquad (13.21)$$

Note that these linking processes are just similar to *Link*1 and *Link*2 introduced in Sect. 13.3.5. Even without the mechanised proof, intuitively, we recognise that Property 3 can be satisfied only if no other event in the minute band occurs between *methane.danger* and *pump.off*, since the total duration of the two events in the second band is 5 seconds. That is, when executing the real program code, the program should directly implement *pump.off* when the methane level is dangerous instead of wasting time on updating the state of water.

13.4.4 Verification

To prove the three properties of the mine pump example by hand is error-prone since a number of obligations are discharged by obvious and intuitive assumptions where security breaches and system holes are usually hidden. However, establishing the mechanical proof in theorem provers is time-consuming, such as PVS [30] in which the semantics of $TCSP_M$ has been embedded and ProofPower [36] in which various theories in UTP are mechanised. The model checker FDR [1] is very successful in efficiently verifying both safety and liveness properties of a system modelled in CSP. Therefore, timed CSP specifications can be implemented by FDR if they are translated into untimed ones. However, regardless of its expressiveness, the miracle cannot be expressed in FDR.

Timed automata [2, 22] are powerful in designing real-time models with explicit clock variables, and a number of tools have been proved to be successful like the popular UPPAAL [21]. Timed automata are transition systems consisting of a set of states along with a set of edges to connect these states, and hence it is potential to express the miracle simply as an unstarted state. The idea of using timed automata to implement $TCSP_M$ or the timebands model is highly inspired by the work [11] in which they define a set of composable timed automata patterns so that timed CSP can be translated to timed automata. Even if it is possible to represent the miracle in timed automata, the mechanism of the timebands model still involves a massive amount of work. For example, we need to develop a sound operational semantics of $TCSP_M$ which is usually described as a labelled transition system. We also have to explore a trace-back technique for executing the model, since the fact that a process will not start if the deadline cannot be satisfied means that the process will go back to the unstarted state if the execution cannot go ahead. In the meantime, the observations which have happened during the execution will be erased, and the process just behaves like it has never started. All in all then, the work of fully analysing the timebands model in timed automata is in progress, and therefore the following verification of the mine pump example in UPPAAL simply provides a flavour to show how it will be possible to prove properties in a model checking approach.

The model checker UPPAAL is based on the theory of timed automata and its modelling language provides expressive features such as urgent edges or locations. The query language of UPPAAL is a subset of TCTL (timed computation tree

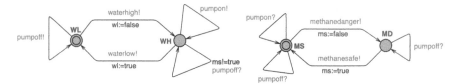

Fig. 13.4 The pump controller without time constraints

logic) [3]. More explanations of UPPAAL will be given along with the modelling of
the mine pump example. First, the process *CONTROL* in (13.7) is modelled as two
timed automata in Fig. 13.4. Locations (or states) of a timed automaton are graphically represented by circles where the overlapped circle is the initial location. Each
location has an invariant which is an expression of conditions, and the program control can stay on this location only if its invariant is satisfied. A transition is a jump
from one location to another through an edge which usually consists of three parts:
guard, synchronisation and update. For example, illustrated in the left automaton of
Fig. 13.4, starting from the location WH (*WATER$_{high}$*), event pumpoff is synchronised (or fired) with another one in the right automaton only if the methane level is
dangerous. As a result, Property 1 holds if the following query is satisfied:

```
A[] METHANE.MS and WATER.WH imply ms==true
```

which means that for all reachable locations, being in the locations METHANE.MS
and WATER.WH implies that ms==true. Since pumpon can be fired only from
the locations MS and WH, the fact that the methane level is always safe guarantees
Property 1.

The behaviour of water and methane in the minute band, *TCW* and *TCM*, are
represented by another two automata in Fig. 13.5. Note that x in both automata is
a local clock that can be reset in the update part of an edge and used in a guard
or an invariant. For example, x is reset during the transition from location TCW to
location HIGH. Unfortunately, the value of a clock is not allowed to be assigned
to any variable in UPPAAL, and that is why we define two integral variables, c1
and c2, to record how long the program control stays on the same location. UP-
PAAL provides pair-wise synchronisation (one sender and one receiver) via regular
channels and broadcast synchronisation (one sender and an arbitrary number of re-
ceivers) via broadcast channels. However, a receiver in a broadcast channel can miss
the synchronisation if it is not ready yet. Obviously, this is not same as the parallel
in timed CSP or *TCSP$_M$*. For example, in the mine pump example, the synchronisation on *pump.on* and *pump.off* involving three different processes cannot be directly
expressed in UPPAAL. The solution is to use a shared variable (e.g. on and off
in Fig. 13.5) that is increased on the edges leading to a location where those events
are ready to happen and is decreased when leaving the location. When the program
stays on a location where all events are ready, a sender can be triggered. For example, the senders for *pump.on* and *pump.off* are defined as two independent automata
in Fig. 13.6.

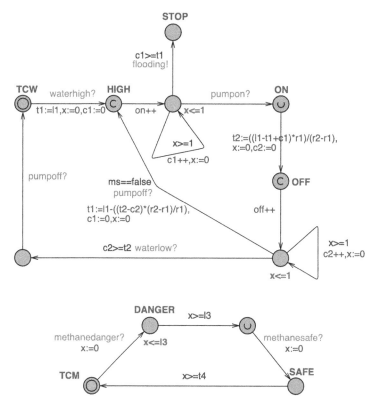

Fig. 13.5 The behaviour of water and methane in the minute band

Fig. 13.6 The senders in a multicast synchronisation

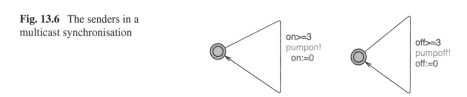

In addition, urgent (labelled with U) and committed (labelled with C) locations are used in Fig. 13.5. Time is not allowed to pass when the program is in any of the two locations, but an urgent location can engage in an interleaving. Notice that the approach to calculate the values of t_1 and t_2 in Fig. 13.5 is different from the one in (13.10) and (13.11) because a recursive process in the timebands model is measured by a descending order. To prove Property 2, we simply need to show the automata can never reach location STOP or event flooding can not be fired if $l_1 > l_3$ and $l_2 < l_4$. Such a query can be expressed as follow:

```
A[] not TCW.STOP
```

which means that it is impossible to reach the location TCW.STOP.

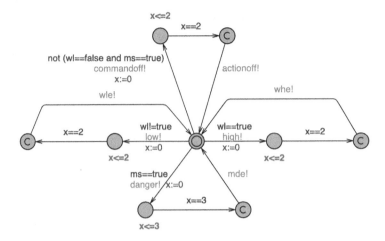

Fig. 13.7 Activities in the second band

Fig. 13.8 The linking
processes in the mapping

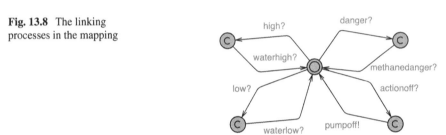

To verify Property 3, we should mechanise the miracle so as to express those processes and operators defined by the miracle. However, the embedding of the miracle
in UPPAAL is still in progress. Here, regarding the mapping only in the mine pump
example, we use an informal scheme to make sure coordination of events and activities in different bands. For example, the process ACT_s, a collection of all activities
in the second band, in (13.20) is described as a timed automaton in Fig. 13.7. The
starting of each activity is guarded by a state variable which denotes whether the
event in the minute band is ready to happen. For example, the bottom loop (corresponding to MD_s) in Fig. 13.7 states that danger can happen only if ms==true,
and then the automaton waits three time units and finishes the activity with event
mde. The safe methane level means that the program control is staying on location MS as Fig. 13.4, and hence methanedanger is ready to occur. The linking
processes like *Link* 3–*Link* 6 are expressed as another automaton in Fig. 13.8. The
instantaneity of events and the signature events of activities is expressed by committed locations which, however, cannot exactly describe this property because a
committed location just means that time is not allowed to reside and an edge must
be fired immediately. If the guard of the edge is not satisfied yet, the automaton is
deadlocked.

We add a new location with a guard in the automaton of $METHANE_{safe}$ in order
to prove Property 3, as illustrated in Fig. 13.9. The guard on the edge to location

Fig. 13.9 The linking
processes in the mapping

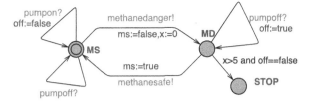

STOP means if the pump has not been switched off within five time units since the
methane level becomes dangerous, the edge can lead to this location. Obviously, we
need to prove the following query to be satisfied:

```
A[] not METHANE.STOP
```

The verifier of UPPAAL shows that the above query holds if we impose a constraint
to exclude any other events between *methane.danger* and *pump.off*.

13.5 Conclusion

In this chapter we have formalised the timebands model using a new timed model
($TCSP_M$) and shown how significantly the model contributes to describing dynamic
behaviours of complex real-time systems at many different time scales. Viewing
a system as a collection of behaviours within a finite set of bands and integrating
these behaviours through linking events and corresponding activities are a natural
and effective approach to separate concerns and identify inconsistencies between
different time bands of the system. We have also demonstrated the potential to use
timed automata to implement the timebands model. Of course, it is still a long way
to go for fully mechanising the timebands model. In future work we will apply
the timebands framework to the analysis of more complex systems such as socio-
technical systems. We believe that the modelling with a time-based hierarchy is able
to help develop a comprehensive foundation to dependable systems.

Acknowledgements   We would like to thank Ana Cavalcanti, Leo Freitas, Andrew Butterfield
and Pawel Gancarski for discussions on the role of reactive miracles in programming logic, and
thank Cliff Jones and Ian Hayes for discussion on the timebands model and possible approaches
to formalisation. This work was partially supported by INDEED project funded by EPSRC:Grant
EP/E001297/1.

References

1. Roscoe A.W.: Model-checking CSP. In: A Classical Mind: Essays in Honour of C.A.R. Hoare.
   Prentice Hall, New York (1994). Chap. 21
2. Alur, R.: A theory of timed automata. Theor. Comput. Sci. **126**, 183–235 (1994)

3. Alur, R., Courcoubetis, C., Dill, D.L.: Model-checking for real-time systems. In: LICS, pp. 414–425 (1990)
4. Bettini, C., Dyreson, C.E., Evans, W.S., Snodgrass, R.T., Wang, X.S.: A glossary of time granularity concepts. In: Temporal Databases, Dagstuhl, pp. 406–413 (1997)
5. Burns, A., Hayes, I.J.: A timeband framework for modelling real-time systems. Real-Time Syst. **45**(1–2), 106–142 (2010)
6. Burns, A., Lister, A.M.: A framework for building dependable systems. Comput. J. **34**(2), 173–181 (1991)
7. Ciapessoni, E., Corsetti, E., Montanari, A., San Pietro, P.: Embedding time granularity in a logical specification language for synchronous real-time systems. In: 6IWSSD: Selected Papers of the Sixth International Workshop on Software Specification and Design, pp. 141–171. Elsevier, Amsterdam (1993)
8. Clifford, J., Rao, A.: A simple, general structure for temporal domains. In: Temporal Aspects in Information Systems, pp. 23–30. AFCET, Paris (1987)
9. Combi, C., Franceschet, M., Peron, A.: Representing and reasoning about temporal granularities. J. Log. Comput. **14**(1), 51–77 (2004)
10. Corsetti, E., Montanari, A., Ratto, E.: Time granularity in logical specifications. In: Proceedings of the 6th Italian Conference on Logic Programming, Pisa, Italy (1991)
11. Dong, J.S., Hao, P., Qin, S., Sun, J., Yi, W.: Timed automata patterns. IEEE Trans. Softw. Eng. **34**, 844–859 (2008)
12. Franceschet, M., Montanari, A.: Temporalized logics and automata for time granularity. Theory Pract. Log. Program. **4**(5–6), 621–658 (2004)
13. Group, T.R.L.: The RAISE Specification Language. Prentice Hall, Upper Saddle River (1993)
14. Hoare, C.A.R.: Communicating Sequential Processes. Prentice Hall International, Englewood Cliffs (1985)
15. Hoare, C.A.R., Jifeng, H.: Unifying Theories of Programming. Prentice Hall International, Englewood Cliffs (1998)
16. Hobbs, J.: Granularity. In: Proceedings of the Ninth International Joint Conference on Artificial Intelligence, Los Angeles, California, pp. 432–435 (1985)
17. Holzmann, G.: Spin Model Checker, the Primer and Reference Manual. Addison-Wesley, Reading (2003)
18. Holzmann, G.J.: The model checker SPIN. IEEE Trans. Softw. Eng. **23**(5), 279–295 (1997)
19. Jifeng, H.: From CSP to hybrid systems. In: A Classical Mind: Essays in Honour of C.A.R. Hoare, pp. 171–189. Prentice Hall International, Hertfordshire (1994)
20. Kramer, J., Magee, J., Sloman, M., Lister, A.: CONIC: an integrated approach to distributed computer control systems. IEE Proc. E, Comput. Digit. Tech. **130**(1), 1–10 (1983)
21. Cardellini, V., Casalicchio, E., Grassi, V., Lo Presti, F., Mirandola, R.: Uppaal—a tool suite for automatic verification of real-time systems. In: Hybrid Systems III. LNCS, vol. 1066, pp. 232–243. Springer, Berlin (1995)
22. Lynch, N., Vaandrager, F.: Action transducers and timed automata. In: Formal Aspects of Computing, pp. 436–455. Springer, Berlin (1992)
23. Montanari, A., Ratto, E., Corsetti, E., Morzenti, A.: Embedding time granularity in logical specifications of real-time systems. In: Proceedings of the Third Euromicro Workshop on Real-Time Systems, Paris, France (1991)
24. Ouaknine, J., Schneider, S.: Timed CSP: a retrospective. Electron. Notes Theor. Comput. Sci. **162**, 273–276 (2006)
25. Roscoe, A.W.: The Theory and Practice of Concurrency. Prentice Hall International, Englewood Cliffs (1998)
26. Sampaio, A., Woodcock, J., Cavalcanti, A.: Refinement in *Circus*. In: FME '02, pp. 451–470. Springer, London (2002)
27. Schneider, S.: Timewise refinement for communicating processes. Sci. Comput. Program. **28**, 43–90 (1997)
28. Schneider, S.A.: Concurrent and Real-Time Systems: The CSP Approach. Wiley, New York (1999)

29. Sherif, A., He, J.: Towards a time model for *Circus*. In: ICFEM '02: Proceedings of the 4th International Conference on Formal Engineering Methods, pp. 613–624. Springer, London (2002)
30. Wei, K., Woodcock, J., Burns, A.: Embedding the timed *Circus* in PVS. Technical report. Available at http://www-users.cs.york.ac.uk/~176kun/, University of York (2009)
31. Wei, K., Woodcock, J., Burns, A.: Formalising the timebands model in timed *Circus*. Technical report. Available at http://www-users.cs.york.ac.uk/~kun/, University of York (2010)
32. Wei, K., Woodcock, J., Burns, A.: A timed model of *Circus* with the reactive design miracle. In: 8th International Conference on Software Engineering and Formal Methods (SEFM), pp. 315–319, IEEE Comput. Soc., Pisa (2010).
33. Woodcock, J., Cavalcanti, A.: The semantics of *Circus*. In: ZB '02: Proceedings of the 2nd International Conference of B and Z Users on Formal Specification and Development in Z and B, pp. 184–203. Springer, London (2002)
34. Woodcock, J., Davies, J.: Using Z: Specification, Refinement, and Proof. Prentice Hall, Upper Saddle River (1996)
35. Yong, X., George, C.: An operational semantics for timed RAISE. In: FM '99: Proceedings of the Wold Congress on Formal Methods in the Development of Computing Systems—Volume II, pp. 1008–1027. Springer, London (1999)
36. Zeyda, F., Cavalcanti, A.: Mechanical reasoning about families of UTP theories. Electron. Notes Theor. Comput. Sci. **240**, 239–257 (2009)

Chapter 14
Software and System Modeling: Structured Multi-view Modeling, Specification, Design and Implementation

Manfred Broy

14.1 Introduction

In this chapter, we develop a theory supporting the structuring of multifunctional systems implemented by networks of distributed components operating concurrently partly in a real time mode with emphasis on interface, architecture, and state. We base our approach on the FOCUS theory—a modular approach to the logical description of distributed interactive systems (see [15]) by their interface behaviors given by relations between their input and output streams.

14.1.1 Central Notion: System

The notion of system is essential both in systems engineering and software engineering. We consider discrete systems. These are systems that interact with their environment via discrete actions and events. In our case we model these actions and events in terms of streams of data elements, called messages.

Our approach uses a specific concept of discrete system with the following notions and principles.

- A discrete *system* has a well-defined boundary that determines its *interface*.
- Everything outside the system boundary is called the system's *environment*. Those parts of the environment that are relevant for the system are called the system's *context*.
- The syntactic interface defines the set of actions that can be performed in interaction with a system. In our case syntactic interfaces are defined by the set of input and output channels together with their types. The input channels define the

M. Broy (✉)
Institut für Informatik, Technische Universität München, München, Germany
e-mail: broy@in.tum.de

M. Hinchey, L. Coyle (eds.), *Conquering Complexity*,
DOI 10.1007/978-1-4471-2297-5_14, © Springer-Verlag London Limited 2012

input actions for a system while the output channels define the output actions for a system.

- By a system's interface it is indicated in which way the system interacts with its context.
- We distinguish between *syntactic interface*, also called *static interface*, which describes the set of input and output actions, which can take place over the system boundary and of *interface behaviour* (also called *dynamical interfaces*), which describes the system's *functionality*; the interface behaviour is captured by the causal relationship between streams of actions captured in the input and output *histories*.
- The behaviour of systems can be described by logical expressions, called *interface assertions*, by *state machines* or it can be further decomposed into *architectures*.
- A system has an internal structure. This structure is described by its state space with state transitions and/or by its decomposition in sub-systems forming its architecture in case the system is decomposed into a number of subsystems, which interact and also provide the interaction with the system's context. The state machine and the architecture associated with a system are called its state view and its structural view respectively.
- Complementary, the behaviour of a system can be described by a set of *traces*, which is a set of scenarios of input and output behaviour of a system. We distinguish between finite and infinite scenarios.

Moreover, systems operate in time. In our case we use discrete time, which seems, in particular, adequate for discrete systems. Sub-systems operate concurrently within architectures.

Especially in software engineering a lot of work is devoted to concepts of *software architecture* (see [3, 20, 21]) as a principle for structuring systems into a family of sub-systems called components (see [19, 26]) for a development method where software systems are composed from prefabricated components. The idea is that main parts of systems can be obtained from appropriate new configurations of reusable software solutions. Thus they do not have to be re-implemented over and over again. Key issues for this approach are precisely specified and well-designed *interfaces* and *system reference architectures*. System architectures describe the structure of distributed systems, composed of components. For handling them, a clean and clear concept using a mathematical model of a system is indispensable.

In software engineering literature the following informal definition of system is found:

> "A system is a physical encapsulation of related functions according to a published specification."

According to this definition we work with the idea of discrete systems that encapsulate either a local state or a set of sub-systems forming a distributed architecture and providing certain functions via its *interface*. We suggest a logical way to write specifications of system functions. We relate these notions to "glass box views", where systems are described by architectures and state machines, to the derived interface abstractions and to system specifications.

We introduce the mathematical notion of a system and on this basis a concept of a system specification. A system specification is a description of a system's syntactic interface and a logical formula that relates input to output histories.

A powerful semantic concept of a system interface is an essential basis for key issues in system development such as well-structured system construction (software and hardware), clear interfaces of systems, proper system architecture, and systematic systems engineering.

In the following we introduce a minimalist's mathematical concept of a system and a syntactic form to describe it by using logic. We show how basic notions of software development such as specification and refinement of systems can be based on this concept. Furthermore, we suggest techniques for specifying, refining, verifying, and implementing systems as well as a framework in which all these activities can be carried out in a model-based way.

Our goal is to have a tight integration between the described views onto a system namely the interface view, the architectural view, and the state view. We provide the following description techniques:

- data models are described by axiomatic data types, type declarations or entity/relationship diagrams
- sets of typed input and output channels together with their types describe syntactic interfaces
- interface assertions specify interface behaviour
- state transition diagrams describe state machines, state transition assertions specify properties of state machines
- graphs with components as nodes and channels as arcs describe architectures; their behaviour is captured by the specification of the interface behaviours of their components; traces (that can be represented by interaction diagrams or message sequence charts) describe the interaction between the components.

These views are related by the following concepts

- *interface abstractions* for state machines and architectures
- *composition* of interface behaviour, state machines, and architectures
- *refinement* to relate system behaviours.

The concepts observe the following principles:

- interface abstraction is *modular* for system composition
- system composition forms architectures
- architectures with all components modeled by state machines are state machines themselves
- refinement relations relate behavioural views.

For an engineering approach we use the following concepts and views:

- A *data model* describes all used data types
- The system functionality is described
  - by a context model that fixes the syntactic interface and how the system is connected to which objects of its environment; the relevant context properties are captured by *assumptions*, the system behaviours by *promises*

- the functionality is described by a *function hierarchy* that contains all the sub-functions offered by a system
- feature interactions between functions are captured with the help of a *mode model*
• The architecture is captured by a decomposition of the system into sub-systems.

We first introduce the basic foundations and afterwards introduce a logical approach where system properties are captured for all the views introduced earlier finally we study engineering issues with emphasis on structured descriptions such that large systems can be captured by the approach and scaling is achieved.

14.1.2 Background, Goals and Structure of the Chapter

Systems are composed of interacting components working concurrently and exchanging messages via communication lines with communication traffic modeled by data streams. FOCUS provides a modular technique for the specification of such systems in terms of their interface behavior and for structuring systems that are composed of components. Each system can be a component of a larger system. We introduce a formal model of comprehensive system functionality structured in terms of *functions* along the lines of [12] where a theoretical basis for the concept of a function is introduced to form function-oriented architectures (see also [10]). This concept is taken as a basis for specifying functional requirements.

The overall goal of this chapter is to work out semantic models of system functionality, architecture, and state machine in terms of functions, composition, state, and their relationships. The goal of this theory is to provide a first basis for an engineering method for the specification of system functionalities, architecture design, and implementation in terms of state machines. For this purpose, the chapter integrates material from a number of publications [6–9, 12, 14] with some more recent results into a more comprehensive approach.

The remainder of the chapter is organized as follows. First, we give an introduction into mathematical models of systems. This includes a simple basis for describing data models on which three fundamental forms of system modeling are based, interface, architecture, and state. For each of the modeling concepts we introduce description techniques based on logic such as interface assertions or state transition tables. This way a mathematical and logical basis is provided that allows us to reason about all three description techniques using predicate logic. We briefly illustrate these techniques by simple examples. In a system development we start by function interface behavior and some basic techniques to specify interfaces, continue by the design of architectures, and finally support their implementation by state machines.

Interface models, composition, and state transition are essential since they support an abstract interface view on systems describing the interface behaviours. Operators for composition of interface behaviour serve as a basis for describing architectures. State transition models describe implementations. All three modeling techniques are related to the notion of a syntactic interface, which is the key to modularity and information hiding. For all three concepts models and description techniques

are introduced such as interface assertions for describing interfaces, graphical notations for describing architectures, and state diagrams as well as state transition rules
for describing implementations.

For a more engineering oriented approach for dealing with this different views
onto systems we introduce context models and functional hierarchies for specification purposes, hierarchical architectures with assumption/promise reasoning for
describing component architectures of systems, and state transition diagrams and
transition tables for describing state machines from which code is generated.

Finally, it is shown how seamless comprehensive system development by these
models can be achieved including concepts of refinement, verification, and tracing.

For the presented approach a tool prototype called AutoFocus is available [11]
(see http://autofocus.in.tum.de).

14.2 Basic Models of Systems

First, we briefly repeat the concepts on which we will base the theory for modeling multifunctional systems. We are dealing with models of discrete systems. We
closely follow the FOCUS approach as described in [15]. A discrete system is a
technical or organizational unit with a clearly specified boundary. It interacts with
its environment over its boundary by exchanging messages in discrete events. In
the case of FOCUS messages are exchanged via channels. In this section we briefly
introduce the syntactic and semantic notion of a system, its interface and that of a
function. This theoretical framework is in line with [12].

14.2.1 Data Models—Data Types

Data models define a set of data types. A *(data) type T* is a name for a data set. Let
TYPE be the set of all data types.

A data type can be specified by an algebraic specification of the following form:

```
SPEC STACK =
{type Stack α,
 estack : Stack α,
 append : α, Stack α → Stack α,
 isestack : Stack α → Bool,
 rest : Stack α → Stack α,
 first : Stack α → α,
 Stack α generated_by estack, append,
 isestack(estack) = true,
 isestack(append(d, s)) = false,
 rest(append(d, s)) = s,
 first(append(d, s)) = d
}
```

Fig. 14.1 Data model (data dictionary) as screenshot from the tool AutoFocus

- ▷ 🗏 BHPPDisplaySignal
- ◢ 🗏 ConsumerDisplaySignal
  - 𝒸 CDStatus(consumedPower:int, loggedOn:boolean)
  - ◉ consumedPower(_D:ConsumerDisplaySignal) : int
  - ◉ is_CDStatus(_D:ConsumerDisplaySignal) : boolean
  - ◉ loggedOn(_D:ConsumerDisplaySignal) : boolean
- ▷ 🗏 ConsumerVPPSignal
- ▷ 🗏 GeneratorProducerSignal
- ▷ 🗏 ProducerDisplaySignal
- ▷ 🗏 ProducerGeneratorSignal
- ▷ 🗏 ProducerVPPSignal
- ▷ 🗏 UserConsumerSignal
- ▷ 🗏 UserProducerSignal
- ▷ 🗏 VPPConsumerSignal
- ▷ 🗏 VPPDisplaySignal
- ▷ 🗏 VPPProducerSignal
- ▷   <Registered Extension Libraries>

It can be implemented (and also directly described) by type declarations of the form:

```
type Stack α = append(first: α, rest: Stack α) | estack
```

Data types provide data elements that are used as messages between systems or as attributes of states. The state space Σ of a state machine is fixed by typed state attributes as in object orientation. Given a set V of typed state attributes, for every state $\sigma \in \Sigma$ and every state attribute $v \in V$ of type T, $\sigma(v)$ denotes the value of attribute v in the state σ. A state space then is described by a set of declarations of its attributes, together with their types.

Large state spaces are described by structured data models along the lines of entity relationship diagrams. Figure 14.1 shows a data model as implemented in our tool AutoFocus.

14.2.2 Syntactic Interfaces

Systems have *syntactic interfaces* that are described by their sets of input and output channels attributed by the type of messages that are communicated over them. Channels are used to connect systems to be able to transmit messages between them. A set of typed channels is a set of channels with a type given for each of its channels.

Definition 14.1 (Syntactic interface) Let I be the set of typed input channels and O be the set of typed output channels. The pair (I, O) characterizes the syntactic interface of a system. The *syntactic interface* is denoted by $(I \blacktriangleright O)$.

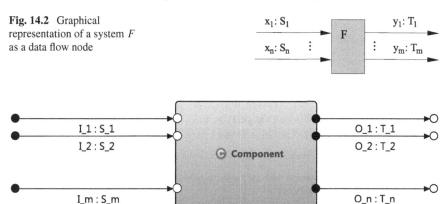

Fig. 14.2 Graphical representation of a system F as a data flow node

Fig. 14.3 System interface as screenshot from the tool AutoFocus

Figure 14.2 shows the syntactic interface of a system F in a graphical representation by a data flow node with its syntactic interface consisting of the input channels $x_1, \ldots, x_n$ of types $S_1, \ldots, S_n$ and the output channels $y_1, \ldots, y_m$ of types $T_1, \ldots, T_m$. Figure 14.3 shows a similar representation from the tool AutoFocus.

To structure functionality, we introduce some auxiliary notions. A fundamental notion is the sub-type relationship between syntactic interfaces.

An *input action* of a system F with syntactic interface $(I \blacktriangleright O)$ is a pair (m, c) where $c \in I$ is an input channel and m is a message of the type associated with channel c. An *output action* of a system F with syntactic interface $(I \blacktriangleright O)$ is a pair (m, c) where $c \in O$ is an output channel and m is a message of the type associated with channel c. By $Act(C)$ we denote the actions of a typed channel set C.

A typed channel set C_1 is called a *sub-type* of a typed channel set C_2 if the following formula holds (we assume that all types stand for non-empty sets of elements):

$$Act(C_1) \subseteq Act(C_2)$$

We write then

$$C_1 \text{ subtype } C_2$$

Thus, a sub-type C_1 of a set C_2 of typed channels carries only a subset of the channel identifiers from C_2 and for each of the channels in C_1 only a subset of the messages it carries in C_2. The idea of sub-types is mainly used for relating functions.

Sub-typing, as introduced, is extended schematically from channel sets to interfaces.

Definition 14.2 (Sub-types between interfaces) If for syntactic interfaces $(I_1 \blacktriangleright O_1)$ and $(I_2 \blacktriangleright O_2)$ both I_1 **subtype** I_2 and O_1 **subtype** O_2 hold, we call the syntactic interface $(I_1 \blacktriangleright O_1)$ a *sub-type of the interface* $(I_2 \blacktriangleright O_2)$ and write:

$$(I_1 \blacktriangleright O_1) \text{ subtype } (I_2 \blacktriangleright O_2)$$

This means that $(I_1 \blacktriangleright O_1)$ includes only a subset of the input and output actions of $(I_2 \blacktriangleright O_2)$.

This definition is chosen to study sub-behaviors working on subsets of input and output actions and stands in contrast to the notions of sub-typing as defined in object-oriented languages. There a functional sub-type requires that its domain type may be increased while its range type may be decreased. Then the usage of functions with sub-types instead of original types does not lead to type errors.

14.2.3 Interface Behavior

Discrete systems show an interface behavior which is modeled by functions mapping the streams of messages received on the system's input channels onto streams of messages sent on its output channels. We call this the *black box behavior* or the *interface behavior* of discrete systems.

14.2.3.1 Streams

In FOCUS, a system encapsulates a state and is connected to its context exclusively by its interface given by its typed input and output channels.

Definition 14.3 ((Non-timed) Streams) Given a set M, by M^* we denote the set of finite sequences of elements of M, by M^∞ the set of infinite sequences of elements of the set M; infinite sequences are formally represented by functions

$$s : \mathbb{N}\setminus\{0\} \to M.$$

By M^ω we denote the set $M^* \cup M^\infty$, called the set of finite and infinite (non-timed) *streams*.

In the following, we work with streams that include discrete timing information. Such streams represent histories of communications of data messages transmitted within a fixed time frame. To keep the time model simple we choose a concept of discrete time where time is represented by an infinite sequence of finite time intervals of equal length.

Definition 14.4 (Timed Streams) Given a message set M of data elements of type T, we represent a *timed stream s* of type T by a mapping

$$s : \mathbb{N}\setminus\{0\} \to M^*$$

In a timed stream s a sequence $s(t)$ of messages is given for each time interval $t \in \mathbb{N}\setminus\{0\}$. In each time interval an arbitrary, but finite number of messages may be communicated. By $(M^*)^\infty$ we denote the set of timed streams.

Special cases of timed streams are of the form

$$s : \mathbb{N}\backslash\{0\} \rightarrow M$$

and (let "–" stand for the empty slot)

$$s : \mathbb{N}\backslash\{0\} \rightarrow M \cup \{\text{"–"}\}$$

They represent special cases of timed streams where exactly one message (represented by a one element sequence) or at most one message (where the empty slot is represented by the empty sequence) are communicated in a time interval. In a number of examples of systems, which we consider in the following, we deal, for simplicity, only with streams with sequences of messages that contain at most one element.

Throughout this chapter we work with a few basic operators and notations for streams that are briefly summarized as follows:

$\langle\rangle$ empty sequence or empty stream
$\langle m \rangle$ one-element sequence containing m as its only element
$a\hat{\ }b$ concatenation of the sequences of streams a and b
$s(t)$ tth element of the stream s (which is a sequence in the case of timed streams)
$s \downarrow t$ prefix of length $t \in \mathbb{N}$ of the stream s (which is a sequence of length t carrying finite sequences as its elements in the case of a timed stream)
$T\copyright x$ stream obtained from stream x by deleting all messages in x that are not members of T
$\#x$ number of elements in stream or sequence x

A (timed) channel history for a set of typed channels C assigns to each channel $c \in C$ a timed stream of messages communicated over that channel.

Definition 14.5 (Channel History) Let C be a set of typed channels; a (total) *channel history* x is a mapping (let $\mathbb{M}$ be the universe of all messages)

$$x : C \rightarrow (\mathbb{N}\backslash\{0\} \rightarrow \mathbb{M}^*)$$

such that $x(c)$ is a timed stream of messages of the type of channel $c \in C$. $\vec{C}$ denotes the set of all total channel histories for the channel set C.

For each history $z \in \vec{C}$ and each time $t \in \mathbb{N}$ the expression $z \downarrow t$ denotes the partial history (the initial communication behavior on the channels) of z until time t. $z \downarrow t$ yields a finite history for each of the channels in C represented by a mapping

$$C \rightarrow (\{1, \ldots, t\} \rightarrow \mathbb{M}^*)$$

$z \downarrow 0$ denotes the history with empty sequences associated with each of its channels.

Fig. 14.4 Example of system interface as screenshot from the tool AutoFocus

14.2.3.2 Interface Behavior Model

The behavior of a system with syntactic interface $(I \blacktriangleright O)$ is defined by a mapping that maps the input histories in $\vec{I}$ onto output histories in $\vec{O}$. This way we get a functional model of a system interface behavior.

Definition 14.6 (Causal Behavior) For a mapping

$$F : \vec{I} \to \wp(\vec{O})$$

we define the set

$$dom(F) = \{x : F(x) \neq \varnothing\}$$

called the *domain* of F. F is called *total*, if $dom(F) = \vec{I}$, otherwise F is called *partial*.

The mapping F is called *causal*, if (for all $t \in \mathbb{N}$ and all input histories $x, z \in \vec{I}$):

$$x, z \in dom(F) \wedge x \downarrow t = z \downarrow t \quad \Rightarrow \quad \{y \downarrow t : y \in F(x)\} = \{y \downarrow t : y \in F(z)\}$$

F is called *strongly causal*, if (for all $t \in \mathbb{N}$ and all input histories $x, z \in \vec{I}$):

$$x, z \in dom(F) \wedge x \downarrow t = z \downarrow t \quad \Rightarrow \quad \{y \downarrow t+1 : y \in F(x)\} = \{y \downarrow t+1 : y \in F(z)\}$$

Causality (for an extended discussion see [15]) indicates a consistent time flow between input and output histories in the following sense: in a causal mapping input messages received at time t do influence future output only after time t; this output is given by messages communicated via output channels at times $\geq t$ (in the case of strong causality at times $> t$, which indicates that there is a delay of at least one time step before input has any effect on output).

Definition 14.7 (I/O-Behavior) A causal mapping $F : \vec{I} \to \wp(\vec{O})$ is called an *I/O-behavior*. By $\mathbb{F}[I \blacktriangleright O]$ we denote the set of all (total and partial) I/O-behaviors with syntactic interface $(I \blacktriangleright O)$ and by $\mathbb{F}$ the set of all I/O-behaviors.

Interface behaviors model system functionality. For systems we assume that their interface behavior is total. Behaviors F may be deterministic (in this case, the set $F(x)$ of output histories has at most one element for each input history x) or non-deterministic.

Fig. 14.5 Composition
$F_1 \otimes F_2$

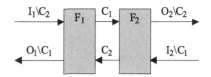

14.2.4 Composition

In this section we describe the composition of systems in terms of their interface behavior. We show how to calculate the interface behavior of a composed system from the interface behaviors of its components.

Definition 14.8 (Composable Interfaces) Two syntactic interfaces $(I_1 \blacktriangleright O_1)$ and $(I_2 \blacktriangleright O_2)$ are called *composable*, if

- the sets I_1 and I_2 of input channels are pairwise disjoint,

$$I_1 \cap I_2 = \varnothing$$

- the sets of output channels O_1 and O_2 are pairwise disjoint,

$$O_1 \cap O_2 = \varnothing$$

- the types of the channels I_1, I_2, O_1, and O_2 are consistent in the sense that equal channel names have equal types.

If channel names are not consistent for a pair of systems to be composed we simply may rename the channels to make them consistent.

Definition 14.9 (Syntactic Composition) Given two syntactic interfaces $(I_1 \blacktriangleright O_1)$ and $(I_2 \blacktriangleright O_2)$ that are composable we define the syntactic composition by syntactic interface $(I \blacktriangleright O)$, where

$I = (I_1 \cup I_2)\backslash(O_1 \cup O_2)$ denotes the set of *input* channels,
$D = (O_1 \cup O_2)$ denotes the set of *generated* channels,
$O = D\backslash(I_1 \cup I_2)$ denotes the set of *output* channels,
$D\backslash O$ denotes the set of *internal* channels,
$C = (I_1 \cup I_2) \cup (O_1 \cup O_2)$ denotes the set of all channels.

By $(I \blacktriangleright D)$ we denote the *syntactic internal interface* and by $(I \blacktriangleright O)$ we denote the *syntactic external interface* of the composition of syntactic interfaces $(I_1 \blacktriangleright O_1)$ and $(I_2 \blacktriangleright O_2)$.

A syntactic architecture forms a directed graph with its components as nodes and its channels as directed arcs as illustrated in the case of two systems in Fig. 14.5.

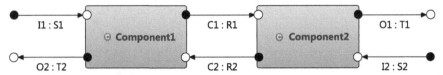

Fig. 14.6 System composition as screenshot from the tool AutoFocus

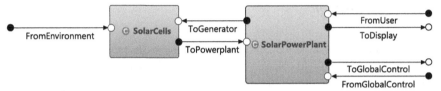

Fig. 14.7 Concrete example of system composition as screenshot from the Tool AutoFocus

Definition 14.10 (Composition of Systems in Terms of Interface Behavior) Given two causal interface behaviors $F_1 \in \mathbb{F}[I_1 \blacktriangleright O_1]$ and $F_2 \in \mathbb{F}[I_2 \blacktriangleright O_2]$, with composable syntactic interfaces we define the composition of F_1 and F_2 involving the feedback channels

$$C_1 = O_1 \cap I_2 \quad \text{and} \quad C_2 = O_2 \cap I_1$$

by the expression

$$F_1 \otimes F_2$$

The interface behavior $F_1 \otimes F_2 \in \mathbb{F}[I \blacktriangleright O]$ of the composed system is defined as follows. Let all definitions of channel sets be as in the definition of composable interfaces. For $x \in \vec{I}$ we define (for a channel valuation $z \in \vec{C}$ and a subset $B \subseteq C$ of channels we denote by $z|B$ the restriction of z to the channels in B):

$$(F_1 \otimes F_2)(x) = \{y \in \vec{O} : \exists z \in \vec{C} : x = z|I \wedge y = z|O \wedge z|O_1 \in F_1(z|I_1) \wedge z|O_2$$
$$\in F_1(z|I_2)\}$$

The composition of systems interface behavior and thus the systems' functionalities as defined above is graphically illustrated in Fig. 14.5.

The composition $\otimes$ works well, in particular, for strongly causal systems and also for composition without feedback (where $C_1 = \varnothing$ or $C_2 = \varnothing$).

In a composed system $F_1 \otimes F_2$, the channels in channel sets C_1 and C_2 are used for internal communication.

The composition of systems with disjoint sets of input channels and disjoint sets of output channels is commutative:

$$F_1 \otimes F_2 = F_2 \otimes F_1$$

as well as associative:

$$(F_1 \otimes F_2) \otimes F_3 = F_1 \otimes (F_2 \otimes F_3)$$

The proof of this these equations is straightforward.

14.2.5 State Machines by State Transition Functions

State machines with input and output describe system implementations in terms of states and state transitions. A state machine is defined by a state space and a state transition.

Definition 14.11 (State Machine with Syntactic Interface $(I \blacktriangleright O)$) Given a state space Σ, a state machine (Δ, Λ) with input and output according to the syntactic interface $(I \blacktriangleright O)$ consists of a set $\Lambda \subseteq \Sigma$ of initial states as well as of a nondeterministic state transition function

$$\Delta : (\Sigma \times (I \to M^*)) \to \wp(\Sigma \times (O \to M^*))$$

For each state $\sigma \in \Sigma$ and each valuation $a : I \to M^*$ of the input channels in I by sequences of input messages every pair $(\sigma', b) \in \Delta(\sigma, a)$ defines a successor state σ' and a valuation $b : O \to M^*$ of the output channels consisting of the sequences produced by the state transition. (Δ, Λ) is a *Mealy machine* with possibly infinite state space. If in every transition the output b depends on the state σ only but never on the current input a, we speak of a *Moore machine*.

14.2.6 Channel Traces

One way to study the behavior of systems are traces. Traces are histories of system channels. As specified, a history is a valuation of a set of typed channels.

Definition 14.12 (Trace of a Set of Channels) A trace for set C of typed channels is given by a valuation $z \in \vec{C}$.

For a system with syntactic interface $(I \blacktriangleright O)$ a trace $z \in \vec{C}$ with $Z = I \cup O$ trace denote runs of the system. Traces $z \in \vec{C}$ of systems with interface behavior F are this way very close to pairs (x, y) input and output histories $x \in \vec{I}$, $y \in \vec{O}$ with $y \in F(x)$ provided $x = z|I$ and $y = z|O$. A set of traces describes properties of systems. Finite traces $z \downarrow t$ can be used to describe test cases.

14.3 Specifying Basic System Views

In this section we show how the basic system views are specified. We introduce both logical techniques and graphical techniques to specify system views.

14.3.1 Specifying Interface Behavior

Interface behavior is described by its properties. We use predicate logic.

Fig. 14.8 Graphical
representation of a function
interface with the set of input
channels I and the set of
output channels O

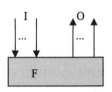

14.3.1.1 Systems and Their Functionality

Systems interact with their contexts via the channels of their interfaces. We identify
both systems by names. A system named k has an interface, consisting of a syntactic
interface $(I_k \blacktriangleright O_k)$ and an interface behavior

$$F_k : \vec{I}_k \to \wp(\vec{O}_k)$$

The behavior may be a combination of a larger number of more elementary sub-
function behaviors. Then we speak of a *multifunctional* system.

Let *SID* be the set of system names. A system named $k \in SID$ is called *statically
interpreted* if only a syntactic interface $(I_k \blacktriangleright O_k)$ is given for k and *dynamically
interpreted* if an interface behavior $F_k \in \mathbb{F}[I_k \blacktriangleright O_k]$ is specified for k.

From a methodological point of view, the concept of a function offered by a
system is closely related to the idea of a use case (see [18]) as suggested for object-
oriented analysis for illustrating one way of using the system for a particular purpose
(e.g., using a mobile phone for taking a digital photo). The use case is described by
a set of interaction scenarios (for instance of taking photos) represented by traces.

14.3.1.2 System Interface Behaviour: Specification by Interface Assertions

The interface behaviour of a system can be specified in a descriptive logical style
using interface assertions.

Definition 14.13 (Interface Assertion) Given a syntactic interface $(I \blacktriangleright O)$ with a
set I of typed input channels and a set O of typed output channels, an interface
assertion is a logical formula with channel identifiers in I and O as free logical
variables denoting streams of the respective types.

We specify the behaviour F_S for a system with name S with syntactic interface
$(I \blacktriangleright O)$ and an interface assertion P by a scheme:

S
_____
in I
out O
_____
P
_____

The scheme specifies the interface behaviour F_S by

$$\forall x \in \vec{I}, y \in \vec{O} : y \in F_S(x) \quad \Leftrightarrow \quad P(x, y)$$

where $P(x, y)$ results from P by replacing all channels c occurring in assertion P by streams $x(c)$ or $y(c)$ respectively.

Notation   Throughout the chapter we use the following notation: Given a predicate

$$p : \vec{C} \to \mathbb{B}$$

we specify for every time $t \in \mathbb{N}$

$$p(x \downarrow t) \equiv \exists x' \in \vec{C} : x \downarrow t = x' \downarrow t \wedge p(x')$$

In other words, assertion $p(x \downarrow t)$ holds if there exists some history x' for which p holds and which is equal to x till time t. This notation is easily extended to n-ary predicates and histories.

This notation can also be understood as a way to extend a predicate on histories to finite prefixes of histories.

Causality can be also defined for interface predicates and assertions.

Definition 14.14 (Causal Interface Assertion) Interface assertion $P(x, y)$ for the syntactic interface $(I \blacktriangleright O)$ is called *causal* if for all $x, x' \in \vec{I}$ and all $t \in \mathbb{N}$

$$x \downarrow t = x' \downarrow t \quad \Rightarrow \quad \forall y \in \vec{O} : P(x, y \downarrow t) \quad \Leftrightarrow \quad P(x', y \downarrow t)$$

and *strongly causal* if

$$x \downarrow t = x' \downarrow t \quad \Rightarrow \quad \forall y \in \vec{O} : P(x, y \downarrow t + 1) \quad \Leftrightarrow \quad P(x', y \downarrow t + 1)$$

We give a first example of a specification.

Example (A Specification Example)   This example illustrates the specification of a simple but relevant example of a concurrent system that is difficult to describe in a procedural programming style. The system offers the function of concurrent reading from and writing to a variable where it is guaranteed that the actions of reading and writing do not mutually constrain each other.

Typically, there are a number of applications where data generated and provided by some source are to be read by some other computing unit, thereby always the freshest value is to be delivered.

This example leads to a typical read/write conflict for a von Neumann type programming style. The value is stored in a storage cell where reading and updating are done in a synchronized atomic mutually exclusive way. Usually, semaphores are used to exclude conflicts. The critical question is not so much the synchronization of concurrent access. The critical question is that by writing read actions are postponed for a long time or by reading updating is not enabled and thus the read values may be out of date.

We treat the example of a system called *Fresh* that always delivers the newest value of the data on stream x. Figure 14.9 shows its syntactic interface.

Fig. 14.9 Syntactic interface

We first define the involved message sets:

$$Write = \{d \in Data\}$$

$$Get = \{get\}$$

$$Val = \{d \in Data\}$$

The logical specification of *Fresh* is defined as follows:

Fresh
---
in $x : Write, z : Get$
out $y : Val$

$\forall t : z(t) = get \Rightarrow y(t+1) = last(x, t)$
   $z(t) = \text{``--''} \Rightarrow y(t+1) = \text{``--''}$

Let d_0 be some fixed initial value:

$$last(x, 0) = d_0$$

$$last(x, t+1) = \textbf{if } x(t) \neq \text{``--''} \textbf{ then } x(t) \textbf{ else } last(x, t) \textbf{ fi}$$

Note that this system is very difficult to describe by synchronized access to shared variables. The reason is that for shared variables interleaving and synchronization as well as timely update is required.

In shared memory system models, reading and writing actions usually cannot be done synchronously but have to be interleaved. However, when interleaving them with the help of semaphores or the concept of indivisible actions we run into the difficulty that due to the restriction to interleaving a high number of writes might block reading for a while and a high number of reading may block writing for a while. Without fairness assumptions, reading or writing may even be blocked out forever. But even under fairness assumption there is no guarantee that the reading of a value is to be carried out within a certain amount of time and that the read value is fresh in the sense that it is not older than a guaranteed amount of time.

Note that the specifying assertion of the example is strongly causal. The specified behaviour is therefore strongly causal, too.

Example (Transmission, Merge and Fork) As simple but quite fundamental examples of systems we specify a merge component *MRG*, a transmission component *TMC*, and a fork component *FRK*. In the examples let $T1$, $T2$, and $T3$ be types (recall that in our case types are simply sets) where $T1$ and $T2$ are assumed to be disjoint and $T3$ is the union of the sets of elements of type $T1$ and $T2$. The specification of the merge component *MRG* (actually the specification relies on the assumption that $T1$ and $T2$ are disjoint, which should be made explicit in the specification in a more sophisticated specification approach) reads as follows:

MRG

in $x : T1, y : T2$
out $z : T3$

$\bar{x} = T1\copyright\bar{z} \wedge \bar{y} = T2\copyright\bar{z}$

In this specification nothing is specified about the time flow and therefore the specification refers only to the time abstractions of the involved streams denoted by the operator $\bar{x}$. The causality of the time flow is considered in detail in the following subsection.

We specify interface assertion $x \sim y$ for timed streams x and y of arbitrary type T; $x \sim y$ is true if the messages in x are a permutation of the messages in y. Formally we define it by the following logical equivalence:

$$x \sim y \equiv (\forall m \in T : \{m\}\copyright\bar{x} = \{m\}\copyright\bar{y})$$

Based on this definition we specify the component *TMC*.

Often it is helpful to use certain channel identifiers both for input channels and for output channels. These are then two different channels, which might have different types. To distinguish these channels in interface assertions, we use a well-known notational trick. In an interface specification, we write for a channel c that occurs both as input and as output channel simply c to denote the stream on the input channel c and c' to denote the stream on the output channel c. Accordingly in the following specification z is the external name of the output channel z and z' is its internal name.

TMC

in $z : T3$
out $z : T3$

$z \sim z'$

This simple specification says that every input message occurs eventually also as output message, and vice versa. Nothing is specified about the timing of the messages. In particular, messages may be arbitrarily delayed and overtake each other. The specification does not exclude that output messages might even be produced earlier than they are received. This paradox is excluded by causality.

The following component *FRK* is just the "inversion" of the component merge.

FRK

in $z : T3$
out $x : T1, y : T2$

$\bar{x} = T2\copyright\bar{z}$
$\wedge\bar{y} = T2\copyright\bar{z}$

Note that the merge component *MRG* as well as the *TMC* component and the fork component *FRK* as they are specified here are "fair" in the following sense. Every input is eventually processed and reproduced as output.

Based on the interface assertion given in a specification of an interface behavior F we may prove properties about F.

14.3.2 Specifying Architectures

In this section, we describe how to form architectures from sub-systems, called the components of the architecture. Architectures are concepts to structure systems. Architectures contain precise descriptions for systems in terms of their sub-systems and how the composition of their sub-systems takes place. In other words, architectures are described by the sets of systems forming their components together with mappings from output to input channels that describe internal communication and form a data flow network.

14.3.2.1 Syntactic Architectures

In the following we assume that each system used in an architecture as a component has a unique identifier k. Let K be the set of identifiers for the components of an architecture.

Definition 14.15 (Set of Composable Interfaces) A set of component names K with a finite set of interfaces $(I_k \blacktriangleright O_k)$ for each identifier $k \in K$ is called *composable*, if the following propositions hold:

- the sets of input channels $I_k, k \in K$, are pairwise disjoint,
- the sets of output channels $O_k, k \in K$, are pairwise disjoint,
- the channels in $\{c \in I_k : k \in K\} \cap \{c \in O_k : k \in K\}$ have consistent channel types in $\{c \in I_k : k \in K\}$ and $\{c \in O_k : k \in K\}$.

If channel names and types are not consistent for a set of systems to be used as components we simply may rename the channels to make them consistent.

Definition 14.16 (Syntactic Architecture) A syntactic architecture $A = (K, \xi)$ with interface $(I_A \blacktriangleright O_A)$ is given by a set K of component names with composable syntactic interfaces $\xi(k) = (I_k \blacktriangleright O_k)$ for $k \in K$.

$I_A = \{c \in I_k : k \in K\} \backslash \{c \in O_k : k \in K\}$ denotes the set of *input* channels of the architecture,

$D_A = \{c \in O_k : k \in K\}$ denotes the set of *generated* channels of the architecture,

$O_A = D_A \backslash \{c \in I_k : k \in K\}$ denotes the set of *output* channels of the architecture,

$D_A \backslash O_A$ denotes the set of *internal* channels of the architecture,

$C_A = \{c \in I_k : k \in K\} \cup \{c \in O_k : k \in K\}$ denotes the set of all channels.

By $(I_A \blacktriangleright D_A)$ we denote the *syntactic internal interface* and by $(I_A \blacktriangleright O_A)$ we denote the *syntactic external interface* of the architecture.

A syntactic architecture forms a directed graph with its components as its nodes and its channels as directed arcs. The input channels in I_A are ingoing arcs and the output channels in O_A are outgoing arcs for that graph.

Definition 14.17 (Interpreted Architecture) An interpreted architecture (K, ψ) for a syntactic architecture (K, ξ) associates an interface behavior $\psi(k) \in \mathbb{F}[I_k \blacktriangleright O_k]$, where $\xi(k) = (I_k \blacktriangleright O_k)$, with every component $k \in K$.

An architecture can be specified by a syntactic architecture and an interface specification for each of its components.

14.3.2.2 Describing the Behavior of Architectures

Behavioral scenarios of architectures can be described by trace sets for the channels of architectures. A logical description can be given by trace assertions.

Definition 14.18 (Architecture Specification) An architecture specification (K, χ) consists of a syntactic architecture (K, ξ) where χ provides an interface assertion $\chi(k)$ for the syntactic interface $(I_k \blacktriangleright O_k)$ for every component $k \in K$.

In the following sections we define an interface behavior for interpreted architectures by composing the behaviors of the components.

14.3.3 Specifying State Machines

State machines are described by state transition diagrams or by state transition tables. We start with a simple example of a system and its specification. We specify a queue. It is a simple basic example out of a rich class of systems for storing and retrieving data. To keep the examples simple, we consider only input histories with at most one (relevant) message per channel in each time interval. For sequences s of messages of length > 1, only their last elements $last(s)$ are considered relevant.

To specify systems, we work with specification templates. A function specification consists of a graphical description of a data flow node that specifies the name of the function, its state attributes including their initial values, and the input and output channels with their types. In addition, a table describes the state transitions.

Example (Queue) A Queue allows us to store elements of type Data and to request them in a first in, first out (FIFO) fashion. A typical application of a device offering such a function might be a PDA that offers the option to store a queue of tasks or dates. We specify the data types involved as follows (*req* is the signal for an output request):

Table 14.1 The system queue as a state transition table

q	a	q'	b
s	d	$s\,\hat{}\,\langle d\rangle$	–
$\langle d\rangle\,\hat{}\,s$	req	s	d

Fig. 14.10 The system queue as data flow node

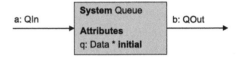

```
type QIn = {req} ∪ Data
type QOut = Data
```

Based on these data types we formulate the specification of the function Queue in Table 14.1.

The specification consists of a state transition table and a data flow node. The data flow node describes the input and output channels, their types, as well as the state attributes and their initial values. The entry "−" in the table indicates empty output (or input) for that channel. The rows in the table describe the state changes. q' denotes the value of the state attribute q after the state transition. For instance, the first row in Table 14.1 represents the state transition rule described by the following formula:

$$(\sigma', \beta) \in \Delta(\sigma, \alpha) \quad \Leftarrow \quad \sigma(q) = s \wedge last(\alpha(a)) = d \wedge \beta(b) = \langle\rangle \wedge \sigma'(q) = s\,\hat{}\,\langle d\rangle$$

There may be different state machines that fulfill the state transition rules. With a table we associate the inclusion-least state transition function that fulfills the rules of the table.

The given table, in fact, is an example of a specification of a partial behavior. If the input stream a has for instance the shape (let $d1, d2 \in Data$)

$$a = \langle\langle req\rangle\rangle\,\hat{}\,\langle\langle d1\rangle\rangle\,\hat{}\,\langle\langle req\rangle\rangle\,\hat{}\,\langle\langle req\rangle\rangle\,\hat{}\,\langle\langle d2\rangle\rangle\,\hat{}\,\langle\langle req\rangle\rangle\,\hat{}\,\dots$$

then the transition rules for input stream a do not apply, since in the initial state q is empty and thus the set of output histories is empty.

For details of how tables describe state machines and how state machine descriptions relate to interface behaviors, see [15].

Figure 14.11 shows a state transition diagram of a nondeterministic state machine representing a storage cell. Arcs represent state transition, labeled by input and output actions and state changes. If the input message is empty represented by "−" the output is "−" and the system remains in its state.

Figure 14.12 shows two state transition diagrams as shown in the tool AutoFocus.

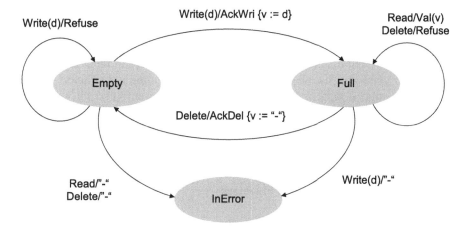

Fig. 14.11 State machine with local attribute v of type data described by a state transition diagram

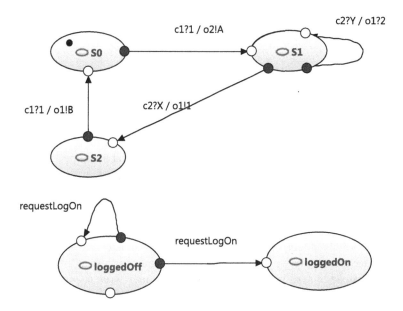

Fig. 14.12 State transition diagrams as screenshot from the tool AutoFocus

14.3.3.1 Specifying Properties of State Machines

Logical properties of state machines are captured by specific formulas of predicate logic. Traditionally temporal logic is used to formulate properties about state transition systems represented by state machines. Usually, in temporal logic state machines without input and output are considered such that the formulas of temporal logic specify properties for the infinite streams of states generated as computations by these state machines. There are several variations of temporal logic including so-called *linear time temporal logic* which talks about the state traces of a state machine and *branching-time temporal logic* which considers the tree of computations defined by a state machine.

Since we are not mainly interested in the states but rather in input and output histories of computations, classical temporal logic is not the right choice for us. Moreover, temporal logic is limited in its expressive power. Although we could introduce a version of temporal logic that talks about input and output of computations, we prefer to talk about the interface behavior in terms of more general and more expressive interface assertions.

14.3.3.2 Assertions About State Machines

Let Q be an *interface interval assertion* which is a formula in predicate logic with x and y as free identifiers for channel valuations that associate messages or finite sequences of messages with each channel; the identifiers s and s' stand for states; we get a kind of temporal logic if we define (for a given system interface with input channels x and output channels y) the classical two operators of linear time temporal logic

$$\Diamond Q \equiv \exists t \in \mathbb{N}_+ : Q[x(t)/x, y(t)/y, \sigma(t-1)/s, \sigma(t)/s']$$

$$\Box Q \equiv \forall t \in \mathbb{N}_+ : Q[x(t)/x, y(t)/y, \sigma(t-1)/s, \sigma(t)/s']$$

This way every system assertion written in temporal logic is translated into a system assertion in classical predicate logic. This is illustrated for a simple formula in temporal logic for a system with an input channel a and an output channel b as follows:

$$\Box(x(a) = \langle\rangle \Rightarrow y(b) = \langle\rangle) \equiv \forall t \in \mathbb{N}_+ : (x(t)(a) = \langle\rangle \Rightarrow y(t)(b) = \langle\rangle)$$

This demonstrates how temporal logic is translated into general predicate logic. This way every formula in temporal logic is translated into an interface assertion.

For better readability we rather write channel names a instead of $x(a)$ and attributes v instead of $s(v)$ in formulas. This way we may write a formula about the queue:

$$\Box(a \in Data \Rightarrow q' = q\hat{}\langle a\rangle \wedge b = \text{``--''})$$

$$\Box(a \in req \wedge \#q > 0 \Rightarrow q = \langle b\rangle\hat{}q')$$

For the state machine in Fig. 14.11 we may formulate the property (assuming x as input channel, y as output channel and two state predicates $s \in empty, full, d \in Data$):

$$\Box(x = write(d) \wedge s = empty \wedge y = AckWri \Rightarrow s' = full \wedge v' = d)$$

This results in specification techniques close to Lamport's TLA (see [1, 2]).

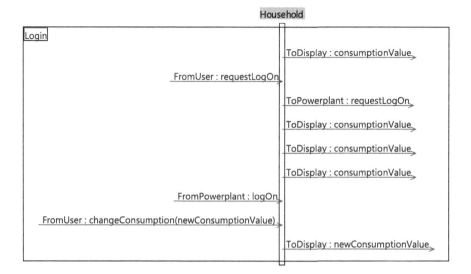

Fig. 14.13 Interaction diagram (message sequence) chart as screenshot from the tool AutoFocus

14.3.4 Specifying Traces

An interaction diagram (also called message sequence chart) describes a trace. The properties of as trace can be captured by a trace assertion along the lines of interface assertions.

A trace assertion over a channel set C is a formula in predicate logic that contains the channels from C as identifiers for streams. The formula may be written also in temporal logic as shown in the previous section.

14.4 Relating System Views

In this section we relate the three basic views: interface behavior, state machines and architectures.

14.4.1 Relating Architectures with Interfaces and Traces

Given a specification of an architecture, which consists of the description of the syntactic network of the architecture as well as the description of the components, we get a description of the behaviour of the architecture. Depending on how the components are described we get different models for views onto the composed system. In particular, if all the components of a particular architecture are described by interface assertions we derive an interface assertion for the composed architecture since the approach we are presenting is modular. For architectures the components may also be represented by state machines or again by architectures.

14.4.1.1 Glass Box Views onto Interpreted Architectures

We first define the composition of composable systems. It is the basis for giving semantic meaning to architectures. We start at the glass box view onto an architecture given by a set of traces for all channels.

Definition 14.19 (Composition of Systems—Glass Box View) For an interpreted architecture A with syntactic internal interface $(I_A \blacktriangleright D_A)$ we define the glass box interface behavior $[\times]A \in \mathbb{F}[I_A \blacktriangleright D_A]$ by the equation (let $\psi(k) = F_k$):

$$([\times]A)(x) = \{y \in \vec{D}_A : \exists z \in \vec{C}_A : x = z|I_A \wedge y = z|D_A \wedge \forall k \in K : z|O_k \in F_k(z|I_k)\}$$

where the operator $|$ denotes the usual restriction operator. Internal channels are not hidden by this composition but the streams on them are part of the output. The formula defines the result of the composition of the k behaviors F_k by defining the output y of the architecture $[\times]A$ with the channel valuation z of all channels. The valuation z carries the input provided by x expressed by $x = z|I_A$ fulfills all the input/output relations for the components expressed by $z|O_k \in F_k(z|I_k)$. The output of the composite system is given by y which is the restriction $z|D_A$ of z to the set D_A of output channels of the architecture $[\times]A$.

For two composable systems $F_k \in \mathbb{F}[I_k \blacktriangleright O_k]$, $k = 1, 2$, we write

$$F_1 \times F_2$$

for $[\times]\{F_k : k = 1, 2\}$. Composition of composable systems is commutative

$$F_1 \times F_2 = F_2 \times F_1$$

and associative

$$(F_1 \times F_2) \times F_3 = F_1 \times (F_2 \times F_3)$$

The proof of this equation is straightforward. We also write therefore with $K = \{1, 2, 3, \ldots\}$

$$[\times]\{F_k \in \mathbb{F}[I_k \blacktriangleright O_k] : k \in K\} = F_1 \times F_2 \times F_3 \times \ldots$$

The glass box view is related to the trace view below by associating with an architecture traces over all its internal and external channels. From the glass box view we can derive the black box view as demonstrated in the following section.

14.4.1.2 Interface Views onto Architectures

The interface view of an architecture is an abstraction of the glass box view.

Definition 14.20 (Composition of Systems—Interface View) Given an interpreted architecture A with syntactic external interface $(I_A \blacktriangleright O_A)$ and glass box interface behavior $[\times]A \in \mathbb{F}[I_A \blacktriangleright D_A]$ we define its interface behavior $F_A \in \mathbb{F}[I_A \blacktriangleright O_A]$ by

$$F_A(x) = (F(x))|O_A$$

Internal channels are hidden by this composition and in contrast to the glass box view not part of the output.

For an interpreted architecture with syntactic external interface $(I_A \blacktriangleright O_A)$, we obtain the interface behavior $F_A \in \mathbb{F}[I_A \blacktriangleright O_A]$ specified by

$$F_A(x) = \{y \in \vec{O}_A : \exists z \in \vec{C}_A : x = z|I_A \wedge y = z|O_A \wedge \forall k \in K : z|O_k \in F_k(z|I_k)\}$$

and write

$$F_A = \bigotimes\{F_k \in \mathbb{F}[I_k \blacktriangleright O_k] : k \in K\}$$

We also write therefore with $K = \{1, 2, 3, \ldots\}$

$$\bigotimes\{F_k \in \mathbb{F}[I_k \blacktriangleright O_k] : k \in K\} = F_1 \otimes F_2 \otimes F_3 \otimes \ldots$$

The idea of the composition of systems as defined above is shown in Fig. 14.5 with $C_1 = I_2 \cap O_1$ and $C_2 = I_1 \cap O_2$. For properties of the algebra, we refer the reader to [5, 15]. In a composed system, the internal channels are used for internal communication.

14.4.1.3 Interface Assertions for Architectures

Given a syntactic architecture $A = (K, \xi)$ and specifying interface assertions S_k for the sub-systems $k \in K$, the specifying assertion for the glass box behavior is given by $\forall k \in K : S_k$, and for the black box behavior by $\exists c_1, \ldots, c_j : \forall k \in K : S_k$, where $\{c_1, \ldots, c_j\}$ denotes the set of internal channels

The set of systems together with the introduced composition operators form an algebra. The composition of systems (more precisely of their behavior in terms of strongly causal stream processing functions) yields systems and the composition of functions yields functions.

Composition is a partial function on the set of all system behaviors. It is only defined if the syntactic interfaces are composable. Syntactic interfaces fit together if there are no contradictions in the channel names and types.

14.4.1.4 Renaming

So far we defined the composition using the names of components to connect them only for sets of components that are composable in the sense that their channel names and types fit together. Often, the names of the components may not fit. Then renaming may help.

Definition 14.21 (Renaming System Channels) Given a system behavior $F \in \mathbb{F}[I \blacktriangleright O]$ a renaming is a pair of mappings $\alpha : I' \to I$ and $\beta : O \to O'$ where the types of the channels are consistent in the sense that c and $\alpha(c)$ as well as e and $\beta(e)$ have the same types for all $c \in I$ and all $e \in O$. By a renaming $\rho = (\alpha, \beta)$ of F we obtain a component $\rho[F] \in \mathbb{F}[I' \blacktriangleright O']$ such that for $x \in \vec{I}'$

$$\rho[F](x) = \beta(F(\alpha(x)))$$

where for $x \in \vec{I}'$ the history $\alpha(x) \in \vec{I}$ is defined by

$$\alpha(x)(c) = x(\alpha(c))$$

for $c \in I$.

Note that by a renaming, a channel in I' or O may be used in several copies in I or O'. Given an interpreted architecture $A = (K, \psi)$ with a set of components $\psi(k) = F_k \in [I_k \blacktriangleright O_k]$ for $k \in K$ and a set of renamings $R = \{\rho_k : k \in K\}$ where ρ_k is a renaming of F_k for all $k \in K$, we call (A, R, ψ) an interpreted architecture with renaming if the set $\{\rho_k[F_k] : k \in K\}$ is well defined and composable. The renamings R define the connections that make A an architecture.

14.4.2 From State Machines to Interface Behaviors

By interface abstraction we may associate an interface behavior with each state machine.

14.4.2.1 Interface Behavior of State Machines

State machines show a particular interface behavior.

Definition 14.22 (Interface Behavior of State Machines) Given a state machine (Δ, Λ) with syntactic interface $(I \blacktriangleright O)$ we define its interface abstraction which relates an interface behavior

$$IA_{(\Delta, \Lambda)} \in \mathbb{F}[I \blacktriangleright O]$$

with machine (Δ, Λ) as follows (let Σ be the state space for (Δ, Λ), $x \in \vec{I}$)

$$IA_{(\Delta, \Lambda)}(x) = \{y : \exists \sigma : \mathbb{N} \to \Sigma : \sigma(0) \in \Lambda \wedge \forall t \in \mathbb{N} : (\sigma(t+1), y(t+1))$$

$$\in \Delta(\sigma(t), x(t+1))\}$$

Note that in computations we start to count states by 0 such that the initial state is $\sigma(0)$ while we count the time intervals starting with 1 such that $x(1)$ and $y(1)$ are the sequences of messages exchanged in interval 1. $IA_{(\Lambda, \Lambda)}$ is called the interface behavior or the interface abstraction of the state machine (Δ, Λ).

By construction $IA_{(\Delta, \Lambda)}$ is causal. If (Δ, Λ) is a Moore machine then $IA_{(\Delta, \Lambda)}$ is strongly causal.

Given a state machine we may perform an interface abstraction. It is given by the step from the state machine to its interface behavior.

Definition 14.23 (Black Box Behavior and Specifying Assertion) Given a state machine $SM = (\Delta, \Lambda)$ with interface behavior IA_{SM} the interface assertion that is equivalent to the proposition $y \in IA_{SM}(x)$ is called the *specifying assertion*.

IA_{SM} is causal by construction. If SM is a Moore machine (that is, the output depends on the state only) then IA_{SM} is strongly causal.

14.4.2.2 The Set of Input/Output Histories of State Machines

With each state machine with input and output we easily associate its set of interface histories. These sets characterize the interface behavior of state machines. It provides an abstraction for computations from the states. Given a state machine (Δ, Λ), where $\Lambda \subseteq \Sigma$ is the set of initial states and

$$\Delta : (\Sigma \times (I \to M^*)) \to \wp(\Sigma \times (O \to M^*))$$

is the state transition function, we define the predicate

$$IC : \vec{I} \times \vec{O} \times \Sigma \to \mathbb{B}$$

that characterizes the set of interface histories in terms of computations for a given state $\sigma \in \Sigma$ as follows:

$$IC(x, y, \sigma) = \forall \phi : \mathbb{N} \to \Sigma : \phi(0) = \sigma \wedge \forall t \in \mathbb{N} : (\phi(t+1), y(t+1))$$

$$\in \Delta(\phi(t), x(t+1))$$

To prove that for some input history x and some output history y the proposition $IC(x, y, \sigma)$ holds we have to construct a stream of states explicitly according to this characterization.

14.4.2.3 Composing State Machines

A syntactic architecture represents a state machine if for each of its components a state machine is specified.

Definition 14.24 (Architecture Implemented by State Machines) An architecture (K, ζ) of a syntactic architecture (K, ξ) that associates a state machine $\zeta(k) = (\Delta_k, \Lambda_k) \in SM[I_k \blacktriangleright O_k]$ with every $k \in K$, where $\xi(k) = (I_k \blacktriangleright O_k)$, defines a state machine for the architecture.

In the following sections we define an interface behavior for interpreted architectures by composing the behaviors of their components.

Definition 14.25 (Composition of State Machines—Glass Box View) For an implemented architecture $R = (K, \zeta)$ for a syntactic architecture $A = (K, \xi)$ we define the composition $(\Delta_R, \Lambda_R) \in SM[I_A \blacktriangleright D_A]$ by the following equations (let $\zeta(k) = (\Delta_k, \Lambda_k)$ with state space Σ_k):
The state space Σ_R is defined by the direct product (let for simplicity $K = \{1, 2, 3, \ldots\}$) of the state spaces

$$\Sigma_R = \Sigma_1 \times \Sigma_2 \times \Sigma_3 \times \ldots$$

the initial state set is defined by the direct product of the sets of initial states

$$\Lambda_R = \Lambda_1 \times \Lambda_2 \times \Lambda_3 \times \ldots$$

and the state transition function Δ is defined by

$$\Delta_R(\sigma, a) = \{(\sigma', b) : \exists z : C \to M^* : b = z|D_A \wedge a = z|I_A \wedge \forall k \in K : (\sigma'_k, z|O_k)$$
$$\in \Delta_k(\sigma_k, z|I_k)\}$$

Internal channels are not hidden by this composition but their messages on them are part of the output.

If the composed state machines are Moore machines, their composition is a Moore machine, too.

14.4.2.4 Architectures as State Machines

If each component of an architecture is given by a state machine, the architecture itself defines a state machine that is the result of the composition of the state machines given for its components. Its state space is the direct product of the state spaces of its components.

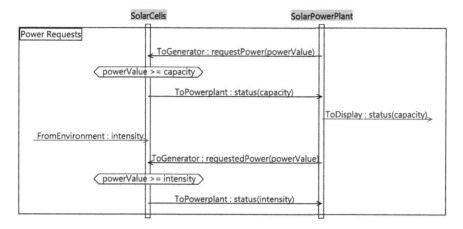

Fig. 14.14 Interaction diagram (message sequence) chart as screenshot from the tool AutoFocus

14.4.3 Traces of Interfaces, State Machines, and Architectures

Traces are histories of system channels.

Definition 14.26 (Trace of an Interface) A trace for a syntactic interface $(I \blacktriangleright O)$ is given by a valuation $z \in \vec{C}$ of channels $C = I \cup O$. For an interface behavior $F \in \mathbb{F}[I \blacktriangleright O]$ the trace $z \in \vec{C}$ is called correct if $z|O \in F(z|I)$.

A finite trace can be used to represent a test case. Systems may be described by sets of traces and illustrated by a finite set of representative traces.

Definition 14.27 (Trace of a State Machine) A trace (z, σ) for a state machine with state space Σ and syntactic interface $(I \blacktriangleright O)$ is given by a valuation $z \in \vec{C}$ of channels $C = I \cup O$ and a stream of states $\sigma : \mathbb{N} \to \Sigma$. A state machine (Δ, Λ) is called correct for the trace if $\sigma(0) \in \Lambda$ and $(\sigma(t+1), y(t+1)) \in \Delta(\sigma(t), x(t+1))$.

Properties of traces of state machines may be described by temporal logic.

Definition 14.28 (Trace of an Architecture) A trace for a syntactic architecture $A = (K, \xi)$ is given by a valuation $z \in \vec{C}$ of channels

$$C = \bigcup_{k \in K} (I_k \cup O_k)$$

For an interpreted architecture (K, ψ) the trace $z \in \vec{C}$ is called correct if $z|O_k \in \psi(k)(z|I_k)$ for all $k \in K$, where $\xi(k) = (I_k \blacktriangleright O_k)$.

Traces of architectures include a trace for each of their component. They can be described by interaction diagrams (see Fig. 14.14). Such traces are snapshots of the glass box view of an architecture.

14.5 Refinement and Verification: Reasoning About System Views

In our approach we formalize the following basic ideas of refinement:

- *property refinement*—enhancing requirements—allows us to add properties to a specification,
- *glass box refinement*—designing implementations—allows us to decompose a system into a distributed system or to give a state transition description for a system specification,
- *interaction refinement*—relating levels of abstraction—allows us to change the representation of the communication histories, in particular, the granularity of the interaction as well as the number and types of the channels of a system (see [4]).

In fact, these notions of refinement describe the steps needed in an idealistic view of a strict hierarchical top down system development. The three refinement concepts mentioned above are formally defined and explained in detail in the following.

14.5.1 System Development by Refinement

In requirements engineering and in the design phase of system development many issues have to be addressed, such as requirements elicitation, conflict identification and resolution, information management as well as the selection of a favorable software architecture (see [20, 21]). These activities are connected with development steps. Refinement relations (see [4]) are the medium to formalize development steps (see [13]) and in this way the development process.

14.5.1.1 Property Refinement

Property refinement is a well-known concept in structured programming. It allows us to replace an interface behavior with one having additional "refused" properties. This way a behavior is replaced by a more restricted one. In FOCUS an interface behavior

$$F : \vec{I} \to \wp(\vec{O})$$

is refined by a behavior

$$F' : \vec{I} \to \wp(\vec{O})$$

if

$$F \approx > F'$$

This relation stands for the proposition

$$\forall x \in \vec{I} : F'(x) \subseteq F(x)$$

Obviously, property refinement is a partial order and therefore reflexive, asymmetric, and transitive. Moreover, the inconsistent specification logically described by false refines everything.

A property refinement is a basic refinement step adding requirements as it is done step-by-step in requirements engineering.

In the process of requirements engineering, typically the overall functionality of a system is specified. Requiring more and more sophisticated properties for systems until a desired behavior is specified, in general, does this.

Example A specification of a system that transmits its input from its two input channels to its two output channels (but does not necessarily observe the order) is specified as follows.

TM2
in $x : T1, y : T2$ **out** $x : T1, y : T2$
$x' \sim x \wedge y' \sim y$

We refine this specification to the simple specification of the time permissive identity *TII* that reads as follows:

TII
in $x : T1, y : T2$ **out** $x : T1, y : T2$
$\bar{x}' = \bar{x} \wedge \bar{y}' = \bar{y}$

TII is a property refinement of *TM2*, formally expressed

$$TM2 \approx> TII$$

A proof of this relation is straightforward (see below).

The verification conditions for property refinement are easily generated as follows. For given interface specifications S_1 and S_2 with interface assertions Φ_1 and Φ_2, the specification S_2 is a property refinement of S_1 if the syntactic interfaces of S_1 and S_2 coincide and if for the interface assertions Φ_1 and Φ_2 the proposition

$$\Phi_1 \quad \Leftarrow \quad \Phi_2$$

holds. In our example the verification condition is easily generated. It reads as follows:

$$x' \sim x \wedge y' \sim y \quad \Leftarrow \quad \bar{y}' = \bar{y} \wedge \bar{x}' = \bar{x}$$

The proof of this condition is obvious. It follows immediately from the definitions of the time abstraction $\bar{x}$ and $x' \sim x$. For an implementation of the calculus in the interactive proof assistant Isabelle (see [22]) see [25].

The property refinement relation is verified by proving the logical implication between the interface assertions.

Property refinement is useful to relate composed systems to systems specified by logical formulas (see also glass box refinement in Sect. 14.5.1.3). For instance, the following refinement relation

$$TII \approx> (MRG \circ FRK)$$

holds. Again the proof is straightforward.

Property refinement is characteristic for the development steps in requirements engineering. It is also used as the baseline of the design process where decisions being made introduce further system properties.

14.5.1.2 Compositionality of Property Refinement

For FOCUS, the proof of the compositionality of property refinement is straightforward. This is a consequence of the simple definition of composition. The rule of compositional property refinement reads as follows:

$$\frac{F_1 \approx> F_1' \quad F_2 \approx> F_2'}{F_1 \otimes F_2 \approx> F_1' \otimes F_2'}$$

The proof of the soundness of this rule is straightforward due to the monotonicity of the operator $\otimes$ with respect to set inclusion. Compositionality is often called *modularity* in system development. Modularity allows for a separate development of systems.

Modularity guarantees that separate refinements of the components of a system lead to a refinement of the composed system.

Example For our example the application of the rule of compositionality reads as follows. Suppose we use a specific component $MRG1$ for merging two streams. It is defined as follows (recall that $T1$ and $T2$ form a partition of $T3$):

$MRG1$

---

in $x : T1, y : T2$
out $z : T3$

$z = \langle\langle\rangle\rangle \char`\^ f(x, y)$
where
$\forall s \in T1^*, t \in T2^*, x \in (T1^*)^\infty, y \in (T2*)^\infty : f(\langle s\rangle \char`\^ x, \langle t\rangle \char`\^ y) = \langle s \char`\^ t\rangle \char`\^ f(x, y)$

Note that this merge component $MRG1$ is deterministic and not time independent. According to the FOCUS rule of compositionality and transitivity of refinement, it is sufficient to prove

$$MRG \approx> MRG1$$

to conclude

$$MRG \circ FRK \approx> MRG1 \circ FRK$$

and by the transitivity of the refinement relation

$$TII \approx> MRG1 \circ FRK$$

This shows how local refinement steps that are refinements of subcomponents of a composed system and their proofs are schematically extended to global proofs.

The composition operator and the relation of property refinement leads to a design calculus for requirements engineering and system design. It includes steps of decomposition and implementation that are treated more systematically in the following section.

14.5.1.3 Glass Box Refinement

Glass Box Refinement is a classical concept of refinement used in the design phase. In this phase, we typically decompose a system with a specified interface behavior into a distributed system architecture or represent (implement) it by a state transition machine. In other words, a glass box refinement is a special case of a property refinement that is of the form

$F \approx> F_1 \otimes F_2 \otimes \ldots \otimes F_n$ design of an architecture for a system with interface behavior F or of the form

$F \approx> IA_{(\Delta, \Lambda)}$ implementation of system with interface behavior F by a state machine

where the interface behavior $IA_{(\Delta, \Lambda)}$ is defined by a state machine (Δ, Λ) (see also [15]) with Λ as its initial states.

Glass box refinement means the replacement of a system F by a property refinement that represents a design step. A design is given by a network of systems $F_1 \otimes F_2 \otimes \cdots \otimes F_n$ or by a state machine (Δ, Λ) with behavior $IA_{(\Delta, \Lambda)}$. The design is a property refinement of F provided the interface behavior of the net or of the state machine respectively is a property refinement of behavior F.

Accordingly, a glass box refinement is a special case of property refinement where the refining system has a specific syntactic form. In the case of a glass box refinement that transforms a system into a network, this form is a term shaped by the composition of a set of systems. The term describes an architecture that fixes the basic implementation structure of a system.

These systems have to be specified and we have to prove that their composition leads to a system with the required functionality.

Again, a glass box refinement can be applied afterwards to each of the systems F_i in a network of systems. The systems $F_1, \ldots, F_n$ can be hierarchically decomposed again into a distributed architecture in the same way, until a granularity of systems is obtained which is not to be further decomposed into a distributed system but realized by a state machine. This form of iterated glass box refinement leads to a hierarchical top down refinement method.

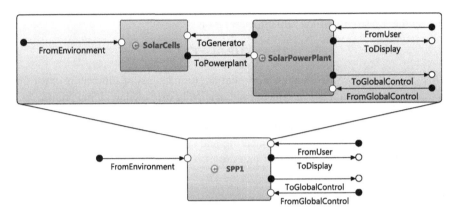

Fig. 14.15 Glass box refinement of a system by an architecture as screen shot from tool AutoFocus

Example A simple instance of such a glass box refinement is already shown by the proposition

$$TII \approx> MRG \circ FRK$$

It allows us to replace the system *TII* by a network of two systems.

Note that a glass box refinement is a special case of a property refinement.

It is not in the center of this chapter to describe in detail the design steps leading from an interface specification to distributed systems or to state machines. Instead, we take a purist's point of view. Since we have introduced a notion of composition we consider a system architecture as being described by a term defining a distributed system by composing a number of systems.

14.5.1.4 Interaction Refinement

In FOCUS interaction refinement is the refinement notion for modeling development steps between levels of abstraction. For a system, interaction refinement allows us to change for a system

- the number and names of its input and output channels,
- the types of the messages on its channels determining the granularity of the messages.

A pair of two mappings describes an interaction refinement for two sets C and C' of channels

$$A : \vec{C}' \rightarrow \wp(\vec{C}) \qquad R : \vec{C} \rightarrow \wp(\vec{C}')$$

that relate the interaction on an abstract level with corresponding interaction on the more concrete level. This pair specifies a development step that is leading from one level of abstraction to the other as illustrated by Fig. 14.16. Given an abstract

Fig. 14.16 Communication
history refinement

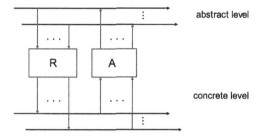

Fig. 14.17 Interaction
refinement (U^{-1}-simulation)

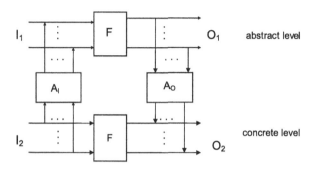

history $x \in \vec{C}$ each $y \in R(x)$ denotes a concrete history representing x. A is called
the *abstraction* and R is called the *representation*. Calculating a representation for
a given abstract history and then calculating its abstraction yields the old abstract
history again. Using sequential composition, this is expressed by the requirement:

$$R \circ A = Id$$

Let Id denote the identity relation. A is called the *abstraction* and R is called the
representation. R and A are called a *refinement pair*. For non-timed systems we
weaken this requirement by requiring $R \circ A$ to be a property refinement of the time
permissive identity formally expressed by the equation(for all histories $x \in \vec{C}$)

$$\overline{(R \circ A)(x)} = \{\bar{x}\}$$

Choosing the system *MRG* for R and *FRK* for A immediately gives a refinement
pair for non-timed systems.

Interaction refinement allows us to refine systems, given appropriate refinement
pairs for their input and output channels. The idea of an interaction refinement is
visualized in Fig. 14.17 for the so-called U^{-1}-simulation. Note that here the systems
(boxes) A_I and A_O are no longer definitional in the sense of specifications, but
rather methodological, since they relate two levels of abstraction. Nevertheless, we
specify them as well by the specification techniques introduced so far.

Given refinement pairs

$$A_I : \vec{I}_2 \to \wp(\vec{I}_1) \qquad R_I : \vec{I}_1 \to \wp(\vec{I}_2)$$
$$A_O : \vec{O}_2 \to \wp(\vec{O}_1) \qquad R_O : \vec{O}_1 \to \wp(\vec{O}_2)$$

Fig. 14.18 Graphical
representation of an
interaction refinement
(U-simulation)

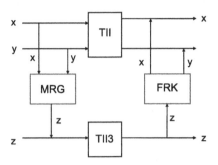

for the input and output channels we are able to relate abstract to concrete channels
for the input and for the output. We call the interface behavior

$$F' : \vec{I}_2 \to \wp(\vec{O}_2)$$

an interaction refinement of the interface behavior

$$F : \vec{I}_1 \to \wp(\vec{O}_1)$$

if the following proposition holds:

$$A_I \circ F \circ R_O \approx> F' \qquad U^{-1}\text{-simulation}$$

This formula essentially expresses that F' is a property refinement of the system
$A_I \circ F \circ R_O$. Thus for every "concrete" input history $x' \in \vec{I}_2$ every concrete output
$y' \in \vec{O}_2$ can be also obtained by translating x' onto an abstract input history $x \in$
$A_I(x')$ such that we can choose an abstract output history $y \in F(x)$ such that $y' \in$
$R_O(y)$.

There are three further versions of interaction refinement. A more detailed discussion of the mathematical properties of U^{-1}-simulation is found in [4].

Example For the time permissive identity for messages of type $T3$ a system specification reads as follows:

TII3
in $z : T3$
out $z : T3$
$\bar{z} = \bar{z}'$

We obtain

$$TII \approx> MRG \circ TII3 \circ FRK$$

as a simple example of interaction refinement by U-simulation with is reverse to
U^{-1}-simulation. The proof is again straightforward.

Figure 14.18 shows a graphical description of this refinement relation.

The idea of interaction refinement is found in other approaches to system specification like *TLA*, as well. It is used heavily in practical system development, although it is hardly ever introduced formally there. Examples are the communication protocols in the ISO/OSI hierarchies (see [17]).

Interaction refinement formalizes the relationship between layers of abstractions in system development. This way interaction refinement relates the layers of protocol hierarchies, the change of data representations for the messages or the states as well as the introduction of time in system developments.

Example In a property refinement, if we replace the component *TII3* by a new component *TII3'* (for instance along the lines of the property refinement of *TII* into *MRG* ∘ *FRK*), we get by the compositionality of property refinement

$$TII \approx> MRG \circ TII3' \circ FRK$$

from the fact that *TII3* is an interaction refinement of *TII*.

Interaction refinement is formulated with the help of property refinement. In fact, it can be seen as a special instance of property refinement. This guarantees that we can freely combine property refinement with interaction refinement in a compositional way.

14.5.2 Proving Properties about Interface Behaviors

Proofs over interface behaviors specified by interface assertions are straightforward using higher order predicate logic.

14.5.3 Proving Properties about Architectures

Given a description of an architecture in terms of composable components with specified interface behaviors we can derive the specification of the interface behavior of the architecture along the following lines in a modular way.

14.5.3.1 Modularity of Composition

The property of modularity of interface specifications may be characterized as follows. Given two system specifications, where P_k are the interface assertions for systems $F_k, k = 1, 2$:

F_k
in I_k
out O_k
P_k

we obtain the specification of the composed system $F_1 \otimes F_2$ as illustrated in Fig. 14.5:

$$F_1 \otimes F_2$$

in $I_1 \backslash C_2 \cup I_2 \backslash C_1$
out $O_1 \backslash C_1 \cup O_2 \backslash C_2$

$\exists C_1, C_2 : P_1 \wedge P_2$

The interface assertion of $F_1 \otimes F_2$ is derived in a modular way from the interface assertions of its components by logical conjunction and existential quantification over channels denoting internal channels.

14.5.3.2 Deriving Interface Specifications from Architecture Specifications

Given an architecture specification (K, χ) for the syntactic architecture (K, ξ) where χ provides an interface assertion $\chi(k)$ for the syntactic $(I_k \blacktriangleright O_k)$ for every component $k \in K$ we get an interface specification for the architecture A described by the specification (let all the channel sets be as in the definition of syntactic interfaces)

$$A$$

in I_A
out O_A

$\exists D_A \backslash O_A : \bigwedge_{k \in K} \chi(k)$

Recall that I_A denotes the set of *input* channels of the architecture, O_A denotes the set of *output* channels, and $D_A \backslash O_A$ denotes the set of *internal* channels of the architecture.

14.5.4 Proving Properties About State Machines

Proving properties about state machines can be tricky and difficult as proving properties about implementations is never easy. State machines basically represent implementations of systems in terms of state transition functions. We can use classical techniques for proving properties about state machines such as invariants. More sophisticated ones are described in [10], where we distinguish between safety and liveness properties. As it is shown, safety properties basically can be proved using invariant techniques, showing that all final prefixes of histories show required properties. Liveness properties can be much more difficult to prove as analyzed in [10].

14.5.5 Proving Properties About Traces

Properties about traces are described by trace assertions. For trace assertions we can use classical predicate logic to work out proofs, similar to interface assertions.

14.5.6 Testing Systems

Verification for systems cannot only be done by proving properties but also by testing properties. A sophisticated test approach for testing the introduced system model is given in [14]. Traces, in particular final traces, can be used to represent test cases. The definition of how test cases are related to system descriptions and how state machines and architectures can be tested is described in [14].

14.6 Engineering Systems: Structuring System Views

In this section we study ways of structuring the interface and the architectural views. We introduce the idea of assumption/promise specifications and that of function hierarchies.

14.6.1 Assumption/Promise Specifications

Specific systems are often only used in restricted contexts. Then the contexts of systems are assumed to fulfill certain properties. Assumptions are properties of the context we can assume about the input along the channels to the system and also about the reactions of the context to outputs produced by the system under consideration (for an extensive presentation, see [9]).

14.6.1.1 Contracts as Interface Assertions by Assumption/Promise

Given a syntactic interface $(I \blacktriangleright O)$, an interface assertion is a Boolean expression $p(x, y)$ where p is a predicate

$$p : \vec{I} \times \vec{O} \to \mathbb{B}$$

and $x \in \vec{I}$ and $y \in \vec{O}$ are input and output histories. Figures 14.19 and 14.20 graphically illustrate the composition. We assume here that context E and system S are composable.

With this modeling the key question is the definition of composition and how we model systems, their properties, their attributes and their behaviour.

Fig. 14.19 Closed
composition $S \otimes E$ of S with
internal channels x' and y'

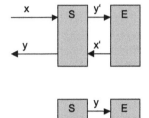

Fig. 14.20 Open
composition $S \times E$ of S with
the context E

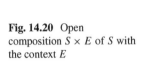

Both Figs. 14.19 and 14.20 illustrate the composition of a system S with context E. Both cases result in composite systems for which the messages on the channels or histories x and y are observable.

An assumption/promise specification (A/P-specification for short) is given by an assumption about the context, which is an interface assertion, and a specification of the system's interface behaviour, which is an interface assertion that holds provided the assumption holds. An A/P-specification is given by a specification of an assumption about the context E

$$Asu(E)$$

and by some promise of the form

$$Pro(E \otimes S)$$

or

$$Pro(E \times S)$$

about the system S if used in a context with property $Asu(E)$. If we understand that the cooperation between context E and system S is captured exclusively in terms of the messages exchanged via the input channels in set I and the output channels in set O then the property $Asu(E)$ of the context can be expressed by an assertion

$$asu(x, y)$$

on histories $x \in \vec{I}$ and $y \in \vec{O}$, while $Pro(E \times S)$ has can be expressed by some assertion

$$pro(x, y)$$

Of course, we assume that assertion $pro(x, y)$ speaks solely about properties of system S if used in the context E. Assertion $asu(x, y)$ has to be a specification indicating which input x is possibly generated by the context E for the system S given some output history y.

14.6.1.2 From A/P-Contracts to Logical Implication

A very useful way to understand A/P-specifications is to see them as special forms of implication. This leads to a very clear and crisp semantic interpretation of A/P-specification formats and allows us to use all of the FOCUS theory in connection with A/P-specifications.

The basic idea is as follows: we write specifications using interface assertions structured into the following pattern:

$$\textbf{assume:} \quad asu(x, y)$$
$$\textbf{promise:} \quad pro(x, y)$$

with the following meaning: if the context fulfills the specification given by the assumption

$$asu(x, y)$$

then the system fulfills the promised assertion

$$pro(x, y)$$

This means that the assertion $asu(x, y)$ is an interface specification for the context and has to follow the rules of system specifications. In fact, $asu(x, y)$ is a specification for the context E. We require of context E the assumption specified by

$$Asu(E) \equiv [\forall x, y : x \in E(y) \;\Rightarrow\; asu(x, y)]$$

and of the system S and its context E the promise specified by

$$Pro(E, S) \equiv [\forall x, y : y \in (E \times S)(x) \;\Rightarrow\; pro(x, y)]$$

The combination of these predicates then specifies a contract

$$Con(S) \equiv [\forall E : Asu(E) \;\Rightarrow\; Pro(E, S)]$$

This equation defines the meaning of a functional contract. Note that the promise speaks about the properties of the system composed with the context while the promise speaks only about properties of the context.

14.6.2 System Use Case Specification: Structuring System Functionality

In the following we study relationships and dependencies between behaviors that are sub-functions of multifunctional systems. Furthermore, we introduce the basic relation between functions called *sub-function relations*.

14.6.2.1 Projections of Histories and Functions

Based on the sub-type relation between sets of typed channels as introduced in Sect. 14.2.2, we define the concept of a projection of a history. It is the basis for specifying the sub-function relation.

Definition 14.29 (History Projection) Let C and G be sets of typed channels with C **subtype** G. We define for history $x \in \vec{G}$ its projection $x|C \in \vec{C}$ to the channels in the set C and to the messages of their types. For channel $c \in C$ with type T we specify the projection by the equation:

$$(x|C)(c) = T © x(c)$$

where for a stream s and a set M we denote the stream derived from s by deleting all messages in s that are not in set M by $M © s$. $x|C$ is called *projection of history x to channel set C*.

To obtain the sub-history $x|C$ of x by projection, we keep only those channels and types of messages in the history x that belong to the channels and their types in C.

Definition 14.30 (Projection of Behaviors) Given syntactic interfaces $(I' \blacktriangleright O')$ and $(I \blacktriangleright O)$ where $(I' \blacktriangleright O')$ **subtype** $(I \blacktriangleright O)$ holds, we define for a behavior $F \in \mathbb{F}[I \blacktriangleright O]$ its *projection* $F\dagger(I' \blacktriangleright O') \in \mathbb{F}[I' \blacktriangleright O']$ to the syntactic interface $(I' \blacktriangleright O')$ by the following equation (for all input histories $x' \in \vec{I'}$):

$$F\dagger(I' \blacktriangleright O')(x') = \{y|O' : \exists x \in \vec{I} : x' = x|I' \wedge y \in F(x)\}$$

In a projection, we delete all input and output messages that are not part of the syntactic interface $(I' \blacktriangleright O')$ and concentrate on the subset of the input and output messages of a system in its syntactic sub-interface $(I' \blacktriangleright O')$. The idea is to derive less complex sub-behaviors that, nevertheless, allow us to conclude properties about the original system.

The following definition characterizes projections that do not introduce additional nondeterminism, since the input deleted by the projection does not influence the output.

Definition 14.31 (Faithful Projection of Behaviors) Let all definitions be as in the definition above. A projection $F\dagger(I' \blacktriangleright O')$ is called *faithful*, if for all input histories $x \in dom(F)$ the following formula holds:

$$F(x)|O' = (F\dagger(I' \blacktriangleright O'))(x|I')$$

In a faithful projection, the sets of histories produced as outputs on the channels in O' do depend only on the messages of the input channels in I' and not on other inputs for F outside I'. A faithful projection is a projection of a behavior to a sub-function that forms an independent sub-behavior, where all input messages in I are included that are relevant for the considered output messages.

14.6.2.2 Sub-functions and Their Dependencies

In the following, we discuss the question, how a given function $F' \in \mathbb{F}[I' \blacktriangleright O']$ that is to be offered by some system with interface behavior $F \in \mathbb{F}[I \blacktriangleright O]$ where $(I' \blacktriangleright O')$ **subtype** $(I \blacktriangleright O)$, relates to the projection $F\dagger(I' \blacktriangleright O')$. This leads to the concept of a *sub-function*.

A given and specified function behavior F' is offered as a sub-function by a multifunctional system with behavior F, if in F all the messages that are part of the function behavior F' are as required in F'. This idea is captured by the concept of a sub-function.

Definition 14.32 (Sub-function Relation) Given $(I' \blacktriangleright O')$ **subtype** $(I \blacktriangleright O)$, function $F' \in \mathbb{F}[I' \blacktriangleright O']$ is a *sub-function* of a behavior $F \in \mathbb{F}[I \blacktriangleright O]$, if for all histories $x \in \vec{I}'$

$$F' = (F\dagger(I' \blacktriangleright O'))$$

We say that *"system with behavior F offers the function F'"* and that *"F' is a sub-function of F"*. We write $F' \leftarrow_{sub} F$.

The sub-function relation forms a partial order.

A system behavior may have many sub-functions. The sub-function relation is significant from a methodological point of view, since it is the dominating relation for function hierarchies.

14.6.2.3 Restricted Sub-functions

The sub-function relation $\leftarrow_{sub}$ introduced so far is rather straightforward. Often, however, functions are actually not sub-functions but only somewhat close to that. Therefore we study weaker relationships between functions $F' \in \mathbb{F}[I' \blacktriangleright O']$ and the projection $F\dagger(I' \blacktriangleright O')$ of a multifunctional system with behavior F.

Let $(I' \blacktriangleright O')$ **subtype** $(I \blacktriangleright O)$ hold; in the remainder of this section we study situations in which the relation

$$F' \leftarrow_{sub} F$$

actually does not hold.

Nevertheless, even in such cases we want to say that the function $F' \in \mathbb{F}[I' \blacktriangleright O']$ is offered by a super-system $F \in \mathbb{F}[I \blacktriangleright O]$, if we restrict the input to F to an appropriate sub-domain $R \subseteq \vec{I}$ of F that excludes the problematic input histories that show dependencies between messages not in I but do influence output on O'.

Definition 14.33 (Restricted Sub-Function Relation) Given behaviors $F' \in \mathbb{F}[I' \blacktriangleright O']$ and $F \in \mathbb{F}[I \blacktriangleright O]$ where $(I' \blacktriangleright O')$ **subtype** $(I \blacktriangleright O)$ holds, behavior F' is called a *restricted sub-function* of behavior F if there exists a subset $R \subseteq \vec{I}$ such that

$$F' \leftarrow_{sub} F|R$$

Here the partial mapping $F|R \in \mathbb{F}[I \blacktriangleright O]$ denotes as usual the restriction of mapping F to subset R of histories in $\vec{I}$ with $(F|R)(x) = \varnothing$, if $x \notin R$, and $(F|R)(x) = F(x)$, if $x \in R$. If R is the largest set for which the relationship $F' \leftarrow_{sub} F|R$ holds then R is called the *domain of F' in F*.

Obviously, if $F' \leftarrow_{sub} F$ holds, then F' is a restricted sub-function of F. The reverse does not hold, in general. The key question in the restricted sub-function relation is, how to get a reliable access to the function F' offered by F. To get access in F to the function described by F', we must not only follow the input patterns in $dom(F')$ but also make sure that the histories are in R. The restricted sub-function relation is a partial order, as well. The restricted sub-function relation as introduced here is weaker and thus more flexible than the sub-function relation.

14.6.2.4 Dependency and Independency of Sub-functions

In this section we specify what it means that a sub-function is independent of another sub-function within a multifunctional system.

For a multifunctional system with behavior $F \in \mathbb{F}[I \blacktriangleright O]$ and syntactic sub-interface $(I_1 \blacktriangleright O_1)$, projection $F\dagger(I_1 \blacktriangleright O_1)$ provides an abstraction of F. If the projection is faithful, then there are no input actions in set $Act(I) \backslash Act(I_1)$, which influence the output actions of O_1 in F. Now we consider the case, where some input action (m, c), with channel $c \in I$ but $c \notin I_1$ has influence on output actions of F on channels of set O_1.

Definition 14.34 (Independency of Projections of Messages) Let channel sets I_2 and O_1 as well as behavior $F \in \mathbb{F}[I \blacktriangleright O]$ be given with I_2 **subtype** I and O_1 **subtype** O; the output actions of channel set O_1 are called *independent* of the input actions of I_2 within F if for all input histories $x, x' \in \vec{I}$ we have

$$x|I' = x'|I' \quad \Rightarrow \quad F(x)|O_1 = F(x')|O_1$$

where I' is the channel set with $Act(I') = Act(I) \backslash Act(I_2)$.

If the projection $F\dagger(I_1 \blacktriangleright O_1)$ is faithful for each set of input channels I_2 with $Act(I_1) \cap Act(I_2) = \varnothing$ we get that for system F channel set O_1 is independent of channel set I_2.

Definition 14.35 (Dependency and Independency of Functions) Let sub-functions $F_1 \in \mathbb{F}[I_1 \blacktriangleright O_1]$, $F_2 \in \mathbb{F}[I_2 \blacktriangleright O_2]$ of $F \in \mathbb{F}[I \blacktriangleright O]$ be given with $(I_1 \blacktriangleright O_1)$ **subtype** $(I \blacktriangleright O)$ and $(I_2 \blacktriangleright O_2)$ **subtype** $(I \blacktriangleright O)$; function F_1 is called *independent* of the function F_2 in system F, if the output actions of the channel set O_1 are independent of the input actions of I_2 within F. If F_1 is *dependent* of the input actions in I_2 within F we write

$$F_2 \rightarrow_{dep} F_1 \text{ in } F$$

Dependency is not a symmetric relation. Function F_1 may be dependent of function F_2 in F, while the function F_2 is independent of the function F_1 in F.

14.7 Models at Work: Seamless Model-Based Development

In the previous sections we introduced a comprehensive set of modeling concepts for systems. We now put them together in an integrated system description approach. In a system specification we capture the interface behaviour of a system. In general, if systems get large the interface behaviour is very difficult to describe because it contains a lot of complexity and therefore, it is practically impossible to describe it in one monolithic way.

If we manage to structure the sub-functions of a system by function hierarchy either in terms of interface assertions, state machines or just by scenarios this is very useful for simulation, validation, or to define test cases for functional tests. We can define both test cases for functional tests but also test cases for testing critical issues for feature interactions.

In architecture design we decompose the system into a syntactic architecture, which results in a network of components and the data flow in that network.

In the component specification each of the components given as a subsystem is specified again. We can use the different types of specifications of components being interface assertions, state machine or a set of traces in terms of scenarios or even informally. A particular interesting way of describing the interface of a component is to give scenarios by traces that are derived from the traces of the architecture of the super-system by projection.

Implementation of components is provided by state machines, from which code can be generated. In addition, we may derive test cases for tests and verification of components. If components are in addition described by interface assertions they can be the basis for verification, either by tests, inspection, or logical verification.

In the integration we use a system integration plan by studying the syntactic architecture. Then for each of the components we may define in which order they are integrated (see [14]). Following this, we can define the integration plan. The integration test can be derived from the architecture description and the incorporation of dummies can also be done by providing test cases for the architecture in terms of traces or by generating test cases from state machines. If interface assertions are given for the components we can derive interface assertions for the channels, which allow us checking certain properties through simulation.

Finally, the test and verification of the system can be based on the function hierarchy applying the tests on the singular function but also by applying tests for testing the feature interactions.

When building a system, in the ideal case we carry out the following steps that we will be able to support by our modeling framework:

- System specification
  - Context Model

- Function Hierarchy
- Definition of Test Cases for System Test.
- Architecture Design
  - Decomposition of the System into a Syntactic Architecture
  - Component specification (enhancing the syntactic to an interpreted architecture)
  - Architecture verification
  - Specification of Test Cases for Component and Integration Test.
- Implementation of the components
  - (Ideally) Code Generation
  - Component (module) Test and Verification.
- Integration
  - System Integration Plan
  - Component Entry Test
  - Integration Test and Verification.
- System Test and Verification.

A *system specification* is given by a syntactic interface $(I \blacktriangleright O)$ and an interface assertion S (i.e., a set of properties) which specifies a system interface behavior $F \in \mathbb{F}[I \blacktriangleright O]$.

An *architecture specification* is given by a composable set of syntactic interfaces $(I_k \blacktriangleright O_k)$ for component identifiers $k \in K$ and a component specification S_k for each $k \in K$. Each specification S_k specifies a behavior $F_k \in \mathbb{F}[I_k \blacktriangleright O_k]$. In this manner we obtain an interpreted architecture.

The *architecture specification is correct* w.r.t. the system specification F if the composition of all components results in a behavior that refines the system specification F. Formally, the architecture is correct if for all input histories $x \in \vec{I}$,

$$\bigotimes \{F_k : k \in K\}(x) \subseteq F(x)$$

Given an *implementation* R_k for each component identifier $k \in K$, the implementation R_k with interface abstraction F'_k is correct if for all $x \in \vec{I}_k$ we have:

$$F'_k(x) \subseteq F_k(x)$$

(note that it does not matter if F'_k was generated or implemented manually). Then we can integrate the implemented components into an implemented architecture

$$F' = \bigotimes \{F'_k : k \in K\}$$

The following basic theorem of modularity is easily proved by the construction of composition (for details see [15]).

Theorem 14.1 (Modularity) *If the architecture is correct (i.e., if $\bigotimes \{F_k : k \in K\}(x) \subseteq F(x)$) and if the components are correct (i.e., $F'_k(x) \subseteq F_k(x)$ for all k), then the* implemented system is correct:

$$F'(x) \subseteq F(x) \quad \text{for all } x \in \vec{I}.$$

Hence, a system (and also a subsystem) is hence called *correct* if the interface abstraction of its implementation is a refinement of its interface specification.

It is worthwhile to stress that we clearly distinguish between

- the architectural design of a system, and
- the implementation of the components of an architectural design.

An architectural design consists of the identification of components, their specification and the way they interact and form the architecture. If the architectural design and the specification of the constituting components is sufficiently precise, then we are able to determine the result of the composition of the components of the architecture, according to their specification, even without providing an implementation of all components! If the specifications address behaviour of the components and the design is modular, then the behaviour of the architecture can be derived from the behaviour of the components and the way they are connected. In other words, in this case the architecture has a specification and a—derived—specified behaviour. This specified behaviour can be put in relation with the requirements specification for the system, and, as we will discuss later, also with component implementations.

The above process includes two steps of verification, *component verification* and *architecture verification*. These possibilities reveal *component faults* (of a component/subsystem w.r.t. its specification) and *architecture faults* (of an architecture w.r.t. the system specification). If both verification steps are performed sufficiently carefully and the theory is modular, which holds here (see [15]), then correctness of the system follows from both verification steps.

The crucial point here is that architecture verification w.r.t. the system specification is enabled *without the need for actual implementations of the components*. In other words, it becomes possible before the implemented system exists. The precise implementation of the verification of the architecture depends of course on how its components are specified. If the specification consists of state machines, then the architecture can be simulated, and simulation results can be compared to the system specification. In contrast, if the component specifications are given by descriptive specifications in predicate logic, then deductive verification becomes possible.

Furthermore, if we have a hierarchical system, then the scheme of specification, design, and implementation can be iterated for each sub-hierarchy. An idealized top-down development process then proceeds as follows. We obtain a requirement specification for the system and from this we derive an architectural design and specification. This results in specifications for components that we can take as requirements specifications for the subsequent step in which the components are designed and implemented. Given a specified architecture, test cases can be derived for integration tests.

Given component specifications, we implement the components with the specifications in mind and then verify them with respect to their specifications. This of course entails some methodological problems if the code for the components has been generated from the specification in which case only the code generator and/or environment assumptions can be checked, as described in earlier work [23].

Now, if we have an implemented system for a specification, we can have either errors in the architecture design—in which case the architecture verification would fail—or we can have errors in the component implementation. An obvious question is that of the *root cause* of an architecture error. Examples of architecture errors include

- connecting an output port to an incorrect input port and to forget about such a connection;
- to have a mismatch in provided and expected sampling frequency of signals;
- to have a mismatch in the encoding;
- to have a mismatch in expected and provided units (e.g., km/h instead of m/s).

One fundamental difference between architecture errors and component errors of course is liability: in the first case, the integrator is responsible, while in the second case, responsibility is with the supplier.[1]

Assume a specified architecture to be given. Then a *component fault* is a mismatch between the component specification, which is provided as part of an architecture, and the component implementation. An *architecture fault* is a mismatch between the behaviour as defined by the architecture and the overall system specification. This way, we manage to distinguish between component faults and architecture faults in an integrated system.

With the outlined approach we gain a number of valuable options to make the entire development process more precise and controllable. First of all, we can provide an architecture specification by a model, called the *architecture model*, where we provide a possibly non-deterministic state machine for each of the components. In this case, we can even simulate and test the architecture before actually implementing it. Thus, we can on the one hand test the architecture by integration tests in an early stage, and we can moreover generate integration tests from the architecture model to be used for the integration of the implemented system. Given state machines for the components we can automatically generate hundreds of test cases as has been shown in [24]. Within slightly different development scenarios this leads to a fully automatic test case generation procedure for the component implementations.

A more advanced and ambitious idea would be to provide formal specifications in terms of interface assertion for each of the components. This would allow us to verify the architecture by logical techniques, since the component specifications can be kept very abstract at the level of what we call a logical architecture. Such a verification could be less involved than it would be, if it were performed at a concrete technical implementation level.

14.7.1 System Specification

In the system specification we specify the syntactic interface of a system, its context model as well as its functionality structured in terms of a function hierarchy.

---

[1] Both architecture and component errors can be a result of an invalid specification and an incorrect implementation. This distinction touches the difference between validation and verification.

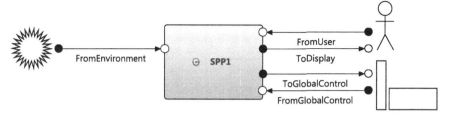

Fig. 14.21 Context model as screenshot from the tool AutoFocus

14.7.1.1 Context Model

A context model defines a syntactic interface and those parts of the environment to which the channels of the system are connected with. A context model additionally introduces all the agents and systems in the environment that are connected to the syntactic interface. This gives a very illustrative view onto the syntactic interface because now we do not only speak of abstract channels, but we also speak of systems of the environment. In addition to the information to which systems the channels are connected we can also provide properties of the context, which we call context assumptions or for short just assumptions. Therefore, we start with a context model, which gives some ideas about the syntactic interface and how the system input and output is connected to agents, users and systems of the environment.

To specify the properties of the context we use assumptions. The specification of the system consists then of promises, which hold only for the cases where the assumptions apply.

Then in the function hierarchy we break down the syntactic interface into sub-interfaces, which characterize, in particular, functionalities. In principle, such functionalities could also be nicely captured informally by use cases. In the end, a function hierarchy is therefore a structured formalized view onto a use case description.

14.7.1.2 Function Hierarchies

A multifunctional system offers a family of functions. The overall interface behavior of the system is modeled by a function $F \in \mathbb{F}[I \blacktriangleright O]$ where the sets I and O may contain many channels carrying a large variety of messages. In this section we show how the functionality and functions offered by F are arranged into function hierarchies. In function hierarchies, names of sub-functions are listed and syntactic interfaces are associated with them where each sub-function uses only a subset of the channels and messages of its super-function.

First we introduce a syntactic concept of a function hierarchy that provides function names and syntactic function interfaces. Based on the concept of a syntactic function hierarchy, we work out interpreted hierarchies where behaviors are associated with the function names.

To begin with, a hierarchy is a simple notion based on graph theory.

Definition 14.36 (Function Hierarchy) Let *SID* be the set of function names. A function hierarchy for a finite set $K \subseteq SID$ of function names is an acyclic directed graph (K, V) where $V \subseteq K \times K$ represents the sub-function relation. For every function with name $k \in K$ the set $\{k' \in K : (k, k') \in V\}$ of function names is called its *syntactic sub-function family*. The nodes in a function hierarchy without successor nodes are called the names of basic functions in the hierarchy. Their sub-function families are empty.

We denote the reflexive transitive closure of the relation V by V^*. On K the relation V^* represents a partial order. Using specific names for the functions of a hierarchy, we get an instance of a function taxonomy, which is a family of function names related by the sub-function relation.

Definition 14.37 (Syntactic Interface Function Hierarchy) A syntactic interface function hierarchy is a function hierarchy (K, V) with a syntactic interface $(I_k \blacktriangleright O_k)$ associated with each function name $k \in K$ in the hierarchy such that for all function names $k \in K$ we have: for every function h in the sub-function family of function k the relationship $(I_h \blacktriangleright O_h)$ **subtype** $(I_k \blacktriangleright O_k)$ holds.

If there is a path in a syntactic function hierarchy from node k to node h then $(I_h \blacktriangleright O_h)$ **subtype** $(I_k \blacktriangleright O_k)$ holds, since the subtype relation is transitive.

The following two properties characterize useful concepts for function hierarchies:

- A syntactic interface function hierarchy is called *complete* if for each function name $k \in K$ each input action in channel set I_k occurs as input action in at least one function of its syntactic sub-function family and each output action in channel set O_k occurs as output action in at least one function of its sub-function family.
- A syntactic interface function hierarchy is called *strict* if for each non-basic function name $k \in K$ each input action in channel set I_k occurs as input action in at most one function of its sub-function family and each output action in channel set O_k occurs as output action in at most one function of its sub-function family.

In complete syntactic interface function hierarchies we only have to provide the syntactic interfaces for the basic functions and then the syntactic interfaces for the non-basic functions can be uniquely derived bottom-up from the basic ones.

In strict syntactic function interface hierarchies every input and every output is owned by exactly one basic function.

Function hierarchies define the decomposition of functions into sub-functions. Syntactic interface function hierarchies associate channels and messages with each function.

14.7.1.3 Structuring Function Specifications by Modes

In this section we introduce a technique to describe sub-functions of a system in a modular way, even in cases where they are not faithful projections. We consider

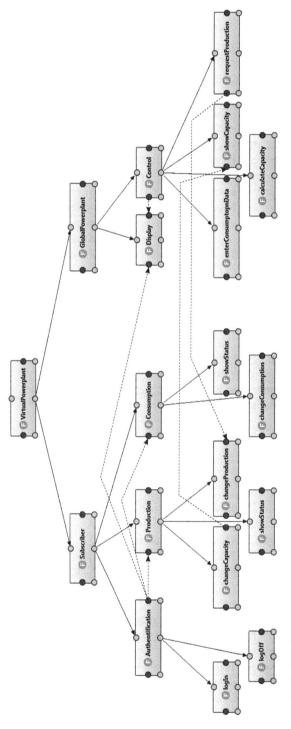

Fig. 14.22 Function hierarchy as screenshot from the tool AutoFocus

a system behavior $F \in \mathbb{F}[I \blacktriangleright O]$ and a sub-interface $(I' \blacktriangleright O')$ where $(I' \blacktriangleright O')$ **subtype** $(I \blacktriangleright O)$ and the projection $F\dagger(I' \blacktriangleright O')$ is not faithful. Let for simplicity

$$I = I' \cup I'', \qquad O = O' \cup O''$$

(where the sets I' and I'' as well as the sets O' and O'' are disjoint) and the types of the channels in I and I' as well as O and O' be identical. In other words, in the sub-interface $(I' \blacktriangleright O')$ we keep certain channels from $(I \blacktriangleright O)$ with the identical types. Furthermore we assume that the projection $F\dagger(I'' \blacktriangleright O'')$ is faithful.

In this case, we cannot describe the sub-function offered by system F over sub-interface $(I' \blacktriangleright O')$ exactly by projection. In fact, we can specify the unfaithful projection $F\dagger(I' \blacktriangleright O')$, but it does not give a precise description of the behavior of the sub-function over sub-interface $(I' \blacktriangleright O')$. To get a precise specification of the sub-function behavior as offered by system F over sub-interface $(I' \blacktriangleright O')$ we need a way to capture the dependencies between the input actions in I'' that influence this sub-function, but are not in I', and the function over sub-interface $(I' \blacktriangleright O')$.

One option to express the influence is the introduction of a channel cm between the over sub-interface $(I' \blacktriangleright O')$ in F and the rest of F to capture the dependencies explicitly (see Fig. 14.23). Let the channel cm occur neither in channel set I nor in channel set O. We define

$$I^+ = I' \cup \{cm\}, \qquad O^+ = O'' \cup \{cm\}$$

Our idea is to decompose the interface behavior F into two behaviors with a precise description of their behavioral dependencies. We specify two behaviors $F^+ \in \mathbb{F}[I^+ \blacktriangleright O']$ and $F^\# \in \mathbb{F}[I'' \blacktriangleright O^+]$ such that for all histories $x \in \vec{I}$, $y \in \vec{O}$ the following formula is valid:

$$y \in F(x) \quad \Leftrightarrow \quad \exists x^+ \in \vec{I}^+, y^+ \in \vec{O}^+ : x|I = x^+|I \wedge y|O'' = y^+|O' \wedge x^+(cm)$$
$$= y^+(cm)$$
$$\wedge \, y^+ \in F^\#(x|I'') \wedge y|O' \in F^+(x^+)$$

This means that $F^\#(x|I'')$ provides on "mode" channel cm exactly the information that is needed from the input on channels in I'' to express the dependencies on messages in I'' for the sub-function on sub-interface $(I' \blacktriangleright O')$ in F. We call cm a *mode channel* and the messages transmitted over it *modes*. In the following we explain the idea of modes in more detail. Later we study the more general situation where both projections $F\dagger(I' \blacktriangleright O')$ and $F\dagger(I'' \blacktriangleright O'')$ are not faithful and mode channels in both directions are introduced.

Modes are a generally useful way to structure function behavior and to specify dependencies between functions. Modes are used to discriminate different forms of operations for a function. Often mode sets consist of a small number of elements—such as enumerated types. An example would be the operational mode of a car being "moving_forward", "stopped", or "moving_backward". Nevertheless, arbitrary sets can be used as mode types. So we may have a mode "Speed" which may be any number in $\{-30, \ldots, 250\}$.

Fig. 14.23 Refinement of
two functions to prepare for
composition

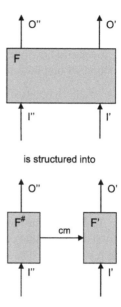

is structured into

Formally a mode is a data element of a data type T where T defines a set of data elements. Each type T can be used as a mode set. For a given type T, we write Mode T to express that we use T as a mode type. We simply assume that type Mode T has the same elements as type T. Each element of type Mode T is called a mode.

A mode (type) can be used for attributes of the state space as well as for input or output channels. For a function we may use several modes side by side.

Example (Modes of a Mobile Phone) A mobile phone is, for instance, in a number of operating modes characterized by Mode Operation:

$$Mode\ Operation = \{SwitchedOff,\ StandBy,\ Connected\}$$

Another mode set may reflect the energy situation:

$$Mode\ Energy = \{BatteryDead,\ LowEnergy,\ HighEnergy\}$$

Both examples of modes are helpful to gain structured views for the functions of a mobile phone.

For functions we use types that are designated as being modes to indicate which channels and attributes carry modes. We use modes in the following to indicate how the messages in a larger system influence the sub-function that do not correspond to faithful projections. This way we eliminate the nondeterminism caused by a non-faithful projection.

We use modes as follows:

- as attributes in state spaces to structure the state machine description of functions—more precisely to structure the state space and also the state transitions; then we use state attributes with mode types called mode attributes. We speak of *internal* modes

- to specify how functions influence each other; then mode types occur as types of input or output channels called *mode channels*. We speak of *external* modes.

For mode channels we assume that in each time interval the current mode is transmitted.

External modes serve mainly for the following purpose: they propagate significant state information from one function to the other functions of the system. If a function outputs a mode via one of its output channels, the function is called the *mode master*, if it receives the mode via one of its input channels the function is called a *mode slave*. Since in a system, each channel can be the output of only one sub-system, there exists at most one mode master for each mode channel.

To describe the modes of a larger system we need a mode model. A mode model is a data model that captures all the mode types that are inside the system. This can be a very large data model, which nevertheless is still an abstraction of the state model.

14.7.1.4 Interpreted Function Hierarchies

In this section we introduce function hierarchies where interface behaviors are specified for each function in the hierarchy. We speak of interpreted function hierarchies.

Definition 14.38 (Interpreted Function Hierarchy) Given a syntactic interface function hierarchy (K, V) where for each $k \in K$ the syntactic interface associated with k is $(I_k \blacktriangleright O_k)$; an *interpreted function hierarchy* is a pair $((K, V), \phi)$, where ϕ is a function $\phi : K \to \mathbb{F}$ that associates a function behavior $\phi(k) \in \mathbb{F}[I_k \blacktriangleright O_k]$ with every function name $k \in K$. The interpreted function hierarchy is called *well-formed*, if for every pair $(e, k) \in V$ the function behavior $\phi(k)$ is a restricted sub-function of $\phi(e)$.

This form of function hierarchy does not indicate on which messages other than the input messages I_k the restricted sub-function $\phi(k)$ depends. This information is included in an annotated function hierarchy.

Definition 14.39 (Dependency Annotated Function Hierarchy) For an interpreted function hierarchy $((K, V), \phi)$ with root r and a dependency relation $D \subseteq K \times K$, $((K, V), \phi, D)$ is called *annotated function hierarchy*, if for function names $k, k' \in K$ with $(k, k') \notin V^*$ we have

$$(k, k') \in D \quad \Leftrightarrow \quad \phi(k) \to_{dep} \phi(k') \text{ in } \phi(r)$$

The relation D documents all dependencies between functions in the function hierarchy. If for a function k there do not exist functions k' with $(k, k') \in D$, then function k is required to be faithful. Note that there can be several dependencies for a function in a function hierarchy.

To give a more precise specification how in a function hierarchy a sub-function influences other functions we use the concept of mode channels that allow us to specify the dependencies of functions in detail.

Definition 14.40 (Function Hierarchy Annotated with Modes) For an annotated function hierarchy $H = ((K, V), \phi, D)$ the pair (H, ψ), where $\psi : K \to \mathbb{F}$, is called *function hierarchy annotated with modes* if

- for each pair $(k, k') \in D$ a mode type $T_{k,k'}$ and a fresh channel $cm_{k,k'}$ with this type that serves as a mode channel is given.
- the syntactic interfaces $(I_k \blacktriangleright O_k)$ of the functions $\phi(k)$ are extended by the mode channels to syntactic interfaces $(I_k^+ \blacktriangleright O_k^+)$ of $\psi(k)$, where

$$I_k^+ = I_k \cup \{cm_{k,k'} : (k, k') \in D\}, \qquad O_k^+ = O_k \cup \{cm_{k',k} : (k', k) \in D\}$$

In an annotated function hierarchy with modes, there is a mode channel $cm_{k,k'}$ for each dependency $(k, k') \in D$ from the function with name k' to the function with name k. In the following section we describe how to decompose the sub-functions via their mode channels.

Relation V is called *vertical*, relation D *horizontal* for the hierarchy. An example of a horizontal relation in a function hierarchy is independency. In a horizontal relationship between two functions F_1 and F_2 we do not deal with sub-function relations (neither F_1 is a super-function of F_2 nor vice versa) but with functions that are either mutually independent or, where supposed to be, there exist specific feature interactions (for the notion of feature interactions see [16]) between these functions that may be specified in terms of modes.

The key idea of the concept of a function hierarchy is that it is useful to decompose the functionality of the system into a number of sub-functions that are specified and validated in isolation. Then dependencies are identified and specified by the horizontal dependency relation and labeled by modes that are used to specify the dependencies.

14.7.1.5 Function and Context

Function hierarchies help to structure large system functionalities in a hierarchy of functions with leaves that are small enough to be specified. In the projection leading to those functions we consider also the context model. This way we get context models for the basic functions where in addition to the channels connected to the context the mode channels are included. In the context model they are connected to the functions being the mode masters—and, if the considered atomic function is a mode master itself, the channels lead to functions that are the mode slaves.

14.7.2 Logical Component Architectures

We describe a logical component architecture by defining a syntactic architecture first. This way components with their names and syntactic interfaces are introduced. In a next step we define the traces of the syntactic architecture (glass box view). This can be done by providing a set of finite traces in terms of interaction diagrams illustrating use cases for the architecture.

We use trace assertions to describe the set of traces of the architecture. The next step is to derive component specifications in terms of interface assertions. These specification have to be chosen such that they are fulfilled by the traces.

The logical component architecture is given by a set K of components together with their interface specifications. It defines the specifications for its components as well as a interface behavior for the overall system. As shown in the following paragraph this leads to the notion of the correctness of an architecture for a system interface specification (specifying the system's required functionality) and the correctness of the component implementations as a basis for component verification.

14.8 Seamless Modeling in System Development

The techniques introduced earlier can be used in a seamless model-based development. This approach is outlined in the next sections.

14.8.1 Combining Functions into Multifunctional Systems

In this section we study sub-function based specifications of multifunctional systems aiming at a structured construction and description of the interface behavior of systems from a user's and requirements engineer's point of view. A structured specification is essential in requirements engineering. The structuring is provided mainly in terms of relations between functions.

Multifunctional systems incorporate large families of different, largely independent functions. Functions are formal models of use cases of systems. Furthermore, we outline how to work out a multifunctional system in a sequence of development steps resulting in a function hierarchy as follows:

(0) Describe a set of use cases informally, identify all sub-functions by introducing names and informal descriptions for them.
(1) Specify (a not interpreted) function hierarchy for the functions identified in (0).
(2) Incorporate all the channels of the system and its functions together with their types (to specify input and output actions) into the hierarchy extending it to a syntactic interface function hierarchy.

Fig. 14.24 Refinement of
two functions to prepare for
composition

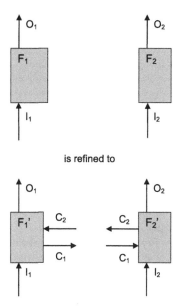

(3) Give behavior descriptions by interaction diagrams, by specifications through assertions, or by state machines for each function; function behaviors are explicitly defined either for the basic function names in the hierarchy or for their parent nodes; in the latter case the behaviors of the sub-functions are derived by projection.
(4) Identify dependencies and introduce the horizontal dependency relation; define mode sets for each of the dependencies. Extend the function specifications for the modes.
(5) Combine the basic functions via their modes into the overall system behavior.

The overall idea is to reduce the complexity of functional specifications of systems by describing each of its basic functions independently by simple state machines. In a first step we do not take into account feature interactions. Only later we combine the specified functions into a function hierarchy and specify relationships between functions by introducing modes to express how the functions influence or depend on each other. Typically, some of the functions are completely independent and are just grouped together into a system. Other functions may depend on each other, often with often just small, not very essential side effects on other functions, while some functions may heavily rely on other functions that influence their behaviors in very significant and often subtle ways.

Understanding the overall functionality of a multifunctional system requires the understanding of its individual functions, but also how they are related and mutually dependent. Functions that are to be combined might not be independent but actually may interfere with each other. This leads to the question of how to handle dependencies between functions and still take advantage of their combination. We illustrate our idea of a systematic combination by Figs. 14.24 and 14.25.

Fig. 14.25 Function
combination by composition

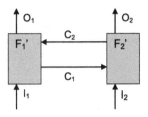

Figure 14.24 shows refinements (for this extended notion of refinement, see [8])
of two functions F_1 and F_2 by introducing additional mode channels. Figure 14.25
shows how they are composed subsequently. Formally, we require that F_1' and F_2'
offer the functions F_1 and F_2 as sub-functions—at least in a restricted form. To
combine functions from sub-functions the channels in C_1 and C_2 carry only mode
types.

Figure 14.24 illustrates the construction starting with functions $F_k \in \mathbb{F}[I_k \blacktriangleright O_k]$,
$k = 1, 2$, and refining these functions by introducing additional channels

$$F_1' \in [(I_1 \cup C_2) \blacktriangleright (O_1 \cup C_1)]$$

$$F_2' \in [(I_2 \cup C_1) \blacktriangleright (O_2 \cup C_2)]$$

such that F_1 and F_2 are restricted sub-functions of F_1' and F_2' controlled by the
messages (being elements of mode types) in the channel sets C_1 and C_2.

Actually our goal is that both F_1 and F_2 are sub-functions or at least restricted
sub-functions of the composed function

$$F = F_1' \otimes F_2'$$

In this construction the functions may influence each other and thus depend on each
other.

Definition 14.41 (Correct Function Hierarchy Annotated with Modes) A mode-
annotated function hierarchy $H = (((K, V), \phi, D), \psi)$ is called *correct*, if for all
$k \in K$:

$$\phi(k) \leftarrow_{sub} \bigotimes \psi$$

In other words every function $\phi(k)$ is a sub-function of the architecture interface
behavior $\bigotimes \psi$. If the $\phi(k)$ are restricted sub-functions of $\bigotimes \psi$ then we speak of
restricted correctness.

In the case of restricted correctness more sophisticated conditions are required
that make use of logical properties of the streams on the mode channels to derive
the set R to restrict the input histories to prove the relationship $\phi(k) \leftarrow_{sub} \psi(k)|R$
of restricted sub-functions.

As the example demonstrates, multifunctional systems can be specified by specifying their basic functions in isolation and combining them into the overall system functions interacting via mode channels. Accordingly, a function hierarchy

$((K, V), \phi, D)$ annotated with modes is called *correct*, if for each non-basic node $k \in K$ its interface behavior $\phi(k)$ is the composition of the interface behaviors $\phi(k')$ of the nodes k' in its sub-function family $\{k' \in K : (k, k') \in V\}$.

14.8.2 Tracing

By tracing in system development the connections and dependencies between requirements, functional specifications, and architectures with their components is addressed. The main goal is to understand for a given functional requirement by which system function it is covered and vice versa. Moreover, we want to understand which of the components contribute to which functions and vice versa. Given this information we can determine the impact of a change of a requirement on the functional specification and the architecture and vice versa.

In this section we define the concept of traces between system level requirements, functional requirements specification, and the component architecture specification. To do that the logical representations of requirements, functional specification, and architectures are used.

14.8.2.1 Logical Representation of Requirements, Specifications and Architectures

According to the modeling of a system, we have the following specifications that all can be represented by a set of logical assertions.

System level requirements (functional requirements) are given by a set $\{R_i : 1 \le i \le n\}$ of requirements. Together they form the requirements specification R as follows

$$R = \bigwedge \{R_i : 1 \le i \le n\}$$

The system level functional specification is given by the functional decomposition of the system behaviour into a set of sub-functions. The system interface behaviour F as specified by the system requirements specification R is structured into a set of sub-interfaces for sub-functions $F_1, \ldots, F_k$ that form the leaves in the function hierarchy and are specified independently by introducing a number of mode channels to capture feature interactions. Each F_i sub-function is described by a syntactic interface and an interface assertion Q_i such that

$$Q \;\Rightarrow\; R$$

where the functional specification is given by

$$Q = \bigwedge \{Q_i : 1 \le i \le m\}$$

The logical component architecture is given by a family of components with interface specifications C_i. The architecture specification is given by

$$C = \bigwedge \{C_i : 1 \leq i \leq k\}$$

where each interface assertion C_i specifies a component. Based on these logical specifications we define the logical dependencies.

14.8.2.2 Correctness

The functional specification is correct with respect to the requirements specification if the following formula is valid:

$$Q \quad \Rightarrow \quad R$$

The component architecture (let be $m_1, \ldots$ mode channels) is correct if the following formula is valid:

$$C \quad \Rightarrow \quad \exists m_1, \ldots, m_i : Q$$

The refinement relations between the requirement specification and the functional specification as well as between the functional specification and the architecture specification define correctness.

14.8.2.3 Relating Logical Views

Let p be a property and R be a set of properties; a subset $R' \subseteq R$ is called *guarantor* for p in R if

$$\bigwedge R' \quad \Rightarrow \quad p$$

A guarantor R' for p is called *minimal*, if every strict subset of R' is not a guarantor. A minimal guarantor is called *unique* if there does not exist a different minimal guarantor. A property $q \in R$ is called *weak guarantor* for p in R if it occurs in some minimal guarantor of p in R. A property $q \in R$ is called *strong guarantor* for p in R if it occurs in every guarantor of p in R (cf. the notion of Primimplikanten a la Quine).

14.8.2.4 Defining Links for Tracing

The relationship between the system level requirements specification and the functional specification in terms of tracing is obtained by the relationship between the requirements R_i and the function specifications Q_i.

In a similar manner we define the relationship between the function specifications Q_i and the components contained in the architecture specified by assertions

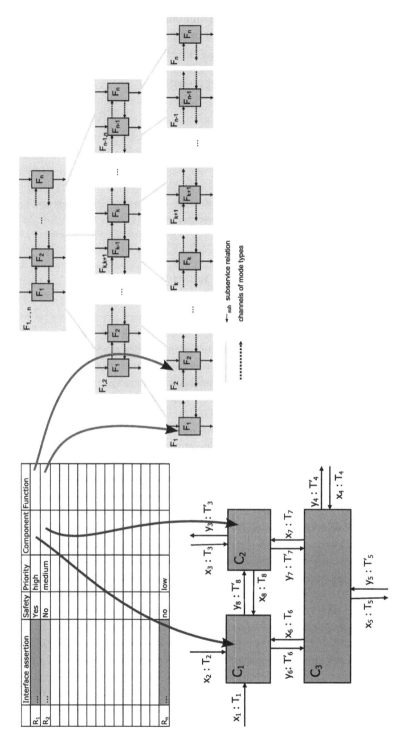

Fig. 14.26 Relationships between requirements, functional specification given by a function hierarchy, and component architecture

C_i. We get a logical relationship between requirements, functional specifications, and components of an architecture as shown in Fig. 14.26. An arrow leading from requirement R_i to function specification F_j expresses that F_j is a weak guarantor for property R_i. An arrow leading from requirement R_i to component specification C_j expresses that C_j is a weak guarantor for property R_i.

14.9 Summary and Outlook

We have introduced a comprehensive theory for describing systems in terms of their interfaces, architectures and states. Starting with basic notions of interfaces, state machines, and composition we have shown how we can form architectures and how to get more structured descriptions of systems step-by-step.

14.9.1 Basics: What Is Needed for Seamless Model Based Development

To describe systems in engineering, pragmatic techniques are needed that provide graphical description techniques and also bring in additional structuring mechanisms. However, these techniques have to be based on firm scientific theories. In our case the technique to decompose the functionality of a system into a number of sub-functions with interactions described by modes, is a way to structure the functionality of systems.

Context models help to gain a more intuitive understanding of the role of the syntactic interface. Then step-by-step by decomposition architectures are formed consisting of a number of sub-systems which in turn can be described by traces, interface specifications, state machines or again by architectures. This gives a highly flexible approach, which supports all kinds of methodologies for the design of systems.

We have introduced a set of basic terms and notions and a theory to capture those. But more has to be done. Modeling theory is needed for capturing following notions

- systems
- interface specifications
- architectures
- quality
- comprehensive architecture
- levels of abstraction
- relationships between levels (tracing)
- artefact model
- structure of work products
- tailoring
- tool support

- artefact based
- automation of development steps

When dealing with typically complex, multifunctional software-intensive systems, the structured specification of their multi-functionality is a major goal in requirements engineering. This task is not sufficiently well supported by appropriate models, so far. In practice today, functional requirements are documented mainly by text. Models are not available and therefore not used. Use cases are applied but not formalized fully by models and not structured in hierarchies.

14.9.2 Further Work

What we have provided aims at a quite comprehensive approach to the seamless model based specification, design, and implementation of systems. It supports the development of distributed systems with multifunctional behaviours including time dependency. It provides a number of structuring concepts for engineering larger systems. Scaling, however, is still an open issue.

There is a large variety of possibilities to support the seamless model-based development by tools. This includes the construction of repositories to capture the models during the seamless development process as well as classical techniques to deal with such repositories in updating and refining models. Many ways of automation can be included for analysis generation, validation, and verification of models in the repository. The approach is by tools as already done by the prototyping tool AutoFocus.

Further work will be done and has to be done to extend the approach to continuous functions over time where systems can be described by differential equations such as in control theory. This way discrete streams are extended to continuous streams represented by continuous functions.

Another open issue is the question as to what extent the described approach is able to cover not only software and software based functionality of systems but also systems with a rich structure in mechanics and electronics.

Acknowledgements   Many members of our Munich software & systems engineering working group have contributed to the material of this chapter. In particular, Sebastian Eder and Andreas Vogelsang have helped with the screenshots and by careful reading draft version and giving feedback. Thanks go to Georg Hackenberg for careful proof reading. Moreover, it is a pleasure to thank Bernhard Rumpe and Alex Pretschner for helpful comments.

References

1. Abadi, M., Lamport, L.: The existence of refinement mappings. Tech. rep., Digital Systems Research Center, SRC Report 29 (1988)
2. Abadi, M., Lamport, L.: Composing specifications. Tech. rep., Digital Systems Research Center, SRC Report 66 (1990)

3. Bass, L., Clements, P., Kazman, R.: Software Architecture in Practice. Addison-Wesley, Reading (1997)
4. Broy, M.: Compositional refinement of interactive systems. Tech. rep., DIGITAL Systems Research Center, SRC 89 (1992). Also in: J. ACM **44**(6), 850–891 (1997)
5. Broy, M.: The 'grand challenge' in informatics: engineering software-intensive systems. IEEE Comput. **39**(10), 72–80 (2006)
6. Broy, M.: Model-driven architecture-centric engineering of (embedded) software intensive systems: modeling theories and architectural milestones. Innovations Syst. Softw. Eng. **3**, 75–102 (2007)
7. Broy, M.: A logical basis for component-oriented software and systems engineering. Comput. J. **53**(10), 1758–1782 (2010)
8. Broy, M.: Multifunctional software systems: structured modeling and specification of functional requirements. Sci. Comput. Program. **75**, 1193–1214 (2010)
9. Broy, M.: Towards a theory of architectural contracts: schemes and patterns of assumption/promise based system specification. Marktoberdorf Summer School (2010)
10. Broy, M.: Verifying of interface assertions of infinite state mealy machines (2011). To appear.
11. Broy, M., Huber, F., Schätz, B.: Autofocus – ein werkzeugprototyp zur entwicklung eingebetteter systeme. Inform. Forsch. Entwickl. **14**(3), 121–134 (1999)
12. Broy, M., Krüger, I.H., Meisinger, M.: A formal model of services. ACM Trans. Softw. Eng. Methodol. **16**(1) (2007)
13. Broy, M., Möller, B., Pepper, P., Wirsing, M.: Algebraic implementations preserve program correctness. Sci. Comput. Program. **7**(1), 35–53 (1986)
14. Broy, M., Pretschner, A.: A model based view onto testing: criteria for the derivation of entry tests for integration testing (2011). To appear
15. Broy, M., Stølen, K.: Specification and Development of Interactive Systems: Focus on Streams, Interfaces, and Refinement. Springer, New York (2001)
16. Calder, M., Magill, E.H. (eds.): Feature Interactions in Telecommunications and Software Systems VI, May 17–19, 2000, Glasgow, Scotland, UK. IOS Press, Amsterdam (2000)
17. Herzberg, D., Broy, M.: Modeling layered distributed communication systems. Form. Asp. Comput. **17**(1), 1–18 (2005)
18. Jacobson, I.: Use cases and aspects-working seamlessly together. J. Object Technol. **2**(4), 7–28 (2003)
19. Leavens, G.T., Sitaraman, M. (eds.): Foundations of Component-Based Systems. Cambridge University Press, New York (2000)
20. Luckham, D.C., Kenney, J.J., Augustin, L.M., Vera, J., Bryan, D., Mann, W.: Specification and analysis of system architecture using rapide. IEEE Trans. Softw. Eng. **21**, 336–355 (1995)
21. Moriconi, M., Qian, X., Riemenschneider, R.A.: Correct architecture refinement. IEEE Trans. Softw. Eng. **21**, 356–372 (1995)
22. Nipkow, T., Paulson, L.C., Wenzel, M.: Isabelle/HOL—A Proof Assistant for Higher-Order Logic, LNCS, vol. 2283. Springer, Berlin (2002)
23. Pretschner, A., Philipps, J.: Methodological issues in model-based testing. In: Broy, M., Jonsson, B., Katoen, J.-P., Leucker, M., Pretschner, A. (eds.) Model-Based Testing of Reactive Systems, Advanced Lectures [The volume is the outcome of a research seminar that was held in Schloss Dagstuhl in January 2004]. LNCS, vol. 3472, pp. 281–291. Springer, Berlin (2005)
24. Pretschner, A., Prenninger, W., Wagner, S., Kühnel, C., Baumgartner, M., Sostawa, B., Zölch, R., Stauner, T.: One evaluation of model-based testing and its automation. In: Roman, G.-C., Griswold, W.G., Nuseibeh, B. (eds.) 27th International Conference on Software Engineering (ICSE 2005), 15–21 May 2005, St. Louis, Missouri, USA, pp. 392–401. ACM, New York (2005)
25. Spichkova, M.: Refinement-based verification of interactive real-time systems. Electron. Notes Theor. Comput. Sci. **214**, 131–157 (2008)
26. Szyperski, C.: Component Software: Beyond Object-Oriented Programming, 2nd edn. Addison-Wesley, Boston (2002)

Chapter 15
Conquering Complexity Through Distributed, Intelligent Agent Frameworks

John A. Anderson and Todd Carrico

15.1 Introduction

New technologies continually emerge and mature as people, organizations, and operational disciplines rapidly adapt to the technology infusion. Innovations are constantly and unpredictably being adopted, rapidly evolving from novelties to conveniences to essential elements of our society and economy. The onset of the Internet, virtual ubiquitous connectivity, and global access to data and people has significantly increased the complexity of individual, commercial, government and military operations. As systems and sensors proliferate on the networks across the world, people are inundated with an ever increasing deluge of information and conflicting considerations for making critical decisions. At exponential rates, our lives, responsibilities and environments are becoming increasingly more complex. Those that can manage or even conquer complexity will remain competitive and survive; those that cannot will perish—either metaphorically or literally.

For an entity to remain competitive, whether that organizational entity is an individual, a business organization, a government agency, or a military operation, it must manage the complexities of its environment and rapidly adapt to the changes imposed. Conquering this complexity challenge can be achieved through the application of frameworks that will support the understanding and organization of the elements along with their individual and/or collective behavior, and their adaptation within that environment.

The frameworks to be applied to conquer complexity will leverage two fundamental concepts in complex systems theory: The concept of organized complexity and the application of complex adaptive systems (CAS) in information technology. For the sake of this treatise, an informal definition of a complex adaptive system is a large network of relatively simple components with no central control, in which emergent complex behavior is exhibited. 'Complex Systems' is a term appropriately

J.A. Anderson (✉)
Cougaar Software, Inc., Falls Church, VA, USA
e-mail: janderson@cougaarsoftware.com

M. Hinchey, L. Coyle (eds.), *Conquering Complexity*,
DOI 10.1007/978-1-4471-2297-5_15, © Springer-Verlag London Limited 2012

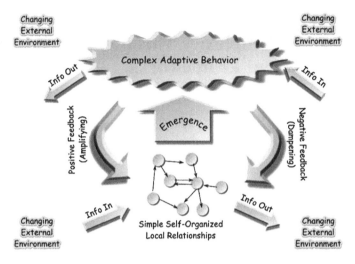

Fig. 15.1 *Complex Adaptive System Behavior.* This classical diagram illustrates the interaction among entities with simple self-organized relationships can result in collective emergent behavior, and that the society of entities can collectively adapt to respond to changes in the external environment

attributed to elements of the organic real world as well as hardware and software-based information systems.

As early as the 1940's, Weaver [11] perceived and addressed the problem of complexity management, in at least a preliminary way, by drawing a distinction between "disorganized complexity" and "organized complexity". Disorganized complexity results from a system having a very large number of parts, where the interaction of the parts is viewed as largely random, but the properties of the system as a whole can be understood using probability and statistical methods. In contrast, organized complexity is non-random (or correlated) interaction between the parts. These correlated relationships create a differentiated structure that can act as a system in itself, and interact with other systems (i.e., existing as a system of systems within a larger system of systems context). At all levels, the systems will manifest properties not necessarily determined by their individual parts (i.e., emergent behavior).

The relationships between individual, self-organized interacting entities and the resultant emergent behavior (which may not be predictable) is illustrated in the 'classical' diagram depicted in Fig. 15.1.[1] As each individual entity exists and operates, it exhibits its own behavior, potentially interacting with and consequently contributing to or responding to changes in its external environment. The changes detected by any individual entity may or may not be a direct result of its interaction with other specific entities. When viewed as a collective system, the behavior of the

---

[1]This diagram has appeared in presentations and literature for several years, but its original source is unknown to the authors. In addition to its availability in http://commons.wikimedia.org/wiki/File:Complex-adaptive-system.jpg, it is referenced in a variety of settings including [2].

individual entities, whether they are directly interacting or not, will result in a complex behavior that may adapt to changes in the external environment. Treated as an organized society, this adaptability can be the critical success criterion for survival.

A CAS is a dynamic network of many agents (which may represent cells, species, individuals, firms, nations) acting in parallel, constantly acting and reacting to what the other agents are doing. The control of a CAS tends to be highly dispersed and decentralized. If there is to be any coherent behavior in the system, it has to arise from competition and cooperation among the agents themselves. The overall behavior of the system is the result of a huge number of decisions made every moment by many individual agents [10].

In Weaver's view, organized complexity results from the nonrandom, or correlated, interaction among the parts. These parts and their correlated relationships create a differentiated structure which can, as a system, interact with other systems. The coordinated system manifests properties not carried by, or dictated by, individual parts. Thus, the organized aspect of this form of complexity is said to "emerge".

Conquering complexity in information systems can be achieved by merging the concepts of CAS and organized complexity. Since any system can potentially be a CAS in itself, and typically operates as a component within a system of systems that is itself complex (and thus may be a CAS at another higher level of abstraction), frameworks are needed to understand, model and manage the organized complexity among the systems at multiple levels of abstraction. A set of mental, organizational and system frameworks can be established that will enable a systems engineer to model entities in the real world, including the interaction among the parts, as naturally as possible. The basic goal for the frameworks is to support the development of complex adaptive information systems that will help users manage the complex adaptive systems that surround them in the environment within which they live and operate.

15.2 Frameworks for Managing Complexity

A variety of frameworks are needed to think about, model, and build such systems. A basic Distributed Intelligent Agent Framework is needed to define the concepts and to specify the structure, organization and behavior of the individual agents, their relationships, and the resulting complex systems at all levels. Such a framework must address the external and internal structure of the agents, and how they will be able to sense, reason, respond and otherwise interact with their environment. The framework must also provide mechanisms for monitoring the resultant emergent behavior of the complex adaptive system as a whole, and for responding to situations that require intervention (that is, allowing the behavior of individual parts to be modified over time—either autonomously or via direct intervention).

The primary framework that will be used for managing complexity and for developing complex adaptive systems is the Distributed Intelligent Agent Framework. Several other complementary frameworks are discussed within the context of the

Distributed Intelligent Agent Framework to address specific aspects of agent behavior, situational reasoning, and systems engineering. The following subsections describe the essential elements of those frameworks and provide references to examples from research and industry. Key topics that the complementary frameworks address include: knowledge representation, situational reasoning, knowledge bases, distributed integrated data environment, and unifying concepts for developing distributed collaborative decision support environments. Each of these framework descriptions incorporate and leverage key elements of the Distributed Intelligent Agent Framework and its properties that support agent definition, emergent behavior, and adaptability.

15.2.1 Distributed Intelligent Agent Framework

It is no coincidence that the terminology for a Distributed Intelligent Agent Framework corresponds to the terms used to define complex adaptive systems. Intelligent agent concepts emerged from the application of complexity theory within the information technology field.

15.2.1.1 Distributed Agent-Based Concepts

The Distributed Intelligent Agent Framework must provide the building blocks and capabilities necessary for agents to be defined in a manner that will support localized reasoning within the agents and collaboration among the agents. Further, the framework must also support the agents in their communication and collaboration, whether they occur within a single node of the environment or distributed across a network. Further, just as the model of CAS emergent behavior illustrates, the agents (collectively or individually) must be able to interact with entities outside of the system.

To address the specific elements of the framework, some basic concepts related to distributed systems [4] and software agents must also be addressed, all of which should be supported by the system development and deployment environments.

A *Distributed System* consists of a collection of autonomous computers, connected through a network and distribution middleware, which enables computers to coordinate their activities and to share the resources of the system, so that users perceive the system as a single, integrated computing facility. The system is comprised of multiple autonomous components that are not shared by all users. Software runs in concurrent processes on (potentially) different processors.

Components access and update shared resources (e.g., variables, databases, device drivers); and the system (or its environment) must be able to coordinate data updates across concurrent processes to ensure the integrity of the system is not violated (e.g., lost updates and inconsistent analysis). The system may have multiple points of control and multiple points of failure. Fault tolerance can be achieved by designing in fault detection and recovery capabilities as well as building redundancy into the system.

Complementing the distributed system concepts are the characteristics of a *Software Agent*. Bradshaw [3] describes a software agent as a software entity which functions continuously and autonomously in a particular environment. A software agent is able to carry out activities in a flexible and intelligent manner that is responsive to changes in the environment. Ideally, software agents are able to learn from their experience, able to communicate and cooperate with other agents and processes in its environment, and potentially able to move from place to place within its environment.

An agent's responsibilities are defined by the behaviors that have been built into it; and agents carry out their activities in a flexible and intelligent manner that is responsive to changes in the environment. Agents can adjust behavior dynamically to fit the current situation, determining how their actions and behaviors should change as events change. Agent-based systems represent the next major advancement in network computing and leverage the strengths of object-oriented, peer-to-peer and service-oriented architectures while providing a process-centric design. The value proposition is that intelligent reasoning occurs at each level of the system to reduce overall system load and increase quality, control, and responsiveness. The key benefits of agent technology come in these areas:

- *Dynamic Re-planning*—The ability to develop and modify distributed workflows using rules and domain knowledge that is appropriate to the current situation. This benefit allows enterprises to create more accurate and appropriate plans and to react more quickly and appropriately when conditions change.
- *Advanced Data Mediation*—The ability to gather and process data from multiple diverse sources into a single environment so that it is appropriate for the current situation.
- *Situational Awareness*—The ability to build and maintain a virtual world representation of the current situation on which intelligent reasoning can occur.
- *Collaborative Information Management*—The ability to easily share information and coordinate changes across your enterprise.
- *Intelligent Reasoning*—The ability to emulate the way humans observe, reason, plan, act, and monitor at computer speeds.
- *Scalable, Distributed Computing*—The ability to handle massive amounts of data across the enterprise while providing more efficient processing.
- *Business Process Adaptation/Evolution*—The ability to allow significant business changes to be implemented quickly and dynamically by actual users who can easily manage adjustments to the business rules or policies—without engaging consultants to significantly alter their systems. This benefit allows enterprises to be agile and adaptive as conditions change, thus saving valuable costs in process re-engineering.

Thus, the characteristics of a distributed system and software agents correspond with the agent concepts defined in the CAS emergent model. This association was highlighted by Franklin and Graesser [5] in their description of an autonomous

Table 15.1 Properties of intelligent agents

Property	Other names	Meaning
Reactive	Sensing and acting	Responds in a timely fashion to changes in the environment
Autonomous		Exercises control over its own actions
Goal-oriented	Pro-active/purposeful	Does not simply act in response to the environment
Temporally continuous		Is a continuously running process
Communicative	Socially able	Communicates with other agents, perhaps including people
Learning	Adaptive	Changes its behavior based on its previous experience
Mobile		Able to transport itself from one machine to another
Flexible		Actions are not scripted
Character		Believable "personality" and emotional state

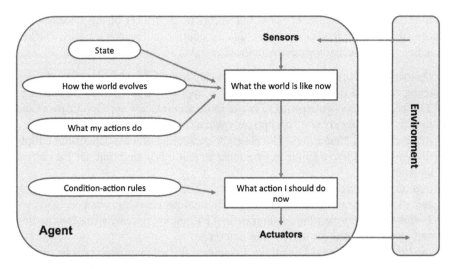

Fig. 15.2 *Reflex (Reactive) Agent.* Example agent structure reflecting its internal processing and interaction with the environment

agent, which spans both domains: An autonomous agent is a system situation within and a part of an environment that senses that environment and acts on it, over time, in pursuit of its own agenda and so as to effect what it senses in the future. The properties of autonomous (or intelligent) agents include those listed in Table 15.1.

Russell and Norvig [9] address Artificial Intelligence in terms of a study of agents that receive percepts from the environment, reason over the data input, and perform actions. The basic structure of an agent emerges from several variations on this theme. For example, Fig. 15.2 illustrates the logical elements of a relatively sophisticated reflex (or reactive) agent, all of which must be addressed by the framework. The agent:

- Can sense a change to the environment
- Can maintain internal states and data
- Can evaluate and reason over conditions related to the environment and the state data maintained
- Can select from multiple potential actions
- Can reason over which actions are appropriate
- Can change the environment based on the input and its internal logic (i.e., execute actuators, including updating data in the external environment).

15.2.1.2 Framework Constructs

The Distributed Agent-Based Concepts described above delineate requirements for a system development and deployment environment. The Distributed Intelligent Agent Framework must support the requirements while establishing a foundation for change management and scalability. The system environment must enable, or more properly, facilitate the development and management of distributed intelligent systems. To ground the discussion, the description will leverage constructs from the Open Source Cougaar (Cognitive Agent Architecture)[2] and the ActiveEdge Platform[3] by Cougaar Software, Inc., both of which are Java-based environments.

System Structure and Agent Definition   Of course, the primary component of the framework is the agent. Developers must be able to define the elements of a system and their interaction in terms of agents. Agents are composed from *Plugin* components, each providing a small piece of business logic or functionality. Plugins can be defined to respond to various stimuli and can execute independent of one another, allowing the agent's behavior to emerge from the composed pieces.

Communities of agents can be defined to present a simple interface to other agents, hiding the internal structure and complexity, and can be composed of multiple potentially collaborating agents and smaller communities. Agents may discover communities within a system, send messages to members of a community, or join and leave a community. Agents within a community can take on specialized roles that help maintain order within the community, including Member, Manager, and Owner.

To fully support the concept of distributed agents, the Framework supports the concept of a Node, which is an *abstraction* of the services and structure required

---

[2] The Cougaar website is here: http://www.cougaar.org/.

[3] ActiveEdge® is Cougaar Software, Inc.'s software development and execution management platform for building complex, distributed, intelligent decision support applications. ActiveEdge extends Open Source Cougaar to provide a more complete and robust framework for building large-scale distributed intelligent decision support applications, simplifying application development, increasing agent functionality, and providing enhanced system capabilities.

to support one or more agents in a single memory space (or Java Virtual Machine (JVM)). Note the Node is a logical construct—it does not necessarily correspond with a particular hardware platform. In fact, a platform may host several nodes from the same system. Nodes can be defined to model logical groupings of agents corresponding to aspects of the application domain, or can be defined to ensure equitable sustainable sharing of computer resource requirements. In some cases, agents from different communities will share a single machine and node to be efficiently collocated near a shared data source. (This concept reinforces the flexibility of the Community concept—agents can be associated with the same community without regard to their location across the network.)

A society, the structural concept with the broadest scope within the framework, is a collection of agents that interact to collectively solve a particular problem or class of problems. In most cases, the society corresponds with the overall distributed system that is under consideration. However, a "system of systems" can be achieved with multiple societies, with cross-society interaction achieved using external interface mechanisms.

Agent Communication—Publish/Subscribe   Communication and information sharing is accomplished via a two-tier concept—agent-to-agent and plugin-to-plugin. Each agent is associated with a blackboard—the blackboard can be viewed as a partitioned distributed collection of objects that may or may not be of interest to any particular plugin. Plugins publish and subscribe to objects on a blackboard. Plugins within an agent can add, change or remove objects from the blackboard and can subscribe to local add, change, or remove notifications. Each agent owns its blackboard and its contents are visible only to that agent. Publish/subscribe facilitates flexibility and promotes scalability for the systems by decoupling senders of messages from their recipients. Thus, plugins can be modified or added to an agent and share data through the blackboard without necessarily requiring modification of existing code.

The blackboard of an agent is part of the distributed blackboard managed by the whole society. Sharing of the blackboard state across agent boundaries is done by explicit push-and-pull of data through inter-agent tasking and querying. Agents communicate with each other as peers, hiding the internal business logic and allowing loosely-coupled, asynchronous, and widely distributed problem solving. A MessageTransport and NameServer is available that provides an API for sending messages to arbitrary agents by name and for registering a client with the Transport so that it can receive messages from other sources. Each agent works independently and asynchronously on messages passed from one another, and responds independently and asynchronously on responses received. Cougaar and ActiveEdge incorporate specific inter-agent communication mechanisms including the concept of a Tasking directive, a Relay, and AttributeBaseAddresses. When an agent allocates a task to another agent, a link between blackboard objects in each agent is established, enabling data to be shared and reasoned over by both participants in the relationship. Relays provide a general mechanism for blackboard objects of one agent to have manifestations on the blackboard of other agents. AttributeBaseAddresses allow messages to be sent to agents based on their attributes rather than their names, which is especially useful for specifying the recipients of a multicast message based on the attributes of the agents within a community (such as a role).

Registration/Discover Services   Registry/Discovery services are provided so that resources can be dynamically bound with an appropriate service, instead of hard-wiring direct calls to specific agents. Society components, communities and service providers can be registered so that they can be discovered and utilized throughout the society. Services are provided to allow registration and lookup of agent addresses, allowing agents to be discovered by any other agent (within the constraints of the security profile) regardless of the network node upon which either resides. A "Yellow Pages" service supports attribute-based queries, permitting agents to register themselves based on their application's capabilities, and allows agents to discover other agents and their services based upon queries for those capabilities. The service discovery mechanism is an alternative to explicitly specifying customer/provider relationships by name. Agents can search and discover a service provider with which to form a relationship.

The Registry/Discovery capability also provides a robust, distributed, and secure environment for defining and managing communities of interest within a society that may contain agents and other communities. Using Registry/Discovery with communities permits agents to be dynamically associated, facilitates resource sharing and control, and allows policies to be apply within controlled contexts.

Inference Rules Engine   To assist in implementation of the reasoning that will be incorporated in the intelligent agents, the Framework includes support from an inference engine. The Framework leverages licensed JESS[4] technology to provide a simple forward-chaining rule engine for identifying patterns in objects on an agent's blackboard or within a situational construct. The Framework supports actions to create rules, group them, and assign them to agents based on scopes.

Interoperability and External Communication   As discussed in the introduction, any CAS can be viewed collectively as a single entity in a higher-level CAS. A system developed with the Distributed Intelligent Agent Framework cannot be managed as an island unto itself—it must be viewed as a component of a constantly changing environment with which it will interact. Modern systems must assume that they will need to operate in a heterogeneous system-of-systems context, leveraging a wide variety of systems and services and interfacing with contemporary and/or other emerging systems.

Interface standards provide clean separation of internal components within a system's architecture and clean integration channels for talking to external systems and components. Internally, the framework supports standards such as:

- *JSR-94: Java™ Rule Engine API*: provides a clean interface layer between the rule engine component and the rest of the architecture, so should a developer

---

[4]The website for the JESS Rule Engine is here: http://www.jessrules.com/.

wish to use a rule engine other than the provided JESS engine, they are free to use any engine supporting the API standard.

- *JSR-168 and JSR-268: Java™ Portlet Specifications*: provides a clean interface specification for any portlet component.

Externally, the framework supports widely supported integration standards including:

- *Simple Object Access Protocol (SOAP) 1.2/Web Services Description Language (WSDL) 2.0 Specification*: provides a clean way for systems to perform transactions using standard protocols against published interface specifications with standard XML content payloads.
- *Java Message Service (JMS) 1.1 Standard*: provides a queue or topic based message interface for passing serialized objects.
- *Extensible Markup Language (XML)*: provides a structured way of representing data structures, usually schema-based, in machine and human readable forms; often used as a payload inside other message protocols.
- *HTTP 1.1/HTML5*: provides a standard web-based data exchange, enabling information render with a standard browser or other browser compatible systems.
- *Remote Method Invocation (RMI) API*: provides a standard invocation protocol for other java-based systems using a payload of serialized objects.
- *Java Database Connectivity (JDBC) API 4.0*: provides a standard means of interfacing with databases and data systems; supported by all the major database providers.

Support for internal and external standards provides significant benefits in development and integration, including reduced learning curve, maturity, tools, and standard usage patterns.

15.2.1.3 Framework Features

Having the capability to define agents and plug-ins, communities, and societies so that they can detect and interpret changes in their environment, reason over information, and collaborate to solve a problem are necessary yet insufficient requirement set for the Distributed Intelligent Agent Framework. The framework must address operational concerns related to the deployment and execution of the agents that will collectively define the system. This section describes some of the key features the development and execution environment must support.

Persistence   The Distributed Intelligent Agent Framework must include the capability for the agent and its data to persist. Persistence differentiates an agent from a simple subroutine: code is not invoked on demand, but runs continuously. This concept allows the agent to keep track of variables over repeated calls, and permits the agents to decide for themselves when they need to perform activities. Persistence allows software agents to be called in a "fire and forget" relationship. Persistence is also essential for system robustness and survivability.

Scalability   Solutions developed with Distributed Intelligent Agent Framework are highly extensible and scalable. The component model, coupled with the agent design approach, allows the easy introduction and upgrade of components and agents, even while the system is running. Additional capabilities, interfaces and behaviors can be introduced into the system to support the evolution of its functionality in the face of a changing environment.

The framework is designed from the bottom up to support applications to a massive scale. Encapsulation and information hiding concepts are designed into each of the constructs described above. By encouraging encapsulation, data hiding, and fine grained information management, coupling among components is minimized, and the information passed between agents can be limited to a bare minimum. The plugin construct leveraging publish/subscribe paradigm through the blackboard allows for building large software systems with much more manageable maintenance and integration costs than traditional architectures. By leveraging peer-to-peer inter-agent communications, exponential growth of interdependencies and interactions among different agents can be avoided.

An effective set of deployment infrastructure and execution management tools should be available to facilitate system deployment and administration. The tools should make it easy to configure how the agents will be deployed across the network and platforms, deploy the societies and/or recall configurations across the network. Such a suite of tools allows agent software to be pushed to available machines, standing up or reconfiguring complex multi-node system configurations straightforwardly. In addition, Agent, community and society configurations should be able to change without impacting other components of the society—supporting both dynamic reconfiguration and a capability for long-term evolution of functionality.

Robustness and Survivability   Distributed systems can be designed to be highly robust and survivable. Leveraging capabilities of the Distributed Intelligent Agent Framework, the system design can utilize redundancy, dynamic monitoring, dynamic reconfiguration and other tools. These tools allow the development of resilient designs which can meet specified failure, recovery and performance requirements.

Ultimately, the system can be designed and provisioned to provide continued operation in the face of hardware, system and network failures and to ensure a level of availability and performance prescribed by the requirements. To that end, the framework constructs and the environment in which they operate must allow systems to be designed in a manner that will allow them to survive the temporary outage of a single Agent, node, or sets thereof. Agents can be configured to persist their internal state, which can be subsequently restored as the Agent is restarted. Other agents in the society may need to be designed to tolerate a long-term absence of a given agent from the society (e.g., due to components being disconnected from the network, agent failure or network outage). The agent logic can be designed to determine the availability of an asset, and to select from various alternatives when a particular resource is unavailable (e.g., time-out and move on with other processing, choose an alternative resource, or wait indefinitely to reconnect appropriately as the unavailable resource rejoins the society).

A distributed system's health can be determined by evaluating the state of all of the nodes in a system. To be fully functional, a Distributed Intelligent Agent Framework must have the capability to query the status of each node of the system and components thereon. Further, there may be a need to manipulate the software assigned to each node to reconfigure the system in response to some changes in the environment or to improve performance.

In the Distributed Intelligent Agent Framework, nodes are actually implemented as distinguished agents, and thus, they may be addressed as message targets, may load additional management logic (via plugins), and may be probed by user interfaces. While most application developers seldom need to focus on the node-level services, many of the robustness and security aspects of highly survivable applications are implemented via NodeAgent components and plugins.

The NodeAgent has the task of providing node-level lifeline and management services to the node. While it does not in itself contain the root objects of the component hierarchy, it does have full control over those objects. Since NodeAgents are true agents, they have a blackboard that may be persisted. Thus, they can retain state across host failures.

Security   The Distributed Intelligent Agent Framework must support a significant degree of commercial-grade security, ensuring that all inter-agent communications are assured to be snoop-proof and tamper-proof. Further, the infrastructure core software, the Plugin modules and configuration information are all designed to be certifiably intact and secure. No properly configured application should be vulnerable to traffic interception, rogue agents or corrupted configuration baseline.

The Framework includes a specific Authentication and Authorization subsystem that is designed to facilitate communications among users in a society by guaranteeing several properties of that communication, providing mechanisms to validate users, encrypt communication, and provide general object permissions management.

The user access control service manages a distributed database of users that can access the system. The service mediates every attempt by a user to access the system, therefore ensuring that only valid and authorized users gain access. Before users can perform an operation, they must provide appropriate credentials, such as a password, certificate or smart card. Password authentication can leverage an underlying certificate-to-user account mapping mechanism. Once users have been authenticated, the user access control service checks whether the user has the privilege to perform the requested operation. If the mediation is successful, the user is allowed to perform the operation.

The Framework allows agent solutions to identify users either through its own identification services or by integrating with other trusted identification services. The system will support simple sign-on such as ID and password, as well as physical and dynamic data tokens, and may also include the capability to support various biometric systems.

Execution Management and Dynamic Reconfiguration   To manage an agent-based complex adaptive system, it is necessary to be able to monitor the health of its components and be able to intervene (manually or autonomously) when conditions call for it. The development and execution environment must provide the infrastructure to monitor status and configuration of components (society, nodes, agents, communities, plugins, etc.) throughout a society, monitor external resources tied to a society, and affect changes to said components and external resources, all in near real time. These services need to implemented and operate efficiently in all societies so that society runtime data can be collected without unreasonable impact on the system.

A robust environment will also facilitate user interaction with these services. In addition to the status data collection mechanisms and distribution mechanisms used to affect changes in the deployment configuration, user interfaces and report generation should be available to offer different ways for users to interact with a society when necessary to effectively audit and manage a running society. To support either autonomic or human execution management and control, the infrastructure will require an events management capability. Events of interest can be published and agents can subscribe to them so that the proper analysis, routing and processing can be assured. The events management capability should be able to notify agents and integrate with user interfaces and external devices so that humans can be notified when necessary for awareness or intervention.

15.2.2 Cognitive Framework for Reasoning

A foundational concept for distributed agent-based system design is to have each agent perform a small logical part of the functionality so that their collective behavior satisfies the requirements for the system. Because each agent has a focused role in the system, changes required for adaptation can be localized to a small part of the system without disrupting the rest. (This is in contrast to a monolithic system that requires human intervention to shut down the system and code changes each time the system requires modification.)

While the Distributed Intelligent Agent Framework provides the essential elements to develop and maintain an agent-based system, it provides maximum flexibility for system component definition. A framework that characterizes appropriately sized components within an overall context would be extremely helpful to system designers and agent developers. Since agents often perform functions on behalf of humans, a model of the human reasoning process has been defined upon which to base agent designs. The Cognitive Framework for Reasoning defines a structure for describing and modeling the *human cognitive model of reasoning and planning*. The components of the Cognitive Framework define patterns for common agent functions that comprise distributed intelligent agent systems. This framework can be used to identify key functions and roles for agents in a CAS.

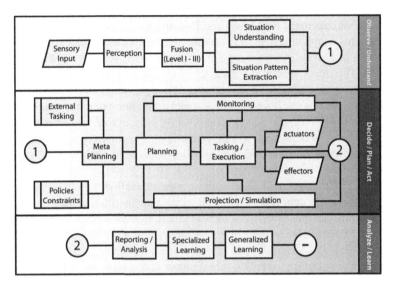

Fig. 15.3 *Cognitive Framework for Reasoning.* Characterizes the elements of reasoning, many of which can be supported by intelligent agents

15.2.2.1 Concept

Developing intelligent agent-based systems involves the development of agents with reasoning components that emulate elements of human cognitive processes. The Cognitive Framework for Reasoning captures the various activities that humans do when they observe, reason, plan, and act. By decomposing these processes into a reference framework, individual elements can be used to define common models and patterns for intelligent agent design. These elements can be considered when designing a system. The Distributed Intelligent Agent Framework can then be used to implement the agents and their interaction. Combining the Cognitive Framework with implementation using the Distributed Intelligent Agent Framework allows applications to emulate the complex processes humans do everyday more realistically and robustly than other traditional technologies.

15.2.2.2 Organizational Structure

Figure 15.3 depicts the Cognitive Framework for Reasoning and its organization into three major processes: Observe/Understand, Decide/Plan/Act, and Analyze/Learn. These processes are comprised of various concurrent and interdependent activities described below. In actuality, humans perform these activities continuously and concurrently on various levels. After we observe and understand an event, we may be making other observations while reacting to the first and/or analyzing other perceptions.

Observe/Understand   In order for people to reason about their condition or their environment, they must use their senses to gather data and information. Correspondingly, for agents to perceive the conditions in their environment, they must intake data and reason over it. A common role for agents in most systems is simply to collect or monitor data sources, whether that process involves tying agents to actual sensors or to databases or to external systems.

Once the data is made available, the first level of reasoning can occur. Data is transformed into actionable information about activities of particular actors by applying business rules to correlated normal and expected activities and their relationships to the dimensions of the potential mission. As data streams in, the activities can be reasoned over and patterns of behavior can be identified. The first focused activity is data fusion.

The Joint Directors of Laboratories (JDL) Data Fusion Working Group created a process model for data fusion which is intended to be very general and useful across multiple application areas. It identifies the processes, functions, categories of techniques, and specific techniques applicable to data fusion. The model is a two-layer hierarchy. At the top level, the data fusion process is conceptualized by sensor inputs, human-computer interaction, database management, source preprocessing, and six key subprocesses [7]:

- Level 0 processing (subobject data association and estimation) is aimed at combining pixel or signal level data to obtain initial information about an observed target's characteristics.
- Level 1 processing (object refinement) is aimed at combining sensor data to obtain the most reliable and accurate estimate of an entity's position, velocity, attributes, and identity (to support prediction estimates of future position, velocity, and attributes).
- Level 2 processing (situation refinement) dynamically attempts to develop a description of current relationships among entities and events in the context of their environment. This entails object clustering and relational analysis such as force structure and cross-force relations, communications, physical context, etc.
- Level 3 processing (significance estimation) projects the current situation into the future to draw inferences about enemy threats, friend and foe vulnerabilities, and opportunities for operations (and also consequence prediction, susceptibility, and vulnerability assessments).
- Level 4 processing (process refinement) is a meta-process that monitors the overall data fusion process to assess and improve real-time system performance. This is an element of resource management.
- Level 5 processing (cognitive refinement) seeks to improve the interaction between a fusion system and one or more user/analysts. Functions performed include aids to visualization, cognitive assistance, bias remediation, collaboration, team-based decision making, course of action analysis, etc.

As the diagram indicates, data fusion in this component of the Cognitive Framework is limited to Levels 1–3; the other levels are included in this section for reference and are achieved across the full continuum of the Cognitive Framework for

Reasoning. Based on the fused data, humans (and agents) can build an understanding of the "world" (or at least the part of the world being represented by that data), or in terms of the model, the situation. People learn to recognize significant events and conditions based on patterns. Pattern recognition and extraction is a key concept in situational understanding.

Decide/Plan/Act   The Decide/Plan/Act process addresses how the human (or agent) reacts to the environment, or at least the situations of interest within the environment. Planning is a process that associates tasks to be executed with conditions and policies. If the appropriate combination of conditions within the situation correlates to particular policies and constraints, an appropriate response (task) can be selected. Meta-planning is the process of combining and associating situational conditions, policies, constraints and tasks. (In essence, meta-planning is determining in advance, that if X occurs, then task Y should be performed.)

Based on the actual data entering the system (note the reference to monitoring), active planning can occur. The dynamics of a changing world preclude knowing all possible outcomes of a task; therefore, once a situation is presented in reality, the outcomes of applying various alternative courses of action are often projected. Based on that analysis, a decision is made to select a course based on some sort of criteria.

Based on this analysis, the course of action (a selected set of tasks) is executed. Particular controls (actuators) may be directed to be changed, or other processes (effectors) may be invoked. As the tasks are executed, the results of those actions are monitored and the process cycle continues.

Analyze/Learn   The Analyze/Learn process of the Cognitive Framework differentiates the human cognitive capabilities from traditional systems and machines. Humans can be retrospective of their actions and relationship with their environment, learn from their successes and mistakes. Humans (and agents) can review the efficacy of their rules, policies, and tasks and adapt accordingly. Alternative approaches can be defined; policies and thresholds can be adjusted; and new rules determined and incorporated into all of the cognitive processes.

15.2.2.3 Application

If one considers the dynamics of a team responsible for an area of operation, there may be a significant number of inputs, conditions of interest, or data sources that need to be collectively monitored and evaluated; multiple actions that need to be planned and executed concurrently; and several areas that require reporting or analysis. Despite its complexity, virtually all of the individual functions of such an environment can be characterized in terms of an element of the Cognitive Framework for Reasoning. Agents designed to perform the individual simple activities within the Cognitive Framework for Reasoning become the building blocks for sophisticated systems engineering. With each agent of the system taking on its assigned role in accordance to this model, the behavior of the overall system can emerge. These building blocks can be combined to achieve more sophisticated objectives, and once built, can themselves be building blocks to address even more complex problems. The rest of the frameworks in this treatise are actually examples of this incremental compilation approach.

15.2.3 Knowledge Base Framework

The Knowledge Base Framework provides transparent and seamless access to different types of knowledge to client components. In a constantly changing network-centric world, not only can the source of information in a system change, but there can be multiple sources of related information available that should be considered. Each of the information sources may have different data formats, and data from multiple sources may need to be fused to determine the facts to be input as a piece of knowledge.

The Knowledge Base Framework provides knowledge access and storage capabilities, irrespective of the location, format and the access mechanism for the knowledge providers. Using the Knowledge Base Framework, knowledge access can be directed (and redirected) without coupling the clients' process logic to the specific location and format of the data being evaluated or stored. Systems can remain operational despite the need to rehost information sources or to reformat files or databases. As systems and logic mature, answers to knowledge queries may be composed by combining and perhaps reasoning over information from multiple heterogeneous data sources.

The Knowledge Base Framework provides an infrastructure that encircles the support of knowledge, the handling of knowledge providers and registrations based on objects that implement the interface with the data sources. The Knowledge Base Framework integrates processing related to data source association, data access, data transformation (i.e., extract/transform/load) between the formats of the data sources and the representations within the system, and access controls. Business rules may be applied to select from multiple data sources based on such criteria as proximity, availability, or provenance.

15.2.4 Integrated Distributed Data Environment Framework

An Integrated Distributed Data Environment provides services to facilitate data exchange and collaboration among agents within a single node of a system, across nodes of a defined society of agents, and across system boundaries. An integrated data environment addresses constancy and availability in a distributed environment and allows authorized users to quickly access and aggregate information from anywhere in the system without waiting for linear processing and transmission of reports. The environment must be database technology agnostic and sensitive to network bandwidth limitations. Autonomously or on command, intelligent agents search across the data environment to locate resources that correspond to their demands. The environment provides data services within the various elements of the system to support both the needs of the node as well as the movement (sharing) of data among nodes.

15.2.5 Situational Reasoning Framework

The ActiveEdge Situational Reasoning Framework (SRF) is a proven commercial intelligent agent-based framework for constructing and maintaining distributed knowledge networks of complex interdependent information. SRF is a complex framework built upon the constructs of the Distributed Intelligent Agent Framework that provides significant value to the development and management of intelligent agent-based systems by encapsulating and organizing logic applicable to most CAS: managing a near-realtime understanding of the environment and the objects of interest therein. Our ever expanding network environment provides access to more and more diverse data inputs, all of which may need to be evaluated and worked into a consistent knowledge model representing "ground truth."

Many operational environments are challenged to monitor conditions of interest and to simply detect and resolve subtle inconsistencies among data from different sources. Raising the level of complexity, systems may be expected to monitor and analyze vast streams of data from multiple sources and to rapidly recognize and raise alerts related to significant events or indicators. When performed manually, these common and relatively mundane activities can consume the bandwidth of literally armies of analysts, and often the processes are error-prone and mind-numbing. Delegating these processes to intelligent agents can significantly improve the speed and quality of the analysis and release vital resources to address more significant challenges.

15.2.5.1 Concept

SRF provides a distributed infrastructure for reasoning about real world scenarios. It combines the strengths of standard Java object models, graph and distributed game theory, and semantic technologies to provide new mechanisms of deep situational reasoning about real world scenarios. This capability utilizes intelligent agents to create a dynamic, intelligent decision support capability that leverages a combination of reasoning, knowledge-based situational representation and simulation analysis to empower decision-makers with information, options and recommendations.

The SRF is used to build a virtual representation of the current situation from various incoming data event streams whether they are random or predictable. This resulting situational model is a rich, object representation of the state of current operations similar to the virtual world representation in a modern video game. Thus,

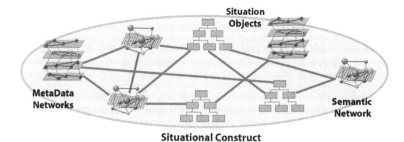

Fig. 15.4 *Situational Reasoning Framework (SRF) Situational Construct (SC).* This notional model of a Situational Construct illustrates the three component models that must be maintained in concert to monitor and reason over changing situations: the Situational Objects, MetaData Networks, and Semantic Network

the system is able to identify and reason on whether data updates entering the system are redundant, conflict with the information from other data streams, or provide new information that will enrich the model. From mediated and pedigree-tagged data, an understandable, real-time representation of the current situation is created, enabling advanced event management, execution monitoring, and collaborative decision support.

15.2.5.2 Organizational Structure

The core unit of processing defined by the SRF is a "scenario" managed within a "Situational Construct," the subsystem implemented using the SRF that encapsulates all of the reasoning and provides an API for clients. A "Situation Construct" (SC), as illustrated in Fig. 15.4, is created to manage the changes associated with a particular set of knowledge constructs. (A sophisticated distributed system may have multiple SCs corresponding with a variety of information domains, events, contexts, etc.) The instance models are configured with reasoners that incorporate and process any new data or information with respect to the current 'understanding' of the situation. The intelligent agents and reasoners in the SRF correlate data updates and resolve interdependencies among the model instances to ensure a consistent view of the situation.

Situational reasoning and representation is more than icons or tracks on a map; it is the union of many aspects of a situation constructed and maintained from the real-time data supporting those aspects, enabling reasoning over the information and their interrelationships. SRF allows system developers to define knowledge networks in terms of three complementary "spaces": the object model (characterizing the state of the objects in the operational environment), a metadata network model (characterizing the metadata about the objects and their class definitions), and the ontological network model (characterizing the business rules that define inferences that can be determined based on relationships between objects of particular classes). Intelligent agents managing the object space and internal networks use efficient graph theory techniques to maintain relationships and consistency among entities in the situation.

Each object space is managed by its own agent, known as an object space controller. Registered with each object space controller are reasoning components which do the bulk of the interesting work of the SRF Situational Construct. (The SRF can be incrementally upgraded over time by adding plug-ins to define additional business rules and nuances among the elements of the operational environment and addressing expanded data availability and refined reasoning.)

The Situational Object Space (SOS)   The Situational Object Space represents the collection of entities of interest that exist in the operating environment. This includes all physical objects as well as abstract concepts and information relevant to the objects and Actors. Scenario actions (e.g., status updates) are validated and manifested as manipulations of objects within this space; information queries result from evaluation of the state of the objects. The SOS contains little, if any, rules. The rules that govern the access and manipulation of objects within this space often rise from reasoning residing in other components within the framework.

The Network Object Space (NOS)   The Network Object Space is a graphical structure layered on top of the SOS. It forms edges representing relationships between SOS objects. The purpose of the NOS is to provide an efficient data structure that makes it a simple task to quickly determine the relationships between sets of SOS objects. The NOS represents the various relationships among the objects in the SOS. SRF components responsible for updating and transmitting portions of the SOS utilize the NOS instead of exhaustive searches through the SOS. The NOS may have one or more instances of graph edges among objects in the NOS (e.g., one denoting distance relationship between the nodes, one denoting parent-child relationship, etc.). Each node in the NOS graph holds a reference to its corresponding original SOS object so that actual retrieval of an asset is possible in future. This is done via using a Unique Object Identifier—UID.

Besides this reference, the NOS also maintains some meta-information about the actual data object, which helps in answering various queries efficiently instead of an exhaustive, potentially expensive search over the SOS space.

Semantic Network Space (SNS)   The SNS provides the strong reasoning and inferencing power from the ontology perspective. The semantic networks, which use Semantic Web concepts and technologies, provide a common ontology for representing and reasoning over domain knowledge. Semantics and data ontologies are essential, providing an understanding of the conceptual meaning of aspects of a situation versus a one-dimensional understanding of individual objects. Thus, situational software permits reasoning over the concepts of the application domain, rather than just the instance—critical for making inferences such as detecting degraded capabilities or assessing alternate resource substitution.

The SNS is very similar in structure to the NOS in that it too has a graph-like structure denoting relationships between various nodes. In the SNS, the nodes represent instances of ontology concepts and the edges denote the property relationships between those instances. In short, the SNS holds an ontology model of the environment characterizing the business rules about the objects in the situation. As the state of objects change, the SNS determines the corresponding rippling effects of those changes, potentially by examining the interrelationships defined in the NOS. In the Distributed Intelligent Agent Framework, this can be easily triggered if the controller is a plug-in that has subscribed to the blackboard and gets invoked when the object that it monitors changes.

The agents managing each SC will perform functions like:

- Updating the knowledge network when new data is received from data sources,
- Projecting consequences within the simulation model on demand or when incoming data causes the data values to cross specified thresholds (e.g., indicating resources have exceeded expected operational ranges),
- Packaging and providing information to the visualization layer of an application for rendering and user interaction,
- Manifesting decision actions and decision events into the SC, as well as determining the implication and effects of those decisions on the situation,
- Maintaining the linkages across SCs where there are constraints, dependencies, allocations or other relationships between elements in different SCs.

15.2.5.3 Application

Functional applications and other intelligent agents within a system subscribe to the situation and associated conditions of interest. Functional applications can use the situation and other services to recognize changes in the environment and respond accordingly. Thus, they can react to changes in the situation to spawn processes, share information, and/or alert other parts of the system or environment that something significant has occurred. In some cases, the process can be cyclic. For instance, in automated supervisory control and data acquisition (SCADA) systems, business rules and processes may be invoked that alter the conditions in the environment (e.g., adjust controls or parameters), which in turn will be detected by the SC(s) and correspondingly recognized by the rest of the system. The agents can evaluate the efficacy of the control adjustments invoked, and respond accordingly (e.g., invoke additional processes such as further adjustment of controls, continue monitoring if within appropriate ranges, or alert operators of exceptional conditions). In a self-regulating system, software agents can even adjust the business rules and processes based on rule patterns and their ability to learn from prior actions.

15.3 Unifying Architectural Frameworks for Developing Distributed Decision Support

Architectural frameworks provide general organizational structures that can be applied to the development of complex systems and their components which will facilitate their design, deployment, and/or management within the operational environment. An architectural framework for complex adaptive systems using distributed intelligent agents should structure the organization of the agents (and/or groups of collaborating agents) within the system, classifying the roles and/or functionality of various agents and establishing the groundwork for system management. An architectural framework facilitates system design and system maintenance, allowing the architect to build in the flexibility for expanding the number of data sources, for modifying interfaces to support additional or alternative user classes, encapsulating transient features of the solution, etc. This section features two architectural frameworks designed by Cougaar Software, Inc. to support agent-based complex adaptive systems that have proven useful: the Shared Situational Awareness (SSA) Architecture Framework and the Adaptive Planning Framework. The descriptions characterize the concepts within the architectural framework, as well as identify the other frameworks that may have been leveraged.

15.3.1 Shared Situational Awareness Architectural Framework

One of the greatest challenges of complex systems is the management of and reasoning over diverse data that is intimately related, and establishing a common awareness (or better, understanding) of the situation as it relates to a variety of users with different roles.

15.3.1.1 Concept

The core concepts behind the SSA Architectural Framework relate to knowledge management; that is, the transformation from raw data to information and eventually knowledge. Distributed intelligent agents collaborate to collect and share data (tagged with metadata), fuse that data into information (possibly analyzing the data to determine ground truth), and disseminate the information to appropriate communities of interest. In addition to simply managing information for dissemination, the framework also recognizes the variety of roles and contexts of the user communities. Similar user classes at different organizational echelons perform similar functions but operate over different data sets, and/or manage changes at different scopes or levels of authority. Additionally, different user groups reason differently over similar data sets. The SSA Architecture Framework must address both challenges.

15.3.1.2 Organizational Structure

As depicted in Fig. 15.5, the SSA Architecture Framework is organized into a four-layer concept, each layer of which includes sets of collaborative intelligent agents. The organization of the agents is only conceptual—it does not imply any constraints related to allocation of agents to any particular physical or virtual node of the deployed system(s). Any number of agents may correspond with a layer or construct within the SSA Architecture Framework. The following paragraphs highlight the purpose of each layer of the framework.

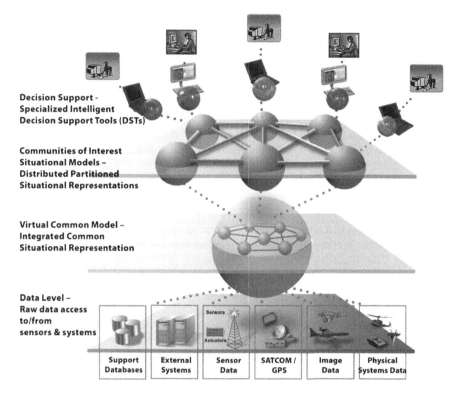

Fig. 15.5 *The Shared Situational Awareness Architecture Framework.* Establishes logical categories for the roles of various intelligent agents across a society to collect, fuse, disseminate and reason over changes in the real world in order to support decision making

Data Level—Raw Data Access to/from Sensors & Systems   The lowest layer in the diagram corresponds with the data interface layer of the architecture. At this level, data and systems are monitored and/or accessed. Data may be found and extracted from support databases, external systems, sensors, knowledge bases, and/or physical system platforms. Distributed intelligent agents can be attached directly to these sources or connected to them via local network devices. The agents continually monitor (i.e., sense) changes to the environment (i.e., changes to the platform states, sensor information, or values in the external systems), tag that data with metadata indicating context and pedigree, and asynchronously update the shared situational model at the level above. In addition to passively monitoring and passing on data updates, agents at this level can monitor the responsiveness of a system by incorporating intelligence based on business processes, policies and rules. Such information can determine system component health and potentially signal that alternative sources or systems should be used. Alternatively, the agents in this data layer may also update system databases, share information with other external systems, and/or interface with system actuators. In the case where actuators are being managed, the agents can report on the responsiveness of changes to those systems to help determine the efficacy of the request, which may lead to further refined responses.

Virtual Common Model—Integrated Common Situational Representation
The Virtual Common Model is an integrated common representation of the situation that collectively represents all of the information of interest within the scope of the complex system. Information is fused from the mediated and pedigree-tagged data collected from the Data Level to establish an understandable data representation of the current situation. The representation is created in near real-time, enabling advanced event management, execution monitoring, and collaborative decision support. The Virtual Common Model is not a centralized database, but a virtual concept composed of information maintained across the network. Agents in this layer have the primary responsibility to detect changes to the situation (based on notifications from the Data Level), normalize that information with other inputs, and forward meaningful status updates to subscribing communities of interest (at the next virtual layer). The Situational Reasoning Framework (SRF) is leveraged to manage the multitude of disparate data inputs that contribute to managing a shared understanding of the situation. The information may actually be managed within Situational Constructs (SCs) corresponding with more than one particular community of interest (described at the next higher level in the SSA Architectural Framework). As changes to elements of the situation are detected, the SCs share the data and *inferences* with other agents across all of the communities of interest to maintain consistent awareness and to empower effective response.

Communities of Interest Situational Models—Distributed Partitioned Situational Representations   Agents at this layer establish and maintain various specialized representations of information which correspond with views for specific communities of interest (e.g., particular roles and/or decision makers). Agents distribute key information across the network to be shared among these communities, offering the right information to the right users at the right time. This information is provided to/accessed by the decision support applications and represent tailored subsets of the situation which are maintained in concert with the rest of the situational information in the Virtual Common Model.

Decision Support—Specialized Intelligent Decision Support Tools (DSTs)
The operational environment (made up of organizations and functions, users, analysts and other decision makers) is reflected at the upper-most level along with the specific decision support tools that support their operations. Planners, analysts, managers and other users in each user class within the communities of interest are assisted by visualization and decision support provided by specialized portal and desktop applications. These decision support tools can reason over the situational updates and orchestrate appropriate analysis and response based on the user's particular role. Applications and portals provide decision support and analytics, data mining, knowledge discovery, and pattern extraction/alerts to the system operators, displaying that information in a format appropriate for their roles. Contrary to the

typical notion of a Common Operating Picture (COP) being a common display of status information shared by all (which implies a 'one size fits all' display design), agents can provide the information in a specialized format appropriate to the particular user. The agents collectively support situational monitoring and analysis, relieving the cognitive burden from the operator. In some operational environments, operators continue to play a key role in selecting from proposed courses of actions, establishing rules, policies and processes, and making key operational and strategic decisions. In some cases, the support tools can actually initiate actions on behalf of the users.

15.3.1.3 Application

Although the architecture framework is described primarily in terms of data flow from the data sources to the operators, the collaboration and information sharing flows in both directions. As decisions are made, directives determined and action is required, that knowledge is shared with others within a community of interest, and relevant information is automatically shared with other communities—human plans, decision and directives are part of the shared situational awareness as well! Just as the event data propagated itself from source to users, plans, decision and directives can be automatically shared across users, translated into data that must be stored, or transformed into system commands and pushed to the device desired.

The SSA Architecture Framework must be considered a notional structure. In some systems, it may be sufficient to have all of the situational reasoning occur in the Communities of Interest layer. In that case, the communities of interest are tied to their specific data sources directly. Information sharing occurs among communities of interest as described above, but the Virtual Common Model is truly notional, it corresponds with the collective information managed by the communities in the society and relies on the communities themselves to maintain appropriately shared awareness.

The primary objective of the framework is to define a society of agents that can effectively remove the human from the low-level processing required to monitor events and data streams, fuse related data into meaningful information, analyze events of interest, and disseminate alerts – allowing operators to reallocate their time from data and event handling to analysis and decision making where necessary. The second, and perhaps as significant objective is to establish an architecture that can be managed in a continuously changing operational environment. As data sources change over time, they can easily be tied to the Virtual Common Model through additional subscriptions and modification of reasoners. Alternative decision support tools can be added to the environment without significant impact on the rest of the system. Thus the architecture framework can be used to structure the design and maintenance of the system as well as facilitate adaptation in the face of continuous change.

15.3.2 Adaptive Planning Framework

The Adaptive Planning Framework (APF) is designed to provide a rich, flexible suite of tools supporting the full range of planning functions from initial planning through plan execution and assessment. The APF supports a broad set of planning roles and allows particular users to have specialized interfaces tailored to their specific organizational needs. These tools support deep, multi-faceted collaborative analysis and planning, and can work together with other tools to form complex, adaptive process chains.

The Adaptive Planning Framework is consistent with the U.S. Department of Defense (DoD) Adaptive Planning and Execution (APEX) concept [1]. The five essential elements of APEX are written specifically to address DoD challenges, but can be generalized for any multi-echelon collaborative planning and execution operational domain[5]:

1. Clear strategic guidance and frequent dialog between senior leaders and planners to promote an understanding of and agreement on planning assumptions, considerations, risks, Courses of Action (COA), and other key factors.
2. Cross-Organizational Connectivity. The APEX concept features early, robust, and frequent discourse between an organization's planners and their external counterparts throughout the planning process.
3. Embedded options, branches and sequels identified and developed as an integral part of the base plan that anticipates significant changes in key planning variables.
4. Parallel planning in a net-centric, collaborative environment across multiple organizational levels and functional areas.
5. "Living Plans" maintained continuously within a networked, collaborative environment with access to current operational, intelligence, logistics and resourcing force management and readiness data and information with automatic triggers linked to authoritative sources that alert leaders and planners to changes in critical conditions, which warrant a reevaluation of a plan's continuing relevancy, sufficiency, or risk that provide for transition to crisis planning.

15.3.2.1 Concept

Figure 15.6 illustrates the key components of an operational system based on the Adaptive Planning Framework. The left side of the figure represents a hierarchical organizational structure with planning teams on each echelon. Teams of decision makers can collaboratively compose plans, execute them, and assess their effectiveness, all of which may be occurring concurrently. A plan may be put into execu-

---

[5]Based on DoD, Adaptive Planning Concept of Operations, Version 3.0 (DRAFT), 15 January 2009. (Paraphrase of significantly longer descriptions in Adaptive Planning Roadmap II.)

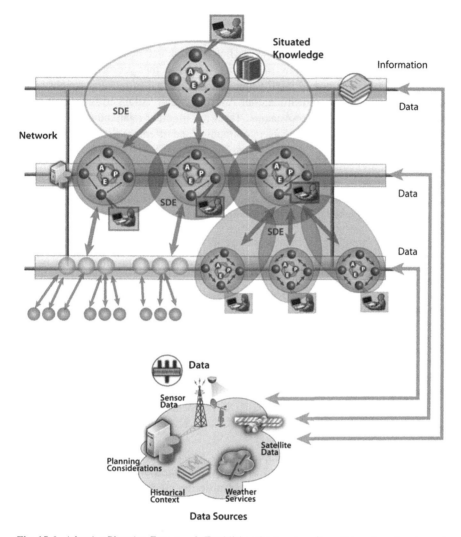

Fig. 15.6 *Adaptive Planning Framework.* Establishes the structure for collaborative planning and execution across organizational and/or geographical boundaries. Leverages the Shared Situational Awareness Architectural Framework to ensure effective dynamic information exchange among interdependent teams

tion while the next phase is being developed. Assessments may occur throughout plan development (e.g., feasibility assessments and simulations), or during execution (e.g., comparing the actual accomplishments to planned outcomes or evaluating the demand and consumption of resources). An organizational team may work together to develop a plan, and can delegate portions of the planning to lower-echelon organizations within their command structure (e.g., a commander may delegate logistics planning to a logistics team, or a contractor may delegate the details of part of a plan to a subcontractor).

The Adaptive Planning Framework links individual decision support tools (DSTs) with data from a variety of sources, tying together sensor data, historical information, status data, and intelligence. As represented in the upper right hand corner of the figure, Shared Situational Awareness data is tagged with meta-data at its source to maintain its provenance, fuses it with other related data to establish and maintain information for the user community, and offers the data/information to DSTs at all echelons and functions across the community. That information is further analyzed and situated by DSTs to support collaborative analysis and planning by decision makers and staff at operational nodes throughout the network. Each node of the planning environment facilitates collaborative Planning, Execution and Assessment (designated as P, E, and A) supported by specialized DSTs and tailored interfaces.

The system infrastructure ensures virtually seamless shared situational awareness among planning staff at all echelons, ensuring the right information is delivered to the right person at the right time in the appropriate context to their function. The situation knowledge shared across the communities consist of more than just operational data tied to the environment, it includes the planning data being produced by analysts and decision makers at each operational node. The Adaptive Planning Framework ensures an appropriate level of visibility at each echelon; planners and analysts share processes and information appropriate for their function and echelon without being overloaded by detail from across the network. The framework facilitates the information sharing to support collaborative planning and operations among interdependent functions at each echelon, while leveraging situated knowledge from lower echelons within their commands.

All of the organizations are supported by a Shared Data Environment (SDE) concept that ensures that the proper information is transported to and from the appropriate nodes via services and publish/subscribe mechanisms. As segments of shared knowledge are updated by one of the operator nodes, the SDE propagates the changes to all the users that participate in the sharing of that knowledge network. It is not unusual to have key knowledge networks, typically representing major plan components or key mission context, to be shared by a large number of users. As illustrated in the figure, these segments of shared knowledge form knowledge spheres, shown using classical Venn fashion, which overlap with the data shared by other unit clusters.

As illustrated in Fig. 15.7, when a planning team tasks another organization with an activity, the request and associated data are logically sent along these command and support channels. Organizations can be tasked to "expand" the plan by performing detailed planning and provide the results back up to the leader who made the assignment. Or organizations may be tasked to "assess" aspects of a plan, which may include feasibility or efficacy assessments. Physically the task is translated to a set of messages to convey them to the target parties in a secure, reliable and survivable manner.

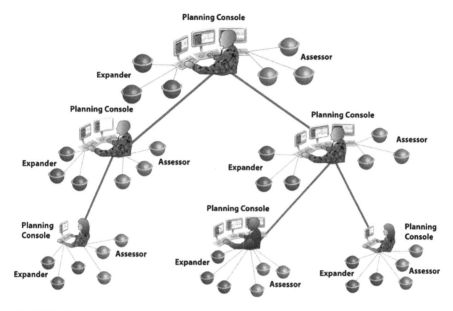

Fig. 15.7 *Hierarchical tasking.* Planners at any level can collaborate and share information with other organizations by delegating planning details and assessments

15.3.2.2 Organizational Structure

The Adaptive Planning Framework is a complex structure that is used to establish decision support tools that enable collaborative planning and plan execution, all the while maintaining share situational awareness of the operating environment and shared planning activities.

Situational Management   As may be expected, the Shared Situational Awareness Architectural Framework is leveraged to maintain a shared understanding of both the operational environment and the plans that are being produced. Implementing an environment supporting shared situational awareness for either of these will be dependent upon a rich data model that represents the information of interest.[6] Both of these situational data models must include some common elements of interest oriented to the plan. The basic elements of a plan have been analyzed for several decades and have been refined into several standard interchange formats (e.g., Joint Consultation, Command and Control Information Exchange Data Model (JC3IEDM)).[7] For discussion purposes, a basic model for planning such as that defined in the Core Plan Representation (CPR) [8] is helpful. The CPR model includes:

---

[6]Cougaar Software, Inc. maintains their Military Logistics Model (MLM) that represents many aspects of military operations, organizations, and battlefield assessments.

[7]General information about the Multilateral Interoperablity Programme (MIP) is available here: https://mipsite.lsec.dnd.ca/Pages/Default.aspx.

- Basic concepts such as Actors, Objective, Resource, and Action, Domain Objects, etc.
- Related information that can be associated with those basic concepts such as Constraints, SpatialPoints, Timepoints, and EvaluationCriterion
- Key associative relationships such as those that associate Plans with Objectives and Actions with Actors, Resources and Spatial and Time Points
- Hierarchical relationships that define the composition (and decomposition) of plan constructs such as Plans and subplans, Objectives and subobjectives, Actors and subactors (i.e., subordinate organizations)
- Additional modifiers that further illuminate a plan such as Annotations, levels of Uncertainty, levels of Precision, etc.

Once an appropriate knowledge reference model has been established, the SSA Architectural Framework can be leveraged to build Situational Constructs to manage the planning and environment situational information. Agents can be designed to manage the specific content of various elements of the plan (e.g., Actors and their status related to readiness, task allocation, resources etc.; Plans and subplans; Tasks, subtasks and associated required resources, etc.)

From a functional point of view, several agent-based applications need to be built to support the plan composition, assessment and execution processes. The Adaptive Planning Framework builds upon the following general applications that when properly configured, work together to establish a planning environment for each user:

Task Planner Application   TaskPlanner is an application with an intuitive graphical user interface for users to develop, assess, and execute various plans for a divers set of actors managed by the system and to handle collaboration among multiple planning agents. The major components of the TaskPlanner focus on the views of the plan from different perspectives including:

- Model Tree Viewer: The Model Tree Viewer is the main model view of the different Actions (or tasks) and the Actors (i.e., organizations or force elements) to which the actions have or may be assigned. The Force-Centric View provides an interface to the hierarchical organization of the actors that can be used to accomplish a plan, and reflects peer and superior/subordinate relationships. The Task-Centric View displays the task/subtask relationships among Actions, any of which can be assigned to the forces in the Force-centric view.
- Gantt Chart: The Gantt Chart is the main view of the Task Planner that graphically displays the task breakdown with their start date and duration. Users can interact with this display to adjust the scheduling of tasks.
- Properties and Status Panels: These components highlight the characteristics and continually changing current and projected status of the tasks and forces. When configured with appropriate assessors, these panels may be configured to indicate that a particular force is not capable of performing assigned tasks, or that a particular task is at risk.
- Collaboration: While the PlanService handles most of the data communication among the groups of planners, the Collaboration component of the TaskPlanner handles the communication among different users affecting the same plan.

- Event Notification: The Event Notification component displays messages that can be filtered by type, priority, keyword or timestamp. Events of interest can relate to a variety of planning challenges, e.g.: changes in the status of forces (e.g., indicating insufficient readiness status for the task assigned), changes in resource availability, or changes in the task assignments in the plans themselves.

Force Builder Application   The Force Builder allows leaders to design and model the various operational units and reporting structures that will perform the tasks that are being planned using the APF. Planners can define force units and their relationships (e.g., subordinate relationships, command/reporting relationships, force levels), as well as associate assets or resources assigned or available to them.

When coupled with its visualizer, the Force Builder presents a panel reflecting the force elements available for the effort, from which the user can assemble his force structure using a drag and drop feature. The force structure can specify a number of command relationships such as supporting vs. supported organizations, and superior vs. subordinates. The new force structure created will carry with it all the responsibilities associated with that force element. Security settings are associated with each of the command elements; when appropriate, a 'commander' can enable or disable aspects of visibility for each command element, or specify which roles can see specific details. The same tool also allows the users to view the status of the force elements during mission execution—identifying the tasks being executed by them, what's in the pipeline, etc. Thus, this application provides a single view of all the command elements and their operations.

Plan Service (Agent)   The Plan Service's responsibility is to create, provide, maintain, persist and dispose of plans in response to different stimulus in the system. The Plan Service acts as a broker between clients and the Plan Knowledge Base Provider, ensuring that requests are valid for a specified agent. The major components of the Plan Service include:

- Plan KnowledgeBase Provider: An instantiation of the Knowledge Base Framework for distributed management of the persistence of plans, subplans, and parts thereof. Utilizing the Knowledge Base Framework allows multiple disparate Plan Service consumers to maintain a globally consistent local object model of the Plan.
- Support Plugins: Abstract plugins are defined for Assessors (which have access to plans, but cannot change the plans in any fashion); Expanders (which support task expansion in response to a person or agent in the system asking for expansion (e.g., when a leader delegates planning to a subordinate); and Exporters, which allow for plans or parts of a plan to be exported into external formats such as excel spreadsheets, images, etc.

15.3.2.3 Application

The Adaptive Planning Framework provides the organizational structure for multi-echelon planning and execution monitoring. To instantiate the system, data sets and reasoner plugins need to be configured together with the Task Planner and Plan Service. Task hierarchies and organizational structures need to be defined based on the knowledge representation model, and incorporated into the system (Task Planner and Force Builder applications can be provided or data can be input via spreadsheets or other external means). Role-based access rules need to be established and associated with the user authorization capabilities in the environment. Based on business rules for organizational and role-based authority, the rules for delegating (expanding) tasking and read/write access need to be defined and integrated into the Plan Service plugins. Plan, Task Force structure and Situational Awareness agents can be implemented to detect and respond to changes in operational environment or planning activities. Finally, the Task Planner application can be configured to leverage the data and controls that have been incorporated into the other segments of the planning system.

15.4 Conclusions

We live in a very complex world in which we are bombarded by ever-increasing volumes of interdependent information. Our minds and current IT systems are incapable of managing all of the inputs and responsibilities, let alone effectively responding to significant changes in our environment. To conquer this complexity and remain competitive, we must be able to effectively adapt to changes in our environment, including having our IT system investments rapidly conform to and support such changes. We can consider this a challenge to establish Complex Adaptive Systems that can respond to changes in the environment with minimal impact.

To meet this challenge, the artificial intelligence concept of distributed agent-based systems has been leveraged to define the Distributed Intelligent Agent Framework, which defines the essential elements of an agent-based system and its development/execution environment. While an agent-based framework is a substantially powerful foundation, additional frameworks can complement the development of adaptive systems.

The Cognitive Framework for Reasoning establishes a basic model of human reasoning and planning that defines the fundamental roles that agents take on when they are part of a larger system. This framework establishes patterns for the composition of agents that will become the building blocks of more sophisticated agent-based systems. The Knowledge Base Framework and Integrated Distributed Data Environment Framework provide general structures for knowledge storage, retrieval and sharing that decouples location, format, and potentially analysis logic from the core business logic of the system, allowing systems to be resilient to data migration. The Situational Reasoning Framework (SRF) provides the infrastructure for detecting, reasoning about and responding to changes in an operational environment.

Building upon all of the basic frameworks, system complexity and change management are further facilitated by architectural frameworks describing common agent-based application domains. The Shared Situational Awareness (SSA) Architectural Framework leverages the SRF to define the overall system organization for collection, fusion, analysis and dissemination of situational information across a network environment. This architectural framework recognizes the diversity of data sources and users that must collaborate over related information, and can be applied in a variety of applications from reconnaissance, to business operations management to SCADA. The Adaptive Planning Framework constitutes an expanded case of applying the SSA Architectural Framework to support collaborative decision making (in this case planning), integrated with shared situational awareness.

Intelligent agents are ideal tools for managing change in a rapidly evolving network-centric world. This chapter focused on the most prominent intelligent agent frameworks available today. Other frameworks will continue to emerge as the challenges to network-centric computing are solved and common patterns and building blocks are identified.

15.5 Dictionary of terms

Table 15.2 Dictionary of terms

Term/acronym	Definition
Common Operational Picture (COP)	A single identical display of relevant information shared by more than one command. A common operational picture facilitates collaborative planning and assists all echelons to achieve situational awareness [6]
Decision Support Tool (DST)	Any functional application or tool employed by one or more user(s) of the S&RL integrated system to collaboratively recognize a given problem, to perform automated analysis and recommendations, and to develop a practical solution through assessment, planning, and execution processes
Software agent	A software entity which functions continuously and autonomously in a particular environment. A software agent is able to carry out activities in a flexible and intelligent manner that is responsive to changes in the environment. Ideally, software agents are able to learn from their experience, able to communicate and cooperate with other agents and processes in its environment, and potentially able to move from place to place within its environment [3]
Living plan	A plan that is maintained continuously within a collaborative environment to reflect changes in guidance or the strategic environment. Automatic triggers linked to authoritative sources, assumptions, and key capabilities will alert leaders and planners to changes in critical conditions that warrant a reevaluation of a plan's continuing relevancy, feasibility, sufficiency, or risk. Living plans provide a solid foundation for transition to crisis action planning [1]
Operator node	Consists of all the DST components on a user's computer or device. This includes the DST environment, cached data and a suite of local DST tools appropriate to the particular function of the user
Shared Data Environment (SDE)	The set of data, information and knowledge shared by a set of users. Can be distributed across multiple platforms

Acknowledgements   The authors wish to acknowledge the contributions of Mr. Kirk Deese. His graphic designs and engineering, as well as technical discussions and review, were instrumental in developing this chapter.

References

1. Adaptive Planning Executive Committee, Office of the Principal Deputy Under Secretary of Defense for Policy PDUSD (P): Adaptive planning roadmap II, March 8, 2008
2. Andrus, D.C.: Toward a complex adaptive intelligence community: the Wiki and the blog. Studies in Intelligence **49**(3) (2005)
3. Bradshaw, J.M. (ed.): Software Agents. AAAI Press, Menlo Park (1997)
4. Emmerich, W.: 1997 Distributed System Principles. Lecture Notes, University College of London, 1997. Downloaded from http://www.cs.ucl.ac.uk/staff/ucacwxe/lectures/ds98-99/dsee3.pdf on December 7, 2010.
5. Franklin, S., Graesser, A.C.: Is it an agent, or just a program? A taxonomy for autonomous agents. In: Müller, J.P., Wooldridge, M., Jennings, N.R. (eds.) Intelligent Agents III, Agent Theories, Architectures, and Languages, ECAI '96 Workshop (ATAL), Budapest, Hungary, August 12–13, 1996, pp. 21–35. Springer, Berlin (1996)
6. Joint Education and Doctrine Division, J-7, Joint Staff: Joint Publication 1-02, Dod dictionary of military and associated terms 08 November 2010, as Amended Through 31 January 2011
7. Liggins, M.E., Hall, D.L., Llinas, J. (eds.): Handbook of Multisensor Data Fusion: Theory and Practice, 2nd edn. CRC Press, Boca Raton (2009)
8. Pease, R.A., Carrico, T.M.: JTF ATD core plan representation. In: Technical Report SS-97-06, p. 95. AAAI Press, Menlo Park (1996)
9. Russell, S., Norvig, P.: Artificial Intelligence: A Modern Approach, 2nd edn. Prentice Hall, Upper Saddle River (2003)
10. Waldrop, M.M.: Complexity: The Emerging Science at the Edge of Order and Chaos. Penguin, Baltimore (1994)
11. Weaver, W.: Science and complexity. Am. Sci. **36**, 536 (1948)

Chapter 16
Customer-Oriented Business Process Management: Vision and Obstacles

Tiziana Margaria, Steve Boßelmann, Markus Doedt, Barry D. Floyd, and Bernhard Steffen

16.1 Motivation

A truly customer-oriented Business Process Management (BPM) approach has been widely acknowledged for several years as an important candidate for driving progress in businesses and organizations. For example, companies such as SAP have spent significant effort in designing more flexible products to serve the market of small and medium enterprises. Products such as MySAP and, more recently, the Business ByDesign on-demand solution are advances in this direction. However, more effort needs to be expended to reach a truly flexible custom solution; one that is really in the hands of the customers. Leaving the market leaders for large and medium enterprises aside (where product life-cycle management reasons may lead the products to not follow the emerging markets so quickly), we see that there are several developing markets for radically different solutions. These solutions come with different needs and motivations:

- *Small enterprises* and even more *microenterprises* have radically different and sometimes peculiar ways of conducting their business that need to be reflected in the BPM software; such users striving for innovation cannot sacrifice their competitive advantage by adapting their business models and processes to standards enforced by some rigid system infrastructure. For these organizations, far reaching inexpensive and easy customization is a necessary requirement.
- Businesses and organizations in *emerging sectors and markets* increasingly choose not to adopt one of the ERP market leaders. This decision happens for reasons of high cost on one side, but also for fear of entering vital dependency relations with products and product management strategies that are outside their own control and have proven critical in the past. For example, Oracle and SAP changed their philosophies underlying the licensing fee models for their own

T. Margaria (✉)
Chair Service and Software Engineering, University of Potsdam, Potsdam, Germany
e-mail: margaria@cs.uni-potsdam.de

M. Hinchey, L. Coyle (eds.), *Conquering Complexity*,
DOI 10.1007/978-1-4471-2297-5_16, © Springer-Verlag London Limited 2012

products and for products of companies they had acquired, resulting in undesirable changes to their clientele. In some cases the user base succeeded in reaching significant amendments to those licensing fee models, but the shock was deep and exposed the vulnerability of the customer. In these fast-growth situations the desire is for a flexible and adaptable solution that does not harness and constrain the organization, but adapts to each customer's shifting requirements and needs as they grow. For creative organizations in sectors and markets still in the course of establishment, potential independence and ease of migration are thus central assets.

- Other organizations, typically in the *public sector*, are concerned and even reluctant to adopt as their technological platforms software products from foreign producers. Some countries that did not have their own world-class solutions strove to migrate to open source operating systems a few years ago. It is also well known that in the BRIC countries[1] as well as in several smaller emerging economies this concern is present for any infrastructure-like kind of software, ERP included. Here, independence and sovereignty are an issue. There is an understandable fear of undisclosed features that might allow information leaks to foreign authorities. These political and performance requirements lead to a diffident attitude towards black boxes, due to the wish to control the information flow boundaries and a fear of unknown unknowns. Empowerment is here reached either through open source solutions, when existing and suitable, or through own local development of suitable alternatives.

In this chapter we look at two major streams of business process development: an aggressive new style of ad-hoc business process development, which is reminiscent of the similar movement in software construction for agile application development like eXtreme Programming [3] and Scrum [11], and the above-mentioned more traditional, largely ERP-dominated business process management. We examine salient aspects from the perspective of the *felt* complexity as discussed in Chap. 10. The point of this investigation is to help align the BP development process to the (business) critical need of agility in an economic way. Unfortunately, both considered streams fail to adequately address the wishes we sketched above. The former because its characteristic lack of structure impairs scalability both in size and along the life-cycle, and the latter because the traditional rigid structure of development impairs agility. Accordingly, the alignment we envision is about combining these two streams in such a way that the outcome retains as much as possible of their individual strengths while overcoming the inherent weaknesses in each. Emphasizing the user perspective, which is a key message of XP and typically underrepresented in classical system design, we consider here how one could enhance the *design by doing* paradigm, which is appealing and successful in the small, with formal-methods based modeling and validation technology so that it becomes better structured, scalable in size, and maintainable and robust along its whole life-cycle.

---

[1]In economics, BRIC is a grouping acronym for the emerging markets of Brazil, Russia, India, and China.

This combination leads to a new form of continuous model-driven engineering [26], based on the eXtreme Model-Driven Development (XMDD) paradigm (see also, Chap. 10 [12, 23]), itself based on organizing the whole process/application life-cycles along one single modeling artifact: the *one thing* of the One-Thing Approach (OTA) [25]. The OTA is in fact designed to provide all stakeholders with adequate views tailored to concisely inform them in real time whenever their input is required.

Seen from a conceptual perspective, XMDD leads to an incremental model of design: the gradually arising one-thing incorporates and documents all the decisions and efficiently propagates conflicts to the responsible stakeholders for discussion and re-decision. This communication discipline improves the classical cyclic developments processes by focused communication between the involved stakeholders in real time, continuously obeying the typically hierarchical responsibility structure, which maintains a waterfall-like organization of priorities in decision. In daily practice though, this same strategy of tight communication and quick feedback closely resembles the pair-programming and 'customer on the lap' philosophy of eXtreme programming, which drastically reduces the felt complexity of BP development because of the agility gained at the development process level. An *agile development process* effectively helps avoid the costly over-engineering that in the traditional style of development is typically employed as a built-in protection against the consequences of misunderstandings or changing requirements. Because agility is now intended and supported in the development process, it no longer needs to be reflected in complex software architectures. Rather, the development should always focus on the *currently known* requirements, without the central preoccupation of guarding against possible or potential change requests, which typically then turn out to be quite different than foreseen. This new approach drastically reduces the felt complexity of the actual development and eases adaptation. Because the software architecture is much simpler, so is its one-thing-oriented change management: maintaining the consistency of the various requirements is inherently supported, and the points of required action for each change are made much more explicitly apparent.

In the following, we first discuss the new style of ad-hoc business process development: this helps us develop our vision in Sect. 16.2 at a global and more conceptual level, and to present XMDD as a way to enhance this style with formal methods-based technology. Subsequently, we look at the state of the art of ERP-centric BPM, which almost naturally exposes typical obstacles of realization in current state of the art environments. In Sect. 16.4 we examine the state of the art of API design. The chapter closes with a brief discussion and statement of future research goals.

16.2 Design by Doing—A Vision for Adaptive Process Management

Modern business process management (BPM) increasingly focuses on enabling ad-hoc changes of running process instances, addressing the need for reacting to changes in business environments in a quick and flexible way. Meanwhile these thoughts have led to a basically different perspective on the engineering of processes, striding away from the traditional two-phased approach of first modeling process templates and afterwards creating process instances for case handling. The new perspective considers processes as being *fluent* in a metaphorical sense, meaning that they are continuously adapted and reshaped to optimally fit the respective concrete case at hand. Consequentially, the more ambitiously this approach is pursued the more the boundary between *engineering* and *use* of processes blurs. The overall goal is to empower business users to create and adapt processes on-the-fly.

These ideas bring a shift from a top-down approach that aims at total control of the workflow by the management towards a bottom-up approach that empowers the process users to align the process models to the actual case at hand [21] and produces new process variants that best suit the actual situation. Ideally, whenever adaptation is needed, managers re-define the needed outcomes, process owners adjust the intersection points, and each process team is able to immediately work in the new, adapted way.

In a sense, this is a form of self-management that is built-in in the new process design philosophy. As desired for self-managed systems, unforeseen exceptions are no longer to be considered as detrimental deviations from the desired canonical workflow. They are rather accepted as an essential part of the variance in everyday business life, and thus considered the new normal case that a good (process) environment must be able to deal with.

Design by doing leads to a process design philosophy which considers changes as welcome variations that ensure response to competitiveness and foster sustainable success. In fact design by doing overcomes the 'classical' burden to foresee and model every potential exception in advance, a goal which is doomed to fail: business changes too rapidly. Moreover, it is exactly the unforeseen changes that typically have the largest impact and the greatest potential for competitive advantage, in particular, when they reflect the customer's perception directly.

Unfortunately, existing approaches based on analyzing the *as-is* process and undergoing the whole stack of BPM life-cycle spanning modeling, simulation, implementation, monitoring, and optimization for one or more *to-be* variants often require too much bureaucratic overhead and implementation time if carried out in business practice. This way of changing often requires a project with business and IT consultants where the task of identifying the *as-is* takes so long that the knowledge gained is obsolete before it can be used to define the *to-be*, resulting in a systematic waste of time and resources. Thus, the investments (costs and response time) are so high that organizations typically afford it only for unavoidable cases such as when laws and regulations mandate new compliances.

16.2.1 Following Recipes Does not Make Good Cooks

Gartner fellow Janelle Hill predicts that

"new BPM technologies will enable the management of more unstructured and dynamic processes to deliver greater business efficiencies and competitive advantage."[2]

Focusing on dynamic and unstructured work results in a process management perspective that is basically different from the traditional focus on routine, i.e. predictable and sequential processes. As Pink [28] observes, predictable, prescribable routines are (in his terminology) algorithmic, and can therefore be scripted, codified in precise processes and then automated or equivalently delegated without running extensive risks. These project types are ones that are well handled by the traditional BPM design approaches. Complex knowledge- and experience-intensive work is on the contrary unpredictable. The underlying processes might even appear chaotic! At minimum they are very sensitive to initial and environmental conditions. This is the realm of the much feared *It depends...* answers, which require creative solutions, and creativity thrives with freedom. Working along a predefined process template implies squeezing and twisting each different case to force it into a standardized way of treatment. This is not the best way to handle creative tasks. Despite the harmonization-oriented advantage of predictability within this approach, forced standardization of knowledge-intensive work reduces business agility instead of increasing it, often resulting in the delivery of significantly less value. In his book *"Mastering the Unpredictable"* Tom Shepherd concludes that

> *"traditional applications, even BPMSs, don't deal well with variability, and it is the knowledge workers that often suffer as a result. [...] We need to move past assembly-line thinking, where we try to eliminate every variation, and focus on how to deal with the reality of work that changes from one situation to the next"* [31].

To support creative processes we need a consistent yet adaptive approach that facilitates a variety of process variants and learns from each special case for future application. Even if a particular case will never be repeated exactly the same way, it contains knowledge that might help solve similar problems still to arise. However, it is a challenge to identify and extract the knowledge that is best suitable to help improve problem solving in future cases. Extracting such knowledge has to do a lot with listening. It is about supporting business users in handling diversity and adapting to customers' needs while at the same time learning from each individual solution and providing it to others as an effective process variant. It is also about creating processes iteratively without the need for a-priori analysis. Gartner fellow Jim Sinur shortly describes it as *Design by Doing* in contrast to the mainstream approach that might rather be seen as *Doing by Design* [32].

Being adaptive is not about predicting a set of variants for how a process will be executed: for realistic processes it is impossible to agree beforehand on all possible alternatives. Instead it is about empowering business users to freely change or create processes on demand within an agreed range, moving from prescriptive control to a form of loose supervision, so that the resulting process is consistent with applicable business rules and well-defined goals. Figure 16.1 shows the main ingredients of an

---

[2]From "Five Predictions for How BPM Will Evolve", 2011, available at: http://www. documentmedia.com.

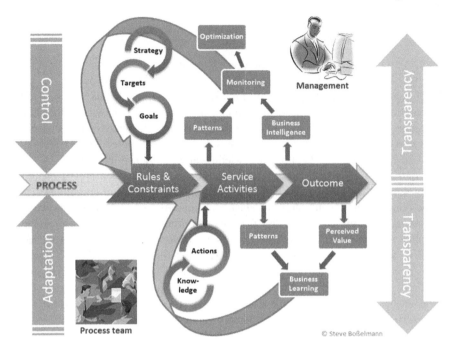

Fig. 16.1 Balancing top-down control and empowerment of process teams

adaptive BPM environment. There, the need of control/supervision and the freedom to adapt, cooperate in a *meet in the middle strategy* that reconciles both top down and bottom up driving forces. Centrally managed business rules make a process as adaptive or rigid as desired, guiding the range of acceptable variance according to stated principles of governance.

From an abstract perspective, both the traditional and the adaptive approach are goal-driven in the sense that they both aim to provide processes for reaching a particular business goal. This is evident in the traditional setting, where every process is developed for achieving a clearly stated outcome. It is true, however, also for the adaptive approach which does not prescribe in detail *how* a certain workflow should proceed, but only *what* has to be achieved in terms of strategic objectives set by executives and the operational targets proposed by management, that are translated to specific goals by process owners.

Thus the difference between prescriptive and adaptive process management approaches is that the *what*-oriented adaptive approach is more flexible to accommodate change than the *how*-oriented traditional approaches, as *what-style* specifications, in contrast to *how-style* specifications, do not enforce premature design decisions. This gives the business process users that carry out a process the necessary degree of freedom in how to achieve their process goals by empowering them to change activity sequences as long as this does not conflict with applicable business rules [8]. More generally, a *formal specification* of process goals and business rules creates a clear framework for user-driven adaptation of processes with which to comply. This formal specification approach facilitates both the adaptation of pre-defined process templates during execution as well as the autonomous creation of sub-processes wherever needed and authorized. This way certain parts of the modeling phase are shifted to the execution phase, leveraging the fact that the actor knows best how to carry out a particular process step to achieve a certain goal. Hence, iterative adaptation transforms a less ordered process state to a structured one by aligning activities that best fit the problem to solve.

The adaptive approach does not search for the one right process that fits all future cases but aims to create alternatives to choose from and to provide guidance for users that might be less experienced. Still, when evaluating performance indicators and the quality of each process' outcome, it is possible to identify and establish guidelines in the form of best practices such as identifying process variants that have proven to be most effective for a certain situation.

16.2.2 Basic Requirements

The set of recommended traits of the proposed approach to adaptive processes can be summarized as follows:

- Empower authorized business users to apply *on-the-fly changes to process instances* during execution. This empowerment includes user-driven creation of new sub-processes.
- Facilitate the definition of *role-based authority to control process change* and of creation as well as execution rights.
- Collect, analyze and *learn from on-the-fly changes of process instances* in order to create knowledge that might influence the execution of upcoming process instances immediately.
- Facilitate the *formal specification of business rules* to be applied to processes and triggered by certain events during process execution. Business rules are constraints that steer decisions and limit user actions. They *enforce compliance to regulations and business principles* of user-created processes. They also define the sphere of autonomy within which the processes can be acceptably defined.
- Facilitate the *formal definition of goals* to replace prescriptive process refinement to the utmost detail. Instead of rigid activity recipes, these goals are the real process drivers because business users will push the concrete process execution towards achieving the required goal.
- Allow *process execution to be completed if all process goals are achieved* instead of requiring a rigid sequence of activities to be executed.
- Facilitate the *partitioning of goals* into formally specified achievements.
- *Link achievements directly to real-world outcomes* so as to be observable as closely to the desired result as possible. Ideally, they should rely on customer feedback instead of statistical extrapolation of abstract performance indicators.
- Facilitate *process optimization based on achievements* to ensure compliance with any Service Level Agreement (SLA) or the cheapest way of process execution according to some applicable measurement of cost or preference.

- Implement *real-time or near-time process analysis* to facilitate immediate reaction to deviations in the expected process outcomes. This real-time analysis induces a self-monitoring component that helps alert and react in a timely fashion.
- *Link processes with process owners and process teams* that span departmental boundaries, thus fostering a collaborative and open culture in the organization.
- Provide *change management functionality for process-related entities* like business rules, contextual data and process content. Nothing is fixed forever, even strategies change, thus an adaptive BPM system needs to be easily evolvable itself.

This process of incremental but continuous explicitation of the tacit knowledge of the actors and of the implicit rules of the context is aligned with the idea of an ideal *enterprise physics* paradigm [24], that helps organizations and enterprises know themselves and their ecosystem in a more systematic way and needs support by adequate process management tools and frameworks that support this incremental formalization style [34].

16.2.3 Challenges

As the adaptive approach gains first ground in industry, some enthusiasts of the first hour like Max J. Pucher—called the *Guru of Adaptive* by the adaptivity community—postulate a radical break from tradition and the transition to a fundamentally different approach of managing processes in organizations in order to leverage an adaptive paradigm. Being less dogmatic and more pragmatic, one might appreciate the advantages of an appropriate integration of both concepts, the traditional approach driven by process-templates as well as the adaptive approach empowering business users. Customers of Business Process Management Systems (BPMS) should not be forced to make an either-or decision, as most processes would best be specified as hybrids between the two worlds comprising structured and unstructured parts and features. The challenge for organizations is to find the right balance between forcing control top-down and empowering business users to adapt processes bottom-up.

The challenge for research—especially in software development—is to create a methodology as well as architectural solutions and behavioral models that provide the required capability, flexibility, and structured guidance in finding this balance. By now, despite the anticipated capabilities, there is little research about an appropriate methodology, although the idea of continuously adapting predefined processes has had proposers for a long time.

The ADEPT2 system [29] focuses on process schema evolution and change propagation to already running instances, which addresses the need of process migration on the fly for long running processes. ADEPT2 processes are modeled by applying high-level change operations with pre- and post-conditions that ensure structural correctness-by-design of the resulting process model. A model-driven approach for the assertion and preservation of semantic constraints has been proposed [18].

Process mining techniques have been used to support business process discovery [9]. They analyze historical information from log files of existing business applications in order to mine actual business processes that might be unknown and hidden.

Finally, process mining techniques have been also incorporated in the ADEPT2 system to mine log files of executing processes for harmonization purposes, in order to extract a single process model from a set of different variants resulting from user-driven changes of existing templates. However, the basic assumptions underlying process mining techniques are that there is a single *exact* process buried under a bunch of more or less structured information in log files, and that these log files are complete and reliable. This is usually not the case even for prescriptive processes designed and enforced in the traditional way. Too many exceptions and variants that in practice are unavoidable and coded into the "canonical" best practice processes implemented in industrial solutions, blur the picture one can extract from real execution logs. Thus,

> *"process mining, in order to become more meaningful, and to become applicable in a wider array of practical settings, needs to address the problems it has with unstructured processes"* [9].

By now, the effort of applying process mining on a set of process variants still presumes a single reference model instead of allowing multiple concurrent process variants of equal value [17].

In order to handle highly adaptive or even ad-hoc processes that gain their structure only at execution time we need research on (automated) learning of complex systems and on reasoning methodologies that can use the information so gained to inform correction or optimization. As depicted in Fig. 16.1 on the right, the assessment of achievements with respect to the goals, produces useful feedback. This information should be learned, and inform the use of flexibility for future cases. As we see in the figure, we propose to do this both from the perspective of business management as well as from the perspective of process actors. This learning and feedback cycle is a self-management loop, and is at the very heart of an adaptive process management approach. In order to deal with it, research has to find innovative ways to capture barely tangible interrelations between process variations and complex business transactions/events. The problems to be solved comprise asking for the reason for changing a particular process, how to determine whether a change is significant or even crucial, and what are the consequences for prevailing process variants.

16.3 Towards Automated Integration to a Virtual Service Platform

Every business process needs to be adapted at some point in time. This has been the reason for introducing a pro-active management of the process life-cycle in classical BPM approaches. However, maximum benefit of the adaptive approach can be achieved in dynamic business environments, especially if individual services are carried out in a custom-tailored or project-driven manner. In this setting innovative processes are crucial for business success. Unfortunately, because of their less-structured nature processes of this kind are barely supported by rigid enterprise systems. On the other hand, these systems are considered essential whenever organizations need to manage complex business processes. Thus Enterprise Resource Planning (ERP) is the key IT system of today's business solutions.

The concerns of ERP users summarized in the motivation are still insufficiently addressed by the large suppliers as well as by smaller ERP vendors. Moreover, open source products run well behind the state of the art of modern software development techniques in their development. Specifically, the three techniques we consider most promising in the context of a future generation of ERP products are as follows:

- *plugin architectures* at the platform level, that help realize a product-line like collection of features
- *service-orientation* for the production and provision of customer-driven and community-specific functionality, combined with
- a *declarative* approach to software assembly and company-level customization.

The three techniques, taken in combination, have the potential to radically change the way ERP systems are conceived, provisioned, and deployed in individual businesses. In particular, as the typical system landscape in enterprises can be extremely heterogeneous, such techniques are even more desirable. This landscape often comprises one or more ERP systems together with many other legacy systems, custom made products, or even spreadsheets, e.g. used as planning and decision making tools. Service-oriented architectures can help in composing all these systems into heterogeneous applications [4, 6, 13, 14, 19, 20, 33] tailored to the particular needs of the users.

The potential of Service Oriented Architectures combined with a declarative approach to software assembly becomes apparent in the XMDD approach [23] (see also, Chap. 10). Corresponding plugin-architecture-oriented development frameworks like the jABC[3] [35] directly support 'safe' user-driven process adaptation by automatic service orchestration from high-level declarative specifications [5, 15, 16, 22].

16.3.1 Import of Third Party Services

Taking SAP-ERP as an example of an ERP system with a large installed base and not designed for business process agility, we show here two ways of integrating SAP services into a business-level service-oriented platform that correspond to the traditional and to the agile approaches of service platform integration, respectively.

---

[3]The jABC Developers' Website is here: http://www.jabc.de.

Fig. 16.2 Architecture of the communication between the SIBs and SAP-ERP

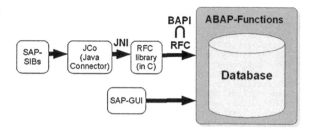

The way to access SAP's functionalities is via a proprietary protocol called Remote Function Call (RFC). The SAP-ERP system plays the role of the service provider (server) and is accessible by a corresponding C library (client). Figure 16.2 shows on the right the SAP-ERP system; for our purposes it can be seen as a database that is surrounded by specialized functionalities that are implemented using the SAP-specific programming language ABAP. SAP-ERP can be used as is by means of the SAP native GUI (as shown on the bottom), or it can be made available to other programming environments by means of specific adaptation/transformation chains, as shown in the variant that goes over RFC and JCo to a service.

We consider now the concrete example of how to define a simple service that adds new material to the ERP system, and we compare two ways of providing access to SAP as a service along the upper tool chain.

16.3.2 The State-of-the-Art Approach to Native Service Integration

The usual way to extend SAP-ERP's native functionalities is by means of programming extensions to it (called 'SAP customization' in the terminology of the many companies that provide this service). This is done by encapsulating the native SAP-ERP services with manually written wrapper code. The wrapped native service can be used directly inside other programs, or deployed as a web service to be orchestrated, for example, by a Business Process Execution Language (BPEL)[4] engine. Adding material to SAP-ERP is a multi-step process: it requires the use of several native SAP-ERP services and the programming of a suitable business logic (actually a small business process) that organizes these steps. The modern way of following the traditional approach requires therefore coding for the wrappers, that encapsulate the native API calls via RFC and make them available for a C or Java or Web service environment, and then additional coding for the workflow (a C or Java program), or a BPEL service orchestration. Assuming that a Java integration is wished, we use the Java Native Interface (JNI) as a middle layer to encapsulate the C code: this is the Java Connector in the middle of Fig. 16.2.

Figure 16.3 shows the (simplified) Java code for calling the Business Application Programming Interface (BAPI) of SAP-ERP's method to add new material.

---

[4]The BPEL TC website is here: http://www.oasis-open.org/committees/wsbpel/.

```
...
JCO.Client client = JCO.createClient("001", "user", "apassword", "EN",
"some.hostname.com", "00");
client.connect();
JCO.Repository repository = new JCO.Repository("myRepository", client);
IFunctionTemplate functionTemplate =
repository.getFunctionTemplate("BAPI_MATERIAL_SAVEDATA");
JCO.Function function = functionTemplate.getFunction();
ParameterList importParameterList = function.getImportParameterList();
JCO.Structure headData = importParameterList.getStructure("HEADDATA");
headData.setValue("M1234", "MATERIAL");
headData.setValue("HAWA", "MATL_TYPE");
headData.setValue("1", "IND_SECTOR");
JCO.Structure clientData = importParameterList.getStructure("CLIENTDATA");
clientData.setValue("PCE", "BASE_UOM_ISO");
clientData.setValue("002", "MATL_GROUP");
JCO.Structure clientDataX = function.getImportStructure("CLIENTDATAX");
clientDataX.setValue("X", "BASE_UOM_ISO");
clientDataX.setValue("X", "MATL_GROUP");
JCO.Parameter tableParameterList = function.getTableParameterList();
JCO.Table descriptionTable = tableParameterList.getTable("MATERIALDESCRIPTION");
descriptionTable.appendRow();
descriptionTable.setValue("e", "LANGU");
descriptionTable.setValue("computer mouse", "MATL_DESC");
client.execute(function);
JCO.ParameterList exportParameterList = function.getExportParameterList();
JCO.Structure returnStructure = exportParameterList.getStructure("RETURN");
if (!(returnStructure.getString("TYPE").equals("") ||
returnStructure.getString("TYPE").equals("S"))) {
        String errorMessage = returnStructure.getString("MESSAGE");
        throw new Exception(errorMessage);
}
System.out.println("Material successfully added!");
client.disconnect();
...
```

Fig. 16.3 The Java code to call a BAPI method

Writing such code is a technical task; the Java Connector works at a quite low application level, however, the depicted code is still much simpler than what would be needed when using this functionality inside a real service implementation.

As one can see, many steps are repeated while invoking a BAPI method (e.g., the creation of the connection, the repository, and the usage of the FunctionTemplate). For the function call itself, the programmer needs concrete knowledge of all the names and acronyms of the parameters as well as all possible values. It is this knowledge and understanding of a cryptical API that makes SAP IT consultants so valuable and integration projects so complicated and costly. In this simple example we need the knowledge that the input data is divided into head data and client data, and that the acronym for the material type is called MATL_TPYE.

Unfortunately, once a method is invoked there is no direct feedback, more programming is needed to analyze the return parameter(s). In case of an error the return parameters contain an error code and a related description. This analysis code is the same for each BAPI method call to invoke.

The global picture of how to provide external access to the SAP functionalities in this setting thus needs low-level programming towards a 'historically grown' API, and repetitive code structures that basically consist of a series of invocations and subsequent checks of the returned items.

16.3.3 The Automated Approach to Service Integration: The Import Wizard

Instead of resorting to programmers to create the function calling code by hand on a case-by-case basis, we can leverage the observation that this code performs the same tasks over and over again, and that the SAP system provides useful meta-information about itself and its functions.

To create a business-level service palette that uses the SAP-ERP native functionalities we can instead apply the XMDD approach to service integration, organize the integration into a dedicated process, and ultimately provide a service that automates these steps and guides the business expert through the import process of a service functionality using a graphical user interface.

The code of Fig. 16.3 can be seen as a kind of pattern collection. It has quite a few technical functions that are generic in the sense that they suffice to reach all goals needed for integration of single functionalities, but which are tedious to manually implement. Ideally, this code should be automatically compiled from something more abstract, and once generated, it should be widely retargetable and reusable. This can be achieved in jABC by generating *parametrized SIBs* for each BAPI call.[5] To generate SIBs with the appropriate parameters, the user only has to be aware of the high-level BAPI layer which is much more familiar than dealing with the low level technicalities of the RFC/JCo view. This means that it suffices that a business expert knows which parameters should be used in order to generate SIB components.

To do so, jABC provides a wizard that exploits the type of service to be encapsulated to support the service import. This wizard collects from the user all the necessary information and generates the SIBs needed to invoke BAPI calls or to show GUI windows that ask for interactive input information or display the feedback information. In our example, if we invoke the method to add new material, the corresponding SIBs should query the user for the material number, type, and description. A screenshot of the wizard's GUI is shown in Fig. 16.4.

Thus, through the use of jABC, no programming is needed; the user enters the name of the BAPI function to be integrated, then the user can access the corresponding help text obtained directly from the SAP-ERP system, and decide about the fields of the business object and the input parameters of interest. In the following steps the user can choose in detail which parts of the export parameters should be taken into account. The output GUI is then configured and the SIBs are generated during the final step. As a result, the business expert obtains the set of ready SIBs that perform all the necessary tasks. The user can now employ them to orchestrate in a relatively simple fashion the processes needed and run these processes within jABC's execution environment as shown in the next section.

The control flow depicted in Fig. 16.5 shows in more detail how the wizard works. By default the wizard creates three SIBs for each BAPI function: one for

---

[5]BAPI is the SAP-specific business-level API, that describes the native business objects.

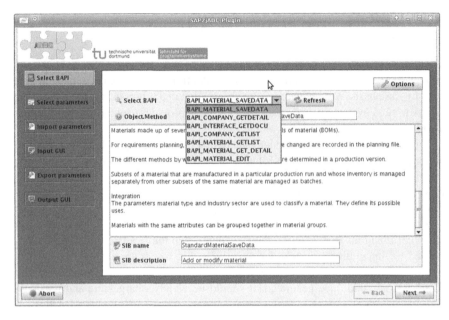

Fig. 16.4 Selection of the BAPI method in the import wizard

an input GUI, one to call the native function and one for the output GUI. Once the wizard has established a connection to the ERP system a concrete BAPI function can be selected and the wizard loads the needed metadata from the Business Object Repository (BOR) of the ERP system. On the first wizard screen the user provides a name and a description for the new SIB. On the second screen the user selects all the relevant parameters of the function and defines for each parameter details like a name and a help text, this whenever the wording from the BOR is either too cryptic or incomplete. The next screen defines the GUI for the input SIB, e.g., the order of the fields or to split them on different tabs. After selecting the output parameters the user can define the user interface for the output SIB. Finally, the generation of the SIB code starts, and the generated code is automatically compiled and loaded into the jABC. The code generation is performed by a Velocity template engine that combines the data provided by the user with static data from a set of code templates and then produces the code for the SIBs.

16.3.4 Practical Impact: Orchestrating SAP Services in an XMDD Style

Using a SIB is fundamentally different than using a Web service (e.g., in BPEL). Using SIBs means choosing ready-to-use business components from a provided collection, whereas using a Web service in a process model means choosing an invoke-activity and then connecting this activity with a certain partner link from

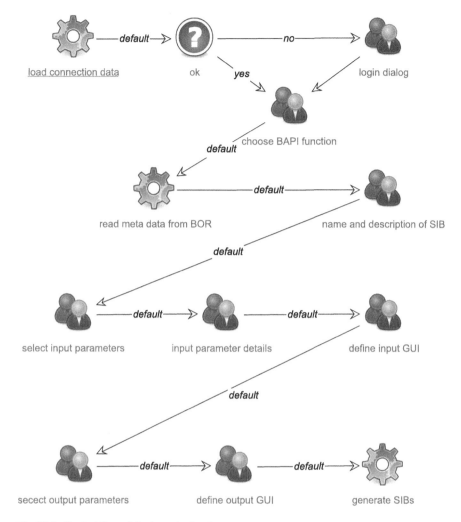

Fig. 16.5 Control flow of the import wizard

some WSDL which can be found at some URI. The latter is still similar to the integration of native APIs just discussed, and not what business users want to do.

Seen from a behavioral point of view, the conceptual mismatch between the two perspectives becomes obvious: a Web service offers a functionality that can be accessed via a conversation with its operations. The conversation requires one or more calls (invoke operations) to it and corresponding answers. The business user, on the contrary, uses a Web service from within the own native context. The user is faced with potentially a series of data adaptation and process mediation steps before the original native request is formulated in a way consumable by the Web service. For each call and answer, this transformation chain strikes. Therefore, the business user does not see in reality the Web service as a single and directly usable unit. Rather

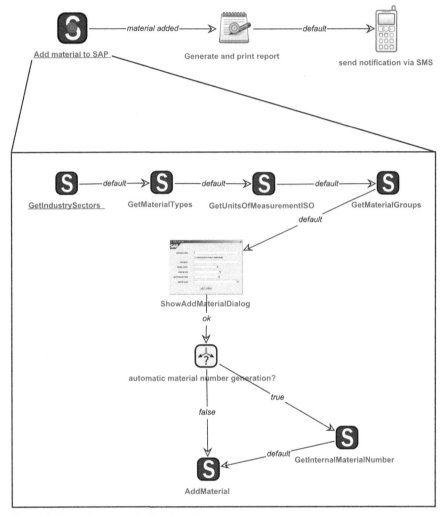

Fig. 16.6 Example process "add material"

he perceives every interaction individually, and sees it as a distant thing at the end of a translation chain. The granularity of the service consumption is thus typically provider-centric: the user sees the calls, not the service in its entirety.

As an example of an overarching process spanning different (service) platforms that an empowered business expert may like to be able to define and execute, we consider the case where a shop owner would like to add new material to shop owner's ERP system, then generate a new list of all materials and notify a colleague that this addition has happened. Figure 16.6 shows the jABC process that implements this on the basis of an SAP-ERP SIB palette generated with the import wizard, OpenOffice to generate and print the report, and the notification services of the IMS Open-SOA platform at Fraunhofer FOKUS in Berlin. The process has a typical structure and consists of two subprocesses, one (shown in the figure) to orchestrate the access to SAP and one within OpenOffice. The last SIB notifies the supervisor of the user via Short Message Service (SMS). Analogously to the SAP integration, also the orchestrated OpenOffice process uses SIBs that are imported third party service components to remotely control the software.

The subprocess of adding the material begins with several SIBs which retrieve data from the SAP system: a list of all industry sectors followed by all material types, the units of measurement and the material groups. All this data is used to prepare the drop-down entries in the GUI which comes as next step and displays this form to the user. Here the domain expert can input all necessary data, and also specify whether the material number should be input manually or generated automatically by the SAP system. This information can be provided here all at once, while in the original SAP-ERP GUI it would be necessary to move around between several masks to find and fill up each field individually. For automatic number generation the SIB automatic material number generation proceeds towards the SIB which asks the SAP system for the next free material number. The last SIB in this process, finally, is the one that actually performs the call of the desired BAPI method.

The following section presents an analysis of native APIs of ERP systems. If these APIs are intended to provide the foundation for the development of services, then it is clear that there are more stringent requirements needed in the definition and design of these APIs than if the designers relied on the intuition and knowledge held by human programmers working to tease out a functional understanding. The perspective of using APIs in an automated, service-oriented environment has led us to identifying a set of domain-independent characteristics that we believe are useful to assess the quality of an ERP's APIs [7].

16.4 Technical Requirements to ERP APIs

The dire status in the ERP commercial product landscape is illustrated in the detailed analysis of ERP APIs for three major ERP vendors done in [7], which we discuss in this section. That analysis concerns market leaders in the segments for large, middle, and small businesses. The authors found, in general, a lack of comprehensiveness and organization both between and within vendor APIs. While much work has been accomplished in designing development rules and guidelines for the user interface, no such guidelines direct the development of APIs so that such resources can be drawn on in a move to a plug-in oriented architecture. The evaluation concerned the APIs of five different solutions: SAP BAPI; SAP eSOA; Microsoft Dynamics NAV Web services; and two versions of Intuit Quickbooks, the online and the desktop edition; along 18 requirements that cover the access provision to 8 key business objects. Other than the work usually done on API analysis, which concerns the adequacy to be dealt with by programmers, this evaluation considers the entire API ecosystem in a systemic and holistic perspective. This work thus includes the aspects of service provisioning, ease of integration and automation, propagation of information to the user.

Fig. 16.7 Requirement
categories (from [7])

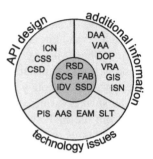

The four categories of requirements are depicted in Fig. 16.7. The *core requirements* in the center are the most important category. They are the central requirements for an enterprise API to support a truly service-oriented development. Usability features are grouped together under *API design*, everything regarding to the underlying technology belongs to *technology issues* and the category *additional information* concerns the possibilities of providing additional data and documentation. These requirements reflect the experience made during the implementation of tools for (semi-) automatic SIB-generation, the feedback and observations from lectures at TU Dortmund University and Potsdam University as well as from the experiences drawn in [10] and [1].

Core requirements A *Registry for service discovery (RSD)* in order to systematically get hold of the services (resp. to provide them) is an obvious must for any service provider, as is the *Soundness and Completeness of Service definitions (SCS)*. Without *Full Accessibility of Business objects (FAB)* the service-oriented design is restricted to the parts made available. Violating the *Stability of Service Definitions (SSD)* drastically impairs the acceptance of provided services: version changes should not break previously working functionality. In contrast, *Input Data Validation (IDV)* is not really a must but still an important feature, in particular for solutions like the SAP solutions, where the formats are 'historically' grown. While the first four requirements of this category are without doubt necessary preconditions for a successful service-oriented development, the last is of lesser importance but still a major factor for gaining acceptance.

API design An *Intuitive and Consistent Naming (ICN)* certainly supports efficiency, in particular in cases where no automatic input validation is supported. The same applies to *Clear and Simple Structure (CSS)*, and to *Complete and Sound Documentation (CDS)*. These three requirements are not really a must, but still of major importance to achieve acceptance.

Technology issues Technology issues concern *Platform Independency through the use of Standards (PIS)*, *API Access Security (AAS)*, *Easy Authentication Mechanism (EAM)*, and *Speed resulting from Latency and Throughput (SLT—not evaluated here)*. While AAS may be easily considered a must, the other requirements are less stringent but certainly characterize features one would expect from a professional solution.

Additional information This class of requirements marks good design and practice: *Documentation Available per API (DAA)* denotes the ability to provide API

Table 16.1 Evaluation overview (from [7]). A plus (+) indicates that the requirement is met, a circle (○) a partial satisfaction, and a minus (−) a full failure

	BAPI	eSOA	NAV	QBOE	QBDE
RSD	−	+	○	○	
SCS	○	+	+	○	
FAB	−	○	+	−	
IDV	+	+	+	+	
SSD	+	+	−	−	
ICN	○	○	+	+	
CSS	○	−	+	+	
CSD	−	○	−	○	
PIS	○	+	○	○	−
AAS	○	○	○	+	○
EAM	+	+	+	−	○
DAA	+	−	−	○	
VAA	+	−	+	+	
DOP	−	+	+	+	
VRA/GIS/ISN	−	−	−	−	

documentation via the API itself. *Value offers Available per API (VAA)* refers to structured ways of data selection beyond text input fields, like drop down menus, in order to free the user from dealing with syntactical details. *Declaration of Optional Parameters (DOP)* means transparency of required vs. optional input.

The *Validation Rules available per API (VRA)*, *Graphical Icons symbolizing the Services (GIS)*, and *Internationalized Service Names (ISN)* requirements are not met by any of the evaluated APIs, but still mark features that would ease the API's use.

16.4.1 Evaluation Profiles

Table 16.1 summarizes the results. It is surprising how far all solutions are from meeting all the requirements, a situation probably due to their individual business profiles.

Looking at the two SAP solutions, the move from the proprietary RFC protocol to platform independent Web services was an important step forward. The number of provided services grew enormously, even though it is incomplete. On the other hand some changes made automation more difficult, e.g., the change to free text input parameters where a menu-driven choice among alternatives would be more suitable (cf. requirement VAA). The overall poor coverage of business object access operations in the SAP solutions witnesses the need to extend the collection of services in a customization phase. Customization is often time-consuming and expensive, and is typical for the SAP business model. Not surprisingly, new SAP services are better implemented on the basis of eSOA, in particular because of the documentation facilities provided by the enterprise service registry and the ES-Wiki.

The Dynamics NAV solution scores with its good coverage of basic CRUD operations on business objects, which makes it a good basis for less demanding customers that can live with the services provided by this ERP-system. On the other hand, Dynamics NAV provides little support for people wanting to develop their own services, which confirms the common opinion that this ERP-system addresses small and medium enterprises with standard requirements.

Quickbooks is Windows-based, and not designed for scale. Its good service documentation API make it nevertheless an attractive and economic solution for small companies with little demand.

It is obvious that none of the evaluated systems is ready yet for truly agile BP development. This is not too surprising for the Quickbooks solution, and the weaknesses the other solutions seem to reflect the current underlying business model. Still, it is possible to build on both SAP's eSOA and Dynamics NAV. For the former the main hurdle is to extend the coverage of the APIs (cf. requirement FAB), whereas Dynamics NAV mostly suffers from lacking stability (cf. SSD). The other weaknesses may be comfortably covered by a surrounding development framework like the jABC.

16.5 Conclusion

We have discussed two major streams of business process development, the aggressive new style of ad-hoc business process development, reminiscent of similar movements for agile application development like eXtreme Programming and Scrum, and the more traditional, largely ERP-dominated business process management. We have argued that both these streams fail to adequately address vital requirements; the former, because the lack of structure hampers scalability, both in size and along the lifecycle, and the latter, because their rigid structure inhibits agility. In addition we have seen that market leading solutions have severe shortcomings concerning their APIs which reflect fundamental failings in the way ERP systems are delivered to the customer.

However, the unacceptably long latency of change with traditional ERP systems is too high to compete with the rapid changes in common business environments. For example, a lot of benefit and value that would be deliverable by small, adaptive day to day changes (akin to a Kanban-style approach [2]) go wasted, because the micro-steps of incremental adaptations are ignored by the traditional holistic approaches.

Research in ERP implementation success point to high failure rates. For example, the Robbins-Gioia Survey (2001) [30] found that 51% of the companies viewed their ERP implementation as unsuccessful and 46% of those companies with ERP systems in place felt that they did not fully understand how to use their systems. In an article analyzing the current status of ERP systems [27], Patrick Marshall states

"The leading cause of ERP angst, some analysts say, is the implicit notion that one system can fit all needs." Marshall reports on a study by IDC's Software Business Solutions Group that found that "in some cases 80 percent of staff members' time is spent working around the system." For example, in an implementation we have been involved with, the software allowed end-users to store finished products within only one location in inventory. Work-arounds to deal with the issue were painful. In an agile environment users that know the business process stream could implement a revised version allowing multiple locations and give value to the organization. As noted, the current culture of end users is to not adapt to system constraints but to find a way to continue to do business in the way they believe is important and to work around any inherent system constraints. Such statistics validate the proposal that a change is mandatory in how ERP systems are constructed and implemented. We believe that available technology in terms of service orientation and model driven development taken in combination have the potential to radically change the way BPM is conceived, provisioned, and deployed in individual businesses and would lead to better success.

Our proposal of putting more emphasis on system development and execution directly into the hands of the key stakeholders, the person responsible for the work and those performing the work, resonates with the current understanding of ERP failure due to excessive system complexity and lack of training and education.[6] Users wish to find ways to make systems simpler and more understandable so that they are able to perform specific tasks as tailored to their needs as possible. They also wish to understand how decisions are made. Both of these concerns are fundamental to the notion of empowerment and are present in our proposal.

The complete bottom-up process definition strategy proposed by ad-hoc methods may however not be the best: while single workers are close to what happens and can be essential in optimizing an existing process, once it is broadly defined, the scope of the entire process is defined at a managerial or strategic level. Thus it is there that the responsibility, the decision power, and the coarse-grain definition need to be homed. As in mission critical software, one distinguishes the goal, the strategic, the tactical, and the operational levels: this is a clear guideline for the organization of autonomy, competence, and design level that matches well the proposed one-thing approach. Clearly such an understanding of the new agile business world requires the ERP industry to master new flexible application environments that support co-innovation to an unprecedented extent.

References

1. Ackermann, A.: Automatische Generierung von Softwarebausteinen zur Modellierung ERP-System übergreifender Geschäftsprozesse. Diploma thesis, Universität Potsdam (2010). In German

---

[6]The Site for Open Source ERP examines the real reasons for failure of ERP systems here: http://www.open-source-erp-site.com/failure-of-erp.html.

2. Anderson, D.J.: Kanban: Successful Evolutionary Change for Your Technology Business. Blue Hole Press, Belize (2001)
3. Beck, K.: Extreme Programming Explained: Embrace Change. Addison-Wesley, Reading (2000)
4. Borovskiy, V., Zeier, A., Koch, W., Plattner, H.: Enabling enterprise composite applications on top of ERP systems. In: Kirchberg, M., Hung, P.C.K., Carminati, B., Chi, C.-H., Kanagasabai, R., Valle, E.D., Lan, K.-C., Chen, L.-J. (eds.) APSCC, pp. 492–497. IEEE Press, New York (2009)
5. Braun, V., Margaria, T., Steffen, B., Yoo, H., Rychly, T.: Safe service customization. In: IEEE Communication Soc. Workshop on Intelligent Network, Colorado Springs, CO (USA), vol. 7, p. 4. IEEE Comput. Soc., Los Alamitos (1997)
6. Kubczak, C., Margaria, T., Steffen, B.: Mashup development for everybody: a planning-based approach. In: SMR2, Proc. 3rd Int. Worksh. on Service Matchmaking and Resource Retrieval in the Semantic Web, Colocated with ISWC-2009, Washington, DC, USA, CEUR-WS, vol. 525 (2009)
7. Doedt, M., Steffen, B.: Requirement-driven evaluation of remote ERP-system solutions: a service-oriented perspective. In: Proc. SEW 2011. IEEE Comput. Soc., Washington, USA (to appear) (2011)
8. Grässle, P., Schacher, M.: Agile Unternehmen Durch Business Rules – Der Business Rules Ansatz. Springer, Berlin (2006)
9. Günther, C.W., Van Der Aalst, W.M.P.: Fuzzy mining: adaptive process simplification based on multi-perspective metrics. In: Proc. of the 5th Int. Conf. on Business Process Management, pp. 328–343. Springer, Berlin (2007)
10. Karla, D.: Automatische Generierung von Softwarebausteinen zur Anbindung von SAP-Diensten an ein Business-Prozess-Management-System. Diploma thesis, Technische Universität Dortmund (2009). In German
11. Ken Schwaber, M.B.: Agile Software Development with Scrum. Prentice Hall, New York (2001)
12. Kubczak, C., Jörges, S., Margaria, T., Steffen, B.: eXtreme model-driven design with jABC. In: Proc. of the Tools and Consultancy Track of the 5th European Conference on Model-Driven Architecture Foundations and Applications (ECMDA-FA), vol. WP09-12 of CTIT Proceedings, pp. 78–99. CTIT, Enschede (2009)
13. Kubczak, C., Margaria, T., Steffen, B., Nagel, R.: Service-oriented mediation with jABC/jETI. In: Jain, R., Sheth, A., Petrie, C., Margaria, T., Lausen, H., Zaremba, M. (eds.) Semantic Web Services Challenge. Semantic Web and Beyond, vol. 8, pp. 71–99. Springer, New York (2009)
14. Lamprecht, A.-L., Margaria, T., Steffen, B.: Bio-jETI: a framework for semantics-based service composition. BMC Bioinform. **10**(10), S8 (2009)
15. Lamprecht, A.-L., Naujokat, S., Margaria, T., Steffen, B.: Constraint-guided workflow composition based on the EDAM ontology. In: SWAT4LS 2010, Proc. 3rd Worksh. on Semantic Web Applications and Tools for Life Sciences (2010)
16. Lamprecht, A.-L., Naujokat, S., Margaria, T., Steffen, B.: Semantics-based composition of EMBOSS services. J. Biomed. Semant. **2**(Suppl 1), 5 (2011)
17. Li, C., Reichert, M., Wombacher, A.: Mining business process variants: challenges, scenarios, algorithms. Data Knowl. Eng. **70**(5), 409–434 (2011)
18. Ly, L., Rinderle-Ma, S., Göser, K., Dadam, P.: On enabling integrated process compliance with semantic constraints in process management systems. Inf. Syst. Front. (2010). doi:10.1007/s10796-009-9185-9
19. Margaria, T., Kubczak, C., Steffen, B.: Bio-jETI: a service integration, design, and provisioning platform for orchestrated bioinformatics processes. BMC Bioinform. **9**(S-4) (2008). doi:10.1186/1471-2105-9-S4-S12
20. Margaria, T., Nagel, R., Steffen, B.: Remote integration and coordination of verification tools in jETI. In: ECBS'05. 12th IEEE Int. Conf. and Workshops on the Engineering of Computer-Based Systems, pp. 431–436. IEEE Comput. Soc., Los Alamitos (2005)
21. Margaria, T., Steffen, B.: Service Engineering: Linking Business and IT. IEEE Comput. **39**(10), 45–55 (2006)

22. Margaria, T., Steffen, B.: LTL guided planning: revisiting automatic tool composition in ETI. In: Proc. SEW 2007, 31st IEEE Annual Software Engineering Workshop, Loyola College, Baltimore, MD, USA, pp. 214–226. IEEE Comput. Soc., Los Alamitos (2007)
23. Margaria, T., Steffen, B.: Agile IT: thinking in user-centric models. In: Margaria, T., Steffen, B. (eds.) ISoLA. Communications in Computer and Information Science, vol. 17, pp. 490–502. Springer, Berlin (2008)
24. Margaria, T., Steffen, B.: An enterprise physics approach for evolution support in heterogeneous service-oriented landscapes. In: 3G ERP Workshop, Copenhagen, DK (2008)
25. Margaria, T., Steffen, B.: Business process modeling in the jABC: the one-thing approach. In: Cardoso, J., Van Der Aalst, W. (eds.) Handbook of Research on Business Process Modeling. IGI Global, Hershey (2009)
26. Margaria, T., Steffen, B.: Continuous Model-Driven Engineering. Computer 42, 106–109 (2009)
27. Marshall, P.: ERP, piece by piece (2010). In GCN, Government Computing News, June 17, 2010. http://gcn.com/Articles/2010/06/21/ERP-evolve-or-die.aspx?Page=1&p=1
28. Pink, D.H.: Drive. Riverhead Books, New York (2009)
29. Reichert, M., Rinderle, S., Kreher, U., Dadam, P.: Adaptive process management with adept2. In: Proc. of the 21st Int. Conf. on Data Engineering (ICDE '05), pp. 1113–1114. IEEE Comput. Soc., Washington (2005)
30. Robbins-Gioia LLC: ERP Survey Results Point to Need For Higher Implementation Success (2002). Press Release, January 28, 2002, Alexandria, Virginia, USA
31. Shepherd, T.: Moving from anticipation to adaptation. In: Swenson, K.D. (ed.) Mastering the Unpredictable: How Adaptive Case Management Will Revolutionize the Way That Knowledge Workers Get Things Done. Meghan-Kiffer Press, Tampa (2010)
32. Sinur, J.: BPM is shifting into high gear. Gartner Blog Network, April 22 (2010)
33. Steffen, B., Margaria, T., Braun, V.: The electronic tool integration platform: concepts and design. Int. J. Softw. Tools Technol. Transf. 1, 9–30 (1997)
34. Steffen, B., Margaria, T., Claßen, A., Braun, V.: Incremental formalization: a key to industrial success. Softw. Concepts Tools 17(2), 78 (1996)
35. Steffen, B., Margaria, T., Nagel, R., Jörges, S., Kubczak, C.: Model-driven development with the jABC. In: Bin, E., Ziv, A., Ur, S. (eds.) Haifa Verification Conference. Lecture Notes in Computer Science, vol. 4383, pp. 92–108. Springer, Berlin (2006)

Chapter 17
On the Problem of Matching Database Schemas

Marco A. Casanova, Karin K. Breitman, Antonio L. Furtado,
Vânia M.P. Vidal, and José A. F. de Macêdo

17.1 Introduction

The problem of satisfiability is often taken for granted when designing database
schemas, perhaps based on the implicit assumption that real data provides a consistent database state. However, this implicit assumption is unwarranted when the
schema results from the integration of several data sources, as in a data warehouse or
in a mediation environment. When we have to combine semantically heterogeneous
data sources, we should expect conflicting data or, equivalently, mutually inconsistent sets of integrity constraints. The same problem also occurs during schema
redesign, when changes in some constraints might create conflicts with other parts
of the database schema. Naturally, the satisfiability problem is aggravated when the
schema integration process has to deal with a large number of source schemas, or
when the schema to be redesigned is complex.

We may repeat similar remarks for the problem of detecting redundancies in a
schema, that is, the problem of detecting which constraints are logically implied by
others. The situation is analogous if we replace the question of satisfiability by the
question of logical implication.

A third similar, but more sophisticated problem is to automatically generate the
constraints of a mediated schema from the sets of constraints of export schemas.
The constraints of the mediated schema are relevant for a correct understanding of
what the semantics of the external schemas have in common.

With this motivation, we focus on the crucial challenge of selecting a sufficiently
expressive family of schemas that is useful for defining real-world schemas and yet
is tractable, i.e., for which there are practical procedures to test the satisfiability
of a schema, to detect redundancies in a schema, and to combine the constraints
of export schemas into a single set of mediated schema constraints. The intuitive
metrics for expressiveness here is that the family of schemas should account for

M.A. Casanova (✉)
Department of Informatics, PUC-Rio, Rio de Janeiro, RJ, Brazil
e-mail: casanova@inf.puc-rio.br

M. Hinchey, L. Coyle (eds.), *Conquering Complexity*,
DOI 10.1007/978-1-4471-2297-5_17, © Springer-Verlag London Limited 2012

the commonly used conceptual constructs of OWL, UML, and the ER model. By a practical procedure, we mean a procedure that is polynomial on the size of the set of constraints of the schema.

As an answer to this challenge, we first introduce a family of schemas that we call *extralite schemas with role hierarchies*. Using the OWL jargon, this family supports named classes, datatype and object properties, minCardinalities and max-Cardinalities, InverseFunctionalProperties, which capture simple keys, class subset constraints, and class disjointness constraints. Extralite schemas with role hierarchies also support subset and disjointness constraints defined for datatype and object properties (formalized as atomic roles in Description Logics). We then introduce the subfamily of *restricted extralite schemas with role hierarchies*, which limits the interaction between role hierarchies and cardinality constraints.

Testing satisfiability for extralite schemas with role hierarchies turns out to be EXPTIME-hard, as a consequence of the results in [1]. However, for the restricted schemas, we show how to test strict satisfiability and logical implication in polynomial time. Strict satisfiability imposes the additional restriction that the constraints of a schema must not force classes or properties to be always empty, and is more adequate than the traditional notion of satisfiability in the context of database design.

The syntax and semantics of extralite schemas is that of Description Logics to facilitate the formal analysis of the problems we address. However, we depart from the tradition of Description Logics deduction services, which are mostly based on tableaux techniques [3]. The decision procedures outlined in the chapter are based on the satisfiability algorithm for Boolean formulas in conjunctive normal form with at most two literals per clause, described in [2]. The intuition is that the constraints of an extralite schema can be treated much in the same way as Boolean implications. Furthermore, the implicational structure of the constraints can be completely captured as a *constraint graph*. The results also depend on the notion of Herbrand interpretation for Description Logics.

The notion of constraint graph is the key to meet the challenge posed earlier. It permits expressiveness and decidability to be balanced, in the sense that it accounts for a useful family of constraints and yet leads to decision procedures, which are polynomial on the size of the set of constraints. This balancing is achieved by a careful analysis of how the constraints interact.

Constraint graphs can be used to help detect inconsistencies in a set of constraints and to suggest alternatives to fix the problem. They help solve the query containment and related problems in the context of schema constraints [10]. They can also be used to compute the greatest lower bound of two sets of constraints, which is the basic step of a strategy to automatically generate the constraints of a mediated schema from the sets of constraints of the export schemas [8]. The appendix illustrates, with the help of examples, how to use constraint graphs to address such problems.

The main contributions of the chapter are the family of extralite schemas with role hierarchies, the procedures to test strict satisfiability and logical implication, which explore the structure of sets of constraints, captured as a constraint graph, and the concept of Herbrand interpretation for Description Logics. The results in the chapter indicate that the procedures are consistent and complete for restricted extralite schemas with role hierarchies, and work in polynomial time. These results extend those published in [8] for extralite schemas without role hierarchies.

There is a vast literature on the formal verification of database schemas and on the formalization of ER and UML diagrams. We single out just a few references here. The problem of modeling conceptual schemas in DL is discussed in [4]. DL-Lite is used, for example, in [5, 6] to address schema integration and query answering. A comprehensive survey of the DL-Lite family can be found in [1]. Techniques from Propositional Logic to support the specification of Boolean and multivalued dependencies were addressed in [9].

When compared with the DL-Lite family [1], extralite schemas with role hierarchies are a subset $DL - Lite_{core}^{\mathcal{HN}}$ with role disjunctions. The restricted schemas in turn are a subset of $DL - Lite_{core}^{(\mathcal{HN})}$ with role disjunctions only, which limits the interaction between role inclusions and cardinality constraints. We emphasize that restricted extralite schemas are sufficiently expressive to capture the most familiar constructs of OWL, UML, and the ER model [4], and yet come equipped with useful decision procedures that explore the structure of sets of constraints.

The chapter is organized as follows. Section 17.2 reviews DL concepts and introduces the notion of extralite schemas with role hierarchies. Section 17.3 shows how to test strict satisfiability and logical implication for restricted extralite schemas with role hierarchies. It also outlines proofs for the major results of the chapter, whose details can be found in [7]. Section 17.4 contains examples of the concepts introduced in Sects. 17.2 and 17.3, and briefly discusses two applications of the results of Sect. 17.3. Finally, Sect. 17.5 contains the conclusions.

17.2 A Class of Database Schemas

17.2.1 A Brief Review of Attributive Languages

We adopt a family of *attributive languages* [3] defined as follows. A *language* $\mathcal{L}$ in the family is characterized by an *alphabet* $\mathcal{A}$, consisting of a set of *atomic concepts*, a set of *atomic roles*, the *universal concept* and the *bottom concept*, denoted by $\top$ and $\bot$, respectively, and the *universal role* and the *bottom role*, also denoted by $\top$ and $\bot$, respectively.

The set of *role descriptions* of $\mathcal{L}$ is inductively defined as

- An atomic role and the universal and bottom roles are role descriptions
- If p is a role description, then the following expressions are role descriptions
    p^-: the *inverse* of p
    $\neg p$: the *negation* of p

  The set of *concept descriptions* of $\mathcal{L}$ is inductively defined as

- An atomic concept and the universal and bottom concepts are concept descriptions

- If e is a concept description, p is a role description, and n is a positive integer, then the following expressions are concept descriptions
  - $\neg e$: negation
  - $\exists p$: existential quantification
  - $(\leq np)$: at-most restriction
  - $(\geq np)$: at-least restriction

An *interpretation s* for $\mathcal{L}$ consists of a nonempty set Δ^s, the *domain* of s, whose elements are called *individuals*, and an *interpretation function*, also denoted s, where:

$s(\top) = \Delta^s$ if $\top$ denotes the universal concept
$s(\top) = \Delta^s \times \Delta^s$ if $\top$ denotes the universal role
$s(\bot) = \varnothing$ if $\bot$ denotes the bottom concept or the bottom role
$s(A) \subseteq \Delta^s$ for each atomic concept A of $\mathcal{A}$
$s(P) \subseteq \Delta^s \times \Delta^s$ for each atomic role P of $\mathcal{A}$

The function s is extended to role and concept descriptions of $\mathcal{L}$ as follows (where e is a concept description and p is a role description):

$s(p^-) = s(p)^-$: the inverse of s(p)
$s(\neg p) = \Delta^s \times \Delta^s - s(p)$: the complement of $s(p)$ with respect to $\Delta^s \times \Delta^s$
$s(\neg e) = \Delta^s - s(e)$: the complement of $s(e)$ with respect to Δ^s
$s(\exists p) = \{I \in \Delta^s/(\exists J \in \Delta^s)/(I, J) \in s(p)\}$: the set of individuals that $s(p)$ relates to some individual
$s(\geq np) = \{I \in \Delta^s/|\{J \in \Delta^s/(I, J) \in s(p)\}| \geq n\}$: the set of individuals that $s(p)$ relates to at least n distinct individuals
$s(\leq np) = \{I \in \Delta^s/|\{J \in \Delta^s/(I, J) \in s(p)\}| \leq n\}$: the set of individuals that $s(p)$ relates to at most n distinct individuals

A formula of $\mathcal{L}$ is an expression of the form $u \sqsubseteq v$, called an *inclusion*, or of the form $u|v$, called a *disjunction*, or of the form $u \equiv v$, called an *equivalence*, where both u and v are concept descriptions or both u and v are role descriptions of $\mathcal{L}$. We also say that $u \sqsubseteq v$ is a concept inclusion iff both u and v are concept descriptions, and that $u \sqsubseteq v$ is a role inclusion iff both u and v are role descriptions; and likewise for the other types of formulas.

An interpretation s for $\mathcal{L}$ satisfies $u \sqsubseteq v$ iff $s(u) \subseteq s(v)$, s satisfies $u|v$ iff $s(u) \cap s(v) = \varnothing$, and s satisfies $u \equiv v$ iff $s(u) = s(v)$. A formula σ is a *tautology* iff any interpretation satisfies σ. Two formulas are *tautologically equivalent* iff any interpretation s that satisfies one formula also satisfies the other.

Given a set of formulas Σ, we say that an interpretation s is a *model* of Σ iff s satisfies all formulas in Σ, denoted $s \models \Sigma$. We say that Σ is *satisfiable* iff there is a model of Σ. However, this notion of satisfiability is not entirely adequate in the context of database design since it allows the constraints of a schema to force atomic concepts or atomic roles to be always empty. Hence, we define that an interpretation s is a *strict model* of Σ iff s satisfies all formulas in Σ and $s(C) \neq \varnothing$, for each atomic concept C, and $s(P) \neq \varnothing$, for each atomic role P; we say that Σ is *strictly satisfiable* iff there is a *strict model* for Σ. In addition, we say that Σ *logically implies* a formula σ, denoted $\Sigma \models \sigma$, iff any model of Σ satisfies σ.

17.2.2 Extralite Schemas with Role Hierarchies

An *extralite schema* with *role hierarchies* is a pair $S = (\mathcal{A}, \Sigma)$ such that

- $\mathcal{A}$ is an alphabet, called the *vocabulary* of S.
- Σ is a set of formulas, called the *constraints* of S, which must be of one the forms (where C and D are atomic concepts, P and Q are atomic roles, p denotes P or its inverse P^-, and k is a positive integer):
  - *Domain Constraint*: $\exists P \sqsubseteq C$ (the domain of P is a subset of C)
  - *Range Constraint*: $\exists P^- \sqsubseteq C$ (the range of P is a subset of C)
  - *minCardinality constraint*: $C \sqsubseteq (\geq kp)$ (p maps each individual in C to at least k individuals)
  - *maxCardinality constraint*: $C \sqsubseteq (\leq kp)$ (p maps each individual in C to at most k individuals)
  - *Concept Subset Constraint*: $C \sqsubseteq D$ (C is a subset of D)
  - *Concept Disjointness Constraint*: $C|D$ (C and D are disjoint atomic concepts)
  - *Role Subset Constraint*: $P \sqsubseteq Q$ (P is a subset of Q)
  - *Role Disjointness Constraint*: $P|Q$ (P and Q are disjoint atomic roles)

We say that a formula of one of the above forms is an *extralite constraint*, the concept subset and disjointness constraints of S are the *concept hierarchy* of S, and the role subset and disjointness constraints of S are the *role hierarchy* of S.

We *normalize* a set of extralite constraints by rewriting:

$$
\begin{array}{ll}
\exists P \sqsubseteq C & \text{as } (\geq 1P) \sqsubseteq C \\
\exists P^- \sqsubseteq C & \text{as } (\geq 1P^-) \sqsubseteq C \\
C \sqsubseteq (\leq kP) & \text{as } C \sqsubseteq \neg(\geq k+1P) \\
C \sqsubseteq (\leq kP^-) & \text{as } C \sqsubseteq \neg(\geq k+1P^-) \\
C|D & \text{as } C \sqsubseteq \neg D \\
P|Q & \text{as } P \sqsubseteq \neg Q
\end{array}
$$

The formula on the right-hand side is called the *normal form* of the formula on the left-hand side. Observe that: a formula and its normal form are tautologically equivalent; the normal forms avoid the use of existential quantification and at-most restrictions; negated descriptions occur only on the right-hand side of the normal forms; inverse roles do not occur in role subset or role disjoint constraints.

Furthermore, we *close* the set of extralite constraints by also considering as an extralite constraint any inclusion of one of the forms

$$
\begin{array}{llll}
C \sqsubseteq \bot & (\geq mp) \sqsubseteq \bot & (\geq mp) \sqsubseteq (\geq nq) \\
P \sqsubseteq \bot & (\geq mp) \sqsubseteq \neg C & (\geq mp) \sqsubseteq \neg(\geq nq)
\end{array}
$$

where C is an atomic concept, P is an atomic role, p and q both are atomic roles or both are the inverse of atomic roles, and m and n are positive integers.

Finally, a *restricted extralite schema with role hierarchies* is a schema $S = (\mathcal{A}, \Sigma)$ that satisfies the following restriction:

Restriction (Role Hierarchy Restriction) *If Σ contains a role subset constraint of the form $P \sqsubseteq Q$, then Σ contains no maxCardinality constraints of the forms $C \sqsubseteq (\leq k\ Q)$ or $C \sqsubseteq (\leq k\ Q^-)$, with $k \geq 1$.*

Note that the normalization process will rewrite the above constraints as $C \sqsubseteq \neg(\geq k+1\ Q)$ and $C \sqsubseteq \neg(\geq k+1\ Q^-)$, with $k \geq 1$.

17.3 Testing Strict Satisfiability and Logical Implication

This section first introduces the notion of constraint graph. Then, it defines Herbrand interpretations for Description Logics. Finally, it states results that lead to simple polynomial procedures to test strict satisfiability and logical implication for restricted extralite schemas with role hierarchies.

17.3.1 Representation Graphs

Let Σ be a finite set of normalized extralite constraints and Ω be a finite set of extralite constraint expressions, that is, expression that may occur on the right- or left-hand sides of a normalized constraint. The alphabet is understood as the (finite) set of atomic concepts and roles that occur in Σ and Ω.

We say that the *complement* of a non-negated description c is $\neg c$, and vice-versa. We denote the complement of a description d by $\bar{d}$. Proposition 17.1 states properties of descriptions that will be used in the rest of this section.

Proposition 17.1 *Let e, f and g be concept or role descriptions, P and Q be atomic roles, and p be either P or P^-. Then, we have:*

   (i) $(\geq np) \sqsubseteq (\geq mp)$ *is a tautology, where* $0 < m < n$.
  (ii) $e \sqsubseteq f$ *is tautologically equivalent to* $\bar{f} \sqsubseteq \bar{e}$.
 (iii) *If Σ logically implies $e \sqsubseteq f$ and $f \sqsubseteq g$, then Σ logically implies $e \sqsubseteq g$.*
  (iv) *If Σ logically implies $P \sqsubseteq Q$, then Σ logically implies $(\geq kP) \sqsubseteq (\geq k\ Q)$ and $(\geq kP^-) \sqsubseteq (\geq k\ Q^-)$.*
   (v) *If Σ logically implies $(\geq 1P) \sqsubseteq \neg(\geq 1\ Q)$ or $(\geq 1P^-) \sqsubseteq \neg(\geq 1\ Q^-)$, then Σ logically implies $P \sqsubseteq \neg Q$.*
  (vi) *If Σ logically implies $e \sqsubseteq f$ and $e \sqsubseteq \neg f$, then Σ logically implies $e \sqsubseteq \bot$.*
 (vii) *If Σ logically implies $(\geq 1P) \sqsubseteq \bot$ or $(\geq 1P^-) \sqsubseteq \bot$, then Σ logically implies $P \sqsubseteq \bot$.*
(viii) *If Σ logically implies $P \sqsubseteq \bot$, then Σ logically implies $(\geq mP) \sqsubseteq \bot$, $(\geq mP^-) \sqsubseteq \bot$, $\top \sqsubseteq (\leq nP)$ and $\top \sqsubseteq (\leq nP^-)$, where $m > 0$ and $n \geq 0$.*

In the next definitions, we introduce graphs whose nodes are labeled with expressions or sets of expressions. Then, we use such graphs to create efficient procedures to test if Σ is strictly satisfiable and to decide logical implication for Σ. Finally, it will become clear when we formulate Theorem 17.2 that the definitions must also consider an additional set Ω of constraint expressions.

To simplify the definitions, if a node K is labeled with an expression e, then $\bar{K}$ denotes the node labeled with $\bar{e}$. We will also use $K \to M$ to indicate that there is a path from a node K to a node M, and $K \nrightarrow M$ to indicate that no such path exists; we will use $e \to f$ to denote that there is a path from a node labeled with e to a node labeled with f, and $e \nrightarrow f$ to indicate that no such path exists.

Definition 17.1 The labeled graph $g(\Sigma, \Omega)$ that captures Σ and Ω, where each node is labeled with an expression, is defined in four stages as follows:

Stage 1:
  Initialize $g(\Sigma, \Omega)$ with the following nodes and arcs:

  (i) For each atomic concept C, $g(\Sigma, \Omega)$ has exactly one node labeled with C.
  (ii) For each atomic role P, $g(\Sigma, \Omega)$ has exactly one node labeled with P, one node labeled with $(\geq 1P)$, and one node labeled with $(\geq 1P^-)$.
  (iii) For each expression e that occurs on the right- or left-hand side of an inclusion in Σ, or that occurs in Ω, other than those in (i) or (ii), $g(\Sigma, \Omega)$ has exactly one node labeled with e.
  (iv) For each inclusion $e \sqsubseteq f$ in Σ, $g(\Sigma, \Omega)$ has an arc (M, N), where M and N are the nodes labeled with e and f, respectively.

Stage 2:
  Until no new node or arc can be added to $g(\Sigma, \Omega)$,
    For each role inclusion $P \sqsubseteq Q$ in Σ,
      For each node K,

  (i) If K is labeled with $(\geq kP)$, for some $k > 0$, then add a node L labeled with $(\geq k\ Q)$ and an arc (K, L), if no such node and arc exists.
  (ii) If K is labeled with $(\geq kP^-)$, for some $k > 0$, then add a node L labeled with $(\geq k\ Q^-)$ and an arc (K, L), if no such node and arc exists.
  (iii) If K is labeled with $(\geq k\ Q)$, for some $k > 0$, then add a node L labeled with $(\geq kP)$ and an arc (L, K), if no such node and arc exists.
  (iv) If K is labeled with $(\geq k\ Q^-)$, for some $k > 0$, then add a node L labeled with $(\geq kP^-)$ and an arc (L, K), if no such node and arc exists.

Stage 3:
  Until no new node or arc can be added to $g(\Sigma, \Omega)$,

  (i) If $g(\Sigma, \Omega)$ has a node labeled with an expression e, then add a node labeled with $\bar{e}$, if no such node exists.
  (ii) If $g(\Sigma, \Omega)$ has a node M labeled with $(\geq mp)$ and a node N labeled with $(\geq np)$, where p is either P or P^- and $0 < m < n$, then add an arc (N, M), if no such arc exists.
  (iii) If $g(\Sigma, \Omega)$ has an arc (M, N), then add an arc $(\bar{N}, \bar{M})$, if no such arc exists.

Stage 4:
  Until no new node or arc can be added to $g(\Sigma, \Omega)$,
      for each pair of nodes M and N such that M and N are labeled with $(\geq 1 P)$
      and $\neg(\geq 1\ Q)$, respectively, and there is a path from M to N
    add arcs (K, L) and $(\bar{L}, \bar{K})$, where K and L are the nodes labeled with P
    and
      $\neg Q$, respectively, if no such arcs exists.

Note that Stage 2 corresponds to Proposition 17.1(iv), Stage 3(ii) to Proposition 17.1(i), Stage 3(iii) to Proposition 17.1(ii), and Stage 4 to Proposition 17.1(v).

Definition 17.2 The *constraint graph that represents* Σ and Ω is the labeled graph $G(\Sigma, \Omega)$, where each node is labeled with a set of expressions, defined from $g(\Sigma, \Omega)$ by collapsing each clique of $g(\Sigma, \Omega)$ into a single node labeled with the expressions that previously labeled the nodes in the clique. When Ω is the empty set, we simply write $G(\Sigma)$ and say that $G(\Sigma)$ is the *constraint graph that represents* Σ.

Note that Definition 17.2 reflects Proposition 17.1(iii).

Definition 17.3 Let $G(\Sigma, \Omega)$ be the constraint graph that represents Σ and Ω. We say that a node K of $G(\Sigma, \Omega)$ is a $\perp$-*node with level n*, for a non-negative integer n, iff one of the following conditions holds:

(i) K is a $\perp$-*node with level 0* iff there are nodes M and N, not necessarily distinct from K, and a positive expression h such that M and N are respectively labeled with h and $\neg h$, and $K \rightarrow M$ and $K \rightarrow N$.
(ii) K is a $\perp$-*node with level n* $+ 1$ iff
   (a) There is a $\perp$-node M of level n, distinct from K, such that $K \rightarrow M$, and M is the $\perp$-node with the smallest level such that $K \rightarrow M$, or
   (b) K is labeled with a minCardinality constraint of the form $(\geq kP)$ or of the form $(\geq kP^-)$ and there is a $\perp$-node M of level n such that M is labeled with P, or
   (c) K is labeled with an atomic role P and there is a $\perp$-node M of level n such that M is labeled with a minCardinality constraint of the form $(\geq 1 P)$ or of the form $(\geq 1P^-)$.

Note that cases (i) and (ii-a) of Definition 17.3 correspond to Proposition 17.1(vi), case (ii-b) to Proposition 17.1(viii), and case (ii-c) to Proposition 17.1(vii).

Definition 17.4 A node K is a $\perp$-*node of* $G(\Sigma, \Omega)$ iff K is a $\perp$-node with level n, for some non-negative integer n. A node K is a $\top$-node of $G(\Sigma, \Omega)$ iff $\bar{K}$ is a $\perp$-node.

To avoid repetitions, in what follows, let $g(\Sigma, \Omega)$ be the graph that captures Σ and Ω and $G(\Sigma, \Omega)$ be the graph that represents Σ and Ω. Proposition 17.2 lists properties of $g(\Sigma, \Omega)$ that directly reflect the structure of the set of constraints Σ. Proposition 17.3 applies the results in Proposition 17.2 to obtain properties of $G(\Sigma, \Omega)$ that are fundamental to establish Lemma 17.1 and Theorems 17.1

and 17.2. Finally, Proposition 17.4 relates the structure of $G(\Sigma, \Omega)$ with the logical consequences of Σ.

Proposition 17.2 *For any pair of nodes K and M of $g(\Sigma, \Omega)$:*

(i) *If there is a path $K \rightarrow M$ in $g(\Sigma, \Omega)$ and if M is labeled with a positive expression, then K is labeled with a positive expression.*
(ii) *If there is a path $K \rightarrow M$ in $g(\Sigma, \Omega)$ and if K is labeled with a negative expression, then M is labeled with a negative expression.*

Proposition 17.3

(i) *$G(\Sigma, \Omega)$ is acyclic.*
(ii) *For any node K of $G(\Sigma, \Omega)$, for any expression e, we have that e labels K iff $\bar{e}$ labels $\bar{K}$.*
(iii) *For any pair of nodes M and N of $G(\Sigma, \Omega)$, we have that $M \rightarrow N$ iff $\bar{N} \rightarrow \bar{M}$.*
(iv) *For any node K of $G(\Sigma, \Omega)$, one of the following conditions holds:*
    (a) *K is labeled only with atomic concepts or minCardinality constraints of the form $(\geq mp)$, where p is either P or P^- and $m \geq 1$, or*
    (b) *K is labeled only with atomic roles, or*
    (c) *K is labeled only with negated atomic concepts or negated minCardinality constraints of the form $\neg(\geq mp)$, where p is either P or P^- and $m \geq 1$, or*
    (d) *K is labeled only with negated atomic roles.*
(v) *For any pair of nodes K and M of $G(\Sigma, \Omega)$,*
    (a) *If there is a path $K \rightarrow M$ in $G(\Sigma, \Omega)$ and if M is labeled with a positive expression, then K is labeled only with positive expressions.*
    (b) *If there is a path $K \rightarrow M$ in $G(\Sigma, \Omega)$ and if K is labeled with a negative expression, then M is labeled only with negative expressions.*
(vi) *For any node K of $G(\Sigma, \Omega)$,*
    (a) *If K is a $\perp$-node, then K is labeled only with atomic concepts or minCardinality constraints of the form $(\geq mp)$, where p is either P or P^- and $m \geq 1$, or K is labeled only with atomic roles.*
    (b) *If K is a $\top$-node, then K is labeled only with negated atomic concepts or negated minCardinality constraints of the form $\neg(\geq mp)$, where p is either P or P^- and $m \geq 1$, or K is labeled only with negated atomic roles.*
(vii) *Assume that Σ has no inclusions of the form $e \sqsubseteq \neg(\geq kP)$ or of the form $e \sqsubseteq \neg(\geq kP^-)$. Let M be the node labeled with $\neg(\geq kP)$ (or with $\neg(\geq kP^-)$). Then, for any node K of $G(\Sigma, \Omega)$, if there is a path $K \rightarrow M$ in $G(\Sigma, \Omega)$, then K is labeled only with negative concept expressions.*

Proposition 17.4

(i) *For any pair of nodes M and N of $G(\Sigma, \Omega)$, for any pair of expressions e and f that label M and N, respectively, if $M \rightarrow N$ then $\Sigma \models e \sqsubseteq f$.*
(ii) *For any node K of $G(\Sigma, \Omega)$, for any pair of expressions e and f that label K, $\Sigma \models e \equiv f$.*

(iii) *For any node K of $G(\Sigma, \Omega)$, for any expression e that labels K, if K is a $\bot$-node, then $\Sigma \models e \sqsubseteq \bot$.*

(iv) *For any node K of $G(\Sigma, \Omega)$, for any expression e that labels K, if K is a $\top$-node, then $\Sigma \models \top \sqsubseteq e$.*

17.3.2 Herbrand Interpretations and Instance Labeling Functions

To prove the main results, we introduce in this section the notion of canonical Herbrand interpretation for a set of constraints. The definition mimics the analogous notion used in automated theorem proving strategies based on Resolution.

Definition 17.5

(i) A set Φ of distinct function symbols is a set of Skolem function symbols for $G(\Sigma, \Omega)$ iff Φ associates:
  (a) n distinct unary function symbols with each node N of $G(\Sigma, \Omega)$ labeled with $(\geq nP)$, denoted $f_1[N, P], \ldots, f_n[N, P]$ for ease of reference;
  (b) n distinct unary function symbols with each node N of $G(\Sigma, \Omega)$ labeled with $(\geq nP^-)$, denoted $g_1[N, P], \ldots, g_n[N, P]$ for ease of reference;
  (c) a distinct constant with each node N of $G(\Sigma, \Omega)$ labeled with an atomic concept or with $(\geq 1P)$, denoted $c[N]$ for ease of reference.
(ii) The Herbrand Universe $\Delta[\Phi]$ for Φ is the set of first-order terms constructed using the function symbols in Φ. The terms in $\Delta[\Phi]$ are called *individuals*.

In the next definition, recall that use $Q \to P$ to indicate that there is a path from a node Q to a node P in $G(\Sigma, \Omega)$.

Definition 17.6

(i) An *instance labeling function for* $G(\Sigma, \Omega)$ *and* $\Delta[\Phi]$ is a function s' that associates a set of individuals in $\Delta[\Phi]$ to each node of $G(\Sigma, \Omega)$ labeled with concept expressions, and a set of pairs of individuals in $\Delta[\Phi]$ to each node of $G(\Sigma, \Omega)$ labeled with role expressions.
(ii) Let N be a node of $G(\Sigma, \Omega)$ labeled with an atomic concept or with $(\geq kP)$. Assume that N is not a $\bot$-node. Then, the Skolem constant $c[N]$ is a *seed term* of N, and N is the *seed node* of $c[N]$.
(iii) Let N_P be the node of $G(\Sigma, \Omega)$ labeled with the atomic role P. Assume that N_P is not a $\bot$-node. For each term a, for each node M labeled with $(\geq mP)$, if $a \in s'(M)$ and there is no node K labeled with $(\geq k \, Q)$ such that $m \leq k$, $Q \to P$ and $a \in s'(K)$, then
  (a) the pair $(a, f_r[M, P](a))$ is called a *seed pair* of N_P triggered by $a \in s'(M)$, for $r \in [1, m]$,
  (b) the term $f_r[M, P](a)$ is a *seed term* of the node L labeled with $(\geq 1P^-)$, and L is called the *seed node* of $f_r[M, P](a)$, for $r \in [2, m]$, if a is of the

form $g_i[J, P](b)$, for some node J and some term b, and for $r \in [1, m]$, otherwise.

(iv) Let N_P be the node of $G(\Sigma, \Omega)$ labeled with the atomic role P. Assume that N_P is not a $\perp$-node. For each term b, for each node N labeled with $(\geq n P^-)$, if $b \in s'(N)$ and there is no node K labeled with $(\geq k \ Q^-)$ such that $n \leq k$, $Q \to P$ and $b \in s'(K)$, then
   (a) the pair $(g_r[N, P](b), b)$ is called a *seed pair* of N_P *triggered by* $b \in s'(N)$, for $r \in [1, n]$, and
   (b) the term $g_r[N, P](b)$ is a *seed term* of the node L labeled with $(\geq 1P)$, and L is called the *seed node* of $g_r[N, P](b)$, for $r \in [2, n]$, if b is of the form $f_i[J, P](a)$, for some node J and some term a, and for $r \in [1, n]$, otherwise.

Intuitively, the seed term of a node N will play the role of a unique signature of N, and likewise for a seed pair of a node N_P.

Definition 17.7 A *canonical instance labeling function for* $G(\Sigma, \Omega)$ *and* $\Delta[\Phi]$ is an instance labeling function that satisfies the following restrictions, for each node K of $G(\Sigma, \Omega)$:

(a) Assume that K is a concept expression node, and that K is neither a $\perp$-node nor a $\top$-node. Then, $t \in s'(K)$ iff t is a seed term of a node J and there is a path from J to K.
(b) Assume that K is a role expression node and is neither a $\perp$-node nor a $\top$-node. Then, $(t, u) \in s'(K)$ iff (t, u) is a seed pair of a node J and there is a path from J to K.
(c) Assume that K is a $\perp$-node. Then, $s'(K) = \varnothing$.
(d) Assume that K is a concept expression node and is a $\top$-node. Then, $s'(K) = \Delta[\Phi]$.
(e) Assume that K is a role expression node and is a $\top$-node. Then, $s'(K) = \Delta[\Phi] \times \Delta[\Phi]$.

Proposition 17.5 *Let s' be canonical instance labeling function for $G(\Sigma, \Omega)$ and $\Delta[\Phi]$. Then*

(i) *For any pair of nodes M and N of $G(\Sigma, \Omega)$, if $M \to N$ then $s'(M) \subseteq s'(N)$.*
(ii) *For any pair of nodes M and N of $G(\Sigma, \Omega)$ that both are concept expression nodes or both are role expression nodes, $s'(M) \cap s'(N) \neq \varnothing$ iff there is a seed node K such that $K \to M$ and $K \to N$.*
(iii) *For any node N_P of $G(\Sigma, \Omega)$ labeled with an atomic role P, for any node M of $G(\Sigma, \Omega)$ labeled with $(\geq mP)$, for any term $t \in s'(M)$, either $s'(N_P)$ contains all seed pairs triggered by $t \in s'(M)$, or there are no seed pairs triggered by $t \in s'(M)$.*
(iv) *For any node N_P of $G(\Sigma, \Omega)$ labeled with an atomic role P, for any node N of $G(\Sigma, \Omega)$ labeled with $(\geq nP^-)$, for any term $t \in s'(N)$, either $s'(N_P)$ contains all seed pairs triggered by $t \in s'(N)$, or there are no seed pairs triggered by $t \in s'(N)$.*

Recall that the alphabet is understood as the (finite) set of atomic concepts and roles that occur in Σ and Ω. Hence, in the context of Σ and Ω, when we refer to an *interpretation*, we mean an interpretation for such alphabet.

Definition 17.8 Let s' be a canonical instance labeling function for $G(\Sigma, \Omega)$ and $\Delta[\Phi]$. *The canonical Herbrand interpretation induced by s' is the interpretation s* defined as follows:

(a) $\Delta[\Phi]$ is the domain of s.
(b) $s(C) = s'(M)$, for each atomic concept C, where M is the node of $G(\Sigma, \Omega)$ labeled with C (there is just one such node).
(c) $s(P) = s'(N)$, for each atomic role P, where N is the node of $G(\Sigma, \Omega)$ labeled with P (again, there is just one such node).

17.3.3 Strict Satisfiability and Logical Implication for Extralite Schemas with Restricted Role Hierarchies

We now ready to prove the main results of the chapter that lead to efficient decision procedures to test strict satisfiability and logical implication for restricted extralite schemas with role hierarchies.

In what follows, let Σ be a finite set of normalized extralite constraints and Ω be a finite set of extralite constraint expressions. Let $G(\Sigma, \Omega)$ be the graph that represents Σ and Ω.

Lemma 17.1 *Assume that Σ satisfies the role hierarchy restriction. Let s' be a canonical instance labeling function for $G(\Sigma, \Omega)$ and $\Delta[\Phi]$. Let s be the canonical Herbrand interpretation induced by s'. Then, we have*:

(i) *For each node N of $G(\Sigma, \Omega)$, for each positive expression e that labels N,* $s'(N) = s(e)$.
(ii) *For each node N of $G(\Sigma, \Omega)$, for each negative expression $\neg e$ that labels N,* $s'(N) \subseteq s(\neg e)$.

Proof Sketch Let s' be a canonical instance labeling function for $G(\Sigma, \Omega)$ and $\Delta[\Phi]$. Let s be the interpretation induced by s'.
(i) Let N be a node of $G(\Sigma, \Omega)$. Let e be a positive expression that labels N.
First observe that N cannot be a $\top$-node. By Proposition 17.3(vi-b), $\top$-nodes are labeled only with negative expressions, which contradicts the assumption that e is a positive expression. Then, there are two cases to consider.
Case 1: N is not a $\bot$-node.
We have to prove that $s(e) = s'(N)$. By the restrictions on constraints and constraint expressions, since e is a positive expression, there are four cases to consider.
Case 1.1: e is an atomic concept C.
By Definition 17.8(b), $s(C) = s'(N)$.
Case 1.2: e is an atomic role P.
By Definition 17.8(c), $s(P) = s'(N)$.

Case 1.3: e is of the form $(\geq nP)$.

Let N_P be the node labeled with P. Then, N_P is not a $\perp$-node. Assume otherwise. Then, by Definition 17.3(ii-b) and Definition 17.4, the node L labeled with $(\geq 1P)$ would be a $\perp$-node. But, by construction of $G(\Sigma, \Omega)$, there is an arc from N (the node labeled with $(\geq nP)$) to L. Hence, N would be a $\perp$-node, contradicting the assumption of Case 1. Furthermore, since N_P is labeled with the positive atomic role P, by Proposition 17.3(vi-b), N_P cannot be a $\top$-node.

Then, since N_P is neither a $\perp$-node nor a $\top$-node, Definition 17.7(b) applies to $s'(N_P)$.

Recall that N is the node labeled with $(\geq nP)$ and that N is neither a $\perp$-node nor a $\top$-node. We first prove that

(1) $a \in s'(N)$ implies that $a \in s((\geq nP))$

Let $a \in s'(N)$. Let K be the node labeled with $(\geq kP)$ such that $a \in s'(K)$ and k is the largest possible integer greater than n. Since $a \in s'(K)$ and k is the largest possible, there are k pairs in $s'(N_P)$ whose first element is a, by Proposition 17.5(iii). By Definition 17.8(c), $s(P) = s'(N_P)$. Hence, by definition of minCardinality, $a \in s((\geq kP))$. But again by definition of minCardinality, $s((\geq kP)) \subseteq s((\geq nP))$, since $n \leq k$, by the choice of k. Therefore, $a \in s((\geq nP))$.

We now prove that

(2) $a \in s((\geq nP))$ implies that $a \in s'(N)$

Since Σ satisfies the role hierarchy restriction, there are two cases to consider.
Case 1.3.1: Σ defines no subroles for P.

Let $a \in s((\geq nP))$. By definition of minCardinality, there must be n distinct pairs $(a, b_1), \ldots, (a, b_n)$ in $s(P)$ and, consequently, in $s'(N_P)$, since $s(P) = s'(N_P)$, by Definition 17.8(c).

Recall that N_P is neither a $\perp$-node nor a $\top$-node. Then, by Definition 17.7(b) and Definition 17.6(iii), possibly by reordering $b_1, \ldots, b_n$, we then have that there are nodes $L_0, L_1, \ldots L_v$ such that

(3) (a, b_1) is a seed pair of N_P of the form $(g_{i0}[L_0, P](u), u)$, triggered by $u \in s'(L_0)$, where L_0 is labeled with $(\geq l_0 P^-)$, for some $i_0 \in [1, l_0]$

or

(4) (a, b_1) is a seed pair of N_P of the form $(a, f_1[L_1, P](a))$, triggered by $a \in s'(L_1)$, where L_1 is labeled with $(\geq l_1 P)$

and

(5) (a, b_j) is a seed pair of N_P of the form $(a, f_{wj}[L_i, P](a))$, triggered by $a \in s'(L_i)$, where L_i is labeled with $(\geq li P)$, $j \in [(\sum_{r=1}^{i-1} l_r) + 1, \sum_{r=1}^{i} l_r]$, with $w_j \in [1, l_i]$ and $i \in [2, v]$

Furthermore, $l_i \neq l_j$, for $i, j \in [2, v]$, with $i \neq j$, since only one node is labeled with $(\geq l_i P)$. We may therefore assume without loss of generality that $l_1 > l_2 > \cdots > l_v$. But note that we then have that $a \in s'(L_i)$ and $a \in s'(L_j)$ and $l_i > l_j$, for each $i, j \in [1, v]$, with $i < j$. But this contradicts the fact that $(a, f_{wj}[Lj, P](a))$ is a seed pair of N_P triggered by $a \in s'(L_j)$ since, by Definition 17.6(iii), there could be no node L_i labeled with $(\geq l_i P)$ with $l_i > l_j$ and $a \in s'(L_i)$. This means that there is just one node, L_1, that satisfies (5).

We are now ready to show that $a \in s'(N)$.

Case 1.3.1.1: $n = 1$.

Case 1.3.1.1.1: a is of the form $g_{i0}[L_0, P](u)$.

Recall that N_P is not a $\perp$-node. Then, by Definition 17.6(iv), $g_{i0}[L_0, P](u)$ is a seed term of the node labeled with $(\geq 1P)$, which must be N, since $n = 1$ and there is just one node labeled with $(\geq 1P)$. Therefore, since N is not a $\perp$-node or a $\top$-node, by Definition 17.7(a), $a \in s'(N)$.

Case 1.3.1.1.2: a is not of the form $g_{i0}[L_0, P](u)$.

Then, by (4) and assumptions of the case, $a \in s'(L_1)$. Since, L_1 is labeled with $(\geq l_1 P)$ and N with $(\geq 1P)$, either $n = l_1 = 1$ and $N = L_1$, or $l_1 > n = 1$ and (L_1, N) is an arc of $G(\Sigma, \Omega)$, by definition of $G(\Sigma, \Omega)$. Then, $s'(L_1) \subseteq s'(N)$, using Proposition 17.5(i), for the second alternative. Therefore, $a \in s'(N)$ as desired, since $a \in s'(L_1)$.

Case 1.3.1.2: $n > 1$.

We first show that $n \leq l_1$. First observe that, by (5) and $n > 1$, $s'(N_P)$ contains a seed pair $(a, f_{wj}[L_1, P](a))$ triggered by $a \in s'(L_1)$. Then, by Proposition 17.5(iii), $s'(N_P)$ contains all seed pairs triggered by $a \in s'(L_1)$. In other words, we have that $a \in s((\geq nP))$ and $(a, b_1), \ldots, (a, b_n) \in s'(N_P)$ and $(a, b_1), \ldots, (a, b_n)$ are triggered by $a \in s'(L_1)$. Therefore, either $(a, b_1), \ldots, (a, b_n)$ are all pairs triggered by $a \in s'(L_1)$, in which case $n = l_1$, or $(a, b_1), \ldots, (a, b_n), (a, b_{n+1}), \ldots, (a, b_{l_1})$, in which case $n < l_1$. Hence, we have that $n \leq l_1$.

Since L_1 is labeled with $(\geq l_1 P)$ and N with $(\geq nP)$, with $n \leq l_1$, either $n = l_1$ and $N = L_1$, or $l_1 > n$ and (L_1, N) is an arc of $G(\Sigma, \Omega)$, by definition of $G(\Sigma, \Omega)$. Then, $s'(L_1) \subseteq s'(N)$, using Proposition 17.5(i), for the second alternative. Therefore, $a \in s'(N)$ as desired, since $a \in s'(L_1)$.

Therefore, we established that (2) holds. Hence, from (1) and (2), $s'(N) = s((\geq nP))$, as desired.

Case 1.3.2: Σ defines subroles for P.

Since Σ satisfies the role hierarchy restriction and defines subroles for P, then Σ has no constraint of the form $e \sqsubseteq \neg(\geq 1P)$ or of the form $e \sqsubseteq \neg(\geq 1P^-)$. The proof of this case is a variation of that of Case 1.3.1.

Case 1.4: e is of the form $(\geq nP^-)$.

The proof of this case is entirely similar to that of Case 1.3.

Case 2: N is a $\perp$-node.

We have to prove that $s(e) = s'(N) = \varnothing$. Again, by the restrictions on constraints and constraint expressions, since e is a positive expression, there are four cases to consider.

Case 2.1: e is an atomic concept C.

Then, by Definition 17.8(b), we trivially have that $s(C) = s'(N) = \varnothing$.

Case 2.2: N is an atomic node P.

Then, by Definition 17.8(c), we trivially have that $s(P) = s'(N) = \varnothing$.

Case 2.3: e is a minCardinality constraint of the form $(\geq np)$, where p is either P or P^- and $1 \leq n$.
We prove that $s((\geq np)) = \varnothing$, using an argument similar to that in Case 1.3. Let N_P be the node labeled with P.
Case 2.1.2.1: N_P is a $\perp$-node
Then, by Definition 17.7(c) and Definition 17.8(c), $s(P) = s'(N_P) = \varnothing$. Hence, $s((\geq np)) = \varnothing$.
Case 2.1.2.2: N_P is not a $\perp$-node.
By Proposition 17.3(vi-b), N_P cannot be a $\top$-node. Then, Definition 17.7(b) applies to $s'(N_P)$.

We proceed by contradiction. So, assume that $s((\geq np)) \neq \varnothing$ and let $a \in s((\geq np))$.

By definition of minCardinality and since $s(P) = s'(N_P)$, there must be n distinct pairs $(a, b_1), \ldots, (a, b_n)$ in $s'(N_P)$. Using an argument similar to that in Case 1.3, there are nodes L_0 and L_1 such that

(6) (a, b_1) is a seed pair of N_P of the form $(g_{i0}[L_0, P](u), u)$, triggered by $u \in s'(L_0)$, where L_0 is labeled with $(\geq l_0 P^-)$, for some $i_0 \in [1, l_0]$

or

(7) (a, b_1) is a seed pair of N_P of the form $(a, f_1[L_1, P](a))$, triggered by $a \in s'(L_1)$, where L_1 is labeled with $(\geq l_1 P)$

and

(8) (a, b_j) is a seed pair of N_P of the form $(a, f_{wj}[L_1, P](a))$, triggered by $a \in s'(L_1)$, where L_1 is labeled with $(\geq l_1 P)$, with $j \in [2, l_1]$

We are now ready to show that no such $a \in s((\geq np))$ exists. Recall that $n > 1$. We first show that $n \leq l_1$. First observe that, by (8) and $n > 1$, $s'(N_P)$ contains a seed pair $(a, f_{wj}[L_1, P](a))$ triggered by $a \in s'(L_1)$. Then, by Proposition 17.5(iii), $s'(N_P)$ contains all seed pairs triggered by $a \in s'(L_1)$. In other words, we have that $a \in s((\geq nP))$ and $(a, b_1), \ldots, (a, b_n) \in s'(N_P)$ and $(a, b_1), \ldots, (a, b_n)$ are triggered by $a \in s'(L_1)$. Therefore, either $(a, b_1), \ldots, (a, b_n)$ are all pairs triggered by $a \in s'(L_1)$, in which case $n = l_1$, or $(a, b_1), \ldots, (a, b_n), (a, b_{n+1}), \ldots, (a, b_{l_1})$, in which case $n < l_1$. Hence, we have that $n \leq l_1$. Since L_1 is labeled with $(\geq l_1 P)$ and N with $(\geq nP)$, with $n \leq l_1$, either $n = l_1$ and $N = L_1$, or $l_1 > n$ and (L_1, N) is an arc of $G(\Sigma, \Omega)$, by definition of $G(\Sigma, \Omega)$. Then, $s'(L_1) \subseteq s'(N)$, using Proposition 17.5(i), for the second alternative. Therefore, $a \in s'(N)$, since $a \in s'(L_1)$. But this is impossible, since $s'(N) = \varnothing$.
Hence, we conclude that $s((\geq np)) = \varnothing$.
Therefore, we have that, if N is a $\perp$-node, then $s'(N) = s(e) = \varnothing$, for any positive expression e that labels N.
Therefore, we established, in all cases, that Lemma 17.1(i) holds.
(ii) Let N be a node of $G(\Sigma, \Omega)$. Let $\neg e$ be a negative expression that labels N. First observe that N cannot be a $\perp$-node. By Proposition 17.3(vi-a), $\perp$-nodes are labeled only with positive expressions, which contradicts the assumption that $\neg e$ is a negative expression. Then, there are two cases to consider.

Case 1: N is not a $\top$-node.

We have to prove that $s'(N) \subseteq s(\neg e)$.

Case 1.1: N is a concept expression node.

Suppose, by contradiction, that there is a term t such that $t \in s'(N)$ and $t \notin s(\neg e)$.

Since $t \notin s(\neg e)$, we have that $t \in s(e)$, by definition. Let M be the node labeled with e. Hence, by Lemma 17.1(i), $t \in s'(M)$. That is, $t \in s'(M) \cap s'(N)$.

Note that M and N are dual nodes since M is labeled with e and N is labeled with $\neg e$. Therefore, since N is neither a $\bot$-node nor a $\top$-node, M is also neither a $\top$-node nor a $\bot$-node, by definition of $\top$-node.

Since Σ satisfies the role hierarchy restriction, there are two cases to consider.

Case 1.1.1: $\neg e$ is not of the form $\neg(\geq nP)$ or $\neg(\geq nP^-)$.

Then, by Definition 17.7(a), $t \in s'(N)$ iff t is a seed term of a node J and there is a path from J to K. Furthermore, by Proposition 17.5(ii), there is a seed node K such that $K \to M$ and $K \to N$ and $t \in s'(K)$. But this is impossible. We would have that $K \to M$ and $K \to N$, M is labeled with e, and N is labeled with $\neg e$, which implies that K is a $\bot$-node. Hence, by Definition 17.7(c), $s'(K) = \varnothing$, which implies that $t \notin s'(K)$. Therefore, we established that, for all terms t, if $t \in s'(N)$ then $t \in s(\neg e)$.

Case 1.1.2: $\neg e$ is of the form $\neg(\geq nP)$ or $\neg(\geq nP^-)$.

Case 1.1.2.1: Σ defines no subroles for P.

Follows as in Case 1.1.1, again using Definition 17.7(a) and Proposition 17.5(ii).

Case 1.1.2.2: Σ defines subroles for P.

Since Σ satisfies the role hierarchy restriction, Σ has no constraint of the form $h \sqsubseteq \neg(\geq nP)$ or of the form $h \sqsubseteq \neg(\geq nP^-)$. Then, by Proposition 17.3(vii), for any node K, if $K \to N$, then K is labeled only with negative concept expressions. Therefore, there could be no seed node K such that $K \to N$. Hence, by Definition 17.7(a), there is no term t such that $s'(N) = \varnothing$, which contradicts the assumption that $t \in s'(N)$.

Therefore, in all cases, we established that, for all terms t, if $t \in s'(N)$ then $t \in s(\neg e)$.

Case 1.2: N is a role expression node.

Follows likewise, using Proposition 17.5(ii) again and Definition 17.7(b).

Thus, in both cases, we established that $s'(N) \subseteq s(\neg e)$, as desired.

Case 2: N is a $\top$-node.

Let $\bar{N}$ be the dual node of N. Since N is a $\top$-node, we have that $\bar{N}$ is a $\bot$-node. Furthermore, since $\neg e$ labels N, e labels $\bar{N}$. Since e is a positive expression, by Lemma 17.1(i), $s'(\bar{N}) = s(e) = \varnothing$.

Case 2.1: N is a concept expression node.

By Definition 17.7(d) and definition of $s(\neg e)$, we have $s'(N) = \Delta[\Phi] = s(\neg e)$, which trivially implies $s'(N) \subseteq s(\neg e)$.

Case 2.2: N is a role expression node.

By Definition 17.7(e) and definition of $s(\neg e)$, we then have $s'(N) = \Delta[\Phi] \times \Delta[\Phi] = s(\neg e)$, which trivially implies $s'(N) \subseteq s(\neg e)$.

Therefore, we established that, in all cases, Lemma 17.1(ii) holds. $\qquad\square$

We are now ready to state the first result of the chapter.

Theorem 17.1 *Assume that Σ satisfies the role hierarchy restriction. Let s be the canonical Herbrand interpretation induced by a canonical instance labeling function for $G(\Sigma, \Omega)$ and $\Delta[\Phi]$. Then, we have*

(i) *s is a model of Σ.*

(ii) *Let e be an atomic concept or a minCardinality constraint of the form $(\geq 1P)$. Let N be the node of $G(\Sigma, \Omega)$ labeled with e. Then, N is a $\bot$-node iff $s(e) = \varnothing$.*

(iii) *Let e be a minCardinality constraint of the form $(\geq kP)$, with $k > 1$. Assume that $G(\Sigma, \Omega)$ has a node labeled with e. Then, N is a $\bot$-node iff $s(e) = \varnothing$.*

(iv) *Let P be an atomic role. Let N be the node of $G(\Sigma, \Omega)$ labeled with P. Then, N is a $\bot$-node iff $s(P) = \varnothing$.*

Proof Sketch Let Σ be a set of normalized constraints and Ω be a set of constraint expressions. Let $G(\Sigma, \Omega)$ be the graph that represents Σ and Ω. Let Φ be a set of distinct function symbols and $\Delta[\Phi]$ be the Herbrand Universe for Φ. Let s' be a canonical instance labeling function for $G(\Sigma, \Omega)$ and $\Delta[\Phi]$ and s be the interpretation induced by s'.

(i) We prove that s satisfies all constraints in Σ.

Let $e \sqsubseteq f$ be a constraint in Σ. By the restrictions on the constraints in Σ, e must be positive and f can be positive or negative. Therefore, there are two cases to consider.

Case 1: e and f are both positive.

Then, by Lemma 17.1(i), $s'(M) = s(e)$ and $s'(N) = s(f)$, where M and N are the nodes labeled with e and f, respectively. If $M = N$, then we trivially have that $s'(M) = s'(N)$. So assume that $M \neq N$. Since $e \sqsubseteq f$ is in Σ and $M \neq N$, there must be an arc (M, N) of $G(\Sigma, \Omega)$. By Proposition 17.5(i), we then have $s'(M) \subseteq s'(N)$. Hence, $s(e) = s'(M) \subseteq s'(N) = s(f)$.

Case 2: e is positive and f is negative.

Then, by Lemma 17.1(i), $s'(M) = s(e)$. and, by Lemma 17.1(ii), $s'(N) \subseteq s(f)$, where M and N are the nodes labeled with e and f, respectively. Since negative expressions do not occur on the left-hand side of constraints in Σ, e and f cannot label nodes that belong to the same clique in the original graph. Therefore, we have that $M \neq N$. Since $e \sqsubseteq f$ is in Σ and $M \neq N$, there must be an arc (M, N) of $G(\Sigma, \Omega)$. By Proposition 17.5(i), we then have $s'(M) \subseteq s'(N)$. Hence, $s(e) = s'(M) \subseteq s'(N) \subseteq s(f)$.

Thus, in both cases, $s(e) \subseteq s(f)$. Therefore, for any constraint $e \sqsubseteq f \in \Sigma$, we have that $s \models e \sqsubseteq f$, which implies that s is a model of Σ.

(ii) Let e be an atomic concept or a minCardinality constraint of the form $(\geq 1P)$. By Stage 1 of Definition 17.1, $G(\Sigma, \Omega)$ always has a node N labeled with e. Since e is positive, by Lemma 17.1(i), $s(e) = s'(N)$.

Assume that N is a $\bot$-node. Then, by Lemma 17.1(i) and Definition 17.7(c), $s(e) = s'(N) = \varnothing$.

Assume that N is not a $\bot$-node. Note that N cannot be a $\top$-node, since N is labeled with the positive expression e. Then, N is neither a $\bot$-node nor a $\top$-node.

By Definition 17.6(ii) and Definition 17.7(a), the seed term $c[N]$ of N is such that $c[N] \in s'(N)$. Hence, trivially, $s(e) = s'(N) \neq \emptyset$.

(iii)–(iv) Follows as for (ii).   □

Based on Theorem 17.1, we can then create a simple procedure to test strict satisfiability, which has polynomial time complexity on the size of Σ:

17.3.4 SAT(Σ)

input: a set Σ of extralite constraints that satisfies the role hierarchy restriction.
output: "YES—Σ is strictly satisfiable"
            "NO—Σ is not strictly satisfiable"

(1) Normalize the constraints in Σ, creating a set Σ'.
(2) Construct the constraint graph $G(\Sigma')$ that represents Σ'.
(3) **If** $G(\Sigma')$ has no $\perp$-node labeled with an atomic concept or an atomic role,

    then return "YES—Σ is strictly satisfiable";
    else return "NO—Σ is not strictly satisfiable".

From Theorem 17.1, we can also prove that:

Theorem 17.2 *Assume that Σ satisfies the role hierarchy restriction. Let σ be a normalized extralite constraint. Assume that σ is of the form $e \sqsubseteq f$ and let $\Omega = \{e, f\}$. Then, $\Sigma \models \sigma$ iff one of the following conditions holds:*

(i) *The node of $G(\Sigma, \Omega)$ labeled with e is a $\perp$-node; or*
(ii) *The node of $G(\Sigma, \Omega)$ labeled with f is a $\top$-node; or*
(iii) *There is a path in $G(\Sigma, \Omega)$ from the node labeled with e to the node labeled with f.*

Proof Sketch Let Σ be a set of normalized constraints. Assume that Σ satisfies the role hierarchy restriction. Let $e \sqsubseteq f$ be a constraint and $\Omega = \{e, f\}$. Let $G(\Sigma, \Omega)$ be the graph that represents Σ and Ω. Observe that, by construction, $G(\Sigma, \Omega)$ has a node labeled with e and a node labeled with f. Let M and N be such nodes, respectively.

($\Leftarrow$) Follows directly from Proposition 17.4.
($\Rightarrow$) We prove that, if the conditions of the theorem do not hold, then $\Sigma \not\models e \sqsubseteq f$.

Since $e \sqsubseteq f$ is a constraint, we have:

(1) e is either an atomic concept C, an atomic role P or a minCardinality of the form $(\geq kp)$, where p is either P or P^-, and
(2) f is either an atomic concept C, a negated atomic concept $\neg D$, an atomic role P, a negated atomic role Q, a minCardinality constraint of the form $(\geq kp)$, or a negated minCardinality constraint of the form $\neg(\geq kp)$, where p is either P or P^-.

Assume that the conditions of the theorem do not hold, that is:

(3) The node M labeled with e is not a $\perp$-node; and
(4) The node N labeled with f is not a $\top$-node; and
(5) There is no path in $G(\Sigma, \Omega)$ from M to N.

To prove that $\Sigma \not\models e \sqsubseteq f$, it suffices to exhibit a model r of Σ such that $r \not\models e \sqsubseteq f$. Recall that $r \not\models e \sqsubseteq f$ iff (i) if e and f are concept expressions, there is an individual t such that $t \in r(e)$ and $t \notin r(f)$ or, equivalently, $t \in r(\neg f)$; (ii) if e and f are role expressions, there is a pair of individuals (t, u) such that $(t, u) \in r(e)$ and $(t, u) \notin r(f)$ or, equivalently, $(t, u) \in r(\neg f)$;

Recall that, to simplify the notation, $e \rightarrow f$ denotes that there is a path in $G(\Sigma, \Omega)$ from the node labeled with e to the node labeled with f, and $e \nrightarrow f$ to indicate that no such path exists.

Since $e \sqsubseteq f$ is a constraint, e must be non-negative and f can be negative or not. Hence, there are two cases to consider.

Case 1: e and f are both positive.

Let s' be a canonical instance labeling function for $G(\Sigma, \Omega)$ and s be the interpretation induced by s'. By Theorem 17.1, s is a model of Σ. We show that $s \not\models e \sqsubseteq f$.

Case 1.1: N is a $\perp$-node.

Since N is a $\perp$-node, by Proposition 17.4(iii), we have that $\Sigma \models f \sqsubseteq \perp$, which implies that $s(f) = \varnothing$, since s is a model of Σ.

By (1), e is either an atomic concept C, an atomic role P or a minCardinality of the form $(\geq kp)$, where p is either P or P^-. By (3), M is not a $\perp$-node. Hence, we have that $s(e) \neq \varnothing$, by Theorem 17.1(ii), (iii) and (iv). Hence, we trivially have that $s \not\models e \sqsubseteq f$.

Case 1.2: N is not a $\perp$-node.

Observe that M and N are neither a $\perp$-node nor a $\top$-node. By assumption of the case and by (4), N is neither a $\perp$-node nor a $\top$-node. Now, by (3), M is not a $\perp$-node. Furthermore, by Proposition 17.3(iv-b), since M is labeled with a positive expression e, M cannot be a $\top$-node.

By Lemma 17.1(i), since e is positive by assumption, by Definition 17.6(ii), (iii) and (iv), and by Definition 17.7(a) and (b), since M is neither a $\perp$-node nor a $\top$-node, we have

(6) $s'(M) = s(e)$. and there is a seed term $c[M] \in s'(M)$, if M is a concept expression node $s'(M) = s(e)$. and there is a seed pair $(t, u) \in s'(M)$, if M is a role expression node

By definition of canonical instance labeling function, we have:

(7) For each concept expression node K of $G(\Sigma, \Omega)$ that is neither a $\perp$-node nor a $\top$-node, $c[M] \in s'(K)$ iff there is a path from M to K For each role expression node K of $G(\Sigma, \Omega)$ that is neither a $\perp$-node nor a $\top$-node, $(t, u) \in s'(K)$ iff there is a path from M to K

By (5), we have $e \nrightarrow f$. Furthermore, N is neither a $\perp$-node nor a $\top$-node. Hence, by (7), we have:

(8) $c[M] \notin s'(N)$, if N is a concept expression node
$(t, u) \notin s'(N)$, if N is a role expression node

Since f is positive, by Lemma 17.1(i), $s'(N) = s(f)$. Hence, we have

(9) $c[M] \notin s(f)$, if f is a concept expression
$(t, u) \notin s(f)$, if f is a role expression

Therefore, by (6) and (9), $s(e) \not\sqsubseteq s(f)$, that is, $s \not\models e \sqsubseteq f$, as desired.

Case 2: e is positive and f is negative.

Assume that f is a negative expression of the form $\neg g$, where g is positive.

Case 2.1: $e \to g$.

Let s' be a canonical instance labeling function for $G(\Sigma, \Omega)$ and s be the interpretation induced by s'. By Theorem 17.1(i), s is a model of Σ. We show that $s \not\models e \sqsubseteq f$.

By Proposition 17.4(i) and (ii), and since s is a model of Σ, we have that $s \models e \equiv g$, if e and g label the same node, and $s \models e \sqsubseteq g$, otherwise. Hence, we have that $s \not\models e \sqsubseteq \neg g$. Now, since f is $\neg g$, we have $s \not\models e \sqsubseteq f$, as desired.

Case 2.2: $e \not\to g$.

Construct Φ as follows:

(10) Φ is Σ with two new constraints, $H \sqsubseteq e$ and $H \sqsubseteq g$, where H is a new atomic concept, if e and g are concept expressions, or H is a new atomic role, if e and g are role expressions

Let r' be a canonical instance labeling function for $G(\Phi, \Omega)$ and r be the interpretation induced by r'. By Theorem 17.1(i), r is a model of Φ. We show that $r \not\models e \sqsubseteq f$.

We first observe that

(11) There is no expression h such that $e \to h$ and $g \to \neg h$ are paths in $G(\Sigma, \Omega)$

By construction of $G(\Sigma, \Omega)$, $g \to \neg h$ iff $h \to \neg g$. But $e \to h$ and $h \to \neg g$ implies $e \to \neg g$, contradicting (5), since f is $\neg g$. Hence, (11) follows.

We now prove that

(12) There is no positive expression h such that $H \to h$ and $H \to \neg h$ are paths in $G(\Phi, \Omega)$

Assume otherwise. Let h be a positive expression such that $H \to h$ and $H \to \neg h$ are paths in $G(\Phi, \Omega)$.

Case 2.2.1: $H \to e \to h$ and $H \to g \to \neg h$ are paths in $G(\Phi, \Omega)$.

Then, $e \to h$ and $g \to \neg h$ must be paths in $G(\Sigma, \Omega)$, which contradicts (11).

Case 2.2.2: $H \to e \to \neg h$ and $H \to g \to h$ are paths in $G(\Phi, \Omega)$.

Then, $e \to \neg h$ and $g \to h$ must be paths in $G(\Sigma, \Omega)$. But, since $g \to h$ iff $\neg h \to \neg g$, we have $e \to \neg h \to \neg g$ is a path in $G(\Sigma, \Omega)$, which contradicts (5), recalling that f is $\neg g$.

Case 2.2.3: $H \to e \to h$ and $H \to e \to \neg h$ are paths in $G(\Phi, \Omega)$.

Then, $e \to h$ and $e \to \neg h$ must be paths in $G(\Sigma, \Omega)$, which contradicts (3), by definition of $\bot$-node.

Case 2.2.4: $H \to g \to h$ and $H \to g \to \neg h$ are paths in $G(\Phi, \Omega)$.

Then, $g \to h$ and $g \to \neg h$ must be paths in $G(\Sigma, \Omega)$. Now, observe that, since $\neg g$ is f, that is, f and g are complementary expressions, g labels $\bar{N}$, the dual node of N in $G(\Sigma, \Omega)$. Then, $g \to h$ and $g \to \neg h$ implies that $\bar{N}$ is a $\bot$-node of $G(\Sigma, \Omega)$, that is, N is a $\top$-node, which contradicts (4).

Hence, we established (12).

Let K be the node of $G(\Phi, \Omega)$ labeled with H. Note that, by construction of Φ, K is labeled only with H. Then, by (12), K is not a $\bot$-node.

By Theorem 17.1(i), r is a model of Φ. Furthermore, by Theorem 17.1(ii) and (iv), and since K is not a $\bot$-node, we have

(13) $r(H) \neq \varnothing$

Since $H \sqsubseteq e$ and $H \sqsubseteq g$ are in Φ, and since r is a model of Φ, we also have:

(14) $r(H) \subseteq r(e)$ and $r(H) \subseteq r(g)$

Therefore, by (13) and (14) and since $f = \neg g$

(15) $r(e) \cap r(g) \neq \varnothing$ or, equivalently, $r(e) \not\subseteq r(\neg g)$ or, equivalently, $r(e) \not\subseteq r(f)$
 or, equivalently, $r \not\models e \sqsubseteq f$

But since $\Sigma \subseteq \Phi$, r is also a model of Σ. Therefore, for Case 2.2, we also exhibited a model r of Σ such that $r \not\models e \sqsubseteq f$, as desired.

Therefore, in all cases, we exhibited a model of Σ that does not satisfy $e \sqsubseteq f$, as desired.

Based on Theorem 17.2, we can then create a simple procedure to test logical implication:

IMPLIES $(\Sigma, e \sqsubseteq f)$

input: a set Σ of constraints satisfies the role hierarchy restriction, and a constraint $e \sqsubseteq f$
output: "YES—Σ logically implies $e \sqsubseteq f$"
             "NO—Σ does not logically imply $e \sqsubseteq f$"

(1) Normalize the constraints in Σ, creating a set Σ'.
(2) Normalize $e \sqsubseteq f$, creating a normalized constraint $e' \sqsubseteq f'$.
(3) Construct $G(\Sigma', \{e', f'\})$.
(4) **If** the node of $G(\Sigma', \{e', f'\})$ labeled with e' is a $\bot$-node, or the node of $G(\Sigma', \{e', f'\})$ labeled with f' is a $\top$-node, or there is a path in $G(\Sigma', \{e', f'\})$ from the node labeled with e' to the node labeled with f',

  then return "YES—Σ logically implies $e \sqsubseteq f$";
  else return "NO—Σ does not logically imply $e \sqsubseteq f$".

Note that **IMPLIES** has polynomial time complexity on the size of $\Sigma \cup \{e \sqsubseteq f\}$. $\qquad\square$

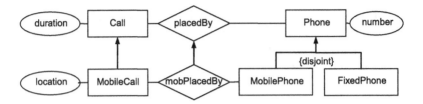

Fig. 17.1 ER diagram of the PhoneCompany1 schema (without cardinalities)

∃ number ⊑ Phone	Phone ⊑ (≤ 1 number)	FixedPhone
∃ number⁻ ⊑ String	Phone ⊑ (≥ 1 number)	⊑ Phone
∃ duration ⊑ Call	Call ⊑ (≤ 1 duration)	MobilePhone
∃ duration⁻ ⊑ String	Call ⊑ (≥ 1 duration)	⊑ Phone
∃ location ⊑ MobileCall	MobileCall ⊑ (≤ 1 location)	MobilePhone
∃ location⁻ ⊑ String	MobileCall ⊑ (≥ 1 location)	| FixedPhone
∃ placedBy ⊑ Call	Call ⊑ (≤ 1 placedBy)	MobileCall
∃ placedBy⁻ ⊑ Phone	Call ⊑ (≥ 1 placedBy)	⊑ Call
∃ mobPlacedBy ⊑ MobileCall	MobileCall ⊑ (≤ 1 mobPlacedBy)	mobPlacedBy
∃ mobPlacedBy⁻ ⊑ MobilePhone	MobileCall ⊑ (≥ 1 mobPlacedBy)	⊑ placedBy

Fig. 17.2 Formal definition of the constraints of the PhoneCompany1 schema

17.4 Examples

17.4.1 Examples of Extralite Schemas

In this section, we introduce examples of concrete, albeit simple extralite schemas with role hierarchies to illustrate how to capture commonly used ER model and UML constructs as extralite constraints.

Example 17.1 Figure 17.1 shows the ER diagram of the PhoneCompany1 schema. Figure 17.2 formalizes the constraints: the first column shows the domain and range constraints; the second column depicts the cardinality constraints; and the third column contains the subset and disjointness constraints.

The first column of Fig. 17.2 indicates that:

- number is an atomic role modeling an attribute of Phone with range String
- duration is an atomic role modeling an attribute of Call with range String
- location is an atomic role modeling an attribute of Call with range String
- placedBy is an atomic role modeling a binary relationship from Call to Phone
- mobPlacedBy is an atomic role modeling a binary relationship from Mobile-Call to MobilePhone

The second column of Fig. 17.2 shows the cardinalities of the PhoneCompany1 schema:

- `number` has maxCardinality and minCardinality both equal to 1 w.r.t. `Phone`
- `duration` has maxCardinality and minCardinality both equal to 1 w.r.t. `Call`
- `location` has maxCardinality and minCardinality both equal to 1 w.r.t. `MobileCall`
- `placedBy` has maxCardinality and minCardinality both equal to 1 w.r.t. `Call`
- (`placedBy⁻` has unbounded maxCardinality and minCardinality equal to 0 w.r.t. `Phone`, which need not be explicitly declared)
- `mobPlacedBy` has maxCardinality and minCardinality both equal to 1 w.r.t. `MobileCall`
- (`mobPlacedBy⁻` has unbounded maxCardinality and minCardinality equal to 0 w.r.t. `MobilePhone`, which need not be explicitly declared)

The third column of Fig. 17.2 indicates that

- `MobilePhone` and `FixedPhone` are subsets of `Phone`
- `MobilePhone` and `FixedPhone` are disjoint
- `MobileCall` is a subset of `Call`
- `mobPlacedBy` is a subset of `placedBy`

Note that the constraints saying that `MobilePhone` is a subset of `Phone` and that `MobileCall` is a subset of `Call` do not imply that `mobPlacedBy` is a subset of `placedBy`. In general, concept inclusions do not imply role inclusions, as already discussed at the end of Sect. 17.2.1.

Example 17.2 Figure 17.3 shows the ER diagram of the PhoneCompany2 schema, and Fig. 17.4 formalizes the constraints, following the same organization as that in Fig. 17.2). Note that:

- `MobilePhone` and `Phone` are disjoint atomic concepts
- `MobileCall` and `Call` are disjoint atomic concepts
- `PlacedBy` is an atomic role modeling a binary relationship from `Call` to `Phone`
- `mobPlacedBy` is an atomic role modeling a binary relationship from `MobileCall` to `MobilePhone`
- the constraints of the schema imply that `PlacedBy` and `mobPlacedBy` are disjoint roles, by the disjunction-transfer rule introduced at the end of Sect. 17.2.1 (see also Example 17.3(b)).

17.4.2 Examples of Representation Graphs

In this section, we illustrate representation graphs and their uses in the decision procedures of Sect. 17.3.3.

Example 17.3 Let Σ be the following subset of the constraints of the PhoneCompany2 schema, introduced in Example 17.2 (we do not consider all constraints to reduce the size of the example):

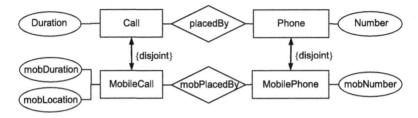

Fig. 17.3 ER diagram of the PhoneCompany2 schema (without card and disjunctions)

∃ Number ⊑ Phone	Phone ⊑ (≤ 1 number)	MobilePhone
∃ Number ⁻⊑ String	Phone ⊑ (≥ 1 number)	| Phone
∃ Duration ⊑ Call	Call ⊑ (≤ 1 Duration)	MobileCall
∃ Duration⁻⊑ String	Call ⊑ (≥ 1 Duration)	| Call
∃ placedBy ⊑ Call	Call ⊑ (≤ 1 placedBy)	
∃ placedBy⁻⊑ Phone	Call ⊑ (≥ 1 placedBy)	
∃ mobDuration ⊑ MobileCall	MobileCall ⊑ (≤ 1 mobDuration)	
∃ mobDuration⁻⊑ String	MobileCall ⊑ (≥ 1 mobDuration)	
∃ mobLocation ⊑ MobileCall	MobileCall ⊑ (≤ 1 mobLocation)	
∃ mobLocation⁻⊑ String	MobileCall ⊑ (≥ 1 mobLocation)	
∃ mobPlacedBy ⊑ MobileCall	MobileCall ⊑ (≤ 1 mobPlacedBy)	
∃ mobPlacedBy⁻⊑ MobilePhone	MobileCall ⊑ (≥ 1 mobPlacedBy)	

Fig. 17.4 Formal definition of the constraints of the PhoneCompany2 schema

(1) ∃placedBy ⊑ Call normalized as: (≥1 placedBy) ⊑ Call

(2) ∃placedBy⁻ ⊑ Phone normalized as: (≥1 placedBy⁻) ⊑ Phone

(3) ∃mobPlacedBy ⊑ MobileCall normalized as: (≥ 1 mobPlacedBy) ⊑ MobileCall

(4) ∃mobPlacedBy⁻ ⊑ MobilePhone normalized as: (≥ 1mobPlacedBy⁻) ⊑ MobilePhone

(5) Call ⊑ (≤1 placedBy) normalized as: Call ⊑ ¬(≥2 placedBy)

(6) MobilePhone | Phone normalized as: MobilePhone ⊑ ¬Phone

(7) MobileCall | Call normalized as: MobileCall ⊑ ¬Call

Figure 17.5 depicts $G(\Sigma)$, the graph that represents Σ, using the normalized constraints. In special, the dotted arcs highlight the paths that correspond to the conditions of Stage 4 of Definition 17.1, and the dashed arcs indicate the arcs that Stage 4 of Definition 17.1 requires to exist, which capture the derived constraint:

(8) mobPlacedBy | placedBy normalized as: mobPlacedBy ⊑ ¬placedBy

Since $G(\Sigma)$ has no ⊥-node labeled with an atomic concept or an atomic role, Σ is strictly satisfiable, by Theorem 17.1. However note that (≥2 placedBy) is a ⊥-node of $G(\Sigma)$.

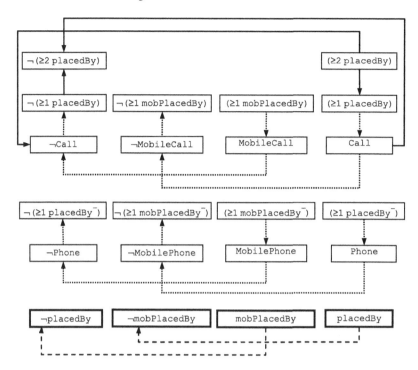

Fig. 17.5 The graph representing Σ

Example 17.4 Let Σ be the following subset of the constraints of the PhoneCompany1 schema, introduced in Example 17.1 (again we do not consider all constraints to reduce the size of the example):

(1) $\exists$placedBy $\sqsubseteq$ Call normalized as: ($\geq$1 placedBy) $\sqsubseteq$ Call
(2) $\exists$placedBy$^-$ $\sqsubseteq$ Phone normalized as: ($\geq$1 placedBy$^-$) $\sqsubseteq$ Phone
(3) Call $\sqsubseteq$ ($\leq$1 placedBy) normalized as: Call $\sqsubseteq$ ¬($\geq$2 placedBy)
(4) MobileCall $\sqsubseteq$ Call
(5) mobPlacedBy $\sqsubseteq$ placedBy

Let Ψ be defined by adding to Σ a new atomic concept, ConferenceCall, and two new constraints:

(6) ConferenceCall $\sqsubseteq$ Call
(7) ConferenceCall $\sqsubseteq$ ($\geq$2 placedBy)

These new constraints intuitively say that conference calls are calls placed by at least two phones. However, this apparently correct modification applied to the PhoneCompany1 schema forces ConferenceCall to always have an empty interpretation. Example 17.5(c) will also show that (6) is actually redundant.

Figure 17.6 depicts G(Ψ), the graph that represents Ψ, using the normalized constraints. Note that there is a path from ConferenceCall to ¬ConferenceCall. Also note that there are paths from the node labeled with ConferenceCall

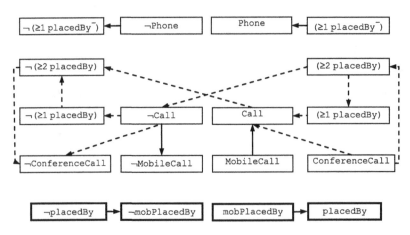

Fig. 17.6 The graph representing Ψ

to nodes labeled with `Call` and `¬Call`, as well as to nodes labeled with (≥ 2 `placedBy`) and ¬(≥ 2 `placedBy`) and nodes labeled with (≥ 1 `placedBy`) and ¬(≥ 1 `placedBy`). The arcs of all such paths are shown in dashed lines in Fig. 17.6.

Hence, the node labeled with `ConferenceCall` is a $\perp$-node of $G(\Psi)$, which implies that Ψ is not strictly satisfiable, by Theorem 17.1. Any interpretation s that satisfies Ψ is such that $s(\text{ConferenceCall}) \subseteq s(\neg \text{ConferenceCall})$ holds, which implies that $s(\text{ConferenceCall}) = \varnothing$.

Example 17.5 This example illustrates the three cases of Theorem 17.2. Let Ψ be the set of constraints considered in Example 17.4 and $G(\Psi)$ be the graph representing Ψ, shown in Fig. 17.6.

(a) Let σ be the constraint `ConferenceCall` $\sqsubseteq$ (≥ 1 `placedBy⁻`). Note that σ is of the form $e \sqsubseteq f$, where $e = \text{ConferenceCall}$ and $f = (\geq 1 \ \text{placedBy}^-)$. Then, $G(\Psi, \{e, f\})$ is equal to $G(\Psi)$, since $G(\Psi)$ already contains nodes labeled with `ConferenceCall` and with (≥ 1 `placedBy⁻`). Recall from Example 17.4 that the node labeled with `ConferenceCall` is a $\perp$-node of $G(\Psi)$, and hence of $G(\Psi, \{e, f\})$. Then, by Theorem 17.2(i), we trivially have

$$\Psi \models \text{ConferenceCall} \sqsubseteq (\geq 1 \ \text{placedBy}^-)$$

(b) Let σ be the constraint `Phone` $\sqsubseteq$ `¬ConferenceCall`. Note that σ is of the form $e \sqsubseteq f$, where $e = \text{Phone}$ and $f = \neg\text{ConferenceCall}$. Since the node labeled with `ConferenceCall` is a $\perp$-node of $G(\Psi, \{e, f\})$, the node labeled with `¬ConferenceCall` is $\top$-node of $G(\Psi, \{e, f\})$. Hence, by Theorem 17.2(ii), we have

$$\Psi \models \text{Phone} \sqsubseteq \neg\text{ConferenceCall}$$

(c) Let σ be the constraint `ConferenceCall` $\sqsubseteq$ `Call`. Note that σ is of the form $e \sqsubseteq f$, where $e = $ `ConferenceCall` and $f = $ `Call`. Since there is a path in $G(\Psi \cup \{e, f\})$ from the node labeled with `ConferenceCall` to the node labeled with `Call` passing through the nodes labeled with (≥ 2 `placedBy`) and (≥ 1 `placedBy`), by Theorem 17.2(iii), we have

$$\Sigma \models \text{ConferenceCall} \sqsubseteq \text{Call}$$

Hence, constraint (6) in Example 17.4 is actually redundant.

17.4.3 Two Applications of Representation Graphs

In this section, we briefly discuss two applications of representation graphs. The first application explores how to use representation graphs to suggest changes to a strictly unsatisfiable schema until it become strictly satisfiable.

Example 17.6 Consider again the modified set of constraints Ψ of Example 17.4. To simplify the discussion, given an expression e, when we refer to node e, we mean the node labeled with e. Recall that Fig. 17.6 shows the graph representing Ψ. Also recall that the sources of the strict unsatisfiability of Ψ are the paths shown in dashed lines in Fig. 17.6.

Note that the arc from node (≥ 2 `placedBy`) to node (≥ 1 `placedBy`) is in $G(\Psi)$ by virtue of the semantics of these minCardinality expressions and, hence, it cannot be dropped (and likewise for the arc from $\neg$(≥ 1 `placedBy`) to $\neg$(≥ 2 `placedBy`)). Therefore, the simplest ways to break the faulty paths are:

(a) Drop the arc from node `ConferenceCall` to node (≥ 2 `placedBy`) (and consequently the dual arc from node $\neg$(≥ 2 `placedBy`) to node $\neg$`ConferenceCall`).
(b) Drop the arc from node `Call` to node $\neg$(≥ 2 `placedBy`) (and consequently the dual arc from node (≥ 2 `placedBy`) to node $\neg$`Call`).

Note that the strict satisfiability of the schema would not be restored by dropping just the arc from node `ConferenceCall` to node `Call` (and its dual arc), or the arc from node (≥ 1 `placedBy`) to node `Call` (and its dual arc).

The representation graph is neutral as to which arc to drop. Thus, we must base our decision on some schema redesign heuristics. Both options are viable, but they obviously alter the semantics of the schema. Option (a) amounts to dropping constraint (7) of Example 17.4, which requires `ConferenceCall` to be a subset of (≥ 2 `placedBy`). This option is not reasonable since it obliterates the very purpose of the redesign step, which was to model conference calls as calls placed by at least two phones. Option (b) means dropping constraint (3), which would alter the semantics of `Call`. However, it is consistent with the purpose of the redesign step and is better than Option (a).

A third option would be to create a second specialization of `Call`, say, `non-ConferenceCall`, and alter constraint (3) of Example 17.4 accordingly. The constraints of Example 17.4 would now include:

(8) $(\geq 1 \ \text{placedBy}) \sqsubseteq \text{Call}$
(9) $(\geq 1 \ \text{placedBy}^-) \sqsubseteq \text{Phone}$
(10) $\text{MobileCall} \sqsubseteq \text{Call}$
(11) $\text{mobPlacedBy} \sqsubseteq \text{placedBy}$
(12) $\text{ConferenceCall} \sqsubseteq \text{Call}$
(13) $\text{ConferenceCall} \sqsubseteq (\geq 2 \ \text{placedBy})$
(14) $\text{nonConferenceCall} \sqsubseteq \text{Call}$
(15) $\text{nonConferenceCall} \sqsubseteq \neg(\geq 2 \ \text{placedBy})$

In view of (13) and (15), note that it would be redundant to include a constraint to force `ConferenceCall` and `nonConferenceCall` to be mutually exclusive. From the point of view of schema redesign practice, this would be the best alternative since it retains the information that there are calls with just one originating place.

The second application we briefly discuss is how to integrate two schemas, S_1 and S_2, which use the same concepts and properties, but differ on their constraints [8]. More precisely, denote by $Th(\sigma)$ the set of all constraints which are logical consequences of a set of constraints σ. Let Σ_1 and Σ_2 be the sets of (normalized) constraints of two schemas, S_1 and S_2, respectively. The goal now is to come up with a set of constraints Γ that conveys the common semantics of S_1 and S_2, that is, a set of constraints Γ such that $Th(\Gamma) = Th(\Sigma_1) \cap Th(\Sigma_2)$.

Example 17.7 Let $G(\Sigma_1)$ and $G(\Sigma_2)$ be the graphs that represent the sets of constraints Σ_1 and Σ_2. Denote their transitive closures by $G*(\Sigma_1)$ and $G*(\Sigma_2)$. Based on Theorem 17.2, we illustrate in this example how to use $G*(\Sigma_1)$ and $G*(\Sigma_2)$ to construct a set of constraints Γ such that $Th(\Gamma) = Th(\Sigma_1) \cap Th(\Sigma_2)$.

Suppose that Σ_1 is the following subset of the normalized constraints of the Phone-Company1 schema of Example 17.1 (again we do not consider all constraints to reduce the size of the example; we also abbreviate the names of the atomic concepts and roles in an obvious way, i.e., pc stands for `placedBy`, etc.):

(1) $(\geq 1 \ \text{pc}) \sqsubseteq \text{C}$
(2) $(\geq 1 \ \text{pc}^-) \sqsubseteq \text{P}$
(3) $\text{C} \sqsubseteq \neg(\geq 2 \ \text{pc})$
(4) $(\geq 1 \ \text{mpc}) \sqsubseteq \text{MC}$
(5) $(\geq 1 \ \text{mpc}^-) \sqsubseteq \text{MP}$
(6) $\text{MC} \sqsubseteq \text{C}$
(7) $\text{MP} \sqsubseteq \text{P}$
(8) $\text{mpc} \sqsubseteq \text{pc}$

Suppose that Σ_2 is the following subset of normalized constraints of the Phone-Company2 schema of Example 17.2:

(9) $(\geq 1\ \text{pc}) \sqsubseteq C$
(10) $(\geq 1\ \text{pc}^-) \sqsubseteq P$
(11) $C \sqsubseteq \neg(\geq 2\ \text{pc})$
(12) $(\geq 1\ \text{mpc}) \sqsubseteq MC$
(13) $(\geq 1\ \text{mpc}^-) \sqsubseteq MP$
(14) $MC \sqsubseteq \neg C$
(15) $MP \sqsubseteq \neg P$

For $i = 1, 2$, let $G(\Sigma_i)$ be the graph that represents Σ_i (Fig. 17.5 depicts $G(\Sigma_2)$). We systematically construct Γ such that $Th(\Gamma) = Th(\Sigma_1) \cap Th(\Sigma_2)$ as follows. Tables 17.1(a) and 17.1(b) show the arcs of $G * (\Sigma_1)$ and $G * (\Sigma_2)$. Note that a tabular presentation of the arcs, as opposed to a graphical representation, is much more convenient since we are working with transitive closures. For example, line 3 of Table 17.1(a) indicates that $G * (\Sigma_1)$ has an arc from the node labeled with $(\geq 1\ \text{pc})$ to the nodes labeled with C and $\neg(\geq 2\ \text{pc})$.

In this specific example, Table 17.1(c) induces Γ as follows:

- Lines 10, 15 and 16 are discarded since they correspond to arcs in just $G * (\Sigma_2)$.
- Lines 1, 5, 6, 9 and 12 are discarded since they have a negated expression on the left-hand side cell.
- Line 4 corresponds to a special case of a $\perp$-node (cf. Theorem 17.2(i)).
- The other lines retain just the arcs that are simultaneously in $G * (\Sigma_1)$ and $G * (\Sigma_2)$.

Table 17.1 shows the final set of constraints in Γ:

(16) $C \sqsubseteq \neg(\geq 2\ \text{pc})$ from line 2
(17) $(\geq 1\ \text{pc}) \sqsubseteq C$ from line 3
(18) $(\geq 1\ \text{pc}) \sqsubseteq \neg(\geq 2\ \text{pc})$ from line 3
(19) $(\geq 2\ \text{pc}) \sqsubseteq \perp$ from line 4
(20) $MC \sqsubseteq \neg(\geq 2\ \text{pc})$ from line 7
(21) $(\geq 1\ \text{mpc}) \sqsubseteq MC$ from line 8
(22) $(\geq 1\ \text{mpc}) \sqsubseteq \neg(\geq 2\ \text{pc})$ from line 8
(23) $(\geq 1\ \text{pc}^-) \sqsubseteq P$ from line 11
(24) $(\geq 1\ \text{mpc}^-) \sqsubseteq MP$ from line 14

Note that it is not entirely obvious that constraints (18), (19), and (22) are in $Th(\Sigma_1) \cap Th(\Sigma_2)$. We refer the reader to [8] for a detailed proof that this construction leads to a set of constraints Γ such that $Th(\Gamma) = Th(\Sigma_1) \cap Th(\Sigma_2)$. Roughly, it corresponds to the saturation strategy in binary resolution.

17.5 Conclusions

We first introduced extralite schemas with role hierarchies, which are sufficiently expressive to encode commonly used ER model and UML constructs, including relationship hierarchies. Then, we showed how to efficiently test strict satisfiability

Table 17.1 Construction of the set of constraints Γ that generates $\Sigma \Delta \Phi$

	(a) $G^*(\Sigma_1)$		(b) $G^*(\Sigma_2)$		(c) $G^*(\Gamma)$	
1	¬MC	¬(≥1 mpc)	¬MC	¬(≥1 mpc)		
2	C	¬(≥2 pc)	C	¬MC ¬(≥1 mpc) ¬(≥2 pc)	C	¬(≥2 pc)
3	(≥1 pc)	C ¬(≥2 pc)	(≥1 p)	C ¬MC ¬(≥1 mpc) ¬(≥2 pc)	(≥1 pc)	C ¬(≥2 pc)
4	(≥2 pc)	⊥	(≥2 pc)	⊥	(≥2 pc)	⊥
5	¬(≥1 pc)	¬(≥2 pc)	¬(≥1 pc)	¬(≥2 pc)		
6	¬C	¬(≥1 pc) ¬(≥2 pc) ¬MC ¬(≥1 mpc)	¬C	¬(≥1 pc) ¬(≥2 pc)		
7	MC	C ¬(≥2 pc)	MC	¬C ¬(≥1 pc) ¬(≥2 pc)	MC	¬(≥2 pc)
8	(≥1 mpc)	MC C ¬(≥2 pc)	(≥1 mpc)	MC ¬C ¬(≥1 pc) ¬(≥2 pc)	(≥1 mpc)	MC ¬(≥2 pc)
9	¬MP	¬(≥1 mpc⁻)	¬MP	¬(≥1 mpc⁻)		
10			P	¬MP ¬(≥1 mpc⁻)		
11	(≥1 pc⁻)	P	(≥1 pc⁻)	P ¬MP ¬(≥1 mpc⁻)	(≥1 pc⁻)	P
12	¬P	¬(≥1 pc⁻) ¬MP ¬(≥1 mpc⁻)	¬P	¬(≥1 pc⁻)		
13	MP	P	MP	¬P ¬(≥1 pc⁻)		
14	(≥1 mpc⁻)	MP P	(≥1 mpc⁻)	MP ¬P ¬(≥1 pc⁻)	(≥1 mpc⁻)	MP
15			pc	¬mpc		
16			mpc	¬pc		

and logical implication for restricted extralite schemas with role hierarchies. The procedures have low time complexity, and they retain and explore the constraint structure, which is a useful feature for a number of problems, as pointed out in the introduction.

Finally, as future work, we plan to investigate the problem of efficiently testing extralite schemas with role hierarchies for finite satisfiability [11].

Acknowledgements   This work was partly supported by CNPq, under grants 473110/2008-3 and 557128/2009-9, by FAPERJ under grant E-26/170028/2008, and by CAPES under grant NF 21/2009.

References

1. Artale, A., Calvanese, D., Kontchakov, R., Zakharyaschev, M.: The DL-lite family and relations. J. Artif. Intell. Res. **36**, 1–69 (2009)
2. Aspvall, B., Plass, M.F., Tarjan, R.E.: A linear-time algorithm for testing the truth of certain quantified boolean formulas. Inf. Process. Lett. **8**(3), 121–123 (1979)
3. Baader, F., Nutt, W.: Basic description logics. In: Baader, F., Calvanese, D., McGuinness, D.L., Nardi, D., Patel-Schneider, P.F. (eds.) The Description Logic Handbook, pp. 43–95. Cambridge University Press, New York (2003)
4. Borgida, A., Brachman, R.J.: Conceptual modeling with description logics. In: Baader, F., Calvanese, D., McGuinness, D.L., Nardi, D., Patel-Schneider, P.F. (eds.) The Description Logic Handbook, pp. 349–372. Cambridge University Press, New York (2003)
5. Calvanese, D., De Giacomo, G., Lembo, D., Lenzerini, M., Poggi, A., Rosati, R., Ruzzi, M.: Data integration through DL-Lite-A ontologies. In: Proceedings of the Third International Workshop on Semantics in Data and Knowledge Bases (SDKB 2008), pp. 26–47 (2008)
6. Calvanese, D., Giacomo, G., Lembo, D., Lenzerini, M., Rosati, R.: Tractable reasoning and efficient query answering in description logics: the DL-Lite family. J. Autom. Reason. **39**, 385–429 (2007)
7. Casanova, M.A., Furtado, A.L., Macedo, J.A., Vidal, V.M.: Extralite schemas with role hierarchies. Tech. rep. MCC09/10, Department of Informatics, PUC-Rio (2010)
8. Casanova, M.A., Lauschner, T., Leme, L.A.P.P., Breitman, K.K., Furtado, A.L., Vidal, V.M.: Revising the constraints of lightweight mediated schemas. Data Knowl. Eng. **69**(12), 1274–1301 (2010). Special issue on 28th International Conference on Conceptual Modeling (ER 2009)
9. Hartmann, S., Link, S., Trinh, T.: Constraint acquisition for entity-relationship models. Data Knowl. Eng. **68**, 1128–1155 (2009)
10. Lauschner, T., Casanova, M.A., Vidal, V.M.P., de Macêdo, J.A.F.: Efficient decision procedures for query containment and related problems. In: Brayner, A. (ed.) XXIV Simpósio Brasileiro de Banco de Dados, 05–09 de Outubro, Fortaleza, Ceará, Brasil, Anais, pp. 1–15 (2009)
11. Rosati, R.: Finite model reasoning in DL-Lite. In: Proceedings of the 5th European Semantic Web Conference on the Semantic Web: Research and Applications, ESWC'08, pp. 215–229. Springer, Berlin (2008)

Index